W9-BFI-527

BOTTOM LINE'S

BREAKTHROUGH TREATMENTS FOR REVERSING DISEASE

The biggest innovations in conventional and alternative medicine that are stopping today's most deadly diseases

BottomLineBooks
BottomLineInc.com

Breakthrough Treatments for Reversing Disease

10 9 8 7 6 5 4 3 2 1

ISBN 0-88723-787-8

Bottom Line Books® publishes the advice of expert authorities in many fields. These opinions may at times conflict as there are often different approaches to solving problems. The use of this material is no substitute for health, legal, accounting or other professional services. Consult competent professionals for answers to your specific questions.

Telephone numbers, addresses, prices, offers and websites listed in this book are accurate at the time of publication, but they are subject to frequent change.

Bottom Line Books® is a registered trademark of Bottom Line Inc.
3 Landmark Square, Suite 201, Stamford, CT 06901

BottomLineInc.com

Bottom Line Books is an imprint of Bottom Line Inc., publisher of print periodicals, e-letters and books. We are dedicated to bringing you the best information from the most knowledgeable sources in the world. Our goal is to help you gain greater wealth, better health, more wisdom, extra time and increased happiness.

Printed in the United States of America

Contents

2 • ALZHEIMER'S DISEASE AND DEMENTIA

3 • ARTHRITIS

4 • CANCER CURES

5 • CHRONIC PAIN

13 • KIDNEY, BLADDER AND LIVER DISORDERS

14 • RESPIRATORY CONDITIONS

15 • STROKE

Preface

We are proud to bring you *Bottom Line's Breakthrough Treatments for Reversing Disease: The Biggest Innovations in Conventional and Alternative Medicine That Are Stopping Today's Most Deadly Diseases*. We trust that you'll find the latest discoveries, best treatments and money-saving solutions to your health concerns.

Whether it's quality medical care, new heart therapies, breakthrough cancer treatments or cutting-edge nutritional advice, our editors talk to the people—from top research scientists to leading medical practitioners—who are creating the true innovations in health care.

How do we find all these top-notch medical professionals? For more than four decades, we have built a network of literally thousands of renowned physicians in both alternative and conventional medicine. These experts are affiliated with the premier medical institutions and the best universities throughout the world. We read the important medical journals and follow the latest research that is reported at medical conferences. And we regularly talk to our advisers in major teaching hospitals, private practices and government health agencies.

Bottom Line's Breakthrough Treatments for Reversing Disease is a result of our ongoing research and contact with these experts, and is a distillation of their latest findings and advice. We trust that you will enjoy the presentation and glean new, helpful and affordable information about the health topics that concern you and your family.

As a reader of a Bottom Line book, please be assured that you are receiving reliable and well-researched information from a trusted source.

But, please use prudence in health matters. Always speak to your physician before taking vitamins, supplements or over-the-counter medication...changing your diet...or beginning an exercise program. If you experience side effects from any regimen, contact your doctor immediately.

The Editors, *Bottom Line Books*, Stamford, Connecticut.

1

Allergies and Autoimmune Diseases

Cure Allergies the Natural Way With Supplements, Nasal Cleansing and Acupressure

Seasonal allergies are most commonly associated with springtime. But the flare-ups that occur in the summer can be just as bad—if not worse—due to the added discomfort caused by unpleasant climate conditions, such as heat and humidity.

Interesting new fact: Allergy symptoms may be lasting even longer due to extended pollen seasons brought on by climate change, according to a recent analysis.

That's why it's more important than ever for the 40 million Americans who suffer from seasonal allergies to use the most effective therapies—with the fewest side effects.

Good news: You don't have to fill your medicine cabinet with powerful drugs that simply temporarily relieve your allergy symptoms and potentially lead to side effects ranging from headache and drowsiness to difficulty breathing. Instead, you can get relief from the natural remedies described in this article.

THE ROOT OF THE PROBLEM

Most doctors treat allergies with a regimen that includes oral antihistamines, such as *loratadine* (Claritin) or *cetirizine* (Zyrtec), to block the release of histamine so that runny noses and itchy eyes will be reduced...and/or inhaled steroids, such as *triamcinolone acetonide* (Nasacort) or flunisolide, to reduce inflammation, mucus production and nasal congestion.

Problem: Aside from the side effects these drugs can cause, many allergy sufferers experience a "rebound effect"—that is, when the drug wears off, the histamine that has been

Richard Firshein, DO, director of the New York City–based Firshein Center for Comprehensive Medicine. He is the author of *Reversing Asthma* and *The Vitamin Prescription*. *FirsheinCenter.com* suppressed by the medication explodes, causing an even bigger allergic reaction.

Important: To transition from medication to the natural regimen described here, first take the natural remedy with the medication, then slowly wean yourself off the medication over a few weeks.

*Try these three simple natural approaches...**

STEP 1—SUPPLEMENTS

Mother Nature has tools that work with your body to stop allergy symptoms. The following naturally occurring substances have few side effects and often are just as effective as over-the-counter and prescription allergy medications.

My advice: Try quercetin, then add others in severe cases.

- **Quercetin is a bioflavonoid,** a type of plant pigment that inhibits histamine-producing cells. It's found in citrus fruits, apples and onions but not in amounts that are sufficient to relieve allergy symptoms. For optimal relief, try quercetin tablets.

Typical dose: Up to 600 mg daily depending on the severity of your symptoms. Quercetin also can be taken as a preventive during allergy season. Discuss the dose with your doctor. Quercetin is generally safe. Rare side effects may include headache and upset stomach. People with kidney disease should not take quercetin—it may worsen the condition.

Good brands: Quercetin 300, 800-545-9960, *www.allergyresearchgroup.com*...or Quercetone, 800-228-1966, *www.thorne.com.*

- **Stinging nettle is a flowering plant that, when ingested, reduces the amount of histamine that the body produces in response to an allergen.** Look for a product that contains 1% silicic acid (the key ingredient).

Typical dose: 500 mg to 1,000 mg once or twice a day depending on the severity of symptoms.

Caution: Some people are allergic to stinging nettle. In rare cases, oral stinging nettle may cause mild gastrointestinal upset.

Good brands: Nature's Way Nettle Leaf, 800-962-8873, *www.naturesway.com*...or Solgar Stinging Nettle Leaf Extract, 877-765-4274, *www.solgar.com.*

- **Fish oil.** The same potent source of omega-3 fatty acids that is so popular for preventing the inflammation that leads to heart disease also helps with allergies. Look for the words "pharmaceutical grade" and "purified" or "mercury-free" on the label. This ensures that the product is potent enough to have a therapeutic effect and has undergone a manufacturing process that removes potential toxins. Choose a brand that provides at least 500 mg of *eicosapentaenoic acid* (EPA) and 250 mg of *docosahexaenoic acid* (DHA) per capsule.

Typical dose: Take 2,000 mg of fish oil per day. Consult your doctor if you take a blood thinner.

Good brands: Nordic Naturals Arctic Omega, 800-662-2544, *www.nordicnaturals.com*... or Vital-Choice fish oils, 800-608-4825, *www.vitalchoice.com.*

STEP 2—NASAL CLEANSING

Inflammation in the nasal passages due to allergies prevents the sinuses from draining and can lead to sinus infection.

Self-defense: Nasal cleansing once daily during allergy season reduces the amount of pollen exposure and can prevent the allergic reaction in the first place.**

One option: Flush your nasal passages with a neti pot. A neti pot looks like a miniature teapot with an elongated spout (available at drugstores for $8 to $30). Add one tablespoon of aloe vera gel and a pinch of salt to the warm distilled water you place in the pot.

What to do: While standing over a sink, tilt your head horizontally, left ear to ceiling, and gently insert the spout into your left nostril. As you slowly pour the mixture into the nostril, it will circulate through the nasal passages and out the right nostril. Continue for 10 seconds, breathing through your mouth, then let the excess water drain. Repeat on the other nostril. Be sure to run your neti pot through the dishwasher or clean with soap and hot water to disinfect it after every use.

*Consult a doctor before trying this regimen if you are pregnant or have a medical condition.

**Nasal cleansing may be irritating for some people. If you experience any irritation, discontinue it immediately.

Alternative: If using a neti pot feels uncomfortable, try using a syringe bulb...or cup warm water (mixed with salt and aloe) in your hand and breathe it in slowly.

Even better: Use a nasal irrigator, which is more thorough and takes less effort than a neti pot. This instrument forcibly expels water—and uses the same aloe/salt/water mixture as you would in a neti pot.

Recommended: The Hydro Pulse, developed by ENT doctor Murray Grossan, 800-560-9007, *www.hydromedonline.com*, $77.95...or SinuPulse Elite Advanced Nasal Irrigation System, 800-305-4095, *www.sinupulse.com*, $97.

STEP 3—ACUPRESSURE OR ACUPUNCTURE

Acupuncture and acupressure can relieve allergies by stimulating certain pressure points to encourage blood flow, reduce inflammation and release natural painkilling chemical compounds known as endorphins.

- **Acupressure.** For 30 to 60 seconds, push (with enough pressure to hold your head on your thumbs) each thumb into the area where each brow meets the nose. Then, press your thumbs just below your eyebrows and slide along the ridges. Finally, press beneath both cheekbones, moving outward with both thumbs toward the ears. Do this sequence three times daily.
- **Acupuncture.** While acupressure helps relieve allergy symptoms, acupuncture is generally more effective. I recommend six to 10 sessions with a licensed acupuncturist during allergy season.

OTHER REMEDIES

- **Allergy shots and drops.** These traditional approaches are in many ways quite natural. Small amounts of an allergen extract are injected. After a number of treatments, you build up a natural resistance to the allergen. Allergy drops (placed under the tongue) are an alternative to allergy shots and work in much the same way.
- **Speleotherapy and halotherapy.** Used for centuries in Europe, these treatments are gaining popularity in the US. With speleotherapy, patients spend time in salt caves. Halotherapy uses man-made salt rooms that simulate caves. The salt ions combined with unpolluted air seem to improve lung function in those with respiratory and sinus ailments as well as allergies.

Salt mines and salt rooms are not always easy to find. Search online under "salt therapy."

Recommended: During allergy season, four to 12 speleotherapy or halotherapy sessions may be helpful. A 45- to 60-minute session typically costs $10 to $15.

Danger in Your Hair

Sonya Lunder, MPH, senior analyst with the Environmental Working Group, a nonprofit environmental health research and advocacy organization in Washington, DC. The Environmental Working Group's Skin Deep website offers safety profiles for more than 80,000 cosmetics, hair-care products and related items. *EWG.org/SkinDeep*

Hair-care products generally are not required to pass government safety tests before being sold in stores or used in salons. Some contain ingredients known to be toxic or to trigger potentially severe allergic reactions. This can be true even of hair-care products labeled "natural" or "hypoallergenic" or that salons insist are perfectly safe.

Sonya Lunder, senior analyst with the Environmental Working Group, a nonprofit organization that provides safety ratings for thousands of hair-care products on its Skin Deep website (*www.ewg.org/skindeep*) has important warnings for men and women...

Chemical hair straighteners usually contain formaldehyde, which can cause skin irritation, allergic reactions and even cancer. This is true even of the hair straighteners used at high-end salons.

Example: The makers of the popular hair straightener Brazilian Blowout claimed that this product did not contain formaldehyde, but tests revealed that it did.

Even if a hair straightener truly does not contain formaldehyde, it likely contains chemicals closely related to formaldehyde that have similar health effects...or chemicals that are not technically formaldehyde but that release formaldehyde when heated by a hair dryer. Some hair straighteners also contain lye and other highly caustic chemicals.

What to do: There is no chemical hair straightener that's safe enough to recommend. Chemical-free heat straightening—that is, straightening blown-dry hair with a flat iron—is safer but, of course, not long-lasting.

"Gradual-change" hair dyes often contain lead acetate. Some men's hair dyes are designed to alter hair color slowly over a period of weeks to make the change less jarring. But gradual-change hair dyes often contain lead acetate, which is extremely toxic and can lead to serious health issues including cancer. These hair dyes actually can cause elevated lead levels throughout the homes of people who use them, triggering health issues for other family members, too.

Examples: Grecian Formula for Men and some Youthair hair dyes have been found to contain lead acetate.

What to do: Avoid hair dyes that list lead or lead acetate as an ingredient. Check the safety rating on the Skin Deep website of any hair dye that claims to change hair color gradually.

Permanent dark hair dyes frequently contain coal-tar ingredients linked to cancer, such as *aminophenols* and/or *pheylenediamines*. (Other hair dyes sometimes contain potential carcinogens and allergens, too.) The European Union recently banned 181 hair-dye ingredients for health reasons, yet many of these remain in use in the US because the FDA does not have to approve the majority of products used in hair salons.

What to do: Consider using temporary or semipermanent hair dyes rather than permanent dyes, particularly with dark-color dyes. These tend to be safer. If you use a permanent dark dye, do full dye jobs as infrequently as possible—just touch up your roots in between.

Wear plastic gloves when applying hair dyes to limit exposure to your skin. Before using any hair dye, enter its name into the Skin Deep site to find out about any potential health risks.

Aerosol hair sprays often are inhaled, because aerosol cans typically distribute a mist of hair spray throughout the area around your head. Inhalation increases the risk for internal exposure and any associated health consequences. Even natural fragrances could trigger allergic reactions when inhaled.

What to do: Choose a hair spray that comes in a pump bottle rather than one that comes in an aerosol can. The spray from pump bottles tends to be less widely dispersed than that from aerosol cans, decreasing the odds of significant inhalation.

Shampoos and conditioners can cause allergies. Shampoos and conditioners tend to be rinsed off relatively quickly, reducing exposure to any problematic ingredients relative to leave-on products. However, some people are allergic to the ingredients in these products, including the chemicals that add fragrance...preservatives and antibacterials that increase a shampoo's shelf life...and surfactants that, for example, work as an antistatic agent in conditioners.

What to do: If your scalp or neck gets itchy or red, look up your shampoo and conditioner on the Skin Deep site. If you discover that one or both contain ingredients known to cause allergic reactions, try a different shampoo or conditioner that doesn't contain these ingredients and see if the condition improves.

Better Care for Allergies

Stress doesn't cause allergy attacks, but it can make them worse, a recent study reports.

Details: Among 179 allergy patients, those who had higher stress levels (as measured by daily online diaries) had more frequent flare-ups.

Why: Stress can disrupt the endocrine and immune systems, which could contribute to allergy episodes.

To reduce stress: Try positive thinking…eat right…get plenty of sleep…exercise regularly—and see a therapist, if necessary.

William Malarkey, MD, associate director, Institute for Behavioral Medicine Research, The Ohio State University, Columbus.

Nasal Allergies Linked to Migraine Frequency

People with migraine headaches who also have allergies such as hay fever were 33% more likely to have frequent migraines than people who had no allergies in a recent study.

Theory: Treating allergy symptoms may relieve migraine symptoms. Talk to your doctor.

Vincent Martin, MD, professor of medicine and codirector of the Headache and Facial Pain Program at University of Cincinnati, is the lead author of a study based on questionnaires from 6,000 people with migraines, published in *Cephalalgia*.

Better Travel with Food Allergies

If you are allergic to certain foods and travel frequently…

- **Learn to say "I am allergic" in the language of your destination**—Je suis allergique in French…Soy alérgico in Spanish…Ich bin allergisch in German. (You can download free allergen-free dining translation cards at *www.GlutenFreePassport.com.*)
- **Use the local language to say what you are allergic to.** Dairy, milk, eggs are aux laitages, au lait, aux œufs in French…a los productos lácteos, a la leche, a los huevos in Spanish…and Milchprodukte, Milch, Eier in German.
- **Eat only foods that you recognize as safe.** When in doubt, do not eat it.
- **Order special airline meals in advance.**
- **Bring plenty of snacks that you know you can eat.**
- **Tell restaurants and hotels of your special dietary requirements.**
- **Take along medicine for a food-related emergency.**

GlutenFree Passport, a health-education company located in Chicago, London, England, and Manly, Australia.

Device for Allergy Emergencies Is Easier to Use Than the Epipen

The Auvi-Q is shaped like a slim smartphone and offers voice instructions that guide a user through the injection process. Just place the device against the outer thigh, push firmly and the needle injects and retracts automatically. Both the Auvi-Q and the EpiPen are equally effective.

Stephen J. Apaliski, MD, is an allergist and immunologist at Allergy & Asthma Centres of the Metroplex, Arlington, Texas, and author of *Beating Asthma* (*Smashwords.com*).

Do You Have a Food Allergy—Or a Different Problem?

Matthew J. Fenton, PhD, division of allergy, immunology and transplantation, National Institute of Allergy and Infectious Diseases, National Institutes of Health, Bethesda.

A number of recent studies have found that most people who believe they have food allergies actually don't—one small study puts that figure as high as 90%! This state of affairs led the National Institute of Allergy and Infectious Diseases (NIAID), part of the National Institutes of Health, to release new guidelines to provide a uniform strategy for diagnosing and managing food allergies. *Matthew Fenton, PhD, chief of the asthma and allergy branch of NIAID, explains the guidelines...*

WHAT'S YOUR REAL PROBLEM?

The new guidelines, which you can see on *The Journal of Allergy and Clinical Immunology* website at *www.jacionline.org/article/S0091-6749(10)01569-1/fulltext*, define a food allergy as "an adverse health effect arising from a specific immune response that occurs reproducibly on exposure to a given food." Or, in easier-to-digest language, most food allergies result from a mistaken response by the immune system, which identifies something you eat as a threat and then creates antibodies to attack it and fight it off. These antibodies usually are what create the allergy symptoms. But, according to Dr. Fenton, what many (if not most) people call food "allergies" are actually more accurately described as "intolerances," especially in the case of lactose, food dyes and chemicals such as MSG.

What's the difference? Intolerances are not caused by the immune system, and they tend to be complex reactions (for instance, causing stomach upset and/or headaches) that worsen as you eat more and more of the food. Allergies, on the other hand, cause symptoms such as redness, itching, tightness in the throat, shortness of breath or anaphylactic shock. Both are troublesome, but it's important to identify whether your reaction is an allergy or intolerance because the two have different consequences—allergies are dangerous while intolerances are merely terribly unpleasant. And they require different treatments.

WHAT IT ALL MEANS

If you suspect that you have a food allergy—or if you now suspect that you don't have a food allergy but rather an intolerance—discuss your concern with your doctor. A detailed medical history and perhaps a skin prick test and/or blood antibody test will help distinguish between intolerance and allergy.

Important! Tests are done on extracts, which are purified, as opposed to foods, which often contain multiple ingredients. Therefore, a negative result to a test using an extract is not really definitive. It is important to be aware that in the real world, foods may contain other ingredients that you may or may not know they contain. Meanwhile, a positive result does not necessarily confirm an allergy. It means that you have a sensitization to a food that could be either an allergy or an intolerance.

THE TRUE TEST

For these reasons, Dr. Fenton suggests that people who believe they have food allergies should get confirmation by having a tightly controlled oral challenge performed by an allergist in a setting where he/she has access to medications and equipment to treat severe reactions. You will be instructed to avoid the suspected food for a certain length of time (usually an hour or two) before your appointment. Then, while you are in the doctor's office, you will consume gradually increasing amounts of the food. Your doctor will monitor your reaction to determine whether you have an allergy or intolerance and, of course, will be able to provide appropriate treatment if your reaction veers into dangerous territory. Since there are no FDA-approved treatments for food allergy at present, you will then have to avoid the food that you are allergic to.

It's good news to learn that foods you are intolerant of—but not allergic to—aren't truly dangerous to your health but, of course, an intolerance produces unpleasant symptoms itself, so it makes sense to follow the very same advice—eat something else. (For more information on food intolerances, see page 13.)

The End of Allergy Shots

The Food and Drug Administration recently approved Oralair, an under-the-tongue medicine, for people allergic to grass pollens. The first dose is taken at a doctor's office, in case of any adverse reaction. Then patients take one pill each day at home. Oralair does not relieve symptoms immediately—it needs time to build up, just as with allergy shots.

Dean Mitchell, MD, is an allergist and immunologist in New York City and author of *Dr. Dean Mitchell's Allergy and Asthma Solution.*

Blood Pressure Drugs Are Linked to Severe Oral Allergy Symptoms

Oral allergy syndrome is characterized by itching and/or swelling of the lips, mouth and throat after eating tree nuts, raw fruits or raw vegetables.

Problem: *Lisinopril* (Zestril), *quinapril* (Accupril) and other ACE inhibitor blood pressure drugs may trigger symptoms such as extreme facial swelling and/or difficulty breathing. See your doctor immediately. Do not stop taking the drug on your own.

Sunit Jariwala, MD, is assistant professor of medicine at Albert Einstein College of Medicine, the Bronx, New York.

Could You Have a Metal Allergy?

Mark A. Stengler, NMD, naturopathic medical doctor and founder and medical director of the Stengler Center for Integrative Medicine in Encinitas, California...adjunct associate clinical professor at the National College of Natural Medicine in Portland, Oregon...the author of many books, including *The Natural Physician's Healing Therapies* and a coauthor of *Prescription for Natural Cures and Prescription for Drug Alternatives.*

Many people are aware of the dangers of metal toxicity and have heard about the process of removing metals from the body.

Another problem caused by metals: A sensitivity or allergy that can have adverse effects on health. *Let me explain...*

Throughout the day, we are exposed to a wide array of metals, including nickel (found in some jewelry, medical prostheses and stainless steel cookware)...mercury (in seafood, some vaccines and dental fillings)...cobalt (in air and water)...and aluminum (in antiperspirants and some food cans).

What many physicians fail to realize: The presence of these metals in people who are sensitive can result in an immune response and inflammation throughout the body—in other words, an allergy.

Symptoms of a metal allergy: Some allergies, such as those to nickel, cause an itchy red rash (known as allergic dermatitis) upon contact with jewelry made with the metal. Other potential symptoms of a metal sensitivity include headache, poor memory, muscle spasms or pain, joint pain, fatigue, anxiety, insomnia, irritability and depression. A metal allergy also may contribute to asthma, multiple autoimmune diseases (such as rheumatoid arthritis), irritable bowel syndrome and chronic fatigue syndrome.

My advice: Consider testing for a metal allergy if you have any of the symptoms or conditions above and are looking for the root cause. Allergic dermatitis can be determined with a skin test, but I use a specific blood test to determine an internal allergy or sensitivity to metal—the memory lymphocyte immunostimulation assay (MELISA). It does not measure the amount of a metal in your blood, but whether your immune system is reacting to it. Even a small amount of metal can trigger an allergic reaction.

If the test comes back positive for a sensitivity to one or more metals, treatment may include detoxification or removal of the metal, such as dental work. The test is sometimes covered by insurance.

If your physician does not use the MELISA test, he/she can find out more about it from Neuroscience, Inc., a company that provides testing (888-342-7272, *www.neuroscienceinc.com).* You also can contact Neuroscience, Inc., to find a physician who administers the test in your area.

Can Your Pollen Allergy Include Fruits and Vegetables?

Hannelore Brucker, MD, is a practicing allergist at the Southdale Allergy and Asthma Clinic in Minneapolis.

It's bad enough that springtime can bring miserable allergy symptoms like itchy eyes, a runny nose and persistent postnasal drip, but more patients seem to be noticing that their pesky pollen allergies are accompanied by a whole other set of seemingly unrelated problems, including allergic reactions to many of the most popular fruits and vegetables—the healthy foods that we thought were supposed to help us!

While seasonal hay fever and food allergies aren't associated in many people's minds, there can in fact be a connection. Practicing allergist Hannelore Brucker, MD, of the Southdale Allergy and Asthma Clinic in Minneapolis, began studying this phenomenon, called "oral allergy syndrome," when she noticed that more of her patients were complaining about strange symptoms, such as an itchy mouth from eating a banana or hives on their skin from peeling potatoes. According to Dr. Brucker, pollen allergies affect about one in five people and, in her practice at least, about one-third of these unfortunate folks also are having allergic reactions to fruits and vegetables and some nuts and herbs.

A SIMPLE CHEMISTRY EQUATION

It sounds mysterious, but there actually is a straightforward explanation as to why this happens. Chemically speaking, some of the proteins in pollen and certain fruits and vegetables (listed on the next page) are very similar—Dr. Brucker calls them "crossover proteins." Their purpose is the same—in pollens and in fruits and vegetables—these proteins help protect against pests that would harm the plants.

As we all know, in some people, the body manufactures antibodies to fight off seemingly benign substances (such as pollen) that it regards as foreign and intrusive. This then sets off a chain reaction that releases histamine, which starts inflammation and produces all those irritating symptoms that make spring and/or fall so very unpleasant for affected individuals.

THE FOOD CONNECTION

What happens with oral allergy syndrome is that when susceptible people are exposed to pollen that irritates them (such as birch tree pollen from March through May...or ragweed pollen from mid-August to the first frost), their bodies not only build up antibodies but, over time, they also begin developing an allergy to the fruits and vegetables that have similar proteins.

For most people, the problem manifests itself as itching in the area of the lips, tongue and throat (hence the name "oral" allergy syndrome). This usually occurs within a few minutes of eating or touching the offending food and almost always vanishes quickly with no intervention—but, Dr. Brucker said, a small percentage of patients experience reactions that are extreme and dangerous, including constriction of the throat or, rarely, anaphylactic shock. If this happens, it is a medical emergency that requires an immediate trip to the hospital.

THE OFFENDING FOODS

Heat (cooking) alters the chemistry of the proteins and makes them no longer problematic, so for the most part these reactions occur only with raw fruits or vegetables. Carrots and celery are frequent offenders, possibly because they often are eaten raw. Peeling potatoes also can make hands itch or produce hives or watery eyes in those who are sensitive.

According to Dr. Brucker, the stronger the pollen allergy, the greater the likelihood that you'll have an oral allergy reaction. Time of year is also relevant since the various pollens are seasonal—if you are allergic to birch, you may be more allergic to its cross-reactive fruits and veggies in the spring, when you are having intense allergies. The reactions may vary among different strains of the same fruit and, as noted above, also will be affected by cooking.

If you are allergic to any type of pollen, now you know to keep track of any adverse reactions you get from eating fruits or vegetables...and then to consider limiting those foods, or at least eating them only cooked, not raw. *For example, here is a list of foods from Dr. Brucker that are known to evoke oral allergy symptoms in people allergic to birch and ragweed...*

Foods Reactive to Birch Allergy

Apples
Pears
Cherries
Peaches
Plums
Apricots
Carrots
Celery
Potatoes (raw)
Kiwi
Hazelnuts
Almonds

Foods Reactive to Ragweed Allergy

All melons, including
Cantaloupe—the most reactive
Watermelon
Honeydew
Cucumbers
Bananas
Zucchini
Chamomile tea
Echinacea (an herb)

A few other interesting facts: There is some indication that yet another common allergen—grass pollen—can lead to oral reactions, for example to tomatoes.

While many people have other types of food allergies, such as to peanuts, fish and shrimp, Dr. Brucker said that these are completely different from, and not related to, pollen allergies and oral allergy syndrome.

WHAT YOU CAN DO

If you're thinking, "hmm...this itchy mouth stuff sounds familiar," Dr. Brucker suggests you schedule an appointment with your allergist.

It's smart to bring along the actual offending raw, fresh food so that your doctor can use it to do an easy skin-prick test, in which the doctor uses a needle to prick the fruit and then the patient's skin and observes the reaction—a test that has the advantage of producing an immediate result that doesn't require sending samples to a lab. (Note: Dr. Brucker said that some doctors use commercial fruit extracts for this testing, but since these products have been heated for sterilization, they may not produce a reliable result.)

And Dr. Brucker has one bit of good news for people who are allergy sufferers and also have oral allergy syndrome—the problem tends to fade away about the same time the pollen does.

When Your Immune System Fights Itself

Noel R. Rose, MD, PhD, director, Autoimmune Disease Research Center, The Johns Hopkins University, Baltimore, and chairman emeritus, National Scientific Advisory Board, American Autoimmune Related Diseases Association, Inc. (AARDA), Eastpointe, Michigan.

Quick—how many autoimmune diseases can you name?

If you're like most Americans, the answer is "none"... and that's a bigger problem than you might guess. Why? Because autoimmune diseases affect as many as one in 20 Americans, and if anyone in your family has one, you are at risk, too. Autoimmune diseases can be quite debilitating, even fatal—and with this type of illness, patient awareness is particularly important.

Scientists have identified more than 100 autoimmune illnesses, and the list includes some names that you surely will recognize—such as multiple sclerosis, diabetes and celiac disease, not to mention rheumatoid arthritis and psoriasis. The American Autoimmune Related Diseases Association (AARDA) is trying to educate people about the fact that all autoimmune diseases are genetically linked to one another...your mother's psoriasis is related to your brother's arthritis and your cousin's Crohn's disease. For information and guidance, we spoke with two experts—Noel R.

Rose, MD, PhD, director of the Autoimmune Disease Research Center at The Johns Hopkins University in Baltimore, and Virginia T. Ladd, president and executive director of AARDA in Eastpointe, Michigan.

CONNECTING THE DOTS

It's not always clear what the trigger is (more about that in a minute), but all autoimmune diseases occur when your immune system attacks your body's own proteins, mistakenly identifying them as invaders and producing antibodies or T cells to overcome them. The result is any one of a number of serious and chronic illnesses that can develop in any bodily system, but most commonly in the nervous, gastrointestinal and endocrine systems, blood, kidneys, lymph nodes, heart and liver.

While their symptoms vary widely, autoimmune diseases share several common threads...

- **They can run in families,** although they may take different forms in different family members. The shared trait is an increased susceptibility to autoimmune disease in general.

- **Women are more susceptible than men as a result of their enhanced immune system.** Three out of four people with an autoimmune disease are women. Ethnicity is a factor, too, with African American, Hispanic and Asian women more prone than Caucasians to certain autoimmune disorders.

- **Environmental factors also can trigger autoimmune disease.** Research has found links with viral and bacterial infections, toxins, drugs, chemicals and even sunlight.

DO THESE SOUND FAMILIAR?

Here are some of the most common autoimmune diseases (you can view a more comprehensive list at *www.aarda.org*)...

Celiac disease: An intolerance for gluten in wheat and other grains.

Crohn's disease: A form of inflammatory bowel disease.

Diabetes type 1: A lifelong endocrine condition resulting from the autoimmune destruction of the cells in the pancreas that manufacture insulin.

Hashimoto's disease: An autoimmune disease in which the thyroid is gradually destroyed.

Lupus: A chronic, inflammatory disorder that damages the joints, skin, kidneys and other parts of the body.

Multiple sclerosis: A crippling autoimmune disease that affects the brain and spinal cord.

Psoriasis: An inflammatory skin disorder characterized by redness and silvery scales.

Rheumatoid arthritis: A painful autoimmune joint disease that involves other organs.

Scleroderma: A disorder in which inflammation infiltrates the skin, esophagus, lungs and other organs.

WATCH THE SYMPTOMS

Many autoimmune disorders have symptoms that are vague, transitory and hard to pin down, which is undoubtedly a factor in a common complaint among people with autoimmune diseases—that doctors don't take them seriously. Ladd said that it's not uncommon for people to see four or five different doctors over a period of five years or so before finding one who pays close attention, orders the appropriate tests and pins down a diagnosis. The process can be incredibly frustrating, especially given that patients often get sicker and sicker before getting any meaningful treatment.

Does any of this sound familiar to you? Are any members of your family struggling with similar stories of disconnected symptoms that are not part of an identifiable disease, or has anyone already been diagnosed with an autoimmune disease? If so, you need to take your symptoms very seriously. *Here are the steps you should take to find the true cause of your symptoms and get a proper diagnosis and treatment...*

- **Research your family's medical history,** and share it with your doctor. Collect information about not just your immediate family, but also grandparents, aunts, uncles and cousins.

• **Write down all your symptoms**—even if they appear unrelated—and tell your doctor about them.

Note: Dr. Rose said that the single most widespread symptom caused by autoimmune diseases is extreme fatigue, which she described as going way beyond ordinary tiredness—it's a state of exhaustion that makes it impossible to do what you need to do.

• **If many of your symptoms fall into a particular category** (say, gastrointestinal distress or joint pain) ask your primary care provider to refer you to an appropriate specialist (such as a gastroenterologist or a rheumatologist). When you see the specialist, share your family history and ask to have autoimmune disease investigated.

• **Get a second opinion**—or a third or fourth one, if necessary, if symptoms continue but no cause is discovered. And... if your doctor doesn't take your concerns seriously, you need a new doctor!

Natural Cures for an Ailing Immune System

Jamison Starbuck, ND, is a naturopathic physician in family practice and a lecturer at the University of Montana, both in Missoula. She is past president of the American Association of Naturopathic Physicians and a contributing editor to *The Alternative Advisor: The Complete Guide to Natural Therapies and Alternative Treatments.*

The immune system is remarkable in its ability to help fight off infections and a wide variety of serious illnesses ranging from flu to staph infections. When our defenses go awry, however, our health can be threatened in a number of ways. For unknown reasons, the body's immune system can attack a part of itself, resulting in autoimmune disease.

Examples: Systemic lupus erythematosus (commonly known as lupus) can affect the kidneys, skin and blood vessels. With Crohn's disease, the immune system strikes the bowel. In patients who have rheumatoid arthritis, the joints are assaulted.

When a patient is diagnosed with an autoimmune disease, conventional doctors generally begin treatment with medication. For lupus and Crohn's disease, prednisone (a steroid drug) is commonly used. For rheumatoid arthritis, medications typically include nonsteroidal anti-inflammatory drugs (NSAIDs), corticosteroids and, most recently, drugs called tumor necrosis factor inhibitors, such as *etanercept* (Enbrel) and *infliximab* (Remicade). While these medications reduce symptoms, they can cause potentially serious side effects, such as liver damage and hypertension. That's why I prefer to treat symptoms naturally whenever possible, reserving strong medications for flare-ups. *My advice for people with autoimmune disease...*

• **Eat an anti-inflammatory diet.** Limit animal food (meat and poultry) to two meals per day and no more than three to four ounces per meal. Also consume at least five one-half cup servings of vegetables daily...one cup of a whole grain, such as brown rice or millet, and/or legumes, such as lentils or split peas... a small handful of nuts...and two or more pieces of fruit.

• **Take an omega-3 supplement.** For most of my patients with an autoimmune disease, I recommend a daily dose of 2,800 mg of inflammation-fighting omega-3 oils from fish oil, 50% of which should be eicosapentaenoic acid (EPA), a fatty acid shown to have strong immune-supportive effects. Omega-3 oils should always be taken with food because they are more readily digested. Check the label to be sure your fish oil source has been tested for heavy metal contamination.

• **Limit your exposure to environmental pollutants and drugs.** Both appear to trigger autoimmune disease in sensitive individuals. Substances that are known to cause this reaction in some people include mercury, cadmium, pesticides, anticonvulsant medications, beta-blockers (taken for heart disease) and estrogens (taken for menopausal symptoms). Talk to your doctor about getting tested for heavy metal toxicity and about taking only those prescription medications that he/she feels are absolutely necessary.

• **Take a vitamin D supplement daily.** An increasing body of scientific evidence links vitamin D deficiency with autoimmune disease. Researchers theorize that vitamin D helps regulate immune cell activity in the body.

My recommendation: A supplement containing 800 international units (IU) to 1,200 IU of vitamin D daily.

The Right Probiotic Can Relieve Autoimmune Conditions

Gary B. Huffnagle, PhD, professor of internal medicine at the University of Michigan School of Medicine in Ann Arbor and coauthor of *The Probiotics Revolution—The Definitive Guide to Safe, Natural Health Solutions Using Probiotic and Prebiotic Foods and Supplements.*

Until recently, probiotics were mostly known for their ability to help prevent or alleviate various digestive problems.

Now: Research has uncovered several other health benefits—for example, these beneficial intestinal microorganisms also boost immunity and reduce the severity of certain autoimmune conditions, such as rheumatoid arthritis and asthma.

What you need to know...

THE RIGHT PROBIOTIC

Consuming probiotics is one of the smartest things you can do for your health.

What you may not know: Some probiotics—available as over-the-counter (OTC) supplements and in certain fermented food products, such as many brands of yogurt and buttermilk—have been found to be more effective than others for treating certain conditions.

What's more, because everyone's intestinal microflora—the term for the many billions of different bacteria and fungi that populate your gut—is unique in its exact makeup, a probiotic that's effective for someone else might not work for you, and vice versa.

Best approach: Try one probiotic product (such as those described in this article) for two weeks and see if you feel better. Probiotics are extremely safe. While some people may experience slight gastrointestinal disturbance, such as intestinal gas or bloating, from a given probiotic, this can be alleviated by reducing the dosage.

If you don't see clear benefits after two weeks, try a different probiotic from the same category (listed on the next page).

Even though most research has focused on the benefits of single types (strains) of microorganisms, many people benefit from combining two or more probiotics, and a number of probiotic products also contain multiple strains.

Once you find a probiotic you respond well to, I recommend taking it daily even in the absence of any specific health complaint—just like a daily multivitamin and mineral supplement.

Choose products from well-known manufacturers, such as Sustenex, Culturelle and Align, that include information on the label about the type of microorganisms and number of viable bacteria, or colony-forming units (CFUs), they contain. Follow the label recommendation on dosage. Studies indicate that probiotics are equally effective when taken with or without food.

FOR DIGESTIVE PROBLEMS

In addition to promoting the growth of beneficial bacteria in the gut, probiotics aid digestion by inhibiting the proliferation of harmful bacteria and other microorganisms in the intestines.

If you suffer from digestive problems, including diarrhea, constipation, bloating, gastroesophageal reflux disease or irritable bowel syndrome (IBS), try one of the following OTC probiotics...

• **Bifidobacterium.** This group, one of the major types of intestinal bacteria, includes Bifidobacterium infantis (found in Align, sold in capsule form)...Bifidobacterium bifidus (a common ingredient of many probiotic supplements, such as those by Source Naturals and Nature's Way)...and Bifidobacterium animalis (contained in Activia yogurt).

Important scientific evidence: In a randomized study of 362 women with IBS, those who took B. infantis in a daily dose of 10 million CFUs showed significant improvement after four weeks, compared with a placebo group.

• **Bacillus coagulans.** This species of bacteria (found in Sustenex Probiotic products, sold in capsule and chewable forms, and Digestive Advantage capsules) can survive for an extended time in the digestive tract, which is believed to increase the probiotic's effectiveness. In a study of 44 people with IBS, those receiving a daily dose of B. coagulans reported significant improvement.

FOR ALLERGIES, ASTHMA, ARTHRITIS, ECZEMA AND MORE

As a first-line probiotic for allergies, asthma, eczema or other autoimmune-related disorders, I recommend trying either B. coagulans—shown in a 2010 study to significantly reduce rheumatoid arthritis pain compared with a placebo—or one of the following...

• **Lactobacillus.** Another major category of probiotics, this genus includes the widely used Lactobacillus acidophilus, contained in many probiotic supplements and yogurt products (including Brown Cow, Stonyfield Farm and some Dannon yogurts)...Lactobacillus GG (the active ingredient in Culturelle capsules and powder)...and Lactobacillus casei (contained in the yogurt drink DanActive).

• **Saccharomyces boulardii.** This probiotic is actually a strain of yeast. Although most people think of yeast as something to be avoided—as in a yeast infection, for example—S. boulardii helps fight disease-causing organisms. S. boulardii is available in capsule form in Florastor and in products by Jarrow Formulas, Nutricology, Swanson, NOW Foods, Douglas Labs and others.

PROBIOTIC-BOOSTING DIET

Certain foods, known as "prebiotics," stay in the digestive tract for an extended period of time, where they stimulate the growth of many types of beneficial bacteria.

Try to include as many of the following prebiotic foods in your diet as possible each day. For example...

• **Foods rich in natural antioxidants**—especially those found in colorful fruits and vegetables, such as berries, citrus fruits, peppers, tomatoes, broccoli, spinach, asparagus and okra...dark beans and nuts...and green tea.

• **Foods high in soluble fiber**—including legumes, such as peas, lentils and pinto beans...oat bran...carrots and Brussels sprouts...apples, pears and prunes...and root vegetables, such as onions and unprocessed potatoes.

To further boost soluble fiber consumption: Talk to your doctor about taking a daily psyllium supplement, such as Carlson Psyllium Fiber Supplement or Metamucil. Follow label instructions.

At the same time, minimize your intake of processed foods containing sugar, white flour and other refined carbohydrates—all of which promote the growth of harmful bacteria in the digestive tract.

Food Intolerances Can Strike at Any Age

Clifford W. Bassett, MD, is on the faculty of New York University School of Medicine and is medical director of Allergy & Asthma Care of New York, both in New York City. *AllergyReliefnyc.com.*

Chew on this—according to a recent report from the National Institute of Allergy and Infectious Diseases, 13% of US adults believe that they are allergic to one or more of the primary allergy-provoking foods, yet only 3% truly are allergic.

One reason: People often confuse food allergy with the more common food intolerance.

There are three major distinctions between the two conditions....

Allergies usually appear in childhood and may disappear over time, whereas food intolerances tend to increase with age.

With an allergy, the immune system mistakes a food for a harmful invader and creates antibodies that provoke a reaction whenever that food is consumed. An intolerance usually is primarily a digestive reaction (rather than an immune response) that occurs when a food irritates the gastrointestinal tract or cannot be properly digested.

Allergy symptoms, which can range from mild to life-threatening, may include itching, flushing, hives, dizziness, nausea, facial swelling and/or difficulty breathing. Intolerance reactions typically are milder and chiefly gastrointestinal (abdominal discomfort, bloating, diarrhea), though they sometimes include skin reactions and other nondigestive symptoms.

Why is it important to recognize the difference? Dr. Bassett explained that with a food allergy, you must assiduously avoid the food, since just a fraction of a teaspoon may bring on a full-blown reaction...and you should keep an epinephrine auto-injector on hand to halt any potentially life-threatening reaction. If you suspect that you have a food allergy (primary culprits include shellfish, fish, peanuts, tree nuts, milk and eggs), consult an allergy specialist for testing.

Referrals: *www.acaai.org*

In the case of a food intolerance, you may be able to identify the trigger by tracking what you eat and when symptoms arise. If you try an "elimination diet" that excludes the suspect food, check food labels so you don't unknowingly ingest something you want to avoid, Dr. Bassett said.

Note: Some people with a food intolerance find that they can have occasional small amounts of that food without bringing on symptoms.

Common food intolerances involve...

- **Lactose, a sugar in cow's milk.** Up to 10% of US adults are lactose intolerant, generally because they have a deficiency of the enzyme lactase required to properly digest lactose. Symptoms typically include abdominal pain, bloating, excessive gas and/or diarrhea. Opting for lactose-free milk or lactase enzyme supplements may allow some intolerant individuals to have more normal digestion, Dr. Bassett said.

- **Gluten,** a protein found in wheat, rye and barley. Gluten intolerance appears to be more common today than it used to be. Patients often experience bloating, gas and intestinal discomfort after eating gluten grains.

Be aware: Gluten is found not only in baked goods and pastas, but also in foods containing grain derivatives—including surprising ones, such as luncheon meats, gravies, sauces, soy sauce, candy, fruit fillings, dairy-free creamer and beer—so you need to be a "food label detective," Dr. Bassett said.

- **Monosodium glutamate (MSG).** Though best known as a flavor enhancer in Asian cuisine, MSG also appears in many frozen, canned and processed foods. Very sensitive people may experience flushing, a burning sensation and pressure in the face, neck and chest, as well as sudden headaches.

Food intolerances you may never have heard of include...

- **Sulfites,** compounds that occur naturally in fermented products (beer, wine, champagne) and that often are added to dried fruit, grape juice, packaged foods, canned goods and other foods as a preservative. Ingesting sulfites may trigger nasal itchiness and congestion, hives and/or swelling. In people with asthma, ingesting sulfites may bring on an asthma attack.

Check labels: Aliases include sodium or potassium bisulfite...sodium or potassium metabisulfite...sulfiting agent...and sulfur dioxide.

- **Tartrazine,** a dye (also called yellow dye #5) used in many beverages, chips, processed vegetables, candies and desserts. Some case reports suggest a link between tartrazine and a rare episodic skin rash. It had been thought that individuals most prone to tartrazine intolerance included those who cannot tolerate aspirin and those with asthma, but more recent research does not confirm this association, Dr. Bassett said.

- **Tyramine,** a naturally occurring compound in aged cheeses, avocados, bananas, beer, chocolate, red wine and tomatoes. In sensitive individuals, Dr. Bassett said, tyramine can bring on headaches, migraines and even an elevation of blood pressure.

Common Chemicals May Increase Food Allergies

Chemicals called dichlorophenols, used to chlorinate public water and found in insect- and weed-control products, can reduce food tolerance and cause food allergies in some people. Avoiding tap water is likely not enough. Limit your exposure to dichlorophenols by buying organic produce and avoiding areas where pesticides have been applied.

Elina Jerschow, MD, MSc, allergist, American College of Allergy, Asthma and Immunology, and leader of a study of 2,211 participants in the US National Health and Nutrition Examination Survey, published in *Annals of Allergy, Asthma and Immunology.*

Not Knowing You Have Celiac Disease Can Kill You

Joseph Murray, MD, professor of medicine and immunology, department of gastroenterology and hepatology, Mayo Clinic, Rochester, Minnesota.

Until the last few years, celiac disease was an obscure, little-known condition and people who had it were extremely limited in terms of what they could eat or even where to turn for help managing their condition. That has changed dramatically with recent studies on celiac disease, abundant online information and support, and a generous selection of gluten-free products, including bread, cookies, cereal and the like in specialty markets. In fact, gluten-free food is one of the fastest-growing categories in today's supermarket.

This is one time food marketers were ahead of the curve. Though it has been recognized that celiac disease (an autoimmune response triggered by gluten, the protein in wheat, rye and barley) is on the rise, the extent came as a surprise to researchers from the Mayo Clinic, who discovered that young people today are more than four times as likely to have celiac disease than was the case 60 years ago.

The study looked for the antibody triggered by celiac in blood samples taken between 1948 and 1954 and compared findings with recent blood tests on two groups of residents of Olmstead County, Minnesota. One group was the same age as those tested in the original study...the other group consisted of people born in the same years as those tested in the original study.

Joseph Murray, MD, professor of medicine and immunology at Mayo Clinic, was the lead author of the study. He explained that this increase undoubtedly is due to environmental causes. One possible factor relates to the fact that wheat has been genetically altered to heighten gluten content. Another might be the huge increase of gluten-containing food products. Gluten is used extensively today because it reduces manufacturing and processing costs of foods.

EVEN WORSE

But there was a second startling finding of the study—people with so-called "silent" celiac have four times greater mortality than people without celiac. To explain...the majority of people with celiac are not diagnosed or treated, so they continue to consume gluten—perhaps with symptoms, and perhaps without. Although the disease can cause severe digestive distress, it also can lead to other conditions that seem unrelated, such as infertility, headaches, osteoporosis (especially early onset) and anemia, or it might cause no apparent problems at all. But even without symptoms, Dr. Murray says that celiac is damaging the intestines and weakening the body, and also may be increasing vulnerability to other diseases, including cancer.

WHAT TO DO

It is possible to develop celiac at any age. Dr. Murray says to consult your doctor about the possibility of celiac in the event of digestive problems, including diarrhea, excess gas and bloating, anemia or accelerated osteoporosis—especially if you have a family history of celiac or if you notice a problem when you eat foods containing wheat, rye or barley. Do not eliminate gluten from your diet before being tested, as this may decrease the accuracy of the tests.

Even in the complete absence of symptoms, some experts advise avoiding wheat, rye and barley in all forms—including such things as soy sauce and many canned soups—entirely to see whether it makes a difference in how you feel. You might feel so much better that you'll learn to live without wheat and wheat products.

Natural Remedies for Celiac Disease

Jamison Starbuck, ND, is a naturopathic physician in family practice and a lecturer at the University of Montana, both in Missoula. She is past president of the American Association of Naturopathic Physicians and a contributing editor to *The Alternative Advisor: The Complete Guide to Natural Therapies and Alternative Treatments.*

The next time a waiter puts a basket of fresh bread on your restaurant table, think twice before you eat it. Experts believe that at least one out of every 100 American adults has celiac disease, a condition that can make sufferers ill after eating even a single slice of bread. The culprit is gluten—a type of protein found in wheat, barley, rye and, in some cases, oats that creates an autoimmune, inflammatory reaction in the small intestine. The usual symptoms are bloating and diarrhea, but some people also experience abdominal pain and/or constipation. In some cases, celiac disease causes only a blistery, itchy skin condition (dermatitis herpetiformis) or fatigue.

If you think you might have celiac disease, discuss it with your doctor. A diagnosis requires specific blood tests and, in some cases, an intestinal biopsy. If you do have celiac disease, your medical doctor will tell you to completely avoid gluten. This may sound like hard work, since gluten is in all sorts of things you might not suspect, such as many kinds of soy sauce, creamed soups and salad dressings. But it is definitely doable and gets easier as you learn where gluten-free products (even bread and pasta) are available—for example, in many health-food stores and a growing number of restaurants.

Payoff: Once you start avoiding gluten, your celiac symptoms will disappear over a period of weeks and months. *Other steps to consider...**

- **Take supplements.** Inflammation in the small intestine interferes with the absorption of key nutrients. I advise my celiac patients to take a daily regimen that includes 5 mg of folic acid...800 international units (IU) each of vitamins E and D...25,000 IU of vitamin A...and 2 mg of vitamin K.

Note: Vitamin K supplements should be avoided by patients taking *warfarin* (Coumadin) or another blood thinner. I also recommend taking a botanical formula that contains one or more of these herbs (in powdered form)—deglycyrrhizinated licorice root, slippery elm and marshmallow root. Follow label instructions and take until inflammatory bowel symptoms abate.

- **Eat healthful fats daily and fish twice a week.** Olive oil, avocado, soy milk and small portions of unsalted nuts (eight to 12) are good sources of healthful fat. (However, celiac patients should avoid peanuts, which can be hard for them to digest.) Fatty fish, such as salmon or halibut, is an easily digested protein source.

Warning: In people with celiac disease, high-fat dairy products, as well as fried foods, tend to worsen diarrhea.

- **Use plant-based enzymes.** Enzyme supplementation helps break down food and reduces post-meal bloating. Plant-based enzymes (available at natural-food stores) are usually derived from pineapple or papaya, and they are safe for just about everyone unless you have ulcers or you are allergic to pineapple or papaya.

Typical dose: One or two capsules per meal.

- **Get support. Avoiding gluten isn't easy,** but you'll feel much better if you do. For more advice, consult the Celiac Sprue Association/USA, 877-272-4272, *www.csaceliacs.org.*

*To minimize inflammation, follow the dietary advice indefinitely—and also continue to take the vitamin supplements to guard against a nutritional deficiency.

Probiotics Help Combat Celiac Disease

Researchers from the National Spanish Research Council have found that probiotics, healthful bacteria, can reduce inflammation and improve the quality of life for patients with celiac disease (CD), a digestive disorder that damages the small intestine and interferes with absorption of nutrients from food. Even people with CD who control the disorder by eating a gluten-free diet can benefit from a probiotic—to help them avoid symptoms when they digest even a small amount of gluten. CD patients can speak to their physicians about taking a probiotic containing healthy bacteria such as Bifidobacteria.

Mark A. Stengler, NMD, licensed naturopathic medical doctor in private practice, Encinitas, California... adjunct associate clinical professor at the National College of Natural Medicine, Portland, Oregon...author of *The Natural Physician's Healing Therapies* and coauthor of *Prescription for Natural Cures*.

7 Steps to Controlling Crohn's Disease

Andrew L. Rubman, ND, director, Southbury Clinic for Traditional Medicines, Southbury, Connecticut. American Society for Microbiology, *ASM.org*.

For people with digestive issues, life tends to revolve around what you can and can't eat and how far away from the nearest bathroom you dare to venture. That's certainly the case with Crohn's disease, which along with ulcerative colitis is one of the two most common forms of inflammatory bowel disease. Symptoms include wrenching stomach pain soon after eating (typically in the lower right side) and relentless diarrhea. It's relatively rare, but a new research finding suggests that people with Crohn's are seven times more apt to carry bacteria that cause a related gastrointestinal disease in cattle. The bacteria—Mycobacterium avium subspecies paratuberculosis or MAP—has been found in milk in American supermarkets, and some studies have found it in meat and cheese, raising the possibility that it may be passed up the food chain to people.

IT'S GUT WRENCHING

Whether or not bacteria such as MAP cause disease in the intestinal tract is largely a matter of threshold, explains *Daily Health News* contributing editor and naturopath Andrew L. Rubman, ND. A person with a healthy, intact digestive tract will likely be able to resist infectious bacteria. But the large intestine is the body's center of immunity, and when the digestive tissue becomes damaged and inflamed, it becomes more susceptible to invasive microorganisms, be it MAP or the increasingly infectious species of E. coli, Salmonella, and other causes of food poisoning. If the balance of healthy versus harmful bacteria is disrupted and/or tissue is damaged, people become less able to resist disease and it becomes more difficult to treat. Dr. Rubman here discusses more about Crohn's disease in general, and about natural support for people with this problem.

Little is known about the causes of Crohn's disease, although family history, an overactive immune system and inflammation response, and environmental triggers are all believed to play a role. It differs from ulcerative colitis (which causes similar symptoms) because inflammation is deeper in the intestinal wall and also potentially affects the entire gastrointestinal tract from mouth to anus. Ulcerative colitis primarily affects the colon and small intestine. There's no known cure for Crohn's and remedies offered by conventional medicine are riddled with problems. In September 2008, the FDA ordered stronger warnings for common Crohn's drugs—*infliximab* (Remicade), *adalimumab* (Humira) and *certolizumab pegol* (Cimzia)—after an association with the risk of developing fungal and yeast infections such as Candidiasis was found. Because conventional treatments have significant side effects—even when they work, and they don't always—more than half of people with Crohn's disease turn to natural therapies.

NATURAL SOLUTIONS

Since Crohn's disease affects different people in different ways, Dr. Rubman individualizes treatment for each patient, working in collaboration with his/her gastroenterologist—a strategy he suggests for all Crohn's patients since a combination of natural and mainstream treatments seems to be most effective.

Dr. Rubman's natural solutions include...

• **Probiotics.** Health requires maintaining a balance between good and bad bacteria in the digestive tract. Poor diet, stress or a digestive disorder such as Crohn's can result in a takeover of the system by "bad" bacteria, resulting in symptoms such as diarrhea and gas. To restore a proper floral balance, Dr. Rubman frequently prescribes a seven- to 10-day course of a probiotic supplement composed of Lactobacillus acidophilus and Bifidobacterium bifidus. However, he notes that it is important to have a stool test before treatment, in order to ensure the proper probiotic formula is administered.

• **Fish oil.** A small British study found that fish oil taken with antioxidants may help reduce the inflammation associated with Crohn's disease. Eat fatty fish such as salmon, mackerel or sardines two or three times a week. In addition, Dr. Rubman often prescribes one or more grams of an EPA-DHA fish oil capsule or liquid daily.

• **Vitamin B-12.** When the bowel has been damaged by Crohn's disease, it may no longer effectively absorb B-12. If you are tired and rundown, ask your doctor to test you. Dr. Rubman prefers to prescribe sublingual B-12 rather than B-12 shots. "It's as effective, less expensive and certainly more comfortable," he notes.

• **Acupuncture.** Acupuncture has traditionally been used to treat inflammatory bowel disease in China and is meeting with increasing mainstream acceptance in the US. A small German study suggests that acupuncture may help improve quality of life and general well-being in people with Crohn's disease by modulating symptoms and may even result in a small decrease in inflammatory markers in the blood. Find an acupuncturist in your area at the website of the American Association of Acupuncture & Oriental Medicine at *www.aaaomonline.org*.

• **Focus on whole foods, fresh fruits and vegetables.** A diet that contains lots of processed and fast foods—like white bread, sugary desserts, etc.—stresses the bowel and may trigger inflammation and worsen symptoms of Crohn's disease. Disease-causing microorganisms thrive on foods like these. Many people with Crohn's report that they feel better when they eliminate or significantly cut back on processed foods and place a greater emphasis on whole foods, fresh fruits and vegetables and moderate amounts of protein. Avoid milk and dairy products as well as trans fats, as they can also irritate the intestinal track.

• **Decompress.** Many people with Crohn's find that their symptoms worsen during stressful periods. If you find this to be the case, take steps to effectively manage stress. Do whatever works best for you—whether that is yoga or meditation or dancing or tennis.

• **Stay away from colonics.** Many people are tempted to turn to this "quick fix," but Dr. Rubman warns that colonics can backfire and worsen symptoms. The large intestine requires a healthy balance of microorganisms to function properly, and colonics indiscriminately wipe out the good with the bad under the thinly supported premise of detoxification.

To feel more in control of your disease and your life, learn more about Crohn's and connect with others who are going through the same things you are. Join message boards, chats, blogs and support groups (online or offline) at websites such as *www.ccfa.org*, or those listed at *http://crohns-disease-and-stress.com/support.html* and *http://ibdcrohns.about.com/od/onlinesupport/a/supportgroups.htm*. Acknowledging that a diagnosis of Crohn's disease is never good news, Dr. Rubman urges those who have the problem to be optimistic—it can often be controlled without drastic drugs or a draconian diet, and quality of life need not suffer.

Tired All the Time? A Doctor's Own Cure for Chronic Fatigue Syndrome

Jacob Teitelbaum, MD, a board-certified internist and medical director of the national Fibromyalgia and Fatigue Centers, headquartered in Austin, Texas. He is author of several books, including the best-selling *From Fatigued to Fantastic!* and *Real Cause, Real Cure* and creator of the free iPhone application *"Cures A–Z." EndFatigue.com*

Do you feel tired all the time? Many people do—and it could be a sign of chronic fatigue syndrome (CFS).

I contracted CFS when I was in medical school and dedicated the next 35 years of my life to finding an effective treatment, treating more than 15,000 CFS patients. I developed a treatment plan that has been proven effective in a scientific study and is regarded by many as the "gold standard" in CFS treatment.

My treatment works because I address the real cause of CFS...

THE REAL CAUSE

In October 2009, *Science* published a study that linked CFS to the XMRV virus (*xenotropic murine leukemia virus*). But study after study failed to replicate the results in *Science*—and subsequent research showed that XMRV probably was nothing more than a laboratory contaminant. In December 2011, *Science* retracted the study.

I'm not surprised. CFS is an energy crisis. When you use more energy than your body can manufacture—usually because of long-term physical and/or mental stresses—your body can "blow a fuse."

That fuse is the *hypothalamus*—the part of the brain that controls sleep...the hormone-producing endocrine system...hunger and thirst...mood...sex drive...blood flow...blood pressure...body temperature and sweating...and bowel function.

The main symptoms of the hypothalamic disorder of CFS are severe chronic fatigue and insomnia. Other symptoms include achiness...forgetfulness...brain fog...increased thirst...bowel disorders...recurrent infections...weight gain...and low libido.

Very important: Don't let your doctor tell you that your symptoms are "all in your head" or that CFS is "not a real disease." Many physicians aren't trained to recognize or treat CFS, and they question its validity. But the National Institutes of Health (NIH), the Centers for Disease Control and Prevention (CDC) and the Food and Drug Administration (FDA) all recognize CFS as real.

THE SHINE PROTOCOL

The hypothalamus isn't damaged in CFS, but it does go into "slow mode" until the energy crisis is treated. The SHINE protocol that I developed can treat the crisis, easing symptoms and restoring vitality in an average of six weeks. SHINE stands for Sleep restoration...Hormonal balancing...Infection treatment...Nutritional supplementation...and Exercise, as able.

Helpful: You may need to find a holistic physician to help you with the SHINE protocol. Go to one of the resource centers listed at *www.fibrocenter.com*, where physicians are up-to-date on CFS research and treatment.

• **Sleep restoration.** Getting enough sleep is critical to feeling better, but getting seven to eight hours of sleep (including deep, non-dreaming sleep, the most refreshing kind) can seem almost impossible.

That's because the hypothalamus controls sleep, and when it is malfunctioning, so is your sleep center. During the first six months of treatment for CFS you may need to try different types of sleep treatments to achieve eight hours of sleep a night—taking a low dose of each rather than a high dose of one. You should do this only under a doctor's supervision.

What to do: You can first try a natural sleep aid such as Revitalization Sleep Formula from Enzymatic Therapy, which contains six relaxing, sleep-inducing herbs. Take two to four capsules nightly, 30 to 90 minutes before bedtime.

If this doesn't work, talk to your doctor about sleeping pills. Be aware that many sleep medications make CFS worse because they cut down on deep sleep. The right types of sleep medication include *zolpidem* (Ambien)...*trazodone*...*clonazepam* (Klonopin)... and/or *pregabalin* (Lyrica).

OTC medications such as *doxylamine* (Unisom) and *diphenhydramine* (Benadryl) also can be effective at a bedtime dosage of 25 mg to 50 mg.

You probably can be weaned off sleep medications after six to 18 months of feeling well. But you may need to take a low dose of sleep medication (or a sleep-enhancing herbal formula) for the rest of your life—particularly during periods of high stress—to prevent a relapse.

• **Hormonal balancing.** The hypothalamus controls the production of hormones throughout your body. When it isn't up to par, you can have all kinds of hormonal imbalances and deficiencies.

What to do: It's helpful to treat CFS with bioidentical (as compared to synthetic) thyroid, adrenal, ovarian and/or testicular hormones, which have been shown to be safer than their synthetic counterparts.

Examples: Bioidentical estrogen and progesterone can help women who have CFS symptoms that worsen around their periods... bioidentical testosterone can benefit men whose blood test results are in the lowest 30% of the normal range...and energizing thyroid hormone can help most people with CFS.

A daily dose of 2.5 mg to 15 mg of natural hydrocortisone (such as prescription Cortef) can help reenergize exhausted adrenal glands. An NIH study found that Cortef caused some patients' adrenal glands to "go to sleep." But the dose in the study was two to three times as high as most patients need. Our studies show that ultra-low-dose Cortef is unlikely to cause adrenal suppression.

• **Infection treatment.** Most people with CFS have weakened immune systems, which can result in infections and a wide range of symptoms.

What to do: The most common infection in CFS is an overgrowth of the fungus Candida albicans. Sinusitis and bowel problems, such as gas, bloating, diarrhea and/or constipation, are common symptoms.

Treatment may include taking the antifungal *fluconazole* (Diflucan) daily for six weeks. Other ways to help banish Candida include a no-sugar diet, taking a daily probiotic supplement, regularly eating acidophilus-rich yogurt and taking an antifungal herbal supplement. (My favorite is Anti-Yeast from NutriElements.)

If after treating Candida your symptoms persist, you may need to be tested and treated for other infections.

• **Nutritional supplementation.** Everyone with CFS needs a therapeutic dose of energizing nutrients, such as B vitamins and magnesium.

What to do: Take Energy Revitalization Formula, the multinutrient powder that I formulated specifically for CFS patients. (All profits from this and other products I have formulated go to charity.)

Also helpful: Supplement your diet with ribose—a healthful sugar and key building block of cellular energy. In studies that my colleagues and I conducted involving nearly 300 people with CFS or fibromyalgia (a similar condition), ribose increased energy by an average of 60% after three weeks. Take five grams, three times a day, for 25 days, then reduce your dose to five grams twice a day.

• **Exercise.** Exercise is energizing for just about everyone, but if people with CFS exercise beyond a certain point, they may be bedridden the next day.

What to do: Begin with light exercise, such as walking or water-walking in a heated pool. Exercise only as much as you comfortably can (or start with five minutes). Increase exercise time by one minute every one to two days, as comfortable. When you get to the point that leaves you feeling worse the next day, cut back a bit to the comfortable level and continue that amount of exercise each day.

Natural Cures for Psoriasis

April Abernethy, ND, a naturopathic physician and interim chief scientific and medical officer at the National Psoriasis Foundation in Portland, Oregon. She is also a member of the board of directors at International Dermatology Outcome Measures, an organization working to establish common measurements of treatment effectiveness and outcomes.

Living day in and day out with psoriasis—known for its silvery scales and itchy, painful red patches (plaques) on the skin—is hard enough for the more than 7.5 million Americans who have the disease.

But researchers are now finding that people with psoriasis also may be more likely to develop other inflammation-based conditions such as diabetes and cardiovascular disease. People with psoriasis should be screened for these conditions and talk to their doctors about ways to reduce other risk factors they may have for these diseases.

Problem: Even though drugs, such as *apremilast* (Otezla) and *adalimumab* (Humira), that inhibit parts of the immune system involved in psoriasis are now available, any therapy that suppresses immunity can increase the risk for infections, gastrointestinal upset and other conditions.

Solution: There's mounting evidence that natural therapies can be used to reduce overall inflammation and help support the immune system. These drug-free approaches can improve the effectiveness of psoriasis medication and sometimes even eliminate the need for it (with your doctor's approval). First, try the dietary approaches in this article—they should result in improvements that increase over time. Supplements also can be used.

PUTTING YOUR DIET TO WORK

Eating the right foods (and using supplements when needed) can increase your ability to fight psoriasis on a systemic level by reducing inflammation and helping regulate your immune system—two key factors linked to psoriasis. *My advice...*

- **Go for anti-inflammatory foods.** Americans eat lots of processed foods—most of which promote inflammation in the body. Meanwhile, whole, nutrient-packed foods such as fresh fruits and vegetables help attack the inflammatory process that is increased in psoriasis.

Good choices: Beets, blueberries, kale or other leafy greens, salmon, garbanzo beans, quinoa, lentils, nuts and ginger. For other food choices, go to *www.psoriasis.org*, and search "anti-inflammatory diet."

- **Get more vitamin D.** People with psoriasis, like many Americans, are often deficient in vitamin D, which is known to help regulate immune function and inhibit inflammation. That's why it's important to consume foods that contain vitamin D, such as oysters, shrimp, salmon, sardines and any fortified milk. Vitamin D supplements also may be needed. If you have psoriasis, ask your doctor for a blood test to check your vitamin D level.

- **Spice things up.** Turmeric, which gives mustard its bright yellow color and curry its distinctive flavor, contains the medicinal compound curcumin.

A 2013 study published in the journal *BioFactors* showed that turmeric helps healthy, new skin cells form more quickly. If you don't like curry or mustard (you would need to eat 1 g to 3 g a day to get the therapeutic effect), you can try turmeric in supplement form—400 mg to 600 mg two to three times a day.

Talk to your doctor first if you take antacids, diabetes drugs or blood thinners, since turmeric may interfere with these medications—and if you have a history of gallstones (turmeric may cause stomach upset in these people).

- **Load up on omega-3s.** Get lots of anti-inflammatory omega-3 fatty acids.

Daily amounts needed to fight psoriasis: Seven ounces of salmon...a small avocado... or two tablespoons of ground flaxseed (store in the refrigerator to prevent spoilage). If you don't like fish and other omega-3–rich foods, consider taking 2 g to 3 g daily of a fish oil supplement. Choose one that has more EPA than DHA, and check with your doctor first if you take a blood thinner or diabetes medication—fish oil could interact with them.

A 2014 study published in the *Journal of the American Academy of Dermatology* found that among many common supplements taken by people with psoriasis, fish oil—which may reduce tumor necrosis factor-alpha (TNF-alpha), a protein associated with systemic inflammation—demonstrated the greatest benefit.

FOR CRACKED SKIN AND PLAQUES

Among the more troubling symptoms of psoriasis are dry, cracked skin (that may even bleed) and the red, scaly, itchy plaques that can develop on the elbows, scalp, torso and other areas.

What works best...

• **Oregon grape root.** When used topically, this powerful, little-known antibacterial herb (also called Mahonia) helps reduce skin irritation and topical infections common to people with psoriasis.

A 2013 research review published in the *British Journal of Dermatology* showed that Oregon grape root reduced the development of red, raised psoriasis plaques and healed psoriasis-related cracked skin.

Oregon grape root is found in tincture form at health-food stores, and you can add two or three drops to your favorite skin cream. The herb also can be found in over-the-counter creams containing 10% Mahonia, which has been shown to help control mild-to-moderate psoriasis plaques.

FOR ITCHING AND FLAKING

Soaking in the high concentration of mineral salts found in the Dead Sea in Israel is a centuries-old remedy for the itching and flaking associated with psoriasis.

What helps: Adding one-quarter to one-half cup of Dead Sea (or Epsom) salts to a warm (not hot) bath has been shown to ease itching skin and remove dead, flaking skin cells. Dead Sea salts have a higher concentration of minerals than Epsom salts and are available online and at health-food stores and spas.

A substantial body of research, including a study published in the *Journal of Dermatological Treatment*, has shown that psoriasis patients who regularly take such baths report significant improvements in itch and irritation levels within three weeks.

For even greater benefits: Mix the salts with colloidal oatmeal, such as Aveeno. Take these baths two to three times a week.

Pycnogenol Helps Psoriasis

Study titled "Improvement in signs and symptoms in psoriasis patients with Pycnogenol supplementation," published in *Panminerva Medica.*

When people talk about the "heartbreak of psoriasis"—a phrase from an old TV commercial—they aren't kidding, because psoriasis is no joke. This autoimmune disorder causes patches of skin to become scaly, red, hard, painful and itchy and to flake off of the body. It also can cause arthritis just about anywhere in the body...and it increases the risk for cardiovascular disease.

Some patients are able to manage their discomfort with skin lotions that soothe the skin and reduce inflammation. In other cases, therapy using light (phototherapy) helps. But sometimes symptoms are so severe that steroids and other powerful medications that suppress the immune system are used.

Problem: These drugs can increase the risk for high blood pressure, high blood sugar, glaucoma, cataracts, osteoporosis and skin cancer.

Possible solution: A supplement made from a particular type of tree can significantly ease psoriasis symptoms, improve quality of life and reduce the need for medication, according to new research. Interestingly, this same supplement has been shown to help with numerous other conditions, from joint pain to diabetes to sexual dysfunction.

BREAKTHROUGH

The 73 participants in the recent study all had moderate-to-severe psoriasis involving 10% to almost 50% of their body surface area and had tried phototherapy and/or systemic treatment (not just topical skin lotions) within the previous year. Throughout the study, all participants received standard psoriasis treatments as needed, prescribed at the discretion of their individual dermatologists...and patients recorded the drugs they used in diaries. In addition to standard care, half of the participants also took 150 mg per day of an oral supplement called Pycnogenol, an extract derived from the bark of the French maritime pine tree.

At the start of the study and again 12 weeks later, participants answered questionnaires about how psoriasis affected their quality of life...for example, whether it made them self-conscious or influenced their clothing choices. Lab tests and exams were done to determine each participant's level of skin moisture (the amount of water and oil in the skin, which is lower than normal with psoriasis)... the disease's severity (indicated by redness, skin hardening and flaking) and spread (the amount of skin affected)...and blood levels of free radicals, a sign of oxidative stress that can worsen symptoms.

By the end of the 12-week study period, participants in both groups showed improvement—not surprising, given that they all had been receiving care from their dermatologists. However, the Pycnogenol group showed significantly greater improvement than the control group. *For instance...*

Severity: By all measures, the Pycnogenol group fared better than the control group. Among Pycnogenol users, the average reduction in redness, skin hardening and flaking was about 45%...whereas in the control group, average reductions for these three symptoms ranged from 16% to 28%.

Spread: The area of skin affected by psoriasis was reduced by 20% in the Pycnogenol group, but by only 8% in the control group.

Moisture levels: Skin moisture rose from abnormally low to within the normal range in the Pycnogenol group, but not in the control group.

Quality of life: On the questionnaires, the Pycnogenol group reported improvement in all 12 areas that assessed quality of life...but the control group showed improvement in only half of the areas.

Standard treatments needed: Compared to the control group, the Pycnogenol users required less medication (as indicated by what their individual dermatologists found it necessary to prescribe). For example, only 31% of Pycnogenol users required topical or systemic steroids, compared with 68% of the control group.

Safety and tolerability: No side effects were reported in the Pycnogenol group and compliance was excellent, with more than 95% of the supplement doses being taken correctly. At the end of the study, 84% of participants in the Pycnogenol group opted to continue using the supplement because they found it beneficial.

HOW IT WORKS

Pycnogenol is a patented amalgam of more than three dozen antioxidants thought to reduce inflammation, swelling and oxidative stress and increase circulation of nutrients to the skin. Supporting this idea is the fact that, in this new study, participants' blood levels of free radicals fell significantly among the Pycnogenol users but not in the control group.

Now, we've all heard of the placebo effect, whereby patients taking a remedy—even if it's just a placebo—tend to improve because they expect the remedy to work. And that certainly could have been a factor in this study, especially given that the Pycnogenol users knew that they were taking a supplement and the control group was not given any placebo to counterbalance the placebo effect. Still, the fact that the Pycnogenol group showed greater improvement in objective measures (such as area of affected skin and moisture levels) and not just subjective measures (such as quality of life) suggests that the supplement had biological and not just psychological effects.

If you have psoriasis: Talk to your dermatologist about adding Pycnogenol to your treatment plan to see whether it improves your symptoms...and possibly even allows you to cut back on medication. The dosage used in this study was 50 mg three times per day.

Pycnogenol's many other uses: Psoriasis isn't the only condition helped by Pycnogenol. Other research has shown that the supplement also benefits people with diabetes, circulatory problems, joint pain, menopausal symptoms, menstrual cramps, chronic low blood pressure, erectile dysfunction and neuropathy.

The Missing Link in Lupus Care

Donald E. Thomas, Jr., MD, an assistant professor of medicine at the Uniformed Services University of the Health Sciences and an instructor of rheumatology at Walter Reed National Military Medical Center, both in Bethesda, Maryland. He is a member of the Medical-Scientific Advisory Council of the Lupus Foundation of America and the author of *The Lupus Encyclopedia*.

Lupus is a stubborn disease that most doctors treat with a variety of medications. If you're lucky, the disease can be controlled with only an antimalarial drug. Other people with lupus need a "cocktail" of powerful medications.

What most people don't realize: To control lupus, medication isn't enough.

Everyone with this disease needs to also manage the triggers that cause flare-ups and can lead to life-threatening complications. Avoiding triggers may allow lupus patients to take smaller doses of stronger immunosuppressant drugs (or even eliminate the need for them) and decrease the frequency and severity of lupus flares.

WHAT IS LUPUS?

About one and a half million Americans—mostly women—are affected with the autoimmune disease known as lupus. With this condition, the body produces antibodies, for unknown reasons, that attack the joints, skin, lungs, kidneys and/or other parts of the body.

About half of lupus patients have a mild form that affects only the joints and the skin. Others have a high risk for organ damage. Systemic lupus erythematosus (SLE), the most serious form of the disease, can affect virtually every part of the body, including not only the skin and kidneys but also the heart, brain and blood vessels.

The signs of SLE differ from patient to patient. One person might have a skin rash but no joint pain.

Someone else might have fatigue and pain but no rash. Others show early signs of heart or kidney disease. This variability makes SLE difficult to recognize—and to treat.

THE DANGER OF UV LIGHT

Even though most people with lupus do take the medication that's prescribed for the disease, they could benefit even more by carefully managing one of the most powerful lupus triggers—ultraviolet (UV) light.

Exposure to UV radiation—both from sunlight and indoor lighting—hurts everyone with SLE. UV light causes chemical changes in skin cells that trigger an increase in immune activity and inflammation. In about 30% of lupus patients, UV exposure causes a red rash on exposed skin (photosensitive rash). A so-called "butterfly" rash (covering the bridge of the nose and cheeks) also commonly occurs during or after sun exposure. Those who don't get a rash may still experience some organ damage.

Even brief exposures to UV light can be dangerous. For example, with the help of her doctor, a woman who continued having symptoms even though she always applied sunscreen before going outdoors discovered that her symptoms were triggered by the light from a photocopy machine.

Best UV protection measures...

- **Apply sunscreen lotion all day, every day.** Use a water-resistant product with an SPF of 30 or higher—and make sure that it blocks both UVA and UVB radiation. Apply it every few hours.

Good products: Anthelios SX by La Roche-Posay and sunscreen brands that contain Helioplex.

Also helpful: Use Rit Sun Guard laundry treatment for your outer garments. It adds an invisible coating to clothing that blocks more than 96% of the sun's harmful rays. The treatment lasts for up to 20 washings.

- **Use sunscreen even when you're indoors or driving.** The sunlight that comes through windows can trigger symptoms. Driving with the car windows up decreases UV penetration in the car.

- **Change the lightbulbs.** Indoor lighting also emits UV radiation. Halogen lights emit the most UV light, followed by fluorescent, including both tubes and bulbs.

Best choice: UV-free LED lights, widely available at hardware stores and online.

• **Don't use the UV drying units after manicures or pedicures.** Let the nail polish dry on its own. Or use a dryer that contains a fan but no light.

WHAT ALSO HELPS

Avoiding ultraviolet (UV) light isn't the only self-care step to follow if you have systemic lupus erythematosus (SLE). *Three other important recommendations...*

• **Boost your vitamin D.** Most people with SLE don't produce enough of this important nutrient, in part because they avoid the sun. (Vitamin D is produced in the skin following sun exposure.) The optimal blood level for a person with lupus is around 40 ng/mL. If you've been diagnosed with SLE, your doctor probably orders blood tests four times a year. Be sure that he/she checks your vitamin D level each time, then prescribes an appropriate dose of vitamin D supplement, as needed.

• **Get more omega-3s.** Everyone with SLE should eat fish and other foods high in omega-3 fatty acids, such as flaxseed and walnuts. These healthful fats are thought to ease excessive immune activity and reduce inflammation in the body.

Also: Studies suggest that food sources of omega-3s are more effective than supplements for this disease. If you're not a fish lover, you can get more omega-3s by drinking protein shakes spiked with ground walnuts and flaxseed. One tablespoon daily of olive oil also has been found to have anti-inflammatory properties.

• **Ask about DHEA.** The naturally occurring hormone dehydroepiandrosterone (DHEA) is converted in the body into testosterone and estrogen. Many patients with SLE have levels that are lower than normal. Some patients who take DHEA may be able to reduce their doses of steroid medications—and thus reduce side effects, such as weight gain, diabetes, brittle bones, glaucoma and cataracts.

Important: Take DHEA only under a doctor's supervision, since it can raise risk for certain cancers in some people. Over-the-counter products can contain much lower amounts of the active ingredient than what's listed on the label. Ask your doctor to write a prescription, and get it filled at a compounding pharmacy

Gentle Touch Offers Remedy for Bell's Palsy, Fibromyalgia and More

Thomas A. Kruzel, ND, who practices CST at the Rockwood Natural Medicine Clinic in Scottsdale, Arizona. He is the former vice president of clinical affairs and chief medical officer at the Southwest College of Naturopathic Medicine in Phoenix.

Can a gentle scalp massage really cure illnesses and injuries as diverse as carpal tunnel syndrome and Bell's palsy—not to mention healing long-ago trauma and emotional distress? As a matter of fact, it can—if you put yourself in the hands of a trained and skilled craniosacral therapist. Of the many alternative therapies, craniosacral therapy (CST) is surely one of the most unusual. CST is a variation of osteopathic and chiropractic medicine, where a therapist gently places his/her hands atop your skull and feels for the oscillation frequency—the small degree of movement that the skull bones naturally retain throughout life. This is a subtle motion of the membrane encasing the cerebrospinal fluid in the brain and spinal cord down to the sacrum, the bone at the bottom of the spine. The therapist gently manipulates the bones to bring them back into proper alignment. It feels like a very gentle massage, but CST is a potent healing therapy for a wide variety of disorders, including chronic pain, headaches, carpal tunnel syndrome, fibromyalgia, learning disabilities, depression, post traumatic stress disorder, vertigo, whiplash injury, TMJ, herniated disc pain and musculoskeletal problems. While surprising and somewhat inexplicable, even many skeptics acknowledge that "sometimes it just works."

HOW CST WORKS

CST is based on research from the early part of the last century by osteopathic doctor William Garner Sutherland, DO. His work centered on the theory that the skull bones have a rhythm that he called the "breath of life" and others call "the vital force." The theory now associated with CST, besides one of treating illness, is that physical or emotional trauma, even from birth, can cause a disturbance in this oscillation that can last for years. Cerebrospinal fluid affects nerves that control all tissues in the body, so any disruption can contribute to a wide range of problems. It's believed that restoring its natural flow enables the body to begin healing itself.

Here in the US, thousands of osteopathic doctors, naturopathic doctors, chiropractors and massage therapists are also CST practitioners. But you probably won't be surprised to learn that the medical world considers CST just this side of loony. Skeptics say its very basis is impossible because the skull bones fuse completely in childhood. CST practitioners respond that this is not so—the skull bones have motion throughout life. They say that even the elderly continue to respond well to CST.

To find out more about this curious and increasingly popular therapy, we spoke with Thomas A. Kruzel, ND, who practices CST at the Rockwood Natural Medicine Clinic in Scottsdale, Arizona. He is the former vice president of clinical affairs and chief medical officer at the Southwest College of Naturopathic Medicine in Phoenix. Dr. Kruzel likens the concept of opening up cerebrospinal fluid flow to the underlying principles of chiropractic in which "communication channels" are realigned throughout the body. CST does not itself heal problems—it releases inertia and congestion, thereby returning homeostasis and enhancing the body's ability to heal and regulate itself.

Dr. Kruzel says the hardest part of his CST training was learning to discern the motion in the skull, which he describes as something like an undulation. When a patient comes to see him, he places his hands on his/her head to get an exact sense of this person's motion. This gives him information he uses in clearing restrictions in the pumping of the fluid through the brain, into the spinal column and the emanating nerve roots. Sometimes he may also gently manipulate the lower part of the spine in an osteopathic fashion to restore tandem movement in the sacrum and the spine.

WHAT WILL YOU FEEL?

Patients don't always feel the change as it is occurring, he says, but they often experience a kind of gastrointestinal release such as a gurgling in the bowels when the fluid is freed up. Constipated patients frequently find that their bowels begin moving again after a treatment. Dr. Kruzel says in older people CST helps reduce risk of stroke and of falling, and that for children it helps with ADD as well as learning disabilities and even possibly autism. Virtually all patients, adults and children alike, find the treatment to be extremely relaxing, he says.

Dr. Kruzel often uses CST to treat Bell's palsy. He says he can correct it very quickly if the patient comes in right after onset. He has used it for hypertension—he says it brings some patients' pressure back to normal. Some parents of newborns bring their baby for a treatment after the emotional and physical rigors of birth. Another frequent reason people come to him is after an athletic or other injury. One patient had been severely injured in a car accident the previous year. She had many broken bones and went through a year of physical rehab, but even after her physical injuries had healed she struggled with depression. When she came to Dr. Kruzel, he found that she had almost no cranial motion because the flow of the fluid had been truncated when her pelvis broke. He treated her regularly for a time and today she is doing very well physically and mentally.

Patients remain fully clothed for CST treatment. Sessions usually last 30 minutes to one hour. Patients may come only one or two times, or several times a week for a number of months. Elderly patients tend to check in for a session once every few months, says Dr. Kruzel. Costs vary by area of the country and many insurance plans cover the cost when treatment is from an osteopathic or naturopathic doctor.

The technique may seem simplistic, even magical—but craniosacral therapy is actually a precise skill a good therapist has trained long and hard to learn. You can find a CST practitioner near you by going to the site of the late osteopathic doctor John Upledger, DO, OMM, *http://www.upledger.com/*. (Dr. Upledger was instrumental in heightening awareness of CST in this country during the 1980s and today his institute trains many people in it.) Another resource is the Craniosacral Therapy Association of North America, which provides CST standards. Since quality may vary widely in the absence of national standards, it's helpful to get a recommendation from someone you trust who has personal experience with a particular therapist.

Fibromyalgia... Make the Pain Go Away

Alan C. Logan, ND, lecturer at Harvard School of Continuing Medical Education in Boston and nutrition editor of the *International Journal of Naturopathic Medicine.* He is coauthor of *Hope and Help for Chronic Fatigue Syndrome* and *Fibromyalgia. DrLogan.com.*

Muscle aches targeting your tenderest spots...fatigue so severe that you can scarcely stand up...sleep disturbances that keep you from ever feeling rested. If these symptoms sound familiar, the problem may be fibromyalgia.

Some doctors claim that fibromyalgia is "all in the head." Yet this potentially debilitating condition is very real to the estimated five million Americans who have it—with women outnumbering men nine-to-one. As yet, it has no known cause or cure. Conventional medical care often fails to bring relief—but many alternative therapies may ease fibromyalgia symptoms. *What you need to know to feel better...*

FIGURING IT OUT

No lab test can detect fibromyalgia, and patients' blood work often appears normal. Diagnosis is based on symptoms—widespread pain that persists for at least three months plus abnormal tenderness at 11 or more of 18 specific spots on the neck, shoulders, chest, back, hips, thighs, knees and elbows. Many patients also experience headache...stiff joints...constipation or diarrhea...depression...sleep problems...and/or sensitivity to lights, sounds or smells.

Theories as to the cause of fibromyalgia include an excess of, or oversensitivity to, the neurotransmitters (brain chemicals) that signal pain...or changes in muscle metabolism and/or hormones that affect nerve activity.

Anti-inflammatory drugs, painkillers and antidepressants are only moderately effective for fibromyalgia symptoms. What's more, because fibromyalgia patients often are very sensitive to medication, they're more likely than other people to experience side effects.

Bottom line: If drugs help you and do not cause side effects, consider complementing your medication with the therapies below. If medication is not effective or appropriate, alternative therapies offer the best chance for relief.

SOOTHING SUPPLEMENTS

The supplements below are listed in the order in which I believe they are likely to be effective for fibromyalgia. All are available at health-food stores and online. Try the first one for six to eight weeks. If it helps, continue indefinitely. If it doesn't help, discontinue use. For greater relief, try the others one at a time for six to eight weeks, continuing with any or all that work for you. They generally are safe and, unless otherwise noted, can be taken indefinitely—but get your doctor's approval before using them. As a general precaution, do not use while pregnant or breast-feeding.

- **Omega-3 fatty acids,** such as ***eicosapentaenoic acid*** (EPA) and *docosahexaenoic acid* (DHA), may ease pain by reducing inflammation.

Source: Fish oil liquid or capsules.

Dosage: 3 grams (g) daily of combined EPA and DHA.

- ***S-adenosylmethionine*** **(SAM-e),** a naturally occurring compound in the body, may reduce fatigue and depression by increasing levels of the neurotransmitter serotonin.

Dosage: 800 mg to 1,200 mg daily. Do not use SAM-e if you take antidepressants or have diabetes.

- ***Coenzyme Q10*** **(CoQ10)**—and *ginkgo biloba,* taken together, may have a synergistic effect. CoQ10, a vitamin-like substance, boosts cellular energy. Ginkgo biloba, an herb, improves blood flow.

Dosage: 200 milligrams (mg) daily of each.

• **Chlorella,** a type of green algae, reduced fibromyalgia pain by 22% in one study.

Possible reasons: It may boost the immune system and/or increase absorption of essential nutrients.

Dosage: 5 g to 10 g daily.

• **Nicotinamide adenine dehydrogenase (NADH), a vitamin-like substance, may increase energy within cells and facilitate production of the neurotransmitter dopamine, which affects mood.**

Dosage: 10 mg daily.

• **Melatonin, a hormone that regulates the "body clock," can improve sleep.**

Dosage: 3 mg daily. Melatonin can affect other hormones, so using it for more than one month requires close medical supervision.

• **Probiotics,** beneficial intestinal bacteria, combat harmful bacteria that cause digestive distress…and may influence inflammatory chemicals that trigger pain and depression.

Dosage: One billion colony forming units (CFU) of lactobacillus and/or bifidobacterium daily.

MORE ALTERNATIVE THERAPIES

Ask your doctor about…

• **Acupuncture.** This involves inserting thin needles into points along the body's meridians (energy pathways) to enhance flow of qi (life force). This may release endorphins that relieve pain.

Referrals: American Association of Acupuncture and Oriental Medicine, 866-455-7999, *www.aaaomonline.org.*

• **Aromatherapy.** This lifts mood, making pain less bothersome.

To use: Place two or three drops of jasmine or lavender essential oil in an aromatherapy diffuser.

• **Mind-body techniques.** These reduce stress.

Try: Meditation, deep breathing, biofeedback. For DVDs and CDs on techniques, contact the Benson-Henry Institute for Mind-Body Medicine (617-643-6090, *www.massgeneral.org/bhi.*

• **Mud packs.** In one study, mud packs were heated to between 104°F and 113°F and applied to patients' sore areas for 15 minutes during 12 separate sessions. Pain, fatigue and physical function all improved.

Theory: Mud draws heat to muscles, reducing pain and stiffness.

Best: Ask a holistic doctor for a referral to a medical spa.

• **Myofascial trigger-point therapy.** This focuses on tender muscle areas that are anatomically similar to acupuncture points. Practitioners inject these "trigger points" with an anesthetic, then stretch muscles to relieve pain.

Referrals: National Association of Myofascial Trigger Point Therapists, *www.myofascialtherapy.org.*

• **Pool therapy.** Exercises done in a heated swimming pool for one hour three times weekly for several months can reduce fibromyalgia pain and increase stamina.

Referrals: Ask a physical therapist.

For a referral to a doctor who specializes in fibromyalgia, contact the National Fibromyalgia Association (714-921-0150, *www.fmaware.org*).

Fibromyalgia Relieved By Water Exercise

In an eight-month study of 33 women with fibromyalgia (characterized by painful muscles, ligaments and tendons), those who participated in a supervised exercise program in a heated swimming pool for 60 minutes three times weekly had fewer symptoms than nonexercisers.

Theory: Warm water induces relaxation, which helps fight pain. Ask your doctor if water workouts are an option for you.

Narcís Gusi, PhD, professor, University of Extremadura, Cáceres, Spain.

Supplement Help for Fibromyalgia

Mark A. Stengler, NMD, licensed naturopathic medical doctor in private practice, Encinitas, California...adjunct associate clinical professor at the National College of Natural Medicine, Portland, Oregon...author of *The Natural Physician's Healing Therapies* and coauthor of *Prescription for Natural Cures*.

Fibromyalgia is a chronic condition characterized by muscle pain and sore spots called tender points. It may be linked to an inability to produce or use adenosine triphosphate (ATP), an energy-carrying molecule essential for muscle function.

Several natural substances improve cellular energy production, reduce pain signals from cells and boost a person's overall energy. They are sold in health-food stores and generally are safe. Try the natural sugar ribose (5 g in powder form, twice daily, mixed with water)...magnesium (250 mg two or three times daily)...malic acid (1,200 mg twice daily)...and vitamin-like coenzyme Q10 (200 mg to 300 mg daily).

The amino acid 5-*hydroxytryptophan* (5-HTP) can relieve musculoskeletal and other symptoms, such as insomnia—take 100 milligrams (mg) three times daily. Do not take 5-HTP if you use an antidepressant or an antianxiety drug.

On this regimen, you should see improvement within two weeks. If not, the cause may be a deficiency of the thyroid hormones needed to stimulate energy production in cells. If blood tests confirm the diagnosis, bioidentical hormone replacement therapy may be warranted.

Sleeping Pill Helps Fibromyalgia and Chronic Fatigue

Relief for fibromyalgia and chronic fatigue symptoms may come from a prescription sleeping pill. Taken at bedtime, Xyrem (chemical name sodium oxybate) can help reduce the pain, fatigue, stiffness, disturbed sleep patterns and other symptoms associated with fibromyalgia and chronic fatigue syndrome (CFS). But Xyrem is not approved for this use—the FDA has approved it only for the treatment of narcolepsy (severe daytime sleepiness)—so insurers may not cover the cost unless it is needed for the FDA-approved purpose.

Less expensive alternative: The dietary supplement D-Ribose, available online and in health-food stores. It is a simple sugar found naturally in the body and may be even more effective than Xyrem.

Jacob Teitelbaum, MD, author of *The Fatigue and Fibromyalgia Solution. EndFatigue.com.*

Fibromyalgia: New Research Helps Unravel the Mystery

Anne Louise Oaklander, MD, PhD, an associate professor of neurology at Harvard Medical School and director of a diagnostic and research laboratory at Massachusetts General Hospital that studies neurological causes of chronic pain and itch, both in Boston. Dr. Oaklander serves on the editorial boards for the journals *PAIN and Neurology Today* and serves on panels for the National Institutes of Health, the Food and Drug Administration and the Institute of Medicine.

For the roughly five million American adults with fibromyalgia, the muscle soreness, body aches and telltale painful "tender points" on the shoulders, neck, back, hips, arms and legs are all too familiar.

But until very recently, the condition was a much maligned mystery illness. In fact, some doctors told patient after patient that the condition was "all in your head" because no cause could be identified.

Now: The medical naysayers are rethinking fibromyalgia because of new research showing that the condition does have an identifiable cause in some patients. Substantial numbers of people with fibromyalgia have been found to have a little-known—but testable—condition that triggers faulty signals from tiny nerves all over the body, possibly causing the symptoms of fibromyalgia.

In addition to chronic widespread pain, sufferers often have various other symptoms, such as fatigue, insomnia, digestive problems (including constipation and nausea), and memory and concentration difficulties commonly known as "fibro fog." People with fibromyalgia also may experience numbness, tingling and/or burning in the hands, arms, feet and/or legs, chronic headaches, depression and even frequent urges to urinate.

WHAT THE NEW RESEARCH HAS UNCOVERED

Even though the American College of Rheumatology has recognized fibromyalgia as an illness since 1990, most doctors have been uneasy about diagnosing it because there has been no way to test for the condition. X-rays and blood tests can rule out other conditions, such as rheumatoid arthritis, but fibromyalgia has been a diagnosis based on symptoms alone. The new research findings may change that.

What important new studies have uncovered: According to several studies published in 2013, one conducted by researchers at Massachusetts General Hospital, nearly half of people with fibromyalgia have evidence of a disease called small-fiber polyneuropathy (SFPN).

A form of peripheral neuropathy, SFPN involves damage to specific nerve cells that can trigger pain and the digestive problems that often accompany fibromyalgia.

How was this discovery made? Skin biopsies were the key tests that uncovered abnormalities in the nerve cells of 40% of SFPN sufferers who were tested.

Meanwhile, researchers at Albany Medical College found another interesting piece of the puzzle—excessive nerve fibers lining the blood vessels within the skin of people with fibromyalgia. Since these fibers control the flow of blood, oxygen and nutrients to muscles during exercise, this abnormality might explain the deep muscle pain of fibromyalgia.

These new findings do not mean that the name has been changed—fibromyalgia (fibro, the Latin term for fibrous tissue...and the Greek words *myo*, meaning muscle...and *algia,* meaning pain) perfectly describes the condition's primary symptoms of chronic, widespread muscle pain.

Even though the discoveries described above don't apply to all fibromyalgia patients, they give researchers some clues to follow toward cracking the disease's formidable mystery.

NEW HOPE FOR BETTER TREATMENTS

Scientists may be intrigued by this new evidence, but what does it mean for people who suffer from fibromyalgia? The most immediate—and significant—implication has to do with testing. Fibromyalgia symptoms can vary widely, so the diagnosis can be challenging even for experienced rheumatologists.

Now that fibromyalgia has been linked to SFPN, people with fibromyalgia symptoms may want to ask their doctors about testing for SFPN. A skin biopsy from the lower leg is currently the best way to diagnose SFPN. The sample can be mailed to an accredited lab—for example, at Massachusetts General Hospital—for analysis. It is usually covered by insurance.

In the meantime, the following medications (in addition to the nondrug approaches described on the next page) can help relieve symptoms of fibromyalgia...

- **FDA-approved medications.** *Pregabalin* (Lyrica), an anticonvulsant...and *duloxetine* (Cymbalta) and *milnacipran* HCI (Savella), both serotonin and norepinephrine reuptake inhibitors (SNRIs), have been shown to reduce pain and improve function for some people with fibromyalgia. Researchers do not know exactly why these drugs work, but some data suggest that they affect pain signaling in the brain and spinal cord.

- **Nortriptyline (Pamelor).** An older tricyclic antidepressant that has also been proven effective for chronic pain relief, nortriptyline is not specifically FDA-approved for fibromyalgia. But it and several other off-label medications, including the anticonvulsant *gabapentin* (Neurontin)—available cheaply as generic drugs—have strong data supporting their use for fibromyalgia.

Nondrug approaches...

Medication isn't the only treatment for fibromyalgia symptoms. *Other good options...*

• **Exercise.** Don't think this is just another plug for exercise. The research showing exercise's effect on fibromyalgia pain is very strong. Whether it's walking, strength training or stretching, exercise improves emotional well-being and lessens muscle wasting, an unfortunate consequence of avoiding exercise due to pain.

• **Vitamin D.** This inexpensive vitamin supplement has just begun to prove its mettle for some people with fibromyalgia. A study published in January 2014 in the journal *Pain* indicates that vitamin D supplements may reduce chronic pain linked to fibromyalgia for those whose blood tests show a low level of the nutrient. The optimal vitamin D dose depends on the level of deficiency.

Key to Fibromyalgia Pain Lies in the Skin of the Palms

Frank L. Rice, PhD, CEO and chief scientist, Integrated Tissue Dynamics, Rensselaer, New York, and former professor, Center for Neuropharmacology and Neuroscience, Albany Medical College, Albany, New York. His study was published in *Pain Medicine. Intidyn.com.*

People with fibromyalgia experience near-constant widespread pain, their hands and feet ache, and they often feel exhausted and foggy-brained. Yet because there is no blood test, lab test or scan that can confirm fibromyalgia, many doctors are skeptical about its very existence and suspect the problem is "all in the patient's head."

Finally, that's about to change—because researchers at last have discovered a surprising key to this confounding and debilitating condition. The problem isn't in patients' heads—it's in the skin of their hands.

BLOOD FLOW BASICS

To understand the new research, you first need to understand some basics about circulation. After leaving the heart, oxygenated blood travels through arteries and then into arterioles (small arteries) before entering the tiny capillaries. Oxygen and nutrients leave the capillaries to get into the body's tissues and cells, and waste enters the capillaries. The blood then enters venules (small veins) and then larger veins, ultimately traveling to the lungs so it can be reoxygenated and filtered. And the cycle constantly repeats.

But not all blood enters the capillaries. Some blood flows directly from arteries into veins via arteriole-venule (AV) shunts, valves that open and close to control the passage of blood. The valves respond to cues from the nervous system, mainly to regulate body temperature. When a person is too hot, the shunts close, forcing the blood into the skin's capillaries, where the heat can leave the body. When a person is cold, the shunts open, allowing the blood to flow into the venules and conserving heat. The parts of the body where AV shunts are most plentiful are the cheeks, nose, soles of the feet and palms of the hands. The skin in those areas is different—smooth, hairless and noticeably more sensitive to heat and cold.

EXAMINING SHUNTS

For the new study, researchers took small samples of skin from the palms of the hands of women with and without fibromyalgia. (Women are more than twice as likely to be diagnosed with fibromyalgia as men, and the hands are particularly painful in fibromyalgia sufferers.) Using special dyes, filters and lenses, the researchers closely examined many structures in the skin that are supplied by nerve fibers, including the AV shunts.

Startling finding: The number of AV shunts didn't differ between the two groups, but their size did. In fact, the AV shunts in women with fibromyalgia were nearly four times larger and had roughly two to eight times as many nerve fibers as those in women without fibromyalgia. This most likely explains why cold exacerbates fibromyalgia symptoms...and it also leads to a compelling theory about the development of fibromyalgia pain and fatigue.

As mentioned before, the AV shunts open and close in response to temperature—but they also regulate blood flow to other tissues, including muscles, when increased blood flow is needed, such as during movement and exercise. If the AV shunts are unable to function properly due to the presence of excessive nerve fibers, the mismanaged blood flow could be the source of the widespread muscle pain, achiness, fatigue and cognitive problems that plague fibromyalgia patients. The researchers are now investigating why there are excess nerve fibers around the shunts. Study leader Frank L. Rice, PhD, explained, "The AV shunts are sites where sensory nerve fibers are intermingled with nerve fibers of the sympathetic nervous system, which is activated by stress. The excess nerves involve mostly the sensory fibers that might be proliferating in response to stress activation of the sympathetic fibers."

GETTING HELP

Hopefully, this new information about fibromyalgia patients will lead to effective treatments…but in the meantime, it's reassuring to know that there is a real pathology involved in the disorder.

Dr. Rice's team is currently investigating whether men with fibromyalgia have a similar pathology to that discovered in women. Preliminary results indicate that women normally have more of the sensory fibers affiliated with the AV shunts, which may put them at greater risk of having excess fibers. Still, fibromyalgia is thought to be vastly underdiagnosed in men. According to recent research from the Mayo Clinic, 19 out of 20 men likely to have the disorder are not being properly diagnosed.

Bottom line: Male or female, if you have symptoms that suggest fibromyalgia and your doctor dismisses them, get a second opinion. To find a health-care provider who is experienced in detecting and treating this disorder, check the National Fibromyalgia Association online directory. For a wealth of information about fibromyalgia and Dr. Rice's ongoing research, visit the website of Integrated Tissue Dynamics.

Lou Gehrig's Disease

Thomas Kruzel, ND, naturopathic physician, Rockwood Natural Medicine Clinic, Scottsdale, Arizona.

Are there any self-care strategies that might help an individual with amyotrophic lateral sclerosis be more comfortable?

ALS, also known as Lou Gehrig's disease, is a rare neurodegenerative disorder that affects nerve cells in the brain and spinal cord. It's a progressive disease and results in total paralysis. But, no two ALS patients will progress at the same rate.

Patients should take a daily multivitamin and mineral supplement without iron that includes B-complex, C, D and E vitamins…and calcium and magnesium to help strengthen the immune system as well as muscle and nerve function.

The progression of muscle weakness, cramping and spasms can be eased with the homeopathic remedies Magnesium phosphoricum, Cuprum metallicum, Plumbum metallicum or nux vomica (follow label instructions for dosage). Alternating hot and cold compresses to areas with muscle cramps will help increase blood flow and reduce pain. Acupuncture can also help relieve symptoms.

How to Fight MS Without Drugs

George Jelinek, MD, an emergency physician with professorial appointments at University of Melbourne and Monash University, both in Melbourne, Australia. He was the founding editor of *Emergency Medicine Australasia* and is author of *Overcoming Multiple Sclerosis: An Evidence-Based Guide to Recovery. OvercomingMultipleSclerosis.org.*

Multiple sclerosis (MS) is one of the most common nerve diseases. It's also among the most frightening because there isn't a cure. Patients imagine a future that includes extreme fatigue, muscle weakness, pain and, in some cases, premature death.

Many patients have a form of MS known as relapsing-remitting, in which the disease generally flares up every year or two. The relapses are followed by periods of remission.

However, there's a way to reduce symptoms and the frequency of relapses by up to 95%. All you need to do is make some lifestyle changes. And these lifestyle changes may be more effective than medications at slowing, and sometimes stopping, the disease's progression.

Numerous studies have shown that people who modify their diets and make other lifestyle changes often can remain symptom-free for decades. I'm a good example—I was diagnosed with MS in 1999, when I was 45. I've had no relapses.

WHAT MS DOES

MS, an autoimmune disease, damages the fatty myelin sheath that surrounds nerves in the brain and spinal cord. The immune system kicks in and produces inflammation that strips away the myelin and causes nerve scarring. This impairs the transmission of nerve impulses.

The central nervous system can sometimes regenerate damaged nerve tissue—but only if there's minimal demyelination. *The key way to reduce MS relapses is to reduce demyelination. Here are the strategies that work best...*

ELIMINATE SATURATED FAT

One long-term study of MS followed the same group of patients for 34 years. At the beginning, participants averaged one to 1.2 relapses a year. This is typical for most MS patients. The patients who switched to a diet that was very low in saturated fat averaged just 0.05 relapses within three years. This translates to about one relapse every 20 years.

MS patients tend to accumulate more saturated fat in their cell membranes than those without the disease. Saturated fat is thought to stimulate the Th1 response, the release of myelin-damaging inflammatory chemicals by immune cells.

Patients who switch to a vegetarian diet—and avoid processed foods, which often are high in saturated fat—can reduce their relapse rate by about 95%. In contrast, most medications achieve only about a 30% reduction.

I advise patients not to eat red meat, commercial baked goods or anything that is deep-fried. They also should avoid eggs (except for the whites) and dairy, including reduced-fat cheese and reduced-fat milk. There's some evidence that a protein in dairy may be just as likely as saturated fat to trigger relapses.

MORE FISH

Patients who consume the most omega-3 fatty acids from fish (or fish-oil supplements) have about 30% fewer relapses than those who get the least. These fatty acids can reduce relapses even in patients who continue to eat meat or other foods that are high in saturated fat. The omega-3s make cell membranes more fluid and flexible. This improves their responsiveness to chemical signals and helps them resist attacks on the immune system. Omega-3s also help the body suppress inflammation.

The optimal amount is thought to be about 20 grams (g)—a little less than three-quarters of an ounce—of fish oil daily. I eat fish three or four days a week. I usually choose oily fish, such as sardines or mackerel. I take fish-oil supplements only on the days when I don't eat fish.

OMEGA-3S FROM FLAX

Flaxseed oil is the best nonfish source of omega-3s. It has a slightly buttery taste that I enjoy. I put it on salads or pasta. It's good for patients who don't like fish or who want a less expensive alternative to fish-oil supplements.

There's been a lot of debate about the use of flaxseed oil as a source of omega-3s. This is because only a small percentage of the alpha-linolenic acid in flaxseed oil is converted in the body into the healthful oils found in fish—EPA (eicosapentaenoic acid) and DHA (docosahexaenoic acid). I recommend two tablespoons of flaxseed oil daily.

VITAMIN D

Patients with MS tend to feel better, and have fewer relapses, when they spend time in the sun. A study published in *Occupational and Environmental Medicine* in 2000 found that people with MS who got the most sun were 76% less likely to die from MS than those without sun exposure.

The body synthesizes vitamin D from sunshine. Vitamin D interacts with the receptors on white blood cells involved in the MS immune response. One study found that MS patients had the lowest relapse rates in mid-to-late summer, when UV exposure from sunlight is highest.

People are understandably nervous about getting too much sun. But in moderation, skin cancer risk is low. I advise patients to get 10 to 15 minutes of all-over sun (by wearing a bathing suit) three to five times a week. If you don't live where you can do that year-round, take a vitamin D supplement.

The long-running Nurses Health Study found that women who took a daily multinutrient that contained 400 international units (IU) of vitamin D were 40% less likely to get MS than those who didn't. Patients who already have MS are less likely to have relapses—and will probably have milder symptoms when they do—if they supplement regularly.

I recommend that MS patients take 5,000 IU of vitamin D on overcast days or on days when they don't get outside. Use the D-3 form—it's similar to the vitamin D from sun exposure.

BOOST ENERGY

Regular exercise improves energy and muscle strength and may reduce MS relapses. It also improves the body's ability to cope with the physical challenges that occur during relapses.

I live in a climate that's warm year-round, so I swim outdoors five or six days a week. It's good exercise, and I get my "dose" of sunshine at the same time.

Bonus: Being in water prevents overheating from exercise, a common problem for people with MS.

MEDITATE

A 2006 review in *Journal of Alternative and Complementary Medicine* found that meditation helps relieve symptoms of autoimmune illnesses. It also improves mood, which helps patients to deal positively with MS.

I meditate every day for 30 minutes, usually when I get home from work. The evidence suggests that people who can find the time to do this twice a day probably get even more benefits.

Meditation doesn't have to be a complex spiritual practice. You can just sit in a comfortable chair, relax and focus on your breathing. If you have stressful thoughts, notice them. Then let them go.

Dr. Terry Wahls's Brain-Boosting Diet Helped Her Conquer Multiple Sclerosis

Terry L. Wahls, MD, an internist and clinical professor of medicine at the University of Iowa Carver College of Medicine in Iowa City and president of the Wahls Foundation, *TerryWahls.com,* which supports research and provides education to the public about managing multiple sclerosis and other chronic diseases. She is the author of *Minding My Mitochondria: How I Overcame Secondary Progressive Multiple Sclerosis and Got Out of My Wheelchair.*

At age 44, I was diagnosed with multiple sclerosis (MS). Three years later, when I became dependent on a wheelchair, my MS was classified as "secondary progressive," meaning that the disease was steadily progressing with no periods of improvement. I kept getting weaker, even though I was receiving widely used treatments for MS including chemotherapy and immune-suppressing medications.

Now: Thanks to the regimen I designed, I haven't needed a wheelchair or even a cane for more than three years. I ride to work on my bicycle, my energy is good and I've stopped taking medication to treat my MS. What happened?

Here's what I credit for my dramatic turnaround—and a description of how it might help you, as well. Because MS is a neurological disease, this program is designed to also help people who are concerned about dementia or Parkinson's disease, have depression or have suffered a traumatic brain injury or stroke.

FINDING A SOLUTION

With the help of my medical training, I began poring over the medical literature and designed my own treatment protocol in 2007 based on my theories of what allowed MS to develop and progress.

In people with MS, immune cells damage the myelin sheath, protein and fatty substances that surround nerve cells in the brain and spinal cord. This results in slower nerve signals, which lead to muscle weakness, a lack of balance and muscle coordination, bladder or bowel spasms, blurred vision and other symptoms.

Medications can reduce symptoms, but they don't accelerate nerve signals. As a result, MS patients battle physical and neurological disability—experienced either episodically or in a steady, unrelenting course. The disease often continues to worsen despite therapy. Within 10 years of initial diagnosis, half of MS patients are unable to work because of disabling levels of fatigue, and one-third need a cane, scooter or wheelchair.

After thoroughly reviewing the research, I decided to put myself on a diet that increases the efficiency of mitochondria, units within cells that supply the energy that's needed for nerve activity. Although the effect of diet on MS was unproven, I firmly believed that this was my best hope for fighting MS.

My eating plan was designed to improve the balance of neurotransmitters and supply the mitochondria with the building blocks needed for healthy nerve activity.

MY BRAIN-HEALTH DIET

People who follow this diet typically notice improvements in neurological symptoms within weeks.*

Because natural foods contain a variety of nutrients that can work synergistically, I recommend taking supplements only when you are unable to get the following nutrients in your diet. Be sure to discuss the supplements (and dosages) with your doctor if you take blood-thinning medication—some supplements may have a blood-thinning effect.

*Consult your doctor before trying the diet and/or supplements described here—especially if you take any medication or have kidney or liver disease.

In addition to taking such general steps as avoiding sugary and/or processed foods that are low in key nutrients, *make sure you get enough...*

- **Sulfur vegetables.** Cabbage, kale, collard greens and asparagus are excellent sources of sulfur, which is used by the body to produce gamma-aminobutyric acid (GABA). This "inhibitory" neurotransmitter counteracts the early brain-cell death that can occur if the neurotransmitter glutamate reaches excessive levels.

My advice: Consume three cups of greens each day, including one to three cups of sulfur-rich vegetables daily.

Also: To get other important nutrients, consume one to three cups of brightly colored vegetables or berries each day.

- **Coenzyme Q-10.** Exposure to environmental toxins, such as detergents, pesticide residues and mercury, has been linked to MS and other neurological conditions, such as dementia and Parkinson's disease. Coenzyme Q-10 is a fat-soluble compound that helps minimize the effects of these toxins while increasing the amount of energy produced by mitochondria.

Organ meats, such as calf liver and chicken liver, are among the best sources of coenzyme Q-10. I particularly recommend organ meats for older adults because coenzyme Q-10 production declines with age. It's also suppressed by cholesterol-lowering statin drugs.

My advice: Eat organ meats at least once a week. If you don't like organ meats, sardines, herring and rainbow trout are also high in coenzyme Q-10. Coenzyme Q-10 is available in supplement form, too.

- **Omega-3 fatty acids.** The omega-3 fatty acids in cold-water fish, such as salmon and sardines, are used by the body to produce the myelin that insulates brain and spinal cord cells. Myelin is also used to repair damage caused by MS. Omega-3s are concentrated in the brain and are necessary to help prevent depression and cognitive disorders.

My advice: To avoid concern about mercury and other toxins in cold-water fish, such as salmon, get your omega-3s from fish oil supplements that are purified.

Recommended dose: 1 g to 3 g daily.

• **Kelp and algae.** These detoxify the body by binding to heavy metals in the intestine and removing them in the stool.

My advice: Take supplements—one to two 500-mg to 600-mg capsules of kelp and one to four 500-mg capsules of algae daily. Or, as an alternative, add about a tablespoon of powdered algae—different types include Klamath blue green algae, spirulina and chlorella—to morning smoothies.

• **Green tea.** It's high in quercetin, an antioxidant that reduces inflammation. Green tea also changes the molecular structure of fat-soluble toxins and allows them to dissolve in water. This accelerates their excretion from the body.

My advice: Drink several cups of green tea daily.

Best choice: Finely milled Matcha green tea. It has more antioxidants than the typical tea brewed with dried leaves.

Note: Most types of green tea contain caffeine—on average, about 25 mg per cup.

Natural Help for Chronic Fatigue

Chronic fatigue is helped by CoQ10. Belgian researchers have found that patients with *myalgic encephalomyelitis* or chronic fatigue syndrome, a range of illnesses characterized by extreme fatigue and muscle weakness, have very low blood levels of coenzyme Q10 (CoQ10), an antioxidant that helps cells function properly. CoQ10 may protect mitochondria, structures in cells that convert nutrients into energy. Patients with these disorders should supplement with CoQ10—other studies have shown it helps fatigue.

M. Maes, et al., "Coenzyme Q10 Deficiency in Myalgic Encephalomyelitis/Chronic Fatigue Syndrome (ME/CFS) Is Related to Fatigue, Autonomic and Neurocognitive Symptoms and Is Another Risk Factor Explaining the Early Mortality in ME/CFS Due to Cardiovascular Disorder," *Neuroendocrinology Letters* (2009).

What Is Sjögren's Syndrome?

Alan Baer, MD, associate professor of medicine and clinical director, Johns Hopkins University Rheumatology Practice, Good Samaritan Hospital, founder and director of the Johns Hopkins Jerome L. Greene Sjögren's Syndrome Center, Baltimore

When tennis superstar Venus Williams announced that she had been diagnosed with Sjögren's syndrome, the tennis world issued a collective gasp. It was followed by the question: What on earth is Sjögren syndrome? Venus had been plagued by, as she put it, an "energy-sucking" disease for some time. She suffered from so much fatigue and joint pain that it was sometimes hard for her to even lift her racket. Fans were incredulous. Venus appeared to be in such good shape and, in fact, had won her first match at the 2011 US Open. But then she withdrew from the competition suddenly. Many were bitterly disappointed and suggested that this was just an excuse for her to drop out of the tournament.

Nothing could be further from the truth. But, the idea that Sjögren's patients are "faking it" or were hypochondriacs is nothing new. That is due to two major factors—the disease is difficult to diagnose, and patients, like Venus, often appear to be perfectly healthy. So let's put this nonsense to rest and finally understand what we can about this mysterious—and serious—autoimmune disease.

FOUR MILLION AMERICANS HAVE THIS DISEASE

Sjögren syndrome is a chronic inflammatory disorder in which disease-fighting white blood cells mistakenly attack the body's own moisture-producing glands, causing symptoms such as dry eyes and dry mouth. The disease can strike children and older adults, but typically, patients develop it between the ages of 40 and the mid-50s. (Venus, who is only 35 years old, got it very young.) Up to four million Americans have Sjögren's (90% of them are female, though doctors aren't sure why), and unfortunately there is no cure. However, it can be managed.

MYSTERY DISEASE

Sjögren's can present many challenges...

- **It's tough to diagnose.** On average, it takes six and a half years for doctors to put the puzzle pieces together.
- **Symptoms seem unrelated.** When the body's immune system attacks the moisture-producing glands, it causes complications all over the body. The eyes and mouth become dry—without the benefit of cleansing saliva teeth develop cavities...and fatigue and joint pain may develop. In women, there may be a lack of vaginal lubrication, which leads to increased risk for infection and pain during intercourse.
- **It's dangerous.** The longer a person goes without getting a diagnosis, the higher the health risks. If the disease advances undetected, it can set off a widespread inflammatory reaction that can harm the lungs, kidney, liver, pancreas and blood vessels as well as the gastrointestinal and central nervous systems. Up to 30% of Sjögren's patients suffer organ damage, and about 5% develop lymphoma (lymph node cancer).

An accurate diagnosis of the syndrome takes into account multiple factors, including a blood test to check for inflammation, antibodies and elevations in immune-related blood proteins. A biopsy from the inside of the lower lip is taken to assess the inflammatory reaction within the small salivary glands. The production of saliva and tears is also tested.

TOP TREATMENTS

Patients can choose from a variety of over-the-counter preparations that are generally very helpful for symptom relief. Lubricants help with vaginal dryness. For dry eyes, there are drops and ointments...and for dry mouth there are sprays, gums, gels, lozenges, mouthwashes and toothpastes.

More powerful prescription drugs can also help dry eyes and mouth. The drug *hydroxychloroquine* (brand name Plaquenil), originally developed to treat malaria, is useful in Sjögren's to relieve fatigue and joint pain. To quiet an overactive immune system, patients can take *methotrexate* (brand name Trexall)—it is used in high doses as chemotherapy, and now it's also used in low doses to treat autoimmune disorders. Methotrexate can be well-tolerated but can also cause some nasty side effects, including mouth sores, stomach upset, skin rash, hair loss and liver toxicity.

One bright spot: Research on drugs for autoimmune diseases is extremely active, and as general awareness of Sjögren's increases, patients are not likely to be left behind.

STEPS FOR QUALITY OF LIFE

Sjögren's can be mild, moderate or severe. Severe cases can cause renal failure, disability due to peripheral neuropathy, impaired vision, hepatitis or pneumonitis. But most cases are mild. To help maintain quality of life, exercise of any kind is important for physical and psychological reasons. An anti-inflammatory diet built on healthy foods is essential—eat plenty of vegetables, fruits, fish and other proteins, and limit processed foods and refined grains. Fish oil supplements and flaxseed oil may help the problem of dry eyes. To maintain a good level of energy, patients need plenty of sleep. They also need to avoid triggers such as extreme heat, fumes, cigarette smoke, dust and winds—all of which can aggravate symptoms.

Quality of life also has much to do with finding doctors who are well-versed in Sjögren's. Rheumatologists are the primary doctors who handle it, but the nature of the disease also requires the involvement of ophthalmologists, otolaryngologists, dentists, neurologists and for women, gynecologists. Ideally, a patient will be treated at a Sjögren syndrome center, such as the one at Johns Hopkins, but these centers are relatively rare. More typically, doctors treat Sjögren's within rheumatology centers, where expertise on autoimmune diseases is available. Once a patient has been diagnosed, his/her primary care doctor will locate an appropriate place for treatment. For an impressive amount of information about the disease and tips for living well with it, go to the Sjögren's Syndrome Foundation website, *www.sjogrens.org*.

Mouth Sores Galore? Don't Ignore This Autoimmune Problem

Neil J. Korman, MD, PhD, professor of dermatology at Case Western Reserve University School of Medicine. He specializes in autoimmune blistering diseases, psoriasis and atopic dermatitis and has published more than 120 articles in peer-reviewed literature.

Eating a bowl of chili one night, Sue felt a burning pain as if she had bitten the inside of her cheek. Oddly, the pain lingered. The next day, she looked in a mirror and saw what appeared to be several canker sores inside her mouth. She shrugged them off at first, but then more sores appeared. No sooner would some heal than others would form. Within a few weeks, her mouth was filled with a multitude of blisters that were so painful she could barely eat a thing.

Her primary-care doctor, dermatologist and dentist were all completely mystified. Finally her periodontist did some digging and came up with the answer—it was an autoimmune disease called *pemphigus*. Yet even with a diagnosis, Sue had to contact numerous dermatologists before finding one who was familiar with the condition and its treatment.

This story is typical of pemphigus patients, since the disorder is uncommon enough that doctors often don't think to check for it. Yet early diagnosis and treatment are crucial because they make this potentially serious condition much easier to control, according to Neil J. Korman, MD, PhD, a professor of dermatology at Case Western Reserve University School of Medicine who specializes in autoimmune blistering diseases.

What is this weird disease? With pemphigus, the immune system makes antibodies that mistakenly attack the proteins in skin cells that keep adjacent cells adhering to one another. This causes cells to separate from each other—to become "unglued," so to speak. Fluid collects between the layers of tissue, forming numerous fragile blisters that rupture easily, shearing away the top layer of skin and leaving open sores.

Of the several types of pemphigus, the most common is pemphigus vulgaris, in which blisters usually appear first in the mouth. Later, blisters may erupt in the mucous membranes of the nose, throat, eyes and/or genitals, as well as on the skin.

Pemphigus occurs most frequently in middle-aged adults and seniors—Sue was in her 70s when it appeared—and women are at somewhat higher risk than men. The disease can develop in people of any ethnicity, though it is more common in those of Mediterranean, Middle Eastern or Ashkenazi Jewish descent.

Getting help: If you have mouth sores that do not heal, seek out a dermatologist or otolaryngologist (ear, nose and throat doctor) who is familiar with pemphigus. If your primary-care physician cannot provide a referral, check the website of the International Pemphigus & Pemphigoid Foundation at *www.Pemphigus.org*. Diagnosis is based on a physical exam, biopsy of affected tissue and a blood test that measures antibody levels.

Pemphigus patients of yesteryear often died when their mucous membranes or skin became so severely damaged that life-threatening infection set in. Today, fortunately, the disease can be controlled with one or more medications. Options include corticosteroids (such as prednisone)...oral immunosuppressants such as *mycophenolate mofetil* (CellCept), which help keep the immune system from attacking healthy tissues...biological therapies such as *rituximab* (Rituxan), which target the white blood cells that produce antibodies...and antibiotics or other drugs as necessary to combat infection.

Because pemphigus is a chronic condition, patients may need to be on medication for life—yet all these drugs can have side effects, so the goal is to find the lowest effective dose. In some cases, patients achieve remission and can withdraw from medications. But as Dr. Korman cautioned, "A remission is not a cure. The blisters can come back."

Your doctor also may advise taking supplements to help minimize medication side effects. Typical recommendations include calcium with vitamin D for patients on steroids and probiotics for patients taking antibiotics.

To minimize mouth pain during a flare-up...

• **Drink beverages at room temperature (not hot or cold),** using a straw so you can guide the liquid away from the sides of your mouth and down your throat.

• **Avoid hard foods in favor of soft ones.** Cook vegetables until they are tender...dip foods in sauces to soften them...accompany each bite of food with a sip of liquid.

• **Keep a list of foods that worsen your pain.** For instance, Sue quickly learned to steer clear of spicy foods, Italian salad dressing and anything with cinnamon. Some pemphigus patients report problems with foods containing *thiols* (such as chives, garlic, leeks, onions and shallots)...*isothiocyanates* (found in broccoli, cabbage, cauliflower and turnips as well as mustard)...*phenols* (in bananas, mangoes, potatoes, tomatoes and milk)...or *tannins* (in ginger, berries, coffee and tea).

• **Dental hygiene can be difficult when mouth tissues are sore and fragile, but remember, it's still important.** Rinse your mouth out with water after eating to remove bacteria...and use a small, soft toothbrush to clean your teeth.

• **Use over-the-counter anesthetic mouth lozenges as needed to reduce discomfort.**

• **For some patients, stress worsens symptoms**—so consider practicing meditation or some other relaxation technique.

Autoimmune Encephalitis: The Brain Disease That Makes People Seem Crazy

Souhel Najjar, MD, associate professor of neurology, director, electroencephalogram laboratory, NYU Langone Medical Center, New York City, and director, Neuroscience Center, Staten Island University Hospital, New York.

Ricki had it all—a great job, great little Manhattan apartment, great life. Only in her early 20s, she already had accomplished much in the fashion world.

But over the course of barely more than a month, all that blew up as Ricki developed increasingly weird and worrisome behaviors.

First, there were memory problems. She couldn't recall simple things, such as where she normally kept her car keys or the names of her coworkers. The following week, her speech slowed, her body felt numb and her movements became awkward. Soon after, Ricki began hallucinating and a psychiatrist put her on medication.

A week later, she had a seizure and was hospitalized. A huge battery of tests, including a spinal tap and brain MRIs, revealed nothing except a little inflammation...doctors were stumped.

Then Ricki began having violent spells, leaping at nurses and orderlies. Said to be psychotic, she was transferred to a psychiatric hospital. And there she might have stayed for the rest of her life—if not for a stroke of luck.

Ricki's father, a retired physician, did not believe that the daughter who had always been so sweet, smart and sane could have become, in a matter of weeks, seriously and irrevocably mentally ill. So he diligently researched her symptoms and discussed her condition with his doctor friends. Fortunately, one of the father's colleagues suggested consulting Souhel Najjar, MD, a neurologist at NYU Langone Medical Center in New York City.

Dr. Najjar gave the young woman a thorough examination, including a special blood test that revealed antibodies targeting certain receptors in the brain—and within days, he had made the diagnosis. Ricki was suffering from a rare autoimmune disorder called anti-NMDA receptor encephalitis.

DEADLY "DEMONIC" DISEASE

Encephalitis, or inflammation of the brain, usually is the result of a viral infection, but it also can be caused by bacteria, fungi or parasites—or, as doctors now realize, by an autoimmune disorder.

In the case of anti-NMDA receptor encephalitis, severe brain inflammation occurs when "the immune system attacks special proteins on the surface of nerve cells in the brain called NMDA receptors. These receptors control various cognitive functions, mood, behavior and personality traits—so when they are compromised, the brain malfunctions.

The resulting symptoms include mood and personality changes, violent outbursts, paranoia, psychosis, memory loss, speech problems, numbness, seizures, involuntary movements, increased heart rate, irregular heart rhythm, slowed breathing and/or decreased levels of consciousness. Patients sometimes sink into an unresponsive catatonic state that may last for weeks. Some experts even suspect that anti-NMDA receptor encephalitis is the true cause underlying many cases of "demonic possession" described in the Bible!

This disease is largely unknown, having first been reported in the medical literature only seven years ago. It typically strikes in early adulthood, but it has been diagnosed in children as young as one and in seniors as old as 85. It can strike both genders, though more than 75% of those affected are female.

We contacted Dr. Najjar to learn more about this disturbing and devastating disease. He said that, though considered rare, anti-NMDA receptor encephalitis may be more common than is currently recognized, with many patients being misdiagnosed with severe psychiatric disorders. "These patients act aggressive, belligerent, violent, psychotic and paranoid. Yet now that we know what the real problem is, we have to wonder how many people have been locked up in psychiatric units for years after they were misdiagnosed," Dr. Najjar said.

Sadly, some patients with anti-NMDA receptor encephalitis die from medical and neurological complications related to irregular heart rhythm, very low blood pressure, slowed breathing, prolonged convulsions and/or persistent coma.

BRAIN-SAVING TREATMENT

The earlier that anti-NMDA receptor encephalitis is diagnosed and treated, the better the outcome tends to be. Treatment includes immunotherapy—a heavy-duty dose of steroids and other drugs aimed at suppressing the body's attack on itself. Typically, Dr. Najjar said, the treatment is effective, and most severe symptoms improve within three to four week after treatment begins. However, patients often need physical, occupational and/or cognitive therapies to regain their ability to walk, talk and function normally, and full recovery may take up to two years.

What causes this disease? That's not entirely clear. As with other autoimmune disorders, such as lupus or rheumatoid arthritis, a genetic predisposition may contribute to an individual's risk, Dr. Najjar said.

A certain type of ovarian tumor called a teratoma appears to play a key role, particularly in females of childbearing age. Bizarrely, teratomas often contain skin, hair, tooth and/or brainlike cells. A recent study from the University of Pennsylvania found that up to 55% of female patients under 18 years of age who had anti-NMDA receptor encephalitis also had teratomas in their ovaries. The body's immune system may be provoked into producing antibodies that attack the abnormal brainlike cells in the tumor, Dr. Najjar explained. Since the antibodies don't distinguish between the brainlike cells in the tumor and cells in the brain itself, the patient's brain becomes a battlefield. If a teratoma is found in a patient's ovary, the ovary needs to be surgically removed.

What's puzzling is that anti-NMDA receptor encephalitis also can develop in patients who do not have teratomas. Such cases may be the result of some kind of virus that damages the blood/brain barrier, allowing antibodies to enter the brain, Dr. Najjar said. These patients are at greater risk for recurrence, even many years after the initial episode. For instance, the University of Pennsylvania researchers reported that, of the 20% of anti-NMDA receptor encephalitis patients who experienced a relapse, most had not had teratomas.

Lucky lady: Ricki is recovering nicely, thanks to timely intervention. *But here's what all of us should remember from her story...*

If a loved one suddenly starts exhibiting psychiatric symptoms that are way out of character, Dr. Najjar said, it is vital to consult a neurologist and ask whether anti-NMDA receptor encephalitis could be the culprit.

Cold Fingers and Toes May Mean Raynaud's Disease

Jamison Starbuck, ND, is a naturopathic physician in family practice and a guest lecturer at the University of Montana, both in Missoula. She is past president of the American Association of Naturopathic Physicians and a contributing editor to *The Alternative Advisor: The Complete Guide to Natural Therapies and Alternative Treatments.*

Cold, numb and tingly fingers and toes are telltale signs of Raynaud's disease. If you have this disorder, you'll experience an extreme reaction to cold and/or psychological stress. Your blood vessels will quickly narrow, reducing blood flow to your extremities. Surprisingly, it doesn't even have to be freezing for symptoms to appear. Simply spending time in an air-conditioned room can be enough to trigger symptoms. When Raynaud's strikes, the hands and feet turn white or even blue/black. After a few minutes, the white extremities turn bright red as blood flow is restored, but it may take up to 30 minutes for coloring to return to normal.

Even though the signs of Raynaud's are fairly straightforward, many people are confused about the condition because there are two forms—primary and secondary. Primary Raynaud's, for which there is no known cause, is the most common. It is really more of a nuisance than a medical disability. Secondary Raynaud's, on the other hand, is caused by an underlying condition—often an autoimmune disease such as lupus, scleroderma or Sjögren's syndrome...an injury from repetitive hand movements such as carpal tunnel syndrome...a disease that causes narrowing of blood vessels, such as diabetes...or even the use of certain medications, including some blood pressure and migraine drugs.

If you have Raynaud's symptoms: The first step is to make an appointment with your doctor so he/she can check for underlying conditions. If you have primary Raynaud's, your symptoms may improve if you just make sure to wear gloves and socks whenever you're exposed to cold and do your best to avoid extremely stressful situations. But if it's secondary Raynaud's, you'll need treatment for the underlying condition (or have any medication that could be causing your Raynaud's reviewed and possibly changed by your doctor). However, both forms of the disorder also can be helped by natural medicine. *What I recommend...**

Targeted vitamins. B vitamins help with nerve function, circulation and stress management.

Typical daily dose for Raynaud's: 100 mg each of B-3, B-5 and B-6 in a tablet or liquid and 1,000 mcg of B-12 in a sublingual (under-the-tongue) form. Vitamin E is also important—it helps with circulation and promotes the health of your blood vessels.

Typical daily dose for Raynaud's: 400 international units (IU) to 800 IU.

Hawthorne. This herb, in supplement form, can help by improving blood flow.

Typical daily dose for Raynaud's: 60 drops of tincture in one ounce of water taken 15 minutes before or after meals, twice daily.

Gentle exercise. As long as you're careful to avoid chilling, activities such as walking, biking and yoga are great ways to reduce stress and enhance circulation—both of which will help you avoid Raynaud's attacks.

Bonus: Even if your cold hands and feet are due to something other than Raynaud's, these steps may help.

*Check with your doctor first if you take any medications.

Surprising Connection Between Autoimmune Disease and Endometriosis

Tine Jess, MD, is a researcher in the department of epidemiology research at the Statens Serum Institut in Copenhagen, Denmark, and lead author of a study on endometriosis and IBD risk published in *Gut.*

What you don't know really can hurt you. So even though today's news isn't exactly welcome, it could ultimately ease the suffering for women with endometriosis. How? By alerting them (and their doctors) to an accompanying increased risk for bowel problems, thus helping them get the treatment they need. *Here's the story...*

With endometriosis, tissue from the uterine lining migrates outside the uterus and implants on other pelvic structures. During menstruation, this displaced tissue bleeds... and the trapped blood inflames surrounding tissues, causing intense pain and internal scarring. Previous studies suggested an association between this inflammatory disorder and various autoimmune diseases. So Danish researchers decided to investigate a possible link between endometriosis and inflammatory bowel disease (IBD), an umbrella term for a group of immune disorders that affect the gut and cause abdominal pain, diarrhea and bloody stools.

The study analyzed data on 37,661 women who were hospitalized for endometriosis between 1977 and 2007. During that 30-year period, 228 of the endometriosis patients also developed ulcerative colitis, a form of IBD that affects the inner lining of the colon...and 92 endometriosis patients also developed Crohn's disease, a type of IBD that affects all layers of both the small and large intestine.

Crunching those numbers: Compared with women in the general population, endometriosis patients were 50% more likely to develop some form of IBD...while those whose endometriosis was verified through surgery had an 80% higher risk for IBD. What's more, the increased IBD risk persisted even 20 years or more after the endometriosis diagnosis.

Why this matters so much: Certain symptoms, notably chronic abdominal pain and diarrhea, are common to both endometriosis and IBD. If a doctor assumes that a patient's ongoing symptoms are solely the result of her endometriosis, he or she may fail to diagnose and treat the woman's IBD—and thus the patient will continue to suffer.

Though it is unclear why endometriosis raises the risk for IBD, researchers suggested that the two conditions might share some underlying immunological features. Or, in some cases, the IBD might be a consequence of treating endometriosis with oral contraceptives (as is commonly done), given that oral contraceptive users are at significantly increased risk for IBD.

Endometriosis patients: If you have persistent abdominal pain or other symptoms, talk with your doctor about this possible link with IBD. Bring this article to your appointment if you think it will help!

How to Keep Your Thyroid Healthy

Jamison Starbuck, ND, is a naturopathic physician in family practice and a guest lecturer at the University of Montana, both in Missoula. She is past president of the American Association of Naturopathic Physicians and a contributing editor to *The Alternative Advisor: The Complete Guide to Natural Therapies and Alternative Treatments.*

Doctor, I think I have a thyroid problem." I hear this from several of my patients each week. It's not surprising. Thyroid problems are quite common, affecting an estimated 27 million Americans.

Thyroid dysfunction can occur in two main ways. For example, hypothyroidism occurs when the thyroid gland is underactive. Common symptoms include fatigue, weight gain unrelated to a change in diet, joint pain, muscle stiffness and depression. Hyperthyroidism is an overactive thyroid, identified by such symptoms as rapid heart rate, diarrhea, anxiety and weight loss. Some of the factors that contribute to thyroid dysfunction often are ignored by conventional doctors. This leaves patients unaware of what they can do to support their thyroid health. *My advice...*

Get appropriate testing. Conventional thyroid screening consists of a blood test known as "TSH"—short for thyroid-stimulating hormone. Unfortunately, most people don't realize that they need more than a TSH test if they are exhibiting signs of thyroid disease. Many patients have a normal TSH level yet abnormal levels of circulating thyroid hormone. If your TSH is normal but you have symptoms that are characteristic of thyroid dysfunction, ask for comprehensive testing that includes both the "bound" and "free" forms of T3 *(triiodothyronine)*...and T4 *(thyroxine)*. Bound T3 is tied to protein molecules, while free T3 is more readily available for metabolic activity in the body.

• **Learn your risk factors.** Did one or both of your parents or grandparents and/or any of your siblings have thyroid disease? If so, you're at greater risk yourself. Hormonal changes, such as those that occur during adolescence, pregnancy and midlife, often precede and hasten the onset of thyroid disease. Even extreme stress, including a divorce, death of a loved one, job loss, sleep deprivation or military service, can trigger thyroid problems. The medication lithium and the hormone supplements estrogen and testosterone can interfere with thyroid function, so anyone receiving one of these treatments should have the comprehensive thyroid testing described above at least once a year.

• **Understand how diet affects thyroid health.** Raw cruciferous vegetables, such as brussels sprouts, cabbage and broccoli, can worsen thyroid health in people with thyroid disorders. However, cooking these healthy vegetables deactivates their antithyroid properties. It's not well known, but wheat can interfere with thyroid health. Research indicates that some patients with celiac disease (an inability to digest gluten, a protein found in wheat, barley and rye) develop autoimmune thyroid disease either in the underactive or overactive form. For these celiac patients, an allergy to wheat—not gluten—is the main problem. Patients with celiac disease or wheat sensitivity should have comprehensive thyroid testing. Many patients with thyroid disease seem to feel better when they avoid wheat.

More from Jamison Starbuck, ND...

Fight Thyroid Disease Naturally

Hypothyroidism is one of those conditions that often hovers just beneath the radar. You feel lousy, then get used to dragging yourself around and may not even think it's important enough to tell your doctor about it. Of course there's a simple blood test for hypothyroidism (underactive thyroid), and treatment—a daily synthetic thyroid replacement hormone pill, or levothyroxine—is fairly straightforward. But in my opinion, thyroid replacement hormone alone usually doesn't take care of the problem, because it helps patients feel better—but not great. That's not good enough!

Here's what most people don't realize: A major cause of hypothyroidism is an autoimmune condition known as Hashimoto's thyroiditis (in some cases, hypothyroidism is due to other causes such as thyroid surgery or thyroid cancer). As an autoimmune disease, Hashimoto's throws the immune system out of whack so that it goes on the attack, for unknown reasons, against the thyroid gland. This means that you've got a bigger problem than an empty gas tank—your whole body needs some tuning up. *If your doctor has told you that you have Hashimoto's, talk to him/her about adding the following natural approaches to your standard thyroid replacement regimen...*

1. Avoid food allergens. Food allergies are linked to autoimmune disease. Gluten and wheat allergies are particularly common in people with thyroid disease. To find out if you have food allergies (believe it or not, many people who have food allergies aren't aware of it), ask your doctor for an IgG blood test. If it's positive, avoiding the foods you're allergic to will increase your vitality and nicely augment your hormone replacement therapy.

2. Try supplements and tweak your diet. Low iodine, zinc and selenium can reduce thyroid hormone production—a bad situation when you already have low thyroid levels. That's why I prescribe low-dose supplements—300 micrograms (mcg) of iodine...30 mg of zinc...and 100 mcg of selenium daily—for my patients with Hashimoto's. (Before trying these supplements, be sure to check with your doctor—especially if you have any other chronic health condition or take medication.) Also, avoid "goitrogens"—foods that suppress thyroid function by interfering with the absorption of iodine, which plays such a key role in keeping this gland healthy. Goitrogens include raw kale and broccoli and soy (in any form). Cooked green veggies are OK—heat deactivates the goitrogenic substances.

3. Get some natural sunlight. When our eyes are exposed to sunlight, it fuels the pineal gland in the brain to produce thyroid hormone. To get this thyroid benefit, take your sunglasses off for at least 30 minutes a day when you're outdoors. (If you have an eye disease, such as glaucoma, this is not advisable.)

4. Do aerobic exercise for 20 minutes, four times a week. Moderate exercise increases thyroid hormone production and boosts the immune system by improving circulation, enhancing cardiac function and relieving stress.

5. Improve circulation to your thyroid gland. Hashimoto's often impairs blood circulation to the thyroid gland. To promote better blood flow, you can try yoga or simply do a "shoulder stand" for a few minutes every day—raise your hips and legs above your head while you lie on your back. (Don't do this if you have glaucoma, high blood pressure or neck problems.)

This Thyroid Disorder Can Be Tricky to Spot

Joshua D. Safer, MD, director of endocrinology fellowship training and endocrinology education at Boston Medical Center and an associate professor of medicine and molecular medicine at Boston University School of Medicine. He has published many articles on thyroid disease in such journals as *Endocrinology and Thyroid.*

You probably know that feeling tired all the time and not being able to lose unwanted weight are classic red flags that you could have an underactive thyroid gland (hypothyroidism), the most common thyroid condition. What you might not realize is that this disease also can cause plenty of other symptoms—some of which seem, at first glance, to be unrelated to the thyroid.

Why is that? The thyroid, a two-inch, butterfly-shaped gland tucked below the voice box, makes hormones that help regulate metabolism—how your body uses energy from the foods you eat—and crucial processes throughout the body such as body temperature, muscle strength and the functioning of such vital organs as the heart and brain.

To ensure that a sluggish thyroid isn't secretly harming your health, here are the facts you need...

• **Symptoms of hypothyroidism can be subtle and often develop gradually.** While you're likely to notice if your bathroom scale shows that you're putting on some unexplained weight, other symptoms of hypothyroidism often are overlooked as normal signs of aging. Symptoms, which are sometimes mild, may include depression, forgetfulness, a puffy face, joint and muscle pain, constipation and dry skin. You might also begin to feel a bit colder than you used to, and your hair may start to thin—typically on the eyebrows, but it may also occur on the scalp. To complicate matters, not everyone with hypothyroidism gains weight.

• **Men can be affected by hypothyroidism, too.** While it's true that 80% to 90% of hypothyroidism cases occur in women, an estimated 1.5 to 3 million men in the US also have the condition. Women are more likely than men to be affected by hypothyroidism because they are more susceptible to autoimmune disease. An autoimmune disorder known as Hashimoto's disease is the main cause of hypothyroidism. With Hashimoto's, the immune system produces antibodies that attack the thyroid gland, interfering with its ability to produce thyroid hormone.

When men develop symptoms of hypothyroidism—especially weight gain, depression and muscle pain—they often are shrugged off as signs of aging. Over time, low levels of thyroid hormone also can interfere with a man's libido and/or lead to premature ejaculation.

• **Medications can cause hypothyroidism.** The use of certain drugs can trigger the disease by interfering with the production of thyroid hormone. These medications include *amiodarone* (Cordarone), a heart drug...*interferon alpha*, a cancer drug...*lithium*, a drug for treating bipolar disorder...and *interleukin-2*, a drug taken for kidney cancer.

Paradoxically, some conditions that cause the thyroid to produce too much hormone also can lead to underproduction. In addition, treatment for overactive thyroid could later make you hypothyroid.

• **Doctors don't routinely test for hypothyroidism.** You may assume that the blood tests you receive at your routine doctor visits always check how well your thyroid is functioning. But that's not true.

Be sure to ask your doctor for a blood test that measures levels of thyroid-stimulating hormone (TSH)—the most accurate indicator of thyroid activity. Higher-than-normal TSH readings indicate hypothyroidism.

Important: Not all TSH testing kits use the same reference ranges—the measurements that are considered normal. For TSH, the most commonly used reference range is 0.5 mIU/L (milli-international units per liter) to 5.0 mIU/L.

However, there is no clear consensus in the medical community on when treatment for hypothyroidism should begin. Some doctors will advise treatment for a reading of 2.5 or above, while others might not unless the reading exceeds 10—the definition of primary hypothyroidism, according to guidelines from the American Association of Clinical Endocrinologists. I typically begin treatment if the TSH level exceeds 4.0 and there is a positive test result for antibodies indicating Hashimoto's. If the test for Hashimoto's is negative, I retest the person's TSH to see if the level normalizes within two to four months before beginning treatment.

Even though there are no definitive answers on when to start treatment, we know that people whose TSH is higher than 2.0 are more likely to eventually develop clear-cut hypothyroidism than those with lower test scores. On the other hand, research has shown that older adults with slightly elevated TSH tend to live longer than those with lower levels.

Tests that may be used in addition to TSH to help diagnose hypothyroidism include those that measure levels of thyroxine (T4) and/or triiodothyronine (T3), two hormones produced by the thyroid...and a thyroid autoantibody test, which looks for antibodies that are markers for Hashimoto's disease.

• **Hypothyroidism can elevate cholesterol levels.** Even in the early stages, low thyroid can cause an increase in LDL "bad" cholesterol. I've seen patients with untreated hypothyroidism whose cholesterol levels were 20 to 50 points higher than they would be otherwise.

Important: If your thyroid levels are low and you also have high cholesterol, be sure to get your thyroid disease treated. It's possible that your cholesterol will fall (sometimes within a matter of weeks) once the thyroid disease is treated.

• **Hundreds of medications interact with the medication used to treat hypothyroidism.** *Levothyroxine* (Synthroid) is a synthetic version of thyroid hormone. Hypothyroidism is typically well controlled with this medication—if it's taken daily as prescribed.

While levothyroxine is unlikely to cause side effects at the proper dose, you can expect to have some side effects until your doctor determines the best dose for you. Too much of the drug can cause increased appetite, shakiness or insomnia. Too little means that your symptoms won't get better. Follow-up blood tests will be needed until the proper dose is determined and periodically repeated thereafter.

Important: More than 500 medications, from antacids to diabetes drugs, can interfere with levothyroxine—and affect the dose you'll need. For a list of these medications, go to *www.Drugs.com* (click on "Interactions Checker" and enter "levothyroxine"). Levothyroxine should be taken first thing in the morning, 30 to 60 minutes before having food, supplements, vitamins or minerals—all of which interfere with the absorption of thyroid hormone. (See "How to Take Your Thyroid Medicine," next page.)

Mysterious Thyroid Problem

Hyperparathyroidism results from a benign tumor on one or two of the four parathyroid glands.

The tumors usually have no identifiable cause. However, in about 2% of cases, parathyroid tumors develop from exposure to radiation to the neck or face 20 to 40 years earlier (for cancer treatments, for example) or even from treatments for acne and recurrent tonsillitis back in the 1950s and 1960s. Some people who had radioactive iodine destruction of their thyroid gland (for Graves' disease) develop a parathyroid tumor 10 to 30 years later. Fortunately, these tumors are nearly always benign and can be removed with a 20-minute outpatient operation.

James Norman, MD, director, Norman Parathyroid Center, Tampa. *Parathyroid.com*

How to Take Your Thyroid Medicine

To make your hypothyroid medication more effective, eat foods rich in selenium, such as Brazil nuts, fish, red meat, chicken, eggs and grains. Selenium helps convert thyroid hormone into a usable form.

Also: Wait at least one hour after taking thyroid hormone before you take antacids containing calcium or aluminum—four hours is even better. Antacids can block the absorption of thyroid hormone. Do not take thyroid hormone at the same time as calcium or iron supplements—wait at least an hour. Talk to your doctor before changing your diet, and tell your doctor and pharmacist about all other drugs you use because some—such as antidepressants—can affect how much thyroid hormone you need.

Theodore C. Friedman, MD, PhD, chairman of internal medicine and chief of endocrinology at Charles Drew University of Medicine and Science, and professor of medicine at University of California, both in Los Angeles. *GoodHormoneHealth.com.*

2

Alzheimer's Disease and Dementia

How to Recognize Early-Stage Alzheimer's Disease

Alzheimer's disease was first identified 100 years ago, but only recently have significant breakthroughs been made in recognizing the sometimes subtle mental deficits caused by the condition.

Important development: With sophisticated new brain scans and neurological tests, doctors are now able to identify telltale signs of this dreaded disease in its early stages, when treatment is potentially most helpful. *What you need to know...*

HOW IT STARTS

With normal aging, our brains begin to shrink a few cells at a time, which slows brain functioning. In patients with early-stage Alzheimer's, however, a much more insidious process occurs. For reasons that are not well understood, abnormal accumulations of protein fragments and cellular material (plaques) that contain an insoluble protein called beta-amyloid develop, as do brain-damaging bundles of neurofibers known as neurofibrillary tangles.

When memory lapses occur as a result of normal aging, the information can almost always be retrieved at some point later. With early-stage Alzheimer's, however, memories of recent events—those that have taken place in past weeks, days or even hours—completely disappear.

Lesser-known symptoms that also characterize Alzheimer's in its early stages...

- **Loss of initiative.** The person may lose interest in what had been favorite activities, such as gardening or taking walks. He/she may become passive and spend more time sleeping or watching television.

Todd Feinberg, MD, chief of the Yarmon Neurobehavior and Alzheimer's Disease Center at Beth Israel Medical Center and professor of clinical neurology and psychiatry at Albert Einstein College of Medicine, both in New York City. He is coauthor of *What to Do When the Doctor Says It's Early-Stage Alzheimer's.*

• **Loss of smell.** One study has linked Alzheimer's to an inability to identify certain smells—specifically, strawberry, smoke, soap, menthol, clove, pineapple, natural gas, lilac, lemon and leather.

• **Language problems.** Finding the right word or phrase becomes increasingly difficult, and vocabulary is diminished.

• **Difficulty reasoning.** This affects a person's ability to do things such as read and understand an instruction manual, balance a checkbook or follow a recipe.

People who have early-stage Alzheimer's also may have trouble making even simple decisions...take longer to perform routine tasks...or experience a change in personality (such as a person who is ordinarily very sociable becoming a recluse).

Important: Many early-stage Alzheimer's symptoms are similar to those caused by depression. Imaging tests, as well as a family history of either condition, can be used to distinguish the two.

During moderate-stage Alzheimer's disease, the patient may become less concerned with personal appearance...confuse the identities of family members (for example, thinking one's wife is one's sister)...hear, see or smell things that are not there...and/or need help with basic hygiene.

Late-stage Alzheimer's is typically characterized by loss of bladder and bowel control...an inability to recognize close family members...difficulties chewing and swallowing...and a need for total assistance with activities of daily living, such as eating, using the toilet, bathing and dressing.

MAKING THE DIAGNOSIS

People who are concerned about memory loss—or experience two or more of the symptoms listed above for early-stage Alzheimer's—should be evaluated by a neurologist, psychiatrist and/or psychologist to rule out treatable conditions that can mimic Alzheimer's. These include nutritional deficiencies (especially those involving vitamin B-12 and folate)...metabolic or hormonal disorders caused by diseases of the liver, pancreas or kidneys...lung problems that reduce oxygen flow, such as emphysema or pneumonia... and alcohol abuse. Certain drugs, such as tranquilizers and antidepressants, also can cause Alzheimer's-like symptoms.

A brain autopsy is the only definitive way to diagnose Alzheimer's disease, but doctors can now make a "probable diagnosis" that is accurate about 90% of the time by using high-tech brain scans and behavior and memory tests.

A computed tomography (CT) or magnetic resonance imaging (MRI) scan is typically used to identify loss of brain tissue and/or decreased brain activity. If results are inconclusive, three-dimensional imaging techniques known as positron emission tomography (PET) or single photon emission computed tomography (SPECT) are used.

EARLY TREATMENT

If a person is diagnosed with Alzheimer's, medication is usually started right away to help slow the progression of the disease as well as curb or stabilize the symptoms. Alzheimer's drugs include *donepezil* (Aricept), *rivastigmine* (Exelon) and *galantamine* (Razadyne). Side effects, such as diarrhea, nausea, appetite loss and insomnia, usually are mild and often diminish within a few months. More recently, *memantine* (Namenda) has been approved for the treatment of moderate and severe Alzheimer's.

PREVENTION

Certain health habits are believed to help protect against Alzheimer's...

• **Control weight, blood pressure and cholesterol levels.** A recent study of nearly 1,500 people in Finland confirmed that risk factors for Alzheimer's and cardiovascular disease are strikingly similar. Researchers found that people who were obese and had high blood pressure and elevated cholesterol levels were six times more likely to develop Alzheimer's than people without those health problems.

• **Eat the right foods.** A nutritious diet rich in brightly colored, antioxidant-rich fruits (blueberries, plums, strawberries, oranges, cherries, raspberries and cranberries) and vegetables (kale, spinach, broccoli, brussels sprouts, red peppers, eggplant and onions) helps curb the damage that brain cells undergo in response to disease-promoting molecules known as free radicals.

• **Stay physically active.** Any kind of physical activity is valuable. But cardiovascular exercise, including walking, is particularly good for overall circulation—and blood circulation to the brain.

5 Surprising Ways to Prevent Alzheimer's—#1: Check Your Tap Water

Marwan Sabbagh, MD, director of Banner Sun Health Research Institute, Sun City, Arizona. He is research professor of neurology at University of Arizona College of Medicine and associate director of the Arizona Alzheimer's Disease Center, both in Phoenix. He is author of *The Alzheimer's Prevention Cookbook: 100 Recipes to Boost Brain Health. MarwanSabbagh MD.com*

Every 68 seconds, another American develops Alzheimer's disease, the fatal brain disease that steals memory and personality. It's the fifth-leading cause of death among people age 65 and older.

You can lower your likelihood of getting Alzheimer's disease by reducing controllable and well-known risk factors (see list on the next page). *But new scientific research reveals that there are also little-known "secret" risk factors that you can address...*

COPPER IN TAP WATER

A scientific paper published in *Journal of Trace Elements in Medicine and Biology* theorizes that inorganic copper found in nutritional supplements and in drinking water is an important factor in today's Alzheimer's epidemic.

Science has established that amyloid-beta plaques—inflammation-causing cellular debris found in the brains of people with Alzheimer's—contain high levels of copper. Animal research shows that small amounts of inorganic copper in drinking water worsen Alzheimer's. Studies on people have linked the combination of copper and a high-fat diet to memory loss and mental decline. It may be that copper sparks amyloid-beta plaques to generate more oxidation and inflammation, further injuring brain cells.

What to do: There is plenty of copper in our diets—no one needs additional copper from a multivitamin/mineral supplement. Look for a supplement with no copper or a minimal amount (500 micrograms).

I also recommend filtering water. Water-filter pitchers, such as ones by Brita, can reduce the presence of copper. I installed a reverse-osmosis water filter in my home a few years ago when the evidence for the role of copper in Alzheimer's became compelling.

VITAMIN D DEFICIENCY

Mounting evidence shows that a low blood level of vitamin D may increase Alzheimer's risk.

A 2013 study in *Journal of Alzheimer's Disease* analyzed 10 studies exploring the link between vitamin D and Alzheimer's. Researchers found that low blood levels of vitamin D were linked to a 40% increased risk for Alzheimer's.

The researchers from UCLA, also writing in *Journal of Alzheimer's Disease*, theorize that vitamin D may protect the brain by reducing amyloid-beta and inflammation.

What to do: The best way to make sure that your blood level of vitamin D is protective is to ask your doctor to test it—and then, if needed, to help you correct your level to greater than 60 nanograms per milliliter (ng/mL). That correction may require 1,000 IU to 2,000 IU of vitamin D daily...or another individualized supplementation strategy.

Important: When your level is tested, make sure that it is the 25-hydroxyvitamin D, or 25(OH)D, test and not the 1.25-dihydroxyvitamin D test. The latter test does not accurately measure blood levels of vitamin D but is sometimes incorrectly ordered. Also, ask for your exact numerical results. Levels above 30 ng/mL are considered "normal," but in my view, the 60 ng/mL level is the minimum that is protective.

HORMONE REPLACEMENT THERAPY AFTER MENOPAUSE

Research shows that starting hormone replacement therapy (HRT) within five years of entering menopause and using hormones for 10 or more years reduces the risk for Alzheimer's by 30%. But a new 11-year study of 1,768 women, published in *Neurology*, shows that those who started a combination of estrogen-progestin therapy five years or more after the onset of menopause had a 93% higher risk for Alzheimer's.

What to do: If you are thinking about initiating hormone replacement therapy five years or more after the onset of menopause, talk to your doctor about the possible benefits and risks.

A CONCUSSION

A study published in *Neurology* in 2012 showed that NFL football players had nearly four times higher risk for Alzheimer's than the general population—no doubt from repeated brain injuries incurred while playing football.

What most people don't realize: Your risk of developing Alzheimer's is doubled if you've ever had a serious concussion that resulted in loss of consciousness—this newer evidence shows that it is crucially important to prevent head injuries of any kind throughout your life.

What to do: Fall-proof your home, with commonsense measures such as adequate lighting, eliminating or securing throw rugs and keeping stairways clear. Wear shoes with firm soles and low heels, which also helps prevent falls.

If you've ever had a concussion, it's important to implement the full range of Alzheimer's-prevention strategies in this article.

NOT HAVING A PURPOSE IN LIFE

In a seven-year study published in *Archives of General Psychiatry*, researchers at the Rush Alzheimer's Disease Center in Chicago found that people who had a "purpose in life" were 2.4 times less likely to develop Alzheimer's.

What to do: The researchers found that the people who agreed with the following statements were less likely to develop Alzheimer's and mild cognitive impairment—"I feel good when I think of what I have done in the past and what I hope to do in the future" and "I have a sense of direction and purpose in life."

If you cannot genuinely agree with the above statements, there are things you can do to change that—in fact, you even can change the way you feel about your past. It takes a bit of resolve…some action…and perhaps help from a qualified mental health counselor.

One way to start: Think about and make a list of some activities that would make your life more meaningful. Ask yourself, Am I doing these?…and then write down small, realistic goals that will involve you more in those activities, such as volunteering one hour every week at a local hospital or signing up for a class at your community college next semester.

The following steps are crucial in the fight against Alzheimer's disease…

- **Lose weight if you're overweight.**
- **Control high blood pressure.**
- **Exercise regularly.**
- **Engage in activities that challenge your mind.**
- **Eat a diet rich in colorful fruits and vegetables and low in saturated fat,** such as the Mediterranean diet.
- **Take a daily supplement containing 2,000 milligrams of omega-3 fatty acids.**

Blood Sugar Problems? Take Action Now to Protect Your Brain

Yutaka Kiyohara, MD, is a professor in the department of environmental medicine in the Graduate School of Medical Sciences at Kyushu University in Fukuoka, Japan, and coauthor of a study on diabetes and dementia risk published in *Neurology*.

Knowledge is power—so even though the news from a recent study on dementia is not exactly welcome, the information is indeed beneficial if it inspires people to take steps that can help keep their brains healthy. The findings are particularly important for people with diabetes...and also, surprisingly, for those with prediabetes, a condition that now affects half of Americans ages 65 and older.

Study details: 1,017 seniors did oral glucose tolerance tests (in which blood sugar is measured after fasting and again after consuming a sweet drink) to determine whether they had normal blood sugar levels...impaired glucose tolerance, a prediabetic condition...or diabetes. Participants were then followed for 15 years to see who developed Alzheimer's disease, vascular dementia (caused by blood vessel damage) or some other form of dementia.

Findings: Compared with participants who had normal blood sugar levels, those with prediabetes were 35% more likely to develop some type of dementia and 60% more likely to develop Alzheimer's. People with diabetes fared even worse, having a 74% higher risk for dementia of any kind, an 82% higher risk for vascular dementia and more than double the risk for Alzheimer's.

The connection: Diabetes and prediabetes can damage blood vessels, causing inflammation and lack of blood flow to the brain, which in turn lead to brain cell death...and/or excess glucose carried through the blood vessels to the brain may allow accumulation of proteins that damage nerve cells.

Self-defense: More research is needed...but for now, maintaining good blood sugar control seems like a sensible way to reduce dementia risk. Ask your doctor about getting screened for prediabetes and diabetes, particularly if you are over age 45, are overweight, have high blood pressure, have a family history of diabetes and/or have a history of diabetes during pregnancy.

If you have prediabetes: According to the American Diabetes Association, you can reduce your odds of developing diabetes by more than half by doing moderate exercise (such as brisk walking) for 30 minutes five days per week and losing 7% of your body weight (about 14 pounds if you currently weigh 200 or about 10 pounds if you weigh 150).

If you have diabetes: Be conscientious about controlling blood sugar through diet, exercise and/or medication...and talk to your doctor about seeing a neurologist if you notice signs of cognitive problems, such as memory loss.

Alzheimer's Indicator

One of the first signs of early-stage Alzheimer's disease is difficulty handling financial affairs. For that reason, people who have even mild symptoms should immediately get help managing their affairs before the disease progresses. They also should speak to their doctors about treatment options.

Symptoms to watch for: Forgetting to pay bills or paying them more than once...difficulty balancing the checkbook or doing simple calculations...increased susceptibility to scam artists.

If you or a loved one is showing any of these signs: A relative or close friend can be given "financial power of attorney" to handle financial duties if it becomes necessary.

Stephen McConnell, PhD, vice president for advocacy and public policy, Alzheimer's Association, Chicago.

Better Way to Find Alzheimer's Trials

The nonprofit Alzheimer's Association recently launched a confidential phone- and Web-based service known as TrialMatch, which connects interested Alzheimer's patients, caregivers and physicians with clinical trials actively recruiting study participants. To learn about the more than 110 ongoing clinical trials for mild cognitive impairment or Alzheimer's disease and related dementias, consult TrialMatch (800-272-3900, *www.alz.org/*

trialmatch). Discuss your findings with your physician.

William Thies, PhD, chief medical and scientific officer, Alzheimer's Association, Chicago.

It Might Not Be Alzheimer's

Jacob Teitelbaum, MD, board-certified internist and founder of Practitioners Alliance Network, an organization for health-care providers dedicated to improving communication among all branches of the healing arts. He is author, with Bill Gottlieb, of *Real Cause, Real Cure.*

Zaldy S. Tan, MD, MPH, assistant professor of medicine at Harvard Medical School and director of the Preventive Health in Aging Program at Brigham and Women's Hospital, both in Boston. He is the author of *Age-Proof Your Mind: Detect, Delay and Prevent Memory Loss—Before It's Too Late.*

If a doctor says that you or a loved one has Alzheimer's disease, take a deep breath and get a second opinion. Studies have shown that between 30% and 50% of people diagnosed with Alzheimer's turn out not to have it.

Bottom line: The symptoms common to Alzheimer's can be caused by other reversible conditions. Problems with memory and other cognitive functions often are linked to what Dr. Jacob Teitelbaum calls MIND—metabolism, infection or inflammation, nutrition or drug side effects—or a combination of these factors. Addressing these can markedly improve cognitive function. Even people who do have Alzheimer's will see improvements.

METABOLISM

Anyone who is experiencing confusion, memory loss or other cognitive problems should have tests that look at the hormones that affect metabolism. In particular...

- **Thyroid hormone.** A low level of thyroid hormone often causes confusion and memory loss. It also increases the risk for Alzheimer's disease. In recent studies, thyroid levels on the low side in the normal range are associated with a 240% higher risk for dementia in women. Borderline low thyroid hormone is associated with as much as an 800% higher risk in men.

Treatment: For most people with unexplained chronic confusion and memory loss, I recommend a three-month trial of desiccated thyroid (30 mg to 60 mg) to see if it helps. It is a thyroid extract containing the two key thyroid hormones. (The commonly prescribed medication Synthroid has just one of the two.) If you have risk factors for heart disease—such as high LDL cholesterol and high blood pressure—your doctor should start you with a low dose and increase it gradually.

- **Testosterone.** This hormone normally declines by about 1% a year after the age of 30. But in one study, men who went on to develop Alzheimer's disease had about half as much testosterone in their bloodstreams as men who did not.

Every 50% increase in testosterone is associated with a 26% decrease in the risk for Alzheimer's.

My advice: Men should ask their doctors about using a testosterone cream if their testosterone tests low—or even if it's at the lower quarter of the normal range. Limit the dose to 25 mg to 50 mg/day. More than that has been linked to heart attack and stroke.

INFECTIONS AND INFLAMMATION

You naturally will get large amounts of protective anti-inflammatory chemical compounds just by eating a healthy diet and using supplements such as fish oil and curcumin (see next page). For extra protection, take aspirin. In addition to reducing inflammation, it's among the best ways to prevent blood clots and vascular dementia, which is as common as Alzheimer's disease. In addition, infections leave us feeling mentally foggy. Have your doctor look for and treat any bladder and sinus infections.

Treatment: Talk to your doctor about taking one enteric-coated low-dose (81-mg) aspirin daily to improve circulation and reduce the risk for ministrokes in the brain. Even people with Alzheimer's may have had a series of ministrokes, adding to their cognitive decline. This is especially important when mental worsening occurs in small distinct steps instead of gradually.

NUTRITION

The typical American diet is just as bad for your brain and memory as it is for your heart. Too much fat, sugar and processed food increase cell-damaging inflammation throughout the body, including in the brain.

In one study, Columbia University researchers studied more than 2,100 people over the age of 65 who consumed healthy foods such as nuts, fruits, fish, chicken and leafy, dark green vegetables and who limited their consumption of meat and dairy. They were 48% less likely to be diagnosed with Alzheimer's over a four-year period.

Especially important…

• **B-12.** Millions of older adults don't get or absorb enough vitamin B-12, a nutrient that is critical for memory and other brain functions. You might be deficient even if you eat a healthful diet due to the age-related decline in stomach acid and intrinsic factor, a protein needed for B-12 absorption.

My advice: Take a multivitamin that contains 500 micrograms (mcg) of B-12 and at least 400 mcg of folic acid and 50 mg of the other B vitamins. If you test low-normal for B-12 (less than 400 ng/ml), also ask your doctor about getting a series of 10 B-12 shots.

Helpful: Have one teaspoon of apple cider vinegar with every meal. Use it in salad dressing, or mix it into eight ounces of vegetable juice or water. It will increase B-12 absorption.

Caution: Vinegar is highly acidic if you drink it straight.

• **Fish oil.** The American Heart Association advises everyone to eat fish at least twice a week. That's enough for the heart, but it won't provide all of the omega-3 fatty acids that you need for optimal brain health. Fish-oil supplements can ensure that you get enough.

Treatment: I recommend three to four servings a week of fatty fish, such as salmon, tuna, herring or sardines. Or take 1,000 mg of fish oil daily. You will need more if you're already having memory/cognitive problems. Ask your doctor how much to take.

• **Curcumin.** Alzheimer's is 70% less common in India than in the US, possibly because of the large amounts of turmeric that are used in curries and other Indian dishes.

Curcumin, which gives turmeric its yellow color, reduces inflammation and improves blood flow to the brain. Animal studies show that it dissolves the amyloid plaques that are found in the brains of Alzheimer's patients.

My advice: Unless you live in India, you're not likely to get enough curcumin in your diet to help, because it is poorly absorbed. Use a special highly absorbed form of curcumin (such as BCM-95 found in CuraMed 750 mg), and take one to two capsules twice a day.

Caution: Taking curcumin with blood thinners can increase the risk for bleeding.

• **Thiamine (vitamin B-1).** Heavy alcohol use, anorexia, bariatric surgery and sometimes rapidly growing malignant tumors can cause a severe deficiency of thiamine (vitamin B-1). If this condition becomes chronic, patients may have difficulty walking straight and will also have cognitive problems that can resemble those of Alzheimer's disease. Severe malnutrition also may cause confusion.

Distinguishing signs: Patients may suffer fatigue, loss of mental alertness, depression and abdominal discomfort. Blood tests will show thiamine levels that are close to zero.

Treatment: Severely low thiamine is an emergency in the acute phase. Patients who receive an intravenous thiamine infusion in time, and maintain adequate thiamine levels afterward, may recover and regain their physical/mental abilities. However, those who continue to have low thiamine (often because of chronic alcohol consumption) may suffer permanent cognitive damage.

TOO MANY DRUGS

Medication side effects are a very common cause of mental decline. This can occur even when you aren't taking drugs with obvious "mind-altering" effects, such as narcotic painkillers. Many drugs—antidepressants, incontinence meds and even simple muscle relaxants—can impair cognitive functions. The risk is higher when you're taking multiple medications and experience drug-drug interactions.

Doctors are far more likely to add medications than to subtract them. Many older adults are taking five or more medications daily.

Treatment: Ask your doctor to review all of your medications. Make sure that you're taking only drugs that you absolutely need—not "leftover" medications that might have been prescribed in the past and that you no longer need. Then ask for a three-week trial off each medication that is considered necessary to see if those drugs are contributing to the dementia (substituting other medications or closer monitoring during those three weeks usually can allow this).

DEPRESSION

Cognitive impairments due to depression are known as *pseudodementia.* Because of a depression-induced lack of attention, which makes it difficult to form and process effective memories, patients may forget appointments or have difficulty remembering names. They also may have trouble concentrating, learning new things and even recognizing faces. This type of dementia, unlike Alzheimer's, is potentially reversible.

Distinguishing signs: Sleep disturbances are more likely to occur with depression than with early-stage Alzheimer's disease. For example, depressed patients may have early morning awakenings or experience difficulty falling asleep at night (typically marked by tossing and turning in bed). They can also have unexplained tearfulness as well as a lack of interest in things that they used to enjoy, a condition called anhedonia.

Treatment: If depression is the culprit, consider talk therapy or an antidepressant, such as *citalopram* (Celexa) or *sertraline* (Zoloft). An antidepressant can usually treat the forgetfulness associated with depression, but it may take several weeks to determine whether a particular drug/dose is going to work. You might also ask your doctor about Saint-John's-wort and other over-the-counter (OTC) natural remedies.

NPH

It's estimated that up to 200,000 older adults in the US have excessive accumulation of fluid on the brain, a condition known as normal pressure hydrocephalus (NPH). The fluid presses on the brain and can cause memory loss and other symptoms that may mimic Alzheimer's.

Distinguishing signs: Most patients with NPH have three main symptoms—an unsteady gait (in the early stages)...followed by urinary incontinence...and cognitive impairments (in later stages). With Alzheimer's, the order is reversed—memory loss and/or other cognitive problems occur first, followed in later stages of the disease by problems with bladder control and gait.

Treatment: NPH can potentially be corrected by inserting a shunt, a tube in the brain that drains excess fluid. However, the surgical procedure is not recommended until after the diagnosis is confirmed by an MRI of the brain and a trial removal of a small amount of fluid through a lumbar tap results in improved memory and/or gait.

STROKE

When a person has a series of mini (warning) strokes, it can lead to a type of vascular dementia known as multi-infarct dementia, which can be mistaken for Alzheimer's.

Multi-infarct dementia occurs when damaged blood vessels in the brain slow (but don't completely stop) normal circulation. Reductions in blood and the oxygen it carries can damage brain cells and impair memory and other cognitive abilities—but usually without the motor deficits that accompany a stroke, such as weakness of a limb or slow and/or garbled speech.

Distinguishing signs: Multi-infarct dementia can cause rapid changes in mental functions, sometimes within a few weeks to a month. With Alzheimer's disease, these changes typically occur slowly but steadily over several years.

Treatment: Multi-infarct dementia usually can be diagnosed with a CT or MRI scan showing characteristic changes in the brain. Unfortunately, existing brain damage can't be reversed, although future damage may be avoided. The goal of treatment is to prevent additional vascular damage and cognitive declines by treating the underlying risk factors, such as high blood pressure.

B-12 Shots Can Fight Alzheimer's

B-12 shots can fight Alzheimer's disease, depression and panic disorders. Vitamin B-12 inhibits a brain enzyme that breaks down chemicals involved in maintaining memory and mood.

But: One-fifth of Americans over age 40 do not produce enough stomach acid to absorb B-12 from protein in food, such as meat, eggs and dairy products, or from oral supplements, so they don't get a sufficient supply of the vitamin. Ask your doctor if monthly B-12 injections would be a good idea for you.

The late Arthur Winter, MD, director of New Jersey Neurological Institute, Livingston, and coauthor of *Smart Food.*

Aspirin—Can It Prevent Alzheimer's?

Even though most people think of aspirin as that "good old drug" that relieves pain and helps prevent heart attack and stroke, researchers now are finding strong evidence that it may fight other devastating medical conditions—including Alzheimer's.

With such positive findings, you might assume that everyone should now be taking aspirin, a nonsteroidal anti-inflammatory drug (NSAID). But aspirin can have certain serious—and sometimes hidden—side effects. *Here's how to safely take aspirin to reduce your risk for Alzheimer's...*

A study of nearly 13,500 people, published in the journal *Neurology*, found that people who regularly used aspirin or some other NSAID were 23% less likely to be diagnosed with Alzheimer's than those who didn't take one of these drugs. It's possible that the drugs reduce the accumulation of plaques in the brain, which have been linked to Alzheimer's.

My advice: Don't take aspirin as an Alzheimer's preventive. The research isn't quite strong enough yet to make it worth risking aspirin's side effects. However, if you regularly take aspirin or another NSAID for some other condition, such as arthritis, you may also be reducing your Alzheimer's risk.

THE DOWNSIDE OF ASPIRIN

About 50,000 Americans die every year from GI bleeding caused in part by aspirin or other NSAIDs. High doses are more likely to cause problems, but even low-dose aspirin can cause bleeding in some patients.

To protect yourself: Be sure to talk to your doctor before taking aspirin—at any dose—on a daily basis. Let him/her know if you develop stomach pain, cramping or other symptoms after taking it.

If you experience symptoms when taking aspirin, ask your doctor about trying the enteric-coated variety. It's less likely to cause stomach upset, and it appears to thin the blood and reduce cancer risks as effectively as regular aspirin. However, enteric-coated aspirin can still cause bleeding in some people.

What most people don't know: Aspirin-related damage to the stomach/GI tract may not cause symptoms. To detect problems: Ask your doctor to perform a fecal occult blood test about three months after you start aspirin therapy and annually thereafter.

If it's more convenient, consider using an over-the-counter test (such as Hemoccult or ColoCARE) that detects small amounts of blood in the stool, which can indicate damage to the GI tract. Discuss this first with your physician.

Caution: Bleeding risk is increased if aspirin is combined with certain prescription medications such as *warfarin* (Coumadin), corticosteroids and some antidepressants, as well as some supplements, including ginkgo biloba, fish oil and willow bark. Taking another NSAID, such as ibuprofen, with aspirin also increases bleeding risk.

Using high doses of aspirin has been shown to cause ringing in the ears (tinnitus) and/or hearing loss in some people, so be sure to have your hearing checked if you notice any changes in your hearing while taking aspirin.

Stefan Gluck, MD, PhD, Sylvester Professor, department of medicine, University of Miami Miller School of Medicine in Miami, Florida.

An Apple a Day Keeps Alzheimer's Away

Apple skins fight Alzheimer's disease and cancer. They contain high levels of quercetin, an antioxidant that may fight cell damage linked with these diseases.

Best: Eat at least one red apple a day. Quercetin also can be found in onions, raspberries, cherries, red wine, red grapes, citrus fruits, broccoli, leafy greens and green and black tea.

Chang Y. Lee, PhD, professor and department chairman, department of food science and technology, Cornell University, Geneva, New York

---

Stay Sharp as You Age—Surprising Causes of Memory Loss

Pamela W. Smith, MD, MPH, MS, a diplomat of the Board of the American Academy of Anti-Aging Physicians and founder and director of The Fellowship in Metabolic, Anti-Aging and Functional Medicine, Boca Raton, Florida. She is author of *What You Must Know About Memory Loss & How to Stop It.*

It is no secret that age and memory are intertwined. But age itself is not the sole reason that we forget things. Memory loss often can be traced to specific factors, including hormonal changes, inflammation and exposure to mercury and other toxins.

Common causes of memory loss—and what you can do to control them...

LOW TESTOSTERONE

After a man reaches age 30, his testosterone goes into free fall. Levels drop by about 1% a year. At least 30% of men in their 70s are hypogonadal, with very low testosterone.

Low testosterone increases the death of brain cells. It also has been linked to an increase in amyloid-B, proteins that are associated with Alzheimer's disease and other forms of dementia.

What to do: If a saliva test shows low testosterone, your doctor may recommend creams, injections or other forms of testosterone replacement. Men who supplement with testosterone have been shown to have improvements in verbal memory (the recall of verbal information) and spatial memory (the part of the memory responsible for recording information about one's environment and spatial orientation).

Important: Women need testosterone, too, and should get tested. Testosterone replacement in women with low levels can help preserve memory.

LOW ESTROGEN

Women often refer to the "brain fog" that occurs during menopause. It's a real phenomenon that is caused in part by declining levels of estrogen. Every brain cell is affected by estrogen, which conducts chemical signals through the hippocampus and other areas of the brain.

Low-dose estrogen replacement can improve brain circulation and reduce the risk for Alzheimer's disease by up to 54%.

Men also depend on estrogen for brain function, although they require smaller amounts than women.

What to do: Both men and women should ask their doctors for a saliva-estrogen test. It measures "free" levels of the three different forms of estrogen (estrone, estradiol and estriol). Free estrogen is the form that is active and available for immediate use in the body.

If your estrogen is low, your doctor may prescribe supplemental hormones. I advise patients to use bioidentical hormones that are made from natural substances. They may be more effective—and cause fewer side effects—than synthetic forms of estrogen.

LOW THYROID

People with low levels of thyroid hormone (hypothyroidism) often experience memory loss. Unfortunately, doctors don't routinely test for it. They mistakenly attribute the symptoms—such as memory loss, fatigue, increased sensitivity to cold, apathy or weight gain—to other conditions, including depression.

What to do: Get a thyroid test if you have any of the above symptoms. A diet high in B vitamins (from meats, whole grains and fortified cereals) and vitamin A (from brightly colored produce) can help improve thyroid function. An adequate intake of iodine (iodized salt is a source) also is important.

If your level of thyroid hormones is too low, your doctor probably will prescribe a thyroid replacement, such as *levothyroxine* (Synthroid) or Armour Thyroid.

IMPAIRED CIRCULATION

If you have high cholesterol or other cardiovascular risk factors—you smoke, have high blood pressure, are sedentary, overweight, etc.—you probably have at least some atherosclerosis, fatty plaques in the arteries that reduce the flow of blood and oxygen to the brain.

What to do: In addition to the obvious—more exercise, weight loss, not smoking—I strongly advise patients to eat a Mediterranean-style diet. This features lots of fruits, vegetables and grains along with healthy amounts of olive oil and fish. A recent study found that people who closely followed this diet were 28% less likely to develop mild cognitive impairment and 48% less likely to get Alzheimer's disease.

Also helpful: Eating more soluble fiber (such as that found in oatmeal, beans, fruit and nuts) or taking a fiber supplement has been shown in both men and women to decrease hardening of the arteries and improve circulation.

EXPOSURE TO MERCURY

Americans are exposed to mercury all the time. It is present in soil, the water supply and some foods, including many fish. It also is used in many dental fillings. Over time, the mercury from fillings and other sources can cause inflammation and oxidative stress in the brain, both of which can damage the neurotransmitters that are essential for memory and other brain functions.

What to do: You can get tested for mercury and other heavy metals, but the tests will be positive only after long-term exposure. I advise patients to reduce their exposure long before it will show up on any test.

If you have dental fillings made of amalgam (an alloy of mercury and other metals), consider replacing them with fillings made from plastics or other materials. The work should be done by an environmental dentist who specializes in the safe removal of mercury.

Also important: Avoid eating shark, swordfish, king mackerel, marlin, orange roughy, ahi tuna and tilefish, which tend to accumulate mercury. Limit canned albacore tuna to three servings or less per month and canned light tuna to six servings or less per month. Best: Cold-water salmon.

Good News for Grandmas!

Postmenopausal women who took care of their grandchildren one day a week had better memory and faster cognitive speed (important for warding off dementia) than those who didn't.

Possible explanation: Active grandparenting includes positive interactions, ongoing learning and mental stimulation—all of which reduce risk for dementia. Careful, though... women who cared for grandchildren five or more days a week had significantly lower cognitive scores, possibly because they felt exhausted.

Cassandra Szoeke, MD, PhD, associate professor of medicine, The University of Melbourne, Australia.

Music for the Brain

In a new study of musicians, researchers found that blood flow to the area of the brain responsible for musical skills also improved language skills. Interestingly, brain blood-flow patterns in non-musicians became similar to those of musicians after only 30 minutes of musical training.

Takeaway: Playing a musical instrument or singing also may help keep your verbal skills sharp.

Georg Meyer, PhD, professor of psychology, University of Liverpool, UK.

Just 10 Hours of Brain Training Can Produce Benefits That Last 10 Years

George W. Rebok, MA, PhD, professor, department of mental health, Center on Aging and Health, The Johns Hopkins University, Baltimore. His National Institutes of Health–funded study was published in *Journal of the American Geriatrics Society.*

Making meals, paying bills, phoning friends, cleaning house, handling personal hygiene—these day-to-day activities may seem mundane. But as we age, the ability to keep doing them is key to our continued independence. When waning brainpower makes it hard to handle such tasks of daily living, quality of life declines... so of course we want to do whatever we can to hang onto our cognitive skills.

Good news: Simple kinds of brain training can help us maintain or even improve our mental skills—and according to an exciting study, training for just 10 hours can bring benefits that last for 10 years!

Participants included 2,832 men and women who at the start of the study had an average age of 74 and were living independently. They were randomly assigned to one of four groups. The control group got no training. The others (the "intervention" groups) were asked to attend 10 training sessions lasting 60 to 75 minutes each, spread over five to six weeks... and some of these participants also attended four additional "booster" sessions one to three years later.

Training was done in small groups and consisted of instruction and practice aimed at improving one of three types of cognitive skills...

- **Speed of processing—**the ability to identify and locate visual information quickly, a skill that allows you to look up phone numbers, drive safely, etc.
- **Reasoning—**the ability to solve problems that follow patterns, such as reading bus schedules or filling out order forms.
- **Memory—**the ability to remember word lists, sequences of items and the main ideas in stories.

Participants' cognitive skills and ability to perform tasks of daily living were assessed through various tests and self-reports at the start of the study and periodically for 10 years thereafter. All the interventions produced immediate improvement in the specific skills in which participants were trained. But what was really stunning was how long-lasting the benefits were, especially considering the training's modest investment of time and effort. After 10 years, participants in all three intervention groups reported having less difficulty with daily tasks than the control group. At an average age of 82, about 60% of intervention group members reported that they were able to handle daily tasks as well as or even better than they had at the start of the study... fewer than half of control group members could make this claim.

On objective tests of skills, the intervention groups again came out ahead...

- **Speed of processing.** After 10 years, 71% of group members were still performing at or above the levels they had demonstrated at the start of the study, compared with only 49% of the control group. Those who had booster training did especially well.
- **Reasoning.** After 10 years, 74% of this group was still performing at or above their

starting level, compared with 62% of the control group. Again, those who had booster training did particularly well.

• **Memory.** Here the results were not as dramatic. Training improved memory for five years...though after 10 years, there was no significant difference between the intervention group and the control group. But five years of better memory for a few hours of work is still a good deal, don't you think?

This study is among the first to show that cognitive training actually translates to improvements in daily functioning—improvements that can help seniors maintain their independence. As the population continues to age, the number of older people with cognitive impairment is expected to skyrocket. The study authors estimate that if interventions were able to delay onset of cognitive impairment by six years, the number of people affected with dementia by the year 2050 would be reduced by more than one-third.

Train your brain: One of the training programs used in this study, speed of processing training, is commercially available from Posit Science. The other two programs, memory training and reasoning training, are not yet commercially available, but an online version of the memory training is currently in development. In addition, a number of universities have faculty involved in mental training research—so you might contact your local university to inquire about such programs.

You can do a lot on your own to protect your brainpower by keeping your mind active and engaged. Just as you might take the stairs instead of an elevator to keep your body strong, think of things that you can do every day to keep your mind strong. Try memorizing the items on your grocery list before you go to the store, then see how many you can remember before you need to refer to the list. Try doing mental calculations in your head before reaching for the calculator. Or read an article and then try to summarize the main points for a friend. Be creative! Anything you can do to challenge yourself mentally may help give your brain a boost.

Yoga Makes You Smarter

In a recent eight-week study, adults over age 55 who took an hour-long class of hatha yoga (the most commonly practiced form of yoga worldwide) three times a week had significantly better memory and attention than adults who simply did stretching and toning exercises. Possible reason: The focus required to hold poses and control breathing during yoga may result in better attention to mental tasks as well.

Neha Gothe, PhD, assistant professor of kinesiology, Wayne State University, Detroit.

CPAP Heals Brain Damage Caused by Sleep Apnea

Study titled "White Matter Integrity in Obstructive Sleep Apnea Before and After Treatment," published in *Sleep*.

If you suffer from obstructive sleep apnea, you may be among the very many people who would rather endure it and its health consequences, such as heart disease, than use a noisy and uncomfortable continuous positive airway pressure (CPAP) machine while you sleep. About 25% of people with sleep apnea refuse to use CPAP.

But now, the time for "blowing off" your CPAP machine has truly passed, because the results of a new study show something chilling: People who don't consistently use their CPAP machines are damaging their brains. That's right—if you don't use CPAP enough, it could be costing you your ability to think and your memory.

Here's why that happens...and how you can recover your lost brain function...

DIRE EFFECT OF SLEEP APNEA

The study was small but well designed. It included 32 men who were in the prime of life (average age 43). Seventeen of them had severe sleep apnea but had never used CPAP...and 15 were healthy men who acted as controls. The researchers used MRI scans to study participants' brains and, in particular, their white matter, which is the part of the brain that conducts nerve impulses and basically allows the different parts of the brain to communicate with each other. The men also took neuropsychological tests to evaluate their attention, reasoning, reaction times and long- and short-term memory.

The results, to put it mildly, were not good for the patients with sleep apnea. Neuropsychological tests taken before CPAP treatment began showed that the men with sleep apnea were simply not as sharp as the other men. Their thinking and reasoning were significantly slower and less accurate than the controls, and their short- and long-term memories were not as good. And the brain scans showed that the patients' white matter was not intact—in other words, neural connections weren't, in fact, connecting as efficiently as they should.

They had decided to delay treatment of their sleep apnea—and now their brains were disintegrating. But there was good news, too.

REGAIN YOUR BRAIN

The saving grace in this study was the following. In tracking the men's functioning over time, researchers discovered that CPAP can reverse the damage to the brain's white matter caused by sleep apnea. In fact, new white-matter connectedness began to be seen after only three months of regular CPAP use. After 12 months of use, a near complete reversal of white-matter damage in all of the affected parts of the brain was seen. This improvement in brain structure was reflected with improvement in memory, attention and other cognitive functions. In fact, scores on a series of neurocognitive tests matched nearly all the scores of the healthy controls. In short, CPAP virtually reversed brain damage caused by untreated sleep apnea.

In an earlier study, the same researchers found the same sort of results when they looked at how CPAP affected the brain's gray matter. Gray matter controls muscle function and the senses.

The bottom line is that, if left untreated, sleep apnea can—no exaggeration—wreck your brain. CPAP therapy is very effective and can save your brain—but only if you use it. Alternatives such as an implantable device and wearable devices that force you to change sleep positions when you roll over onto your back (which can set off sleep apnea) are alternatives that do not work as well as CPAP but are better than no treatment at all.

Also, new CPAP designs that are more comfortable and quieter are becoming available. Your doctor can also adjust the CPAP machine that you already have to make sure it fits comfortably. So, no more excuses...save your heart and your brain by doing what you can to manage your sleep apnea.

Exercise Prevents a Shrinking Brain

Exercise prevents brain shrinkage, according to a recent, small study from the Cleveland Clinic. People who have the APOE epsilon4 allele (e4 gene) are at increased risk for Alzheimer's disease. Consistent exercise may reduce risk.

Recent finding: After 18 months, the brain scans of people with the e4 gene who exercised moderately a few times a week showed dramatically less shrinkage in the hippocampus—which is associated with Alzheimer's—compared with people with the gene who were not physically active.

Stephen Rao, PhD, is a professor and director of Schey Center for Cognitive Neuroimaging, Cleveland Clinic, and leader of a study of 97 people, published in *Frontiers in Aging Neuroscience.*

Shocking Stats on How TV Shortens Your Life...and Hurts Your Brain

J. Lennert Veerman, MD, PhD, MPH, is a senior research fellow at the Centre for Burden of Disease and Cost-Effectiveness in the School of Population Health at the University of Queensland in Australia, and leader of a study published in *British Journal of Sports Medicine*.

Robert Friedland, MD, professor of neurology, Case Western Reserve University, Cleveland, and leader of a study of activity level and Alzheimer's incidence in 551 people, presented at the International Conference on Alzheimer's Disease and Related Disorders.

You know that vegging out in front of the boob tube isn't good for you. But have you heard about a disturbing study from Australia suggesting that TV's negative effects on life span are even worse than you probably imagined?

For the study, researchers analyzed data from an observational survey of more than 11,000 people ages 25 and older that began in 1999, cross-referencing against mortality figures for 2008.

Findings: People who spent a lifetime average of six hours per day watching television died 4.8 years sooner, on average, than people who watched no TV. Also, every single hour of TV viewed after age 25 reduced the average viewer's life expectancy by 22 minutes!

Explanation: It is an indirect link, according to study leader J. Lennert Veerman, MD, PhD, MPH, of the School of Population Health at the University of Queensland in Australia. The more time a person spends watching television, the less time she (or he) has for healthy behaviors proven to promote longevity, such as exercising and socializing. Also, Dr. Veerman noted, while researchers in this study adjusted for the effects of diet quality and waist circumference, other studies show that TV viewing typically is associated with a worse diet.

In another recent study out of Case Western Reserve University in Cleveland, researchers found a link between television and the brain. Alzheimer's risk increases by 30% for each hour of daily TV viewing. Watching TV doesn't cause Alzheimer's, but it is a marker of an inactive lifestyle, which can contribute to the disease. Mental and physical activity enhance brain health and help prevent diseases associated with aging.

Bottom line: TV's harmful effects on longevity may be comparable to the effects of major chronic disease risk factors such as obesity and physical inactivity—a fact worth remembering next time you are tempted to camp out in front of the boob tube.

Common Vitamin Slows Alzheimer's Symptoms

When people with mild-to-moderate Alzheimer's took a high dose of vitamin E—2,000 international units (IU) daily—they had slower declines in activities of daily living, such as dressing and bathing without help, than people who didn't take the vitamin or took the Alzheimer's drug memantine (Namenda). Vitamin E provided just over a six-month delay in the disease's progression over a two-year period.

Note: A doctor should be consulted before this therapy is tried—vitamin E may increase risk for bleeding and/or interact with medications.

Maurice Dysken, MD, geriatric psychiatrist, Minneapolis VA Health Care System, Minnesota.

Alzheimer's Slowed by Statins

In a three-year study of 300 Alzheimer's patients, the disease progressed more slowly (loss of 1.5 points in a 30-point mini mental status exam, or MMSE) in those who took a cholesterol-lowering drug than it did in those not taking the medication (loss of 2.5 points in MMSE).

Theory: High cholesterol levels increase the deposition of proteins that can impair brain function.

Florence Pasquier, MD, PhD, professor of neurology, University Hospital, Lille, France.

Don't Trust These Tests

Beware of online tests for Alzheimer's disease.

Recent finding: When 16 online Alzheimer's tests were evaluated by two panels of experts, the tests were found to be misleading and their results invalid...and some of the tests did not disclose that they were associated with companies that market products and services to people who have dementia.

Study of 16 online Alzheimer's tests by researchers at British Columbia University, Vancouver, Canada, presented at the Alzheimer's Association International Conference in Boston.

Bacteria for Alzheimer's

In a novel approach to Alzheimer's, a bacterial virus (phage) is introduced through the nose, goes to the brain and dissolves disease-causing plaques. Mice given the phage for one year had 80% fewer plaques than untreated mice.

American Friends of Tel Aviv University, *AFTAU.org.*

Ask Your Doctor About Memory Loss

Very early stages of Alzheimer's disease may show up in memory issues that are too small for doctors to notice or test for—but that are apparent to the person experiencing them. People should trust what they observe about themselves and talk to their doctors if they are concerned about their memory. Signs of Alzheimer's disease include memory changes that are disruptive to daily life...challenges in planning or solving problems...and difficulty completing familiar tasks.

Rebecca Amariglio, PhD, is a clinical neuropsychologist at Harvard Medical School and Brigham and Women's Hospital, both in Boston. Her study of brain changes in 189 people was presented at the Alzheimer's Association International Conference.

More Than Half of Alzheimer's Cases Could Be Prevented with Lifestyle Changes

Many of the biggest risk factors for Alzheimer's disease are modifiable—lack of physical activity, depression, smoking, midlife hypertension, midlife obesity and diabetes. Changing or eliminating these risks could potentially prevent 2.9 million Alzheimer's cases in the US.

Deborah Barnes, PhD, MPH, associate professor of psychiatry, University of California, San Francisco, and leader of a comprehensive review published online in *The Lancet Neurology.*

Midlife Stress Linked to Late-Life Dementia

Among 800 women tracked for nearly 40 years, those who experienced significant stress (divorce, widowhood, loss of a child or mental illness in a loved one) were 21% more likely to develop Alzheimer's disease.

Why: Stress may cause structural and functional changes in the brain, which may linger for years after a stressful event.

If you're facing midlife stress: Try psychotherapy, meditation and/or yoga.

Lena Johansson, PhD, researcher, University of Gothenburg, Mölndal, Sweden.

The Spice That Could Keep Alzheimer's Away

Muralidhar Hegde, PhD, research scientist, and Sankar Mitra, PhD, professor of biochemistry and molecular biology, University of Texas Medical Branch, Galveston, Texas.

Curcumin, a phytochemical that is found in the spice turmeric, may be the super-spice your brain needs, according to recent research. This intriguing study comes from the University of Texas Medical Branch in Galveston—it was published in *Journal of Biological Chemistry*. We've been learning for years that this phytochemical can prevent and treat many diseases, such as certain cancers, but this is the first study to suggest that curcumin is also beneficial to the brain.

SWEEPING AWAY METALS

Lead study author Muralidhar Hegde, PhD, and senior author Sankar Mitra, PhD, noted that our bodies naturally contain trace amounts of certain metals, including copper and iron. In small amounts, these metals are not only harmless but essential for good health. But some people's brain cells—for reasons that scientists don't yet completely understand—start accumulating large amounts of copper or iron, which can wreak havoc.

If you have a large amount of iron and copper in your brain cells, the extra "free" metals overwhelm the proteins that are supposed to store them and start causing two major problems. First, they initiate chemical reactions that lead to DNA damage. And then, to make matters worse, Dr. Hegde and colleagues found, they also interfere with DNA repair enzymes that attempt to fix the damage. Since too much unrepaired DNA damage can lead to neurodegenerative disorders, that's one scary situation.

THE WONDER SPICE

But it's not all doom and gloom. The researchers tested several chemicals called metal chelators and natural dietary and/or plant components in petri dishes to see if any of the substances would help keep iron and copper stored so they wouldn't interfere with the DNA repair enzymes. All the substances tested worked to some extent, but there was one that worked better than all the rest—curcumin. "Curcumin appeared to stop the metals from blocking the DNA repair by more than 90% to 95%—so it essentially reversed the damage to the genetic material," said Dr. Hegde.

A natural remedy that may help stave off Alzheimer's disease is exciting to think about—but, said Dr. Hegde, it's important to keep the nature of this particular finding in context. Animal testing is in order to confirm that curcumin is an effective treatment and to know exactly how much curcumin belongs in the ideal dose, then researchers can move on to human studies.

In the meantime, since what we are talking about is just a common spice, what can't hurt—and might greatly help—is to consume greater quantities of curcumin in foods like Indian and Asian dishes.

An MRI May Reveal Alzheimer's

By using arterial spin labeling (ASL), which can be done by all modern MRI scanning machines, it may be possible to detect very subtle blood flow changes in parts of the brain linked to memory. Early detection could make it possible to start medicines to slow decline.

Sven Haller, MD, is a senior physician in clinical neuroradiology at Geneva University Hospital, Switzerland, and leader of a study published online in *Radiology*.

How to Cut Your Risk for Alzheimer's...by 50%: "Brain Fitness" Activities Help Ward Off Cognitive Decline

Pierce J. Howard, PhD, a leading cognitive researcher and cofounder and director of research at the Center for Applied Cognitive Studies in Charlotte, North Carolina. He is the author of *The Owner's Manual for the Brain: Everyday Applications from Mind-Brain Research.*

It's easy to blame fading memory and waning cognitive skills on advancing age. But in reality, age doesn't hurt the brain as much as unhealthful habits, such as a sedentary lifestyle...poor food choices...excessive alcohol use...and chronic health problems, such as heart disease, high blood pressure, diabetes, obesity and depression.

Latest development: Although the evidence is not yet definitive, a growing body of scientific research suggests that people who incorporate a steady dose of mental challenges into their daily activities are less likely to suffer cognitive decline—including that associated with Alzheimer's disease.

For example, a landmark study of 678 nuns found that although autopsies revealed some of them had late-stage Alzheimer's disease upon death, those who were mentally active did not develop behavioral symptoms of the disease while they were alive—perhaps because they had reserves of brain cells.

While some neurologists recommend crossword puzzles and the popular number-placement game Sudoku to help promote brain fitness, there are a variety of other activities that are less well-known but perhaps just as effective—if not more so. By varying your brain-fitness workout, you will maximize the benefits.

My five favorites...

1. Adopt a "back-to-school" attitude. Until recently, scientists believed that we had a finite number of brain cells. Now, research shows that we are able to generate new brain cells (neurons) and connections (synapses) between them. Acquiring new knowledge and skills—no matter what your age—is one of the best ways to stimulate brain activity.

Even if you do develop the classic brain changes associated with Alzheimer's disease, having a ready supply of additional brain cells may help protect you from the signs and symptoms of dementia. The key is to learn something brand new and mentally challenging.

What to try: If you enjoy books, read about an unfamiliar topic and grapple with it until you understand it. If you play music, learn a new piece—or better yet, a new instrument—and practice until you master it. Learning a foreign language (CDs are available at most public libraries) also promotes brain health.

Helpful: Devote the first part of the day to learning. At that time of day, you are less likely to be fatigued, and your attention will be better. During the day, review the material and other information you learned on previous days.

Smart idea: You can study a wide variety of subjects, ranging from pure science and the humanities to architecture and engineering, by enrolling in one of the 1,800 free college-level online classes offered by the Massachusetts Institute of Technology. To learn more, go to MIT OpenCourseWare at *http://ocw.mit.edu.* To learn a new vocabulary word each day, sign up for A.Word.A.Day at *www.wordsmith.org.*

2. Involve others in your brain workouts. Research shows that people who interact socially on a regular basis are less likely to suffer cognitive decline—perhaps due to the soothing effects of the brain chemicals serotonin and endorphins, which are secreted during positive interactions with others. This, in turn, reduces levels of the hormone cortisol, which contributes to deterioration of the hippocampus, the brain's memory storage center. By involving other people in your brain activities, you not only challenge your cognitive abilities but also increase your social connections, thus further protecting your brain.

What to try: Chess, bridge, backgammon or board games, such as Stratego or Risk, that test your ability to strategize.

Also helpful: Increase your social interactions by joining a book club, a civic organization or a religious group. Or get involved in volunteer work.

3. Do brain-sharpening exercises online. For times when you are alone, online brain-training games are a good option. Researchers at the University of Michigan in Ann Arbor recently found that people who performed computer-based brain-training exercises for about 30 minutes daily boosted their ability to reason and solve new problems.

What to try: Play different games on different days. This helps to thicken the myelin sheath (fatty tissue surrounding nerve fibers) on existing neural pathways and fosters the emergence of new synapses. For a wide variety of free online games and brain teasers, go to *www.gamesforthebrain.com* or *www.sharpbrains.com.*

4. Surprise your brain with new habits. Experts call these exercises "neurobics," activities that jar the brain into forming new synapses by creating new associations. The idea is to do something familiar—but in an unfamiliar way. A good plan for doing this is to tweak one old habit every week. Find a pattern that works for you. Later, disrupt the pattern—to keep yourself on your toes!

What to try: Drive a different route to work...eat a type of ethnic food you've never experienced...if you wear your watch on your left wrist, try putting it on your right...switch the part in your hair to the other side...and brush your teeth or hold eating utensils with your nondominant hand.

5. Preserve your brain's equilibrium. As we age, changes occur in our sense of balance, which is controlled by signals that the brain receives from certain sensory systems. To adapt gradually to this change, we need to force ourselves to experiment with unaccustomed postures, which helps us become familiar with our new "internal gyroscope."

What to try: Whenever you're waiting in line, lift one foot off the ground and balance your weight on the other foot for as long as possible. Then, switch feet and rest your weight on the other foot. A good sense of balance helps prevent falls and preserves the brain's equilibrium.

Caution: If you feel unsteady on your feet, do not attempt this activity unless you can support yourself by holding on to a counter or railing.

Delaying Retirement May Protect Your Brain

For each additional year that a person worked before retiring, dementia risk dropped by 3%. That means someone who retired at age 60 had a 15% greater chance of developing dementia, on average, than someone who retired at 65. Theory: The mental stimulation and social connections at work may keep the brain healthy.

Analysis of the records of more than 400,000 retired workers in France by researchers at National Institute of Health and Medical Research, Paris, presented at the 2013 Alzheimer's Association International Conference.

Are You Shrinking Your Brain?—Surprising Ways to Stay Mentally Sharp

Daniel G. Amen, MD, a brain-imaging specialist and assistant clinical professor of psychiatry and human behavior at the University of California, Irvine, School of Medicine. He is the author of several books, including *Use Your Brain to Change Your Age: Secrets to Look, Feel, and Think Younger Every Day.*

When scientists talk about memory and learning, the hippocampus, a small, seahorse-shaped structure located deep inside the brain, gets most of the credit for these vital cognitive functions.

What you don't hear much about: The prefrontal cortex (PFC), a much larger part of the brain located just behind and slightly beneath the forehead. Known as the "executive" part of the brain because it controls judgment, insights and impulse control, the PFC is just as important when it comes to staying sharp mentally, learning new information and controlling processes involved in memory.

Unfortunately, millions of Americans don't follow simple lifestyle habits that promote optimal functioning of the PFC. Result: Lapses in judgment (such as making risky maneuvers when driving)...disorganized thinking (including an inability to prioritize tasks)...shorter attention spans (resulting in difficulty with reading and other activities that require focus)...and impairments in learning and memory.

IMPROVE YOUR BRAIN—LIVE LONGER

The PFC needs good "fuel" to thrive. That's why people with healthful habits tend to have a larger PFC than those who don't take good care of themselves. As a result, they're more likely to live longer (because their judgment about risks is better), and they're less likely to develop Alzheimer's disease.

Important finding: A 2007 study of Catholic nuns and priests found that those who had the most self-discipline were 89% less likely to develop Alzheimer's disease. Self-discipline is one of the traits that is enhanced when you have a robust PFC.

POWER UP YOUR "WIRING"

People with healthful habits have less damage to myelin, the fatty coating on brain cells, than people who are less conscientious about their health. Brain cells that are sheathed in myelin work 10 to 100 times faster than unmyelinated cells. People with healthful habits also tend to have better blood circulation in the brain, which improves thinking as well as memory.

To protect your PFC—and other key parts of the brain...

- **Rethink your alcohol intake.** Millions of Americans drink a glass or two of red wine a day because it's good for the heart. But the cardio-protective properties of alcohol—it raises HDL "good" cholesterol and reduces clots, thus reducing the risk for a heart attack—may be offset by the damage it can do to the brain. Alcohol decreases the size and functioning of the PFC. What's more, even moderate drinking (two drinks daily for men and one for women) can impair brain circulation.

My advice: If your doctor agrees that you can forgo the cardiovascular benefits of drinking wine, limit your intake to no more than two or three alcoholic beverages per week.

- **"Water" your brain.** The brain is 80% water. People who don't drink enough water or who drink a lot of dehydrating liquids, such as alcohol or caffeinated coffee or tea, often have impairments in cognition and judgment, which can occur when the PFC is damaged.

My advice: Drink plenty of water—eight glasses (64 ounces) of water every day is typically sufficient. If you like, add a splash of lemon or lime juice for flavor.

- **Slow down on the omega-6s.** Most Americans get far too many inflammation-promoting omega-6 essential fatty acids in their diets—primarily from cooking oils (such as corn and vegetable), fatty red meats and processed foods—that are harmful to the brain. That's why a plant-based, anti-inflammatory diet is among the most effective ways to reduce damage to the PFC and other areas of the brain.

My advice: Eat lots of greens—including salads—along with vegetables, fruit, whole grains and legumes. Approximately three servings of lean protein daily will help balance blood sugar and keep you feeling sharp. Also, eat at least three servings weekly of cold-water fish such as salmon, mackerel and sardines. The omega-3s in these fish have potent anti-inflammatory effects. Fish oil supplements (1 g to 3 g daily) are also helpful. Check with your doctor first if you use a blood thinner.

- **Aim to change your diet so that your intake of omega-6 fatty acids** is no more than three times higher than your intake of omega-3s.

Good rule of thumb: A plant-based diet that's high in fish provides the ideal 3:1 (or lower) ratio of omega-6s to omega-3s.

• **Try green tea and rhodiola.** Distractibility, disorganization and poor impulse control are commonly associated with children who may be suffering from attention-deficit/hyperactivity disorder (ADHD), but many adults (who may or may not have ADHD) also struggle with such symptoms.

Often linked to low activity in the PFC, these symptoms can be reversed, in part, with green tea and rhodiola, a plant-based supplement frequently used as an energy booster. In one study, researchers at my clinic did brain scans before and after giving patients green tea and rhodiola. Two months later, scans showed a significant increase in circulation in the PFC.

How it helps: Green tea appears to benefit the PFC by increasing the availability of dopamine, a brain chemical that controls the brain's reward and pleasure centers. It also helps regulate emotional responses, such as the motivation to take positive actions. Rhodiola is an "adaptogen," a substance that normalizes the body's functions by boosting blood flow to the brain and raising dopamine and serotonin levels.

My advice: Take 200 mg of rhodiola and drink two to three cups of green tea daily (avoid drinking it in the evening since the tea's caffeine can interfere with sleep...or drink decaffeinated green tea).

• **Keep your BMI in check.** People who are overweight—with a body mass index (BMI) of 25 or higher—have less circulation in the PFC than those of normal weights. Excess body weight is associated with atherosclerosis, diabetes and other conditions that impede circulation throughout the body.

Danger: A high BMI can cause the brain to shrink. Research has shown that people who are obese typically have about 8% less brain tissue than normal-weight adults.

My advice: At least once a year, check your BMI by using an online calculator, such as the National Heart, Lung and Blood Institute's *www.nhlbi.nih.gov/health/educational/lose_wt/BMI/bmicalc.htm.* A BMI of 18.5 to 24.9 is considered normal. If your BMI is 25 or higher, you need to lose weight.

• **Don't ignore sleep problems.** An estimated 18 million Americans have sleep apnea, a condition in which breathing intermittently stops during sleep. Unfortunately, the condition is undiagnosed in most of these people.

Why does this matter? Scans on patients with sleep apnea show brain changes that resemble early Alzheimer's disease. Poor sleep decreases blood flow to the PFC and other parts of the brain. Snoring, daytime fatigue and morning headaches are common symptoms of sleep apnea. Your doctor may recommend tests in a sleep laboratory.

My advice: If you're overweight, sleep apnea can often be reduced or even eliminated with weight loss. Many patients also benefit from continuous positive airway pressure (CPAP) units, which help keep the airways open during sleep.

Also important: Avoid sleepless nights. Patients with chronic insomnia have a higher risk for cognitive declines than people who sleep well. To prevent insomnia, follow the tried-and-true strategies—relax in a warm bath before bed...reduce arousal by not watching TV or using a computer in the hour before bedtime...and go to bed and wake up at the same times every day.

Also helpful: Melatonin. The standard dose of this sleep hormone supplement is 1 mg to 6 mg taken a half hour before bed. Start with the lower dose and increase it over a period of weeks, if necessary.

Check with your doctor first if you take an antidepressant, blood pressure medication, blood thinner, steroid or nonsteroidal anti-inflammatory drug—melatonin may interact with these medications.

Insulin vs. Alzheimer's

A clinical trial of 104 adults with mild cognitive impairment or Alzheimer's disease found that insulin, delivered via a nasal spray, delayed memory loss.

Theory: Insulin abnormalities may contribute to the brain damage that leads to Alzheimer's. Larger clinical trials are expected.

National Institute on Aging.

Hormone Replacement Therapy (HRT) May Reduce Alzheimer's Risk

Women who take hormones within five years of menopause have a 30% lower risk for Alzheimer's, compared with women who never take them. The issue of HRT remains complex and controversial—discuss your personal situation with your doctor.

Study of 1,768 women by researchers at Johns Hopkins Bloomberg School of Public Health, Baltimore, published in *Neurology*.

New Alzheimer's Danger?

Animal studies show that a type of protein, known as tau, that accumulates in the brains of Alzheimer's patients increases when body temperatures fall, such as when patients are given anesthesia. Recommended: Avoid "optional anesthesia," such as for minor dental procedures.

Federation of American Societies for Experimental Biology.

Walk Away Alzheimer's

Walking six miles weekly may prevent Alzheimer's.

Recent finding: In a study of 426 adults with or without cognitive decline, those who walked at least six miles weekly were half as likely to develop Alzheimer's disease over 13 years as nonwalkers. Among those with cognitive impairment, walking five miles a week reduced cognitive decline by more than half.

Theory: Exercise improves blood flow to the brain, which helps keep neurons healthy. To help preserve brain health: Aim to walk at least three-quarters of a mile daily.

Cyrus Raji, MD, PhD, physician-scientist, department of radiology, University of Pittsburgh.

Herbs for Alzheimer's?

Extracts made from spearmint and rosemary were found in animal studies to improve learning and memory. Human studies are now being planned.

Saint Louis University School of Medicine.

Niacinamide for Alzheimer's

Is it true that large doses of niacinamide can help "cure" Alzheimer's disease?

Niacinamide is a water-soluble form of vitamin B-3 that actually is niacin, known to reduce cholesterol. A 2008 University of California, Irvine, study conducted on mice with Alzheimer's that were given niacinamide showed cognitive deficits restored by the supplement. To date, no study has shown that niacinamide supplementation in humans helps Azheimer's disease, although there currently is a study in the works at UC Irvine. Research does show that people who consume higher amounts of niacin (not niacinamide) from food and multivitamin sources have a lower risk of developing Alzheimer's disease, compared with people who consume less niacin. Until study results are available, eating foods that are high in niacin, including fish, nuts, beans, coffee and niacin-fortified grains and cereals, may help stave off Alzheimer's.

Mark A. Stengler, NMD, founder and medical director, Stengler Center for Integrative Medicine, Encinitas, California, and author of the *Health Revelations* newsletter and *The Natural Physician's Healing Therapies. MarkStengler.com*

Cold Sores May Be Linked to Alzheimer's Disease

Research has shown that a herpes simplex infection—the virus that causes cold sores—increases the amount of amyloid precursor protein, the parent protein of the plaque associated with Alzheimer's disease.

Self-defense: Treat cold sores quickly with an antiviral agent to minimize the amount of time that the virus remains active.

Elaine Bearer, MD, PhD, Harvey Family Professor and vice-chair for research, departments of pathology and neurosurgery, University of New Mexico School of Medicine, Albuquerque, and principal investigator in a study published in *PLoS One.*

Dementia: When It's Not Alzheimer's

Muriel R. Gillick, MD, an associate professor in the department of ambulatory care and prevention at Harvard Medical School/Harvard Pilgrim Health Care, and staff geriatrician at Harvard Vanguard Medical Associates, all in Boston. She is the author of *Tangled Minds: Understanding Alzheimer's Disease and Other Dementias.*

Memory-robbing Alzheimer's disease is the most common form of dementia, affecting more than five million Americans.

What you may not know: One-third to one-half of patients with dementia suffer from a non-Alzheimer's neurological disease that typically starts with symptoms other than memory loss.

In advanced stages, the symptoms of these other dementias resemble those of Alzheimer's disease. Besides suffering from memory loss, patients eventually have minimal ability to speak and/or limited ability to move.

Anyone who has problems with walking, planning activities or mood (such as apathy or depression) should be evaluated by a neurologist or geriatrician, who may suggest treatments that can help improve symptoms.

Non-Alzheimer's dementias...

VASCULAR DEMENTIA

It's the second most common form of dementia in older adults, and the one that's potentially the most preventable.

Key symptoms: Difficulty performing mental tasks, such as balancing a checkbook or planning an activity, and problems with walking, bladder control and/or vision. Although memory loss is one of the first symptoms experienced by people with Alzheimer's disease, it typically occurs later in most patients with vascular dementia.

Vascular dementia can be caused by a single large stroke, multiple small strokes or narrowing of small blood vessels to the brain due to plaque formation (atherosclerosis).

Some patients experience symptoms of vascular dementia abruptly—for example, immediately after a stroke. More often, damage to the brain occurs over a period of years. A magnetic resonance imaging (MRI) scan of the brain often shows abnormalities in people with vascular dementia.

The same conditions that increase the risk for stroke—elevated blood pressure, diabetes and high cholesterol—also increase the risk for vascular dementia. Treating these conditions won't reverse cognitive changes but can play a significant role in prevention.

Recent finding: European researchers followed a group of patients age 60 and older for four years. All had hypertension, but none had signs of dementia. Those who were given the drug *nitrendipine*—a calcium channel blocker similar to the US drug *nifedipine* (Procardia)—to control hypertension were half as likely to develop vascular dementia over a four-year period as those who weren't given the drug.

Treatment: Alzheimer's drugs known as cholinesterase inhibitors, such as *donepezil* (Aricept) and *rivastigmine* (Exelon), may reduce symptoms of vasculardementia in some patients.

LEWY BODY DEMENTIA

Lewy body dementia, which typically occurs in adults age 65 and older, is named for Dr. Friederich H. Lewy, the scientist who discovered the disease's characteristic abnormal protein deposits that form inside nerve cells in the brain.

Key symptoms: Some are typical of Alzheimer's disease, such as memory loss and confusion...others resemble those caused by Parkinson's disease, such as muscle rigidity. Lewy body dementia also causes visual hallucinations (seeing objects or people that are not really there)...delusions (a false belief that cannot be altered by a rational argument)... and fluctuations in alertness.

No one knows exactly what causes Lewy body dementia. The protein deposits are often present in patients with Alzheimer's and Parkinson's diseases, suggesting that the conditions may be linked in some way.

To diagnose Lewy body dementia, doctors look for a progressive decline in cognitive abilities, along with intermittent episodes of hallucinations, a lack of alertness and Parkinson's-like symptoms.

Treatment: Parkinson's disease drugs, such as *carbidopa* and *levadopa* (Sinemet), to improve motor symptoms.

Warning: In some Lewy body patients, Sinemet may worsen hallucinations.

For hallucinations and delusions, low doses of antipsychotics, such as *quetiapine* (Seroquel) or *olanzapine* (Zyprexa), if necessary.

Warning: The antipsychotic drugs *haloperidol* (Haldol) and *risperidone* (Risperdal) worsen Parkinson's-like symptoms in patients with Lewy body dementia.

FRONTOTEMPORAL DEMENTIA

This is a rare form of dementia in which portions of the brain shrink, causing extreme changes in personality. Unlike other forms of dementia, which are most common in older adults, frontotemporal dementia typically appears between ages 40 and 60.

Key symptoms: Inappropriate public behavior, such as getting undressed in public...rude comments...lack of inhibition...apathy or a loss of interest in everyday life...short-term memory loss...and compulsive behavior, such as constantly shutting doors.

No one test can diagnose frontotemporal dementia. Imaging studies of the brain, such as MRI, will sometimes show shrinkage of the frontal or temporal lobes. There are no treatments that can stop frontotemporal dementia or slow its progression. Most patients die within two to 10 years after the initial diagnosis.

Treatment for symptoms: Antipsychotic drugs (preferably low-dose) may be used to reduce agitation or compulsive behavior. However, research shows that these drugs are not very effective for this purpose and may even hasten death in older dementia patients.

Is This Parkinson's Disease Cure on Your Spice Rack?

Kalipada Pahan, PhD, professor of neurological sciences, Floyd A. Davis Professor of Neurology, Rush University Medical Center, Chicago. His study appeared in the *Journal of Neuroimmune Pharmacology.*

The Bible makes several references to it. The ancient Egyptians used it to preserve their mummies. The ancient Greeks and Romans used it to help them digest their feasts of lamb and wine. We know it's great for diabetes and glycemic control.

And now we find out that this substance fights Parkinson's disease. What is it?

"Cinnamon," said Kalipada Pahan, PhD, professor of neurologic sciences at the Rush University Medical Center in Chicago. "Besides being a commonly used spice, cinnamon has a long history as a medicine. Medieval physicians used it to treat arthritis, coughing, hoarseness and sore throats. In fact, it was once so valuable, wars were fought over it."

Dr. Pahan has shown that cinnamon can prevent symptoms of Parkinson's disease that include tremors, slow, jerky movement, stiffness and loss of balance. Or at least he's shown that cinnamon has this effect in mice acting as experimental models of Parkinson's disease.

Mouse studies often translate to humans when further research is done—so, given how devastating Parkinson's disease can be...and how familiar and safe cinnamon is...these cinnamon studies merit our attention right now. As Dr. Pahan put it, "If these results are repeatable in Parkinson's disease patients, it would represent a remarkable advance in the treatment of this neurodegenerative disease."

The first thing to know is that we are not talking about just any kind of cinnamon, but a specific, authentic kind.

Two types of cinnamon are sold in the United States—Chinese cinnamon (sometimes sold as Saigon cinnamon) and Ceylon cinnamon. Chinese cinnamon, or cassia, is the more common, less expensive type of cinnamon and is what you generally find in supermarkets. You know it—the usual cinnamon powder or that hard, aromatic curl of wood that you plunk into hot apple cider or cocoa. But this is not really "true" cinnamon and does not have its health benefits. Ceylon cinnamon is true cinnamon, and its sticks are softer and flakier than those of Chinese cinnamon. The powder is also lighter and sweeter smelling. There is virtually no way of knowing whether the powdered cinnamon you buy is true cinnamon or cassia or a mix unless it is specifically marked. Ceylon cinnamon is what Dr. Pahan is referring to when he talks about the spice. So even just for general health, keep that in mind the next time you head out to the grocery store to replenish your spice rack—you may need to go to a higher-end market or even order online to get Ceylon cinnamon.

HOW DOES IT WORK?

As you may know, cinnamon is loaded with antioxidants. It may be therapeutic in Parkinson's disease because its antioxidant effects counteract nitric oxide, a free radical that attacks proteins essential to supporting adequate levels of dopamine. Dopamine is the chemical in our brains that not only makes us feel happy and motivated but also controls many of our muscle and limb movements.

It's known that the amount of proteins like DJ-1 and Parkin decrease in the brains of patients with Parkinson's disease. "We have found that these proteins also decrease in the brains of mice with Parkinson's disease because of nitric oxide production," said Dr. Pahan. He found that after the mice ate ground cinnamon, their livers turned the cinnamon into an element, or metabolite, that cinnamon breaks down into during digestion, called sodium benzoate. Once the sodium benzoate got to the brain, it decreased the production of nitric oxide, which stopped the loss of Parkin and DJ-1, protected brain cells and allowed the mice to move around more normally, with steadier legs and less need for rest and downtime. According to Dr. Pahan, it's possible that cinnamon could also prevent or lessen the symptoms of other diseases, such as types of palsy and Lewy body dementia, which are also caused by dopamine dysfunction.

HOW TO USE CINNAMON

Dr. Pahan's findings are potentially great news for people with Parkinson's disease and those who worry that they carry the potential for it in their genes. As it stands, Parkinson's disease patients must rely on drugs, such as levodopa, to replace dopamine, but these drugs neither cure nor change the course of the disease. They only provide temporary relief. Over time, symptoms become increasingly harder to control, and the drugs often have a wide range of serious side effects.

"Cinnamon, however, and its metabolite sodium benzoate, could potentially be among the safest approaches to stop the progression of Parkinson's disease once it's diagnosed," said Dr. Pahan.

You've already heard of sodium benzoate. It's a common food preservative found in salad dressings, juices, condiments and cosmetics. The National Institutes of Health's National Center for Complementary and Alternative Medicine has concluded that sodium benzoate and true cinnamon are safe and that true cinnamon is safe even in large amounts—but this is not true for cassia (Chinese cinnamon) because it contains coumarin, which, besides being a blood thinner, can damage the liver.

Unless you're allergic to cinnamon, Dr. Pahan suggests taking one teaspoon a day. But don't attempt to just swallow a teaspoon of dry cinnamon powder "straight-up"! It will make you gag and could cause you to cough and inhale the powder into your lungs, which is dangerous. Instead, mix cinnamon into food or drink.

You can bet there's much more research coming on cinnamon and Parkinson's—meanwhile, generous helpings of this richly antioxidant spice could be well worth trying.

Simple Way to Test Yourself for Dementia

Douglas W. Scharre, MD, associate professor of neurology and director, division of cognitive neurology, Wexner Medical Center, The Ohio State University, Columbus. His research was published in *Journal of Neuropsychiatry and Clinical Neuroscience.*

Having trouble finding the right words... showing up for visits on the wrong day...getting confused while balancing a checkbook. For people who are getting on in years, such experiences can spark worries about whether cognitive skills are starting to slip.

Still, no one likes to think that dementia might be on the horizon—which is one reason why cognitive decline often goes undiagnosed in the early stages. In fact, patients typically don't mention such problems to their doctors until three or four years after symptoms begin. What's more, doctors themselves often fail to pick up on the early, subtle signs of dementia during routine medical exams... and many doctors don't do the time-consuming tests necessary to diagnose cognitive impairment until the problem has progressed to later stages. That's too bad—because early intervention may help delay the progression of mild cognitive impairment and/or provide the best opportunities for patients and their loved ones to make appropriate plans for the future regarding caregiving, finances, legal matters, etc.

Game changer: Now there's a simple screening test for cognitive impairment or dementia that you or a loved one can take anywhere, using just paper and pencil. It takes only about 10 minutes to complete, and it provides your doctor with the info he/she needs to determine whether more thorough testing is needed.

DIY SCREENING ADVANTAGE

Professionally administered screening tests for mild cognitive impairment do exist, but many take lots of time and attention—which is one reason why more than 40% of people with mild cognitive impairment are not diagnosed by their primary doctors. In addition, some tests place too much emphasis on memory and too little on evaluating other cognitive skills. There also are Web-based tests that people can take on their own, but many people are not comfortable enough with computers to use these...and often such tests have not been validated.

To address these problems, researchers from The Ohio State University developed a screening tool called the Self-Administered Gerocognitive Examination (SAGE). The test was designed to identify mild cognitive impairment (which sometimes progresses to full-blown dementia) as well as dementia. In studies, SAGE has been shown to detect cognitive problems as accurately as other established but more time-consuming screening tools, correctly identifying nearly 80% of people with cognitive impairment and excluding 95% of those without impairment.

SAGE was designed to be a self-administered exam, with simple instructions written in plain language. It is a four-page, 12-question test that looks at abilities in six different areas that can be used as early predictors of mild cognitive impairment—orientation, language, reasoning/computation, spatial ability, problem solving and memory.

Some examples: Test takers are asked to name certain objects...do simple math...draw lines that follow a pattern...remember one easy task...and so forth. The test takes about 10 to 15 minutes to complete (though there is no time limit), and scoring can be done in less than one minute.

The maximum score possible is 22 points. A score of 17 to 22 is classified as normal cognitive ability...a score of 15 or 16 is classified as mild cognitive impairment...a score of 14 or less is classified as possible dementia. To compensate for age and education level, the researchers suggest adding one point to the score when the test taker is over age 80...and adding one point when the person has 12 years or less of education.

Recently the test designers recruited more than 1,000 volunteers over age 50 from venues such as health fairs, senior centers, assisted-living facilities and educational talks, and gave them the SAGE test.

Results: 72% scored in the normal range...10% scored in the mild cognitive impairment range...and 18% scored in the dementia range. These percentages, the researchers said, are typical for the population that was tested.

HOW TO TEST YOURSELF

SAGE can be taken in the privacy of your own home or at your physician's office, without supervision or special instruction. Simply download the test from *www.sagetest.osu.edu* and print it out. No calendars or clocks should be available during test-taking, but you can spend however much time you need completing it.

Of course, there's nothing to stop you from scoring your own test or from asking a loved one to score it for you. But in actuality, the test is intended to be scored and interpreted by your physician—so take your test paper with you the next time you see your doctor (scoring instructions can be downloaded from the same website). If you've done fine, ask your doctor to save the test in your file for future comparison. If your score suggests that some impairment has already occurred, talk with your doctor about getting a complete cognitive evaluation. Remember, the sooner such impairment is diagnosed, the more and better options you will have.

Having a Purpose in Life Prevents Dementia

Patricia A. Boyle, PhD, neuropsychologist, Rush Alzheimer's Disease Center, and associate professor, department of behavioral sciences, Rush University Medical Center, both in Chicago. Her study was published in *Archives of General Psychiatry.*

You already know that staying physically and mentally active may help stave off dementia, but researchers have found yet another protective trick—having a purpose in life.

This doesn't mean having a goal that has a definite end point, such as telling yourself that you'll run a marathon or write a novel.

For brain protection, having a purpose in life is a little bit different.

What are some examples of "purposes," and how can you figure out what yours is if you don't already have one?

WARDING OFF BRAIN FOG

Figuring out your life's purpose is not that hard to do. *Here's what the study found...*

Researchers analyzed 246 senior citizens who received annual cognitive testing for about 10 years. Each was asked questions to determine whether he or she had a strong purpose in life. When participants died, they underwent brain autopsies.

What the researchers found was that in participants who had a lot of plaques and tangles in their brains—abnormal structures in and around the brain's nerve cells that are hallmarks of Alzheimer's disease—the rate of cognitive decline had been about 30% slower for people who had a strong purpose in life compared with those who had had a weaker purpose or no purpose at all.

What these findings might mean: The stronger your purpose in life, the less likely you'll suffer cognitive decline as you age, even if your brain is affected by Alzheimer's signs. I hope that's true because it means that you can preserve your cognitive ability by making sure that you have a purpose.

Of course, it could be the other way around—it could be that some people have a biological problem that makes them less able to cope with brain plaques and tangles and, also, less able to feel that their lives have purpose.

GO FOR IT ANYWAY

This study doesn't prove whether purposefulness helps our brains work better or is simply a side effect of a brain that is already working better. Maybe research will determine that one day. But on the other hand, since having a sense of purpose seems to make people happier, she said, why not cultivate one?

Based on the work with the study subjects, a life purpose is defined as "the sense that one's life has meaning and direction—that one is intentional and motivated to engage in activities that one finds important and fulfilling." In other words, it's what gets you out of bed each day and makes you feel that life is worth living.

A purpose doesn't have to be ambitious or complicated. In fact, many purposes are simple. It just can't have a definite end point—it has to last throughout your life. For example, some purposes include spending time every day with loved ones...helping other people (for example through long-term volunteer work)... learning something new every day...or passing down a certain set of knowledge or skills to a younger generation. If you love running marathons or writing novels, as I mentioned earlier, make sure that your goal is to continue pursuing those activities through life—and not just run one marathon or write one novel.

It's not so much what your purpose is, Dr. Boyle said—what's critical is how it makes you feel. If it stirs you up inside and makes you feel passionate, energetic and excited, then you've found it!

What Really Causes Dementia

Peter V. Rabins, MD, MPH, Richman Family Professor for Alzheimer's and Related Diseases, vice-chair for academic affairs, department of psychiatry and behavioral sciences, Johns Hopkins University School of Medicine, and coauthor of *The 36 Hour Day.*

What really causes dementia? What a relief it would be to know the answer, since many aging individuals worry about whether the occasional "senior moment" or "brain fog" is a sign that something more serious is going on. With the incidence of dementia rising worldwide, scientists are studying this issue from every possible angle, trying to learn what illnesses, lifestyle habits and environmental factors are at play—but, to be honest, as yet no one knows for sure.

Making this particular challenge even more difficult (or rewarding) is that dementia researchers seem to find new associations with every rock they turn over. Having a big head? Exposure to bright lights? Both may be protective. Living a sedentary lifestyle, smoking and having high cholesterol at midlife? Trouble lies ahead.

WHAT WE DO KNOW

Let's take a quick trip through some of the more recent research findings.

Healthy habits that seem to protect against dementia...

• **Using your brain, living a full life.** A study of 951 older, dementia-free patients found that those who reported having a purpose in life at the study's start were half as likely to have Alzheimer's disease seven years later...while numerous studies showed that engaging in mentally stimulating activities, such as doing crossword puzzles, playing cards and attending movies and plays, holds back development of dementia.

• **Good nutrition—including taking tea.** A four-year study of 2,258 dementia-free New Yorkers found 40% lower risk for Alzheimer's among those who followed the Mediterranean diet (lots of fruit, vegetables, fish, olive oil, legumes and cereals and moderate alcohol intake) than for those whose diets weren't as healthy. Studies have also found that drinking tea regularly is protective—for instance, one 14-year study found that tea drinkers were 37% less likely to develop dementia than those who don't drink tea.

• **Exercise.** A vast body of research finds regular exercise is protective. For instance, one study found that those who engage in active exercise, such as doing yard work or biking, had a 29% lower risk for dementia than people who got little or no exercise.

Meanwhile, signs that point to increased risk for other health problems are also associated with a higher risk for dementia...

• **Vitamin D deficiency.** An international group that assessed cognitive decline of 858 seniors over six years found that people deficient in vitamin D were more than 60% more likely to have experienced significant cognitive decline and 31% more likely to have problems with executive function (which includes thinking, learning and memory) than those with healthy levels of vitamin D.

• **Cardiovascular risk factors.** One large study that followed almost 10,000 people over age 40 found that even marginally high cholesterol (200 mg/dL to 239 mg/dL) at middle age increased risk for late-life dementia by about 50%, while other studies have correlated high blood pressure with dementia.

• **First- and secondhand smoking.** Beyond the countless studies linking smoking and cognitive impairment, a six-year study of almost 5,000 nonsmoking adults by researchers from the Universities of Cambridge and Michigan found that those who reported long-term exposure (30 years or more) to secondhand tobacco smoke were about 30% more likely to develop dementia than those who reported no regular exposure.

And if you already have certain diseases, odds are higher that you'll get dementia, too...

• **Diabetes.** Substantial research has found diabetes is a risk factor for dementia. For example, a new study by London's Institute of Psychiatry found that participants with diabetes were nearly three times as likely as nondiabetics to develop dementia.

• **Depression.** Several studies find depression increases dementia risk. Of nearly 1,000 elderly participants from the 62-year Framingham Heart Study, those who were depressed when first examined had almost double the risk for dementia 17 years later.

IS THERE A THEME HERE?

It makes sense, in practical terms, to summarize risk factors for dementia as being pretty much inclusive of everything that we already know is bad for your heart. But when it comes to prevention—frustratingly—the massive amount of research has so far produced "no strong evidence that we can 'prevent' dementia by doing anything in particular," said Peter V. Rabins of Johns Hopkins University.

A major problem is that most of the studies have some basic limitation or flaw in research design. For instance, most of the existing research compares people who develop dementia with those who don't...but new research indicates that dementia may be present decades before symptoms are noticeable enough to make a diagnosis, so it may be that some of those patients weren't actually dementia-free.

Another flaw: Healthier people tend to take better care of themselves, so it's hard to tease out which factors or habits are responsible for cognitive health.

IN THE MEANTIME

What scientific advice can be offered, based on what is known at this point? When it comes to preventing dementia, the odds clearly favor those who live a healthy lifestyle. For instance, since 10% to 20% of dementia in the US is known to have vascular causes, we can infer that eating a healthy diet, exercising and managing stress are beneficial. The fact that only 30% to 60% of dementia risk is thought to be genetic means that there is plenty of reason to do all you can to reduce environmental risk—another argument for health-promoting habits and choices.

The search for the cause or cure will certainly continue, but reviewing what we already do know says quite a lot. Living well and with joy seems to boost the odds that you will remain cognitively intact, whereas all those things that are bad for you...are bad for you.

Say No to Benzodiazepines to Cut Dementia Risk

Mark A. Stengler, NMD, founder and medical director, Stengler Center for Integrative Medicine, Encinitas, California, and author of the *Health Revelations* newsletter and *The Natural Physician's Healing Therapies. MarkStengler.com*

If you, like many Americans, rely on Xanax, Valium, Ativan or Klonopin to reduce anxiety, panic, insomnia or another problem, this news might be just the incentive you need to find a healthier alternative. These drugs, known as benzodiazepines or sedative hypnotics, have now been shown to have a lasting negative effect on users' thinking and memory...and to increase risk of Alzheimer's disease. There is a right way and wrong way to use these drugs...and there are safer, natural alternatives to soothe anxiety and panic symptoms. *Here's what you need to know to protect your mind...*

THE ALZHEIMER'S CONNECTION

The brain danger of benzodiazepine sedatives is linked to how long a person uses them, according to a study that compared six years' worth of medical records of elderly people who did and did not use benzodiazepines. Because benzodiazepines are often prescribed for known symptoms of Alzheimer's disease, such as anxiety, depression and insomnia, the question, in earlier, similar studies, was whether benzodiazepine use was, in fact, a risk factor for Alzheimer's or whether benzodiazepines were merely given to people who already had or were destined for Alzheimer's disease. The researchers of the current study attempted to control for this by making sure that none of the study participants had Alzheimer's disease at the start of study...and that more than five years had elapsed between getting a benzodiazepine prescription and a diagnosis of Alzheimer's to better ensure that the participants were not getting the drugs for early symptoms of dementia.

The results: In patients who took the drugs for more than six months, the risk of Alzheimer's was a whopping 84% higher than for people who did not take benzodiazepines! The risk was 32% higher for folks who took benzodiazepines for three to six months.

People in the study who had taken benzodiazepines for up to three months did not seem to be affected by them as far as Alzheimer's risk went. Their risk was not increased over people who never took benzodiazepines. And the fact of the matter is that these drugs are not supposed to be used for more than three months, according to treatment guidelines set up by health-care standard-setters, because they are addictive. The longer they're used, the longer it takes to wean a person off them without triggering withdrawal symptoms that can include seizures, psychosis, agitation and rapid heartbeat. What's more, long-term use of these drugs for symptoms such as insomnia or agitation is not backed up by science. Regardless, doctors routinely give them to people as a more or less open-ended prescription.

NATURAL ALTERNATIVES TO SEDATIVES

So, the wrong way to use benzodiazepines is for more than three months, whereas these drugs appear to be safe and useful to get symptoms under control when used for three months or less. But if you or a loved one are taking a benzodiazepine and want to stop after reading this, don't go cold turkey. Patients on benzodiazepines should never stop therapy abruptly because withdrawal symptoms are very real. You need to work with your physician or psychiatric therapist to slowly taper off the drug. You'll also want guidance on alternative remedies. *Dr. Mark Stengler, NMD, one of the country's top naturopathic physicians, often prescribes the following options...*

- **Amino acids.** Certain amino acids help promote calm instead of anxiety and, in fact, anxiety and panic can be caused by being deficient in certain amino acids. Dr. Stengler uses either gamma-aminobutyric acid (GABA) or L-theanine. His patients may be prescribed 250 mg to 500 mg of GABA three times daily. For L-theanine, Dr. Stengler often prescribes 200 mg three times daily. But ask your doctor about an appropriate dose for you. These supplements should be taken on an empty stomach so that your body most effectively absorbs them.

- **Nutrient supplements.** Another option is a nutrient called inositol, which has been shown to reduce panic attacks and ease anxiety. Dr. Stengler may prescribe up to six grams twice daily. Another antianxiety nutrient, 5-hydroxytryptophan (5-HTP), helps boost serotonin levels in the brain, which helps memory and mood (and promotes restful sleep). Dr. Stengler finds that 100 mg three times daily benefits many of his patients. Don't take either of these nutrients if you are still taking an antianxiety medication or an antidepressant because the nutrients will interact with such drugs.

Sleep problems often go hand-in-hand with anxiety and other mood disorders. Because benzodiazepines are often prescribed for insomnia, Dr. Stengler has found one or another of these sleep-enhancing alternatives beneficial...

• **Melatonin.** This naturally occurring hormone, which is produced by the pineal gland, helps regulate the body's sleep/wake cycle. Dr. Stengler prefers sublingual melatonin supplements (lozenges placed under the tongue) to capsules or tablets, saying that the sublingual lozenges generally are faster acting and therefore more effective at helping a person fall asleep. He typically prescribes 1.5 mg of sublingual melatonin 30 to 45 minutes before bedtime. If no improvement is seen after three nights, the dose can be increased to 3 mg, said Dr. Stengler.

• **Herbs and medicinal plants.** Chamomile, passionflower and lemon balm teas can help bring on sleep, as can 300 mg of valerian root supplement taken 30 minutes before bed. But don't take valerian if you are also taking a sedative drug because it might make for a double-punch of sedation and may also harm your liver. Also, if you are scheduled for surgery, stop taking valerian at least two weeks before surgery to prevent it from interacting with anesthesia. Also avoid taking valerian at the same time that you are taking anithistimines, statins or oral antifungals because they can stress the liver.

• **5-HTP.** As mentioned above, 5-HTP is another option for sleep-enhancement. Dr. Stengler often prescribes 100 mg about an hour before going to bed.

Sleep Deprivation Can Cause Brain Damage

According to a recent study, after one night without sleep, study participants' blood samples showed increased concentrations of molecules that are known to spike when brain damage is present.

Theory: Pulling an all-nighter deprives the brain of the restorative time it needs to clean out these toxic molecules.

Study led by researchers at Uppsala University, Sweden, published in *Sleep.*

Nutrients That Prevent Dementia

Gabriele Nagel, MD, MPH, an epidemiologist and professor of medicine, and Christine von Arnim, MD, a neurologist and professor of medicine, both at the University of Ulm, Germany. They are leading authors of a study published in *Journal of Alzheimer's Disease.*

You've probably heard that pirates and sailors of yore stocked up on vitamin C-rich citrus fruits to prevent scurvy.

But it's possible that those seafaring men also kept their minds sharper for longer (assuming that they went easy on the rum).

Yes, it turns out that we can learn a thing or two from Blackbeard and the like!

A new study found that senior citizens who consume plenty of vitamin C—plus another easy-to-find nutrient—may be less likely to develop dementia with age.

BRAIN-BOOSTING VITAMINS

Here's how this research came about. A group of German scientists knew that oxidative stress—which restricts the use of oxygen in the body, causing cells to break down—plays an important role in the aging process, where all of our body's systems (including the neurological system) begin to slowly break down. Dementia occurs when the brain degenerates more aggressively than normal. So the researchers wanted to see whether antioxidants, vitamins that can fight off the damage caused by oxidative stress, might help prevent brain degeneration.

For the study, researchers analyzed data on more than 1,500 men and women between the ages of 65 and 90—some had mild dementia and some were healthy. People with dementia had significantly lower blood levels of vitamin C and another antioxidant, beta-carotene, than people without dementia. And this held true after controlling for body mass index, education levels, smoking status, alcohol consumption and current dietary supplement use. The researchers also tested the blood for concentrations of several other antioxidants, including coenzyme Q10, lycopene and vitamin E—but they found no similar connection between those other antioxidants and a reduced dementia risk.

ASSESSING ANTIOXIDANTS

So does this mean that eating more foods containing vitamin C and beta-carotene helps prevent dementia? It's a possibility, although that's not what this study proved. It showed only an association, meaning that some other relationship could have caused the results—for example, it's possible that people with dementia tend to consume less of those particular antioxidants.

On the other hand, vitamin C and beta-carotene are not (of course) exotic and dangerous substances...they're healthful nutrients found naturally in certain wholesome foods...so if we want to think of this dementia study as another reason to eat these foods, there's no harm done!

STOCK UP ON "C" AND BETA-CAROTENE

Beta-carotene is found in high amounts in (as you know) carrots—but also in sweet potatoes, kale, winter squash, cabbage and pumpkins. Good sources of vitamin C include not only citrus fruits but also spinach, strawberries, kiwi, bell peppers, broccoli, cauliflower and Brussels sprouts—and that's certainly better eating than you'd find on any pirate ship!

Watch for Anemia to Avoid Dementia

Study titled "Anemia and risk of dementia in older adults: Findings from the Health ABC study," published in *Neurology*.

These days, people are increasingly able to live long lives—even to 100. But it's not enough to live long...we all want to live well, sound in mind and body. So concerns about dementia haunt us—considering that at least 44% of us are destined to fall victim to it once we hit our early 80s.

The good news is that protecting yourself against a common blood condition—one that you've surely heard about but have probably not given much thought—might dramatically reduce your risk of ever getting dementia.

That blood condition is nothing exotic...it's anemia! So how could something as run-of-the-mill as anemia have such a profound effect on brain health?

THE DEMENTIA-ANEMIA LINK

Anemia—a shortage of oxygen-carrying red blood cells—is fairly common in older adults, affecting up to 24% of people age 65 and older. Meanwhile, Alzheimer's disease, the most common form of dementia, affects 15% of people age 65 to 74 and 44% of people age 75 to 84. And now studies have shown a link between the two disorders, and that's good news. Looking out for and addressing one (anemia) may have a strong impact on avoiding the other (dementia).

In one small study, the risk of dementia doubled within three years of an anemia diagnosis and, in another, anemia was associated with a 60% increased risk of Alzheimer's disease within 3.3 years. But while small studies are all well and fine to get a glimpse into new ways of seeing health problems, larger studies are needed to really make a strong case. And that's what an international team of researchers has done.

The team followed 2,552 people, age 70 to 79, who participated in an 11-year study called *Health, Aging and Body Composition*.

Over the course of the study period, all of the participants were given memory tests to check for signs of dementia and blood tests for anemia. None of them had dementia at the start of the study, and 15% of them had anemia. By the end of the study, 18% of participants had Alzheimer's or another form of dementia. When the researchers compared rates of dementia between people who had or didn't have anemia, they discovered that having anemia was associated with a 41% higher risk for Alzheimer's or another form of dementia.

WHAT TO DO

How anemia is linked to dementia is not completely understood. Possible factors include simply being in poor health, not getting enough oxygen to the brain (those red blood cells!) or having an iron or vitamin B-12 deficiency. Whatever the connection, in case it is anemia that is actually causing dementia, you'll want to do whatever you can to recognize and treat the symptoms of anemia—and, of course, prevent anemia from ever happening in the first place.

Signs of anemia can be subtle at first and include fatigue, weakness, pale skin, fast or irregular heartbeat, trouble breathing, chest pain, trouble with memory and concentration, cold hands and feet and headache. So if you've been feeling fatigued and don't know why or have other symptoms just mentioned, make an appointment with your doctor, who will order a blood test to check for anemia.

If anemia is found, additional tests will be done to find the exact cause, and the results will determine treatment.

Although rare or hereditary forms of anemia require blood transfusions, others are corrected by treating the underlying cause, whether it be loss of blood from a bleeding ulcer or complications from an infection or a medication side effect. Fortunately, the most common form of anemia—that caused by an iron or B-12 deficiency—is managed with good nutrition and vitamin and mineral supplements. It might be a simple correction that lets you avoid a horrific outcome.

PREVENTING ANEMIA

Since prevention is best, keep your diet rich in iron, folate, vitamin B-12, and vitamin C (which is essential for iron absorption). Foods that will give you the iron you need include red meat, beans, dried fruit, and green leafy vegetables, such as spinach. Besides vitamin C, citrus fruits provide folate. Other good sources of folate include green leafy veggies, beans and bananas. As for vitamin B-12, rely on salmon, shellfish, beef and dairy. And if you are vegan or vegetarian (or have a large B-12 deficiency), you likely already know that you need to get B-12 from supplementation.

REM Sleep Disorder Is a Warning Sign for Dementia

Study titled, "Breakdown in REM sleep circuitry underlies REM sleep behavior disorder," published in *Tren.*

Do you sleep next to (or barely sleep because of) someone who acts out dreams—or has your bed partner told you that you're the nasty bump in the night? If a nightly "wrestlemania" is just starting or getting worse over time, you may be chalking it up to aging. Don't do that! Restless dreaming—that is, lots of physical movement, including sleep walking, during rapid eye movement (REM) sleep—is not a natural part of aging. It may be REM sleep behavior disorder, which researchers are now learning is a warning sign that dementia, Parkinson's or another neurological disease may be coming to get you.

Consider this…a neurodegenerative disease will be diagnosed in 50% of people with REM sleep behavior disorder within five years and 80% within 15 years, according to a recent University of Toronto study. Within the years between diagnosis of REM sleep behavior disorder and a full-fledged neuro problem, subtle yet growing signs of neurodegeneration, such as difficulty recognizing smells and colors and not being able to think or walk straight, are likely to crop up. This might sound like a nightmare, but it might be a boon in more than one respect. It means scientists can even more fully study how neurodegenerative diseases begin and progress in people—and that means getting closer to cures for Alzheimer's disease, Lewy body dementia, and Parkinson's and Lou Gehrig's diseases. It also means that, until a cure is found, you and an informed and forward-thinking doctor can take action to quickly recognize and slow down a neurodegenerative disease before it sets in.

WHAT TO DO

First, know what REM sleep behavior disorder is. It's a condition in which the body's safety catch that keeps us from physically acting out dreams doesn't kick in properly. People with this disorder risk seriously hurting themselves or their bed partners. Instead of staying still, their bodies act out whatever they are doing in their dreams—be it picking flowers, fighting dragons or making love. So this is just another important reason not to ignore this annoyance if it is happening to you or someone dear to you. And given what we now know—that restless dreaming is closely tied to dementia and other neurological diseases—it is even more crucial not to delay getting a diagnosis for REM sleep behavior disorder.

If you know or suspect that you experience restless dreaming, your first step is to discuss it with a primary care physician, who will most likely refer you to a neurologist. The neurologist will set up a sleep study at a hospital or sleep disorders clinic. The essentials of a sleep study are a video polysomnogram, which videotapes you sleeping and records your brain waves, and an electromyogram, which records the electrical activity of your muscles to see whether the movements you make are consistent with those of REM sleep behavior disorder.

If it turns out that the neurologist says, yes, you have REM sleep behavior disorder, he or she may suggest a treatment that will reduce the symptoms, such as the antiseizure medication clonazepam or the sleep aid melatonin. If your neurologist doesn't bring up the link between this sleep disorder and the very high risk of neurodegenerative disease down the road, you must bring up this link and make a plan with this neurologist—or another one you have confidence in, if necessary—for monitoring and staving off symptoms of neurodegeneration.

To learn more about REM sleep behavior disorder and other sleep disorders, visit the website of the National Sleep Foundation at *www.sleepfoundation.org.*

How Blood Pressure Changes Affect Memory

Blood pressure fluctuations may lead to memory loss. In a study of 5,400 adults over age 70, those with the greatest fluctuations in blood pressure performed worse on tests of memory, attention and reaction time than those with more stable levels, even if blood pressure was high. Extreme swings in blood pressure are also associated with brain microbleeds, which may contribute to cognitive decline.

Possible explanation: Unstable blood pressure can disrupt blood flow to the brain, which could lead to dementia over time.

Simon Mooijaart, MD, PhD, director, Institute for Evidence-Based Medicine in Old Age, Leiden University Medical Center, the Netherlands.

Blood Pressure Drugs May Fight Dementia

According to a recent finding, people treated for hypertension with beta-blockers had less brain atrophy...fewer signs of small strokes...and a lower level of plaques associated with Alzheimer's disease than people who were not taking the medications.

Study by researchers at Pacific Health Research and Education Institute, Honolulu, presented at the annual meeting of the American Academy of Neurology in San Diego.

Is the Drug You're Taking Triggering Dementia?

Armon B. Neel, Jr., PharmD, a certified geriatric pharmacist, adjunct instructor in clinical pharmacy at Mercer University College of Pharmacy and Health Sciences in Atlanta. Dr. Neel is also coauthor of *Are Your Prescriptions Killing You? How to Prevent Dangerous Interactions, Avoid Deadly Side Effects, and Be Healthier with Fewer Drugs. MedicationXpert.com*

When your doctor pulls out his/her prescription pad, you probably assume that your health problem will soon be improving. Sure, there may be a side effect or two—perhaps an occasional upset stomach or a mild headache. But overall you will be better off, right?

Not necessarily. While it's true that many drugs can help relieve symptoms and sometimes even cure certain medical conditions, a number of popular medications actually cause disease—not simply side effects—while treating the original problem.

Here's what happens: Your kidney and liver are the main organs that break down drugs and eliminate them from your body. But these organs weaken as you age. Starting as early as your 20s and 30s, you lose 1% of liver and kidney function every year. As a result, drugs can build up in your body (particularly if you take more than one), become toxic, damage crucial organs such as the heart and brain—and trigger disease, such as dementia.

Older adults are at greatest risk for this problem because the body becomes increasingly less efficient at metabolizing drugs with age. But no one is exempt from the risk.

To protect yourself—or a loved one...

- **Many drugs can cause symptoms of dementia,** such as short-term memory loss, confusion and agitation, that patients (and physicians) frequently mistake for dementia. The main offenders are anticholinergic medications, which treat a variety of conditions by blocking the activity of the neurotransmitter acetylcholine.

- **Hundreds of medications are anticholinergic,** and it's likely that any class of drugs beginning with anti- is in this category—for example, antihistamines and antispasmodics. Cholesterol-lowering statins also can cause dementia-like symptoms.

Other offenders: Beta-blockers (for high blood pressure or cardiac arrhythmias)...benzodiazepines (for anxiety)...narcotics...tricyclic antidepressants...anticonvulsants...muscle relaxants...sleeping pills...fluoroquinolone antibiotics...heartburn drugs (H2 receptor antagonists and proton-pump inhibitors)...antipsychotics...nitrates (for heart disease)...and sulfonylurea derivatives (for diabetes).

My advice: If you or a loved one has been diagnosed with dementia, the patient should immediately undergo a comprehensive medication review—drug-induced dementia usually can be reversed by stopping the offending drug (or drugs). A competent physician or consultant pharmacist can always find an alternative drug to use.

Surprising threat: Even general anesthesia can cause weeks or months of dementia-like confusion (and an incorrect diagnosis of Alzheimer's) in an older person, as the drug slowly leaves the body.

The anesthesia is collected in the fat cells in the body, and normal cognition may take months to return. The longer a person is under anesthesia, the longer it takes to recover.

THE VERY BEST DRUG SELF-DEFENSE

If you're over age 60—especially if you take more than one medication or suffer drug side effects—it's a good idea to ask your physician to work with a consulting pharmacist who is skilled in medication management. A consulting pharmacist has been trained in drug therapy management and will work with your physician to develop a drug management plan that will avoid harmful drugs. These services are relatively new and may not be covered by insurance, so be sure to check with your provider.

To find a consulting pharmacist in your area, go to the website of the American Society of

Consultant Pharmacists, *www.ASCP.com,* and click on "Find a Senior Care Pharmacist."

Also helpful: Make sure that a drug you've been prescribed does not appear on the "Beers Criteria for Potentially Inappropriate Medication Use in Older Adults." Originally developed by the late Mark Beers, editor of *The Merck Manual of Medical Information*, the list has been recently updated by The American Geriatrics Society. To download the list for free, go to *AmericanGeriatrics.org/health_care_professionals/clinical_practice/clinical_guidelines_recommendations/2012.*

Hearing Loss Raises the Risk for Dementia

A recent study that tracked more than 600 adults for approximately 12 years found that every 10 decibels of hearing that is lost made participants 20% more likely to develop cognitive problems associated with dementia and Alzheimer's. Researchers are trying to determine whether hearing loss is really a cause of dementia or a symptom.

Frank R. Lin, MD, PhD, assistant professor, division of otology, neurotology and skull base surgery, Johns Hopkins School of Medicine, Baltimore.

A Caregiver's Guide for Alzheimer's and Dementia

Judith Fox, a photographer and writer whose award-winning photographs have been exhibited in shows in Los Angeles, New York City and major cities in Virginia. She is the author/photographer of *I Still Do: Loving and Living with Alzheimer's.*

After her 72-year-old husband was diagnosed with Alzheimer's disease, Judith Fox became a caregiver in addition to being a wife. At age 56, she joined the ranks of the estimated 45 million Americans who provide care to a sick spouse, elderly parent or other family member or friend.

The needs of a person with Alzheimer's are among the most challenging to meet of all chronic conditions. Affecting nearly half of all Americans over age 85, the devastating neurodegenerative disease typically leads to memory loss, confusion, apathy, personality changes and psychiatric disturbances, such as hallucinations.

Over time, Fox not only took over more and more of the household duties, but also found herself trying to anticipate the smallest of day-to-day details that could possibly affect her husband's well-being ("Will he trip on the lamp cord?").

After more than 10 years, Fox made the difficult decision to move her husband to the dementia unit in a full-care facility, where she now visits him almost every day. Fox worked hard to make the transition relatively easy, and her husband adjusted surprisingly well to the move.

Throughout her caregiving journey, Fox gradually integrated her work as a fine art photographer and writer with the demands of tending to the needs of her husband.

Her advice to anyone caring for a person with Alzheimer's or any other form of dementia...

• **Keep him/her engaged.** Ed had been a surgeon, a pilot and a university president. All people with dementia crave mental stimulation—even while their mental abilities are declining. Given Ed's background, this was particularly important.

At the facility where he now lives, Ed attends lectures given by a college professor who volunteers his time once a week...I also make sure that Ed has DVDs on topics that might interest him, such as documentaries about the space program. He can watch those for hours but won't remember that he had previously seen them. They're "new" each time he views them.

• **Lighten up when you can.** Even as the disease progresses, most people with Alzheimer's keep their sense of humor. Find things to laugh about. For Ed, humor is a welcome distraction that allows him to feel normal again.

• **Live in the moment.** It's all that you have when you live with someone with any form of dementia. Your loved one can sound almost normal one minute—but completely out of it the next. Don't assume that the bad will stay bad or that the good is a harbinger of better things ahead. Just take the moments as they are.

• **Enter their world.** Many Alzheimer's patients experience hallucinations, in which they hear or see things that aren't there. Sometimes the hallucinations are frightening, but they can also be very pleasant.

Ed and I spent lovely hours attending parties, discussing what's on the buffet table and gossiping about the people in the room. None of it was real—but he experienced it all as though it were. I was there with him, and we had a great time!

• **Touch.** Ed and I hold hands all the time. That means a lot to both of us. When we touch, I'm able to look beyond the disease and remember how much of Ed's essence is still there. When he's anxious or frightened, just touching him will often make him calmer.

• **Encourage friendships.** Dementia, more than most illnesses, fosters alienation.

Some people with the disease avoid gatherings because they're embarrassed that their minds are slipping and that they may say something inappropriate. Ed and I have stayed in touch with friends long after the time when he was fully able to follow the conversations—or even remember who the other people were. But he has enjoyed those moments.

• **Love a pet.** I recommend this for everyone with Alzheimer's or any other form of dementia. Dogs and cats enjoy cuddling, and they give unconditional love. There's never the fear that they'll judge you or let you down. Ed and I both love our cat, Honey, but she and Ed have formed a special bond because of his illness.

Finally...There's a Way to Connect with a Loved One Who Has Dementia

Gerontologist Tom Brenner, MA, cofounder, with his wife, Karen Brenner, MA, of Brenner Pathways, a consulting and educational company in Chicago that specializes in the Montessori Method for Positive Dementia Care. He and his wife are also coauthors of *You Say Goodbye and We Say Hello: The Montessori Method for Positive Dementia Care.*

One of the most heartbreaking and frustrating aspects of caring for a loved one with dementia is the loss of meaningful interaction.

But there's good news on this front: The Montessori Method for Positive Dementia Care, a nondrug approach (often used in combination with medication), is now being used by some caregivers in home-care settings and nursing homes with dramatic results.

Through basic Montessori principles (see below), this method offers ways to be in the moment with a dementia patient and possibly have a deep connection. Patients become more secure, confident and calm. And caregivers are less likely to get frustrated.

Recent research: In a study involving nine residential facilities in Melbourne, Australia, dementia patients were two times more actively engaged when participating in Montessori-based activities than when they were not doing these activities.

Background: Developed more than 100 years ago as a method of teaching "unreachable" children with learning disabilities, the Montessori approach encourages the use of all five senses to stimulate different areas of the brain and the use of "muscle memory"* to develop small-muscle coordination and promote confidence. The Montessori method also advocates an environment that meets the specific physical and emotional needs of those using it.

*Sometimes called procedural memory, this involves physical movements fixed into memory through repetition (think of riding a bike or playing a musical instrument).

Key Montessori tenets and how they can help dementia patients...

• **Emphasis on environment.** The surroundings of the dementia patient should be familiar and comforting and designed to foster as much independence as possible. For example, the layout of the living space should be uncomplicated so there is less potential for confusion. Clutter should be minimized, but the use of natural elements—such as plants, pictures of nature, natural lighting, etc.—can induce a feeling of calm.

• **Muscle memory stimulation.** While the mind of a dementia patient might be faltering, the muscles often "remember" how to do an activity that was done repetitively and enjoyably in the past. The key is to discover a patient's unique strengths, passions and interests—not only tapping muscle memory but strong emotions as well. A caregiver might take a former golfer to the driving range to jump-start his muscle memory. Or an artist might be given pastels and a sketch pad so she can tinker. These activities also build muscle coordination and can simply make life more pleasant and enriching for a dementia patient.

• **Sharing stories.** This is one of the most effective tools for helping dementia sufferers stay connected. Moments when patients share their stories, even if the time is fleeting, can enable the patient and caregiver to feel a deep connection, boosting the patient's sense of security.

To encourage a patient to share a story: A caregiver might give him a meaningful object to hold—something important from the patient's life or an object from nature. This simple act can help spark a memory and get the patient talking.

• **Art therapy.** Painting, singing and playing an instrument can provide patients new avenues of self-expression and strengthen their spirits. These activities also can give patients the opportunity to engage their senses.

Good activity: Flower arranging. Patients are encouraged to feel and smell the flowers, cut stems and pour water. This exercise calls on small motor skills, essential for independence and range of motion. Key areas of the brain are also exercised when deciding how to arrange the flowers.

• **The Knobbed Cylinder.** This classic Montessori tool—a long wooden block with 10 different-sized holes in which the user places matching cylinders—builds focus and small-muscle coordination. Dementia patients might be asked to fill only two holes—the point is for the patient to feel success and build confidence through this activity.

• **Finish a phrase.** Old sayings may never leave our minds. With this technique, the caregiver holds up the first half of a statement on a piece of paper ("The whole nine...") and asks the patient to finish the saying ("...yards"). It's astonishing to see dementia sufferers suddenly become very vocal and involved.

Benefits for the caregivers: The Montessori method gives the caregiver more tools to care for a dementia patient. It encourages the caregiver to use his imagination and allows him to act more like a guide than a director. Plus, patients are less agitated and aggressive, so they are easier to be with. All this helps minimize caregiver burnout and frustration.

Try out a few of these exercises with your loved one. To find a facility that offers this specific approach, you'll need to ask the director of the center you are considering.

Help for Alzheimer's Patients and Their Families

The best websites include Alzheimer's Association (*www.alz.org*), which lists warning signs, disease stages, treatments, care options and financial-planning advice. Alzheimer's Disease Education and Referral Center (*www.nihseniorhealth.gov*), from the National Institute on Aging, has information on the latest studies about the disease's causes and possible cures. And PBS offers a 90-minute documentary on Alzheimer's patients and their families (*www.pbs.org/theforgetting*). Finally, This Caring Home (*www.thiscaringhome.org*), from Weill Cornell Medical College, gives room-by-room safety recommendations and solutions to problems.

Kiplinger's Retirement Report. Kiplinger.com

3

Arthritis

Natural Cures for Arthritis: Research Shows They Really Work!

If you have arthritis, you may have shied away from natural medicine in the past because you didn't think that it would relieve your pain.

After all, there is no rigorous scientific evidence to back up these remedies, right?

Wrong.

Now: While it's true that many nondrug approaches for pain relief have been based primarily on their thousands of years of use by Asian, Indian and other traditional cultures, there is now an impressive body of scientific evidence that makes natural medicine a smarter choice than ever before for many arthritis sufferers. (These therapies have been studied most often for osteoarthritis but may also relieve pain due to rheumatoid arthritis. Check with your doctor.)

PAIN RELIEF WITH LESS RISK

Millions of Americans depend on high-dose pain relievers that cause side effects, including gastrointestinal upset or bleeding, in up to 60% of patients.

What you may not realize is that some natural therapies, which are far less likely to cause side effects, work just as well as the powerful pain-relieving drugs that are so commonly used for arthritis.

Many Americans take glucosamine (a dietary supplement that stimulates production of key components in cartilage) to help fight arthritis. However, arthritis pain symptoms improve only slightly or moderately in some patients—even when they take glucosamine sulfate, the most widely studied form of this supplement. (Research currently indicates that adding chondroitin, a supplement derived from shark or

Steven Ehrlich, NMD, a naturopathic physician and founder of Solutions Acupuncture & Naturopathic Medicine in Phoenix. He has spent the last decade using natural medicine to treat chronic pain and illness. Dr. Ehrlich has also taught naturopathic techniques to both conventional and alternative medicine practitioners.

bovine cartilage or produced synthetically, isn't necessarily helpful for arthritis.)

In my practice, I often recommend the following regimen (with or without glucosamine) to relieve arthritis pain—the typical arthritis patient might start with curcumin and fish oil (pain relief should begin within one week to a month). *Ginger can be added if more pain relief is needed...**

- **Curcumin.** A chemical compound in the spice turmeric, it helps inhibit inflammatory enzymes and reduces joint pain without the gastrointestinal side effects that often occur with aspirin and related drugs.

Scientific evidence: A study published in *The Journal of Alternative and Complementary Medicine* found that curcumin reduced arthritis pain and improved knee function about as well as *ibuprofen* (Motrin).

How to use curcumin: To obtain a concentrated dose of the active ingredient, try curcumin supplement capsules with a standardized curcuminoid complex (rather than kitchen turmeric, which would be difficult to consume in therapeutic amounts). Follow the label instructions—typically taking it three times daily during flare-ups. Between arthritis episodes, you can take half this amount to prevent inflammation.

Caution: Curcumin can inhibit the ability of blood to clot. Use this supplement only under a doctor's supervision, particularly if you're also taking a blood-thinning medication such as *warfarin* (Coumadin) or aspirin.

- **Fish oil.** The omega-3 fatty acids in fish oil supplements increase the body's production of inhibitory prostaglandins, substances that prevent inflammation.

Scientific evidence: A study published in *Arthritis & Rheumatism* discovered that some arthritis patients who took fish oil improved so much that they were able to discontinue their use of conventional painkillers.

How to use fish oil: The amount of omega-3s found in dietary sources is insufficient for pain relief. Use a fish oil supplement—doses range from about 2,000 mg to 6,000 mg daily. Start with the lower dose, then gradually increase it until you notice improvement in pain and stiffness (the rate at which the dose is increased depends on the patient). If you take more than 2,000 mg of fish oil daily, you should be monitored by a physician—this supplement has a blood-thinning effect.

- **Ginger.** This spice has compounds that inhibit the effects of cyclooxygenase, an inflammatory enzyme.

Scientific evidence: A study that looked at 261 patients with knee arthritis discovered that those who took ginger supplements had less pain—and required fewer painkillers—than those taking placebos.

How to use ginger: Ginger spice will not provide enough of the active ingredient, so use a ginger supplement. The standard dose is 250 mg taken four times daily. Talk to your doctor before trying ginger—especially if it's used with a blood-thinning drug, curcumin and/or fish oil. Ginger can increase the risk for bleeding in some patients.

OTHER THERAPIES THAT HELP

The following approaches can accelerate and increase the pain-relieving effects offered by the supplements described earlier...

- **Balance Method acupuncture.** Acupuncture can be extremely effective because it increases the flow of blood and oxygen into painful areas while accelerating the removal of inflammatory chemicals.

Scientific evidence: A study involving more than 3,500 patients with chronic hip and/or knee arthritis found that those given acupuncture (in addition to conventional care, including doctor visits and use of painkillers) had fewer symptoms and a better quality of life than those given only conventional treatments.

My advice: Consider trying Balance Method acupuncture. Rather than inserting needles above or near the painful areas (as occurs with standard acupuncture), the practitioner will use points on your arms or legs

*Consult a doctor before trying these supplements—especially if you have a chronic condition or take medication. To find a physician near you with experience prescribing botanical medicines, consult the American Association of Naturopathic Physicians at *www.naturopathic.org*.

that "remotely" affect the joints. It seems to be more effective than standard acupuncture.

How acupuncture is used: Virtually all arthritis patients improve by the end of the third session—some after the first session. Most practitioners advise an initial series of 12 to 15 sessions, given once or twice a week, followed by monthly "tune-ups."

• **Meditation.** Meditation works in part by lowering levels of stress hormones. This decreases inflammation as well as the perception of pain. Patients who do meditation may still have pain, but it won't bother them as much as it did before.

Scientific evidence: In a study reported at an American College of Rheumatology meeting, arthritis patients who did meditation for 45 minutes a day, six days a week for six months had an 11% decrease in symptoms, a 46% decrease in erythrocyte sedimentation rate (a measure of inflammation) and a 33% reduction in psychological stress.

How meditation is used: Practice meditation for five to 10 minutes, once or twice a day—even during symptom-free periods.

Helpful: "Tapping meditation," which incorporates elements of acupressure as the patient taps different areas of his/her body. It has been especially helpful for arthritis patients in my practice. Most health practitioners who recommend meditation can teach you how to perform tapping meditation.

• **Yoga.** Any form of exercise is helpful for arthritis as long as it doesn't put excessive pressure on the joints. Yoga is particularly beneficial because it gently stretches and strengthens the muscles. It also increases the movement of synovial (lubricating) fluid across bone surfaces.

Scientific evidence: Researchers recently found that patients with knee osteoarthritis who took a weekly yoga class had improvements in pain and mobility after just eight weeks.

How yoga is used: The yoga that's practiced in many health clubs and yoga studios may be too aggressive for patients who have arthritis. Start with a beginner's class, preferably one that's taught by an instructor who specializes in therapeutic yoga, which is designed to treat specific medical conditions. To find a yoga instructor who specializes in therapeutic yoga, consult the International Association of Yoga Therapists at *www.iayt.org*.

---

5 Myths About Arthritis

C. Thomas Vangsness, Jr., MD, professor of orthopaedic surgery and chief of sports medicine at Keck School of Medicine at University of Southern California, Los Angeles. He is author, with Greg Ptacek, of *The New Science of Overcoming Arthritis: Prevent or Reverse Your Pain, Discomfort and Limitations.*

About one in six Americans will have to cope with osteoarthritis* during their lifetimes. But even though so many people have it, there's still a lot of misinformation about it. *What's true about osteoarthritis—and what's not...*

MYTH: Running causes arthritis.

It would seem likely that the pounding the body receives during running could damage cartilage and increase the risk for arthritis. Not true.

A study that followed nearly 75,000 people for seven years found that those who ran 1.2 miles a day were 15% less likely to develop osteoarthritis and 35% less likely to need a hip replacement than those who merely walked.

Even though runners strike the ground with a force that equals eight times their body weight, they take longer strides (and require fewer steps) than walkers. The cumulative jolts caused by running actually appear to be similar to the slower-speed impacts among walkers.

That said, if you have, say, an arthritic knee, you should consult with a medical professional before beginning a running program. The joint stress from running could increase the progression in an already-damaged joint.

MYTH: Don't move when you're hurting.

The traditional arthritis advice is to give your joints total rest during flare-ups. Don't believe it.

*The advice in this article may help with rheumatoid arthritis, too. Talk to your doctor.

You obviously don't want to overdo it when a joint is inflamed. But gentle movements keep joints mobile, flush out inflammatory chemicals and improve the flow of oxygen and nutrients to damaged tissues.

On "good" days, you could swim, lift weights, jog, etc. Yoga is an excellent exercise because it strengthens muscles and joints in a controlled fashion. Tai chi is another excellent form of gentle exercise.

Important: If you have more pain than usual, talk to your doctor or physical therapist before starting—or continuing—exercise. You might need to adjust your workouts, including stopping/starting particular exercises.

MYTH: It's an age-related disease.

This is one of the most pervasive myths. Over the last few decades, people have begun to get osteoarthritis at younger and younger ages. Today, the average age at which symptoms start is 45—and the downward trend is likely to continue.

Experts aren't sure how to explain the increase in younger adults. Americans are heavier than they used to be, and obesity is strongly associated with arthritis. Also, injuries to joints during sports can lead to joint pain down the road. Ongoing inflammation increases cartilage destruction in the joint.

Important: If you have had a joint injury—a torn meniscus in the knee, for example—at any age, there's a good chance that you eventually will develop arthritis in the same joint. Work with a physical therapist to strengthen the muscles and tendons that surround the joint before symptoms start.

MYTH: A little extra weight is OK.

Studies have shown that people who are obese have more inflammation, less joint mobility and more cartilage damage than those who are lean. But what if you're just a few pounds overweight?

It's still a problem. People tend to exercise less when they're overweight. Reduced movement leads to less joint mobility—and more pain. Also, even a small amount of extra weight increases pressure on the joints. Every 10 pounds that you add above the waist generates an extra 70 to 100 pounds of pressure on the knees when you walk.

Research has shown that women who lose about 11 pounds can reduce their risk of developing arthritis symptoms by more than 50%.

MYTH: You can't stop it.

Arthritis may be persistent, but it's rarely hard to treat. Most patients get good relief without high-tech treatments or expensive medications.

Though the American College of Rheumatology advises patients with knee and/or hip arthritis to start with acetaminophen (Tylenol), I tell my patients that acetaminophen is an effective painkiller, but it doesn't help with inflammation.

My advice: Take one of the NSAIDs (nonsteroidal anti-inflammatory drugs) such as aspirin, ibuprofen or naproxen. They reduce pain as well as inflammation. Follow the dosing directions on the label, or ask your doctor for advice.

Helpful: To reduce stomach irritation (a common side effect of all the NSAIDs), take an anti-ulcer medication, such as *cimetidine* (Tagamet). I also have been prescribing a newer medication, *misoprostol* (Cytotec), for stomach irritation. Ask your doctor whether either of these might help you.

Healing Tea for Arthritis

Bring one-half cup of water to a boil. Add fresh ginger, cut into thin slices—you can use as much as you like—and let simmer for five minutes. Remove and discard the ginger. Turn off the heat, and add one-quarter teaspoon of turmeric powder, one tablespoon of unflavored gelatin and one tablespoon of coconut oil. Stir until the gelatin is dissolved, then add one-half to one cup of calcium-enriched orange juice. Drink this tea once or twice a day.

Lydia Wilen and Joan Wilen are sisters who are folk-remedy experts based in New York City. The sisters are coauthors of many books, including *Bottom Line's Secret Food Cures* and *Household Magic Daily Tips.*

Milk Does Your Body Good

Milk may slow the progression of knee osteoarthritis in women.

Recent finding: The more low-fat or fat-free milk women drank, the more slowly the disease progressed. The same benefit was not found in men.

But: Increased intake of cheese made knee osteoarthritis progress more quickly. Yogurt was not found to have any effect.

Study of 1,260 women and 888 men with knee arthritis by researchers at Brigham and Women's Hospital, Boston, published in *Arthritis Care & Research.*

Thunder God Vine—Can a Chinese Medicine Remedy Help Your Arthritis?

Study titled "Comparison of Tripterygium wilfordii Hook F with methotrexate in the treatment of active rheumatoid arthritis (TRIFRA): a randomized, controlled clinical trial," published in *Annals of the Rheumatic Diseases.*

Thunder god vine extract has been a staple in the treatment of rheumatoid arthritis in China for hundreds of years. In fact, about two-thirds of patients with rheumatoid arthritis in China are treated with this time-tested remedy. Nowadays, though, most people in China are treated with the extract in combination with low doses of *methotrexate*, a powerful chemotherapeutic drug that tends to be used in the United States only when rheumatoid arthritis is severe and all other remedies have failed.

PUTTING IT TO THE TEST

Scientists already know that thunder god vine extract can help your body keep a lid on the inflammation familiar to rheumatoid arthritis. But does it work just as well without methotrexate? And how does it stack up in comparison to methotrexate anyway?

Researchers enrolled 207 patients with rheumatoid arthritis and divided them into three groups. Each group was given methotrexate at a dosage of 7.5 milligrams (mg) weekly to start, which could be increased up to 12.5 mg weekly if needed...or 20 mg of thunder god vine extract three times a day...or a combination of both the methotrexate and the extract. Patients were examined before and at various times during the study to track whether their treatment was working.

What the researchers found: Patients who received both methotrexate and thunder god vine extract fared the best—by far. In fact, after 24 weeks, 77% of that group saw their symptoms improve by at least 50%. In comparison, just 55% who received only thunder god vine extract improved that much...and only 46% of the patients who received only methotrexate improved that much. The natural product also worked faster than methotrexate in reducing the erythrocyte sedimentation rate, a marker of inflammation that is measured in blood tests.

By the fourth week of the study, participants in the thunder god vine extract group had improved significantly more than those in the methotrexate group, who didn't see a major improvement until the very end of the study period. This all sounds great for thunder god vine extract...but although the amount of methotrexate that these Chinese patients were getting was less than what an American patient would normally get. In America, the dosage can be increased to up to 25 mg a week—double the dose that it was increased to in the Chinese study. This basically means that the Chinese patients may have been getting less than the optimum dosage of methotrexate than they really needed, which might explain why the methotrexate wasn't as effective or as fast to work as thunder god vine extract.

Bottom line: More research is needed—but these preliminary findings are promising...

- **Maybe there will be a place someday soon for thunder god vine** in your doctor's bag of remedies for rheumatoid arthritis, and...
- **Maybe Western researchers will discover that methotrexate can be used at lower doses** in combination with products like thunder god vine for different levels of

rheumatoid arthritis, not just the severe, nothing-else-works kind.

ALL-NATURAL DOESN'T MEAN SIDE EFFECT-FREE

Of course, side effects can and do occur with natural remedies, and thunder god vine extract is no exception. In the study that compared thunder god vine extract to methotrexate, side effects occurred slightly less often for patients receiving only the extract compared with those receiving only methotrexate. The most common side effects were gastrointestinal (abdominal discomfort, nausea, and loss of appetite). Also, because thunder god vine extract is known to cause irregular periods in women and affect reproductive hormones in both men and women, Chinese doctors recommend that it not be used in women of child-bearing age. It also might not be the best choice for people who have or are at risk for osteoporosis because the extract decreases bone mineral density.

Should you give thunder god vine a go? The active ingredient is carefully extracted from the skinned root of the vine, but other parts of the plant, including its leaves, flowers and the root skin that's removed, are very poisonous and can cause death—so manufacturing must be precise. If you would like to try this remedy, it's imperative to do so under the supervision of a knowledgeable integrative physician (such as a rheumatologist in-the-know about alternative health), a naturopathic doctor or a specialist in herbal medicines.

Traditional Chinese Moxibustion for Arthritis Pain Relief

Study titled "Effectiveness of moxibustion treatment as adjunctive therapy in osteoarthritis of the knee: a randomized, double-blinded, placebo-controlled clinical trial," published in *Arthritis Research & Therapy.*

The pain and limitations of arthritis, together with the risks of nonsteroidal anti-inflammatory drugs, send many arthritis sufferers in search of alternative treatments, such as traditional Chinese medicine. The "proof" of effectiveness of traditional remedies often is simply that they've been used, literally, for ages. If they did not provide a benefit, the thinking goes, they would've been dropped by the wayside a few hundred years ago. But in today's world—in our Western world, at least—credibility demands cold, hard evidence.

The more East meets West, the more scientists are putting traditional Chinese medicine remedies to the test. And they just did that with a remedy that has been part of traditional Chinese medicine for at least 2,000 years and used for everything from turning breech babies to curing constipation to—you guessed it—relieving arthritis pain. It's not a form of acupuncture or an herbal extract. It's something even more exotic—moxibustion.

UP IN SMOKE

Moxibustion is a cross between acupressure and old-fashioned herbalism—but with fire. It involves burning moxa (the herb Artemisia vulgaris, also known as mugwort) very close to the skin at acupoints—acupuncture meridian points. In one common moxibustion technique, the moxa is packed into a very small pillar that sits in a hollow cylindrical base that is placed on an acupoint. Tiny holes in the base allow smoke and heat from the burning moxa to escape and make contact with the acupoint.

To prove by Western standards that moxibustion is effective for pain relief of knee osteoarthritis, Chinese researchers recruited 110 people with painful knee osteoarthritis. Half of the participants received real moxibustion treatments, as I described above, and the other half received a sham procedure three times per week for six weeks. Moxa was burned in its cylinder in the sham procedure, but the holes at the base of the gadget were covered by a hidden, internal membrane that blocked the escape of smoke and heat. None of the participants knew whether they were getting real moxibustion or a sham treatment. The practitioners providing the treatments also were kept in the dark by the study researchers about whether they were providing a real or sham moxibustion so that they wouldn't unconsciously or consciously perform treatment or record results in a biased way.

NOT JUST BLOWING SMOKE

Three weeks into the study, the moxibustion group reported a 25% reduction in pain, on average, whereas the sham treatment group reported a mere 3% reduction. By the end of treatment, reduction in pain more than doubled—to 53%—in the moxibustion group and improved to 24% in the sham group. These results held up for quite some time after treatment ended. At 24 weeks, patients in the moxibution group reported 51% less pain than before the study, and patients in the sham group reported 20% less pain.

There was improvement in use of the knee, too. Function increased by 39% after six weeks of moxibustion treatment and by 51% after six more weeks went by. Meanwhile, function improved by only 13% after six weeks of sham treatment and did not improve anymore after that.

For anyone hoping to improve an arthritic knee, here's an important time marker—the level of improvement in function began to slip after 18 weeks had gone by, suggesting that the healing effects of six weeks of moxibustion for knee osteoarthritis could last 4.5 months.

And the only complication of moxibustion was temporary redness at the acupoint site.

These are wonderful results, clearly. No one knows how moxibustion works, but one theory is that the heat generated by the burning moxa stimulates the skin at the acupoint, which, in turn, stimulates the nervous system to release feel-good hormones called endorphins, which block the sensation of pain. Another possibility is that the heat generated by the moxa, which is not quite strong enough to cause injury, is irritating enough to trigger the body to launch a healing response anyway. If you are asking why moxa is used instead of any number of herbs, the answer is tradition. In Chinese medicine, burning mugwort is thought to have a therapeutically warming effect on the body that promotes blood circulation and pain relief.

If you're interested in giving moxibustion a try, you can find a licensed provider through the National Certification Commission for Acupuncture and Oriental Medicine.

How People With Arthritis Can Avoid Joint Replacement

Kimberly Beauchamp, ND, licensed naturopathic doctor and health and nutrition writer. Her blog, Eat Happy, helps take the drama out of healthy eating. *AskDoctorMama.com/category/eat-happy*

Arthritis is easily the most common cause of physical disability in America. A recently released report from the National Institutes of Health (NIH) says that nearly 50 million Americans have doctor-diagnosed arthritis (including both osteoarthritis, or OA, and rheumatoid arthritis, or RA) and predicts that that number will soar to 67 million in the next 20 years. That's a lot of stiff, painful knees, hands, shoulders and feet!

While some folks joke that they're headed straight for joint replacement, the truth is that arthritis responds well to many natural therapies, including dietary supplements. *Here are supplements and natural therapies that many arthritis patients find helpful...*

- **Zyflamend.** This proprietary blend of supplements contains 10 anti-inflammatory plant extracts that can be helpful for many people with both OA and RA. Kimberly Beauchamp, a naturopathic doctor in Kingtown, Rhode Island, has patients take one capsule twice daily with meals. (Available online at *www.NewChapter.com* and at many health-food stores.)

- **Red Seaweed Extract.** Red seaweed extract (Lithomanion calcarea) can help people with OA. One study reported in *Nutrition Journal* and funded by Marigot, the company that makes Aquamin (a patented red seaweed extract), found that taking the extract for one month was associated with a 20% reduction in arthritis pain. Patients also reported less stiffness and better range of motion and were able to walk further than those taking a placebo. A typical dose would be 2,400 mg of seaweed extract in capsule form each day, Dr. Beauchamp said. (*Note*: Seaweed contains iodine in amounts that may be dangerous to thyroid patients.)

• **Vitamin D.** New research indicates that vitamin D may play a key role in slowing the development and progression of both OA and RA. If you have either, it's a good idea to get your blood level of vitamin D checked, said Dr. Beauchamp. If you are deficient, she suggests taking at least 1,000 IU of vitamin D-3 (cholecalciferol) each day.

• **Peat/Peloid Packs (also called balneotherapy).** Commonly used in Europe, this is a form of thermal mud therapy that holds heat particularly well. Peat (or peloid packs that are sheets of peat mud on fabric) is applied to the aching area for about 20 minutes. The treatment can be done at home, but Dr. Beauchamp said it is far better to work with a physical therapist or doctor who is knowledgeable in the technique, as the packs are cumbersome and must be carefully applied to protect the skin from burning. Peat therapy treatments are typically administered over the course of several visits, declining in frequency as the patient's pain begins to ease—the results are long-lasting and you can resume treatment if and when the pain returns.

Better Arthritis Treatment

In an 18-month study of 110 people with an undetermined form of arthritis characterized by painful and stiff joints, those who took weekly doses of *methotrexate* for 12 months were less likely to develop rheumatoid arthritis, one of the most debilitating forms of the disease—and more likely to go into remission—than those who took a placebo.

Theory: Methotrexate, a drug used to treat some cancers and severe psoriasis, works, in part, by curbing activation of white blood cells, which may play a role in causing rheumatoid arthritis.

Caution: For treatment of rheumatoid arthritis, methotrexate is taken once a week, not once a day, as it is for the treatment of cancer.

Study titled "Effectiveness of moxibustion treatment as adjunctive therapy in osteoarthritis of the knee: a randomized, double-blinded, placebo-controlled clinical trial," published in *Arthritis Research & Therapy.*

Best Shoes for Arthritis

In a study of 16 adults with knee osteoarthritis, clogs and foot-stabilizing shoes (athletic shoes) put significantly more stress on the knees than flat walking shoes, flip-flops and walking barefoot.

Theory: Shoes that promote a natural foot motion may allow for a better transfer of the body's weight as the foot hits the ground.

If you have knee arthritis: Speak to your doctor about appropriate footwear.

Najia Shakoor, MD, assistant professor of internal medicine, section of rheumatology, Rush Medical College, Chicago.

Spice Eases Arthritis

Frankincense is a traditional arthritis treatment that blocks the production of inflammatory molecules and helps protect joint cartilage.

Cardiff University.

Qigong Eases Arthritis

Practitioners of qigong use traditional Chinese medicine techniques—such as mind-body breath work, acupressure, therapeutic touch and focused attention—to stimulate the healing flow of qi (energy).

New study: Among patients with knee osteoarthritis, those who participated in five or six qigong sessions reported 13% to 26% greater reduction in pain and 13% to 28% more improvement in function than patients who got placebo treatments.

Results vary depending on the practitioner—so look for an experienced practitioner when starting out, then take classes to learn to practice qigong on your own.

Resources: National Qigong Association, 888-815-1893, *www.nqa.org*...Qigong Research Society, 856-234-3056, *www.qigongresearchsociety.com*.

Kevin W. Chen, PhD, MPH, associate professor, Center for Integrative Medicine, University of Maryland, Baltimore, and coauthor of a study of 106 arthritis patients, published in *Clinical Rheumatology*.

Cod Liver Oil Benefits Rheumatoid Arthritis Sufferers

Study: People taking 10 grams of cod liver oil a day can cut their reliance on nonsteroidal anti-inflammatory drugs (NSAIDs), such as ibuprofen, by more than 30%. The reduction in drug use wasn't associated with any worsening of pain or the disease.

Caution: Avoid oil with added vitamin A—it may lead to consuming unsafe amounts of that vitamin.

Jill Belch, MD, head of the Cardiovascular and Lung Biology Centre, Ninewells Hospital, University of Dundee Medical School, Dundee, Scotland.

Cherry Pills Ease Arthritis Pain

In a new study of 20 patients with osteoarthritis of the knee, more than half the patients experienced significant improvement in knee pain after taking tart-cherry supplements daily for eight weeks.

Theory: Cherry extracts contain flavonoids and anthocyanins, which have been shown to have anti-inflammatory effects.

If you have osteoarthritis: Ask your doctor about trying tart-cherry supplements.

John J. Cush, MD, rheumatologist, Baylor Research Institute, Dallas.

Dance to Avoid Arthritis

Women in their 70s who reported no stiff or painful joints at the start of a three-year study and who engaged in moderate exercise, such as dancing or brisk walking, for a little more than one hour a week reduced their risk of developing arthritis symptoms by 26%. Women who did at least two hours per week of moderate exercise reduced their risk by 46%.

Other good options: Tai chi, yoga and swimming.

Kristiann Heesch, DrPh, research fellow, School of Human Movement Studies, University of Queensland, Australia, and researcher on a study of 8,750 women, published in *Arthritis Research & Therapy*.

This Juice Helps Arthritis

Fight osteoarthritis with pomegranate juice. It has antioxidants and an anti-inflammatory effect that can block enzymes involved in cartilage deterioration by up to 68%. It also may protect against cancer and heart disease. Pomegranate juices are available at health-food stores.

Best: Mix at least two tablespoons of 100% pomegranate juice with another juice or seltzer daily.

Tariq Haqqi, PhD, is professor of medicine and director of rheumatology research at Case Western Reserve University in Cleveland. His study was published in *Journal of Nutrition*.

Ginger Relieves Arthritis Pain

Ginger supplements soothe osteoarthritic joints by inhibiting production of pain-causing prostaglandins.

Best: Take a 100-mg supplement, such as Gingerforce, one to three times a day.

Sung Woo Kim, PhD, professor of nutrition and digestive physiology, department of animal and food sciences, Texas Tech University, Lubbock, and leader of a study published in *Journal of Medicinal Food.*

The Spice That Treats Arthritis Better Than NSAIDs

Ajay Goel, PhD, director of epigenetics and cancer prevention, Baylor Research Institute, Baylor University Medical Center, Dallas.

You might think that you've heard everything there is to hear about curcumin, the compound found in turmeric (the yellow spice used in curry). But you haven't.

For those who are unfamiliar, research has shown, for example, that curcumin may help alleviate symptoms of irritable bowel syndrome and ulcerative colitis and that it might even help prevent and treat certain cancers.

Now a new study suggests that curcumin can help with yet another serious condition—rheumatoid arthritis.

This is very promising when you consider how painful and debilitating rheumatoid arthritis can be...and when you consider that the main treatments—nonsteroidal anti-inflammatory drugs (NSAIDs) such as diclofenac sodium, ibuprofen and *celecoxib* (Celebrex)—have serious side effects, including liver damage and gastrointestinal bleeding.

Could curcumin offer effective and safe relief? Let's see what the research is saying...

A NATURAL ANTI-INFLAMMATORY

Researchers decided to study curcumin because, in the human body, it's believed to tamp down inflammation, and rheumatoid arthritis is driven by inflammation.

Ajay Goel, PhD, a coauthor of the study, split participants into three groups. For eight weeks, one group took curcumin in supplement form...one group took diclofenac sodium...and the third group took a combination of the two.

In terms of relief from painful and swollen joints, all three groups saw similar results. In fact, the people taking only curcumin saw slightly more relief than the others did. But when you think about it, that's a staggering result—because the curcumin created none of the dangerous side effects caused by the NSAID. Not a single patient in the curcumin-only group or the combo group dropped out of the study due to intolerable side effects, while 14% of those taking only the NSAID did.

One limitation of the study is that it didn't include a placebo group as a control. Dr. Goel noted that this is common in a Phase 1 clinical trial such as this one. In further studies, a control group will be included.

SAFETY FIRST

It's understood why curcumin may have helped relieve symptoms—it's an anti-inflammatory. But why is it better tolerated by patients?

It has to do with how the treatments work within the body, Dr. Goel said. In simple terms, a pharmaceutical NSAID completely blocks one inflammatory pathway, while curcumin blocks many inflammatory pathways—and blocks each only a little, taking a balanced approach as opposed to an "all or nothing" approach.

"Some levels of inflammation are actually required for normal functioning of healthy cells in our body. So when you completely block a pathway, that's what can trigger undesirable side effects. As a result, curcumin seems to be more gentle on the body," said Dr. Goel.

FOR RELIEF: CONSUME MORE CURCUMIN

Most Americans, he said, don't eat enough curcumin. Even if you eat an Indian meal once or twice a week or occasionally sprinkle the spice on soup, meat or eggs, you're not likely to reach the amount needed to get the anti-inflammatory benefit.

So if you have rheumatoid arthritis, Dr. Goel suggests talking to your doctor about taking a curcumin supplement (about $25 for 60 250-milligram capsules, a month's supply). In his study, the curcumin dose that helped the study subjects was 500 milligrams of curcumin a day, but ask your doctor about the appropriate dose for you.

For people with arthritis who are not yet treating the condition, this supplement might be a good first step, said Dr. Goel. For those already treating the condition with an NSAID, ask your doctor if it's OK to gradually start taking a curcumin supplement instead.

"Curcumin is very safe for most people," said Dr. Goel, who gives the supplement to his nine- and seven-year-old children. But he added that people on certain drugs, such as anticoagulants, may not want to use it, because curcumin also has anticoagulant properties. Also, it may negatively interact with certain chemo drugs, and people with bile duct obstruction, gallstones or stomach ulcers may want to avoid using it. To be safe, check with your doctor before using it.

Prevent Knee Arthritis

Women who exercised vigorously for 20 minutes every day for 14 days had more cartilage in their knees than women who did not exercise. Healthier cartilage protects against degenerative diseases, such as osteoarthritis.

For healthy joints: Do regular strenuous weight-bearing exercise, such as brisk walking, jogging or cycling.

Fahad Hanna, PhD, department of epidemiology and preventive medicine, Monash University, Clayton, Australia, and lead author of a study of 176 women, published in *Menopause.*

Surprising Risk for Knee Arthritis

Researchers measured leg lengths of 3,026 adults who had knee osteoarthritis or were at risk for it (due to factors such as family history or obesity).

Results: Adults with one leg that was at least 0.4 inches shorter than the other were 1.5 times more likely to develop knee arthritis within 2.5 years than those without the leg-length disparity.

Theory: The shorter leg travels farther to reach the ground and strikes with greater force, setting the stage for arthritis.

If you're at risk for knee arthritis: Have your doctor measure your leg lengths. If they differ, ask about corrective measures, such as shoe inserts and physical therapy.

William F. Harvey, MD, assistant professor of medicine, Tufts Medical Center, Boston.

Herbs That Help Treat Arthritis

Devil's claw has an anti-inflammatory component that may relieve pain.

Suggested dose: 750 mg of standardized 3% iridoid glycosides three times a day.

- **Extract of avocado and soybean oil can reduce pain and stiffness**—300 mg a day.
- **Phytodolor, a mixture of ash, aspen and goldenrod, may also reduce symptoms**—30 drops three times a day.
- **Niacinamide can ease pain and swelling**—100 mg three to four times a day.
- **Tart cherry juice. A daily cup can ease mild arthritis.**

Note: Check with your doctor before taking any dietary supplements.

Andrew Heyman, MD, adjunct clinical instructor in family medicine, University of Michigan Medical School, Ann Arbor.

Slow Rheumatoid Arthritis with Early Detection

Beth L. Jonas, MD, is an assistant professor of medicine and rheumatology and director of the Rheumatology Fellowship Program at the University of North Carolina Thurston Arthritis Research Center in Chapel Hill.

An elderly neighbor has fingers so gnarled and painful that she can scarcely hold a fork. The cause, she told me, is rheumatoid arthritis (RA). When she told her doctor that her middle-aged daughter was starting to show signs of the disease, he urged, "Tell your daughter to see a doctor right away."

Why the rush? Because now—unlike when my neighbor first developed RA decades ago—there are ways to limit the disease's progression, most notably with disease-modifying antirheumatic drugs (DMARDs). But these work best when treatment begins within six to 12 weeks of the onset of symptoms.

Unfortunately, many RA sufferers postpone seeking medical care...and once they do, doctors may not accurately diagnose the disease or may fail to refer patients to rheumatologists, the specialists best equipped to treat RA. In a recent study in *Arthritis & Rheumatism*, 69% of RA patients did not see a rheumatologist within those crucial first 12 weeks—and the delay contributed to a 30% faster rate of joint destruction and an 87% lower likelihood of remission, compared with patients who saw a specialist promptly.

Permanent joint damage can occur at a very early stage of the disease. Medication can slow and sometimes prevent joint destruction—but once damage is done, we can't reverse it. New concern: Some research links the high levels of inflammation associated with RA to cardiovascular disease.

What about people who have already missed that window of opportunity for early treatment? Avoiding further delay is vital because the new medications still can help somewhat...whereas RA sufferers left untreated face a significantly increased risk of becoming disabled.

SPOTTING THE SIGNS

With RA, the immune system attacks the synovial membranes that line the joints. This lining becomes inflamed and thickened... fluid builds up...ligaments and tendons weaken and stretch out...cartilage is destroyed...and bone is damaged. Over time, patients develop crippling chronic pain and joint deformity.

Women are two to three times more likely than men to get RA. The disease can arise at any time but usually appears in midlife. While genetics may play some role, most RA patients have no close relatives with the disease—so we all should be on the lookout for RA. See your doctor without delay if you experience any of the following...

- **Pain, tenderness and/or stiffness in any of the small joints—fingers, wrists, toes, ankles—**usually occurring symmetrically on both sides of the body. (As RA progresses, the neck, shoulders, elbows, hips and/or knees also may be affected.)

- **Morning stiffness that lasts for more than 30 minutes.**

- **Redness, swelling and/or sensations of heat at the joints.**

- **Numbness, tingling or burning sensations in the hands or feet.**

Confirming an RA diagnosis can be tricky because the symptoms mimic those of lupus, Lyme disease and other forms of arthritis. Diagnosis is based on a physical exam... blood tests for antibodies (including rheumatoid factor and anti-cyclic citrullinated peptide) plus various markers of inflammation... and imaging tests (ultrasound, MRI, X-ray).

So if your doctor suspects RA, ask to be referred to a rheumatologist or get a referral through the American College of Rheumatology (visit *www.rheumatology.org* and click on "Find a member").

Can This Patient Be Cured? Rheumatoid Arthritis

Mark A. Stengler, NMD, licensed naturopathic medical doctor in private practice, Stengler Center for Integrative Medicine, Encinitas, California...adjunct associate clinical professor at the National College of Natural Medicine, Portland, Oregon...author of many books including *The Natural Physician's Healing Therapies. MarkStengler.com*

Sandy had been suffering from rheumatoid arthritis for 16 years. This inflammatory disease is characterized by joint pain on both sides of the body, most often in the hands, wrists and knees. It is an autoimmune condition—that is, the body's immune system attacks its own tissue, causing the cartilage in the joints to degrade over time. Sandy, a 43-year-old homemaker, had constant pain and inflammation in her hands and wrists.

When I first saw her, she was taking two prescription anti-inflammatory medications —*methotrexate*, which also is used as a chemotherapy agent, and *hydrochloroquine* (Plaquenil). To make matters worse, she had been in a car accident a year before, which injured her hands and back, further aggravating her condition. In addition to her pain, Sandy's digestion was not good—she was prone to diarrhea, gas and bloating—and for the past five years, she had not slept well.

Understandably, Sandy was concerned about the potential toxicity of her medications. For example, methotrexate can cause liver damage and anemia.

Sandy and I discussed the potential triggers of rheumatoid arthritis—stress (which was high in her life), food sensitivities, hormone imbalances, poor digestion, environmental toxins and nutritional deficiencies.

I started Sandy on enzymes that aid digestion, fish oil, a proteolytic enzyme (to reduce inflammation) and a formula containing the hormone melatonin and the amino acid 5-hydroxytryptophan to help her sleep. I had her tested for hormone imbalances as well as food and environmental sensitivities. I also tested the absorption status of her small intestine.

The tests showed that she had a mild problem with malabsorption—the food she ate was not being broken down and absorbed properly. This validated my prescription for supplements that support digestion. Hormone testing showed that her thyroid was underactive, so I prescribed natural thyroid hormone. The allergist I work with found that Sandy had several food sensitivities—to wheat, tuna, onions, yams and other foods. I suggested that she rotate these foods, since it is difficult to avoid them indefinitely. To reduce the reactions triggered by her overactive immune system, I also recommended that she take desensitization drops, with a homeopathic dilution of the foods to which she was sensitive.

On her follow-up visit two months later, Sandy reported that she no longer had any symptoms of arthritis in her joints and had stopped her medications (with her rheumatologist's knowledge). She did experience a mild flare-up midway through her menstrual cycle, indicating a hormone connection. For this, I prescribed the homeopathic remedy Pulsatilla, known for its hormone-balancing properties. Now, a year later, Sandy experiences only minor, occasional arthritis flare-ups and has been able to reduce the number of supplements she uses.

Ancient Arthritis Pain Relief

Acupuncture can reduce arthritis pain and stiffness.

Recent study: People with arthritis of the knee who received acupuncture twice a week for eight weeks reported 40% more improvement than those who did not receive acupuncture. Subjects took their regular pain medication throughout the study.

To find a certified acupuncturist: Contact the American Association of Acupuncture & Oriental Medicine, 866-455-7999, *www.aaaomonline.org*.

Brian M. Berman, MD, professor of family medicine, director, Center for Integrative Medicine, University of Maryland School of Medicine, Baltimore, and leader of a study of 570 arthritis patients, published in *Annals of Internal Medicine.*

Psoriatic Arthritis

Mark A. Stengler, NMD, licensed naturopathic medical doctor in private practice, Stengler Center for Integrative Medicine, Encinitas, California...adjunct associate clinical professor at the National College of Natural Medicine, Portland, Oregon...author of many books, including *The Natural Physician's Healing Therapies* and coauthor of *Prescription for Natural Cures. MarkStengler.com*

After four stressful months at work, Tiffany, a 55-year-old businesswoman, was diagnosed with psoriatic arthritis. This is a chronic condition in which psoriasis causes inflammation of the joints. Tiffany had suffered from psoriasis of the scalp for many years. This autoimmune condition causes skin cells to replicate too quickly, resulting in patches of red, swollen skin and silvery or white scales on the skin's surface. Psoriatic arthritis caused Tiffany's hands and feet to swell. She had pain in one knee and shoulder, and her muscles ached. She also was experiencing hot flashes due to menopause.

To confirm the diagnosis, her internist used the erythrocyte sedimentation rate (ESR) test, which can measure the degree of inflammation in the body and help diagnose autoimmune conditions. Tiffany's ESR level was very high.

She was taking 12 pills of ibuprofen (Advil) every day, a common first-line treatment for arthritis pain. Her internist wanted to give her a steroid or *methotrexate* (Trexall), a drug commonly used to treat rheumatoid arthritis by suppressing immune function. But Tiffany was concerned about side effects and didn't want to take stronger medication.

Tests I ran indicated that her vitamin D levels were low, which can cause inflammation. Menopause also was taking a toll, resulting in low levels of the hormones estrogen... testosterone...progesterone...dehydroepiandrosterone (DHEA), an anti-inflammatory hormone produced by the adrenal gland... and cortisol, which, when low, can impair immune function.

I created a treatment protocol for Tiffany consisting of 5,000 international units (IU) daily of vitamin D and bioidentical hormone replacements for DHEA, testosterone, cortisol, estrogen and progesterone, all of which I have found can help reduce inflammation in menopausal women.

I also put Tiffany on a pH-balanced diet to further reduce inflammation. (The diet consists of lots of vegetables, lean protein and small amounts of starch.) To help her joint pain, I recommended 4,000 mg of an anti-inflammatory form of sulfur called methylsulfonylmethane (MSM) twice daily and fish oil containing 3,000 mg of combined eicosapentaenoic acid (EPA) and docosahexaenoic acid (DHA). To reduce flaking, I prescribed a vitamin D cream for her scalp.

Four weeks later, Tiffany felt better, but while the MSM helped her arthritis symptoms, she still was in acute pain and taking Advil. As the months went on, the swelling in her hands and feet continued to decrease—and she reduced her use of Advil until she was taking it once every two to three weeks. The bioidentical hormones helped her hot flashes, and her ESR now is in the normal range.

Because the protocol helped, Tiffany has stayed on it. Even her internist is impressed with her progress, although he has expressed no interest in knowing exactly what treatments I have prescribed for her.

Prolotherapy Sugar Injections Relieve Knee Arthritis Pain

David Rabago, MD, assistant professor and associate research director, department of family medicine, University of Wisconsin School of Medicine and Public Health, Madison. His study was published in *Annals of Family Medicine*.

If you find yourself gingerly maneuvering up and down stairs and in and out of chairs because your knees are so painful and stiff, your doctor may have diagnosed osteoarthritis, the "wear and tear" type of arthritis. Exercise helps alleviate the stiffness but can be too uncomfortable for some sufferers...and painkilling drugs provide only temporary relief while carrying a risk for potentially serious side effects. The good news: There's promising new evidence that an alternative treatment requiring just a few visits to a doctor's office can ease symptoms for a year or more. It makes use of a substance you normally wouldn't consider to be therapeutic—sugar!

The treatment involves injecting a solution into and around painful joints. Called prolotherapy, the technique has been around for at least 75 years. However, it isn't broadly accepted because there haven't been many high-quality studies demonstrating its effectiveness and clarifying which type of solution works best. *With the recent publication of a study from the University of Wisconsin School of Medicine, that may be about to change...*

SWEET SOLUTION

The study included 90 adults with osteoarthritis of the knee and moderate-to-severe pain that had lasted for at least three months and had not responded well to other treatments. At the start of the study, all participants completed questionnaires that assessed, using a 100-point scale, the severity of their arthritis in terms of pain, stiffness and loss of function.

Next, participants were randomly assigned to one of three groups. One group was instructed in knee exercises and encouraged to practice them at home, gradually working their way up over the course of 20 weeks until they were doing the exercises three times during the day, five days per week.

Participants in groups two and three received prolotherapy sessions at weeks one, five and nine...and at weeks 13 and 17 if the participant and his/her physician thought the additional treatment would be helpful. Group two received injections of a saline (salt) solution... group three received injections of a dextrose (sugar) solution. Each session included up to 15 injections. Because this was a "blinded" experiment, neither the participants nor the doctor giving the injections knew which type of solution was being used on any given patient.

At several points during the treatment and a year after the start of the study, participants again filled out the symptom questionnaires to score their pain, stiffness and function.

Results: The dextrose prolotherapy group had the best improvement by a significant margin. Nine weeks into the study, after the third round of prolotherapy, the dextrose group's symptom score had improved by 13.9 points, on average. In comparison, the saline prolotherapy group had improved by 6.8 points...and the exercise group improved by an average of just 2.5 points.

Even more encouraging was the fact that the relief seemed to be long-lasting. Though the final injections were given at week nine, 13 or 17 (depending on the patient), at week 52 the dextrose prolotherapy group still reported an average improvement of 15.3 points compared with their pretreatment symptom scores. This degree of improvement on the 100-point scale has been determined to be "clinically robust" in prior studies, the researchers said. In comparison, the saline prolotherapy group wound up with an average improvement of just 7.6 points, while the exercise group ended up with an 8.2-point improvement.

How it works: No one knows exactly how prolotherapy helps or why the sugar solution would work better than the salt solution. The basic theory, though, is that the injections provoke minor, temporary inflammation, causing the body to send more blood and nutrients to the area and thus promoting a healing response.

NOT-ENTIRELY-PAINLESS PAIN TREATMENT

Although the anesthetic lidocaine was used to minimize the discomfort of the injections, participants reported short-term mild-to-moderate pain as the shots were given. No other adverse side effects were noted. The temporary discomfort seemed to be worth it, though—among participants who received dextrose prolotherapy, 91% said that they would recommend the treatment to other people with knee arthritis.

The procedure also can hurt the wallet—because most insurance providers do not cover prolotherapy, considering it to be experimental. If paying out-of-pocket, you can expect dextrose prolotherapy to cost from about $150 to $500 per session, depending on the provider and location. Still, you may consider that money well spent if it brings significant relief from pain and allows you to once again participate in everyday activities and favorite pastimes.

Prolotherapy should be administered by a physician (an MD, ND or DO) trained in the procedure. Ask your primary care doctor for a referral, or check the provider locator of the American Association of Orthopaedic Medicine, then call the doctor you are considering to find out whether he uses dextrose solution. You may be advised to temporarily reduce or discontinue anti-inflammatory drugs (aspirin, ibuprofen, naproxen) while undergoing prolotherapy—but acetaminophen is OK if it's otherwise safe for you. If you take blood thinners or other drugs, tell the doctor because extra precautions may be warranted.

Relief for Knee Osteoarthritis

Researchers performed magnetic resonance imaging (MRI) scans of the knee joints of 265 people with osteoarthritis of the knee to determine cartilage loss over a 30-month period and also measured the strength of the patients' quadricep (upper thigh) muscles.

Result: Patients who had stronger quadriceps had less cartilage loss behind the kneecap.

Theory: Strong quadriceps may help prevent excessive wear and tear on knee cartilage. If you have knee osteoarthritis: Ask your doctor about quadricep exercises.

Shreyasee Amin, MD, MPH, assistant professor of medicine, Mayo Clinic College of Medicine, Rochester, Minnesota.

Rhus Toxicodendron—A Soother for Arthritis and Shingles

Mark A. Stengler, NMD, licensed naturopathic medical doctor in private practice, Stengler Center for Integrative Medicine, Encinitas, California...adjunct associate clinical professor at the National College of Natural Medicine, Portland, Oregon...author of many books, including *The Natural Physician's Healing Therapies* and coauthor of *Prescription for Natural Cures*. *MarkStengler.com*

Rhus toxicodendron (pronounced roos tox-ih-ko-den-dron) is the homeopathic dilution of poison oak. We know this as a plant that causes a nasty, blistering rash. However, this homeopathic is one of the best skin remedies for relieving symptoms in people who have touched poison ivy. It is also effective in treating eczema, where the skin is very itchy and feels better after the application of very hot water.

I have also used this for people with shingles. The itching, burning pain of the shingles blisters can be relieved in a few days with rhus tox.

Dosage: The typical dosage for rhus tox is 30C potency taken two to three times daily for a day or two for conditions such as stiffness from overexertion. For long-term use for eczema or arthritis, I generally start with a lower dose such as 6C taken two to three times daily.

What are the side effects? While rhus tox has few side effects, some people may experience skin irritation. People with chronic eczema or arthritis may experience a flare-up of their condition at the beginning of treatment. This is usually a sign that the remedy is working (known as a healing aggravation).

If you do have a flare-up and you begin taking the rhus tox less frequently, you'll probably notice that the flare-up subsides. Soon after, you'll probably notice an improvement in your condition.

If you are not sure whether you should use rhus tox, consult a homeopathic practitioner.

Recommendations for...

• **Arthritis.** Rhus tox is commonly used for osteoarthritis and rheumatoid arthritis. This is probably the right remedy for you if you notice certain characteristics about your symptoms—they are worse in the morning, improve with motion and activity during the day and then get worse again at night while in bed.

Rhus tox is also a good remedy if these arthritic symptoms flare up before a storm or in damp weather. It's probably the right remedy for you if hot baths and showers also provide joint pain relief.

• **Flu.** Rhus tox is a good remedy for the type of flu that makes your joints and muscles stiff.

• **Herpes.** Cold sores on the mouth or face, or genital herpes outbreaks can be helped greatly with rhus tox.

• **Shingles.** This dormant chicken-pox virus erupts when the immune system is weakened. Many elderly people suffer from excruciating pain that is often not relieved with conventional medicines. Rhus tox has worked wonders in several cases I have treated.

• **Strains.** Rhus tox should be used when ligaments and tendons are strained. It helps speed up the recovery process. Athletes should have a supply of rhus tox available at all times.

• **Urticaria.** Urticaria is a fancy way of saying hives. For hive breakouts that do not require emergency treatment (such as when the throat closes), rhus tox helps to relieve the itching and works to heal the lesions more quickly. It is also effective for relieving itching caused by mosquito bites.

Quick Yoga Cures for Arthritis and Foot Cramps

Tara Stiles, the founder and owner of Strala Yoga in New York City. She is the author of two books, *Yoga Cures* and *Slim Calm Sexy Yoga.* Stiles has also created several yoga DVDs with Jane Fonda, Deepak Chopra and others. *TaraStiles.com*

Yoga aficionados know that this ancient practice can tone muscles and calm the mind. But few people are aware of yoga's ability to cure everyday ailments that can cause pain and sap our energy.

If you suffer from arthritis or foot cramps, consider trying the single, carefully chosen yoga pose described here. This can help other treatments, such as medication, work more effectively—or, in some cases, the pose alone may alleviate the problem. *Best single-pose yoga cures (stay in each pose for five to 10 deep, long breaths)...**

ARTHRITIS

Pose to try: "Hands and knees fist release." For many people, this pose helps the swelling, joint pain, stiffness and limited range of motion that accompanies rheumatoid arthritis and osteoarthritis—especially in the hands.

What to do: Gently, get on your hands and knees. Make tight fists with both hands. Bend your elbows out to your sides, and place the tops of your hands on the ground, with your knuckles facing each other. Begin to straighten your elbows, but keep your fists tight and only do as much as you can without causing pain. You should feel a stretch on the tops of your wrists.

How it works: Whether you have arthritis or just sit at a desk all day, which dramatically limits your range of motion, this move

*If you have a chronic medical condition, check with your doctor before doing the poses, which should be done on a mat or carpeted floor.

increases flexibility in the wrists, hands, arms and back—important in easing arthritis pain.

FOOT CRAMPS

Pose to try: "Runner's stretch."

What to do: Gently, move into a low lunge with your right foot forward. Tuck the toes of your left foot so that they point forward, and lower your back knee to the ground. Shift your hips back to sit on your back heel to stretch the arch of your foot. Relax your torso over your right leg. Stay in the pose for five long, deep breaths. Then do the pose with the other leg.

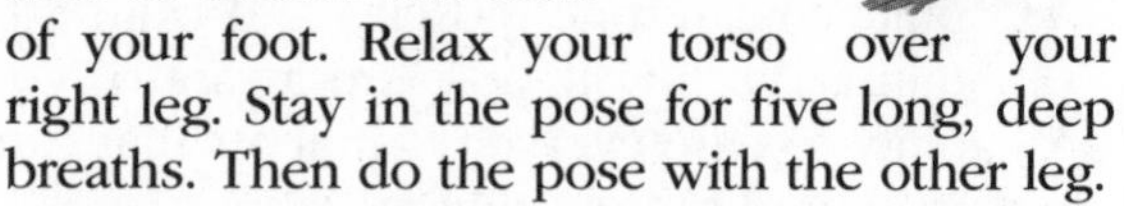

How it works: Foot cramps typically respond quickly to the even pressure this pose places on the foot and arch. This move also helps maintain the foot's flexibility, which is important for balance.

Photos: Thomas Hoeffgen

Finally...an Arthritis Therapy That Works

Vijay Vad, MD, sports medicine physician specializing in minimally invasive arthritis therapies at the Hospital for Special Surgery in New York City. He is a professor of rehabilitation medicine at Weill Medical College of Cornell University, also in New York City, and author of *Arthritis Rx.*

Only about half of the people who suffer from osteoarthritis pain obtain significant relief from aspirin, *ibuprofen* (Advil, etc.) or other nonsteroidal anti-inflammatory drugs (NSAIDs)—and each year, an estimated 16,000 Americans die from gastrointestinal bleeding or other side effects from these medications.

New approach: Up to 80% of people who have osteoarthritis can experience a significant improvement in pain and mobility—and reduce their need for medication and surgery—when they combine dietary changes, supplement use and the right kind of exercise. This program provides significant relief within six weeks.

DIET RX

Inflammation in the body has been implicated in heart disease, diabetes and kidney disease—and it also contributes to osteoarthritis.

The incidence of arthritis has steadily risen since the early 1900s, when processed foods, such as packaged crackers, cereals, bread and snack foods, began to dominate the American diet—and more people started becoming obese. Most of these foods actually promote inflammation, which can cause joint and cartilage damage and aggravate arthritis pain.

Studies suggest that adding more foods with anti-inflammatory effects to the average American diet—and reducing the foods that promote inflammation—can reduce inflammation by approximately 20% to 40%.

Best anti-inflammatory foods...

- **Apricots and berries contain large amounts of antioxidants,** chemical compounds that reduce inflammation.
- **Almonds have fiber,** vitamin E and monounsaturated fats to curb inflammation.

Other important steps...

- **Increase omega-3s.** These inflammation-fighting essential fatty acids are mainly found in cold-water fish, such as salmon, tuna, mackerel and sardines. At least three three-ounce servings of fish per week provide adequate levels of omega-3s.

People who don't like fish, or don't eat it often, can take fish-oil supplements or flaxseed oil.

My advice: Use 2 to 3 grams (g) daily of a fish-oil supplement which contains eicosapentaenoic acid (EPA) and docosahexaenoic acid (DHA)...or one to three tablespoons daily of flaxseed oil.

Caution: Because fish oil taken at this dosage can trigger a blood-thinning effect, check with your doctor if you take a blood-thinning medication, such as *warfarin* (Coumadin).

- **Reduce omega-6s.** Most Americans get far too many of these inflammation-promoting fatty acids in their diets. A century ago, the ratio of omega-6 to omega-3 fatty acids was about 2:1 for the typical American. Today, it's about 20:1. This imbalance boosts levels of a chemical by-product, arachidonic acid, that triggers inflammation.

My advice: Because the omega-6s are found primarily in red meats, commercially processed foods (described earlier) and fast foods, anyone with arthritis should avoid these foods as much as possible.

- **Give up nightshades.** Although the reason is unknown, tomatoes, white potatoes, eggplant and other foods in the nightshade family have been found to increase arthritis pain. It has been estimated that up to 20% of arthritis patients get worse when they eat these foods.

My advice: If you eat these foods and have arthritis pain, give them up completely for six months to see if there's an improvement.

SUPPLEMENT RX

Americans spend billions of dollars annually on supplements to ease arthritis pain, but many of them are ineffective. *Best choices...*

- **Ginger.** The biochemical structure of this herb (commonly used as a spice) is similar to that of NSAIDs, making it a powerful anti-inflammatory agent. A study of 250 patients at the University of Miami School of Medicine found that ginger, taken twice daily, was as effective as prescription and over-the-counter drugs at controlling arthritis pain.

My advice: Add several teaspoons of fresh ginger to vegetables, salads, etc., daily or take a daily supplement containing 510 milligrams (mg) of ginger.

Caution: Ginger thins the blood, so consult with your physician if you take blood-thinning medication.

- **Glucosamine and chondroitin.** Taken in a combination supplement, such as Cosamine DS, these natural anti-inflammatories inhibit enzymes that break down cartilage and enhance the production of glycosaminoglycans, molecules that stimulate cartilage growth.

My advice: Take 1,500 mg of glucosamine and 1,200 mg of chondroitin daily. Or consider using a product called Gingerflex (formerly Zingerflex), which contains both glucosamine and chondroitin as well as ginger.

Caution: If you have diabetes, consult your doctor before using glucosamine. It can raise blood sugar. Do not take glucosamine if you are allergic to shellfish.

EXERCISE RX

Osteoarthritis pain weakens muscles, which diminishes joint support. The result is more inflammation and pain, and faster progression of the underlying disease.

Common exercises, including both running and traditional forms of yoga, actually can increase pain by putting too much pressure on the joints. Patients will benefit most from medical exercise, which includes modified variations of common strengthening and stretching exercises, supervised by a physical therapist.*

It's best to perform medical exercises under the guidance of a physical therapist for one to two months before beginning an exercise program at home. *Best choices...*

- **Medical yoga** improves joint strength and flexibility by strengthening muscles and moving joints through their full range of motion. Unlike conventional yoga, it does not require poses that put undue stress on the joints.

- **Pilates** combines yoga-like stretching and breathing control to strengthen the "core" muscles in the lower back and abdomen, as well as muscles in the hips. Like medical yoga, it puts very little pressure on the joints.

- **Healthy breathing.** Most of us take shallow breaths from the upper lungs—a breathing pattern that increases levels of stress hormones and heightens pain.

Better: Deep breathing, which promotes the release of pain-relieving chemicals known as endorphins. Patients who breathe deeply for five minutes daily have less pain for several hours afterward. Practice deep breathing in addition to a regular exercise program.

Here's how...

- **Sit in a chair with both feet flat on the floor.** Close your mouth, place one hand on your stomach and breathe deeply through your nose until you can feel your stomach expanding. Hold your breath for 10 seconds.

*To locate a physical therapist in your area, contact the American Physical Therapy Association at 800-999-2782 or *www.apta.org*.

• **Exhale through your nose,** contracting your stomach until you've expelled as much air as possible. Hold the "emptiness" for a moment before inhaling again.

• **Repeat the cycle for at least five consecutive minutes daily.**

New Treatment for Arthritis Pain

Flavocoxid is a natural supplement that is a combination of flavonoids (anti-inflammatory plant chemicals). Like nonsteroidal anti-inflammatory drugs (NSAIDs), flavocoxid suppresses pain-producing enzymes but is less likely to cause such side effects as gastrointestinal bleeding, so it is helpful for people who experience problems taking aspirin. It is sold at pharmacies as a capsule under the brand name Limbrel and requires a prescription. If you have osteoarthritis and can't use NSAIDs, ask your doctor about flavocoxid.

Caution: It may not be covered by insurance and can cost $4/day.

UC Berkeley Wellness Letter, 500 Fifth Ave., New York City 10110.

4

Cancer Cures

Starve Cancer to Death with the Ketogenic Diet

A 65-year-old woman with brain cancer had surgery to remove the tumor, but the operation couldn't remove it all. The woman started following the ketogenic diet—a diet very high in fat, moderate in protein and very low in carbohydrate. She also had chemotherapy and radiation. After six weeks on the diet, a brain scan showed that the tumor had disappeared. A brain scan five months later showed it was still gone. However, the patient stopped the diet—and a scan three months later showed that the tumor had returned.

Yes, a special diet called the ketogenic diet can fight cancer. It is being used to manage brain cancer and advanced (metastatic) cancer, which is when the disease has spread beyond the original tumor to other parts of the body (such as breast cancer that spreads to the liver and bones). It may be effective in fighting most, if not all, cancers, but it must be done under the supervision of an experienced oncological nutritionist.

Here, what you need to know about this little-known therapy for cancer…

HOW IT WORKS

The ketogenic diet is very high in fat—the ratio is four grams of fat to one gram of protein/carbohydrate. It has long been used to control epilepsy and is offered as an epilepsy treatment at hundreds of hospitals and clinics around the world, including The Johns Hopkins Epilepsy Center, Mayo Clinic and Mattel Children's Hospital at UCLA.

It eases epilepsy by stabilizing neurons (brain cells). It does so by reducing glucose (blood sugar), the main fuel used by neurons, and increasing ketones (beta-hydroxybutyric acid and acetoacetic acid), a by-product of fat

Thomas N. Seyfried, PhD, a professor of biology at Boston College and author of *Cancer as a Metabolic Disease: On the Origin, Management, and Prevention of Cancer.*

metabolism used by neurons when glucose levels are low. Reducing glucose and increasing ketones play key roles in fighting cancer as well.

The typical American diet is about 50% to 60% carbohydrate (fruits, vegetables, breads, cereals, milk and milk products, and added sugars in sweetened foods and beverages). The body turns carbohydrate into glucose, which is used for energy.

Cancer cells gorge on glucose. Eating a ketogenic diet deprives them of this primary fuel, starving the cells, which stop growing or die. Also, ketones are a fuel usable by normal cells but not by cancer cells, so this, too, helps stop cancer growth. *In addition, the diet...*

- **Puts you into a metabolic state similar to that of fasting**—and fasting has repeatedly been shown to arrest cancer.
- **Lowers levels of insulin (the glucose-regulating hormone) and insulin-like growth factor**—both of which drive tumor growth.

CASE HISTORIES

The first case report about the ketogenic diet for cancer appeared in *Journal of the American College of Nutrition* in 1995. The ketogenic diet was used by two children with advanced, inoperable brain cancer who had undergone extensive, life-threatening radiation and chemotherapy. They both responded remarkably well to the diet.

A case report that I coauthored, published in *Nutrition & Metabolism* in 2010, told the story (see beginning of this article) of the 65-year-old woman with glioblastoma multiforme—the most common and most aggressive type of brain tumor, with a median survival of only about 12 months after diagnosis. Standard treatment—surgery to remove as much of the tumor as possible, plus radiation and/or chemotherapy—extends average survival time only a few months beyond that of people who aren't treated.

My viewpoint: In animal research, the ketogenic diet is the only therapeutic approach that deprives tumors of their primary fuel...stops tumor cells from invading other areas...stops the process of angiogenesis (blood supply to tumors)...and reduces inflammation, which drives cancer. The diet also could reduce the need for anticonvulsant and anti-inflammatory medications in brain cancer patients.

Considering how ineffective the current standard of care is for brain cancer (and for metastatic cancer), the ketogenic diet could be an attractive option for many cancer patients.

WORKING WITH AN EXPERT

The ketogenic diet for cancer is not a diet you should undertake on your own after reading a book or other self-help materials. It requires the assistance of an oncological nutritionist or other health professional who is familiar with the use of the regimen in cancer patients. Ask your oncologist for a referral.

Important aspects of the ketogenic diet include...

- **Measuring glucose and ketone levels.** For the management of cancer, blood glucose levels should fall between 55 mg/dL and 65 mg/dL, and ketone levels between 3 mmol and 5 mmol. In order to monitor those levels—and adjust your diet accordingly—you need to use methods similar to those used by patients with diabetes. These methods include glucose testing several times a day with a finger stick and glucose strip...daily urine testing for ketones...and (more accurate) home blood testing for ketones, perhaps done weekly.
- **Starting with a water-only fast.** If you are in relatively good health (aside from the cancer, of course), it is best to start the ketogenic diet with a water-only fast for 48 to 72 hours, which will quickly put you in ketosis—the production of a therapeutic level of ketones. This fast should be guided by a health professional.

If you are fragile or in poor health, you can skip the water fast and initiate ketosis with the ketogenic diet, reducing carbohydrates to less than 12 grams a day. This should produce ketosis within two or three weeks.

- **Macronutrient ratios and recipes.** Working with a nutritionist, you will find the fat/protein/carbohydrate ratio that works best for you to lower glucose and increase ketones...and the recipes and meal plan that consistently deliver those ratios. A food diary, a food scale and the use of a "KetoCalculator" (available on websites such as *www.keto-calculator.ankerl.com*) are necessary tools to implement the ketogenic diet.

Helpful: The oncological nutritionist Miriam Kalamian, EdM, MS, CNS, managed her own son's brain tumor with the ketogenic diet, and she counsels cancer patients around the world in the implementation of the diet. You can find more information on her website, *www.dietarytherapies.com.*

CLINICAL TRIALS

Currently, there are several clinical trials being conducted using the ketogenic diet for cancer.

• **Brain cancer.** There are trials at Michigan State University and in Germany and Israel testing the diet's efficacy as a complementary treatment with radiation for recurrent glioblastoma...and by itself to improve the quality of life and survival time in patients with brain cancer. Michigan State University currently is recruiting patients for its trial.

Contact: Ken Schwartz, MD, 517-975-9547, e-mail: *ken.schwartz@ht.msu.edu.*

• **Metastatic cancer.** The VA Pittsburgh Healthcare System is recruiting patients with metastatic cancer for a study of the effect of the ketogenic diet on quality of life, tumor growth and survival.

Contact: Jocelyn Tan, MD, 412-360-6178, e-mail: *jocelyn.tan@va.gov.*

You can find out more about these trials at *www.clinicaltrials.gov.* Enter "Ketogenic Diet" into the search engine at the site for a complete listing of cancer trials and trials testing the ketogenic diet for other conditions, including epilepsy, amyotrophic lateral sclerosis (ALS), Lafora disease (a severe neurological disease), Parkinson's disease and obesity.

More from Dr. Seyfried...

Can the Diet Prevent Cancer?

Cancer survivors and people with a family history of cancer may wonder if they should go on the ketogenic diet as a preventive measure. It is not necessary for people to follow the diet if they do not have cancer. A six-to-seven-day water-only fast done once or twice a year—under a doctor's supervision—can be effective in reducing the risk for recurrent cancer in survivors and in those individuals with a family history of cancer. Fasting reduces glucose and elevates ketones.

Vanishing Cancers

Keith I. Block, MD, director of integrative medical education at University of Illinois College of Medicine and medical director of Block Center for Integrative Cancer Treatment in Evanston, Illinois. He is author of *Life Over Cancer. BlockMd.com*

A common belief about cancer is that it is an irreversible process. Normal cells become malignant and grow uncontrollably. The only way to stop the process is to remove or kill the cancer through surgery, chemotherapy and/or radiation. Cancer cannot just disappear.

That belief is proving to be untrue. In a recent study in *Archives of Internal Medicine*, researchers from Norway and the US analyzed the six-year incidence of invasive breast cancer in two very similar groups of Norwegian women.

About 119,000 of the women had mammograms every two years. Another 110,000 women in the study had not had mammograms and then had one mammogram.

To the surprise of the researchers, the six-year incidence of breast cancer in the two groups was quite different. The more frequently screened group had a 22% higher incidence of breast cancer.

So, what caused less cancer to be found in the second group? The intriguing theory is that cancer did indeed start in this group at an equal rate...and then spontaneously disappeared without ever being noticed (because the women were not being screened).

Other research has shown that spontaneous regression of cancer occurs in cases of advanced melanoma, advanced kidney cancer and neuroblastoma (a childhood cancer of nerve tissue). Regression also occurs in colonic adenomas (precancerous growths of the colon) and in precancerous lesions of the cervix.

Keith I. Block, MD, one of America's top integrative cancer therapy experts, explains that the number of documented cases of spontaneous cancer remission is quite low. He estimates that only one in 500 cancer tumors regress without surgery, chemotherapy or radiation.

However, he suggests that the unalterable, one-way trajectory of cancer is an outdated paradigm.

Cancer is not only mutagenic—propelled by damage to DNA—it also is mitogenic and the growth (mitogenesis) of cancer cells may be stopped by inhibiting molecular signaling and correcting disruption in the body's internal biochemical environment. This can be influenced by lifestyle factors that are alterable through personal choices.

WHY CANCERS VANISH

There are three main factors that can cause a cancer to regress...

- **Innate biology.** Some people are born with a naturally stronger constitution that is capable of stopping a cancer before it takes firm hold.
- **Transformation of the body's biochemical and molecular environment.** Many lifestyle factors influence the body's inner biochemical and molecular environment, including what you eat, how much you exercise and how much stress you're under.

The latest research shows that positive lifestyle factors can influence genes by turning on the tumor-suppressor genes and turning off the tumor-promoting genes.

- **Better communication.** This includes two types of communication—biochemical communication between cells and emotional communication with yourself and others.

What happens: In a normal biochemical environment, one cell sends a message to another: Don't grow, I'm using this space. One reason tumor cells can divide and grow is that they don't receive this message.

The breakdown in communication is fundamental in the biology of cancer in other ways. Studies show that meditation—one way to communicate with your inner spirit—reduces cancer-causing inflammation.

Close personal relationships also are relevant. A preclinical study from researchers at The University of Chicago suggested that social isolation and its impact on stress resulted in a greater than threefold increase in the onset of breast cancer.

STEPS YOU CAN TAKE

Various lifestyle factors can strengthen you against cancer...

- **Exercise and fitness.** Numerous studies link increased physical activity to lower incidence of cancers of the colon, lung, prostate, testicles, breast, ovaries and uterus.

Exercise counters many cancer-causing biological factors, including cancer-fueling molecules called growth factors...oxidative stress (a kind of internal rust)...a weakened immune system...and poor response to inflammation. Aim for a minimum of 30 minutes of aerobic exercise daily, which can be divided into multiple sessions.

- **Whole-foods diet.** The right diet deprives a tumor of the compounds it most likes to feed on and supplies you with nutrients that help your body keep malignant cells in check.

Example: The Japanese have long had a diet rich in land and sea vegetables and fish—and low in meat, refined sugars and high-fat foods. Japan also has lower cancer rates than the US and better survival rates. For instance, men in Japan and the US are equally likely to have very early prostate cancer—the kind that never causes clinical problems—but American men have much higher rates of the clinical type that can lead to advanced prostate cancer.

Bottom line: If you eat too much dietary fat and refined carbohydrates, you run the risk of increasing body fat and weight while weakening your immune system and increasing oxidative stress, inflammation and blood levels of substances that promote tumors.

- **Power foods.** There are "power foods" rich in phytochemicals that are uniquely anticancer. These include turmeric...grapes (with the phytochemical resveratrol)...green tea...milk thistle...ginger...and pomegranate.

But to get enough turmeric, resveratrol and all the rest, you would have to eat curry and guzzle grape juice until you exploded.

Best: Supplements and concentrates, such as "green drinks," often sold in health-food stores. Talk to your doctor about the best supplements for you.

• **Stress reduction.** Chronic anxiety and stress contribute to cancer's ability to thrive in your body.

What happens: Stress triggers biochemistry that is procancer—high levels of certain growth factors...an excess of oxidation-causing free radicals...high blood sugar...and raging inflammation.

Techniques such as relaxed abdominal breathing, progressive muscle relaxation and calming imagery can help you create emotional ease.

IF YOU HAVE CANCER

The fact that a cancer can vanish without conventional treatments is important knowledge for a person diagnosed with cancer and for his/her doctor. However, a patient should never simply wait for a cancer to disappear. Getting started quickly on a plan of care can be essential for one's survival—losing time can be detrimental, even life-threatening.

New Drug for Colorectal Cancer?

Fingolimod (Gilenya), a drug now used for multiple sclerosis, blocks an enzyme involved in inflammatory bowel disease and colitis-associated cancers. It could someday be used to treat such malignancies.

Cancer Cell.

Best Ways to Beat Cancer Now

Isaac Eliaz, MD, an integrative physician and medical director of the Amitabha Medical Clinic & Healing Center in Santa Rosa, California, an integrative health center specializing in cancer and chronic conditions. *DrEliaz.org*

Radiation, chemotherapy and surgery are widely known to be the main treatments for cancer. But to fight the disease more effectively and to maximize the odds of recovery, doctors and patients are increasingly turning to integrative oncology.

This approach combines the conventional treatments mentioned above with natural or alternative treatments that can minimize the complications and side effects from cancer treatments, help relieve pain and improve overall health, increasing chance of survival.

Here are integrative treatments that scientific studies and my clinical experience show are likely to be effective for a wide range of cancer patients...

EXERCISE

Research shows that cancer patients who walked three to five hours a week improved their outcomes, compared with cancer patients who didn't exercise.

My advice: Try to exercise every day. Walking is usually best—it's easy to do on a regular basis and is proven to work. Other helpful exercises include yoga, tai chi and qi gong, all of which stretch and strengthen muscles, relax the body and even improve immunity.

Caution: Too much strenuous exercise can produce inflammation, thought to be a factor in cancer development, and cause wear and tear on the body. Do not exercise to the point of exhaustion.

STRESS MANAGEMENT

Stress management is essential for cancer patients—stress, anxiety and even pessimism weaken immunity and may spark inflammation, possibly spurring the progression and aggressiveness of cancer. In my clinical experience, cancer patients who practice stress management often have better outcomes than those who don't.

New finding: Women with breast cancer who practiced mindfulness-based stress reduction, including meditation, indicated that they were better able to cope with stress, anxiety and panic, were more confident and had improved personal relationships, reported researchers in *Complementary Therapies in Clinical Practice.*

My advice: Regular meditation—even 10 minutes a day—is a proven stress-reduction technique with results comparable to or better than antidepressants and antianxiety medications. Strong social support and social networking also can reduce stress and improve outcomes in cancer patients. Creative outlets—such as drawing or painting, writing, playing an instrument and dancing—also help ease stress and improve emotional well-being.

DIET

Dietary needs vary from patient to patient. For example, some cancer patients may require a high-protein diet (those who are weak), while others may need a diet emphasizing plant foods (those who are overweight). But all cancer patients should follow these essential basics…

A low-glycemic diet that minimizes or eliminates refined carbohydrates such as sugar and white flour, both of which fuel inflammation and may promote the growth and aggressiveness of tumors…and avoidance of processed trans fats and fried foods, which spur inflammation and damage DNA. Also, eat as much organically grown food as possible—it's free of synthetic pesticides, many of which are linked to cancer in humans…and drink eight eight-ounce glasses of filtered water every day to stay hydrated and eliminate toxins.

SUPPLEMENTS

Here are four supplements that research and my own clinical experience confirm are uniquely effective for cancer—all are available at health-food stores, well-tolerated and safe for adults, the elderly and children…*

- **Honokiol.** This extract from the bark of the magnolia tree interferes with the growth and spread of cancer and can increase the effectiveness of chemotherapy and radiation. Studies have shown that honokiol may be useful for many types of cancer, including leukemia and cancer of the brain, breast, bone, colon, pancreas, skin and stomach.

- **Artemisinin.** The herb Artemisia annua (commonly called sweet wormwood) is as powerful as quinine in treating malaria. Recent research shows that artemisinin, a compound derived from the herb, has strong anticancer effects, reducing tumor size and blocking metastases.

- **Modified citrus pectin (MCP).** This substance, derived from citrus fruit peels and apples, controls galectin-3, a protein linked to cancer formation and metastases. MCP also boosts the immune system and safely removes heavy metals and other toxins from the body.

New research: Combining MCP with chemotherapy was more effective in killing prostate cancer cells than chemotherapy alone, reported researchers in *Cell Biology International.*

- **Mushroom extracts.** Extracts from medicinal mushrooms such as coriolus, reishi, cordyceps, maitake and shiitake can boost immunity…improve digestion…increase energy…and help prevent side effects from chemotherapy and radiation as well as improve their effectiveness.

Standout scientific evidence: In a study of patients who had undergone surgery for liver cancer, those who took active hexose correlated compound (AHCC), an extract of shiitake, had a longer time to recurrence and a higher survival rate.

ACUPUNCTURE

Acupuncture can help cancer patients in many ways, including providing relief from pain and nausea. It also has been shown to reduce inflammation and boost immune function.

New research: In an analysis of 15 studies on acupuncture published in *Supportive Care in Cancer*, researchers found that combining acupuncture with drug therapy was 36% more effective in relieving pain in cancer patients than drug therapy alone.

To find an integrative physician: Online, go to Cancer Decisions (*www.cancerdecisions.com*), and click on "Professional Associates"…or go to the Society for Integrative Oncology (*www.integrativeonc.org*).

*Consult an integrative physician before taking any of these supplements. He/she can advise you on the best supplements for your cancer, dosage and possible side effects. Inform your doctor of all drugs/supplements you are taking to avoid possible interactions.

Natural Cancer Treatments That Really Work

Keith I. Block, MD, medical director of Block Center for Integrative Cancer Care in Skokie, Illinois...director of Integrative Medical Education at University of Illinois College of Medicine, Chicago...and scientific director of the Institute for Integrative Cancer Research and Education, Evanston. He is editor of *Journal for Integrative Cancer Therapies*. He is author of *Life Over Cancer*.

Many cancer patients augment conventional medical treatment with complementary medicine, such as nutritional or herbal supplements. The newest research and decades of successful clinical use show that some of these natural treatments work very effectively to fight cancer and reduce side effects.

Here are the best science-based complementary treatments for cancer. It's usually fine to take several of these supplements simultaneously, but be sure to talk to your doctor first. For help finding an integrative practitioner, go to *http://nccam.nih.gov/*, then click on "How to Find a Practitoner."

ANTIOXIDANTS

Cancer specialists often advise patients not to take antioxidant supplements, such as vitamin A or vitamin E, during chemotherapy and radiation treatments.

Reason: One way chemotherapy and radiation destroy cancer cells is by causing oxidative stress. According to one theory, antioxidants may be counterproductive because they might have the ability to protect against this oxidative damage.

But new scientific research shows that the opposite is true—antioxidant supplements aren't powerful enough to counter chemotherapeutic medicines or radiation, but they can reduce the side effects of those treatments and also may battle tumors and extend life.

Recent study: Researchers from the University of Illinois at Chicago and the Institute for Integrative Cancer Research and Education analyzed 19 studies involving 1,554 cancer patients who took antioxidants during chemotherapy. They concluded that most cancer patients are better off using antioxidants in conjunction with chemotherapy and radiation than not using them.

Typical doses...

- **Vitamin A.** 7,500 daily international units (IU), which should only be taken under a doctor's supervision—patients should have their liver enzymes monitored on an ongoing basis.
- **Vitamin E.** 400 IU daily, taken under a doctor's supervision (patients should have their platelet counts monitored). It's best to divide the dose, taking half in the morning and half in the evening. Ideally, take it on an empty stomach.

ASTRAGALUS

The herb astragalus has been used in traditional Chinese medicine for thousands of years. Scientific studies show that it strengthens the immune system, increasing the activity of cancer-fighting cells and inhibiting the activity of immune cells that increase inflammation and thereby worsen cancer. Research shows that the herb also can boost the power of some types of chemotherapy.

Recent study: Researchers from the School of Public Health at the University of California, Berkeley, analyzed 34 studies involving 2,815 patients with non-small-cell lung cancer who were treated with chemotherapy alone or who were treated with chemotherapy and astragalus. The patients taking astragalus had a 33% lower risk for death after 12 months and a 24% to 46% better tumor response than those not taking the herb.

Typical dose: 750 milligrams (mg) to 2,500 mg a day of astragalus extract.

GINSENG

Extracts from the root of this herb often are used as a natural stimulant—to boost mental and physical energy, improve athletic performance and relieve fatigue. Ginseng also may boost energy in cancer patients.

Recent study: Doctors from the North Central Cancer Treatment Group at the Mayo Clinic gave either a placebo or ginseng—at daily doses of 750 mg...1,000 mg...or 2,000 mg—to 282 cancer patients. Those taking 1,000 mg or 2,000 mg of ginseng had more energy and vitality and less fatigue. Those taking 750 mg or a placebo had no such improvement. The patients taking the higher doses of ginseng also reported greater physical, mental, emotional and spiritual well-being.

Typical dose: 500 mg to 1,000 mg twice daily of American ginseng (not Asian red ginseng). Medical supervision is needed for the higher dosage, particularly if you are taking blood-thinning medication.

GLUTAMINE

Chemotherapy can damage the mucous lining of the digestive tract, which stretches from the inside of the mouth to the rectum. One common result is oral mucositis (OM), a condition in which the mucous lining of the mouth and throat becomes inflamed, painful, ulcerated and prone to infection. The amino acid glutamine fuels the daily maintenance of the mucous lining of the digestive tract—and supplemental glutamine helps limit or stop its destruction by chemotherapy.

Recent study: Researchers at the University of Connecticut Health Center gave either glutamine powder or a placebo to 326 cancer patients undergoing chemotherapy who were developing OM. Those taking glutamine experienced a significant reduction in the severity of the condition compared with those taking the placebo. In fact, many of those taking glutamine didn't develop OM at all during their second cycle of chemotherapy.

Typical dose: 5 grams (g) to 10 g, twice daily.

OMEGA-3 FATTY ACIDS

Chronic inflammation is known to fuel the growth of tumors. Omega-3 fatty acids, nutrients abundant in fish oil and flaxseed, are potent anti-inflammatories that slow tumor growth and shrink tumors in animal studies. Recent research shows that omega-3 fatty acids may do the same for men with prostate cancer.

Recent study: Researchers at Duke University Medical Center, the University of Michigan and the University of North Carolina studied 140 men with prostate cancer who were scheduled to undergo prostate surgery in 30 days. They divided the men into four presurgical groups—some took 30 g (about one ounce) of ground flaxseed daily...some ate a low-fat diet and took the flaxseed...some just ate a low-fat diet...and a control group used none of the regimens. After the surgery, researchers found that the tumors of the men who took flaxseed had grown more slowly—at a 30% to 40% slower rate than those of the other men. The men mixed the ground flaxseed in drinks or sprinkled it on yogurt and other foods. The study was reported at the 2007 annual meeting of the American Society of Clinical Oncology.

Typical dose: One ounce of ground flaxseed...or 3 g of fish oil.

ACUPUNCTURE

Acupuncture is a healing technique from traditional Chinese medicine. An acupuncturist inserts tiny needles into the skin along meridians (energy channels in the body) in order to restore and enhance chi, the fundamental force of health and well-being.

Recent study: Doctors at the Osher Center for Integrative Medicine at the University of California, San Francisco, studied 138 cancer patients undergoing surgery, dividing them into two groups. One group received acupuncture and massage after surgery, along with standard care, such as pain-relieving medications. The other group received standard care only. The acupuncture and massage group had 58% less postsurgical pain and less depression, reported the doctors in the March 2007 issue of *Journal of Pain and Symptom Management*. It's hard to tell specifically what role acupuncture played and what role massage played, but other studies that look at acupuncture and massage alone show that each has benefits, including reducing surgical pain.

Other studies show acupuncture may help prevent or relieve chemotherapy-induced nausea and fatigue...chemotherapy-induced decrease in white blood cell count...radiation-induced dry mouth...shortness of breath...and insomnia and anxiety.

The Anticancer Formula—Combine Conventional Treatments with Unconventional Treatments

Raymond Chang, MD, a faculty member at Weill Cornell Medical College, New York City, and a pioneer in the use of complementary and alternative treatments in oncology. He is author of *Beyond the Magic Bullet—The Anti-Cancer Cocktail: A New Approach to Beating Cancer.*

Researchers are discovering that multiple treatments given simultaneously can be far more effective at fighting cancer than any single treatment. That's because a typical cancer involves an average of 63 genetic mutations, each of which works in different ways. A single treatment is unlikely to affect more than a few of these processes.

Better approach: Cancer "cocktails" that simultaneously attack abnormal cells in a multitude of ways.

Examples: A deadly form of blood cancer, multiple myeloma, now is routinely treated with drug combinations that have doubled survival rates. A French study, published in *The New England Journal of Medicine*, found that patients with pancreatic cancer who were given a combination of four drugs lived about 60% longer than those given standard chemotherapy.

For the most part, the conventional treatment strategy for cancer involves using one or two traditional treatments—surgery, radiation, chemotherapy or hormone therapy—one after the other. Only on occasion are different treatments used in combination simultaneously such as when radiation and chemotherapy are administered following a patient's surgery.

Many oncologists now believe that it's better to hit cancers all at once with a barrage of treatments—including, in some cases, unconventional treatments, such as vitamins, herbs, supplements and medications typically prescribed for other health problems.

Example: I might advise a cancer patient getting conventional treatments to include the arthritis drug *celecoxib* (Celebrex), which makes cancer cells more sensitive to radiation...the hormone melatonin (which decreases the growth of some cancers)...and vitamin D-3 (which may reduce cancer recurrence).

GETTING STARTED

Here's how to make this approach work for you...

- **Keep an open mind.** Ask your doctor if there are safe and effective treatments that he/she recommends that may be unconventional, including "off-label" drugs—medications that haven't been approved by the FDA specifically for your type of cancer.

Doctors often know about new treatments that seem to work for a given cancer. They share stories with their colleagues about treatments that appear to be effective but that haven't yet been completely validated. When you have cancer, there's no reason not to try innovative approaches as long as they are safe.

Important: Don't try any treatment without first checking with your doctor to make sure that it is safe for you. If it is, he can recommend the right dose and tell you when you should take it.

- **Start with conventional care.** I never advise patients to forgo appropriate standard cancer treatments such as chemotherapy and/or radiation. These approaches have been proven to improve survival. You can then supplement these approaches with off-label medications, herbs and/or supplements to help increase effectiveness.

- **Define your goals.** A cure isn't the only reason to use a medley of treatments. The right cocktail also can reduce treatment side effects and improve your quality of life.

Example: Patients with breast cancer may be given hormonal treatments that reduce tumor growth, but in premenopausal women, these treatments also induce early menopause—and the accompanying hot flashes, night sweats and "brain fog." To be more comfortable during the posttreatment period, you can take vitamin E to reduce hot flashes...ginkgo to improve memory...and herbs such as black cohosh to reduce vaginal dryness and night sweats.

INGREDIENTS TO CONSIDER

Ask your doctor what you can add to your current treatments to increase their effectiveness. Some of the most common medications in the US have been shown to help cancer patients, as have supplements. *Here, some unconventional treatments that can help...*

• **Vitamin D.** Studies have shown that vitamin D induces apoptosis, the death of cancer cells. This is important because one of the characteristics of cancer cells is the ability to avoid cell death. Using vitamin D along with chemotherapy, surgery and/or radiation could improve your outcome.

The ulcer medication *cimetidine* (Tagamet) strengthens the immune system so that it can fight cancer cells. Studies have shown that patients who start taking cimetidine a few days before colon cancer surgery may be less likely to have a recurrence of the cancer.

• **Aspirin.** An analysis of data from the Harvard Nurses' Health Study found that breast cancer patients who took aspirin reduced the risk of the cancer spreading (metastasis) by nearly 50%.

• **Curcumin,** the active compound in the spice turmeric. Like aspirin, it's an anti-inflammatory that can reduce the invasion and spread of cancer cells. It also can inhibit angiogenesis, the development of blood vessels that nourish tumors.

• **Green tea.** This is one cancer-cocktail ingredient that everyone can "take." One cup of green tea has approximately 45 milligrams (mg) of epigallocatechin 3-gallate (EGCG), a compound that appears to reduce the growth of cancer cells. Dozens of studies have shown that green tea may be effective.

Example: A Mayo Clinic study found that the majority of leukemia patients who took EGCG showed clear improvement. Other studies have shown that it can reduce prostate-specific antigen (PSA), a substance that is elevated in patients with prostate cancer.

I recommend eight cups of green tea a day to fight cancer.

• **Red yeast rice.** This type of yeast, taken in supplement form, contains monacolin K, the same active compound that is used in lovastatin, one of the cholesterol-lowering statins. Red yeast rice is an anti-inflammatory that also affects immune response and cell signaling—actions that can help prevent and possibly treat some cancers.

Laboratory studies indicate that red yeast rice (as well as statins) might increase the effectiveness of radiation and chemotherapy.

As for statins, in studies involving nearly a half-million patients, the drugs have been shown to significantly reduce the incidence and recurrence of colon, breast, lung and prostate cancers.

GO SLOW

Mix the cocktail slowly. It's not good to start many treatments at the same time. You need to know if a particular ingredient is causing side effects.

Example: I might advise a patient to use Chinese herbs for a week. If he/she is doing well, I might add a second ingredient and then a third.

Mistletoe Extract Helps Fight Cancer

Mark A. Stengler, NMD, licensed naturopathic medical doctor in private practice, Stengler Center for Integrative Medicine, Encinitas, California...adjunct associate clinical professor at the National College of Natural Medicine, Portland, Oregon...author of many books, including *The Natural Physician's Healing Therapies* and coauthor of *Prescription for Natural Cures. MarkStengler.com*

It's not often that there is a proven natural treatment to recommend to the approximately 12 million people in the US who currently have cancer. I'm talking about an extract made from European mistletoe (*Viscum album*), a plant that grows on apple, oak, maple and other trees. (You know it as a decoration for holiday kisses.)

Mistletoe extract has become one of the most well-studied compounds in complementary cancer therapy (with more than 120 published studies). It is widely used in Europe, particularly in Germany, Austria and Switzerland. In fact, in Germany, mistletoe extract is a licensed medicine that is partly reimbursable through the health-care system...and more than 50% of cancer patients are treated with the plant in some form. In Switzerland, it is fully reimbursable through health insurance.

Mistletoe extract has been used in medicine for centuries. It had multidimensional uses, including treating headache, menstrual symptoms, infertility and arthritis. Interest in mistletoe extract as a treatment for cancer was ignited in the 1920s.

Today several companies manufacture mistletoe extract under the brand names Iscador, Helixor, Isorel and others. One of the most studied formulations is Iscador.

Available from conventional medical and holistic doctors in the US and around the world, mistletoe extract is most often used in conjunction with standard cancer treatments such as chemotherapy and/or radiation. It has been found to increase the effectiveness of, and reduce the side effects from, conventional therapies and to improve patients' immunity and quality of life, including vitality, sleep and appetite.

I regularly prescribe mistletoe extract to my patients—to help those with cancer battle the disease and as a postcancer treatment.

Find out what mistletoe extract can do...

HOW IT CAN HELP

Medicinally, mistletoe extract's active compounds seem to be related to two main components—viscotoxins, proteins that exhibit cell-killing activity and stimulate the immune system...and lectins, molecules that bind to cells and induce biochemical changes in those cells. However, since the extract is made from the whole plant, including leaves, stems and berries, it contains hundreds of active compounds.

Studies have shown that mistletoe extract can help in a number of ways and with several different types of cancers. *What some studies have found...*

- **Patients with cancer of the colon,** rectum, stomach, breast or lung who took Iscador in addition to the conventional therapies reviewed in the study (chemotherapy and/or radiation) lived about 14 months, or 40%, longer than those who did not take mistletoe extract, according to a study published in 2001 in *Alternative Therapies in Health and Medicine.*

- **Mistletoe extract extended** survival time in patients with malignant melanoma in a 2005 study published in a German journal. Patients had significantly lower rates of metastases compared with the control group.

- **Patients with colorectal cancer** who were treated with Iscador in addition to conventional treatment experienced fewer adverse side effects...better symptom relief...and improved disease-free survival rates compared with those treated with only conventional therapy, according to a 2009 study in the *Journal of Clinical Oncology.*

- **At last year's American Society for Clinical Oncology meeting in Washington, DC,** researchers presented the results of a Phase I clinical trial that tested the safety of Helixor and the drug *gemcitabine* (Gemzar) in patients with advanced solid tumors of the breast, pancreas or colon.

Finding: 48% of patients taking both Helixor and Gemzar benefited from enhanced immune function and an increase in infection-fighting cells. Helixor also may allow for higher doses of chemotherapy.

- **Mistletoe extract improved the quality of life of 270 breast cancer patients undergoing chemotherapy,** says a German study published in *Phytomedicine.* Physicians rated improvements in general well-being (87% of patients), mental health (71%) and disease coping (50%). Patients also reported improved appetite and sleep and less pain. Well-being is believed to result from mistletoe extract's anti-inflammatory effect, which can reduce pain and boost energy.

In addition, mistletoe extract has been found to inhibit growth of malignant cells and cause cancer-cell death (apoptosis)...and protect cell DNA.

HOW IT IS USED

Mistletoe extract typically is given by injection. It also is available as a tincture and can be given intravenously—however, all the studies used the injection form. Cancer patients should use only the injection form because that's the form that has been studied. I teach my patients how to give themselves the injection in the abdomen or upper side of the thigh three times a week. We begin after a diagnosis and before surgery and/or chemotherapy/radiation. Even if mistletoe extract is not given immediately after diagnosis, it can be started at any time during the course of conventional cancer treatment.

Different species of mistletoe extract can treat different types of cancer. Doctors can use varying strengths depending on patients' responses to mistletoe extract. I like to have patients take mistletoe extract for five years after being diagnosed because it optimizes the immune system to continue fighting cancer. As with most natural substances, the US Food and Drug Administration has not approved mistletoe extract as a cancer treatment. However, in this country, injectable mistletoe is available as a prescription. Any licensed primary care doctor can order and prescribe it. It costs about $200 a month and is not covered by insurance.

Cancer patients should have this treatment only while being supervised by a doctor.

Side effects are uncommon but can include headache, dizziness, fatigue and itching. An allergic reaction is rare but possible. A normal reaction may include mild fever for one to two days after the first injection, swelling of local lymph nodes and redness or swelling at the injection site for 48 hours. Doctors look for this reaction—it means that the treatment is working and is prompting an immune response.

People who have an autoimmune disease such as rheumatoid arthritis or multiple sclerosis...high fever...active tuberculosis... or hyperthyroidism should be attentive to any symptoms that might occur because mistletoe extract can aggravate these conditions. Transplant patients and others who take immune-suppressing drugs should not use mistletoe extract.

Don't eat any part of the mistletoe plant—some species are toxic. For more information on mistletoe extract, speak to a holistic doctor who has experience using it.

Potent Cancer Fighters

Onions and garlic fight cancer. Both reduce risk of colorectal, ovarian, prostate, breast, renal, esophageal, oral-cavity and throat cancer.

Possible reason: The sulfur compounds that give onion and garlic eaters bad breath may inhibit tumor growth. Onions and garlic also are rich in antioxidant flavonoids. Garlic provides even more protection than onions.

Carlo LaVecchia, MD, professor of epidemiology, Instituto di Ricerche Farmacologiche, Milan, Italy, and leader of an analysis of data on almost 10,000 cancer patients and 15,000 healthy people, published in *American Journal of Clinical Nutrition.*

Herb for Lung Cancer

A substance extracted from the herb milk thistle can help prevent the spread of lung cancer cells in mice. This finding may help scientists develop new treatments for lung cancer.

Molecular Carcinogenesis.

New Personalized, Precision Approach to Lung Cancer Treatment

Peter Bach, MD, epidemiologist and lung cancer specialist, Memorial Sloan-Kettering Cancer Center, New York City. He has done extensive research and development on lung cancer prediction models and has authored numerous articles on lung cancer for medical journals.

Prasad Adusumilli, MD, thoracic surgeon and researcher, Memorial Sloan-Kettering Cancer Center, New York City. He has researched and published extensively on lung cancer topics, including the personalization of lung cancer surgical resection procedures.

The odds of surviving lung cancer admittedly still aren't great, but these days a lung cancer diagnosis is not an automatic death sentence—even in the case of late-stage cancer. We have many more options for treating the disease than we did just a decade ago... and treatment today is more personalized and precise than ever.

For instance, doctors now can look at the individual characteristics of a tumor, including particular cell patterns and genetic mutations. This information helps them to set treatment plans that are more likely to work—and to avoid recommending treatments with low chances of success. In fact, Peter Bach, MD, an epidemiologist and pulmonologist at Memorial Sloan-Kettering Cancer Center in New York City, said that he is "extremely enthusiastic" about the progress that's been made over the past decade.

The problem: Despite the remarkable advances, not all hospitals have the needed tools in their arsenals...and not all doctors understand which patients will benefit from such a personalized approach.

SECRETS FOUND IN CELL PATTERNS

The term lung cancer actually is misleading because the disease is not just one entity. Rather, there are two major types of lung cancer, each with different risk factors, probable prognoses and treatments. And then even within one of those types, different tumors can have different characteristics that affect how aggressive the cancer may be and which treatment may work.

The majority of lung cancers fall in to the non–small cell category. *Adenocarcinoma* is the most common non–small cell cancer, accounting for about half of all lung cancers. It's the type found most often in current and former smokers—and also in people who never smoked.

When adenocarcinoma is detected before it has had a chance to spread, it's treated surgically. Most of the time, the surgeon performs a lobectomy by removing the entire lobe that has the cancer in it (a pair of lungs has five lobes, three on the right side and two on the left). In some cases, the surgeon does a limited resection, removing just part of the affected lobe.

Tricky: The decision about which procedure to do can be a tough one, according to Prasad Adusumilli, MD, a thoracic surgeon and scientist at Memorial Sloan-Kettering Cancer Center. That's because the surgeon wants to remove enough lung tissue to prevent a cancer recurrence, but at the same time leave enough tissue to preserve lung function. Until now, there hasn't been an evidence-based system to guide surgeons, so the size and location of the tumor (for example, how far the tumor is from the edge of the lung) often have been used as criteria in deciding how much to remove.

Breakthrough: Surgeons at Memorial Sloan-Kettering perform about 1,000 of these operations each year. With all the data they have accumulated over the years, Dr. Adusumilli and his research team have developed an algorithm to help surgeons decide which operation is best for patients with adenocarcinoma.

The research that led to the new algorithm was complicated, but basically the researchers performed microscopic examinations of many hundreds of samples of early-stage adenocarcinoma, classifying each according to the proportion of the five major cell patterns (acinar, papillary, lepidic, micropapillary and solid) seen in the tumor. Then they analyzed the follow-up data to determine the chances of cancer recurrence based on the cell pattern and the type of surgery that was done.

Overall, the five-year incidence of cancer recurrence was 21% for patients who had a limited resection and 15% for patients who had a lobectomy. When the specific cell patterns were analyzed, though, it became clear that tumors with a higher percentage of cells showing a micropapillary pattern had a much higher risk for recurrence within the same lobe if patients underwent limited resection.

Bottom line: Doctors can now use this knowledge about cell patterns to opt for the tissue-sparing limited resection procedure in patients whose tumors do not have the aggressive micropapillary pattern...and save the more extensive lobectomy for patients whose cell pattern indicates a high risk for recurrence.

Only a limited number of hospitals have the expertise needed to determine a lung tumor's cell pattern right on the spot, in the operating room, at the time of the actual surgery. "This requires expert pathological experience and a large volume of tumors for the pathologists to get experienced," Dr. Adusumilli explained. At hospitals that do not currently have this ability, some patients who get a limited resection may end up needing another operation later if their cancer subsequently is found to have the micropapillary pattern...or, worse, they may have a cancer recurrence.

Hopefully, that will change soon. Dr. Adusumilli and his team of researchers are now trying to develop tools that can more easily determine the cell's pattern—preferably before surgery—sparing patients the need to go under the knife a second time.

SECRETS FOUND IN GENETIC MUTATIONS

When lung cancer is diagnosed after it has spread to the lymph nodes or beyond, as it is most of the time, treatment involves more than just surgery—it also requires medication. Now, in what Dr. Bach refers to as a "very exciting" development, the particular medications that will work best often can be determined based on specific genetic mutations in the tumors.

How it started: About 10 years ago, during clinical trials for two new lung cancer drugs, doctors observed that some people receiving the drugs *gefitinib* (Iressa) and *erlotinib* (Tarceva) had a much better response than others—even though all the patients had advanced adenocarcinoma. This led to the discovery that the patients who responded well had tumors that showed a specific mutation in the epidermal growth factor receptor (EGFR) gene. People with the mutation survived nearly twice as long on the drug regimen as those without it. It turns out that the mutation is present in about 20% of people diagnosed with advanced adenocarcinoma.

A few years later, researchers discovered another mutation on the anaplastic lymphoma kinase (ALK) gene, which is present in 7% of people with adenocarcinoma. A drug that inhibits ALK activity, called *crizotinib* (Xalkori), is very effective in people who have that particular mutation.

All three of these drugs have been approved, and the required genetic testing is available. Many experts now recommend that all patients with advanced adenocarcinoma have their tumors analyzed for mutations of EGFR and ALK—including patients who have mixed cancer types, even with just a small component of adenocarcinoma. Referring to molecular testing in its entirety, not just for EGFR and ALK, Dr. Bach said, "Now, 60% to 70% of adenocarcinomas have important molecular information that affects therapeutic choices. That's huge! Lung cancer might be the poster child for this kind of precision, personalized medicine."

If you are diagnosed with lung cancer: If at all possible, see an oncologist at a hospital associated with a university, Dr. Bach advised. Academic medical centers usually have the technology and expertise to take advantage of these new tests and procedures. If you live too far away to see a doctor there regularly, consider having a consultation with an appropriate expert at such a facility—that person can advise you and your doctor on the best treatment for you.

Thyroid Cancer—Epidemic...or Overdiagnosis?

Juan Pablo Brito, MBBS, assistant professor and health-care delivery scholar in the division of endocrinology, diabetes, metabolism and nutrition at the Mayo Clinic, Rochester, Minnesota, where he also is co-investigator of the Knowledge and Evaluation Research Unit. He is lead author of "Thyroid Cancer: Zealous Imaging Has Increased Detection and Treatment of Low Risk Tumours," which appeared in *BMJ.*

Any increase in cancer is worrisome, but the dramatic rise in thyroid cancer is particularly troubling. In just 30 years, the incidence in the US has more than tripled, from 3.6 cases per 100,000 people in 1973 to 11.6 per 100,000 in 2009.

It is among the fastest-growing diagnoses in the US. This is an alarming trend—but not for the reason you might think.

Experts have concluded that the vast majority of thyroid cancers were there all along. Better imaging tests such as ultrasound and magnetic resonance imaging (MRI) now make it possible to detect minuscule cancers that would have been missed before. What looks like an increase in disease actually is an increase in diagnosis.

Isn't it good to detect cancers when they're still small? Not in this case. The most common type of thyroid cancer grows slowly—if it grows at all. Most patients would never have symptoms or need treatment. But once you know you have cancer, you want that thing out of there. Unfortunately, the treatments often cause more problems than they solve.

MORE SCREENING, MORE CANCER

There's a saying in medicine, "When you have a new hammer, everything looks like a nail."

In the 1980s, ultrasound was the new hammer. Endocrinologists used it routinely during office visits. Even if you came in with vague symptoms that could be caused by just about anything, such as fatigue from insomnia, you would likely be given a neck ultrasound and possibly an MRI or a computerized tomography (CT) scan. These tests can detect nodules as small as 2 millimeters (mm) in diameter.

In many cases, tests that were ordered for other conditions happened to detect a growth in the thyroid. More cases of thyroid cancer are diagnosed incidentally than when doctors actually are looking for them. Doctors call these unexpected findings "incidentalomas."

Does finding small cancers save lives? Despite the tremendous increase in diagnosed thyroid cancers, the death rate has scarcely budged—it was 0.5 per 100,000 people a generation ago, and it is virtually the same today. All that has changed is the ability to detect them.

THE RISK OF KNOWING

About 90% of diagnosed thyroid cancers are small papillary cancers. They usually are indolent—cancers that are unlikely to grow or cause problems. Two Japanese studies and one American study have tracked nearly 1,500 patients who did not receive active treatment for papillary cancers less than one centimeter. After an average of five years, none of these patients has died.

Yet most people who are diagnosed with papillary thyroid cancers opt for treatment—usually a complete thyroidectomy, the removal of the thyroid gland. Once the gland is removed, patients require lifelong treatment with thyroid-replacement medications. Some suffer nerve damage that causes permanent voice changes. When surgery is followed by radioactive iodine therapy, patients face additional risks.

SYMPTOMS OF THYROID CANCER

Thyroid cancer typically doesn't cause any signs or symptoms early in the disease. As thyroid cancer grows, it may cause...

- **A lump that can be felt through the skin on your neck**
- **Changes to your voice, including increasing hoarseness**
- **Difficulty swallowing**
- **Pain in your neck and throat**
- **Swollen lymph nodes in your neck**

MORE DANGEROUS THYROID CANCERS

There are other types of thyroid cancer—follicular, medullary and anaplastic—that are more serious. These typically require surgery, usually the total removal of the thyroid gland and sometimes the removal of lymph nodes in the neck. Patients with these cancers typically are given postsurgical radioactive iodine to destroy remaining parts of the gland and any cancer cells that were left behind during surgery.

WHAT TO DO

Experts don't recommend widespread screening for thyroid cancer. A neck ultrasound is recommended only for specific patients—people who have a family history of thyroid cancer...had previous exposure to head/neck radiation...or a nodule that can be felt during an exam. If a test reveals a nodule that is one centimeter or more in diameter, a biopsy often is performed to determine the seriousness of the growth.

Also important...

• **Question the ultrasound.** If your doctor recommends neck ultrasonography during a routine checkup or because you're experiencing somewhat vague symptoms (such as fatigue), ask if you really need it and what the benefits and risks are if you do the test or don't do the test. You should clearly understand the goal of doing the test and how you will benefit.

Consider a second opinion before agreeing to surgery. According to data from the US National Cancer Institute, death rates in patients who didn't have immediate surgery for papillary cancers were virtually the same as for those who did have surgery. Watchful waiting—forgoing treatment but getting checkups every six months at the beginning and then every year after that to see if a tumor has grown—usually is the best approach for these cancers.

Keep your emotions in check. It is emotionally difficult to know that you have a cancer and not do something about it. You will want it gone whether it poses a threat or not. But most thyroid cancers—like the majority of slow-growing prostate cancers—are simply not dangerous. Some experts believe that they shouldn't even be called cancer. An alternative, less frightening term that has been proposed is papillary lesions of indolent course (PLIC).

• **Get the treatment that fits you.** If you have a papillary cancer that does need treatment, ask your doctor if you can have a partial rather than a total thyroidectomy. The partial procedure is safer and, for most papillary cancers, just as effective.

Don't agree to postsurgical treatment with radioactive iodine unless your doctor insists that you need it. It usually is not recommended for low-risk thyroid cancers because it can cause serious side effects, including an altered sense of taste and inflamed salivary glands. The treatment also has been linked to a 5.7-fold increase in the risk for leukemia.

Drug for Advanced Prostate Cancer Also Helps If Used Early in the Course of the Disease

When the drug *abiraterone acetate* (Zytiga) was added to the standard therapy given to men whose disease had not spread beyond the prostate gland, tumors disappeared in 10% of the men and were significantly smaller in 24%. Zytiga slows the production of testosterone, which fuels tumor growth.

Study by researchers at Dana-Farber Cancer Institute, Boston, presented at the annual meeting of the American Society of Clinical Oncology in Chicago.

Prostate Cancer Biopsy

Prostate cancer patients should not rely on a conventional biopsy when deciding between surgery and active surveillance.

Reason: A conventional "blind" biopsy may fail to reveal the true extent of the cancer.

Better: A targeted biopsy, which fuses an MRI with a 3-D ultrasound to more accurately determine the grade of the cancer and help doctors decide whether treatment or surveillance makes the most sense.

Jesse Le, MD, is resident physician in the department of urology at UCLA's David Geffen School of Medicine, California.

Men with Prostate Cancer Need This

Men with prostate cancer who should get CT, MRI and bone scans often do not... and many prostate cancer patients who don't need these scans do get them, exposing them to unnecessary radiation. Men diagnosed with prostate cancer are classified as low, intermediate or high risk. But in a recent study, 39% of high-risk men who should get scans did not. And 36% of low-risk and 49% of intermediate-risk men did get the scans, even though the chance of the disease spreading beyond the prostate in those patients was very low.

Self-defense: If diagnosed with prostate cancer, ask your doctor what your classification is and which scans are appropriate.

Sandip Prasad, MD, urologic oncology fellow, The University of Chicago, and leader of a study of 30,183 men diagnosed with prostate cancer in 2004 and 2005, presented at a recent Genitourinary Cancers Symposium.

Slow Down Prostate Cancer

Prostate cancer can be slowed with diet changes and stress management.

Recent finding: Men who followed a plant-based diet and decreased their stress levels had a significant reduction in the rate of increase in levels of prostate-specific antigen (PSA), an indicator of prostate cancer. The men were asked to increase their intake of whole grains, cruciferous and leafy vegetables, beans, legumes and fruits, as well as decrease their intake of meat, poultry and dairy. Stress-management training included meditation, yoga and t'ai chi.

Gordon Saxe, MD, PhD, assistant professor of family and preventive medicine, University of California, San Diego, School of Medicine, and lead author of a study of prostate cancer, published in *Integrative Cancer Therapies.*

Better Breast Cancer Treatment

An analysis of 17 randomized trials involving 10,801 women found that those who had breast-conserving surgery plus radiation had a 10-year recurrence rate of 19.3%, compared with 35% in the group that received surgery but no radiation. Risk for death after 15 years was 21.4% in the radiation group and 25.2% in the nonradiation group. This means that one death is prevented for every four recurrences.

Sarah C. Darby, PhD, professor of medical statistics, University of Oxford, UK.

Good News for Women with Breast Cancer—Five Recent Advances Are Dramatically Changing Treatment Approaches…

Jill Dietz, MD, director of the Hillcrest Breast Center, Cleveland Clinic Foundation. She is a fellow of the American College of Surgeons and member of several professional organizations, including the American Society of Breast Surgeons and Society of Surgical Oncology.

Women who have breast cancer are now living longer than they did only five years ago—and not simply due to improved mammography techniques.

Reason: New scientific evidence is changing the way physicians can treat the disease—making these treatments much more selective and effective. *Key findings breast cancer patients need to know about…*

• **New thinking on double mastectomy.** Many women with breast cancer opt to surgically remove the breast with the malignancy and the healthy breast. Their decision to remove both breasts is driven by the fear that a new breast cancer will develop in the healthy breast. But new research suggests that double mastectomy for these women may be overused.

Recent scientific evidence: Researchers who followed up with 1,525 early-stage breast cancer patients four years after they had received mastectomy, double mastectomy or lumpectomy (a breast-conserving procedure that removes only the malignancy and surrounding tissue) found that women who had both breasts removed would have had a very low risk of developing cancer in the healthy breast.

Who should consider having a double mastectomy? According to the Society of Surgical Oncology, it may be warranted for a woman who is at increased risk for breast cancer because she has two or more immediate family members (a mother, sister or daughter) with breast or ovarian cancer...or has tested positive for mutations in the BRCA1 or BRCA2 gene. These criteria apply to women who have early-stage breast cancer as well as those who haven't developed the disease.

Self-defense: If you don't have a family history or genetic predisposition to develop breast cancer, carefully review your reasons for considering a double mastectomy.

• **Better results with tamoxifen.** Doctors have long advised certain breast cancer patients to use an estrogen-blocking drug (tamoxifen) for about five years to stave off future breast malignancies.

Recent scientific evidence: For more than 15 years, researchers followed 6,846 breast cancer patients who took tamoxifen for an additional five years after five years of initial use while another group stopped the drug at five years.

Result: Those who used the drug for 10 years had a significantly reduced risk for breast cancer recurrence and death.

The benefits of longer-term tamoxifen use apply primarily to premenopausal women. That's because postmenopausal women have the option of taking another class of drugs called aromatase inhibitors, including *letrozole* (Femara), which are slightly more effective than tamoxifen at preventing future breast cancers but do not, for unknown reasons, offer the same benefit to premenopausal women. Research has not yet determined whether postmenopausal women would benefit from taking letrozole for 10 years rather than the standard five-year recommendation.

Self-defense: If you're a premenopausal woman with breast cancer (especially if the tumor was large and/or you had lymph nodes that tested positive for cancer), ask your doctor about the risks and benefits of taking tamoxifen for more than the standard five years. Using the drug increases risk for endometrial cancer and pulmonary embolism.

• **Less invasive treatment may improve survival for early-stage breast cancer.** Women with early-stage breast cancer perceive mastectomy to be more effective at eliminating their future risk for breast cancer, but research shows that this is probably not true.

Recent scientific evidence: In an analysis of more than 112,000 women with stage I or stage II breast cancer who were tracked for an average of 9.2 years, those who received lumpectomy plus radiation had odds of survival that were as good as or better than those who underwent mastectomy.

Self-defense: If you are diagnosed with stage I or stage II breast cancer, ask your doctor about lumpectomy plus radiation.

• **More women could benefit from reconstruction.** With breast reconstruction, a woman who has received a mastectomy (or, in some cases, a lumpectomy) can have her breast shape rebuilt with an implant and/or tissue from another part of her body (typically the abdomen, back or buttocks). When a patient opts for reconstruction, it is ideally performed with the initial breast cancer surgery for the best cosmetic result.

Breast reconstruction does not restore the breast's natural sensation or replace the nipple. However, a new "nipple-sparing" mastectomy, a technically difficult procedure in which the surgeon preserves the nipple and areola (the brownish or pink-colored tissue surrounding the nipple), is gaining popularity with women whose malignancy does not interfere with this type of surgery.

Recent scientific evidence: Even though breast reconstruction can offer cosmetic and psychological advantages, not very many women choose to have it. In a study of more than 120,000 women who underwent mastectomy, fewer than one in four of the women with invasive breast cancer opted for reconstruction, while only about one in three of those with early-stage disease got it. Almost all women are candidates for reconstruction, which does not impact survival rates. In some cases, women require one or more subsequent surgeries to fine-tune the reconstruction.

Self-defense: Ask about reconstruction before your treatment begins. If you're a candidate, the breast surgeon can coordinate with a plastic surgeon. Breast reconstruction is often covered by insurance, but some insurers may require a co-pay.

- **Targeted therapies save lives.** Until 40 years ago, breast cancer was treated almost uniformly with radical mastectomy, radiation and some form of hormone therapy.

Recent scientific evidence: Using new genomic DNA–based tests, doctors are now able to customize treatment based on tumor biology, helping them better predict a patient's risk for recurrence and response to particular treatments. This may help thousands of women avoid chemotherapy, including anthracyclines, which are linked to heart damage and leukemia.

Self-defense: Ask your doctor whether you could benefit from genomic testing to help determine which breast cancer therapies would be most effective for you.

Less Invasive Breast Cancer Treatment May Be Better for Some Women

Over a 14-year study period, early-stage breast cancer patients 50 years old and older who chose a lumpectomy plus radiation were 13% less likely to die from breast cancer and 19% less likely to die from any cause than similar women who had more invasive mastectomies.

Study of 112,154 women by researchers at Duke Cancer Institute, Durham, North Carolina, and the Cancer Prevention Institute of California, Fremont, published in *Cancer.*

Vitamin D for Breast Cancer

Breast cancer patients benefit from vitamin D. Researchers from the University of Rochester Medical Center in New York have found that women with aggressive, difficult-to-treat breast cancer often are deficient in vitamin D. The study is one of the first to assess vitamin D deficiency and poor prognosis. It's a good idea to have your doctor check your vitamin D level—especially if you are a cancer patient—and supplement accordingly.

Mark A. Stengler, NMD, licensed naturopathic medical doctor in private practice, Stengler Center for Integrative Medicine, Encinitas, California…adjunct associate clinical professor at the National College of Natural Medicine, Portland, Oregon.

Ovarian Cancer Life-Saving Breakthroughs

Krishnansu S. Tewari, MD, associate professor of gynecologic oncology at the University of California, Irvine Medical Center. Dr. Tewari is the principal investigator for the Gynecologic Oncology Group at UCI, and cochair of the Clinical Trials Protocol Review & Monitoring Committee at UCI's Chao Family Comprehensive Cancer Center.

Ovarian cancer is known as a deadly malignancy that typically causes no symptoms or ones that are so subtle they are easily overlooked. For this reason, the cancer is already widespread in 75% of newly diagnosed cases.

Now: Tests are being developed that help detect ovarian cancer before it reaches advanced stages—and scientists are hopeful that a breakthrough treatment will extend survival times in women diagnosed with the disease.

Recent developments that could help save your life or that of someone you love…

WHO IS AT GREATEST RISK

No one knows what causes ovarian cancer. But it is known that risk increases with age—90% of cases occur after age 45—as well as with...

• **Ovulation.** Every time an egg ruptures through the surface of the ovary during normal ovulation, the body repairs the damage. Each repair brings the possibility of DNA mutations that can set the stage for ovarian cancer. That's why taking a break from ovulation—by using birth control pills, for example, or having children—reduces the risk for ovarian cancer.

Who can benefit: Women of child-bearing age who do not have contraindications to birth control pills and are at high risk for ovarian cancer.

• **Genetic susceptibility.** Women who carry an inherited mutation in the BRCA1 and BRCA2 genes (most commonly associated with breast cancer) are 10 to 27 times more likely to develop ovarian cancer than women without this mutation.

Women who should consider testing for BRCA mutations: Those who are of Ashkenazi Jewish descent—they are at increased risk for breast cancer and ovarian cancer... those who have multiple relatives affected by cancer, especially ovarian and breast...and/or have a first-degree relative, such as a parent, sibling or child, who developed any cancer before age 50.

Important: Having a mutation means an increased risk, not a guarantee of cancer.

In addition to increasing surveillance—via ultrasound and a blood test for the protein cancer antigen 125 (CA-125)—women with genetic susceptibility may want to consider having their ovaries and fallopian tubes removed. Fallopian tubes also are susceptible to developing cancer from BRCA mutations. This surgery, known as salpingo-oophorectomy (SO), is recommended only if a woman has completed childbearing or when she reaches age 35—the age at which most women have decided whether they want to have children.

Because small bits of tissue could be left behind, SO significantly reduces, but doesn't eliminate, the risk for ovarian cancer. This surgery may sound drastic, but many women prefer this approach to living with an elevated threat of cancer.

What's new: Researchers have found a new genetic marker of ovarian cancer—a mutation on a variant of the cancer gene known as KRAS. In one study, the KRAS variant was present in more than 25% of women with ovarian cancer.

What's more, the KRAS variant was present in 61% of women with ovarian cancer who did not have BRCA1 or BRCA2, adding a new piece to the genetic cancer puzzle. More clinical research is needed before the test for the KRAS gene variant can be approved by the FDA.

WHAT'S NEW IN DETECTION

If a suspicious ovarian tumor is discovered—during a pelvic exam or ultrasound, for example—a gynecologist will usually order a CA-125 blood test. Typically, high levels of CA-125 protein in these women signal the presence of ovarian cancer. The test also is used to screen for cancer in women with known genetic mutations and to catch signs of cancer recurrence after treatment.

However, the test has not been used for general screening of women without tumors because it has a high rate of false positives—even regular menstruation can increase CA-125 levels. False positives often lead to unnecessary and expensive follow-up testing, occasionally surgery and, of course, fear and distress for the patients.

What's new: An effective and low-cost way to use CA-125 to screen for ovarian cancer in the general population. An eight-year study followed more than 3,000 postmenopausal women (ages 50 to 74) who had no family history of breast or ovarian cancer. Researchers took a baseline reading of CA-125, and then the women were categorized by risk level based on a mathematical model called the Risk of Ovarian Cancer Algorithm (ROCA). Each woman ended up with her own CA-125 profile, which was used to determine when additional testing was warranted. For example, if an individual woman's CA-125 increased by a certain amount, then she would get an ultrasound.

Exciting finding: Among the more than 3,000 women studied, this method of CA-125 testing found three invasive ovarian cancers, which were detected at an early stage. If approved for general use, this method will provide a cost-effective way to screen women for ovarian cancer, just as the Pap test screens for cervical cancer.

Another new development: The OVA1 blood test was recently approved by the FDA. OVA1 is a panel of five marker proteins, including CA-125, which are combined to give an overall composite score, like a cancer risk report card. OVA1 is used in women with a tumor to assess whether it is likely to be malignant and whether biopsies/surgery should be recommended or avoided.

In some cases, oncologists order three tests—OVA1, CA-125 and another test called HE4, which detects an additional ovarian cancer marker—to determine whether a mass is likely to be malignant. Because OVA1 gives a composite score, not an individual value for each of the five proteins, it can be helpful to also order CA-125 individually.

EXCITING TREATMENT ADVANCE

This is the first year in more than a decade that a breakthrough has occurred in the treatment of ovarian cancer. Up to now, ovarian cancer has typically been treated only with surgery and chemotherapy.

What's new: Research has shown that a drug called *bevacizumab* (Avastin)—also used to treat malignancies such as those of the colon and breast—delays the progression of advanced ovarian cancer. Bevacizumab is an antiangiogenic drug, which starves tumors by preventing the growth of new blood vessels.

Women who took bevacizumab during and up to 10 months after chemotherapy lived an average four months longer than those not taking it.

Bevacizumab is not FDA approved for ovarian cancer but can be used for this condition at a doctor's discretion. For this reason, insurance may not cover the cost of the drug—a year's supply can exceed $50,000. The drugmaker is expected to apply soon for FDA approval to use bevacizumab in the treatment of ovarian cancer.

GET THE BEST CARE

- **If you have one or more symptoms of ovarian cancer and they don't subside with treatment,** ask for proof of the diagnosis. For example, if your doctor says that you have a urinary tract infection, ask if a urine culture was performed. Don't give up until your symptoms improve.
- **If your doctor suspects ovarian cancer,** be sure to see a gynecologic oncologist to confirm the diagnosis. These doctors have specialized training that helps ensure your best chances for survival. To find a specialist in your area, consult the Women's Cancer Network (*www.wcn.org*).
- **If you are diagnosed with ovarian cancer,** try to get treated at one of 40 Comprehensive Cancer Centers in the US that are designated by the National Cancer Institute (NCI). These centers provide cutting-edge therapy and offer access to clinical trials. To find an NCI-designated cancer center near you, go to *http://cancercenters.cancer.gov* and click on "Cancer Centers."

Ovarian Cancer Risk

Women with irregular periods may have double the risk for ovarian cancer, compared with women who have regular monthly periods.

Best: If you have irregular periods or if you have a condition called polycystic ovarian syndrome, ask your doctor if you should be screened for ovarian cancer.

Study of more than 14,000 women led by Barbara A. Cohn, PhD, MPH, director of Child Health and Development Studies at the Public Health Institute in Oakland, California, presented at the annual meeting of the American Association for Cancer Research, San Diego.

Clinical Trials Can Help

Did you know that experimental cancer treatments are more beneficial than previously thought? In a recent study, the largest and most comprehensive to date, about 11%—and in some cases, 27%—of patients in Phase 1 cancer trials responded positively. Previous reviews showed that only 4% to 6% benefited.

Christine Grady, RN, PhD, department of clinical bioethics, WG Magnuson Clinical Center, National Institutes of Health, Bethesda, Maryland.

A Common Diabetes Drug Can Fight Cancer

In one study, metformin, used to control blood sugar in people with type 2 diabetes, slowed tumor growth by 32% in men with prostate cancer. A second study suggests that metformin may extend the lives of people with pancreatic cancer.

Studies by researchers at Princess Margaret Hospital/University Health Network, Toronto, and University of Texas MD Anderson Cancer Center, Houston.

Aspirin: The Cancer Pill

Aspirin cuts cancer deaths significantly, says Peter Rothwell, MD, PhD.

Recent finding: Taking low-dose aspirin daily for five years decreased gastrointestinal cancer deaths by up to 54% and overall cancer mortality by 34%. The longer aspirin is used, the greater the benefit. The mechanism by which aspirin helps prevent cancer deaths is not yet fully understood.

Peter Rothwell, MD, PhD, is professor of clinical neurology, Oxford University, England, and senior author of an analysis of studies of 25,570 patients, published in *The Lancet.*

A New Blood Test Detects Pancreatic Cancer Earlier

Early detection and tumor removal can help increase life expectancy for pancreatic cancer patients. Currently the five-year survival rate is less than 5%. Further testing is needed before the test becomes available.

Study of 271 patients and volunteers by researchers at Kobe University Graduate School of Medicine, Japan, published in *Cancer Epidemiology, Biomarkers & Prevention.*

Mushroom Extract May Hold Key to Curing Pancreatic Cancer

Daniel Sliva, PhD, senior investigator, Cancer Research Laboratory, Methodist Research Institute, Indiana University Health, Indianapolis. His study was published in *International Journal of Oncology.*

Michael Landon, Luciano Pavarotti, Sally Ride, Jack Benny, Patrick Swayze. Those are familiar names of people who have died from pancreatic cancer. You probably know someone who has succumbed to it as well, given that it is the fourth-leading cause of cancer-related deaths in the US.

Pancreatic cancer moves fast—many of its victims die within months of being diagnosed, and the five-year survival rate is dismal, not even reaching 5%. That's why any good news about pancreatic cancer is most welcome. So it's heartening to learn that a traditional Asian remedy made from mushrooms may hold the key to winning the battle against this dreaded disease, according to a new laboratory study.

MAGIC MUSHROOMS?

Poria cocos is a type of mushroom that grows on pine trees. Among practitioners of traditional Asian medicine, the mushroom has been used for many years as a sedative, diuretic and stomach settler. Recent studies suggested that bioactive compounds in mushrooms might protect against breast and skin cancer...

so researchers set out to discover whether they also might hold promise against pancreatic cancer, for which there is no known cure.

For the new study, normal pancreatic cells and pancreatic cancer cells were laid out in culture trays in a laboratory, then treated with extracts from the Poria cocos mushroom to see how the cells would react.

Exciting: Within just one day, the mushroom extract inhibited several different mechanisms by which pancreatic cancer proliferates—so that the cancer cells acted less aggressively and didn't multiply as rapidly as they usually would. For instance, the mushroom extract seemed to silence one particular gene, MMP-7, that is overactive in pancreatic cancer cells. Importantly, the mushroom extract had minimal effect on the normal pancreatic cells.

Of course, these findings do not mean that pancreatic cancer patients can be cured by eating pine tree mushrooms. But scientists are already working on the next phase of research to determine exactly how the mushroom extract turns down the MMP-7 gene...and whether the extract has the same effects in real life as it does in the lab.

Cause for hope: The potent drugs morphine, penicillin and *paclitaxel* (Taxol, which is used to treat lung, breast and ovarian cancers) were derived from poppy plants, mold and Pacific yew tree bark, respectively. So it's not at all farfetched that a mushroom might eventually prove to play a pivotal role in curing deadly pancreatic cancer.

Bladder Cancer: How to Get the Right Care

Karim Chamie, MD, MSHS, a postdoctoral fellow in urologic oncology and health services research at the University of California, Los Angeles. He led the team of researchers from UCLA's Jonsson Comprehensive Cancer Center that studied physician compliance with bladder cancer treatment guidelines.

It may surprise you to learn that bladder cancer is one of the most commonly diagnosed cancers in the US. Every year, about 70,000 Americans are diagnosed with bladder cancer, and approximately 15,000 die from it.

Good news: While bladder cancer has among the highest recurrence rates of any malignancy, it's often diagnosed long before it has a chance to spread. Patients who are treated according to the recommended clinical practice guidelines usually make a full recovery.

Not-so-good news: The majority of patients do not receive this level of care. In a recent study published in the journal *Cancer*, researchers analyzed the treatment records of 4,545 patients who had been diagnosed with high-grade (aggressive) non-muscle-invasive bladder cancer and found that only one was treated according to the full guidelines.* Specifically, nearly half of the urologists in the study had not performed important recommended follow-up tests or a single instillation of a cancer-killing drug in the bladder in the first two years after diagnosis—all of which are included in treatment guidelines.

If you or someone close to you is diagnosed with bladder cancer, it is essential that you know the recommended treatments to ensure that the most effective care for this eminently treatable cancer is being given...

EARLY WARNINGS

Bladder cancer is not a "death sentence" for most patients. The five-year survival rate for those diagnosed with early-stage cancer is more than 85%. One reason for this is that symptoms typically occur before the disease has spread—and because the symptoms are alarming enough that most people see a doctor right away.

Main symptom: Blood in the urine. The urine may appear bright red...it can also be dark yellow or the color of coffee. Less often, the urine may appear normal but will contain trace amounts of blood that can be detected under a microscope and is often picked up incidentally during a routine urine test.

Other symptoms may include frequent or painful urination, an unusually urgent need

*Treatment guidelines included in the study were set by the American Uroogical Association, National Comprehensive Cancer Network and European Association of Urology.

to urinate or getting up frequently at night to urinate.

Important: These symptoms are nonspecific. They can be caused by any type of irritation in or near the bladder, including prostate problems in men or urinary tract infections in women. Don't assume that you have cancer—but do make an appointment to see a doctor, who may refer you to a urologist if there is a problem.

Warning for women: Women with bladder cancer are often diagnosed later than men because they assume that the blood they see in the toilet or on the tissue is vaginal in origin.

GETTING TESTED

Blood in the urine and/or changes in urinary habits should always be brought to the attention of a doctor. Depending on your symptoms and whether you have a history of bladder cancer, your doctor may recommend one or more of the following tests...

- **Urine cytology.** A sample of urine is examined under a microscope to look for cancer cells.
- **Cystoscopy.** A narrow tube equipped with a camera and fiber-optic lights is inserted through the urethra into the bladder to look for changes that could indicate cancer. A biopsy (small sample of cells) may be taken. The procedure is done with a local anesthetic and takes about five to 20 minutes.
- **CT scan.** Some patients with pain or other symptoms may be given a CT scan or other imaging tests to look for abnormalities in the kidneys, bladder or ureters, the tubes that carry urine from the kidneys to the bladder.

TREATMENT OPTIONS

About 90% of bladder cancers are transitional cell carcinomas. They arise in the cells that line the inner wall of the bladder. Two other types of bladder cancer—squamous cell carcinoma and adenocarcinoma—are rare in the US.

Three-quarters of patients who are diagnosed with bladder cancer have an early, non-muscle-invasive form, meaning that the cells haven't migrated into the underlying muscle. This type of bladder cancer can be treated by surgically excising the tumor and instilling cancer-killing drugs inside the bladder.

However, more than one-third of patients in this group have a high-grade cancer, with a strong potential to spread. This type of cancer is treated by administering chemotherapy directly into the bladder. If necessary, chemotherapy is also used to treat any cancer cells that have spread to other sites. After treatment, patients should receive both cytoscopy and cytology every three to six months for two years after the initial treatment.

Virtually all patients who have been diagnosed with bladder cancer will require surgery to remove the abnormal cells. If the cancer has spread, the entire bladder may need to be removed. For small cancers, a transurethral resection is usually performed. In this type of surgery, a wire loop inserted into the bladder is used to burn away cancer cells.

Larger cancers that have invaded bladder muscle are typically treated with radical cystectomy, the total removal of the bladder and adjacent organs, and diversion of urine to either a new bladder created from a small piece of the colon or a pouch with a tube that is drained through an opening in the skin. Radiation and/or other types of chemotherapy may be needed, depending on the type and extent of the cancer.

PREVENTION

You definitely have the power to reduce your own risk for bladder cancer...

- **Stop smoking.** Between 60% and 70% of bladder cancer patients are current or former smokers. After lung cancer, bladder cancer is the second-leading cause of smoking-related malignancy.

Recent study: The National Cancer Institute found that cigarette smokers have an even higher risk for bladder cancer than was previously reported—four times the risk of nonsmokers compared with a threefold increased risk in previous studies.

If you smoke, quit. It takes at least 10 years after stopping smoking for the risk for bladder cancer to decline.

- **Reduce exposure to workplace carcinogens.** About one-third of bladder cancer cases are due to workplace exposure to carcinogenic chemicals, including chemicals that are used in types of businesses where there may not be a high awareness of the danger, such as auto shops.

Also be careful with hair dye: Studies show that hair colorists in salons have an elevated risk for bladder cancer. Wearing gloves is essential when using these dyes.

Carcinogens from tobacco and the workplace are absorbed into the bloodstream, then filtered out into the urine via the kidneys. The carcinogens then sit in the bladder until the individual urinates, exposing the bladder lining to the toxins for many hours during the day.

- **Drink more water.** A study that looked at nearly 48,000 men over a 22-year period found that those who drank a little more than two-and-a-half quarts of water a day were less likely to get bladder cancer than those who drank smaller amounts. This makes sense because people who drink a lot of water urinate more and, as a result, they both dilute and excrete toxins more rapidly than those who don't drink water regularly.

Stress Fuels Cancer Spread

In laboratory studies, stress was shown to increase the spread (metastasis) of breast cancer cells to the bone. Stress-reducing therapies appear to decrease levels of a molecule that promotes cell migration.

PLOS Biology.

Sitting Too Long Causes Cancer

Prolonged sitting increases risk for colon cancer. Men who were sedentary for more than 11 hours a day were 45% more likely to have a recurrence of colorectal adenomas—benign lumps associated with increased colon cancer risk—than men who were sedentary for fewer than seven hours.

Analysis of two studies of 1,730 people by researchers at Columbia University Mailman School of Public Health, New York City, presented at a meeting of the American Association for Cancer Research.

New Prep-Free At-Home Colon Cancer Test

In a recent study, the Fecal Immunochemical Test (FIT), an inexpensive stool test, detected 79% of cancers. The standard fecal occult blood test detects up to 50% of cancers, and colonoscopy detects more than 95%. FIT may be appropriate for people who are unwilling to undergo the bowel preparation the night before a colonoscopy...or are afraid of an invasive procedure.

Jeffrey Lee, MD, a gastroenterology fellow at University of California, San Francisco, and leader of an analysis of 19 studies of FIT screening, published in *Annals of Internal Medicine.*

Now You Can Get Your Own Lab Results

Deven McGraw, director of the Health Privacy Project at the Center for Democracy & Technology, a nonprofit organization, Washington, DC. *CDT.org*

Have you ever gone for a blood test and then had to wait weeks for your doctor to call you back...or maybe you never heard from him/her at all?

Well, soon you can have direct access to your lab results. A recent federal ruling will require medical labs to provide test results directly to patients who request them. Previously, patients in most states had to wait for labs to send results to their doctors, then for those doctors to contact them.

This ruling could not only help you obtain your lab results faster but also improve the odds that you will get your results at all. A recent study published in *Archives of Internal Medicine* showed that medical providers neglect to inform patients about potentially problematic test results 7% of the time.

Waiting to receive lab results from the doctor may be the best option for you. (Call your doctor if you don't hear back.) It ensures that you have a doctor's help interpreting potentially confusing results.

But for a patient who has a chronic condition that requires frequent tests from the same lab, obtaining results directly from the lab could be an effective way to keep track of a health issue. Many people with chronic conditions have learned to interpret their own lab results.

Labs had to comply with this new rule no later than October 6, 2014. The federal ruling supersedes existing state rules that previously prohibited labs from providing results directly to patients in 13 states.

High Doses of Selenium Double Risk for Prostate Cancer

In a recent study, men who had moderate or high levels of the antioxidant selenium at the start of the study and who then took daily supplements of 200 mcg of selenium doubled their prostate cancer risk.

What to do: Limit your selenium intake to no more than the recommended daily intake (RDI) of 55 mcg.

Alan Kristal, DrPH, is associate program head of the Cancer Prevention Program at Fred Hutchinson Cancer Research Center, Seattle, and leader of a study published in *Journal of the National Cancer Institute.*

Best Treatment for Skin Lesions

Precancerous skin lesions are better treated with photodynamic therapy (PDT) than with cryotherapy. In cryotherapy, lesions are frozen with liquid nitrogen. With PDT, the entire treatment area is "painted" with medication and then a special light is directed on it to activate the drug that kills the precancerous cells. Patients may require up to three sessions. Studies show that PDT is 14% more likely to completely clear the area in three months.

Daniel Eisen, MD, is clinical professor of dermatology at University of California Davis Health System, Sacramento.

Beware of Nail Salon Dryers

Dryers with lights, especially those used for gel manicures, emit ultraviolet (UV) rays. Multiple exposures can result in premature age spots, wrinkles and a slightly increased risk for skin cancer on the hands and fingers.

Self-defense: Apply sunscreen before using the dryer. Or wear special manicure gloves (available online).

Chris G. Adigun, MD, is clinical assistant professor and attending nail clinic physician at New York University Langone Medical Center, New York City.

New Ways to Fight Deadly Melanoma

Albert Lefkovits, MD, an associate clinical professor of dermatology at Mount Sinai School of Medicine and codirector of the Mount Sinai Dermatological Cosmetic Surgery Program, both in New York City.

Melanoma is the most dangerous form of skin cancer. It's particularly frightening because it's more likely than other cancers to spread (metastasize) to other parts of the body. More than 76,000 Americans are diagnosed with melanoma each year, and between 8,000 and 9,000 will die from it.

Good news: New technology increases the chances that a melanoma will be detected early—and when it is, you have a 95% to 97% chance of surviving. The prognosis is worse after the disease has spread, but two new drugs can significantly increase survival times—and medications that may be even more effective already are in the pipeline.

WHO'S AT RISK?

A study published in *Journal of Investigative Dermatology* found that melanoma rates increased by 3.1% annually between 1992 and 2004—and the incidence continues to rise.

The increase is due to several reasons. The US population is aging, and older adults are more likely to get melanoma (though it is a leading cause of cancer death in young adults). Public-awareness campaigns have increased the rate of cancer screenings (though officials would like the screening rates to be even higher), and more screenings mean an increase in melanoma diagnoses.

If you are a fair-skinned Caucasian, your lifetime risk of getting melanoma is about one in 50. The risk is lower among African Americans, Hispanics and Asians, but they're more likely to die from it because they often develop cancers on "hidden" areas (such as the soles of the feet), where skin changes aren't readily apparent.

Important: Don't be complacent just because you avoid the sun or use sunscreen. Many cancers appear in areas that aren't exposed to the sun, such as between the toes or around the anus.

STATE-OF-THE-ART SCREENING

Melanomas grow slowly. Patients who get an annual skin checkup are more likely to get an early diagnosis than those who see a doctor only when a mole or skin change is clearly abnormal.

Doctors used to depend on their eyes (and sometimes a magnifying glass) to examine suspicious areas. But eyes-only examinations can identify melanomas only about 60% of the time.

Better: An exam called epiluminescence microscopy. The doctor takes photographs of large areas of skin. Then he/she uses a device that magnifies suspicious areas in the photos. The accuracy of detecting melanomas with this technique is about 90%.

The technology also allows doctors to look for particular changes, such as certain colors or a streaked or globular appearance, that indicate whether a skin change is malignant or benign. This can reduce unnecessary biopsies.

Few private-practice physicians can afford the equipment that's used for these exams. You might want to get your checkups at a medical center or dermatology practice that specializes in early melanoma detection. If this isn't possible, ask your doctor if he/she uses a handheld dermatoscope. It's a less expensive device that's still superior to the unaided eye.

NEW TREATMENTS

In the last two years, the FDA has approved two medications for patients with late-stage melanoma. These drugs don't cure the disease but can help patients live longer.

- **Ipilimumab** (Yervoy) is a biologic medication, a type of synthetic antibody that blocks a cellular "switch" that turns off the body's ability to fight cancer. A study of 676 patients with late-stage melanoma found that those who took the drug survived, on average, for 10 months after starting treatment, compared with 6.4 months for those in a control group.

- **Vemurafenib** (Zelboraf) may double the survival time of patients with advanced melanoma. It works by targeting a mutation in the BRAF V600E gene, which is present in about 50% of melanoma patients. Researchers who conducted a study published in *The New England Journal of Medicine* found that more than half of patients who took the medication had at least a 30% reduction in tumor size. In about one-third of patients, the medication slowed or stopped the progression of the cancer.

- **Combination treatment.** Each of these medications attacks tumors in different ways. They can be used in tandem for better results. For example, a patient might start by taking the first drug, then, when it stops working, he/she can switch to the second drug. This approach can potentially extend survival by up to a year.

Both drugs can have serious side effects. For now, they're recommended only for a select group of patients.

SELF-PROTECTION

Take steps to protect yourself…

• **Check your skin monthly.** It's been estimated that deaths from melanoma could be reduced by 60% if everyone would do a monthly skin exam to look for suspicious changes. Look for asymmetric moles in which one part is distinctly different from the other part…moles with an irregular border…color variations…a diameter greater than 6 millimeters (mm), about one-quarter inch…or changes in appearance over time.

• **Get a yearly checkup with a dermatologist.** It's nearly impossible to self-inspect all of the areas on your body where melanoma can appear. I advise patients to see a dermatologist every year for full-body mapping. The doctor will make a note (or photograph) of every suspicious area and track the areas over time.

Important: New moles rarely appear in people over the age of 40. A mole that appears in patients 40 years and older is assumed to be cancer until tests show otherwise.

• **Use a lot of sunscreen.** Even though melanoma isn't caused only by sun exposure, don't get careless. Apply a sunscreen with an SPF of at least 30 whenever you go outdoors. Use a lot of sunscreen—it takes about two ounces of sunscreen (about the amount in a shot glass) to protect against skin cancer. Reapply it about every two hours or immediately after getting out of the water.

• **Don't use tanning salons.** Researchers who published a study in *Journal of the National Cancer Institute* found that people who got their tans at tanning salons—that use tanning lamps and tanning beds that emit UV radiation—at least once a month were 55% more likely to develop a malignant melanoma than those who didn't artificially tan.

Pain or Itching Could Be Skin Cancer

Pain or itching can be signs of skin cancer. People often are told to be on the lookout for visual changes to their skin, but it is important not to overlook changes in how skin feels.

Recent findings: More than one-third of skin cancer lesions itch—these can be a sign of basal cell carcinoma. About 30% are painful, and these can indicate squamous cell carcinoma.

Gil Yosipovitch, MD, is chair of dermatology at Temple University School of Medicine and director of Temple Itch Center, both in Philadelphia, and leader of a study published in *JAMA Dermatology.*

Better Esophageal Cancer Treatment

In a study of 178 early-stage esophageal cancer patients, the five-year rate of death (about 20%) was comparable whether patients had their esophagus removed (esophagectomy) or the malignant cells shaved off through a scope inserted into the esophagus (endoscopic mucosal resection).

Advantage: The endoscopic procedure is performed on an outpatient basis, while esophagectomy typically requires a one-week hospitalization and has a 30% to 50% rate of complications (such as lifelong dietary restrictions).

If diagnosed with esophageal cancer: Ask your doctor about the endoscopic procedure.

Ganapathy Prasad, MD, consultant, department of gastroenterology and hepatology, Mayo Clinic, Rochester, Minnesota.

Wheat Germ Seed for Cancer

Mark A. Stengler, NMD, licensed naturopathic medical doctor in private practice, Stengler Center for Integrative Medicine, Encinitas, California...adjunct associate clinical professor at the National College of Natural Medicine, Portland, Oregon...author of many books, including *The Natural Physician's Healing Therapies* and coauthor of *Prescription for Natural Cures. MarkStengler.com*

The vast majority of products that are promoted on the Internet to "cure cancer" are scams. When you look carefully at these products, you will find that they have not been studied in clinical trials, and with those that have been, the tests were done in the laboratory or with animals but not humans.

Several reputable natural products have been studied and do have anticancer properties, such as fermented wheat germ extract (from the wheat germ seed), which has been found to promote cancer cell destruction...Coriolus versicolor (a mushroom used in Japan and China) and maitake (a Japanese mushroom), which both have been found to aid cancer regression and ease the effects of chemotherapy. This does not mean that these remedies cure cancer on their own. Instead, certain natural remedies are most wisely used as a component of a multifaceted, integrated approach to cancer treatment. In fact, the majority of cancer patients who come to see me for natural treatments also receive conventional cancer therapy, such as chemotherapy, surgery and radiation.

Keep Cancer from Coming Back

Julie K. Silver, MD, who cofounded Oncology Rehab Partners, a Northborough, Massachusetts–based firm that trains and certifies hospitals and cancer centers in evidence-based cancer rehabilitation, and developed its Survivorship Training and Rehabilitation (STAR) Program. Dr. Silver is the author of *After Cancer Treatment: Heal Faster, Better, Stronger. StarProgramOncologyRehab.com*

This year, an estimated 1.4 million Americans will be diagnosed with cancer. The primary cancer therapies—surgery, chemotherapy and/or radiation—are more effective than ever before, but these powerful weapons often leave cancer survivors weak and exhausted.

Until recently, doctors told cancer patients to go home following treatment and wait—sometimes for weeks or months—for their bodies to recover.

Now: Cancer specialists and physiatrists (doctors trained in rehabilitation medicine) have identified the best ways for cancer survivors to achieve a faster, fuller recovery—and perhaps even improve their odds against a recurrence.

As a physiatrist, I have worked with thousands of cancer survivors. But in 2003, when I was diagnosed with breast cancer, I experienced firsthand the debilitating effects of lifesaving cancer therapies. Medical research and my personal experience have convinced me that a positive outlook...supportive family and friends...a strong spiritual life...and effective pain relief all aid recovery.

How to have an even greater impact on cancer recovery...

EAT THE RIGHT FOODS

While attacking malignant tumors, chemotherapy and radiation treatments also kill normal cells. Your diet plays a crucial role in helping your body heal and replace lost and damaged tissue. *In addition to eating at least five daily servings of vegetables and fruits... whole grains at most meals...and legumes at least once daily, be sure your diet includes...**

- **Protein.** During treatment and for several weeks afterward, increase your intake of protein. It helps prevent infection and repair damaged cells. How much protein do you need? Divide your weight in half and eat that many grams of protein daily.

Example: If you weigh 150 pounds, aim for 75 g daily.

Best protein sources: Fish, poultry, eggs and low-fat dairy products. Protein from plant sources, including most beans, nuts and seeds, also aids healing by providing cancer-fighting phytochemicals.

*If your cancer therapy makes you tired or nauseated, it is best to start these practices after your treatment ends.

• **Organic foods.** The potential danger of pesticides is still being debated. But why take a chance? While your body is healing, protect it from potentially toxic pesticides by choosing organic fruits, vegetables and meats. (Look for "certified organic" on the label.)

While increasing your intake of the foods mentioned earlier, it's equally important to avoid...

• **Soy.** Soy and chickpeas, as well as licorice and tea (black and green), are rich sources of plant chemicals known as flavonoids, which may contain components that resemble the hormone estrogen. In many people, these foods help fight a variety of diseases, including some types of cancer, but if you have a hormone-dependent tumor, such as a breast or prostate malignancy, it's best to avoid flavonoid-rich foods.

• **Alcohol.** Relatively small amounts of alcohol have been linked to some types of malignancies, including colon, pancreatic and breast cancer. Limit your intake of alcohol to social occasions, or abstain altogether.

STAY ACTIVE

Exercise improves mood, and there's increasing evidence that it also reduces the risk for breast, colon and possibly prostate cancer—and may help prevent a recurrence of these malignancies. *Your exercise program should include...*

• **Cardiovascular exercise.** Even while you're undergoing treatment, start using a pedometer to track how far you walk. These devices, which cost $15 or more at most sporting-goods stores, record the number of steps you take throughout the day.

Smart idea: Write down your daily step total (a mile equals about 2,000 steps) and aim to increase it by 10% a week until you reach 10,000 steps, or five miles a day.

When you feel strong enough, begin formal workout sessions. Use a treadmill and/or stationary exercise bike—or simply take brisk walks or swim. The American Cancer Society recommends working up to a 30-minute moderate-intensity workout (the equivalent of brisk walking), five days a week. Forty-five minute workouts may be even more beneficial.

Important: If you were active before your cancer diagnosis, aim for your earlier fitness level. If you were sedentary, simply try to exercise regularly for whatever period of time you are able to do so.

Helpful: Several shorter sessions each day—for example, three 10-minute sessions of brisk walking—may be less tiring than a single sustained workout.

• **Strength training.** Lifting weights or using resistance-type exercise machines, such as those made by Nautilus or Cybex, rebuilds muscle mass that is lost during inactivity and treatment, strengthens the bones and immune system, and improves balance.

Strength training should be performed two to three times per week to allow time for your muscles to recover between sessions.

During each workout...

• **Focus on all major muscle groups and on strengthening your "core" (middle section of the body)**—the core muscles support the rest of your body.

• **Find the maximum weight you can lift 10 times**—your "10 RM" (repetition maximum). Start by lifting 50% of this amount 10 times. Rest for one to two minutes or longer, then lift 60% of the same weight 10 times. After another one- to two-minute rest, lift 80% of the weight 10 times. Increase the weight as you grow stronger—a reasonable goal is 10% per week until you reach a plateau.

• **Flexibility exercises.** This type of exercise is less important than cardiovascular and strength training, but it will improve comfort and mobility, and make you more resilient and less prone to injury.

Tai chi and yoga are good forms of stretching exercise if you avoid movements that are painful.

Important: Before you start an exercise program, check with your doctor and consider working with a physical therapist or personal trainer. To avoid fatigue and injury, listen to your body. If you feel you're doing too much, cut back.

Although unstructured physical activity—for example, walking from your car to the mall, taking the stairs or gardening—is usually good for health, it provides less benefit than regular, structured exercise. Preserve your energy for exercise sessions by avoiding activities that tire you.

GET ENOUGH REST

Poor sleep compounds the fatigue that often follows radiation and chemotherapy. Research shows that sleep is vital to the cells and chemicals of the immune system, fortifying the body against infection and cancer growth.

Helpful: Plan for seven to eight hours of sleep a night, and follow the rules of "sleep hygiene"...

- **Avoid heavy meals and limit fluids within two to three hours of going to bed.** Stop drinking caffeine and alcohol (if you drink it) four to six hours before bedtime.
- **To "train" your body to sleep, go to bed and get up at the same time each day—including the weekend.**
- **Keep your bedroom dark and quiet, at a comfortable temperature.**
- **Don't watch television,** play computer games or exercise within one to two hours of going to bed. Allow an hour to unwind with music, reading, quiet conversation or a warm bath.

If worries about your health keep you awake, try meditation or relaxation exercises to lower anxiety. Talk out your concerns with friends and family. Counseling can teach you techniques to ease worrying.

If you find yourself sleeping more than 10 hours a night, tell your doctor—this could indicate depression or an underlying health problem. And if you have trouble falling asleep or staying asleep, ask your doctor about sleep aids (including natural remedies, such as low-dose melatonin).

Five Supplements That Help Prevent Cancer Recurrence

Lise N. Alschuler, ND, board-certified naturopathic oncologist in practice at Naturopathic Specialists in Scottsdale, Arizona. A breast cancer survivor, she is coauthor of *The Definitive Guide to Thriving After Cancer: A Five-Step Integrative Plan to Reduce the Risk of Recurrence and Build Lifelong Health. DrLise.net*

It's a top question on the minds of many cancer survivors: What will help keep the cancer from coming back? Unfortunately, conventional medicine often doesn't have much of an answer beyond, "Take care of yourself, and try not to worry." Naturopathic medicine, however, does have some specific recommendations for cancer survivors—and dietary supplements play a key role.

The reason: "Dietary supplements are able to fit into the 'nooks and crannies' of our biochemical pathways, creating specific changes that influence our bodies on a cellular level," said Lise Alschuler, ND, a breast cancer survivor and coauthor of *The Definitive Guide to Thriving After Cancer.*

The five supplements listed below comprise what Dr. Alschuler calls a "foundational supplement plan" for just about every cancer survivor—and for just about every person who wants to reduce the odds of ever getting cancer in the first place. *Each of the five supplements helps reduce cancer risk through five key pathways...*

- **Boosting immune system function**
- **Reducing inflammation**
- **Improving insulin sensitivity**
- **Supporting digestion and detoxification**
- **Reducing stress-induced hormone imbalances**

Although dietary supplements are available over-the-counter, before you start taking them, it is essential to check with a naturopathic doctor (ideally one with additional board certification in naturopathic oncology) or an integrative medical doctor with specific expertise in integrative cancer care. These providers have training in nutritional biochemistry as it relates to cancer. They can confirm that the following supplements are appropriate for you and determine the dosages and the specific brands that will best suit your needs.

For her own post-cancer patients, Dr. Alschuler typically prescribes all five of the following supplements, to be taken daily starting as soon as conventional treatment is completed. "Some patients may be advised to start taking some of these supplements during their conventional treatment, but that should be done only under the guidance of an integrative health-care physician," she said.

The top five cancer fighters include…

• **Omega-3 fatty acids.** These essential fatty acids—found in supplements of fish oil, flaxseed oil and algae-based oil—positively influence all five of the key pathways mentioned above. However, they are especially important for reducing chronic inflammation, which is one of the precursors of cancer. "Think of inflammation as a burning ember in your body that can change your tissues in ways that favor the growth of abnormal cells. Omega-3s quench that fire," Dr. Alschuler said.

Though omega-3s are helpful for survivors of all types of cancer, studies show particular benefits for patients who have battled colon, prostate, breast or lung cancer. A typical daily dosage is 1,000 mg to 3,000 mg of omega-3 oil.

Caveat: Omega-3s can increase bleeding, so it's vital to get your doctor's OK before taking omega-3s if you are on blood-thinning medication or are anticipating any surgery.

• **Probiotics.** Beneficial bacteria in the intestinal tract help metabolize nutrients, bind waste products for removal in stool and regulate immunity. When beneficial bacteria are depleted, the digestive tract is overrun with harmful bacteria and a condition called dysbiosis develops. This negatively impacts all five of the body's key pathways, contributing to an increased risk for cancer recurrence. Studies have shown that supplementing with beneficial intestinal bacteria called probiotics can reduce the risk for infection after surgery and improve the immune system's response.

You can get some probiotics from eating yogurt and fermented foods such as fresh sauerkraut, miso, tempeh and kefir. However, to fully support her patients' beneficial digestive bacteria, Dr. Alschuler typically prescribes a supplement that combines several types of probiotics at a dosage of at least one billion colony-forming units (CFU) daily.

Caution: Probiotics are not appropriate for people whose white blood cell count is below normal—some evidence suggests that probiotics can increase the risk for blood infection in those individuals.

• **Polyphenols.** Healthful, colorful fruits and vegetables get their rainbow hues from the naturally occurring plant compounds called polyphenols (also referred to as flavonoids). According to Dr. Alschuler, three polyphenols are particularly important in the fight against cancer…

• Green tea catechins, which may lower the risk for cancers of the digestive tract, breast, bladder, lung, blood and prostate.

• Curcumin, the bright yellow flavonoid found in turmeric root, which appears to inhibit cancer formation in a variety of ways, helping protect against the majority of cancer types.

• Resveratrol, which gives color to red grapes and some berries, has shown promise against breast, colorectal and liver cancers by activating tumor suppressor genes and increasing the rate of apoptosis (normal programmed cell death).

Your doctor may prescribe a combination supplement that contains all three of these polyphenols, or you may take each one separately. "Many high-quality brands also include other polyphenols. But watch out for what I call 'window-dressing' supplements that list 20 to 30 different polyphenols—because the amount of each one will be so small that you might as well just eat a salad," Dr. Alschuler said.

• **Antioxidants.** "Look at metal that's been exposed to rain and sunlight—it starts to rust because it's being oxidized. That's essentially what happens to our bodies from exposure to 'free radicals,' or oxidative toxins," Dr. Alschuler said. Antioxidants guard against this by binding to oxidative toxins so they can be eliminated…and they also stimulate cell repair and normal apoptosis. Cancer treatment can deplete your antioxidant capacity because cancer drugs themselves exert their cancer-killing effects via oxidation. *A plant-based diet provides antioxidants, but cancer survivors should get additional support by taking...*

• **Glutathione,** the body's "master antioxidant," which is critical for the elimination of environmental toxins. A typical dosage is 250 mg to 500 mg daily.

• **Coenzyme Q10 (CoQ10),** which is associated with decreased risk for breast and thyroid cancer, as well as melanoma, studies show. A typical daily dosage is 30 mg to 100 mg.

• **Vitamin D.** Numerous studies have shown the cancer-preventing potential of this vitamin, which promotes proper cell maturation and regulates inflammation, among other activities. "Without adequate levels of vitamin D, it's hard for our bodies to maintain good blood sugar control or reduce inflammation," said Dr. Alschuler.

Although it's often called the sunshine vitamin, many people in the northern hemisphere cannot get enough vitamin D just from being outdoors, especially during cooler seasons. Ask your doctor to measure your blood level of vitamin D—that information will help determine the right dosage for you.

Caution: If you take the heart medication digoxin, be especially sure to talk with your doctor before taking vitamin D because the combination could lead to abnormal heart rhythms.

Important: "Dietary supplements are called 'supplements' for a reason—they are meant to supplement the diet, not to replace healthy eating," Dr. Alschuler said. "Over time, they provide targeted molecular support that gently but radically alters the terrain in your body, creating an environment that impedes cancer recurrence...so you can get back to the business of living your life."

After Cancer: You Really Can Get Back to Normal

Julie K. Silver, MD, who cofounded Oncology Rehab Partners, a Northborough, Massachusetts–based firm that trains and certifies hospitals and cancer centers in evidence-based cancer rehabilitation, and developed its Survivorship Training and Rehabilitation (STAR) Program. Dr. Silver is the author of *After Cancer Treatment: Heal Faster, Better, Stronger. StarProgramOncologyRehab.com*

Until relatively recently, there was no such thing as "cancer rehab" to help cancer patients cope with the grueling and sometimes lasting physical and psychological effects of chemotherapy, radiation, surgery or other treatment.

Now: Just as patients who have suffered a heart attack or stroke are likely to receive guidance on how to cope with the aftereffects of treatment, more and more cancer patients are beginning to get the help they need to regain the quality of life they had before getting sick.

Who can benefit: Of the 12.6 million cancer survivors in the US, an estimated 3.3 million continue to suffer physical consequences of their treatment, such as fatigue and/or chronic pain...and another 1.4 million live with mental health problems, such as depression and/or a form of mild cognitive impairment known as "chemo brain."

Latest development: As cancer rehab becomes more prevalent throughout the US—hundreds of facilities nationwide offer such programs—there is mounting evidence showing how this type of care can help accelerate recovery, improve a patient's quality of life and perhaps even reduce risk for cancer recurrence.* In fact, the American College of Surgeons' Commission on Cancer now requires cancer centers in the US to offer rehab services in order to receive accreditation.

WHEN CANCER REHAB HELPS

Even though it was first conceived as a resource for patients immediately after their acute phase of treatment, cancer rehab can help long after treatment has taken place. For

*To find a medical center near you that offers cancer rehab services, consult Oncology Rehab Partners, *StarProgramOncologyRehab.com*

example, people who were treated years ago and are now cancer-free—but not free of side effects from treatment—can benefit from cancer rehab. Just because you went for, say, physical therapy two years ago after you finished cancer treatment, it doesn't mean that you can't get more help now for the same problem or a different one.

Insurance picks up the tab: Because the benefits of cancer rehab are now so widely accepted, insurance generally covers the cost—regardless of when you were treated for cancer—including consultations with physiatrists (medical doctors who specialize in rehabilitation medicine), physical therapists, occupational therapists, speech language pathologists and others.

Even though cancer rehab therapies tend to be short term (typically requiring two to three sessions weekly in the provider's office for a period of a few weeks), insurance plans often limit the number of visits for such therapies. Be sure to check with your insurer for details on your coverage.

Each cancer patient's situation is different, but here are some common problems and how they are treated with cancer rehab…

MILD COGNITIVE IMPAIRMENT ("CHEMO BRAIN")

Cancer patients who have received chemotherapy often complain that they don't think as well and that they have less energy and decreased attention spans. If anxiety or hot flashes due to chemo interfere with sleep, that can decrease cognitive functioning, too.

How cancer rehab helps: A physical therapist might work with a cancer patient by using a specific therapeutic exercise plan. Exercise has been shown to improve cognitive functioning—perhaps by improving blood flow to the brain.

An occupational therapist or speech therapist may recommend strategies to help concentration, attention and memory. This may involve computer-based programs that improve short-term memory.

ANEMIA AND FATIGUE

Anemia is common with many hematological (blood) cancers, such as leukemia and lymphomas.

How cancer rehab helps: In a young person who has just undergone a bone marrow transplant, for example, if there is a low red blood cell count (an indicator of anemia) or a risk for infection, a tailored exercise program can build strength and endurance to help fight fatigue.

For an older adult, exercise is also a key part of a fatigue-fighting regimen that improves endurance and overall fitness. If fatigue results in problems with balance and gait, an occupational therapist can help the patient remain independent at home by suggesting a smartphone-based monitoring device such as a motion sensor that notifies a family member or friend if the patient falls.

BREATHING PROBLEMS

Difficulty breathing and feeling short of breath are common problems in lung cancer survivors. These patients also may experience pain after surgery and have trouble exercising and performing their usual daily activities due to shortness of breath.

How cancer rehab helps: In addition to improving strength and physical performance through targeted exercises, a cancer patient who is having breathing problems would need to improve his/her ability to get more air into the lungs. This may involve "belly breathing" exercises that will allow him to complete his daily activities without getting out of breath so quickly.

CANCER "PREHAB" CAN HELP, TOO

Cancer "prehab" is useful during the window after a patient is diagnosed with cancer but before treatment begins to help boost his/her physical and emotional readiness for cancer treatment. A nutrition program may be used to improve a patient's nutritional status before treatments that may sap appetite or lead to nutrition problems such as anemia. Working with a psychologist can help identify and deal with anxiety and stress before treatment starts. Cancer prehab usually is offered at centers that provide cancer rehab services.

5

Chronic Pain

Best Pain Relievers for Headache, Arthritis, Backache, More

Most of us turn to *acetaminophen* (Tylenol) and *ibuprofen* (Advil, Motrin) for pain relief—but there can be more effective approaches, including combining conventional and natural pain relievers.

Caution: Check with your doctor before taking any new medication or supplement.

ARTHRITIS

There are two types of arthritis—osteoarthritis, in which cartilage between bones wears away...and rheumatoid arthritis, an autoimmune disease that inflames joints. For relief, people with either type often take nonsteroidal anti-inflammatory drugs (NSAIDs), such as aspirin, ibuprofen and *naproxen* (Aleve, Naprosyn)—but 16,000 Americans die annually from side effects of these drugs. Another estimated 55,000 died from taking the recalled Vioxx, Bextra and other COX-2 inhibitors (a class of NSAIDs). *Instead, try...*

FOR OSTEOARTHRITIS

- **Glucosamine sulfate.** Take 1,500 milligrams (mg) of this supplement—made from chitin, which is derived from shellfish—with 3 grams (g) a day of methylsulfonylmethane (MSM), a natural substance in the human body. These nutrients repair cartilage, reducing arthritis pain within six weeks. For maximum tissue repair, take these supplements for two to five months. For chronic arthritis, you may continue for up to a year.
- **Lidoderm.** Put a patch, available by prescription, on the joint. It contains the anesthetics Novocain and Lidocaine. Wear it for about 12 hours a day (one lasts that long) for two to six weeks. For a large area, some people may

Jacob Teitelbaum, MD, director of The Annapolis Center for Effective CFS/Fibromyalgia Therapies in Maryland. For 25 years, he has researched ways to relieve pain. He is author of *Pain Free 1-2-3!* and *From Fatigued to Fantastic! EndFatigue.com* use as many as four patches (the package says three). Many patients experience a 30% to 50% decrease in pain within two weeks.

• **Willow bark and Boswellia.** These herbs are as effective as Vioxx and Motrin. Take 240 milligrams (mg) of willow bark and 1,000 mg of Boswellia daily. It can take six weeks to work. For chronic arthritis, you may need to take these for up to a year to feel the full effect.

For rheumatoid arthritis...

• **Fish oil.** Studies show that fish oil (one to two tablespoons a day for at least three months) can reduce inflammation and pain. Eskimo-3, available at health-food stores, and Enzymatic Therapy (800-783-2286, *www.enzymatictherapy.com*) don't have the high levels of mercury that may be present in other brands. Keep taking the fish oil after the pain is gone as a preventive measure.

BACK PAIN

Back pain can occur for no apparent reason and at any point on your spine.

• **Lidoderm.** For low-back pain, apply a Lidoderm patch in the morning and remove it in the evening. Expect relief in two to six weeks.

• **Colchicine.** About 70% of back pain can be eliminated without surgery, with six intravenous injections of the gout medicine colchicine. It enters the space between the discs of the vertebrae and reduces inflammation. Colchicine's main risk is a rare but severe allergic reaction (similar to that caused by penicillin).

CARPAL TUNNEL SYNDROME

When a nerve passing under a ligament through two bones in the wrist becomes swollen and pinched, it causes pain, numbness and tingling in the hand or forearm. For relief...

• **Vitamin B6 and thyroid hormone.** Take 250 mg a day of B6. Also ask your doctor about a prescription for natural thyroid hormone. The combination of B6 and thyroid hormone decreases swelling and usually clears up the problem after six to 12 weeks. You can stay on this treatment for six months to prevent recurrence. During treatment, wear a wrist splint at night and, if possible, during the day.

HEADACHES

Tension headaches begin and end gradually. They can last for minutes or sometimes hours. The pain comes from tightened muscles across the forehead and/or at the base of the skull.

Ultram (*tramadol hydrochloride*) is an often-overlooked but effective prescription pain reliever. Take up to 100 mg as many as four times a day.

Migraines—severe headaches that may be preceded by lights flashing before your eyes and accompanied by nausea, vomiting, sweating and dizziness—can last for hours, even days. Natural remedies are more effective than prescription drugs at preventing migraines...

Butterbur, from the butterbur plant, can prevent—and even eliminate—migraines. Take 50 mg three times a day for one month, then one 50-mg dose twice a day to prevent attacks. Take 100 mg every three hours to eliminate an acute migraine. Use only high-quality brands, such as Enzymatic Therapy (800-783-2286, *www.enzymatictherapy.com*) and Integrative Therapeutics' Petadolex (800-931-1709, *www.integrativeinc.com*).

• **Sumatriptan (Imitrex).** When a migraine is developing, 75% of patients experience tenderness and pain around the eyes. Sumatriptan knocks out 93% of migraines when taken before the pain around the eyes occurs. When it is taken later, it helps in only 13% of cases. Therefore, if you have a migraine, it is best to take sumatriptan within the first five to 20 minutes.

• **Magnesium.** In the doctor's office or the hospital emergency room, intravenous magnesium can eliminate a migraine in five minutes.

IRRITABLE BOWEL SYNDROME

Irritable bowel syndrome (IBS), also known as spastic colon, is a digestive disorder characterized by bloating, abdominal cramps and diarrhea and/or constipation. *Consider...*

• **Peppermint oil.** For symptomatic relief, take one or two enteric-coated peppermint oil capsules three times a day. Peppermint oil decreases spasms of the bowel muscles. Effective brands include Enzymatic Therapy (800-783-2286, *www.enzymatictherapy.com*)

and Mentharil, available at most health-food stores.

• **Hyoscyamine** (Anaspaz, Levsin). Take this prescription antispasmodic as needed. It relaxes the muscular contractions of the stomach and intestines. Dosages range from 0.125 mg to 0.375 mg, taken 30 to 60 minutes before a meal.

SHINGLES

This itchy, blistering rash—from herpes zoster, the virus associated with chicken pox—strikes in middle or old age and usually afflicts one side of the upper body. The virus affects the nerves, so it can leave victims in chronic pain, a condition called postherpetic neuralgia (PHN). *Discuss these options with your doctor...*

• **Ketamine.** This prescription anesthetic can decrease shingles pain within days in 65% of cases. Apply a gel of 5% ketamine two to three times daily to the painful area.

• **Lidoderm.** Place a patch over the area of maximum pain.

• **Neurontin.** This prescription medication also can reduce pain. To avoid side effects, start with 100 mg to 300 mg, one to four times a day.

• **Tricyclic antidepressant.** A prescription tricyclic such as *amitriptyline* can relieve nerve pain. To avoid side effects, use a low dose of 10 mg to 50 mg.

More Natural Ways to Curb Your Pain

Mark A. Stengler, NMD, licensed naturopathic medical doctor in private practice, Stengler Center for Integrative Medicine, Encinitas, California...adjunct associate clinical professor at the National College of Natural Medicine, Portland, Oregon...author of many books, including *The Natural Physician's Healing Therapies* and coauthor of *Prescription for Natural Cures. MarkStengler.com*

Not long ago, a 60-year-old woman came to my office suffering from severe arthritis pain in both hands. I gave her a bean-sized dab of a homeopathic gel that she applied directly to the skin on her hands. After a few applications in the span of 30 minutes, her pain was reduced by 90%. She did not need to apply the gel again for two weeks.

I witnessed a similar result with a retired National Football League player. He had severe chronic hip pain from past injuries. With one application of the gel, his pain was relieved by 70% for two full days.

The relief that these people experienced has given them each a new lease on life. But here's the best news—unlike pharmaceutical pain relievers, which often cause gastrointestinal upset or damage to internal organs, natural therapies can reduce pain without adverse effects.

WHAT ARE YOU TAKING FOR PAIN?

Most Americans take too many pharmaceutical pain relievers. An estimated 175 million American adults take over-the-counter (OTC) pain relievers regularly. About one-fifth of Americans in their 60s take at least one painkiller for chronic pain on a regular basis.

People who use painkillers on a regular basis are at risk of dangerous side effects. For instance, people who rely on acetaminophen increase their risk of developing stomach ulcers, liver disease and kidney disease. If you regularly take Celebrex or an OTC nonsteroidal anti-inflammatory drug (NSAID), such as aspirin or *naproxen* (Aleve), you run the risk of kidney and stomach damage. Regular use of NSAIDs also increases risk of heart attack, according to the FDA.

BETTER RESULTS, FEWER RISKS

Before you take any remedy, it's important for your doctor to identify what is causing your pain. What if your back hurts? You may need a pain reliever—but back pain also can be a signal that you're harming your body by bending or sitting the wrong way. You may need to address the underlying cause to prevent further injury. Pain receptors are found in the skin, around bones and joints—even in the walls of arteries. If a muscle is torn, for example, a pain signal is released from fibers in the shredded tissue.

In light of the dangers from prescription and OTC drugs, what safe alternatives are available to you? There are many natural supplements that I recommend.

NATURE'S PAIN RELIEVERS

If you take prescription or OTC pain medication, work with a naturopathic physician, holistic medical doctor or chiropractor who will incorporate natural pain fighters into your treatment regimen. With his/her help, you may be able to reduce your dosage of pain medication (natural pain relievers can be used safely with prescription or OTC painkillers)—or even eliminate the drugs altogether.

Natural pain-fighting supplements are even more effective when combined with physical therapies, such as acupuncture, chiropractic, magnet therapy or osteopathic manipulation (a technique in which an osteopathic physician uses his hands to move a patient's muscles and joints with stretching, gentle pressure and resistance). Physiotherapy (treatment that uses physical agents, such as exercise and massage, to develop, maintain and restore movement and functional ability) also is helpful.

Here are—in no special order—the best natural pain relievers, which can be taken alone or in combination...

• **White willow bark extract is great for headaches, arthritis, muscle aches and fever.** In Europe, doctors prescribe this herbal remedy for back pain, and recent research supports this use. One study conducted in Haifa, Israel, involved 191 patients with chronic low-back pain who took one of two doses of willow bark extract or a placebo daily for four weeks. Researchers found that 39% of patients taking the higher dose of willow bark extract had complete pain relief, compared with only 6% of those taking a placebo. The participants who benefited the most took willow bark extract that contained 240 mg of the compound salicin, the active constituent in this herbal remedy. (Aspirin is made from acetylsalicylic acid, which has many of the chemical properties of salicin.) However, aspirin can cause gastrointestinal ulceration and other side effects, including kidney damage. Willow bark extract is believed to work by inhibiting naturally occurring enzymes that cause inflammation and pain.

I recommend taking willow bark extract that contains 240 mg of salicin daily. In rare cases, willow bark extract can cause mild stomach upset. Don't take willow bark if you have a history of ulcers, gastritis or kidney disease. It also should not be taken by anyone who is allergic to aspirin. As with aspirin, willow bark extract should never be given to children under age 12 who have a fever—in rare instances, it can cause a fatal disease called Reye's syndrome. Willow bark extract has blood-thinning properties, so avoid it if you take a blood thinner, such as *warfarin* (Coumadin). For low-back pain, you may need to take willow bark extract for a week or more before you get results.

• **Methylsulfonylmethane (MSM)** is a popular nutritional supplement that relieves muscle and joint pain. According to Stanley Jacob, MD, former professor at Oregon Health & Science University who has conducted much of the original research on MSM, this supplement reduces inflammation by improving blood flow. Your cells have receptors that send out pain signals when they're deprived of blood. That's why increased blood flow diminishes pain.

MSM, a natural compound found in green vegetables, fruits and grains, reduces muscle spasms and softens painful scar tissue from previous injuries. A double-blind study of 50 people with osteoarthritis of the knee found that MSM helps relieve arthritis pain.

Start with a daily dose of 3,000 mg to 5,000 mg of MSM. If your pain and/or inflammation doesn't improve within five days, increase the dose up to 8,000 mg daily, taken in several doses throughout the day. If you develop digestive upset or loose stools, reduce the dosage. If you prefer, you can apply MSM cream (per the label instructions) to your skin at the painful area. This product is available at health-food stores and works well for localized pain. MSM has a mild blood-thinning effect, so check with your doctor if you take a blood thinner.

• **S-adenosylmethionine (SAMe)** is a natural compound found in the body. The supplement is an effective treatment for people who have osteoarthritis accompanied by cartilage degeneration. SAMe's ability to reduce pain, stiffness and swelling is similar to that of NSAIDs such as ibuprofen and naproxen, and the anti-inflammatory medication Celebrex. There's also evidence that SAMe stimulates cartilage repair, which helps prevent bones from rubbing against one another. A 16-week study conducted at the University of California, Irvine, compared two groups of people who were being treated for knee pain caused by osteoarthritis. Some took 1,200 mg of SAMe daily, while others took 200 mg of Celebrex. It took longer for people to get relief from SAMe, but by the second month, SAMe proved to be just as effective as Celebrex.

Most patients with osteoarthritis and fibromyalgia (a disorder characterized by widespread pain in muscles, tendons and ligaments) who take SAMe notice improvement within four to eight weeks. Many studies use 1,200 mg of SAMe daily in divided doses. In my experience, taking 400 mg twice daily works well. It's a good idea to take a multivitamin or 50-mg B-complex supplement daily while you're taking SAMe. The vitamin B-12 and folic acid contained in either supplement help your body metabolize SAMe, which means that the remedy goes to work faster.

- **Kaprex is effective for mild pain caused by injury or osteoarthritis.** It is a blend of hops, rosemary extract and oleanic acid, which is derived from olive leaf extract. Rather than blocking the body's pain-causing enzymes, these natural substances inhibit pain-causing chemicals called prostaglandins.

In a study sponsored by the Institute for Functional Medicine, the research arm of the supplement manufacturer Metagenics, taking Kaprex for six weeks reduced minor pain by as much as 72%. I recommend taking one 440-mg tablet three times daily. Kaprex is manufactured by Metagenics (800-692-9400, *www.metagenics.com*), the institute's product branch. The product is sold only in doctors' offices. To find a practitioner in your area who sells Kaprex, call the toll-free number. Kaprex has no known side effects and does not interact with other medications.

- **Proteolytic enzymes, including bromelain, trypsin, chymotrypsin, pancreatin, papain** and a range of protein-digesting enzymes derived from the fermentation of fungus, reduce pain and inflammation by improving blood flow. You can find these natural pain fighters at health-food stores in products labeled "proteolytic enzymes." Take as directed on the label. Bromelain, a favorite of athletes, is available on its own. Extracted from pineapple stems, bromelain reduces swelling by breaking down blood clots that can form as a result of trauma and impede circulation. It works well for bruises, sprains and surgical recovery. If you use bromelain, take 500 mg three times daily between meals.

Repair is a high-potency formula of proteolytic enzymes that I often recommend. It is manufactured by Enzymedica (to find a retailer, call 888-918-1118 or go to *www.enzymedica.com*). Take two capsules two to three times daily between meals. Don't take Repair or any proteolytic enzyme formula if you have an active ulcer or gastritis. Any enzyme product can have a mild blood-thinning effect, so check with your doctor if you take a blood thinner.

Pain Med is the homeopathic gel that gave such quick relief to the patients I described at the beginning of this article. It is remarkably effective for relieving the pain of arthritis, muscle soreness and spasms, sprains, strains, stiffness, headaches (especially due to tension) as well as injuries, including bruises.

Pain Med is a combination of nine highly diluted plant and flower materials, including arnica, bryonia, hypericum and ledum. Like other homeopathic remedies, it promotes the body's ability to heal itself. A bean-sized dab works well for anyone who has pain. It should be spread on the skin around the affected area. Following an injury, use it every 15 minutes, for a total of up to four applications. As the pain starts to diminish, apply less often. Do not reapply the gel once the pain is gone. Pain Med does not sting, burn or irritate the skin. It is clear, has no odor, does not stain and dries quickly. Because it has so many uses and works so rapidly, Pain Med is a good first-aid remedy to have on hand. To order, contact the manufacturer, GM International, Inc., at 800-228-9850 or *www.gmipainmed.com.*

Homeopathy and Acupressure for Pain

Mark A. Stengler, NMD, licensed naturopathic medical doctor in private practice, Stengler Center for Integrative Medicine, Encinitas, California...adjunct associate clinical professor at the National College of Natural Medicine, Portland, Oregon...author of many books, including *The Natural Physician's Healing Therapies* and coauthor of *Prescription for Natural Cures. MarkStengler.com*

When something hurts, you want to feel better quickly. Often that means reaching for an over-the-counter or prescription drug. But there are natural pain stoppers that offer the same relief—without the risks.

Caution: Severe pain, or mild pain that gets suddenly worse, can be a sign of a serious injury or other medical problem.

Best: Seek medical attention immediately.

HOW TO USE NATURAL REMEDIES

For each common pain problem discussed here, I give more than one treatment. You may have more success with, or simply prefer, a particular treatment. If something has worked for you in the past, start there. If you don't get much relief from a treatment, try another option. If you get only partial improvement, try adding another supplement. Because natural remedies have a very low risk for serious side effects, it's usually safe to use them in combination with prescription or nonprescription medications, such as for high blood pressure—and over the long run, they can help reduce the need for these drugs entirely. Check with your doctor before starting a natural regimen or changing your drug regimen.

Natural remedies also work well in combination with pain-relieving "body work," such as chiropractic, physical therapy and acupuncture.

HELP A HEADACHE

Migraines and other headaches are often set off by food sensitivities—most commonly, to red wine, caffeine, chocolate and food additives, such as monosodium glutamate. Other triggers, such as lack of sleep or hormonal fluctuations, can also leave you with headache pain.

Best: Pay attention to patterns and avoid your triggers.

Fortunately, headaches are usually very responsive to natural remedies...

- **Mild (tension) headaches.** First, try acupressure. This ancient Chinese technique uses gentle pressure and light massage on specific points.

In traditional Chinese medicine, chi (chee) is the vital energy of all living things. Your chi flows along 12 meridians that run through your body and nourish your tissues. Each meridian is associated with a particular organ, such as the liver or gallbladder. Along each meridian are specific points, designated by numbers, that are the spots where the flow of chi can be affected. *For headaches, the standard acupressure points are...*

- **Gallbladder 20**—the small indentation below the base of the skull, in the space between the two vertical neck muscles. Push gently for 10 to 15 seconds, wait 10 seconds, then repeat five to 10 times.
- **Large intestine 4**—located in the webbing between the thumb and index finger. Push gently for 10 to 15 seconds (as described above). Do this on one hand, then switch to the other.
- **Yuyao**—the indentation in the middle of each eyebrow (straight up from the pupil). Push gently for 10 to 15 seconds (as described above) on both points simultaneously.

If you don't feel relief within several minutes after trying a particular pressure point, move on to a different one.

Another option for mild headaches: A cup of peppermint tea, or a dab of peppermint oil on the temples, can banish a mild headache quickly.

Note: Peppermint essential oil is highly concentrated—don't take it internally.

To brew peppermint tea, make an infusion using one to two teaspoons dried peppermint leaf in eight ounces of boiling water. Let steep for five minutes. You may find relief after one cup. Drink as much and as often as necessary.

• **Migraine headaches.** The herb feverfew has been used effectively for centuries to treat migraines. Take a feverfew capsule standardized to contain 300 micrograms (mcg) of the active ingredient parthenolide every 30 minutes, starting at the onset of symptoms.

Maximum: Four doses daily or until you feel relief.

Prevention: Take a feverfew capsule standardized to contain 300 to 400 mcg of parthenolide—or 30 drops of a standardized tincture, either in a few ounces of water or directly on your tongue, every day. In about three months, you should notice dramatically fewer migraines, and/or less severe symptoms.

Note: Feverfew may thin blood, so consult your doctor if you are taking a blood thinner, such as *warfarin* (Coumadin).

SOOTHE SORE MUSCLES

Natural remedies can help an aching back or sore, cramped muscles. Here, too, acupressure is valuable. Zero in on the points that are most tender and then gently press on them and release, or massage for 10 to 15 seconds, at 10-second intervals, five to 10 times. If you can't reach a spot, have someone do it for you.

For some people, an ice pack on the affected area helps. Others prefer warmth from a hot compress or heating pad. For acute injuries, use cold (within 24 hours). Otherwise, use warmth or alternate warmth and cold. *Other remedies that help sore muscles...*

• **Herbal arnica cream or tincture** can soothe sore muscles and is also great for bruises. It reduces swelling, which helps lessen pain. Rub a small amount on the affected area. Repeat as needed.

Caution: Don't use on broken skin because it is not intended for internal use.

• **Homeopathic Rhus toxicodendron** is especially helpful in relieving low-back pain. Take two pellets of 30C potency twice daily for two or three days.

EASE ARTHRITIC JOINTS

The stiff, swollen joints of osteoarthritis are a major cause of doctors' visits for people over age 45. *But with natural remedies, the pain and joint damage can be kept to a minimum...*

• **Glucosamine sulfate** helps rebuild damaged cartilage in arthritic joints and works as well as or better than many of the drugs doctors recommend. It can take several weeks to feel the benefits. Begin by taking 1,500 to 2,000 mg daily for three months. After that, cut back to 500 to 1,000 mg daily. If symptoms worsen, go back to the higher dose. It's OK to continue with anti-inflammatory drugs, but be sure to tell your doctor if you're using glucosamine.

• **Boswellia,** an herb used in Ayurveda, traditional medicine from India, is a powerful anti-inflammatory that's very helpful for arthritis. Take 1,200 to 1,500 mg of a standardized extract containing 60% to 65% boswellic acids, two to three times daily.

• **Bromelain,** an enzyme derived from pineapple stems, is very effective at reducing pain and swelling. Bromelain supplements come in two designations—MCU (milk-clotting units) and GDU (gelatin-dissolving units). Use either formula, choosing a product that's standardized to either 2,000 MCU per 1,000 mg or 1,200 GDU per 1,000 mg. Take 500 mg three times daily between meals.

Caution: If you take a blood-thinning medication such as warfarin, skip the bromelain—it could thin your blood too much.

Any of these supplements can be used alone or in combination. Natural pain stoppers can be effective alternatives to drugs, but pain is also your body's way of telling you that something is wrong. If your pain is very sudden or severe, and/or accompanied by other symptoms—such as weakness, nausea, redness and swelling in the painful area, shortness of breath or fever—get medical attention immediately.

Conquer Pain Safely

Vijay Vad, MD, a sports medicine physician and researcher specializing in minimally invasive arthritis therapies at the Hospital for Special Surgery in New York City. Dr. Vad is an assistant professor at Weill Medical College of Cornell University and founder of the Vad Foundation, an organization that supports medical research on back pain and arthritis. He is the author of *Stop Pain: Inflammation Relief for an Active Life. VijayVad.com*

What's the first thing you do when you're hurting? If you're like most people, you reach for aspirin, *ibuprofen* (Advil, Motrin), *naproxen* (Aleve) or a similar non-steroidal anti-inflammatory drug (NSAID). Each day, more than 30 million Americans take these popular medications. Another roughly 7 million take a different class of painkiller, *acetaminophen* (Tylenol) each day.

The risks most people don't think about: Even though NSAIDs are as common in most American homes as Band-Aids and multivitamins, few people realize that these medications often cause stomach and intestinal bleeding that leads to up to 20,000 deaths every year in the US. And while previous studies have suggested that these drugs also threaten heart health, an important new meta-analysis found that the risks are more significant than once thought. In fact, ibuprofen and other NSAIDs—taken in doses that many people consider normal—increased the risk for "major vascular events," including heart attacks, by about one-third.

SAFER PAIN RELIEF

The good news is, it's still fine to take an NSAID for arthritis, a headache or other types of short-term pain up to two or three times a week. It is also safe, with your doctor's approval, to take a daily low-dose aspirin (81 mg) to prevent heart attacks and stroke.

What not to do: It is never a good idea to depend on these drugs to relieve chronic pain. As a doctor who specializes in treating arthritis pain, I rarely recommend these medications for long-term use because there are safer analgesics that are just as effective.

My favorite alternatives to oral NSAIDs (ask your doctor which might work best for your pain)...

ANALGESIC CREAMS

You've probably seen over-the-counter pain-relieving creams, such as Zostrix and Capzasin. These products contain capsaicin, which causes a mild burning sensation and appears to reduce substance P, a neurotransmitter that sends pain signals to the brain. Capsaicin products work well for some people suffering from osteoarthritis or rheumatoid arthritis, back pain, shingles and diabetic nerve pain (neuropathy). *Many people, however, get better results from...*

- **Voltaren Gel.** In the heart study mentioned earlier, oral *diclofenac* (Voltaren) was one of the riskiest NSAIDs. But a topical version, Voltaren Gel, which is available by prescription, is less likely to cause side effects, even though it's just as effective as the tablets. Voltaren Gel is good for pain in one joint, but if your pain is in several joints, supplements (see below) will offer more relief.

How it's used: Apply the gel (up to four times a day) to the area that's hurting—for example, your knee or wrist.

Helpful: Apply it after a bath or shower, when your skin is soft. More of the active ingredient will pass through the skin and into the painful area. Voltaren Gel should not be combined with an oral NSAID.

PAIN-FIGHTING SUPPLEMENTS

If you need even more pain relief, consider taking one or more of the following supplements. Start with the first one, and if pain has not decreased after eight weeks, add the second, then wait another eight weeks before adding the third, if necessary.

Important: Be sure to check first with your doctor if you take blood thinners or other medications because they could interact.

- **Curcumin.** There's been a lot of research on the anti-inflammatory and painkilling effects of curcumin (the compound that gives the curry spice turmeric its yellow color). One study found that it reduced pain and improved knee function about as well as ibuprofen.

Typical dose: 1,000 mg, twice daily.

• **Fish oil.** A huge amount of data shows that the omega-3 fatty acids in fish oil have analgesic and anti-inflammatory effects.

Scientific evidence: One study found that 60% of patients with neck, back and joint pain who took fish oil improved so much that they were able to stop taking NSAIDs or other medications.

Typical dose: 2,000 mg daily.

• **Boswellia.** Boswellia (or frankincense) is an herbal medicine that reduces both pain and inflammation. It's effective for all types of joint pain, including osteoarthritis and rheumatoid arthritis.

Scientific evidence: In one study, patients with knee arthritis took boswellia or a placebo for two months, then switched to the opposite treatment for another two months.

Results: The people taking boswellia had less pain and more knee mobility than those taking placebos.

Typical dose: 300 mg to 400 mg, three times daily.

HOW TO USE TYLENOL FOR PAIN

If you prefer an oral medication over the options mentioned above, ask your doctor about switching from NSAIDs to *acetaminophen* (Tylenol). It's not an anti-inflammatory, but it's an effective pain reliever that doesn't cause stomach upset or bleeding—or trigger an increase in cardiovascular risks. I've found that people who limit the dosage of acetaminophen are unlikely to have side effects.

Caution: Taking too much of this drug can lead to liver damage, particularly if it's used by someone who consumes a lot of alcohol or has underlying liver disease, such as hepatitis.

My recommendation: No more than 2,000 mg daily of acetaminophen (this dosage is lower than the limits listed on the label).

Important: In calculating your total daily dose, be sure to factor in all sources of acetaminophen. More than 600 prescription and over-the-counter drugs, including cold and flu medications and allergy drugs, contain the active ingredient acetaminophen. For a partial list of medications that contain acetaminophen, go to *www.knowyourdose.org/common-medications.*

To be safe: Get a liver function test (usually covered by insurance) every six months if you regularly take acetaminophen.

5 Steps to Relieve Chronic Pain Without Drugs

Ingrid Bacci, PhD, a certified craniosacral therapist (a manual therapy that treats chronic pain and other conditions) and a licensed teacher of the Alexander Technique (a movement therapy). She is the author of *Effortless Pain Relief.*

Contrary to popular belief, an injury or accident is hardly ever the only cause of chronic pain—be it a backache, throbbing knee, or stiff neck or shoulder.

Surprising: Chronic pain generally results from lifestyle habits, such as the way we breathe, stand, move or hold tension in our bodies. These habits involve patterns of physical stress—expressed as muscle tension—that either can be the cause of pain or can turn injuries into long-standing problems.

For example, someone with a back injury may find that it's more comfortable to stoop forward slightly or lean to one side. Even when the original injury is healed, the body position can become a habit—and cause excessive muscle stress and pain.

KNOW YOUR BODY

If you suffer any type of chronic pain, it's essential for you to develop a heightened awareness of how your body feels…recognize physical habits that cause muscle tension…and move in ways that enhance flexibility and comfort. Even if you have severe chronic pain that requires other treatment, such as medication, the strategies described in this article also may be used to promote healing.

My advice…

STEP 1: "Scan" your body. Yoga, meditation and many other relaxation techniques recognize that simply observing your body's sensations without judgment can often encourage your body to spontaneously relax. When we worry about pain, we unconsciously tighten our muscles. The key is to accept whatever you feel.

Solution: When you are in bed at night, or relaxing on a sofa during the day, start by observing the sensations in your feet, then gradually travel up your entire body. Just observe your sensations. While you may feel momentary discomfort as you become aware of areas of tension, this tension will gradually dissipate, leaving you feeling more relaxed both physically and emotionally.

STEP 2: Practice breathing deeply. The diaphragm, located just below the lungs and heart, is a large muscle responsible for about 75% of the work involved in breathing.

Interesting fact: Because the diaphragm is attached via connective tissue and muscles to the low back and hips, tension in the diaphragm can contribute to low back pain. In addition, when the diaphragm does not work optimally—contracting and releasing fully—secondary respiratory muscles in the upper torso must kick in to improve breathing. This contributes to upper torso fatigue and pain. People whose diaphragms are contracted and rigid tend to breathe shallowly. They are known as "chest breathers."

Solution: To relieve muscle tension, practice diaphragmatic breathing. As you breathe in this way, you will notice your breath becoming softer, deeper and slower. *What to do...*

- **While sitting or lying on your back,** put one hand on your chest and the other on your stomach.
- **Slowly inhale through your nose**—or keep your lips slightly parted and breathe slowly through your mouth.
- **If you notice that your chest is expanding,** focus more on breathing "into the belly." Your stomach should rise more than your chest with each breath.

Practice diaphragmatic breathing as often and for as long as you like. The more you practice, the more it will become your preferred way of breathing.

Helpful: If you're not sure that you are breathing in a relaxed, fully diaphragmatic way, count the number of breaths you take in one minute. If you're breathing more shallowly than you're capable of doing, you may take as many as 11 to 20 breaths a minute. If you're breathing deeply and diaphragmatically, you will take as few as four to 10 breaths a minute.

STEP 3: Work on body alignment. As a result of years of sedentary living, most adults have poor body alignment. Since we stand and sit a great deal of the time, it is particularly important to improve alignment in these postures.

Interesting fact: Improving alignment isn't about squaring back your shoulders and being stiff. It's about using your body in more comfortable ways.

Solution: A few simple steps can help improve the way that you stand and sit, reducing pain and fatigue. *Examples...*

- **Bend your knees slightly when standing.** It reduces stress on the low back.
- **Keep your weight distributed evenly over both legs when standing**—and keep both feet pointed in the same direction, instead of turning them in or out.
- **When walking, roll from heel to toe,** pushing off through the ball of the foot and keeping the weight evenly distributed between the inside and outside of the foot.
- **When you get in and out of a chair,** bend fully at the knees and hips, keeping your torso relaxed and straight.

STEP 4: Stretch your body. Few adults move enough of their muscles regularly to stay limber.

Interesting fact: Certain animals, such as cats, stretch their whole bodies each time they get up, which helps keep them limber.

Solution: Spend 15 to 30 minutes daily fully stretching your body. You can do this through a formal discipline, such as yoga, or through an activity such as free-form dancing. Put on some music you enjoy, close your eyes and move to the beat, freeing up every stiff muscle. Or simply lie on the floor and stretch in any way that feels good.

STEP 5: Release body tension. To reduce chronic pain, it is important not only to pay close attention to your body and recognize muscle tension as it occurs, but also to let it go whenever you can.

Interesting fact: Once people learn how their bodies should feel, they're better able to make other physical changes that reduce muscle tension.

Solution: Don't ignore muscle tension. Learn how to move more "intelligently"—using minimum effort to achieve maximum results.

Examples: Grip your car steering wheel less tightly...notice whether you tense your muscles when having a stressful conversation or work long hours at a desk. Then try to relax a little bit. The more you relax, the less pain you will have.

Back Pain Cured!

Jack Stern, MD, PhD, a surgeon who specializes in spine neurosurgery and is author of *Ending Back Pain: 5 Powerful Steps to Diagnose, Understand, and Treat Your Ailing Back. DrJackStern.com*

The ability to diagnose and treat the different types of back pain has improved tremendously over the years. A wide variety of conventional and complementary therapies has made this possible. The fortunate result is that the vast majority of patients don't need invasive procedures or powerful drugs.

Fact: The majority of people with back pain can make a full recovery with conservative treatments. These include integrative approaches such as acupuncture and other so-called "complementary" techniques.

When I went to medical school, the term integrative medicine was unknown. Now, more than one-third of Americans use some form of alternative medicine, often on the advice of their doctors.

Which of these therapies is best for back pain? *What the evidence shows...*

EXERCISE

• **Exercise isn't an alternative therapy per se,** but it's such an effective one and so often underutilized that it's important to include here. It's difficult to exercise when your back hurts, but people who don't exercise tend to have more pain and are more susceptible to future problems. Even if you've been diagnosed with sciatica—the shooting nerve pain often caused by a herniated disk—exercise is among the best ways to feel better.

How it helps: Exercise triggers the release of endorphins, natural opiates produced by the body. It improves circulation and flushes inflammatory chemicals from damaged tissues. It increases muscle strength and flexibility and helps people use their bodies in ways that take pressure off the spine.

One study found that people who exercised four days a week had less back pain than those who worked out less frequently (or not at all). A recent study published in *Clinical Rehabilitation* found that simply walking two to three times a week (for 20 to 40 minutes each time) reduced pain and increased mobility as well as more complicated programs did.

My advice: Work with a physical therapist initially. There are many different causes of back pain. Exercise has to be customized to each patient. In general, low-impact workouts—such as walking, using a stationary bike and swimming—are safe for most people with back pain.

LUMBAR STABILIZATION

This form of exercise changes proprioception, the awareness of where your spine and other joints are positioned. Patients who do lumbar-stabilization exercises learn to maintain a "neutral" spine, using positions that reduce tension on spinal ligaments and joints. You can do the exercises at home, but I recommend working with a physical therapist first to learn to do them correctly. Examples...

• **Pelvic tilt.** Lie on the floor with your knees bent and your feet flat on the floor. Tighten the abdominal muscles so that your lower back is pulled toward the floor. Hold for about 10 seconds, relax for a moment, then repeat the movement five to 10 times.

• **Ball bridges.** Lie on your back with your legs straight and your feet propped on an exercise ball. Keeping your spine straight, lift your buttocks off the floor. You'll have to use muscles in the abdomen and back to stay balanced and keep the ball from moving.

ACUPUNCTURE

Many people think of acupuncture as too "out there" for them. But they shouldn't.

A study in *JAMA Internal Medicine* compared traditional Chinese acupuncture for low-back pain to conventional treatments using drugs, exercise and physical therapy. They also compared Chinese acupuncture to sham treatments that mimicked real acupuncture.

The seven-week study, which involved a total of 10 treatments, showed that acupuncture was twice as effective for pain relief as conventional therapy. Curiously, the "fake" treatments were almost as effective as the real ones, possibly because they triggered brain changes that altered pain perceptions. There's some evidence that electro-acupuncture, in which small electrical currents are transmitted through the needles, may be somewhat more effective than traditional acupuncture.

My advice: Go to a certified acupuncturist who has met your state's training standards. A good resource is the National Certification Commission for Acupuncture and Oriental Medicine (*www.nccaom.org*).

ALEXANDER TECHNIQUE

I often recommend this for patients with back pain that is caused by poor body mechanics—how they stand, sit, walk, hold their necks, etc. In my experience, about 50% of people with chronic back pain have poor body mechanics.

The Alexander technique (named after F.M. Alexander who developed it) involves analyzing an individual's body mechanics and then designing a plan to improve them. A study in *British Medical Journal* looked at 579 patients with chronic or recurrent lower-back pain. Those patients who were treated with the Alexander technique had less pain than those given massage or conventional treatments recommended by their doctors.

The Alexander technique is somewhat expensive (typically $60 to $125 per session) and unlikely to be covered by insurance. You can save money by signing up for group lessons.

My advice: Try one session. If you like it and feel comfortable, sign up for a series of 10. You can use the American Society for the Alexander Technique website (*www.amsatonline.org*) to find a practitioner in your area.

CHIROPRACTIC

Many conventional doctors view chiropractic as an unproven treatment—or even fraudulent. But that's not true.

Spinal manipulations and "adjustments" by chiropractors are meant to restore the spine's structural integrity and stimulate the body's natural ability to reduce pain. I've had a number of patients with herniated disks who reported significant improvement after getting chiropractic treatments.

A randomized, double-blind study conducted last year found that back-pain patients who were treated with chiropractic therapy in addition to standard medical care had less pain and better physical functioning than those who received standard care alone.

Bonus: People who see chiropractors tend to rate their care as very good or excellent. Most chiropractors spend a lot of time with patients. They take a detailed history, watch how patients move and give advice on using the back in healthier ways. It's possible that patients who receive the extra attention are able to change their perceptions of pain—a phenomenon known as the attention placebo effect.

My advice: Chiropractors are the frontline treaters of low-back pain. They are knowledgeable, and a qualified chiropractor will know when your specific problem requires additional attention.

The Right Bed Can Ease Back Pain

Baljinder Bathla, MD, cofounder of Chicago Sports & Spine, a pain-management practice. He is certified in physical medicine, rehabilitation and pain management. *ChicagoSportsSpine.com.*

People with back pain often think that a very firm mattress is best. Not true. In a study published in *The Lancet*, 313 individuals with low-back pain slept on either a firm or a medium-firm coil mattress. After 90 days, the participants with the medium-firm mattresses had less pain in bed, upon rising and during the day than those with firm mattresses. *Other misconceptions about beds and back pain...*

MISCONCEPTION: Everyone with back pain feels the pain when he/she first wakes up—so you can't tell if the mattress is a problem or not.

Fact: Most back pain is mildest in the morning, before you get out of bed and begin moving. If you wake up stiff and sore, your mattress may be to blame. Try sleeping on a different mattress—in the guest room, at a friend's, in a hotel—and see if you notice an improvement when you get up.

MISCONCEPTION: Heavier people with back pain need soft beds.

Fact: Everyone needs enough support during the night to keep the spine in a normal position. If the spine sinks into a sagging bed, the muscles are strained. Heavier people and those who sleep on their backs tend to need firmer mattresses. Side and stomach sleepers need softer beds.

MISCONCEPTION: A foam pad or an entire mattress made of foam helps relieve back pain.

Fact: There are two kinds of foam generally available—egg-crate and memory foam. Egg-crate foam creates a layer of softness but does not change the support beneath. Memory foam is sensitive to temperature and conforms to the body. However, there is no scientific evidence that either kind of foam reduces back pain.

MISCONCEPTION: Adjustable beds can ease back pain.

Fact: Some adjustable beds are filled with air or water that can be pumped in or out. Other types have joints that allow parts of the bed to be propped at different angles. There are no authoritative studies showing that adjustable beds help reduce back pain.

MISCONCEPTION: You can't tell in the store if the mattress is right for you.

Fact: Trying out a mattress in the store can help you determine if it's comfortable. Lie on each mattress for at least five minutes. Start on your back, without a pillow. Your hand should fit snugly in the small of your back. Lying on your side, you shouldn't notice significant pressure on your hips or shoulders. Choose a retailer that will allow you to return a mattress if it isn't comfortable. These include Sleepy's and *www.1800mattress.com.* (You may have to pay an exchange fee.)

Drink Water to Prevent Back Pain

Depending on your age and spinal health, the shock-absorbing discs in your spine are 70% to 90% water. If a person is not adequately hydrated, increased back stiffness may result.

Self-defense: Drink about one-half ounce of water per pound of body weight.

Also: Use proper lifting techniques (bend with your knees and keep the object as close to you as possible)...and maintain a healthy weight. If back pain is severe or accompanied by leg weakness, numbness or fever, seek immediate attention. This could be a sign of a disc herniation, circulatory problems, infection or cancer.

Daniel A. Shaye, DC, certified chiropractic rehabilitation doctor, Williamsburg, Virginia.

How to Wreck Your Back

David Borenstein, MD, clinical professor of medicine at The George Washington University Medical Center in Washington, DC, and a partner at Arthritis and Rheumatism Associates, the largest rheumatology practice based in Washington/Maryland. He is host of Speaking of Health with Dr. B, a weekly radio program on *WomensRadio.com*, and author of *Heal Your Back*. *DrBHealth.org*

As many as 80% of Americans will suffer an episode of back pain at some time in their lives. Back problems are among the main reasons for doctor visits, and they can be excruciatingly slow to heal.

What people don't realize is that most back injuries are predictable and how to avoid them might surprise you. *Here are the six worst mistakes that people make that hurt their backs...*

WEIGHT AND EFFORT MISMATCH

I see this all the time. Suppose you lift a box that is heavier than you expected. You get it a few inches off the floor and then realize that it's really heavy. It's going to crash back down if you don't bring all of your strength into play. The sudden contraction of unprepared back muscles can cause an instant strain.

Or maybe you're lifting a box that you think is heavy but turns out to be as light as a feather. All of the muscle force that you generated causes a "snap" in the muscles (and the box goes flying).

Self-protection: Before you lift something, test the weight. Slide it a few inches, or lift just a corner. You have to know what you're dealing with. If it's heavy, get your legs under you...use the muscles in your legs more than the muscles in your back. If it's light, lift with a smooth motion—you won't need that initial hard jerk to get it moving.

OVERHEAD BIN REACH

If you think that the cramped, knees-to-chest seating in today's airplanes is hard on your back, wait until you use the overhead bins. You will pay in pain what you saved on checked luggage.

Travelers often overstuff their carry-ons. A 20-pound bag that's easy to carry (or wheel) can feel like 50 pounds when you're off-balance and reaching overhead. Unloading also is a hazard. You probably had to angle, wedge and stuff your bag to get it to fit. You will have to give it a hard yank to get it out, a motion that is very hard on the back.

Self-protection: Pack light. If you're in reasonable shape, you probably can manage, say, a 10-pound bag when your arms are extended and you're standing on tiptoe. Use both hands to place the bag in the bin...don't swing it up with one arm. Store it with the handle facing out. That way, you can grip the handle with one hand and use your other hand for support. For anything much heavier, put it in checked baggage—it's worth it even if you have to pay.

SUPER-SOFT CHAIR RECLINE

It feels good to sink into a soft chair or sofa—but it is hard to extricate yourself from the pillowy depths.

Surprising fact: Sitting in a soft chair is hard work.

When you sit in a firm chair, your back is supported, so it relaxes. But a soft chair doesn't provide the same sensory input, so the muscles stay contracted. After an hour or so, you might notice that your back is hurting even though you haven't done anything more strenuous than read a book or work the TV remote.

Self-protection: When you're settling in, choose a chair that provides a decent amount of back support. It doesn't have to be hard, but it should be firm.

Also helpful: If you have a history of back problems, you probably will do better if you stand up for one to two minutes now and then—say, every 15 or 20 minutes.

THE CAR TRUNK LEAN

How many times have you felt a "pinch" when you lift a suitcase or a sack of groceries from a car's trunk or cargo area? It's not so much the weight that causes problems but your position. When you bend over and lift, you are at a mechanical disadvantage. You are not using the big muscles in your legs. Your back muscles aren't very strong. Their job is to stabilize your spine, not help with heavy lifting.

Self-protection: Get as close to the vehicle as you can before pulling the item to the front of the trunk and taking it out. This allows you to bring your leg muscles into play. Most people stand back from the rear of the car because they don't want to get their clothes dirty. Step in closer. It's easier to clean your clothes than to deal with a month or two of back pain.

TWIST AND SHOUT

"Twist and shout" is what I call the stab of pain that occurs when people use a twisting motion to bend over. Suppose that you're picking something up off the floor that's a little bit off to your side. You might pivot at the hips and swing one hand down to snag it. Don't! This is an unnatural motion because the spinal joints are designed to shift from front to back, not side to side. Twisting strains the soft tissues and can lead to sprains and spasms.

Self-protection: Before you pick something up, take a fraction of a second to move into a position of strength. With both feet facing the object, squat down and pick it up. Face it square, and use your legs more and your back less.

SHOVELING ANYTHING HEAVY

Back specialists see a lot of new patients in the spring after they have been working in the yard shoveling mulch, dirt or gravel. The same is true after snowstorms. Even when snow looks light and fluffy, each shovelful packs a lot of weight—and you never move just one shovelful.

Self-protection: Warm up before picking up the shovel. Walk around the house for a few minutes. Stretch out the muscles in your back, legs and arms.

Once you're outside, let your legs do the work. Bend your knees when you load the shovel, then straighten them when you lift. Don't bend your back any more than you have to. And don't take the heaviest shovelfuls that you can manage—if you're grunting, it's too much.

Also helpful: Home-supply stores stock a variety of ergonomic shovels that make it easier to stand upright when you're shoveling.

Ahhh...Safe, Quick Relief from Hemorrhoid Pain—You Don't Need Surgery!

Mark A. Stengler, NMD, licensed naturopathic medical doctor in private practice, Stengler Center for Integrative Medicine, Encinitas, California...adjunct associate clinical professor at the National College of Natural Medicine, Portland, Oregon...author of many books, including *The Natural Physician's Healing Therapies* and coauthor of *Prescription for Natural Cures. MarkStengler.com*

"My hemorrhoids are driving me crazy," said Don, a 55-year-old man who recently visited me for a consultation. "The bleeding and itching have been really bad this year, so my doctor is recommending surgery. What do you think?"

I could tell that Don was desperate for relief, but I felt obligated to share my concerns about the procedure.

"Have you ever spoken with someone who has had hemorrhoid surgery?" I asked.

"Well, no," Don replied.

"Believe me, it's the last thing you want to consider," I said. "The pain can be excruciating for several days, or even weeks, afterward, and the hemorrhoids can return."

I presented Don with an alternative to surgery—he could change his diet, take nutritional supplements and get more exercise (physical activity improves circulation and promotes bowel regularity). Don agreed to try the plan, and after two months, his pain and bleeding were completely eliminated. He thanked me for saving him from the ordeal of surgery.

COMMON CAUSES OF HEMORRHOIDS

According to the National Institutes of Health, an estimated 50% of American adults develop hemorrhoids by age 50. However, when you speak with proctologists (medical doctors who specialize in diseases of the rectum, anus and colon), they will tell you that everyone has at least some hemorrhoidal tissue, even though many people don't experience symptoms. Problematic hemorrhoids are found equally in men and women, and the prevalence of this condition peaks between ages 45 and 65.

Hemorrhoids, also known as piles, occur when veins and soft tissue around the anus or lower rectum become swollen and inflamed as a result of pressure from straining or carrying extra body weight and/or irritation due to diet. The most common culprits are constipation (especially when a person strains to pass stools)... obesity (extra body weight bears down on veins in the lower rectum, causing pressure)...and pregnancy/childbirth (the fetus increases pressure on the pelvic and rectal tissues, and hormonal changes make blood vessels more lax). Diarrhea associated with inflammatory bowel diseases, such as Crohn's disease and ulcerative colitis, can cause irritation that predisposes sufferers to hemorrhoids.

Hemorrhoids are often the cause of bleeding from the anus. This is due to the rich network of veins in tissues of the rectum and anal canal. Besides pain, other common hemorrhoidal symptoms include itching and burning in the anal area.

Caution: If you experience excessive or recurrent rectal bleeding, discuss it with your doctor. Although hemorrhoids are a common cause of such bleeding, other conditions, such as colon cancer, may trigger it.

CONVENTIONAL TREATMENT OPTIONS

There are a variety of conventional therapies for hemorrhoids. They include ointments, creams and suppositories, all of which provide temporary relief from rectal pain and itching. Common over-the-counter topical treatments include ointments and suppositories, such as Anusol and Preparation H, as well as Tucks medicated wipes. Stool softeners such as *docusate sodium* (Colace) are commonly recommended. These treatments can provide temporary relief, but they don't address the root causes of hemorrhoids.

Internal hemorrhoids that are confined to the anal canal become a problem if they prolapse and bulge from the anus. If this occurs, they are candidates for several procedures, each of which destroys the affected tissue and leaves a scar at the treatment site. The procedures include ligation (putting a rubber band around hemorrhoids so that the tissue dies)...sclerotherapy (injecting chemicals into the hemorrhoid, causing shrinkage)...heat coagulation (using heat from lasers to destroy hemorrhoidal tissue)...and cryotherapy (freezing of hemorrhoidal tissue).

Large hemorrhoids that protrude from the anal canal and/or cause bleeding that is difficult to control are commonly removed by surgery. Hemorrhoidectomy involves surgical removal of internal and/or external hemorrhoids from the anal canal by cutting out the hemorrhoidal tissue and stitching the site. Postsurgical pain is a major problem with this procedure, and strong pain medications are required for days to weeks. Patients are also told to sit on a large, soft "donut" to ease pressure after the surgery.

Even so, I remember one patient telling me that his postsurgical rectal pain was so intense that for two days, even with the strongest of painkillers, he lay in his bed, knocking his head against a wall. Patients don't typically return to work for two to four weeks. Other complications may include painful bowel movements, difficulty urinating, hemorrhaging, infection, narrowing of the anus (due to scarring) and bowel incontinence. Obviously, this type of surgery should be used only as a last resort.

AN IMPROVED DIET TO THE RESCUE

Hemorrhoids are yet another result of the typical Western diet. People who live in countries where fiber intake is high, such as Japan, have a very low incidence of hemorrhoids. The problem is that the average American consumes only about 15 g of fiber daily. For efficient bowel movements, a person should consume about 25 g to 30 g of fiber daily.

Insoluble fiber, which is found mainly in whole grains and vegetables, bulks up the stool and allows for better elimination. In addition to increasing your intake of these foods, it is imperative that you drink enough water, which allows for easier bowel movements by preventing dryness and adding weight to stool. If you are prone to constipation, drink 64 ounces of water daily, spread throughout the day. As I have mentioned before, ground flaxseed is an excellent source of insoluble fiber. I recommend using one to two tablespoons daily of ground flaxseed (grind fresh flaxseed in a coffee grinder for five seconds or buy preground flaxseed, known as flaxmeal) on cereal, yogurt, salads, etc. It adds a delicious, nutty flavor. Drink at least 10 ounces of water immediately after consuming flaxseed. As an alternative to flaxseed, people who are prone to hard stools or straining should use one to two tablespoons of flaxseed oil—it lubricates stool. Take flaxseed oil with meals or add it to salads or shakes.

Researchers have confirmed the importance of fiber for the treatment of hemorrhoids. A study published earlier this year in the *American Journal of Gastroenterology* reviewed seven trials involving a total of 378 patients who received either fiber or a nonfiber placebo over the course of one to 18 months. Compared with people who received a placebo, the fiber group's risk of persistent hemorrhoidal symptoms decreased by 47% and their risk of bleeding decreased by 50%.

Not surprisingly, certain foods can aggravate hemorrhoids. These include coffee and other caffeine-containing products, alcohol, spicy foods and high-sugar products, such as soft drinks and candy. In addition, patients who are prone to repeated hemorrhoidal flare-ups usually do better when they reduce or eliminate their intake of tomatoes, cow's milk, citrus fruit, wheat and peanuts. No one knows exactly why these foods and drinks are problematic, but they most likely cause veins to swell.

SOOTHING SUPPLEMENTS WORK WONDERS

I consistently find the following nutritional supplements to be effective in treating and preventing hemorrhoids. If you have an acute flare-up, I recommend taking the first two or more supplements for quicker healing. After symptoms subside, continue taking them for two months to prevent a recurrence. If your symptoms don't improve after using the first two supplements for 30 days, consider taking the others listed below (individually or in a combination formula) for a more aggressive approach. All of the products are available at health-food stores and some pharmacies.

Horse chestnut improves circulation to the rectal area and reduces swelling of hemorrhoidal tissue. One of the herb's most important active constituents is aescin. It is believed to strengthen the vein walls and capillaries—and helps with the functioning of vein valves—so that swelling is less likely to occur. Take 400 mg to 600 mg of horse chestnut three times daily. Choose a product that contains 40 mg to 120 mg of aescin per capsule.

Important: Because horse chestnut may have a mild blood-thinning effect, it should not be used by anyone taking a blood thinner, such as *warfarin* (Coumadin).

Butcher's broom is an herb that reduces hemorrhoidal symptoms, such as bleeding and pain. Ruscogenins, a primary constituent, are believed to have an anti-inflammatory effect on hemorrhoidal tissue. Take a total daily dose of 200 mg to 300 mg of butcher's broom with 9% to 11% ruscogenins. This supplement is very safe, with only rare reports of nausea.

Bilberry, an herbal supplement that's well known for promoting eye health, also helps hemorrhoids, most likely because it strengthens blood vessel walls and improves circulation. A four-week, double-blind, placebo-controlled study of 40 hemorrhoid patients showed that bilberry significantly reduced hemorrhoidal symptoms. In my practice, I've received good results with virtually all my hemorrhoid patients who try bilberry. I recommend taking 320 mg daily of a 25% anthocyanoside extract. Bilberry can be used during flare-ups or on an ongoing basis for prevention.

Psyllium seed husks are used as a supplement to treat constipation. Some people find that taking psyllium capsules is more convenient than adding flaxseed to food. Take 3 g to 4 g of psyllium in capsule form with 8 ounces of water twice daily. People who are prone to digestive upset should start with 1 g and slowly work up to 3 g over a period of three weeks.

Caution: Do not use psyllium within two hours of taking a pharmaceutical medication—it can hinder absorption of the drug.

Witch hazel, an astringent derived from the bark of the witch hazel shrub, works well as a topical treatment to soothe inflamed, bleeding hemorrhoids. It's available in cream and liquid forms. Use a cotton ball to dab it on the hemorrhoid three or four times daily and after bowel movements during flare-ups.

A SECRET HEMORRHOID CURE

For about three decades, Steve Gardner, ND, DC, has been the nation's foremost expert in natural hemorrhoid therapies. Dr. Gardner holds degrees in naturopathic medicine and chiropractic. For close to 15 years, he has been an assistant professor at the National College of Natural Medicine in Portland, Oregon, teaching proctology. Patients with acute and chronic hemorrhoid problems come to his clinic near Portland from all over the world to benefit from his noninvasive therapy for internal and external hemorrhoids.

More than a decade ago, I treated patients with him at his clinic. Many had experienced the horrors of hemorrhoid surgery and were unwilling to go through such an ordeal again. Many patients told me of the seemingly miraculous relief they had experienced with Dr. Gardner's therapy.

Dr. Gardner and a limited number of doctors (mostly naturopathic and chiropractic physicians) use a procedure known as the Keesey Technique. Wilbur Keesey, MD, developed this technique in the 1930s and never reported a severe complication in more than 700 individual treatments. (Dr. Gardner has performed this therapy several thousand times.) The technique is not FDA approved, but it has a strong history of clinical efficacy.

During this outpatient procedure, known as hemorrhoidolysis, the doctor touches the protruding hemorrhoids with an electrode that conducts a galvanic (electrical) current. This type of current causes the hemorrhoids to shrink. The Keesey Technique leads to only slight discomfort, hemorrhage rarely occurs and infection is rare. Because hemorrhoidal tissue is shrunk through the use of this technique, hemorrhoid recurrence is uncommon. There is no loss of time from work, no special preoperative treatment is required, and the procedure costs about $1,500 to $2,000 less than hemorrhoid surgery.

For patients with moderate to severe hemorrhoids, Dr. Gardner usually gives a series of six to 10 treatments with one to two treatments a week. Patients typically have one or two more treatments three months later as a routine follow-up. The cost is $95 per treatment. Dr. Gardner states that about half of his patients' health insurers cover the treatments.

The Keesey Technique offers relief even for people who have extensive hemorrhoidal swelling that does not respond to dietary changes, supplement use and regular exercise. Dr. Gardner has found that less than 5% of the patients he treats require a referral for surgery.

To find a doctor who uses the Keesey Technique, contact the American Association of Naturopathic Physicians, 866-538-2267, *www.naturopathic.org*. Or see Dr. Gardner or one of his colleagues at his Sandy Blvd. Hemorrhoid Clinic East in Portland, Oregon, 503-786-7272 or 888-664-6662, *www.hemorrhoidhelp.com*.

Alleviate Neck and Back Pain with Fish Oil

In a recent finding, when neck and back pain sufferers took a fish-oil supplement (1,200 mg daily) for 75 days, 60% reported significant pain relief that allowed them to decrease or discontinue use of painkillers.

Theory: The omega-3 fatty acids found in fish oil block the inflammation that can lead to neck and back pain. Fish oil also may help relieve joint pain.

If you have neck or back pain: Ask your doctor about taking fish oil. Do not use fish oil if you take *warfarin* (Coumadin) or another blood thinner.

Joseph Maroon, MD, vice chairman of neurological surgery, University of Pittsburgh.

Simple Stretches That Really Do Relieve Pain

Ben Benjamin, PhD, a sports medicine and muscular therapy practitioner since 1963. He is the author of several books, including *Listen to Your Pain: The Active Person's Guide to Understanding, Identifying, and Treating Pain and Injury.*

If you suffer from pain or stiffness due to an injury, arthritis or even a neurological disorder, such as Parkinson's disease or multiple sclerosis, a type of bodywork known as Active Isolated Stretching (AIS) may give you more relief than you ever thought possible.

What makes AIS different: While most other stretching techniques recommend doing each stretch for 30 seconds or longer, AIS uses brief, two-second stretches that are done eight to 10 times each.

What's the advantage of quick, repeated stretches? This approach gives the muscle a full stretch without triggering its stretch reflex—an automatic defense mechanism that causes the muscle to contract and ultimately undo many of the stretch's benefits. The result is that muscles stretch more efficiently and avoid the buildup of waste products that lead to muscle soreness.

Developed by American kinesiologist Aaron Mattes about 35 years ago, AIS also stretches each muscle group at a variety of different angles, thus stretching all muscle fibers equally.

A MINI REGIMEN

To get a sense of AIS, try the stretches in this article. While doing each one, slowly count to yourself "one-one thousand, two-one thousand"—never any longer than two seconds. Always exhale while performing the stretch and inhale as you return to the starting position.

The first repetition of each stretch should be gentle...the second should go up to the point where you begin to feel resistance. Subsequent repetitions should push just beyond this point (with the help of your hands, a rope or other aid, if necessary) to go a few degrees further each time, thus providing a maximum stretch. If you feel discomfort during a stretch, stop the stretch at that point. If a stretch feels painful from the start, then skip it.

Daily AIS exercises that help relieve common types of pain...*

SHOULDER STRETCHES

Purpose: To help prevent muscle strain and joint sprain by increasing flexibility.

1. With your right elbow bent, position your right arm at a 90° angle in front of your body. Place your right palm on the back of your right shoulder. Exhale and extend your flexed arm upward as far as possible. Gently assist the stretch with your left hand. Repeat eight to 10 times on each side.

2. With your right elbow bent and your right arm positioned at a 90° angle in front of your body, place your right palm on the back of your right shoulder. Drop a two- to three-foot rope over your right shoulder and grasp the bottom of it with your left hand. Gently pull the rope to move your right arm upward behind your neck at a 45° angle for a maximum stretch. Return to the starting position after each repetition. Repeat eight to 10 times on each side.

NECK STRETCHES

Purpose: To help prevent neck injuries, relieve stiffness and improve range of motion.

1. Tuck your chin as close to your neck as possible. Put both your hands on the back of your head and, while keeping your back straight, gently bend your neck forward, bringing your chin as close to your chest as you can. Return to starting position. Repeat 10 times.

2. Gently bend your head to the right side, moving your right ear as close as possible to the top of your right shoulder. Exhale and place your right hand on the left side of your head to gently extend the stretch. Keep your left shoulder down. Focus your eyes on a point directly in front of your body to keep your head in an aligned position. Repeat 10 times on both sides.

GETTING STARTED

For people who are new to AIS, I advise working with an AIS practitioner for hands-on instruction. If the movements are done incorrectly, you will get no benefits and could even hurt yourself. To find a practitioner near you, go to *www.stretchingusa.com* and click on the "Find a Therapist" link. Sessions are not typically covered by insurance and usually range from $50 to $150 per session. The website also offers books, including *Specific Stretching for Everyone*, and DVDs if you prefer to learn a complete AIS regimen on your own.

*Check with your doctor before performing these movements.

Ginger Eases Muscle Pain and Inflammation Caused by Exercise

Ginger eases muscle pain and inflammation caused by exercise.

Recent finding: Exercisers who consumed two grams (about one teaspoon) of raw or heated ginger had 23% to 25% less pain after exercise than those who did not consume ginger. Volunteers consumed the ginger daily for eight days prior to exercising and three days afterward.

Recommendation: Add fresh ginger to your diet for faster workout recovery.

Christopher D. Black, PhD, assistant professor, department of kinesiology, Georgia College and State University, Milledgeville, and leader of a study published in *The Journal of Pain.*

Ginger vs. Sumatriptan for Migraine Relief

Study titled "Comparison between the efficacy of ginger and sumatriptan in the ablative treatment of the common migraine," published in *Phytotherapy Research.*

Migraine. The sound of the word is like nails on a chalkboard for sufferers. If you deal with these headaches, the mere hint of an attack probably drives you to the medicine cabinet in search of any number of oral, inhaled or injectable drugs despite their dreadful side effects, because nothing matters except relief. But what if instead of rushing to the medicine cabinet, you could get relief from a safer, natural food supplement?

That supplement is ginger, and new research shows that it offers a natural alternative to *sumatriptan* (Imitrex), a commonly prescribed migraine medication. *But you have to know exactly how to use it...*

The Face-off: Ginger vs. Sumatriptan.

A team of neuroscientists compared ginger and sumatriptan in 100 men and women who had suffered migraines for an average of seven years. The participants were randomly assigned to take one capsule of either ginger (at a dose of 250 mg) or sumatriptan (50 mg) as soon as a migraine started. Participants didn't know whether they were taking ginger or sumatriptan until the end of the study, which lasted for one month.

For each headache that occurred during that month, participants recorded the time the headache began, headache severity before taking the remedy and degree of pain relief from the remedy at 30, 60, 90 and 120 minutes as well as 24 hours after taking it.

The results: Sumatriptan and ginger both, on average, decreased the severity of headache by 44% within two hours. Slightly more people in the sumatriptan group—70% versus 64%—achieved 90% migraine relief after two hours had elapsed.

Now think about that for a minute. Regular old ginger darn near matched the prescription pharmaceutical sumatriptan for migraine headache relief.

The biggest difference in the study results, as you might guess, had to do with side effects. Twenty percent of patients taking sumatriptan reported dizziness, drowsiness, vertigo or heartburn. Meanwhile, 4% of those taking ginger had some indigestion.

The doses of ginger and sumatriptan used in the study were moderate. Oral sumatriptan is generally prescribed in doses of 25 mg, 50 mg or 100 mg depending on the severity of migraine that a person suffers. If no relief occurs within two hours, another dose can be taken, but the maximum dosage allowed per day is 200 mg. Mild side effects include pressure or a heavy feeling in any part of the body, feeling hot or cold, dizziness, vertigo, drowsiness and nausea or other gastrointestinal problems. And serious adverse events, such as heart attack, stroke and seizure, can occur. That's enough for me to look for an alternative!

Although the most effective dosage of ginger for migraine has yet to be established, dosages of ginger at 250 mg four times per day have been safely used in research studies of morning sickness and arthritis. Ginger supplements are widely available in stores, usually in doses higher than 250 mg, and are considered "generally safe" by National Institute of Health standards, but people taking blood thinners, such as *warfarin* (Coumadin), high blood pressure medications, especially *nifedipine* (Procardia), or insulin should speak with their doctors before taking ginger supplements because ginger can interfere with their medications. Because ginger is a natural blood thinner, people with bleeding disorders should also shy away from ginger supplements or take them only under a doctor's supervision.

Although earlier studies have shown that ginger can reduce or deactivate a migraine, this was the first study to pit ginger against a big-name migraine drug. The robustness of the results are encouraging so, if you have concerns about taking sumatriptan for migraine relief, ask your doctor about whether a ginger supplement might be a safe and effective alternative remedy.

Migraine Relief

Eliminate migraine pain with pepper. Capsaicin, an ingredient in cayenne pepper, cuts off neurotransmitters in the brain that cause headache pain.

Best: Dissolve one-quarter teaspoon of cayenne powder in four ounces of warm water. Dip a cotton swab into the solution, and apply the liquid inside your nostrils. It will burn—and by the time the burning stops, the headache pain will be reduced and sometimes gone altogether.

Eric Yarnell, ND, assistant professor, department of botanical medicine, Bastyr University, Kenmore, Washington.

Landmark Study Shows 6 Exercises Can Relieve Neck Pain

Gert Bronfort, DC, PhD, vice president of research at Northwestern Health Sciences University in Bloomington, Minnesota. A leading researcher on chiropractic and complementary and alternative medicine, Dr. Bronfort has authored several systematic reviews of the literature on treating neck, back and headache pain. Dr. Bronfort is coauthor, with Roni Evans, DC, of the neck pain study in *Annals of Internal Medicine*. Dr. Evans also contributed to this article.

If you suffer from neck pain, chances are you've tried heating pads, painkillers and perhaps even repeated visits to a physical therapist, osteopath or chiropractor.

But new research shows that simple neck exercises can relieve neck pain.

Important new research: In a landmark study published in *Annals of Internal Medicine*, researchers followed 272 people suffering from neck pain of less than three months' duration with no specific known cause. One group received pain medication and muscle relaxants for 12 weeks...another had 12 weeks of spinal manipulation sessions...and a third group did 12 weeks of special daily neck exercises.

Findings: Spinal manipulation was more effective than medication at improving neck pain by the end of 12 weeks of treatment and one year later—and participants who did home neck exercises experienced improvement in their pain similar to that achieved with spinal manipulation.

WHY THESE EXERCISES WORK

Various factors contribute to neck pain, including chronic strain on the joints and ligaments due to poor posture, minor trauma and excessive work in front of a computer.

The neck exercises used in the neck pain study described above were adapted from a program developed by New Zealand physical therapist Robin McKenzie. The "McKenzie Method" brings the neck into normal alignment by reinforcing its natural curves and rebalancing supporting muscles. Through numerous gentle repetitions, these exercises help you develop a healthier posture, eliminating stress on the neck's joints and ligaments.

HOME EXERCISE PROGRAM

If you suffer from neck pain or stiffness, the following sequence of exercises should be performed six to eight times throughout the day (a total of about 30 to 40 minutes daily).*

Keep doing the routine as long as your neck pain continues to improve. Once you reach a plateau, do the exercises just once a day to maintain a healthy neck and prevent a recurrence.

All of the exercises should be done while sitting on a straight-backed chair or stool, except for the two lying-down versions. As you hold each position, take one full, deep breath—inhaling, then exhaling and relaxing.

EXERCISE 1: Head retraction. While sitting in a relaxed position and looking straight ahead, slowly move your head backward as far as you can. Next, tuck in your chin as much as possible toward your throat while continuing to look straight ahead. Hold this position for three seconds, then return to starting position. Repeat 10 times.

If this exercise is too difficult: While lying on your back on a bed (without a pillow), tuck in your chin toward your throat. Hold this position as you push your head backward into the bed for three seconds. Repeat 10 times.

EXERCISE 2: Head retraction with extension. Tuck in your chin and pull your head backward, as in Exercise #1. While keeping your head pulled back, lift your chin up and tilt your head back as far as you can. Hold this position for three seconds as you rotate your head a half inch to the right and then a half inch to the left. Return to the starting position. Repeat the sequence 10 times.

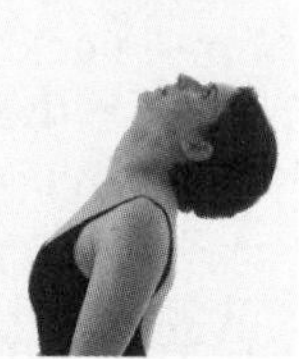

If this exercise is too difficult: While lying on your back on your bed with your head, neck and the tops of your shoulders extending off the bed, support your head with one hand. Next, tilt your head backward as far as you can. Hold this position for three seconds as you rotate your head a half inch to the right and then a half inch to the left. Return to the starting position. Repeat the sequence 10 times.

EXERCISE 3: Head retraction with side bending. Tuck in your chin and pull your head backward, as in Exercise #1. While continuing to look straight ahead, put your right hand on your head and gently tilt your head so that your right ear moves as far as possible toward your right shoulder. Hold this position for three seconds, then return to the starting position. Repeat five times on each side.

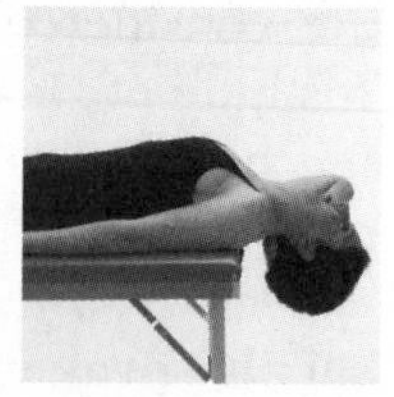

EXERCISE 4: Head retraction with rotation. Tuck in your chin and pull your head backward, as in Exercise #1. While maintaining this posture, turn your head to the right as far as you can and hold this position for three seconds, then return to the starting position. Repeat five times on each side.

EXERCISE 5: Head flexion. Relax completely, then let your head fall forward so that your chin drops to your chest.

Put your hands behind your head, then let your arms relax so your elbows point downward and the weight of your arms gently pulls your chin even closer to your chest. Hold this position for three seconds, then return to the starting position. Repeat five times. After completing Exercise #5, do 10 additional repetitions of Exercise #2.

EXERCISE 6: Scapular retraction. This exercise strengthens the shoulders' scapular muscles, which help support the base of the neck. Hold your arms at your sides with your elbows bent at 90° angles. While maintaining this position and continuing to look straight ahead, pull your elbows back behind you until you feel a squeezing

*Check with your doctor before trying these exercises. If your neck pain worsens as a result of the exercises, stop them and see your doctor for advice.

between your shoulder blades. Hold for three seconds, then return to the starting position. Repeat five times.

Exercise photos: courtesy of Spinal Publications New Zealand Ltd.

Ointments vs. Oral Drugs for Pain

Painkilling ointments are as effective as oral drugs for certain types of pain.

Recent finding: Topical NSAIDs treated pain associated with osteoarthritis in the knee and hand and musculoskeletal injuries, such as tendinitis, as effectively as oral NSAIDs. Topical NSAIDs are absorbed through the skin, so there is little risk for gastrointestinal bleeding. Currently, only three are available, all by prescription—Voltaren Gel, the Flector Patch and liquid Pennsaid.

Roger Chou, MD, associate professor of medical informatics and clinical epidemiology, and medicine, School of Medicine, Oregon Health & Science University, Portland.

Abdominal Pain

Mark A. Stengler, NMD, licensed naturopathic medical doctor in private practice, Stengler Center for Integrative Medicine, Encinitas, California...adjunct associate clinical professor at the National College of Natural Medicine, Portland, Oregon...author of many books, including *The Natural Physician's Healing Therapies* and coauthor of *Prescription for Natural Cures. MarkStengler.com*

By the time he consulted me, 57-year-old Shawn was fed up. For four decades, he had suffered from unpredictable bouts of burning abdominal pain that occurred about once a month and lasted for days. Each attack was accompanied by excessive burping and a bitter taste.

Over the years, Shawn had consulted half a dozen gastroenterologists and had numerous tests—including ultrasound and endoscopy—but no abnormalities had been found. Six years ago, he had taken antibiotics for several months after being diagnosed with an infection of *Helicobacter pylori* (the bacterium that causes stomach ulcers), but relief was temporary. Shawn also took *pantoprazole* (Protonix), a prescription heartburn drug that reduces stomach acid. It did ease his heartburn but did not alleviate his sporadic abdominal pain.

A stool test showed undigested meat fibers, indicating poor protein digestion. This made sense, since Shawn was still taking the acid-suppressing medication. It also showed an overgrowth of the fungus *Candida albicans*—a common side effect of antibiotics, which destroy beneficial bacteria in the digestive tract that keep fungi in check.

Blood tests showed no signs of a food allergy but did show a deficiency of vitamin B-12, which is common in people with low levels of the stomach acids that promote absorption of certain nutrients. A B-12 deficiency also can result from excessive alcohol use—clearly the case for Shawn, who had several alcoholic drinks per day. Shawn also smoked four cigars daily and sometimes indulged in sweets and spicy foods—all of which contribute to inflammation, especially of the digestive system.

Since Shawn's abdominal pain was not the result of any single cause, we took an integrated approach. He agreed to reduce his smoking by half, cut back to three alcoholic drinks weekly, avoid spicy fare and limit foods that contain simple sugars, such as soda and white bread. He began taking a daily B-12 supplement and, to reduce inflammation, an ingestible blend of aloe vera juice plus deglycyrrhizinated licorice root (DGL), available at health-food stores. (These shouldn't be used while pregnant or nursing.) I prescribed the homeopathic remedy Chelidonium majus (from the juice of a plant with the same name), to take at the first sign of abdominal pain (from Remedy Source, 301-610-6649, *www.remedysource.com*).

A month later, Shawn reported that the Chelidonium majus brought quick relief during bouts of pain. His attacks were less frequent and milder, and the burping and bitter taste had disappeared—all results of improved digestion and decreased stomach irritation. I prescribed a supplement of antifungal herbs, including oregano oil and pau d'arco (from the taheebo tree), to halt the Candida overgrowth. After several months, Shawn was able to stop using his heartburn medication—and his abdominal pain became a thing of the past.

Got Wrist Pain That Won't Go Away?

Randall W. Culp, MD, an orthopedic surgeon at The Philadelphia Hand Center, *HandCenters.com*, and a professor of orthopedic surgery at the Jefferson Medical College of Thomas Jefferson University, both in Philadelphia. He is on the board of directors of the nonprofit Hand Rehabilitation Foundation, *HandFoundation.org*

Millions of Americans have had hip, knee or shoulder replacements to relieve pain and improve their mobility.

Now: A similar procedure can be done on the wrist, a joint that used to be considered too complex to remove and replace.

With wrist replacement, or arthroplasty, patients can achieve pain relief while retaining more mobility than was possible with earlier procedures.

What you need to know...

A NEW APPROACH

Approximately 27 million American adults suffer from osteoarthritis—a condition that frequently affects the wrist. Millions more have rheumatoid arthritis or osteoporosis, conditions that also can lead to permanent damage to the wrist and other joints.

Until recently, the main surgical treatment for arthritic and damaged wrists was fusion, in which wrist bones are permanently fused to prevent the bones from rubbing together and causing pain. Fusion is very effective at easing pain but, depending on the procedure, allows for little or no joint movement.

Unlike the hip and knee joints, which have only two bones each, the wrists have eight bones—10 if you count those in the forearm. The challenge for manufacturers was to design an artificial joint that gave patients a wide range of movement but also was durable enough to justify the risks and discomfort of surgery.

WHO SHOULD CONSIDER A WRIST REPLACEMENT?

Wrist replacement is a good choice for people whose persistent pain and stiffness interferes with their daily activities, and who have not been helped by medical treatments such as rest, splinting, stretching exercises and/or the use of anti-inflammatory medications.

Important: There isn't enough data to predict how long the new wrist replacements will last. We think they'll last 10 to 15 years—but no one knows for sure.

Because of this, I advise patients—particularly those who are younger and have decades of life ahead of them—to wait as long as they possibly can before having surgery. When a wrist replacement wears out, pain results and a new artificial wrist joint or fusion will be required.

Cost is also a factor. A total wrist replacement costs significantly more than wrist fusion. For this reason, patients with limited or no insurance might decide that the lower cost of a fusion procedure justifies having less wrist mobility.

Exception: If you've already had one wrist fused and need treatment for the other wrist, I always recommend joint replacement. You need at least one mobile wrist for many of the activities of daily living, such as brushing your teeth, buttoning a shirt, etc.

GETTING A WRIST REPLACEMENT

If you're considering a wrist replacement, look for an orthopedic hand surgeon with experience in wrist replacements.*

Wrist replacement is typically a 45-minute outpatient surgery that doesn't require general anesthesia—a nerve block is used to numb the arm.

The surgeon makes a two- to three-inch incision on the back of the wrist and removes the arthritic/damaged joint. The artificial joint, made of plastic and steel, is then inserted. There is a separate component that attaches to the radius, one of the bones in the forearm.

New development: We've found that many younger patients do just as well when they

*To find a hand surgeon near you, consult the American Society for Surgery of the Hand, *www.assh.org*.

have a hemiarthroplasty, which involves replacing only half of the joint.

Hemiarthroplasty is a less extensive procedure that leaves more of the carpal bones in the wrist in place. This is important because an implant on the carpal bones is more likely to loosen and become unattached from those bones than other parts of the joint.

Unlike hip and knee replacements, arthroplasty usually doesn't use bone cement. The prosthesis has a roughened surface that allows the body's natural bone to grow into and anchor the steel parts, a process known as porous in-growth. It's stronger and more stable than cement.

Long-term complications (after 10 to 15 years), including joint loosening or damage to the components, occur in 2% to 3% of arthroplasty cases. A revision replacement or fusion is required to treat the pain that occurs in these patients.

Postsurgical infection is possible but is no more likely with wrist replacement than with other surgical procedures.

WHAT TO EXPECT AFTER SURGERY

Patients regain, on average, about half of their normal wrist motion, usually within three to four months of wrist-replacement surgery. This range of motion, accompanied by a roughly equal level of fine control, is typically enough to do just about anything you want, including activities such as gardening, golf and tennis. In some cases, patients may regain up to 75% of their normal wrist motion following wrist replacement.

However, as a precaution, I advise my patients who have undergone wrist replacement not to lift anything heavier than about 10 pounds for the rest of their lives to avoid loosening the joint.

For four weeks following wrist- replacement surgery, a splint or cast is worn to keep the joint stable while it heals.

After that, patients meet regularly with a physical therapist—usually twice weekly for about two to four months—to perform stretching and strengthening exercises.

Caution: Unlike hip and knee replacements, the smaller devices used in wrist replacement may not set off scanners at airports—but we've had reports that they will set off scanners used in other settings, such as in courtrooms. Ask your doctor for a card that explains that you've had the procedure.

Also important: Bacteria can readily proliferate on foreign material in the body, including artificial joints. A lingering infection, even if you don't have symptoms, can loosen the implant.

Be sure to mention to your dentist and all of your doctors that you have an artificial joint. You may be advised to take antibiotics for a few days prior to dental and medical procedures to help avoid infection.

Amazingly Simple Pain-Relief Trick

Beth Darnall, PhD, clinical associate professor, division of pain medicine, Stanford University.

UK scientists have started to develop simpler tricks that people with any kind of pain can do themselves—no mirrors needed (no drugs either)—to "fool" their brains into perceiving less pain. It involves simply touching your own body in a certain way. It sounds so appealing—does it really work?

THE BRAIN'S POINT OF VIEW

According to Beth Darnall, PhD, at the Oregon Health & Science University, this works because of a process that scientists call "brain signaling." An ample body of research has shown that often the brain does not distinguish between what is real (that you can see and touch) and what it just believes to be true based on experience. Furthermore, she said, research shows that just thinking negatively about pain can create biochemical changes that show up in MRI brain scans when areas associated with pain light up. In other words, people can literally grow their pain through their thoughts—so it also makes sense, Dr. Darnall says, that people can use their brains to banish it.

MIND OVER PAIN

So what can we do with this intriguing research finding? *Here's Dr. Darnall's advice on how to put it to use right now...*

The first step is to become aware of the extent to which chronic pain triggers anxiety and catastrophic thinking (chronic thoughts and feelings of helplessness and doom). This increases stress and worsens pain, so it is crucial to establish ways to calm and center your body and mind—otherwise you'll be "at the mercy of anything in the environment, including your own body," said Dr. Darnall. She suggested that a type of counseling called cognitive behavior therapy can be a good way to learn how to eliminate anxiety and catastrophic thinking, noting that studies show that such therapy actually can change—physically change—the neural networks of the brain and make them healthier.

As far as the self-touch method for pain relief, Dr. Darnall discussed a technique she developed called "bilateral tactile stimulation" that you can learn to use on yourself for pain relief—though it's important to start with a practitioner in order to experience how it is properly done.

Note: Psychotherapists trained in either Eye Movement Desensitization Reprocessing (EMDR) or Emotional Freedom Technique (EFT) are the ones most likely to be familiar with this technique.

How it works: Sitting in front of the client, the therapist leads him/her through a guided visualization or deep-relaxation exercise while lightly and rapidly tapping one side and then the other of (for example) the back of the knees or hands—a place that is easy to reach and comfortable but not the painful spot. *This is done for one to three minutes. According to Dr. Darnall, this works to reduce pain in the following ways...*

Tapping while also doing a guided visualization seems to help patients encode positive images, feelings and thoughts more quickly.

In turn, this helps put a stop to the cycle of pain, stress and the body's inflammatory response by keeping the brain from focusing on helplessness and how much it hurts.

Lastly, this technique can help deepen the relaxation response, thereby releasing the muscle tension that pain causes and, with it, the pain itself. In other words, the tapping helps to encode and anchor information in the brain, including the information that the patient is fully relaxed and pain-free.

THE AT-HOME VERSION

Once you are familiar with the process and feel ready to try it on yourself, Dr. Darnall suggests an at-home process to follow...

• **Sit or lie down in a comfortable position.** Because it is crucial to feel calm before using this technique, listen to a relaxation-response CD (many are available online and at health-food stores), meditate or do some diaphragmatic breathing to first get centered.

Once you are relaxed and calm, focus on envisioning positive images. Create an image of yourself hurting less and functioning better. Concentrate on how good it feels to move without pain...to experience joy...or to accomplish goals you set for yourself.

Now, alternating one side of the body and the other, tap your knees, legs or upper arms—whatever location you have chosen where you can easily reach and you have sensation (no numbness). Using the opposite hand (e.g., left hand on right knee, right hand on left knee), tap at a rate of two or three taps per second, all the while continuing your positive imagery, as described above. Start with sessions of about three minutes, and gradually add more time in later sessions if you wish.

As you become more practiced at this simple pain-relief technique, Dr. Darnall suggested trying to expand your vision of yourself, creating new visualizations where you picture yourself moving more easily around your life, pain-free, exercising and engaging in other activities you enjoy. Keep tapping as you do this...consider it a source of positive energy that you can "tap" at any time you wish!

How to Cure Chronic Pelvic Pain—For Women and Men...

Geo Espinosa, ND, LAc, a naturopathic doctor and acupuncturist who specializes in prostate disorders, male sexual health and chronic pelvic pain. He founded the Integrative Urology Center at New York University (NYU) Langone Medical Center in New York City. *DrGeo.com*

It is one of the most common but least talked about medical conditions. Chronic pelvic pain (CPP)—dull aching, cramping and/or sharp pains in the area between the navel and the hips—is mostly thought of as a woman's disorder. But men account for approximately 20% of the 11 million Americans who suffer from CPP.

It's a tricky condition to diagnose because the symptoms—which in women and men may include painful intercourse, difficulty sleeping, low energy and/or alternating constipation and diarrhea—can be caused by many different conditions, such as endometriosis in women... or prostate enlargement in men. In both women and men, infection of the urethra or bladder and food sensitivities can trigger CPP.

And even though the condition is chronic—that is, lasting for six months or longer—it might wax and wane daily...or you might have a weeklong flare-up after a pain-free month.

WHERE TO START?

Every woman with CPP symptoms should see a gynecologist, who will perform a thorough pelvic exam to look for such problems as abnormal growths and tension in the pelvic muscles. Men affected by CPP symptoms should be seen by a urologist. Specific testing will depend on what your physician finds—or suspects—during the initial exam as the underlying cause of CPP.

Examples: Ultrasound to examine the organs for abnormalities such as ovarian cysts in women and prostate enlargement in men... and laboratory tests to look for infections. In some cases, a woman may also undergo laparoscopy, the insertion of a thin tube into the abdomen to look for endometriosis.

Some patients get relief once the underlying problem is identified and treated, but many patients don't.

Reason: Within just months, CPP can trigger sometimes permanent changes in the spinal cord that allow the persistent passage of pain signals to the brain—even when the underlying cause of the pain has been corrected.

THE NEXT STEP

Patients with CPP can improve with conventional treatments (such as the use of painkillers or surgery to remove growths), but these approaches won't necessarily give them the greatest odds of adequately relieving their pain.

Better: Taking a complementary approach that combines conventional and alternative treatments.

Best therapies to try—in addition to mainstream treatments...

- **Relax trigger points.** Most women and men with CPP have one or more trigger points (areas of knotted muscle) somewhere in the pelvic area—for example, on the lower abdomen or on the upper thighs. Trigger points themselves can be excruciatingly painful and can transmit pain throughout the pelvic region.

Example: Vaginal pain could be caused by a trigger point elsewhere on the pelvis.

Massage therapists are typically trained to identify and treat trigger points. Simply pressing on one of these points for 20 to 30 seconds—and repeating the pressure several times during an hour-long massage—can relax the tension and help ease the pain. Having a weekly massage for several months sometimes can eliminate symptoms of CPP.

To find a massage therapist who specializes in trigger point treatment, go to *www.massagetherapy.com*, click on "Find a Massage Therapist" and select "Trigger Point Therapy."

Drawback: Pressure on a trigger point can be painful. You can get the same relief, with less discomfort, with electroacupuncture. Two or more hair-width acupuncture needles are inserted into the skin above the trigger point.

Then, a mild electrical current is administered, which causes the muscle to relax.

Treatment for CPP will typically require about six to 20 sessions of electroacupuncture. Many acupuncturists are trained in electroacupuncture. However, because the technique is less well-studied than standard acupuncture, it may not be covered by your health insurer. Electroacupuncture typically costs about $70 to $100 per session.

Electroacupuncture should not be used on patients who have a history of seizures, epilepsy, heart disease, stroke or a pacemaker.

• **Try standard acupuncture.** Even if you don't have trigger points, acupuncture is among the most effective treatments for CPP. A study of 67 women who had bacterial cystitis (infection of the bladder wall that commonly causes CPP) found that 85% of them were virtually pain-free after receiving 20-minute acupuncture sessions, twice weekly for four weeks. Reinfection rates were also reduced.

Acupuncture is believed to help block the transmission of pain signals. It's also an effective way to reduce muscular as well as emotional stress, both of which increase all types of chronic pain. Most CPP patients will need 10 to 20 treatments. Acupuncture is often covered by insurance.

• **Identify food sensitivities.** Many women and men with CPP are sensitive to one or more foods, particularly wheat and dairy. What happens: When these patients eat "problem" foods, they have increased intestinal permeability, also known as "leaky gut" syndrome. Large, undigested food molecules that are normally contained within the intestine pass into the bloodstream, where they trigger the release of inflammatory chemicals that can cause pain throughout the body and in the pelvic region, in particular.

A blood test known as ALCAT (antigen leukocyte cellular antibody test) can identify specific food sensitivities. Although it is reasonably reliable, the test usually isn't covered by insurance because it is considered an "alternative" diagnostic tool. It costs about $400.

Another option: An elimination-challenge diagnostic diet.

What to do: Quit eating wheat, dairy and other likely food triggers, such as soy, wine and sugar, for 21 days. If your symptoms improve, at least one of the foods was a problem. Then, reintroduce the foods, one at a time over a period of weeks, to see which food (or foods) causes symptoms to return.

Patients may get frustrated, initially, because they feel like there are few foods left to eat, but many of the foods that they give up during the test will turn out to be harmless. Foods found to cause problems should be given up indefinitely.

• **Take probiotics.** Because infections, such as those described earlier, are a common cause of pelvic pain, patients often receive multiple courses of antibiotics. Antibiotics eliminate infection, but they also kill beneficial bacteria in the intestine. This can lead to digestive problems such as irritable bowel syndrome and leaky gut syndrome—both of which are linked to CPP.

Helpful: A daily probiotic supplement with a mix of at least 10 billion live, beneficial organisms, such as Acidophilus and Lactobacillus. A probiotic supplement should be taken indefinitely.

Also helpful: Glutamine—100 mg to 200 mg, taken twice daily until symptoms improve. It nourishes the cells that line the intestine and can help prevent leaky gut syndrome. People with liver or kidney disease should not take glutamine.

Caution: Do not take a B-complex nutrient if you're suffering from CPP. In my practice, patients who take B vitamins have more CPP symptoms for reasons that aren't clear.

• **Learn to relax.** Emotional stress doesn't cause CPP, but people who are stressed and anxious tend to be more aware of their pain. Women and men who practice stress-reduction techniques—such as deep breathing and meditation—report about a 50% reduction in CPP symptoms, on average.

Very helpful: Yoga. It is probably the best workout if you have CPP. That's because it relaxes muscle tension as well as trigger points...increases levels of painkilling endorphins...and promotes overall relaxation.

Antibiotics May Relieve Chronic Low-Back Pain

Nearly half the people whose pain is caused by a herniated disk later develop a bacterial infection. For those people, a 100-day course of the antibiotic amoxicillin reduced pain by up to 80% in a recent study. If you have had severe low-back pain for at least three months...have a damaged vertebra and swelling...and other treatment options have failed, ask your doctor whether an extended course of antibiotics is worth trying.

Study of 61 people with back pain by researchers at University of Southern Denmark, Odense, published in *European Spine Journal.*

Real Relief for Prostate Pain

H. Ballentine Carter, MD, professor of urology and oncology and director of adult urology at Johns Hopkins University School of Medicine, Baltimore. He is coauthor, with Gerald Secor Couzens, of *The Whole Life Prostate Book: Everything That Every Man—at Every Age—Needs to Know About Maintaining Optimal Prostate Health.*

More than one-third of men over 50 have this chronic condition.

A man who goes to his doctor with prostate-related pain will probably be told that he has prostatitis and that he needs an antibiotic for the infection that is assumed to be causing his discomfort.

In most cases, that diagnosis would be wrong. He probably doesn't have an infection, and antibiotics won't make a bit of difference.

Only 5% to 10% of men with prostate-related symptoms have a bacterial infection. Most have what's known as chronic nonbacterial prostatitis/chronic pelvic pain syndrome (CP/CPPS). It's a complicated condition that typically causes pain in the perineum (the area between the testicles and the anus) and/or in the penis, testicles and pelvic area.

The pain can be so great—and/or long lasting—that it can significantly interfere with a man's quality of life. *Here's how to ease the pain...*

A COMMON PROBLEM

More than one-third of men 50 years old and older suffer from CP/CPPS, according to the National Institutes of Health. In this age group, it's the third most-common urological diagnosis, after prostate cancer and lower urinary tract conditions.

CP/CPPS isn't a single disease with one specific treatment. The discomfort has different causes and can originate in different areas, including in the prostate gland, the ejaculatory ducts, the bladder or the muscles in the pelvic floor. It can affect one or all of these areas simultaneously.

If you have pelvic pain that has lasted three months or more, you could have CP/CPPS. The pain typically gets worse after ejaculation and tends to come and go. Some men will be pain-free for weeks or months, but the discomfort invariably comes back.

THE UPOINT EXAM

A man with CP/CPPS might not get an accurate diagnosis for a year or more. Many family doctors, internists and even urologists look only for a prostate infection. They don't realize that CP/CPPS can be caused by a constellation of different problems.

You may need to see a urologist who is affiliated with an academic medical center. He/she will be up-to-date on the latest diagnostic procedures and treatments for ongoing pelvic pain.

Recent approach: Researchers recently introduced the UPOINT (urinary, psychosocial, organ specific, infection, neurologic/systemic and tenderness of skeletal muscles) exam. It categorizes the different causes of CP/CPPS and helps doctors choose the best treatments.

Your doctor will perform a physical exam and take a detailed history. He will ask where the pain is, how often you have it and how severe it is. He also will ask if you've had recurrent urinary tract infections, sexually transmitted diseases, persistent muscle pain, etc.

Important: Arrive for your appointment with a full bladder. You might be asked to perform a two-glass urine test. You will urinate once into a container to test for bacteria/cells in the bladder. Then you will urinate a second time (following a prostate "massage") to test for bacteria/cells from the prostate gland.

NEXT STEPS

What your doctor looks for and what he may recommend...

• **Infection.** Even though it affects only a minority of men with pelvic pain, it's the first thing your doctor will check.

Consider yourself lucky if you have an infection: About 75% of men with bacterial prostatitis will improve when they take an antibiotic such as *ciprofloxacin* (Cipro).

The discomfort from an acute infection—pain, fever, chills—usually will disappear within two or three days. You will keep taking antibiotics for several weeks to ensure that all of the bacteria are gone.

In rare cases, an infection will persist and become chronic. Men who experience symptoms after the initial antibiotic therapy will need to be retested. If the infection still is there, they will be retreated with antibiotics.

• **Urinary symptoms.** These include frequent urination, urinary urgency and residual urine that's due to an inability to completely empty the bladder. Your doctor might prescribe an alpha-blocker medication, such as *tamsulosin* (Flomax), to relax muscles in the prostate and make it easier to urinate.

Also helpful: Lifestyle changes such as avoiding caffeine and limiting alcohol...not drinking anything before bedtime...and avoiding decongestants/antihistamines, which can interfere with urination.

• **Pelvic pain.** It is the most common symptom in men with CP/CPPS. It's usually caused by inflammation and/or tightness in the pelvic floor, a group of muscles that separates the pelvic area from the area near the anus and genitals. The pain can be limited to the pelvic area, or it can radiate to the lower back, thighs, hips, rectum or bladder.

Helpful treatments...

• **Kegel exercises to ease muscle tension and pain.** The next time you urinate, try to stop the flow in midstream—if you can do it, you're contracting the right muscles. To do a Kegel, squeeze those muscles hard for about five seconds...relax for five seconds...then squeeze again. Repeat the sequence five or 10 times—more often as the muscles get stronger. Do this five times a day.

• **Mind-body approaches,** including yoga and progressive relaxation exercises, can help reduce muscle spasms and pelvic pain.

• **Anti-inflammatory drugs,** such as ibuprofen or aspirin, as directed by your doctor. If you can't take these medications because of stomach upset or other side effects, ask your doctor about trying quercetin or bee pollen supplements. They appear to reduce inflammation in the prostate gland. Follow the dosing instructions on the label.

• **Sitz bath** (sitting in a few inches of warm water) can relieve perianal/genital pain during flare-ups. Soak for 15 to 30 minutes.

• **Treatment for depression,** anxiety or stress. Therapy and/or stress reduction are an important part of treatment because both approaches can reduce muscle tension. Also, patients who are emotionally healthy tend to experience less pain than those who are highly stressed.

Helpful: Cognitive behavioral therapy, which helps patients identify negative thought patterns and behaviors that increase pain.

I also strongly advise patients to get regular exercise. It's a natural mood-booster that helps reduce stress, anxiety and pain.

You Can Relieve Prostate Pain Naturally

Mark A. Stengler, NMD, licensed naturopathic medical doctor in private practice, Stengler Center for Integrative Medicine, Encinitas, California...adjunct associate clinical professor at the National College of Na tural Medicine, Portland, Oregon...author of many books, including *The Natural Physician's Healing Therapies* and coauthor of *Prescription for Natural Cures. MarkStengler.com*

When it comes to men's health, we hear a lot about enlarged prostate and prostate cancer. But there is another prostate ailment that gets much less attention yet affects many men. Prostatitis, a very painful condition, is inflammation of the prostate gland. It can be difficult to diagnose because its symptoms (persistent pain in the pelvis or rectum...discomfort in the abdomen, lower back, penis or testicles...difficult, painful or frequent urination or painful ejaculation) are similar to those of other conditions such as an enlarged prostate or a urinary tract infection.

It is estimated that almost half of all men will be affected by prostatitis at some point in their lives. If the condition lasts for three months or longer, it's considered to be chronic prostatitis.

Mainstream medicine often is unsuccessful in treating chronic prostatitis, leaving men in pain and without hope of feeling better. In my practice, I have had lots of success treating chronic prostatitis as both an inflammatory condition (which it always is) and as a possible fungal infection.

REASONS BEHIND PROSTATITIS

For a long time, it was thought that prostatitis could be caused only by bacterial infection. That view was dispelled when several studies found that the bacteria in the prostates of both healthy men and men with prostatitis were essentially identical. It's now understood that most prostatitis cases are not caused by bacteria. Still, most mainstream physicians routinely prescribe antibiotics for it—a treatment that is appropriate only if your case is one of a very small number actually caused by bacteria.

Although prostate inflammation is not well understood, the inflammation could be the result of inadequate fluid drainage into the prostatic ducts...an abnormal immune response...or a fungal infection.

PROSTATITIS TREATMENT PLAN

If you experience any of the symptoms of prostatitis mentioned above, see your doctor. Your visit should include a rectal exam to check for swelling or tenderness in the prostate...and a laboratory test of prostatic fluid to check for bacterial infection. (Fluid is released during prostate gland massage.) I also recommend that you have your doctor order a urine culture to test for fungal infection (most medical doctors don't test for this).

In a small number of cases, the lab test does reveal a bacterial infection, and an antibiotic is appropriately prescribed. But if there is no bacterial infection, then I recommend that men with this condition follow an anti-inflammatory, antifungal treatment plan for two months. If symptoms subside but don't disappear, continue for another two months. Even if you don't have a test for fungal infection, I often advise following the antifungal portion of the program (along with the inflammation portion) to see if it helps to relieve symptoms.

FOODS THAT BATTLE PROSTATITIS

- **Anti-inflammatory diet.** Eating a diet of whole foods and cutting out packaged and processed foods go a long way to reducing inflammation in general and prostate inflammation in particular.

Eat: A variety of plant products to maximize your intake of antioxidants, which are natural anti-inflammatories...coldwater fish such as salmon, trout and sardines, which are high in omega-3 fatty acids...and pumpkin seeds, which are high in zinc, a mineral that helps reduce prostate swelling.

Don't eat: Foods that are high in saturated fat, such as red meat and dairy, which can make inflammation worse. Avoid alcohol, caffeine, refined sugar and trans fats, all of which tend to contribute to inflammation.

- **Antifungal diet.** If you already are following the anti-inflammatory diet above, then you have eliminated refined sugar from your diet. (Fungi thrive on sugar!) Also try eliminating all grains (including whole grains and rice) from your diet. Fungi thrive on these foods.

PROSTATE-PROTECTIVE SUPPLEMENTS

The following supplements have targeted benefits for prostate inflammation. They are safe to take together, and there are no side effects. Many men feel much better within two weeks of taking these supplements.

- **Rye pollen extract.** Studies show that rye pollen extract can relieve the pain of chronic prostatitis. In one study published in *British Journal of Urology,* men with chronic prostatitis took three tablets of rye pollen extract daily. After six months, 36% had no more symptoms and 42% reported symptom improvement. Follow label instructions. The pollen component in rye pollen does not contain gluten, but if you have celiac disease or a severe allergy to gluten, look for a certified gluten-free product.

• **Quercetin.** This powerful flavonoid helps reduce prostate inflammation.

Dose: 1,000 milligrams (mg) twice daily.

• **Fish oil.** In addition to eating anti-inflammatory foods, these supplements are a rich source of inflammation-fighting omega-3 fatty acids.

Dose: 2,000 mg daily of combined EPA and DHA.

ANTIFUNGAL SUPPLEMENTS

Many patients benefit from taking one or more antifungal remedies. Several herbs—such as oregano, pau d'arco, garlic and grapefruit seed extract—have potent antifungal properties. They are available in capsule and liquid form. For doses, follow label instructions. Most patients feel better within two to four weeks of taking antifungal supplements.

Remedies That Relieve Genital Pain in Women

Joel M. Evans, MD, clinical assistant professor, Albert Einstein College of Medicine, New York City, and founder and director, The Center for Women's Health, Stamford, Connecticut. Dr. Evans is the coauthor of *The Whole Pregnancy Handbook. CenterForWomensHealth.com*

Ladies, have you ever worn too-tight jeans that rubbed your crotch raw...developed an itchy all-over rash that really did go everywhere...or had a sore or an infection (or even a cut from shaving the bikini area) that made your private parts painful or tender?

When discomfort occurs "down there"—especially when there is an open sore or when pain is accompanied by other symptoms that could indicate an infection, such as a fever or vaginal discharge—of course you need to contact your doctor so he or she can diagnosis the complaint and prescribe treatment. To relieve simple chafing or other minor injuries or irritations, though, there often are steps you can take at home that bring relief. In some cases, the remedies suggested below also can alleviate discomfort while you wait for your doctor-prescribed treatment to take effect.

Complaint: A cut or sore in the genital area...

If you've nicked yourself shaving your bikini area or otherwise injured your genital area, you'll need to give yourself some TLC for a few days to let the problem heal—not easy in an area where everything rubs together. If you've got genital herpes, you'll have already discussed how to handle outbreaks with your doctor, such as by taking oral antiviral medication. But with herpes sores, as with cuts, it's important to keep the area very clean.

To that end, after using the toilet, wipe yourself thoroughly but gently with moistened toilet paper, then pat the area dry with clean toilet paper. Do use disposable premoistened wipes because these may contain irritating chemicals.

To soothe sores or cuts as they heal, apply a topical ointment containing aloe, calendula or shea butter twice daily. If your discomfort is severe or extremely distracting, ask your doctor about using a prescription topical cream that contains a painkilling agent, such as lidocaine, for a few days.

Complaint: External itchiness, irritation, inflammation or rash...

Chafing (for instance, from very tight pants or overzealous cycling) and allergic reactions or sensitivities (to laundry products, personal-care products, clothing fabrics, even toilet paper) are two main reasons why women can end up with a hot, itchy rash or other type of irritation in the genital area. Your first order of business is to do some detective work to figure out the cause. Go over everything you've done in the past few days that is different from your normal routine. If you identify a possible suspect, such as a new type of shower gel or new brand of laundry detergent or toilet paper, your course of action is clear—stop using it!

In the meantime, for relief, apply an ice pack to the affected region for 15 minutes or so two or three times daily. You can use an icy gel pack (available at drugstores)...create your own ice pack by placing ice chips in a plastic bag and wrapping it in a towel...or use a bag of frozen peas (peas are small enough to mold comfortably to the shape of your body). Whatever you use, do not apply the ice pack directly to the skin because this could damage the skin—instead, put a thin cloth between you and the ice pack.

It's also helpful to take a cool oatmeal bath once or twice daily—the oatmeal soothes, moisturizes and coats irritated skin. You can buy ready-made oatmeal bath products (such as Aveeno Soothing Bath Treatment Colloidal Oatmeal Skin Protectant or a similar generic brand)...or make your own by running a cup of whole oats through the blender and adding them to the bath water. Soak for 10 to 20 minutes, using only your hands to wash yourself (no soap, washcloth or loofah, which could cause further irritation). Then dry off gently but thoroughly.

Until the area is healed, wear all-cotton underwear (no thongs)...opt for thigh-high or knee-high hose rather than pantyhose...and stick with loose-fitting cotton clothing as much as you can. Avoid panty liners and pads, which can trap moisture, slowing down healing.

Complaint: Internal vaginal itching or irritation...

Though a common culprit here is a recurrent or chronic yeast infection, you don't want to make assumptions. It's best not to use an over-the-counter anti-yeast product on your own because you cannot be sure that you have a yeast infection without going to the doctor. Yeast infections are often confused with bacterial infections, and the treatments are vastly different.

Until you can get to the doctor's office, for temporary relief, try taking frequent baths or sitz baths (using a plastic bowl that sits on top of your toilet seat so you can soak your pelvic area without getting your whole body wet). Use cool water, and soak for about 10 to 20 minutes two or three times daily. Bathing helps soothe the internal irritation and the itching because it dilutes the offending agent.

If it turns out that you are prone to chronic or recurrent yeast infections, for long-lasting relief, you and your doctor will need to work together to determine the underlying cause and find a solution. For example, you might start by trying to identify a trigger, such as latex condoms, and see whether switching to a nonlatex brand helps. Lifestyle changes—such as avoiding sugar, white flour and alcohol...reducing stress...and getting more sleep—also may help with chronic yeast infections. Your doctor also may suggest one week of nightly use of a natural douche or vaginal suppositories made with boric acid to help correct the vaginal pH. Recommended products: Arden's Powder Vaginal Cleansing Douche and Yeast Arrest boric acid suppositories.

Important: If you notice any painless genital symptom—lesion, bump, cyst, discharge—that does not go away within a few days, contact your doctor. Certain sexually transmitted diseases and genital cancers cause no pain at the outset but absolutely must be treated.

Cheers to This Remedy!

Beer may cut risk for rheumatoid arthritis. Women who drink two to four beers weekly have 31% less risk of developing the chronic condition than women who never drink beer. Moderate use of any form of alcohol is linked to 21% lower risk for RA. Alcohol consumption also may improve symptoms in people who already have the disease.

Possible reason: RA is an inflammatory disease—and alcohol has a known anti-inflammatory effect.

Bing Lu, MD, DrPH, is assistant professor of medicine at Brigham and Women's Hospital and Harvard Medical School, both in Boston, and lead researcher for a study of 238,131 women, published in *Arthritis & Rheumatology.*

Got Pain in Your Heel, Knee or Elbow?

Sabrina M. Strickland, MD, an orthopedic surgeon and specialist in sports medicine at the Hospital for Special Surgery and an assistant professor at Weill Cornell Medical College, both in New York City. She is also chief of orthopedics at the Bronx Veterans Affairs Medical Center in Bronx, New York.

Virtually all adults suffer a bone or joint (orthopedic) injury at some point in their lives. Often complicated by damage to nearby muscles or ligaments, orthopedic complaints can severely limit movement and sometimes cause excruciating pain.

Although surgery is available to correct most orthopedic injuries, about 80% of cases can be treated with appropriate home care, such as rest, anti-inflammatory drugs and applications of ice and/or heat.

Best treatments for some of the most common orthopedic complaints...

BONE SPURS

Bone spurs (osteophytes) are bony outgrowths that can form on the spine or a joint—in your knees, hips, elbows, fingers or feet. Although no one knows what causes bone spurs, people with osteoarthritis have a higher risk of getting them, so it's possible that they're a normal part of aging.

Nonsteroidal anti-inflammatory drugs (NSAIDs) can be used if bone spurs cause pain. If the spurs interfere with your ability to perform everyday activities, surgery may be considered (the specific type of surgery would depend on the location of the bone spur).

Heel spurs, which form where the connective tissue of the foot (fascia) joins the heel bone (calcaneus), are one of the most common types of bone spur.

Important: Plantar fasciitis, inflammation of the plantar fascia (the arch tendon of the foot), is an injury that often occurs as a result of overuse. This condition, which causes heel pain that may radiate forward into the foot, differs slightly from a heel spur, which can result from repetitive pulling of the plantar fascia.

Main treatment: For heel spurs, place a silicone heel cup, available at pharmacies for $5 to $10, in your shoe. It cushions the heel and reduces pain. Use the heel cup daily—especially when wearing hard shoes—then gradually taper off its use. This approach, along with physical therapy, relieves the pain within a few months. A heel cup may also improve symptoms of plantar fasciitis.

Surgical option: Plantar fasciotomy, in which all or part of the fascia is separated from the heel bone, is performed when the pain from heel spurs or plantar fasciitis is intense and doesn't improve within nine months with other treatments. In rare cases, nerve injury to the foot or infection can occur.

KNEE PAIN

The meniscus is a C-shaped piece of cartilage that helps stabilize the knee. People who suddenly twist or rotate the knee can tear a meniscus. In younger adults, a torn meniscus is usually caused by traumatic injury—from playing sports, for example. In people who are middle-aged and older, it's more likely to be caused by age-related degeneration of the cartilage.

Symptoms: A "popping" sensation in the knee, followed by pain and swelling within a day. Magnetic resonance imaging (MRI) studies in knee patients show that about one-third have meniscal tears that don't cause discomfort or loss of mobility. These tears do not require treatment.

Main treatment: Patients with mild symptoms, such as pain and/or swelling, are often given an injection of cortisone and/or assigned to physical therapy. This approach often eliminates symptoms within four to six weeks, even if the meniscus doesn't completely heal.

Also helpful: The supplements glucosamine (1,500 mg daily) and chondroitin (1,200 mg daily) may improve symptoms in people who also have arthritis. Combination formulas are available. I tell patients to use glucosamine and chondroitin for three months while trying other nonsurgical treatments.

Caution: Glucosamine supplements may not be safe for people with seafood allergies.

Surgical option: Between 25% and 35% of patients with a torn meniscus will require surgery to regain normal knee motion and stability. In some cases, the meniscus can be repaired. More often, the torn portion is trimmed away. People who have had the surgery usually regain all or most of their normal knee function within four to six weeks. Risks, though rare, include infection and injury to nerves or blood vessels in the knee.

TENNIS ELBOW

About 90% of patients who get tennis elbow (lateral epicondylitis) do not play tennis. The condition is caused by overuse of the extensor tendon, which runs from the wrist to the elbow. People who flex the wrist repeatedly—from prolonged hammering or painting, for example, or from poor tennis form—are at greatest risk.

Symptoms: Pain that radiates from the elbow to the forearm and/or wrist...pain when bending the wrist...or tenderness on the outside of the elbow.

Medical experts used to think that tennis elbow was mainly due to inflammation.

New finding: The real problem is a condition in the cells of the tendon, known as tendonosis, in which wear and tear is thought to cause degeneration of the tendon. Experimental treatments, such as injecting platelet-rich plasma, are meant to promote tissue repair rather than fight inflammation.

Main treatment: About 90% of people with tennis elbow recover with rest and the use of ice. Also, patients should use a counterforce brace, which limits stress on the proximal part of the tendon (near the elbow). Avoid painful activities for two weeks, then gradually resume them with use of the brace.

Helpful: An exercise that lengthens the muscle and accelerates healing.

What to do: While keeping the wrist straight, hold a hammer in the hand of the affected arm. With the palm facing down, slowly bend the wrist downward. At the bottom of the movement, switch the hammer to the other hand to avoid lifting the weight with your bad arm. Repeat eight to 10 times, a few times a day.

Surgical option: Fewer than 10% of patients with tennis elbow will require surgery. The goal is to remove dead tissue from the area to encourage the formation of new blood vessels and healthy tissue.

Patients typically are able to resume most activities in four to six weeks, and to resume tennis and other sports in four to six months. In rare cases, nerve and/or ligament damage may occur.

The Real Reason Your Joints Won't Stop Hurting

Harris H. McIlwain, MD, a pain specialist who is board-certified in internal medicine, rheumatology and geriatric medicine. With a private practice in Tampa, Dr. McIlwain is the author of 28 books on topics including arthritis, osteoporosis, back pain and fibromyalgia.

That stabbing, aching pain in your joints may mean that you just have a touch of garden-variety osteoarthritis. Or so you tell yourself.

What most people don't realize: When osteoarthritis wears down the cartilage covering the ends of your bones, it can lead to bony growths known as osteophytes, an often undetected source of severe joint pain.

Commonly known as bone spurs, these smooth or pointed growths on normal bone tissue also can form in response to stress on a joint—as may occur from repetitive motion activities, such as running or typing. Regardless of the trigger, bone spurs can rub against other bones, ligaments, tendons or nerves and are marked by painful inflammation.

Why this matters: It's important to distinguish bone spurs from run-of-the-mill arthritis so that you can take the necessary steps to stay ahead of potentially debilitating joint inflammation. If not dealt with in the right way (and at the right time), bone spurs often require powerful additional treatment to control the pain, and this treatment can have bad side effects. You want to deal with bone spurs early.

What you need to know to determine whether you have bone spurs—and the therapies that help most...

MORE THAN ARTHRITIS

How do you tell whether your joint pain is partly or completely due to bone spurs?

Clues to watch for: Osteoarthritis pain tends to come and go gradually—like the general stiffness that affects a large area of your body, such as your lower back, in the morning but eases by afternoon.

A bone spur, on the other hand, may cause chronic localized pain that's bad enough to make you not want to move your back, neck, hip, finger or some other joint that may be affected. You may have bone spurs in more than one place, but one spur could cause more pain, depending on its location and the amount of physical activity in that area.

The more sudden and severe the pain, the more likely that a bone spur is the culprit. Numbness, tenderness and weakness may also occur. If a parent or sibling has suffered from bone spurs, you're at increased risk, too—research suggests there is a genetic component.

HOT SPOTS FOR BONE SPURS

Any joint can develop a bone spur, but here are the most common locations and how the pain and other symptoms may vary in each part of your body...

- **Knees.** Bone spurs in the knee—a common location for those that occur with osteoarthritis—often resemble a pointy bird's beak on X-rays. The resulting discomfort is typically a blend of arthritis and bone spur pain—both sore and sharp.
- **Feet and/or heels.** Acute pain that occurs with every step—the kind that makes you want to avoid walking—can signal bone spurs in the feet and/or heels (often called "heel spurs"). Corns and calluses may also build up over heels or toes as the body tries to protect the area by providing added padding. Therefore, if you have pain along with corns and/or calluses, ask your doctor to check for a bone spur.
- **Hips.** Arthritis in the hips generally produces a deep aching and stiffness that occurs when you stand or walk. Bone spurs at the side of the hip—where the bony prominence can sometimes be felt—trigger pain when the hip is flexed, such as when riding a bike.
- **Hands and/or shoulders.** Jabbing pain (rather than a dull throb) is the telltale sign.
- **Neck and/or spine.** Bone spurs at these locations usually do not cause pain unless accompanied by arthritis, but they can pinch the spinal cord and irritate surrounding nerves.

GETTING DIAGNOSED

If you have one or more bone spurs, the usual arthritis treatments—including nonsteroidal anti-inflammatory drugs (NSAIDs), such as *ibuprofen* (Motrin) and *naproxen* (Aleve)... stretching...and warm heat—often don't make a dent in your joint pain.

Because bone spurs usually are not large enough to feel externally, an X-ray is the easiest way to diagnose them. In certain areas, such as the neck, more advanced imaging tests, such as MRI or CT scans, may be needed to diagnose them.

My advice: If your joint pain doesn't respond to the therapies described earlier and you suspect that you may have bone spurs, you don't need a definitive diagnosis provided by an X-ray. Ask your physician whether you may have bone spurs, and get his/her OK to promptly try the approaches below. If you don't start treatment quickly, the serious pain that bone spurs typically cause may limit your use of the joint, progressively weakening muscles surrounding it and creating an even worse problem.

FINDING THE BEST TREATMENT

Among the best therapies for joint pain due to bone spurs...

- **Alternate heating pads and ice packs in 20-minute intervals.** Use ice first to ease acute pain, then moist heat to penetrate inflamed areas. Do this twice a day.
- **Get acupuncture.** Acupuncture has been shown to reduce pain and improve functional mobility. Your acupuncturist will tailor a treatment plan for your bone spur.
- **Eat inflammation-fighting foods.** Processed foods promote inflammation, while certain whole foods, such as salmon, nuts, beets, leafy greens, olive oil and berries, fight

it. Include as many of these foods in your daily diet as possible.

- **Use targeted supplements.** These include fish oil, turmeric and ginger. There is strong research showing that these supplements help fight painful inflammation. My advice: You can take one or all of these supplements, depending on the intensity of your pain. Daily dosages are up to 3 g of fish oil…three 400-mg to 600-mg tablets or capsules of turmeric…and two 500-mg to 1,000-mg capsules of ginger, taken with food. It usually takes about two months for turmeric to work.

Caution: Talk to your doctor before using any of these supplements if you take any type of medication (especially a blood thinner) or have a chronic medical condition.

- **Try ultrasound therapy.** Ultrasound uses sound waves that can penetrate more than two inches into the body to reach the painful area. Often used for shoulder or heel pain caused by bone spurs, it can be administered by a medical doctor or physical therapist. Caveat: The pain relief provided by ultrasound may be long-lasting but sometimes lasts only a few weeks.

WHEN TO CONSIDER SURGERY

One of the biggest misconceptions about bone spurs is that they need to be removed surgically. The truth is, when strategies such as those described in this article are used, the inflammation may lessen after a period of weeks or months even though the spur does not go away.

In determining the need for surgery, location of the bone spurs is the key factor. For example, bone spurs located in the neck can press on nerves or even the esophagus, which can interfere with swallowing.

Generally, however, the risks associated with surgery, such as infection, outweigh the benefits for most bone spurs. If you have tried the regimen described above for bone spurs for about a year but still have not gotten adequate pain relief, then ask your primary care doctor for a referral to an orthopedic surgeon.

New Relief for Back Pain: Vitamin D

Stewart B. Leavitt, PhD, editor of *Pain Treatment Topics (Pain-Topics.org)*. *Pain Treatment Topics* provides access to news, information, research and education for a better understanding of evidence-based pain-management practices. Neither the author nor sponsor has a vested interest in nutritional supplements or offers vitamin D prescribing advice for individual patients.

Do you have back pain that is not linked to a specific injury or nerve problem? According to new research, the root cause may be as simple as a deficiency of vitamin D and, if so, the solution may be equally simple—a daily dose of this effective and inexpensive nutrient.

HOW VITAMIN D HELPS BACK PAIN

Stewart B. Leavitt, PhD, editor of the website *Pain Treatment Topics* (*www.pain-topics.org*), believes that most people are functionally deficient in vitamin D. As we know, the body manufactures vitamin D from sunlight exposure or gets it from food sources such as salmon, tuna, eggs and fortified dairy foods. Often though, this is not enough for optimal health. Insufficient levels of this nutrient affect the body's ability to absorb calcium from foods. This, in turn, can negatively affect bones, muscles and nerve function, leading to back pain among other problems.

In reviewing 22 clinical investigations for his peer-reviewed report, "Vitamin D—A Neglected 'Analgesic' for Chronic Musculoskeletal Pain," Dr. Leavitt found that people with chronic body aches and back pain usually had low levels of vitamin D. The good news is that once they began getting enough of this nutrient, aches and pains diminished or even disappeared. By restoring calcium balance throughout the body, extra vitamin D helps maintain healthier bones and muscle strength. Vitamin D also acts as a hormone, necessary for the health of many tissues and organs in the body. Because it addresses the underlying cause of pain rather than the pain itself, it may take weeks or even months before there is noticeable improvement.

ABC'S OF VITAMIN D

Generally speaking, Dr. Leavitt says that the amount of vitamin D (400 to 800 IU) in regular multivitamins is insufficient. Experts believe the body requires at least 1,000 IU of vitamin D daily and that people with chronic musculoskeletal pain need even more—2,000 or more IU daily. (*Note:* Supplemental vitamin D should only be taken under physician oversight.) Vitamin D comes in two forms—D-2 and D-3. Dr. Leavitt favors D-3, which is also known as cholecalciferol. More good news: Vitamin D is inexpensive—typically no more than 10 cents a day.

Vitamin D should be viewed as a helping hand, not a miracle worker. It may not replace other medications for people suffering from chronic pain, but it may decrease your discomfort and reduce your need for pain medications. That said, if you suffer from an aching back, it's worth taking a second look at this "neglected analgesic." Consult your doctor for further advice about your specific level of need.

Will Surgery Help Your Back Pain—Or Make It Worse? How to Tell

David Hanscom, MD, board-certified orthopedic spine surgeon, Swedish Medical Center, Seattle. He is the author of *Back in Control: A Spine Surgeon's Roadmap Out of Chronic Pain. DrDavidHanscom.com*

Does your back hurt...and has your doctor suggested that surgery might help? If so, don't be too quick to take the bait. Instead, take 10 seconds to check out a simple chart that can help you determine whether you are a good candidate for back surgery—or not.

Why this is so important: In today's profits-before-people health-care environment, patients who complain of back pain often get hooked into having operations that they don't need and that probably won't help. Even worse, back surgery can carry risks for infection and nerve damage that can cause sexual dysfunction, incontinence or even paralysis.

As a consumer, you can and must take a proactive stance to ensure that you aren't pushed into unnecessary and potentially catastrophic surgery. Spine procedures are costly and surprisingly ineffective, statistically speaking—surgery for nonspecific lower-back pain has a success rate of less than 30%—yet for the hospitals and physicians involved, these operations are highly profitable.

Take spinal fusion, for instance, a procedure in which two or more vertebrae are joined together. With more than 450,000 spinal fusions being done in the US each year, the operation has become more common than hip replacement—though it seldom helps. What's more, new research shows that as many as half of these surgeries are done on people who do not meet the medical criteria for needing them.

Statistically, 15% to 20% of patients having spinal fusion require another surgery within one year. Dr. Hanscom cited research showing that, in his home state of Washington, only 15% of workers who underwent spinal fusion for lower-back pain had enough reduction in pain a year later to be able to return to their jobs.

SUCH A SIMPLE SOLUTION

Back pain affects four out of five people at some point. Despite how common the problem is, though, its treatment often is shrouded in mystery, Dr. Hanscom said. In his view, factors that contribute to the current crisis in back-pain care include deficiencies in physician training and understanding as to what does and doesn't help with back pain...an emphasis on the bottom line rather than patient welfare (because of course, surgeons make their money by performing surgery, not by steering patients away from operations)...and patients who have grown so desperate for help that they will agree to anything that they think might relieve their suffering.

But often, the reality boils down to one key point. "The main thing to understand is that if a back problem cannot be 'visualized'—meaning seen via an imaging test—then there should be no operation regardless of what other treatments have or have not already been tried. And in the vast majority of cases,

YOUR LIFESTYLE \ YOUR SYMPTOMS	You have a back abnormality that is visible via medical imaging **AND** Your symptoms are consistent with abnormality	Medical imaging has revealed no visible back abnormality **OR** Your symptoms are vague or inconsistent with your back abnormality
Your general health is good **AND** You sleep 7 hours or more per night **AND** You have normal, reasonable levels of stress	You are a good candidate for back surgery with minimal rehab.	Surgery will not help—but your body is well-positioned to heal itself naturally.
Your general health is not good **AND/OR** You sleep poorly or for less than 7 hours per night **AND/OR** You have high stress (from problems with your finances, job, family, etc.)	**Surgery may help fix your physiological abnormality, but your poor health and/or lifestyle puts you at high risk for complications, including chronic pain that may be much worse than your current discomfort.**	**Do not have back surgery! Not only will it fail, but it quite likely will make you even more miserable.**

Source: David Hanscom, MD

back pain cannot be visualized because it has nonspecific causes and is located in soft tissue, which means that surgery cannot solve the problem," Dr. Hanscom said.

When surgery won't help, Dr. Hanscom recommends that his patients follow a "structured care program" that he devised called Defined, Organized, Comprehensive Care (DOCC). First though, let's take a look at the clear and simple formula that he developed to help patients and their doctors determine whether it makes sense to even consider back surgery.

AN INTERSECTION OF SYMPTOMS AND LIFESTYLE

Back pain is complicated, with many potential causes. Absent a clear cause such as an injury or a defect of the spine, most cases of back pain eventually resolve on their own without treatment. But other factors, including the nature of the pain...your overall health...your stress level...and even how well you sleep can have a huge impact.

If your back pain does not go away on its own and if an imaging study reveals damage or an abnormality, surgery may help—or it may make matters worse. So to increase the odds that you will make the right decision, check out the chart above and choose the description that best fits you with regard to your symptoms and your lifestyle...then find the intersection of the two to see whether or not you're a good candidate for back surgery. (Of course, all patients should discuss the potential benefits and risks of surgery with their own doctors, so after you find your place on the chart, take this information to your doctor to discuss your particular situation.)

THIS CARE PLAN CAN HELP

Regardless of where you fall on the chart, the odds are that your back pain will improve dramatically if you learn and practice the techniques involved in Dr. Hanscom's DOCC structured program. Its basic premise is that pain is a perception rooted in neurological pathways, and understanding this allows you to gain control of what you feel. He outlines a step-by-step program that calms the nervous system so it can heal...while also retraining your brain so you literally no longer feel the pain. For details on Dr. Hanscom's DOCC program, visit *www.drdavidhanscom.com.*

When to Try "Keyhole" Surgery

David F. Jimenez, MD, FACS, chairman and professor in the department of neurosurgery at The University of Texas Health Science Center at San Antonio. He is the editor and a coauthor of *Intracranial Endoscopic Neurosurgery,* a textbook published by the American Association of Neurological Surgeons.

No one likes the thought of undergoing brain or spine surgery. Traditionally, a neurosurgeon would create a four- to six-inch incision and peel back the scalp before drilling through the skull to expose the brain…or make a similar-sized incision in your back, where muscles are then moved to expose the spine.

Recent development: Endoscopic, or minimally invasive, surgery, which has long been offered for such common procedures as gallbladder removal and knee surgery, is now widely available at major US medical centers for neurosurgical operations that involve the brain, spine and peripheral nerves.

Whether it's the removal of a brain tumor or the repair of herniated disks, spinal stenosis or carpal tunnel syndrome, neurosurgeons can now use sophisticated instruments to operate through an incision that's smaller than a dime or even through a natural opening such as a nostril.

This approach allows for a faster recovery and less pain and swelling than the traditional "open" procedures. Older patients frequently respond better to surgery that has minimal blood loss and requires less time under general anesthesia.

Why this matters: Even though endoscopic (sometimes known as "keyhole") neurosurgery is now available, not all surgeons have the training and experience to perform it. This means that you may not be offered endoscopic neurosurgery when it would be a better option than a traditional procedure—or a surgeon may attempt the endoscopic operation without adequate training and/or experience. *What you need to know…*

A NEW GENERATION OF NEUROSURGERY

What makes most types of surgery so challenging has less to do with repairing a problem—whether it's replacing a joint or removing an appendix—than simply getting access to the specific body part.

With endoscopic neurosurgery of the brain, the surgeon makes one or two incisions ranging from one-third to three-quarters of an inch and drills into the skull. A tube (endoscope) is passed through the narrow opening. Everything that's needed to complete the procedure, such as a lighted camera and cutting and scraping tools, is guided into place through the endoscope. Surgeons enter through the nostrils or above the eyebrow to operate on pituitary adenomas and tumors in the front of the brain.

The benefits of endoscopic surgery are largely due to the smaller incision, which is obviously less painful than a large one and has less risk for infection. Since there is less blood loss, there is less need for blood transfusion—another benefit.

Because endoscopic procedures can usually be done faster than traditional surgeries, patients also spend less time under general anesthesia, which reduces postoperative complications, such as cognitive dysfunction and nausea, and improves recovery.

In my practice, at least 30% of brain surgeries (including treatment for hydrocephalus—buildup of fluid in the brain that is drained via a shunt…and removal of skull-base tumors) are minimally invasive. Deep areas of the brain cannot be accessed with endoscopic neurosurgery. Most of our spine surgeries and virtually all carpal tunnel procedures are done this way.

Examples of when endoscopic neurosurgery can be used…

- **Herniated disk.** Computerized image guidance creates a three-dimensional image of the spine so surgeons can achieve a superb view of the operating field with an endoscopic incision that's barely more than a half-inch long. They use microinstruments to remove the damaged part of the disk.

• **Spinal stenosis.** This narrowing inside the spinal canal (usually due to arthritis) often causes leg pain or other symptoms. It's relatively easy to "open up" the spinal space with endoscopic surgery. Patients often make a full recovery within a month—and may be symptom-free almost immediately—while traditional surgery usually requires a recovery period of at least three months.

IS IT FOR EVERYONE?

In general, endoscopic surgery is a good option for most patients, especially those who are too old, ill or frail to have traditional surgeries.

One patient's story: My oldest patient was a 96-year-old woman whose spinal stenosis was so bad she could barely walk. She might not have done well with a lengthy open procedure, but I knew that I could complete the operation in about 90 minutes—half the usual time. Her pain was gone almost instantly—and a month later, she was bowling and dancing with her boyfriend.

The complication rate (infections and/or bleeding) for endoscopic surgery is at least as good as—and sometimes better than—that of traditional procedures. The numbers will only get better as surgeons gain experience and new approaches and technologies are developed.

FINDING THE RIGHT SURGEON

Before agreeing to any type of neurosurgery, ask the surgeon whether the procedure will be open or minimally invasive. While some operations, such as certain brain tumors, still require a traditional approach, most do not.

Chances are that you'll recover much more quickly—and experience less postoperative pain—if you go with endoscopy. If your surgeon doesn't do endoscopic surgery, get a second opinion. You can find a surgeon at the American Association of Neurological Surgeons, *www.aans.org*.

Experience and training are crucial for surgeons who perform endoscopic surgeries. Compared with traditional operations, endoscopic surgeries require the surgeon to overcome such issues as poor depth perception (from the endoscopic camera) and limited range of motion to manipulate surgical instruments. Make sure your surgeon has several years of experience in performing the procedure you'll be getting and has received endoscopic neurosurgical training.

Torn Meniscus? Think Twice Before Surgery

Kenneth Fine, MD, orthopedic surgeon, The Orthopaedic Center, Rockville, Maryland, and assistant clinical professor of orthopedics, George Washington University School of Medicine and Health Sciences, Washington, DC. *TheOrthoCenterMD.com*

Your knee is killing you and the pain won't quit, so you consult an orthopedist. He says that you've torn your meniscus, one of two C-shaped pieces of cartilage in the knee that serve as shock absorbers and help lubricate the joint. Then he recommends arthroscopic surgery to repair or trim back the tear, assuring you that it's a very common and minimally invasive procedure.

Do you say OK to the operation? Hold your horses! Even though this surgery is the most frequently performed orthopedic procedure in the US, there's growing evidence that in many cases—or even in most cases—it simply doesn't help. In fact, according to a new study, the procedure works no better than fake surgery! *Here's what your knees need you to know...*

REAL DEAL VS. A SHAM

The common treatment for a torn meniscus is an arthroscopic partial meniscectomy, in which a video camera and instruments are inserted through a few tiny incisions in the knee so the damaged portion of the meniscus can be trimmed away and smoothed out. It's the bread-and-butter procedure for many orthopedic surgeons, with 700,000 such procedures done each year in the US alone, at a cost of $4 billion.

The new study, which was done in Finland and published in *The New England Journal of Medicine*, included 146 men and women. All had knee pain consistent with a degenerative tear—the most common type, caused by the "wear and tear" of aging rather than a sudden injury—of the meniscus. They were divided into two groups. The first group got the real operation...the second group got a sham procedure in which the surgeon simply pretended to operate.

With the real meniscectomy, the damaged and loose parts of the meniscus were removed with tiny instruments, including a shaver to smooth the torn edges. For the sham operation, the surgeon asked for the same surgical instruments, manipulated the knee as if he were operating, pushed the shaver (without the blade) on the outside of the knee and used suction. Either way, participants were kept in the operating room for the same amount of time. Afterward, all were given the same postoperative walking aids and instructions for a graduated exercise program to promote recovery. Neither the patients nor the doctors with whom they followed up after surgery knew which procedure—real or sham—each patient had undergone.

Startling results: When patients were evaluated a year later, both groups reported equal levels of improvement in their knees. There were no significant differences in pain scores for the two groups, and both groups were equally satisfied with the outcome of their procedures—in fact, 93% of the surgery group and 96% of the sham group said that, given the chance, they would have the same procedure again.

In other words, the fake surgery was just as effective as the real deal!

IS THE TEAR CAUSING THE PAIN...OR NOT?

What does this mean? In many cases, a torn meniscus could be an early sign of arthritis rather than the source of knee pain. It would be the arthritis—not the tear in the meniscus—causing the pain.

Arthritis of the knee is extraordinarily common, with more than 9 million men and women in the US having x-ray evidence of the disease and symptoms. Up until a few years ago, many people with arthritis of the knee had an operation to "clean out" the joint—until several studies showed that the operation is just not helpful. In fact, some studies suggested that arthritis progresses more rapidly in people who have had an arthroscopic meniscectomy.

A basic principle is that surgery is good for fixing mechanical problems but not for curing pain. People with knee pain can become frustrated, and they want to 'do something'—but often surgery is just not the answer.

WHAT HELPS WHEN SURGERY WON'T

When Dr. Fine sees patients with knee pain and meniscus tears, especially the degenerative type, he first treats them conservatively. "My initial interventions don't do anything directly to the meniscus, but they can help maintain the basic overall functioning of the knee," he said. Typically he uses some or all of the following approaches...

Temporary "activity modification"—for instance, if you play a lot of tennis, you may need to cut back on your time and/or intensity until your knee feels better.

Ice packs applied for 20 minutes at a time, several times a day.

Strengthening exercises for the quadriceps and hamstring muscles that help support the knee, such as those recommended by the American Academy of Orthopaedic Surgeons.

Physical therapy to further strengthen muscles and extend the range of motion.

Oral anti-inflammatory medications, such as aspirin or ibuprofen, as needed.

A cortisone injection in the knee to reduce inflammation.

Weight loss, if appropriate.

WHEN IS AN OPERATION WARRANTED?

This is not to say that meniscus surgery is never justified. An operation may well be the best bet for...

Patients with degenerative tears that have resulted in a small piece of cartilage getting curled up under itself or a flap of cartilage literally getting stuck in the joint. An MRI sometimes can reveal such a problem, but often the doctor must make a clinical judgment as to its likelihood.

Patients who have acute tears (rather than degenerative tears) of the meniscus—the type typically associated with sports injuries or other trauma. For one thing, acute tears sometimes can be repaired effectively with sutures instead of being trimmed. For another thing, addressing such injuries helps keep the rough torn edge of the meniscus from damaging the joint surface...and this is particularly important in younger people, who generally have firmer cartilage than older people do, Dr. Fine said. In contrast, degenerative tears tend to be smoother and the cartilage softer, so they usually do no additional harm to the knee.

Bottom line: If you've been told that you need surgery for a torn meniscus, ask your doctor about the findings in this article...and if he doesn't make a clear case that your meniscus damage warrants surgery, get a second opinion before deciding whether to have the operation. You can get a referral from the American Academy of Orthopaedic Surgeons. After all, there's no point in putting yourself through the expense, inconvenience and risks that go along with any surgery if your knee is likely to improve just as much with some smart noninvasive therapies...plus time and patience.

Marijuana: A Safer Solution to Chronic Pain Relief?

Study titled "Medical Cannabis Laws and Opioid Analgesic Overdose Mortality in the United States, 1999-2010," published in *JAMA Internal Medicine.*

Don't kid yourself—if you use an opioid-based pain drug, such as OxyContin, Percocet, or Dilaudid, it could kill you. Thousands of people who use opioids for pain control die from overdose each year—and the number is increasing. In fact, opioid-overdose deaths have quadrupled within 10 years, according to the Centers for Disease Control and Prevention, and three out of four of these deaths involve prescription pain medications, not street drugs. Most of the people who die—60%—aren't using the drugs illegally either. They have legitimate prescriptions. Houston, we have a problem. But how to get a handle on it?

Enter medical marijuana. A recent study has revealed some very interesting facts about medical marijuana and relief of chronic pain and patient safety. Meanwhile medical marijuana is becoming legal in more and more states. *Here's why you should be thinking about it if you or a loved one suffers from chronic pain...*

MAKING THE CONNECTION

A team of investigators from the University of Pennsylvania decided to take a look at the incidence of opioid-related deaths in states that have legalized medical marijuana. They reasoned that since pain control is a major reason why people use medical marijuana, states that have legalized or decriminalized the herb might have lower rates of opioid-related deaths.

To test its theory, the team analyzed medical marijuana laws and 10 years' of death certificates from the entire United States. The research team discovered that, in states that allowed medical marijuana, the overall average annual death rate from opioid overdose was almost 25% lower than it was in states where medical marijuana remained illegal. Not only that, but the relationship grew stronger over time. When average death rates were looked at on a year-to-year basis, the researchers discovered that deaths from opioids decreased by an average 20% in the first year of medical marijuana legalization...25% by the second year...and up to 33% by the fifth and sixth years after medical marijuana was legalized.

Keep in mind that, whatever you might think of marijuana as a recreational drug, we are not talking about recreational use here—we are talking about marijuana as an alternative to potentially dangerous and addictive drugs that often lose effectiveness with long-term use and, thus, lead people with chronic pain to up their dosages to get the same effect.

Now, it's true that the University of Pennsylvania study doesn't show the degree to which the decline in opioid death rates in states with legal medical marijuana is due to patients switching from opioids to marijuana. More research is needed on that issue. And the study is not a carte blanche invitation for everyone with chronic pain to start using marijuana. Marijuana is not an across-the-board solution for everyone with intractable pain. But the study does provide yet more scientific evidence in support of marijuana as a medical treatment. At minimum, it suggests that rather than being a so-called "gateway drug" to opiate use, as we were told years ago, marijuana can be a lifesaving alternative to opiates.

When Neck Pain Means a Serious Problem

Seek medical attention if neck pain precedes or accompanies a headache—it could indicate an impending stroke or heart attack... when the pain radiates to your shoulders or arm or is accompanied by leg weakness or difficulty walking—this may be a sign of a herniated disk...if the pain worsens at night or is accompanied by fever or weight loss—this may indicate an infection or another serious condition, such as cancer.

Mayo Clinic Health Letter. *HealthLetter.MayoClinic.com*

Natural Help for Back Pain

Back pain can be helped by topical herbal remedies with fewer side effects. The remedies—capsaicin (cayenne) and a wintergreen/peppermint oil combination—are available over the counter. Apply the product to the painful area three times a day, following directions on the package insert. The remedies have shown promising results, but direct testing comparing the herbal remedies to standard painkillers is needed.

Charles H. Hennekens, MD, DrPH, the first Sir Richard Doll Professor and senior academic adviser to the dean in the Charles E. Schmidt College of Medicine at Florida Atlantic University, Boca Raton.

Self-Help for Painful Heels

Jim Johnson, PT, is a physical therapist and clinical instructor at Emory University Hospital in Atlanta. He is the author of 11 books, including *The 5-Minute Plantar Fasciitis Solution* and *Treat Your Own Knee Arthritis*. *BodyMending.com*

Ouch! Have you been recently plagued by a debilitating sharp pain in one or both heels? You most likely have plantar fasciitis (PLAN-tar fash-she-EYE-tis), a condition characterized by persistent, stabbing pain in one or both heels.

Physical therapist Jim Johnson, PT, a clinical instructor at Emory University Hospital, says that plantar fasciitis results from injury to and incomplete healing of the plantar fascia, a thick band of tissue that runs along the sole from heel to toes to help support the arch of the foot when a person stands or walks. Plantar fasciitis can afflict anyone but usually arises from some sort of physical stress—for instance, playing more tennis than you're accustomed to...taking up a new sport...or even just being on your feet a lot, especially on hard surfaces. Stiff ankles and/or excess weight contribute to the problem by putting pressure on the plantar fascia.

If you have heel pain, your podiatrist or physical therapist can confirm the plantar fasciitis diagnosis. Often the condition eventually goes away on its own, Johnson said—but since this can take months, you'll want to know what you can do to alleviate pain and hasten healing. *What helps...*

- **Stretch the plantar fascia.** Do this before getting out of bed and twice more during the day, continuing until symptoms are gone. Sit on the edge of your bed or in a chair and rest the ankle of the affected foot on the opposite knee. With either hand, grasp the base of the toes and gently pull the toes back toward the shin until you feel a stretch through the sole. Hold for 10 seconds...rest...repeat 10 times. For detailed instructions and illustrations, see Johnson's book, *The 5-Minute Plantar Fasciitis Solution*.

• **Stretch your calves.** Increasing calf muscle flexibility helps support the plantar fascia. Four times daily: Stand on the bottom step of a stairway, facing the stairs and holding the railing. Place the ball of each foot on the edge of the step so your heels hang off. Keeping knees straight, slowly lower your heels until you feel a mild stretch in your calves. Hold for 20 seconds...rest...repeat three more times.

• **Use shoe inserts that support the arch and cushion the heel.** These change the way your feet sit in shoes, reducing stress on the feet as you stand or walk. The inserts sold at drugstores for about $15 to $20 generally work as well as more expensive custom-made inserts, Johnson noted. Put inserts in both shoes even if only one heel hurts and use them daily for eight to 12 weeks.

• **Wear a night splint.** Tissues in the sole tend to constrict and tighten at night, which is why plantar fasciitis patients often experience pain upon arising in the morning. The night splint, which looks like a big plastic boot, prevents constriction by keeping the ankle and foot at a 90° angle overnight, Johnson explained. Unless you have pain in both feet, it's OK to wear just one splint. Use it nightly for 12 weeks. Night splints start at about $30 and are sold at medical-supply stores and online (for instance, check *www.footsmart.com/c-night-splints-20.aspx*).

Johnson advised that surgery on the plantar fascia be considered only as a last resort. And even then, beware—surgery can cause the arch to drop and compromise foot stability and there is no conclusive evidence that it helps. A better medical treatment option is extracorporeal shockwave therapy, in which a machine sends ultrasonic waves through the sole, causing micro-injuries that are thought to increase the flow of blood and healing nutrients to the tissues. Fortunately, though, for most patients the aforementioned self-help techniques are enough to make heel pain a thing of the past.

Coffee Relieves Pain

The caffeine in coffee raises the body's level of dopamine, which causes pleasurable sensations that counteract pain. Caffeine also narrows swollen blood vessels in the brain that are associated with certain types of headaches, such as migraines. If you usually drink one cup of coffee a day, a second one may make you feel better when you get a headache.

Robert Kaniecki, MD, director, The Headache Center, University of Pittsburgh School of Medicine.

Pain in Your Big Toe? You May Have Gout

Robert T. Keenan, MD, MPH, a rheumatologist and assistant professor of medicine in the division of rheumatology at Duke University School of Medicine and medical director of the Infusion Center at Duke University Medical Center, both in Durham, North Carolina.

Approximately six million Americans suffer from gout, the most common form of inflammatory arthritis. Although gout is most often associated with pain, it is now thought that the condition also increases risk for hypertension and cardiovascular disease.

AGONIZING ATTACKS

Gout often strikes at the base of the big toe, causing pain that increases for eight to 12 hours and subsides within three to 10 days without treatment. Other joints can also be affected. The attacks are intermittent and unpredictable. They may occur every few weeks or months, once or twice a year or every few years. But without treatment, the attacks generally increase in duration as well as frequency.

The risks: Untreated gout can cause permanent joint damage. Some patients progress from recurrent gout to tophaceous gout, a severe form in which lumps of urate crystals form in and around joints or even under the skin. Gout increases the risk for kidney stones, and patients who don't achieve good control of their elevated uric acid levels are more likely to develop cardiovascular disease than those without gout.

EASY TO DIAGNOSE

Patients who are suspected of having gout are usually advised to have a blood test to measure uric acid. However, some asymptomatic patients have high levels of uric acid, while those in the midst of an attack may have apparently normal levels (3 mg/dL to 7 mg/dL). Typically, the uric acid level peaks around two weeks after an acute attack.

Joint aspiration is the best test for gout, especially in its early stages. Your doctor will insert a needle into the inflamed joint (lidocaine and numbing sprays minimize the pain of the needle) and withdraw fluid, which is then examined under a microscope. The presence of urate crystals means that you have gout, regardless of the uric acid concentrations in your blood.

Ultrasound is now used by some doctors to diagnose gout. It's painless and completely noninvasive. It's good for detecting gout (which may not be evident with a physical exam), but harder to diagnose in the early stages without joint aspiration.

BEST TREATMENTS

Treating gout is a two-step process. Depending on the severity of the attack, various medications can be used to reduce pain and inflammation.

Examples: Nonsteroidal anti-inflammatory drugs, such as *ibuprofen* (Motrin)...*colchicine* (Colcrys), the oldest medication used for treating gout...and corticosteroids, which serve as fast-acting anti-inflammatories.

To reduce uric acid, medications such as the following are taken one to two weeks after a gout attack (using these drugs during a gout attack can worsen symptoms)...

- **Febuxostat (Uloric)** is the first new oral drug for gout in 40 years. Taken daily, it can reduce uric acid to an optimal level within a few weeks. Most people with gout need to continue taking this drug indefinitely, but in rare cases it can be discontinued after about a year without subsequent flare-ups.
- **Allopurinol** (Zyloprim, Aloprim), like febuxostat, reduces uric acid concentrations. It's much less expensive than febuxostat ($40 versus $185 for 30 tablets), and it works well for most patients. It usually takes at least six to eight weeks to see a reduction in uric acid levels and may take subsequent dose increases to reduce uric acid to an appropriate level. An older gout drug, allopurinol is more likely to cause kidney problems than febuxostat.
- **Probenecid** (Probalan) increases the excretion of uric acid by the kidneys. Most patients who take it can achieve reductions in uric acid levels within two weeks. Potential side effects include kidney stones, gastrointestinal upset and rash. Probenecid can't be taken by patients with kidney disease.
- **Pegloticase** (Krystexxa) has just been approved by the FDA for the treatment of refractory gout, which can't be managed with other approaches. It's given by intravenous infusion once every two weeks. Side effects may include nausea, confusion and vomiting.

LIFESTYLE APPROACHES

People with gout were traditionally advised to avoid foods high in purines (such as anchovies and organ meats), which are metabolized to form uric acid. Research shows that this approach reduces uric acid levels only minimally, but in combination with drug therapy, exercise and weight loss, may help to prevent attacks. *Other strategies...*

- **Consume low-fat dairy.** Research shows that a high intake of low-fat milk and low-fat yogurt reduced the risk for gout by 50%. The benefit was mainly seen in those who consumed two or more eight-ounce glasses of skim milk daily—milk proteins reduce uric acid levels.
- **Avoid beer and liquor.** Both can raise uric acid and precipitate gout attacks. Beer contains the greatest amount of purines. Wine is thought to have antioxidant compounds that may mitigate the effects that alcohol has on gout.
- **Eliminate high-fructose corn syrup (HFCS).** This sweetener, commonly used in snacks, soft drinks and other processed foods, raises uric acid.

To minimize intake of HFCS: Eat whole, natural foods such as fresh vegetables, fruits and grains.

• **Get enough vitamin C.** Consuming at least 500 mg of vitamin C daily can reduce uric acid, but it may take large doses (at least 1,500 mg daily) to significantly reduce levels. Use caution, however, because high-dose vitamin C may cause upset stomach, diarrhea and kidney stones.

Best option: Dietary sources such as strawberries (one cup fresh contains 98 mg of vitamin C).

• **Eat cherries.** A 2010 study showed that one tablespoon of cherry juice concentrate (the equivalent of 45 to 60 cherries) twice a day cut gout attacks by more than 50%.

WHAT IS GOUT?

Gout occurs when uric acid, a by-product of metabolism, is produced in excessive amounts or when it is not excreted efficiently by the kidneys. A buildup of uric acid causes the formation of urate crystals in the fluid that lubricates joints. These crystals can trigger an immune response that causes inflammation and excruciating pain.

Promising New Treatment for Painful Heels

Luca M. Sconfienza, MD, is a radiologist at Policlinico San Donato in Milan, Italy, and lead author of a study of 44 people, presented at a meeting of the Radiological Society of North America.

If you dread getting out of bed because it hurts to put weight on your heel (particularly in the morning or after standing for a long time), chances are that you have plantar fasciitis—persistent, painful inflammation of a large ligament on the bottom of the foot. Usually it is treated with rest, exercises, splints and arch supports...steroid injections...a series of shockwave treatments (often uncomfortable)...or surgery.

Encouraging: A recent study investigated a new single-treatment therapy. Under ultrasound guidance, after injecting local anesthesia, researchers repeatedly punctured affected areas with a needle, creating a bit of bleeding (which hastens healing by increasing blood flow to the area)...then injected an anti-inflammatory steroid. Results: 95% of study participants were symptom-free within three weeks and remained so throughout the four- to six-month follow-up period.

Best: If you have severe plantar fasciitis that has not responded to noninvasive therapies, talk to your podiatrist about this technique, called dry-needling with steroid injection. More research is needed before it could become standard protocol—but results are promising.

Licorice Licks Pain

A dissolving oral patch shrinks painful canker sores by 90%, while untreated sores often get bigger. The patch, cankermelts, releases licorice root extract for two to six hours—and eases pain in about 10 minutes.

Ivanhoe Newswire.

Looking for Pain Relief? Try Prolotherapy

Allan Magaziner, DO, director of Magaziner Center for Wellness in Cherry Hill, New Jersey, and a clinical instructor at University of Medicine and Dentistry of New Jersey in New Brunswick. His website is *DrMagaziner.com.*

A medical procedure that "tricks" the body into healing itself, prolotherapy treats acute or chronic pain from damaged ligaments, tendons and cartilage. Some studies show significant improvement in patients with injuries or arthritis, especially in the joints, back, neck or jaw. Prolotherapy is used as a first-line therapy or when other treatments fail.

• **How it works.** A physician injects a solution, typically of dextrose (a sugar) and lidocaine (an anesthetic), into the painful area. This provokes minor, temporary inflammation...

causing the body to send more blood and nutrients to the spot...which hastens healing.

• **What to expect.** Each session lasts 15 to 30 minutes and includes from one to 20 injections, depending on the areas treated. Patients experience slight discomfort during injection and mild soreness for several days after. Minor pain might need one session...severe pain might require 10 sessions spread over several months.

• **Cautions.** Your doctor may advise you to temporarily reduce or discontinue anti-inflammatory drugs—aspirin, *ibuprofen* (Motrin), *naproxen* (Aleve)—while undergoing prolotherapy. *Acetaminophen* (Tylenol) is okay. If you take blood thinners or other drugs, tell your doctor—extra precautions may be warranted.

• **Finding a practitioner.** Prolotherapy should be administered by a physician trained in the procedure—preferably through the American Association of Orthopaedic Medicine, *www.aaomed.org*) or Hackett Hemwall Foundation (*www.hacketthemwall.org*). Visit these websites for referrals.

Cost: $100 to $400 per session. Because prolotherapy is considered experimental, insurance seldom covers it.

Gua Sha...Pain Relief

Arya Nielsen, PhD, licensed acupuncturist and gua sha researcher, department of integrative medicine, Continuum Center for Health and Healing, Beth Israel Medical Center, New York City. Dr. Nielsen, considered the Western authority on gua sha, is the author of *Gua Sha: A Traditional Technique for Modern Practice. GuaSha.com*

You may never have heard of *gua sha*—but if you experience recurrent muscle or joint pain, particularly in the back, neck or shoulder, this drug-free hands-on therapy is certainly worth learning about.

An East Asian healing technique, gua sha (pronounced *gwah sah*) is typically performed by an acupuncturist, but no needles are used. Instead, the practitioner uses a round-edged, handheld instrument on a particular area of the body to repeatedly "press-stroke" (stroke while applying gentle pressure) without breaking the skin.

"The purpose is to alleviate what in Chinese medicine is called 'blood stagnation.' This represents a kind of contraction of capillaries near the skin's surface and is associated with fixed or recurrent pain and sometimes illness. Moving the congested blood improves circulation to the muscles, tissues and organs directly beneath the area being treated. The patient experiences immediate changes in pain, stiffness and mobility," said Arya Nielsen, PhD, an authority on gua sha who practices at the Beth Israel Medical Center's Department of Integrative Medicine and who is the author of *Gua Sha: A Traditional Technique for Modern Practice.*

Dr. Nielsen explained that the press-stroking motion forces red blood cells out of the tiny capillaries and into the surrounding tissues. The capillaries are not broken and there is no external bleeding. However, numerous tiny reddish spots of blood called petechiae do appear just beneath the skin's surface, giving the area a rashlike appearance. (This is not the same as bruising, she said—a bruise represents traumatic damage to the tissue and can take a week or more to heal, but with gua sha the tissue is not damaged.) The red blood cells immediately begin to be reabsorbed. The resulting breakdown of hemoglobin (the oxygen-carrying pigment of red blood cells) increases the response of a particular enzyme and the bile pigments bilirubin and biliverdin—all of which are anti-inflammatory and stimulate the immune system, promoting healing over a period of days.

IF YOU WANT TO GIVE GUA SHA A TRY

Gua sha often is done on the back, neck, shoulders and hips, Dr. Nielsen said, though it can be used on other parts of the body. Sometimes the area treated is the painful spot itself, but other times it is an area that corresponds with a certain organ or body channel (meridian), according to the traditions of Eastern medicine.

A gua sha session usually lasts about 10 minutes. First the practitioner palpates an area to assess whether there is "sha" (stagnation) present in the tissue. The area to be treated is then lubricated with oil or a product like Badger Balm.

Next comes the press-stroking. Traditionally the Chinese used a smooth-edged soup spoon, but modern practitioners typically use a handheld instrument that looks like a metal cap with a smooth lip. "There is a small but real risk of exposure to blood-borne pathogens, so gua sha instruments should not be reused on other patients. Simple metal caps that can be disposed of after one use are recommended, rather than the outdated spoon, coin, jade, stone or bone tool," Dr. Nielsen said. Each particular narrow section of skin, or "stroke-line," is press-stroked with about six to 10 strokes. Where there is no blood stagnation, the skin simply turns pink…but where stagnation has occurred, gua sha causes the tiny red petechiae to appear.

"To the patient, gua sha feels invigorating. It does not hurt if done correctly. I have even treated babies and children without a problem," Dr. Nielsen said. The red marks raised on the skin immediately begin to change and fade and are completely gone within a few days. After a session, it is best to drink water and moderate your activity. Dr. Nielsen said, "I tell my patients, 'No drugs, booze, sex, fasting, feasting or hard labor, including working out, for the rest of the day after treatment.' In other words, mellow mode."

The number of sessions needed varies based on patients' conditions. Some people experience lasting relief after just one or two sessions. For patients with chronic conditions, Dr. Nielsen typically recommends three sessions one week apart, followed by sessions every other week as appropriate. The cost of treatment depends on the training of the practitioner and your location, as with most medical treatments. Check your insurance—it may pay for the treatment if it covers care by an acupuncturist.

Gua sha often can be safely used even on people who have a condition such as diabetes, who are pregnant or who use anticoagulant medication, Dr. Nielsen said—but for safety's sake, it is essential to be treated by a qualified licensed practitioner who is trained in gua sha. Acupuncturists often have such training, as do some physical therapists and massage therapists. To find a practitioner, Dr. Nielsen recommended contacting licensed acupuncturists in your area and asking about their level of experience with the technique. You can find nearby acupuncturists and verify their licensure through your state's department of public health, office of consumer affairs, office of professional regulators or similar agency.

Relief at Your Fingertips

Michael Reed Gach, PhD, founder of the Acupressure Institute in Berkeley, California, and author of self-healing instructional DVDs and CDs and many books, including *Acupressure's Potent Points, Acupressure for Lovers* and *Arthritis Relief at Your Fingertips. Acupressure.com*

You've probably heard of acupuncture, but there's something similar that you can do yourself—no needles involved—called acupressure. Acupressure can alleviate many physical, mental and emotional problems in only a few minutes—and it is free.

Acupressure involves stimulating acupoints on the body with fingertips or knuckles and is based on the principles of acupuncture, an ancient healing technique used by practitioners of Traditional Chinese Medicine (TCM). The acupoints often have ancient descriptive names, such as "Joining the Valley" and "Mind Clearing." Acupressure increases blood flow to the treated area and triggers the release of endorphins, pain-relieving brain chemicals.

Here are the acupressure techniques for various health problems. Unless otherwise noted, daily acupressure sessions, three times a day, are the best way to relieve a temporary or chronic problem.

ARTHRITIS PAIN

Joining the Valley is a truly amazing acupoint because it can relieve arthritis pain anywhere in the body.

Location: In the webbing between the thumb and index finger, at the highest spot of the muscle when the thumb and index finger are brought close together.

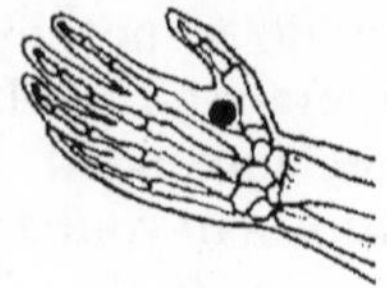

What to do: Rhythmically squeeze the acupoint. As you're squeezing, place the side of your hand that is closest to the little finger on your thigh or a tabletop. Apply pressure in the webbing as you press downward. This allows you to angle more deeply into the point, increasing the benefits.

Also good for: Headache, toothache, hangover, hay fever symptoms, constipation.

Caution: This point is forbidden for pregnant women because its stimulation can cause premature contraction in the uterus.

LOWER BACK PAIN

To help prevent and relieve lower back pain, practice this exercise for one minute three times a day. You can do it standing or sitting.

Location: Place the backs of your hands against your lower back, about one inch outside the spine.

What to do: Briskly rub your hands up and down—about three inches up and six inches down—using the friction to create heat in your lower back.

If you're doing the technique correctly, you'll need to breathe deeply to sustain the vigorous rubbing, and you'll break out in a slight sweat.

Also good for: Food cravings, especially sugar cravings, chronic fatigue, sexual problems, chills, phobias and fibromyalgia symptoms.

HEADACHES

The acupoints Gates of Consciousness relieve a tension headache or migraine.

Location: Underneath the base of your skull to either side of your spine, about three to four inches apart, depending on the size of your head.

What to do: Using your fingers, thumbs or knuckles, press the points under the base of your skull.

At the same time, slowly tilt your head back so that the angle of your head relaxes your neck muscles. Press forward (toward your throat), upward (underneath the base of your skull) and slightly inward, angling the pressure toward the center of your brain. Continue to apply pressure for two minutes, breathing.

Also good for: Neck pain, insomnia, high blood pressure.

Illustrations courtesy of Michael Reed Gach, PhD.

Extra Sleep May Help You Withstand Pain

American Academy of Sleep Medicine, news release.

Getting more sleep improves daytime alertness and reduces pain sensitivity in healthy adults, according to a small recent study.

STUDY DETAILS

The research included 18 mildly sleep-deprived volunteers who spent four nights getting either their normal amount of sleep or extending their sleep time to 10 hours per night. The extended sleep group slept an average of 1.8 hours more per night than those in the normal sleep group.

Tests showed that the nightly increase in sleep time was associated with increased daytime alertness and less pain sensitivity.

The length of time that people in the extended sleep group were able to keep their finger on a heat source increased by 25%, the investigators found. That increase is greater than what was found in a previous study when participants took 60 milligrams of the painkiller codeine before undergoing the same pain sensitivity test.

IMPORTANCE OF SLEEP AGAINST PAIN

The study, published in the journal *Sleep*, is the first to show that extended sleep in mildly sleep-deprived people reduces their pain sensitivity, according to the researchers. This and previous findings suggest that lack of sleep increases pain sensitivity.

"Our results suggest the importance of adequate sleep in various chronic pain conditions or in preparation for elective surgical procedures," said study lead author Timothy A. Roehrs, PhD, director of research at the Sleep Disorders and Research Center of Henry Ford Health System in Detroit. "We were surprised by the magnitude of the reduction in pain sensitivity, when compared to the reduction produced by taking codeine."

For more information about sleep, visit the website of the US National Institute of Neurological Disorders and Stroke, *www.ninds.nih.gov*, and search "understanding sleep."

Acupuncture for Pregnancy Pain

Acupuncture relieves pain during pregnancy. Pregnant women tend to arch their backs to balance their growing abdomens, creating extra strain on back and pelvic muscles.

Recent study: 60% of pregnant women who receive acupuncture report relief from discomfort in the back and pelvis.

Victoria Pennick, MHSc, senior clinical research project manager, Institute for Work and Health, Toronto, and lead author of a study of 1,305 pregnant women, published in *The Cochrane Library.*

Myotherapy: Drug-Free Help for Pain

The late Bonnie Prudden, who helped create the President's Council on Youth Fitness in 1956 and was one of the country's leading authorities on exercise therapy for more than five decades. In 2007, she received the Lifetime Achievement Award from the President's Council on Physical Fitness and Sports. She wrote 18 books, including *Pain Erasure.*

Can you imagine living well into your 90s and being able to eliminate virtually all of the aches and pains that you may develop from time to time?

Bonnie Prudden, a longtime physical fitness advocate, stayed pain free till her death at 97—even though she had arthritis that led to two hip replacements—by using a form of myotherapy ("myo" is Greek for muscle) that she developed more than 30 years ago.

Now: Tens of thousands of patients have successfully used this special form of myotherapy, which is designed to relieve "trigger points" (highly irritable spots in muscles) that develop throughout life due to a number of causes, such as falls, strains or disease.

By applying pressure to these sensitive areas and then slowly releasing it, it's possible to relax muscles that have gone into painful spasms, often in response to physical and/or emotional stress.

A simple process: Ask a partner (a spouse or friend, for example) to locate painful trigger points by applying his/her fingertips to parts of your body experiencing discomfort—or consult a practitioner trained in myotherapy.*

If you're working with a partner, let him know when a particular spot for each body area described in this article is tender.

Pressure should be applied for seven seconds (the optimal time determined by Prudden's research to release muscle tension) each time that your partner locates such a spot.

On a scale of one to 10, the pressure should be kept in the five- to seven-point range—uncomfortable but not intolerable.

The relaxed muscles are then gently stretched to help prevent new spasms.

If you prefer to treat yourself: Use a "bodo," a wooden dowel attached to a handle, and a lightweight, metal "shepherd's crook" to locate trigger points and apply pressure. Both tools are available at 800-221-4634, *www.bonnieprudden.com,* for $8 and $39.95, respectively.

For areas that are easy to reach, use the bodo to locate trigger points and then apply pressure to erase them. For spots that are difficult to reach, use the shepherd's crook to find and apply pressure to trigger points.

*To find a practitioner of Bonnie Prudden's myotherapy techniques, go to *www.bonnieprudden.com* or call 800-221-4634. If you are unable to find a practitioner near you, call local massage therapists and ask whether they are familiar with the technique.

As an alternative to the specially designed tools, you can use your fingers, knuckles or elbows on areas of the body that can be reached easily. *Common types of pain that can be relieved by this method...***

SHOULDER PAIN

Finding the trigger point: Lie face down while your partner uses his elbow to gently apply pressure to trigger points that can hide along the top of the shoulders and in the upper back. If you are very small or slender, your partner can use his fingers instead of his elbow.

Place one of your arms across your back at the waist while your partner slides his fingers under your shoulder blade to search for and apply pressure to additional trigger points. Repeat the process on the opposite side.

While still lying face down, bend your elbows and rest your forehead on the backs of your hands. With his hands overlapped, your partner can gently move all 10 of his fingers along the top of the shoulder to locate additional trigger points.

Pain-erasing stretch: The "shrug" is a sequence of shoulder exercises performed four times after myotherapy and whenever shoulder tension builds.

From a standing or sitting position, round your back by dropping your head forward while bringing the backs of your arms together as close as possible in front of your body. Extend both arms back (with your thumbs leading) behind your body while tipping your head back and looking toward the ceiling.

Next, with both arms at your sides, raise your shoulders up to your earlobes, then press your shoulders down hard.

LOW-BACK PAIN

Finding the trigger point: Lie face down while your partner stands to your right and reaches across your body to place his elbow on your buttocks in the area where the left back pocket would appear on a pair of pants. For seven seconds, your partner should slowly apply pressure to each trigger point—not straight down but angled back toward himself.

Repeat on the other side. If the pressure causes slight discomfort, your partner has found the right spot! If not, your partner should move his elbow slightly and try the steps again. Two to three trigger points can typically be found on each buttock.

Pain-erasing stretch: Lie on your left side on a flat surface (such as a bed, table or the floor). Bend your right knee and pull it as close to your chest as possible.

Next, extend your right leg, keeping it aligned with the left leg and about eight inches above it.

Finally, lower the raised leg onto the resting one and relax for three seconds. Perform these steps four times on each leg.

HIP PAIN

Finding the trigger point: The trigger points for hip pain are often found in the gluteus medius, the muscle that runs along either side of the pelvis.

Lie on your side with your knees slightly bent. Using one elbow, your partner should scan for trigger points along the gluteus medius (in the hip area, roughly between the waist and the bottom seam of your underpants) and apply pressure straight down at each sensitive spot for seven seconds.

The same process should be repeated on the opposite side of your body.

Pain-erasing stretch: Lie on your left side on a table with your right leg hanging off the side and positioned forward. Your partner should place one hand on top of your waist and the other hand on the knee of the dangling right leg.

This knee should be gently pressed down eight times. The stretch should be repeated on the opposite side.

**Check with your doctor before trying this therapy if you have a chronic medical condition or have suffered a recent injury.

Sex Can Ease Migraine Pain

Women who have sex when they feel a migraine coming on experience less head and neck pain, fatigue and moodiness. Nearly one-third of women who had sex at the start of a migraine reported reduced symptoms...and for 12%, sex stopped the migraine completely.

Possible reason: Sex and orgasm boost levels of the pleasure hormone serotonin—which is known to be low in migraine sufferers.

James R. Couch, MD, PhD, professor and former chair of neurology, University of Oklahoma Health Sciences Center, Oklahoma City, and leader of a study of 82 women with migraines, published in *Headache: The Journal of Head and Face Pain.*

Do-It-Yourself Pain Relief With a Tennis Ball

Mark A. Stengler, ND, naturopathic physician in private practice, Encinitas, California...adjunct associate clinical professor at the National College of Natural Medicine, Portland, Oregon...author of many books, including *The Natural Physician's Healing Therapies* and coauthor of *Prescription for Natural Cures.*

When patients come to me with sore or stiff muscles, one of the first things I suggest is a simple home remedy—self-massage with tennis balls. It is remarkably easy to do and effective. It is based on bodywork techniques such as myofascial release and acupressure, in which pressure is applied at the point or points of tenderness. I spoke with Mark H. LaBeau, DO, who specializes in family medicine and osteopathic manipulative medicine (a type of therapy that involves physical contact) at the Center for Advanced Medicine in Encinitas, California. Try it out—you'll find that this technique eases your muscle pain in minutes.

WHICH BALL IS BEST?

While using a tennis ball is more common, Dr. LaBeau also encourages patients to experiment with a golf ball, which often is easier to use because it's smaller. Try both—and see which works best for you. To relieve discomfort in two nearby areas, place two balls in a sock and arrange them at the points of tenderness.

SO EASY TO DO...

Even though we're using the word "massage," the technique actually involves just lying on or pressing on a tennis ball (not rolling over it). As you'll see, the pressure of your body's weight on the ball is all you need to relieve tension. The back, neck and feet are the places most helped by tennis ball massage, but you can place a ball under any muscle or muscle area in which there is tenderness or a knot.

Repeat each exercise multiple times a day, but limit the duration of each time to no more than 10 minutes. Doing it longer than that can irritate the tissue.

Caution: Ongoing muscle discomfort that lasts for about a week or more may be a sign of a more complex condition, such as a muscle tear or tendonitis, and should be evaluated by your doctor.

FOR THE BACK

Lie comfortably on the floor, and position the ball under the area or areas where you are experiencing any tenderness or pain. Adjust as needed. You should feel relief of some or all of the pain within five minutes. Remain with the ball in place for up to 10 minutes.

FOR THE NECK

Lie on the floor or a bed, and position the ball in the natural curve at the back of the neck...at the base of the neck...or on either side of the neck that is sore. You should feel relief of some or all of the pain within five minutes. Remain with the ball in place for up to 10 minutes.

FOR THE FOOT

Sit in a comfortable chair with your feet on the floor in front of you. Place a ball under your arch or any place that you feel pain. You can either press your foot into the ball—or roll over the tender point. (This is one time when rolling over the ball can help!)

Natural Ways to Get Relief from Painful Muscle Cramps

Jamison Starbuck, ND, is a naturopathic physician in family practice and a guest lecturer at the University of Montana, both in Missoula. She is past president of the American Association of Naturopathic Physicians and a contributing editor to *The Alternative Advisor: The Complete Guide to Natural Therapies and Alternative Treatments*.

As a kid, I loved the funny sound of "charley horse." Somewhere along the line, I learned that the term may have originated from a baseball pitcher who played in the late 1800s—Charley "Old Hoss" Radbourn evidently suffered from excruciating muscle cramps while playing baseball. Nowadays, I know how painful a muscle cramp can be, and as a naturopathic physician, I disagree with my medical doctor colleagues who believe that a muscle cramp is just one of those things you must "learn to live with." The truth is, muscle cramps usually result from one of three causes—dehydration, muscle overuse or mineral deficiency. *To protect yourself...*

• **Get enough fluids.** If you don't get enough fluids, your risk for muscle cramps increases, especially while exercising. Soda, juice, coffee, diet drinks and even sweetened electrolyte-replacement beverages are no substitute for plain water.

For adequate hydration: I recommend drinking one-half ounce of water per pound of body weight per day.* So, if you weigh 150 pounds, you should drink 75 ounces. It's wise to increase your total daily water intake by 16 to 32 ounces if you are doing vigorous exercise (such as hiking, biking or running)...are out in hot weather (above 80°F)...are pregnant (a risk factor for muscle cramps)...are flying long distances (through two or more time zones)...or if you are starting a new project, such as gardening or house painting, involving physical activity that stresses the muscles in new ways.

• **Stretch your muscles properly.** Sometimes we can't avoid overusing our muscles. But we can stretch. This should be done before overusing your muscles, but if you forget, then do so afterward and again before bed.

What to do: Immediately after vigorous activity, spend 10 minutes elongating the muscles you used, especially those of the thigh, calf and low back, which are most likely to suddenly spasm. For example, try forward bends (bend from the waist to touch the floor, if possible—use a table edge for support if you feel unsteady)...and calf stretches (put your hands on the wall while standing about three feet away from it—lean in, elongating the calf muscles).

• **Get the right minerals.** Inadequate blood levels of such minerals as magnesium, potassium and sodium will increase your risk for muscle spasms. Most people get plenty of sodium in their diets but lose much of it when they perspire during exercise and/or are out in hot weather. Potassium and magnesium in vegetables, whole grains, beans, nuts, seeds and fresh fruit are most readily available for absorption. However, if you suffer from muscle spasms, talk to your doctor about taking daily mineral supplements of potassium and magnesium to ensure adequate levels. Be sure to consult your doctor first if you have kidney or heart disease or take any type of medication.

• **Try homeopathy.** The homeopathic remedies Mag phos (6x) and Kali phos (6x), taken together, often relieve muscle cramps. The remedies, manufactured by Hyland's/Standard Homeopathic, are available in stores selling natural medicines. Dissolve two pellets of each remedy (four pellets total) under the tongue. Repeat the same dose every 10 minutes for up to one hour until the pain is gone.

*Talk to your doctor before significantly changing your daily water intake.

Treating Low Testosterone May Relieve Pain

Shehzad Basaria, MD, associate professor of medicine, Harvard Medical School, and medical director, Section of Men's Health, Aging and Metabolism, Brigham & Women's Hospital, both in Boston.

Men feel less pain than women. That's not a judgment call—tests have proven it. For instance, among patients who have chronic pain conditions (such as arthritis or nerve damage) or who undergo identical surgical procedures (such as a knee replacement), women tend to experience more pain than men.

It's not just that men generally are raised to be more stoic or that women are raised to be more sensitive. Rather, a key element in this discrepancy seems to be the hormone testosterone. Though women do produce some testosterone, men naturally produce much more of it. Animal studies support this idea that testosterone protects against the perception of pain. Male mice whose production of testosterone is blocked demonstrate increased sensitivity to pain...and when the animals' testosterone levels are returned to normal, their response to painful stimuli is reduced.

What does this mean for people whose testosterone levels are abnormally low? They may have increased pain perception. And ironically, opioids—the very drugs that are often used to relieve pain—can significantly reduce testosterone levels, creating a vicious cycle in which patients may require more and more medication to deal with their pain. *Now a fascinating new study suggests a possible way to break this cycle...*

TESTING TESTOSTERONE

Men produce testosterone in their testicles, and their normal range of serum testosterone (the total amount in the blood) is between 300 nanograms per deciliter (ng/dL) and 1,000 ng/dL. In women, testosterone is produced in the ovaries, and their normal serum testosterone range is 15 ng/dL to 75 ng/dL. Opioid pain-relieving medications such as morphine, codeine, fentanyl and *oxycodone* (Oxycontin) are known to reduce testosterone production, sometimes decreasing it to undetectable levels in the blood.

For the new study, researchers enrolled men who were taking opioid medication for chronic pain and whose average testosterone level was 228 ng/dL. Before treatment, all the men underwent various tests to measure their perception of and tolerance for pain. Then they were randomly assigned to one of two groups. In one group, each man used a transdermal (applied to the skin) testosterone gel daily to bring his testosterone level up in the desired range of 500 ng/dL to 1,000 ng/dL. The other group of men used a placebo gel.

After 14 weeks, the tests were repeated to gauge any changes in the men's reactions to...

- **Mechanical pain.** For this test, blunt-edge pins were applied to the forearm. Compared with their scores at the start of the study, the placebo users reported an average increase in perceived pain of eight points on a 100-point scale, while the testosterone users reported a decrease in pain of five points, on average.
- **Pressure pain.** A device called an algometer was placed on the thumb or on the upper back. The algometer exerted increasing amounts of pressure, measured in watts, until a participant said that he could not tolerate the discomfort any longer. In the placebo group, the men's ability to withstand the pain decreased by an average of 70 watts from the start to the end of the study...but among the testosterone users, tolerance increased by 25 watts.
- **Cold tolerance.** Here the challenge for each man was to keep his hand immersed in ice-cold water for as long as possible. At the end of the study, the men who had received testosterone were able keep their hands in the water an average of 10 seconds longer than men who had received the placebo.

IF YOU ARE IN PAIN

This study could hold a clue as to why people often become dependent on opioid medication. A cycle is created in which the drug reduces testosterone levels, thereby increasing pain...which in turn leads to a need for even more medication and increases the risk for addiction. It's possible that testosterone replacement therapy could help break this cycle by reducing pain perception and increasing pain tolerance. Additional studies are needed to confirm that theory.

Not all cases of low testosterone are due to opioid use. Other possible causes include obesity, various endocrine disorders, certain inflammatory diseases, excess iron in the blood, and chemotherapy or radiation for cancer treatment. Whether testosterone replacement also might help alleviate pain in these conditions remains to be seen.

Important: The findings from this study do not suggest that patients with normal hormone levels should be given extra testosterone to treat their pain. Excess testosterone can increase the risk for sleep apnea and heart disease and may lead to elevated red blood cell counts.

However, if you have a chronic painful condition or if you experience pain that seems out of proportion to an injury or illness, it is worthwhile to talk with your doctor about having your testosterone level checked and treated if it turns out to be too low.

Ginkgo vs. Nerve Pain

Neuropathic pain—in which damaged nerves send erroneous pain signals in response to harmless stimuli such as a light touch—is hard to treat. Common causes include diabetes and shingles. Among rats with neuropathic pain, those given a ginkgo biloba herbal extract showed significantly lower pain responses to cold and pressure than those given a placebo. Human studies are needed.

Hae-Jin Lee, MD, chief/professor of anesthesiology, Catholic University of Korea, Seoul, Republic of Korea, and leader of an animal study.

Chronic Pain Linked to Low Vitamin D

Chronic pain is the leading cause of disability in the US. In a recent study, it was found that patients with low vitamin D levels required twice as much narcotic pain medication to manage symptoms as those with adequate levels.

Theory: Vitamin D deficiency leads to low bone density, which can create achy pain throughout the body.

Best: Ask your doctor about testing your blood level of vitamin D and supplementing if it is below 20 nanograms per milliliter.

Michael Turner, MD, department of physical medicine and rehabilitation, Mayo Clinic, Rochester, Minnesota, and lead author of a study of 267 people.

Why Uncoated Aspirin Is Better for Pain Relief and Heart Health

An enteric coating delays pain relief by as much as four hours and may interfere with aspirin's ability to inhibit clotting—the reason low-dose aspirin is used for cardiovascular health.

University of California, Berkeley Wellness Letter. *BerkeleyWellness.com*

Better Pain Relief After Sinus Surgery

Thirty-four patients received either the nonnarcotic drug *ketorolac* or the narcotic fentanyl immediately after undergoing endoscopic sinus surgery.

Result: Ketorolac was just as effective for pain relief as fentanyl but did not have the side effects of a narcotic drug, such as nausea, vomiting and drowsiness.

Self-defense: To avoid the side effects of narcotics, ask your doctor if ketorolac is an option following sinus surgery. It is also used in cardiac and orthopedic surgeries.

Kevin Welch, MD, assistant professor of otolaryngology, Stritch School of Medicine, Loyola University Chicago.

Device for Chronic Pain

The Calmare pain therapy treatment relieves chronic neuropathic pain from diabetes, shingles, herniated discs, chemotherapy, reflex sympathetic dystrophy (RSD) and other causes. The FDA-approved device uses electrodes applied to the skin to transmit "no-pain" messages to the brain. Patients usually undergo 10 to 12 daily treatments, each lasting less than one hour. For a list of centers that offer Calmare therapy, go to *www.calmarett.com/locations.html.*

C. Evers Whyte, MS, DC, is a pain expert and founder and director of the New England Center for Chronic Pain, Stamford, Connecticut. *NECCP.com*

Meditation Offers Rapid Pain Relief

After practicing 20 minutes of meditation daily for just four days, study participants found that meditation reduced their perception of pain by up to 57%.

Fadel Zeidan, PhD, postdoctoral researcher, Wake Forest University School of Medicine, Winston-Salem, North Carolina, and leader of a study of meditation and pain, presented at a recent meeting of the Society for Neuroscience.

Try Self-Hypnosis for Drug-Free Pain Relief

Bruce N. Eimer, PhD, psychologist and owner/director of Alternative Behavior Associates in Huntingdon Valley, Pennsylvania, and author of *Hypnotize Yourself Out of Pain Now!*

Chronic pain is the leading cause of disability in the US, affecting more than 90 million Americans. Painkillers, including morphine and related drugs, invariably cause side effects (ranging from constipation to confusion), can be addictive and are only marginally effective for many patients.

Better: Self-hypnosis. It doesn't eliminate pain, but it improves your ability to cope with it. It also lowers levels of pain-causing stress hormones and increases the body's production of endogenous opioids, substances with morphinelike effects.

The practice of hypnotism has been distorted in movies and stage shows. You can't be hypnotized against your will, and you can't be made to do things that you don't want to do.

A hypnotic trance is merely an altered state of consciousness. It involves entering a physical and mental state of relaxation from which you redirect your attention to achieve certain goals—including the reduction of pain.

SIMPLE METHOD

Once you've learned to induce hypnosis, you can do it on your own once or twice a day—preferably for 10 minutes in the morning and 10 minutes at night (if you have trouble judging the time, set a timer with a quiet alarm). You might need more frequent hypnosis sessions if you are in severe pain. Most people notice a significant reduction in pain within two months—some improve after a single session.

One common technique to induce hypnosis is The Zarren Marble Method, developed by the noted hypnotist Jordan Zarren...

- **Sit in a comfortable chair, and hold a marble between your thumb and other fingers.** Roll it around and notice the texture, colors, patterns and tiny imperfections.

• **Notice how relaxed you are.** You're probably blinking more...your eyelids are getting heavy.

• **At this point, close your eyes and close your hand around the marble so that it doesn't drop.** Now you are in a state of deep relaxation. If you find that you're thinking of something else, just bring your mind back to the marble.

Once you've entered this hypnotic trance, you can use a number of mental techniques to reduce pain. Try the techniques below and see which ones work best for you...

DEEP RELAXATION

No one can consciously experience multiple sensations simultaneously. When the sensation of relaxation is dominant, you'll feel less pain.

How to do it: First, before you enter a hypnotic state, choose two or three positive thoughts that you want to implant in your mind. These might include things such as My body is relaxed or With each breath that I take, I relax more and more.

Then go into a hypnotic state, and mentally focus on the thoughts that you've chosen. If your mind drifts, bring it back to the thoughts.

Dwelling on the positive produces physical changes in the body, including a reduction in muscle tension and lower levels of cortisol and other stress hormones. Even when the pain isn't gone, you'll react to it less strongly.

DECATASTROPHIZING

Decatastrophizing means to stop blowing things out of proportion. This helps separate pain from suffering. Example: Someone might feel that life is worthless because of the pain. You can decatastrophize by limiting these negative thoughts or feelings. This can stop the transmission of pain signals.

How to do it: While under hypnosis, reframe how you think about pain. Rather than dwelling on hopelessness, for example, consider the possibility that pain has a purpose—that it can alert you that you need to do something to heal. Dwelling on pain's purpose can make you feel stronger and more in control.

You also can practice disputation—interrupting negative thoughts about pain by redirecting your attention to a thought that reduces stress. Say to yourself, My pain is bad today, but I'm still going to get a lot done.

DIRECTION

During self-hypnosis, dwell on thoughts that emphasize your sense of control. *Examples...*

• **When you notice an increase in pain,** tell yourself, I know I can handle this. I've dealt with worse before.

• **If the pain gets stronger,** repeat positive thoughts, such as, I will not let the pain get the best of me. I know I can do things to make it more tolerable.

• **Handle the worst moments with thoughts such as,** This is only temporary. I will get through it.

When the pain subsides, remind yourself that you coped well—and that you now have a plan to help make it easier the next time.

Important: Minimize physical "pain behaviors," such as grimacing, groaning and complaining. These reinforce the pain and increase disability.

DISTRACTION

Because the mind can process only a limited amount of information at one time, you can introduce sensations that compete with pain sensations.

How to do it: Create physical sensations (such as rubbing the place where it hurts) that are more pleasant than the pain sensations. Or distract yourself with mental exercises, such as listening to the sound of your breathing.

Try this: Go into a hypnotic trance, and pay attention only to your breathing. Listen to the sounds. Note the rhythm and the ways in which your breathing naturally changes.

The mental activity will reach your brain ahead of the pain sensations. This can close the "pain gate" so that you experience less pain.

MORE HELP

If you want to consult with a professional hypnotist, you can find one in your area by contacting the American Society of Clinical Hypnosis (ASCH), 630-980-4740, *www.asch.net.*

6

Depression and Suicide

Drug-Free Ways to Overcome Depression

Everyone feels blue occasionally, but for the many who are depressed, feelings of sadness and hopelessness persist for months or years.

Conventional treatment for depression includes medication, most often with a selective serotonin reuptake inhibitor (SSRI), such as *fluoxetine* (Prozac), or a selective serotonin/norepinephrine reuptake inhibitor (SSNRI), such as *venlafaxine* (Effexor). The mechanism is unclear, but these drugs may work by blocking reabsorption of the brain chemicals serotonin and/or norepinephrine, leaving more of these mood-lifting neurotransmitters in the brain.

Problem: Antidepressants' side effects can include lowered libido, weight gain, headache, fatigue, anxiety, zombie-like moods and even suicidal tendencies.

Finding: An analysis of numerous clinical studies concluded that SSRIs were not significantly more effective than a placebo against mild-to-moderate depression. Other studies are more favorable for antidepressants, and medication is a vital part of treatment for some patients—but given the concerns about antidepressants, many experts believe that these drugs are overprescribed.

Better: A natural approach that treats depression with minimal side effects.

GETTING STARTED

Research demonstrates the mood-elevating effects of regular exercise, proper diet, sufficient sleep and moderate sunshine—yet depression can erode motivation to pursue healthful habits.

Hyla Cass, MD, a board-certified psychiatrist and nationally recognized expert on integrative medicine, Pacific Palisades, California. She is a frequent TV and radio commentator, author or coauthor of 10 books, including *Natural Highs: Feel Good All the Time,* and a board member of the American College for Advancement in Medicine. *CassMD.com*

What helps: Certain dietary supplements are natural mood enhancers, combating depression by correcting biochemical imbalances and increasing motivation to make healthful lifestyle changes.

Important: Before using supplements, check with a doctor knowledgeable about natural medicine, especially if you take medication, have a medical condition or are pregnant or breast-feeding. *Best...*

- **If you are not depressed...**take the nutrients listed below under "Mood Boosters for Everyone" to maintain healthful neurotransmitter levels.
- **If you are depressed but are not taking an antidepressant...**try natural remedies before considering drugs.
- **If you take an antidepressant but see no improvement in mood and/or suffer from side effects...**ask your doctor about weaning off the drug and starting natural therapies. Do not discontinue drugs on your own!
- **If an antidepressant is helping you and side effects are minimal...**continue your medication and ask your doctor about also taking supplements.

Supplements below are available in health-food stores and online.

Guideline: Begin at the low end of each recommended dosage range. If symptoms do not improve within a week, gradually increase the dosage.

MOOD BOOSTERS FOR EVERYONE

The following supplements are appropriate for most adults. Take all of them indefinitely to prevent or treat depression. They are safe to take while on antidepressants.

- **Omega-3 fatty acids.** These are essential for production of neurotransmitters that affect mood and thinking. Most effective are eicosapentaenoic acid (EPA) and docosahexaenoic acid (DHA), found in fish oil. Take 1,000 milligrams (mg) to 2,000 mg of combined EPA/DHA daily.

Caution: Fish oil may increase bleeding risk in people taking a blood thinner, such as *warfarin* (Coumadin).

- **B vitamins and magnesium.** The B vitamins help carry oxygen to the brain and produce neurotransmitters. They work best together and are absorbed best when taken with magnesium. Take a daily multivitamin or a vitamin-B complex that includes the following—25 mg each of vitamins B-1 and B-2...20 mg each of vitamins B-3 and B-6...50 mg each of B-5 and magnesium...and 100 micrograms (mcg) each of B-12 and folic acid.

Caution: Avoid supplements of B-3 if you have diabetes, gout or liver problems...avoid B-6 if you take L-dopa for Parkinson's disease.

- **Vitamins C, D and E.** These aid neurotransmitter production and/or protect brain cells. Take a daily multivitamin that includes 500 mg to 1,000 mg of vitamin C...2,000 international units (IU) of vitamin D...and 400 IU of vitamin E.

FOR EXTRA HELP

If you still are depressed after taking the nutrients above for seven to 10 days, also take either of the following supplements. If symptoms do not improve within two weeks, switch to the other supplement. If you still see no improvement, take both.

Important: Though many patients are successfully treated with a combination of these supplements and antidepressants, this requires close medical supervision. Theoretically, the combination could lead to the rare but potentially fatal serotonin syndrome, caused by excess serotonin. Symptoms include headache, increased body temperature, fast heart rate, blood pressure changes, hallucinations and/or kidney damage.

Once you find an effective regimen, continue for several months. Then reduce your dose by one-quarter for one week. If symptoms return, resume the former dose. Otherwise, continue reducing until you find an effective maintenance dose or can stop completely.

- **St. John's wort**. This herb raises serotonin and possibly the neurotransmitter dopamine, and may calm nerves. With breakfast, take 300 mg to 900 mg daily of a standardized extract of 0.3% hypericin (the active constituent).

Caution: Side effects may include digestive distress and a sun-sensitivity rash. St. John's wort may interact with some drugs, including *warfarin*, the heart drug *digoxin* and birth control pills.

• **5-HTP (5-hydroxytryptophan) or L-tryptophan.** These are forms of the amino acid tryptophan, which converts to serotonin. With fruit juice, take either 50 mg to 100 mg of 5-HTP or 500 mg to 1,000 mg of L-tryptophan once or twice daily.

Caution: Occasional side effects include nausea and agitation.

TO REV UP

If your symptoms include low energy and sleepiness, add either of the following to your regimen for as long as necessary. They may be taken with an antidepressant under close medical supervision.

• **Tyrosine.** This amino acid aids production of energizing adrenaline, dopamine and thyroid hormone. Take 500 mg to 1,000 mg before breakfast and in mid-afternoon.

Caution: Tyrosine may raise blood pressure—talk to your doctor. Do not use tyrosine if you have melanoma—it may worsen this cancer.

• **SAMe (s-adenosyl-methionine).** This compound boosts neurotransmitters and energy. Take on an empty stomach no less than 20 minutes before or after eating or taking any other supplement.

Dosage: Take 200 mg to 400 mg once or twice daily.

Caution: It may cause irritability and insomnia. Do not take SAMe if you have bipolar disorder—it could trigger a manic phase.

TO WIND DOWN

If depression symptoms include anxiety and/or insomnia, try...

• **Valerian.** This herb enhances activity of gamma-aminobutyric acid (GABA), a calming neurotransmitter. Take 150 mg to 300 mg one-half to one hour before bed. After one to two months, stop for a week. If insomnia returns, resume use. It is safe to take with an antidepressant.

Caution: Don't take valerian while using sedatives, such as muscle relaxants, antihistamines or alcohol.

6 Foods Proven to Make You Happy

Tonia Reinhard, MS, RD, a registered dietitian and professor at Wayne State University in Detroit. She is the program director for the Coordinated Program in Dietetics, course director of clinical nutrition at Wayne State University School of Medicine and past president of the Michigan Academy of Nutrition and Dietetics. She is author of *Superfoods: The Healthiest Foods on the Planet* and *SuperJuicing: More Than 100 Nutritious Vegetable & Fruit Recipes.*

You can eat your way to a better mood! Certain foods and beverages have been proven to provide the raw materials that you need to feel sharper, more relaxed and just plain happier. *Best choices...*

HAPPY FOOD #1: CHOCOLATE

Chocolate can make you feel good—to such an extent that 52% of women would choose chocolate over sex, according to one survey.

Chocolate contains chemical compounds known as polyphenols, which interact with neurotransmitters in the brain and reduce anxiety. An Australian study found that men and women who consumed the most chocolate polyphenols (in the form of a beverage) felt calmer and more content than those who consumed a placebo drink.

Chocolate also boosts serotonin, the same neurotransmitter affected by antidepressant medications. It triggers the release of dopamine and stimulates the "pleasure" parts of the brain.

Then there's the sensual side of chocolate—the intensity of the flavor and the melting sensation as it dissolves in your mouth. The satisfaction that people get from chocolate could be as helpful for happiness as its chemical composition.

Recommended amount: Aim for one ounce of dark chocolate a day. Most studies used dark chocolate with 70% cacao or more.

HAPPY FOOD #2: FISH

Fish has been called "brain food" because our brains have a high concentration of omega-3 fatty acids—and so does fish. These fatty acids have been linked to memory and other cognitive functions. In countries where people eat a lot of fish, depression occurs less often than in countries (such as the US) where people eat less.

The omega-3s in fish accumulate in the brain and increase "membrane fluidity," the ability of brain-cell membranes to absorb nutrients and transmit chemical signals.

A study in *Archives of General Psychiatry* looked at patients diagnosed with depression who hadn't responded well to antidepressants. Those who were given 1,000 mg of EPA (a type of omega-3 fatty acid) daily for three months had significant improvements, including less anxiety and better sleep.

Recommended amount: Try to have at least two or three fish meals a week. Cold-water fish—such as sardines, mackerel and salmon—have the highest levels of omega-3s. Or choose a supplement with 1,000 mg of EPA and DHA (another omega-3 fatty acid) in total.

HAPPY FOOD #3: DARK GREEN VEGGIES

Dark green vegetables such as spinach, asparagus, broccoli and Brussels sprouts are loaded with folate, a B-complex vitamin that plays a key role in regulating mood. A Harvard study found that up to 38% of adults with depression had low or borderline levels of folate. Boosting the folate levels of depressed patients improved their mood.

Dark green vegetables are particularly good, but all vegetables and fruits boost mood. Researchers asked 281 people to note their moods on different days. On the days when the participants consumed the most vegetables and fruits, they reported feeling happier and more energetic. Folate certainly plays a role, but self-satisfaction may have something to do with it as well. People feel good when they eat right and take care of themselves.

Recommended amount: The minimum you should have is five servings of vegetables and fruits a day.

Bonus: Middle-aged men who had 10 servings a day showed reduced blood pressure.

HAPPY FOOD #4: BEANS (INCLUDING SOYBEANS)

Beans are rich in tryptophan, an essential amino acid that is used by the body to produce serotonin, the neurotransmitter that affects feelings of calmness and relaxation.

Beans also are loaded with folate. Folate, as mentioned in the veggies section, plays a key role in regulating mood.

In addition, beans contain manganese, a trace element that helps prevent mood swings due to low blood sugar.

Recommended amount: For people not used to eating beans, start with one-quarter cup five days a week. Build up to one-half cup daily. This progression will help prevent gastrointestinal symptoms such as flatulence.

HAPPY FOOD #5: NUTS

Nuts are high in magnesium, a trace mineral involved in more than 300 processes in the body. People who don't get enough magnesium feel irritable, fatigued and susceptible to stress.

The elderly are more likely than young adults to be low in magnesium—because they don't eat enough magnesium-rich foods and/or because they tend to excrete more magnesium in their urine.

Also, many health problems can accelerate the depletion of magnesium from the body.

Examples: Gastrointestinal disorders (or bariatric surgery), kidney disease and sometimes diabetes.

Recommended amount: Aim for one ounce of nuts a day. Good choices include almonds, walnuts, cashews, hazelnuts and peanuts (the latter is technically a legume). If you don't like nuts, other high-magnesium foods include spinach, pumpkin seeds, fish, beans, whole grains and dairy.

HAPPY FOOD #6: COFFEE

The caffeine in coffee, tea and other caffeinated beverages is a very beneficial compound. One study found that people with mild cognitive impairment were less likely to develop full-fledged Alzheimer's disease when they had the caffeine equivalent of about three cups of coffee a day.

Caffeine can temporarily improve your memory and performance on tests. It enhances coordination and other parameters of physical performance. When you feel energized, you feel happier. Also, people who feel good from caffeine may be more likely to engage in other happiness-promoting behaviors, such as seeing friends and exercising.

Recommended amount: The challenge is finding the "sweet spot"—just enough caffeine to boost mood but not so much that you get the shakes or start feeling anxious. For those who aren't overly sensitive to caffeine, one to three daily cups of coffee or tea are about right.

WHAT NOT TO EAT

Some people turn to food or drink for comfort when they're feeling down. *Here's what not to eat or drink when you've got the blues...*

- **Alcohol.** Alcohol is a depressant of the central nervous system. When you initially consume alcohol, it produces a euphoric effect and you become more animated and less inhibited. But as you continue drinking and more alcohol crosses the blood-brain barrier, the depressant effect predominates.
- **Baked goods.** When you eat high-sugar, high-fat carbs such as cookies, pastries and donuts, you tend to want more of them. The food gives you a temporary "good feeling," but the excess food intake that typically results causes drowsiness and often self-loathing.

Natural Mood Elevators

Mark Blumenthal, founder and executive director, American Botanical Council, and editor, *HerbalGram*.
Eric Yarnell, ND, core faculty member, department of botanical medicine, Bastyr University, and in private practice. He is author of *Clinical Botanical Medicine*.

Ads for antidepressants make it seem as though the most logical solution for a case of the blues is to seek a prescription. Pharmaceutical drugs may be helpful—even necessary—for people with severe depression, but for others, there are natural solutions that may work even better, with less risk of adverse side effects. Dietary supplements and lifestyle changes can be used to naturally lift your spirits.

"I think that a lot of our modern-day fatigue and depression has to do with the fact that we're totally separated from nature," says Eric Yarnell, ND, core faculty member in the department of botanical medicine at Bastyr University and author of *Clinical Botanical Medicine*. "People don't eat well, they watch huge amounts of television and don't spend much time relating to people or the outdoors." He believes that eating plenty of whole, unprocessed foods and getting regular exercise are the first steps to take in attempting to boost your mood and energy level. "Also, I tell people to turn off their televisions," he says, noting that replacing TV with even 15 minutes of daily outdoor activity and sunlight will help, as will getting enough sleep.

SUPPLEMENTS THAT HELP

Eating whole foods with little or no added sugar, exercising (even a bit) and getting some moderate sun exposure are all highly effective ways to beat the blues and lift the spirits. Some people, however, still feel like there are times when they need a more controllable lift—and for them, Dr. Yarnell says there are natural supplements that really do help. Research supports three, in particular—St. John's wort (Hypericum perforatum), goldenroot (Rhodiola rosea) and eleuthero (Eleutherococcus senticosus).

- **St. John's wort.** A meta-analysis published in the *British Medical Journal* in 1996 reviewed 23 trials on St. John's wort involving more than 1,700 patients, with researchers reporting it was more effective than a placebo at treating mild to moderately severe cases of depression. "The evidence is very strong that St. John's wort is an effective natural antidepressant for people whose depression is mild," says Mark Blumenthal, founder and executive director of the nonprofit American Botanical Council. This distinction is an important one, he notes—you might recall that the reputation of St. John's wort was sullied by a 2001 study published in the *Journal of the American Medical Association*, calling it ineffective. Blumenthal explained that this particular study had examined a group of patients that included those who had already been unresponsive to treatment with a conventional antidepressant drug, so their depression was quite severe.

Caveats for people interested in using St. John's wort to elevate their mood: Those with severe depression should seek medical advice to ensure proper treatment and monitoring. Also, cautions Blumenthal, "St. John's wort interacts with a whole suite of conventional pharmaceutical drugs so you must check with your health care provider about any possible interactions before taking it." Your prescriber will quite likely recommend preparations standardized to contain 0.3% hypericin, a naturally occurring compound in St. John's wort to which manufacturers standardize their extracts for quality-control purposes. And, if you are scheduled to have elective surgery, make sure you discontinue this supplement ahead of time.

- **Rhodiola rosea/golden root.** In Europe, Rhodiola rosea or R. rosea, the best known and most studied of different species of Rhodiola (also called goldenroot), has a long history of being used to treat chronic fatigue, especially in Sweden and Russia. One interesting study tested the effect of 170 mg of R. rosea root extract on 56 physicians who were on stressful night-call duty. R. rosea brought about a statistically significant reduction in general fatigue for the first two weeks—but the positive effect seemed to fade by six weeks, suggesting it might be a good short-term solution that is helpful for acute stressful conditions but not for chronic stress. An experienced naturopath can provide advice on what's the best dosage in your case.

As for depression, a clinical trial found that R. rosea can also work as an antidepressant and mood elevator. In this Swedish study, R. rosea extract was found to not only help reduce symptoms of depression in patients with mild to moderate depression, but also to enhance their cognitive and sexual function, as well as mental and physical performance under stress.

- **Eleuthero.** There is some debate about eleuthero, also known as Siberian ginseng (although it is no longer marketed under that name in the US). Blumenthal is not enthusiastic about eleuthero, calling it "not great" for fatigue, but Dr. Yarnell believes it's effective, doesn't have significant adverse effects and works "to balance people's systems." One clinical study evaluated 96 adults who had complained of fatigue for at least six months. They were given four capsules per day of eleuthero. While some reported their fatigue lessened considerably, the results were not statistically significant...though two sub-groups in the population—those with longstanding fatigue and those with less severe fatigue—experienced some effect from the treatment after two months.

ASK YOUR DOCTOR

Natural supplements aren't necessarily risk-free and so it is vitally important to seek supervision by a physician experienced in their use, advice that rings as true when talking about moods as with physical ailments. You may find these products can be very beneficial and produce less adverse effects than pharmaceutical products...but use them responsibly.

Use Mindfulness to Overcome Depression

Zindel V. Segal, PhD, Cameron Wilson Chair in Depression Studies, University of Toronto, Ontario, Canada, and head of the Cognitive Behavioral Therapy Unit at the university's Centre for Addiction and Mental Health. He is coauthor of *The Mindful Way Through Depression: Freeing Yourself from Chronic Unhappiness. http://mbct.co.uk*

Most people who experience depression—or even just a bout of the blues—try to "fix" it with an antidepressant or something else to make them feel better.

A different but highly effective approach: Do not try to fix the uncomfortable feelings. That's a key aspect of mindfulness—which involves paying special attention to what's going on in our minds and bodies in a nonjudgmental way. With this approach, many people who have battled depression or sadness have experienced significant improvement in their symptoms.

For anyone who has ever suffered the pain of depression or low moods, this approach may sound wrongheaded. But the truth is it works. Of course, there are instances in which antidepressants may be needed. However, when people stop taking the drugs, depression often returns.

Important finding: People with a history of depression who used mindfulness in an organized program had half as many recurrences as people not on the program.

Here's what you need to know to use mindfulness to cope with sadness or depression...*

THE OLD WAY DOESN'T WORK

Most people don't realize that it's not the sad thoughts and feelings that cause us to spiral downward. It's what we do about them that matters. Two of the most common coping mechanisms to get out of a bad mood—trying to think our way out of a problem or trying to avoid painful feelings—actually trap us in the darkness.

Why thinking doesn't help: We are accustomed to believing that we can think our way out of any problem. So it's only natural to regard a dark mood as a problem to be solved. When we're in this dreary state, we might ask ourselves questions such as Why do I feel this way? How can I change my life? What should I be doing differently? We believe that if we think hard enough, we'll find a solution.

But the opposite is true. Dwelling on how bad you feel, on the distance between the way things are and the way things should be, just reinforces your mood. Your mind begins running in an endless circle—and it seems as though there is no way out.

Why ignoring feelings doesn't help: We often think that if we ignore painful feelings, they will go away. When we try to push away these strong emotions, they rebound, stronger than ever.

Think about it this way: If someone told you not to think about a white bear, guess what you would do. You couldn't help but think about a white bear or how you shouldn't think about it. Suppressing thoughts or feelings doesn't work.

*Consult a doctor before trying this approach if you have experienced suicidal thoughts or your depression interferes with your ability to perform daily activities.

WHAT TO DO INSTEAD

The practice of mindfulness enables you to look at your thoughts and feelings in a different way. Instead of dwelling on how bad you feel and struggling to do something about it, you simply experience what's going on.

Mindfulness encourages you to be aware of your emotions, thoughts and bodily sensations without judging or interpreting them. You "watch" them...identify them...and acknowledge them instead of lingering over each one.

To get an idea of what mindfulness feels like, apply it to an ordinary activity that you do every day. While washing the dishes, for instance, notice how the warm water feels on your hands...how your hands and arms feel as you turn a dish over and rinse it off. Make washing dishes the full focus of your attention, not a task to get past. If your mind wanders, bring your focus back to the dishes. What you've done is to bring physical sensations into the realm of mindfulness.

Next, take thoughts and feelings into the realm of mindfulness. Being aware of your thoughts and feelings without reacting to them is the key to keeping negative emotions from cascading. This can be particularly challenging, which is why it's helpful to begin as though thoughts are sounds that you are simply listening to.

Here's how: While sitting quietly, let your attention shift to your hearing. Open your mind to sounds from all directions, near and far, subtle as well as obvious sounds. Be aware of these auditory sensations without thinking about where they're coming from or what they mean. Note the way they appear and fade. When you realize that your attention has drifted, note where it has gone and gently come back to the sounds.

After trying this a few times with sounds, shift your awareness to your thoughts. Let your mind "hear" them as if they were coming from outside, noting how they arise, linger and move on.

Helpful: Imagine your thoughts projected on a screen at the movies...or see them as clouds passing across a clear sky. When a thought provokes strong emotions or physical feelings, notice this as well but only notice it, without trying to draw any conclusions from it.

Acknowledge if a feeling is particularly unpleasant. Does it cause any physical sensations or discomfort? Instead of ignoring the thought or the discomfort because it's unpleasant and you don't want to deal with it, sit with it for a little while. This can be difficult to do.

Helpful: Notice your thought patterns. If you are feeling like this—I'll never be happy again or I feel like a failure—you can say to yourself, There's that "never-be-happy-ever" feeling again.

How often to practice: It is recommended that you set aside 30 minutes every day to practice mindfulness. You can do this in a variety of ways—lying on the floor comfortably and focusing on your breathing...or walking and focusing on how your legs and arms feel as they move.

Even incorporating mindfulness for just five minutes at a time into routine daily activities—such as showering...brushing your teeth...or taking out the garbage—can help. The point is to be able to focus on what you are doing when you are doing it.

When you practice mindfulness regularly, it makes it easier to use the technique when you need it most—when you are upset because you are stuck in traffic...are in the middle of a heated argument...or begin to feel a bout of depression coming on.

Yes, Homeopathy Can Help Depression

Mark A. Stengler, NMD, naturopathic medical doctor and leading authority on the practice of alternative and integrated medicine. He is author of *The Natural Physician's Healing Therapies*, founder and medical director, Stengler Center for Integrative Medicine, Encinitas, California, and adjunct associate clinical professor, National College of Natural Medicine, Portland, Oregon. *MarkStengler.com*

This statistic saddens me—more than one out of every 20 Americans experiences depression at any given time, yet fewer than one-third seek help from a mental health professional for this condition.

I use homeopathy to treat many of my patients who have depression—and I closely follow the work of one of the leaders in the field, Dana Ullman, MPH, a consultant, author and founder of Homeopathic Educational Services, a nationally known resource for homeopathy (*www.homeopathic.com*). *Here's what he had to say about how homeopathy can help depression...*

Pharmaceutical drugs for depression are designed to force the body chemistry to act in certain ways—for example, to artificially increase the effects of brain chemicals known as neurotransmitters. These drugs may reduce symptoms of depression, but they don't address the root cause of this type of mental health problem.

Homeopathy, by its very nature, requires holistic practitioners to take into account the whole person. After an extensive interview with a patient, a practitioner will consult a repertory, a catalog of symptoms and the homeopathic remedies associated with relieving those symptoms. The correct remedy is believed to stimulate the body's natural healing response.

FOR HELP WITH DEPRESSION

Holistic doctors see firsthand how effective homeopathy can be for treating depression, but you need to know how to take these remedies because they work differently from other types of medicines.

There are dozens of homeopathic remedies to choose from based on an individual's personality, symptoms and disposition.

The challenge: To find the remedy that works best for your profile. Four of the most common remedies used to treat depression are described below. You can begin with the one that best matches your symptoms. As you will see, some of the symptoms overlap.

Homeopathic remedies can be dispensed in different dosing amounts. One dose with a high potency, such as 200C or higher, usually is prescribed by a holistic practitioner (this high dose should not be taken by a patient on his own). The patient then waits a month or two to see if it has helped. Sometimes patients feel much better after taking just one high dose.

Lower doses (such as 6C or 30C) can be taken by a patient on his own. Lower doses usually are taken once or twice daily for about two to four weeks. If one homeopathic remedy doesn't start to relieve symptoms within that time, stop taking it and try another remedy. These remedies have no known side effects.

- **For acute depression following grief,** such as after the loss of a loved one or a job, the breakup of a relationship or a recent experience of abuse…

Symptoms: Sighing, a lump in the throat, frequently alternating moods.

Remedy: Ignatia amara, derived from the seeds of the St. Ignatius bean tree.

- **For depression that arises following a humiliating experience,** insult or loss of pride…

Symptoms: Bouts of anger aimed at yourself or someone else.

Remedy: Staphysagria, derived from the herb stavesacre.

- **For depression related to loss or grief,** particularly if you tend to dwell in the past, suppress your grief or have haunting memories…

Symptoms: You are an emotional individual who does not like to express his emotions and rejects sympathy.

Remedy: Natrum muriaticum derived from sodium chloride (table salt).

- **For chronic depression,** including depression marked by feelings of despair and lack of meaning in life…

Symptoms: You engage in self-condemnation, self-reproach and self-criticism. You imagine that obstacles are in your way and impede the reaching of goals. You expect bad news and things to go wrong.

Remedy: Aurum metallicum, derived from gold.

If none of the treatments above helps you, there are many more homeopathic remedies to try. A trained practitioner can pick up the nuances of your symptoms and match you to the most helpful remedy.

To find a licensed homeopathic practitioner in your area, contact the American Institute of Homeopathy (*http://homeopathyusa.org*). A practitioner can work with you and your doctor to help you make the transition from antidepressant drugs to homeopathic remedies.

Caution: Do not stop taking an antidepressant drug on your own—this can be dangerous. If you have severe depression or suicidal thoughts, you should be under the care of a psychiatrist.

Saffron Tea for the Blues

According to recent studies, saffron can be as effective as some medications to treat depression. It contains B vitamins and flavonoids, which may be behind its mood-boosting powers, although researchers aren't quite sure. So to lighten a heavy heart, try some saffron tea.

All you need is one-half teaspoon of saffron threads that you would use for cooking. Steep in just-boiled water for 10 minutes, and add honey and/or cinnamon to taste. Or, if you don't want to pay the high price of high-quality saffron, you can purchase saffron tea bags at your local health-food store or online at *www.amazon.com*…or, if it's OK with your doctor, you can take saffron extract supplements, also available at health-food stores or online.

Lydia Wilen and Joan Wilen, folk-remedy experts, New York City. The sisters are coauthors of many books, including *Bottom Line's Secret Food Cures* and *Household Magic*.

Exercise Can Work Better Than Drugs for Depression

Jordan D. Metzl, MD, sports medicine physician, Hospital for Special Surgery, New York City. The author of *The Exercise Cure: A Doctor's All-Natural, No-Pill Prescription for Better Health & Longer Life*, Dr. Metzl maintains practices in New York City and Greenwich, Connecticut, and is a medical columnist for *Triathlete Magazine*. He has run in 31 marathons and finished 11 Ironman competitions.

Exercise really is nature's antidepressant. Several studies have shown that working out is just as effective, if not more so, than medication when it comes to treating mild-to-moderate depression. Exercise also can help reduce the amount of medication needed to treat severe cases of depression... and even prevent depression in some people.*

A Norwegian study that tracked about 39,000 people for two years found that those who reported doing moderate-to-high physical activity, including daily brisk walks for more than 30 minutes, scored significantly lower on depression and anxiety tests compared with nonexercisers.

There are many effective antidepressant drugs, but they are frequently accompanied by bothersome side effects, including sexual dysfunction, nausea, fatigue and weight gain. And while most of these drugs can take a month to work, a single exercise session can trigger an immediate lift in mood, and consistent aerobic exercise will make an even more lasting positive impact.

What to do: The key is to boost your heart rate high enough to trigger the release of endorphins, feel-good chemicals that elicit a state of relaxed calm. Spend 30 to 45 minutes at a level of exertion where carrying on a conversation is quite difficult due to panting—do this three to five days a week, to benefit.

You also may want to try exercising outdoors. A study published in *Environmental Science & Technology* found that outdoor exercise produces stronger feelings of revitalization, a bigger boost of energy and a greater reduction in depression and anger than exercising indoors.

Strength training also is effective in treating depression—lifting weights releases endorphins and builds a sense of empowerment. For a strength-training program, ask your doctor to recommend a physical therapist or personal trainer.

If it's difficult to motivate yourself to exercise when you're depressed, relying on a personal trainer—or a "workout buddy"—can help.

*Be sure to check with your doctor before starting any fitness program. If your condition is severe, he/she may initially want you to use exercise as an adjunct to medication, not as a replacement. Never stop taking a prescribed drug without talking to your doctor. *Caution*: With this or any workout, seek immediate medical attention if you experience chest pain, shortness of breath, nausea, blurred vision or significant bone or muscle pain while exercising.

Down and Depressed? Acupuncture Can Help

Daisy Dong, LAc, OMD, chief acupuncturist, The Center for Integrative Medicine, University of Colorado Hospital, Aurora, and professor, Southwest Acupuncture College, Boulder. Her private practice, Colorado Boulevard Acupuncture, is based at Colorado Boulevard Chiropractic Centers in Denver.

Mention acupuncture and many people think of therapy for physical aches and pains...but what if the problem is the persistent inner ache of sadness? The ancient healing technique of acupuncture also is used as a complementary treatment for various types of depression—including the notoriously tricky bipolar disorder (manic-depressive disorder), in which patients cycle between deep depression and manic episodes.

Though Western-style research studies on the topic are somewhat limited, clinical trials have reported significant findings. *For instance, here is evidence for acupuncture's effectiveness in treating...*

• **Major depression.** A study published in *Psychological Science* found that 70% of women with mild-to-moderate depression who underwent 12 acupuncture sessions experienced at least a 50% reduction in symptoms—results comparable to the success rates of antidepressant medication, but without the drugs' risk for side effects. Other studies have shown greater improvement in patients treated with acupuncture alone or with acupuncture plus antidepressants than in patients treated with antidepressants alone.

• **Bipolar disorder.** In two studies from Purdue University, all bipolar patients who received eight to 12 weeks of acupuncture sessions (in addition to their usual medication) showed improvement in their symptoms. This was true regardless of whether they entered the study during a phase of depression or a phase of mania.

• **Depression during pregnancy.** In a study published in *Journal of Affective Disorders*, 69% of pregnant participants got significant relief after 12 sessions of acupuncture in which depressive symptoms were specifically addressed...in a control group that received massage therapy instead of acupuncture, only 32% of patients improved. A similar study in *Obstetrics & Gynecology* reported comparable results.

According to Daisy Dong, LAc, OMD, a licensed acupuncturist and herbalist in private practice in Denver and a professor at Southwest Acupuncture College, for patients with various types of depression, acupuncture treatment generally brings increased energy... greater calmness...reduced anxiety...more positive thoughts and fewer negative ones... and improved sleep. For bipolar patients, acupuncture also helps to stabilize moods. When performed by a qualified professional, acupuncture has no adverse effects other than perhaps mild temporary discomfort at the needle sites. In contrast, antidepressant medications carry a risk for side effects including nausea, weight gain, fatigue and sexual problems...in bipolar patients, drugs must be very carefully managed to avoid triggering mania...and during pregnancy, there are concerns about potential negative effects of drugs on the fetus.

If you decide to give acupuncture a try: The first visit generally takes about an hour, with subsequent sessions lasting 30 to 45 minutes depending on the complexity of the case. Depression patients typically receive one or two treatments per week. Some people notice improvement after the first treatment, but for many people, it takes several treatments before results are seen—and sustained improvement generally requires about 10 sessions.

Acupuncture treatment for depression costs the same as acupuncture for other ailments—about $60 to $120 per session, depending on your location and the individual practitioner. Some health insurance policies cover acupuncture, so check your plan.

If you are taking medication for depression or bipolar disorder: It is very important that you not simply stop taking the drugs on your own even if you start feeling better after beginning acupuncture. Depending on your condition, you may indeed be able to reduce or even discontinue your medication—but this must be done under the supervision of your prescribing physician.

To find a qualified acupuncturist: Ask your doctor or mental health professional for a referral...talk to friends who have used acupuncture...or check the online databases of the American Association of Acupuncture and Oriental Medicine (*www.aaaomonline.org*) or the National Certification Commission for Acupuncture and Oriental Medicine (*www.nccaom.org*). Practitioners' database profiles may or may not specify the types of conditions they specialize in, but you can phone or check providers' websites to find out whether they treat your type of depression.

Light Therapy: Not Just for Wintertime Blues

Michael Terman, PhD, psychologist and director, Center for Light Treatment and Biological Rhythms, Columbia University Medical Center, and professor of clinical psychology, Columbia University College of Physicians and Surgeons, both in New York City. He also is president of the Center for Environmental Therapeutics and director of clinical chronobiology at the New York State Psychiatric Institute. *ColumbiaPsychiatry.org*

The short days of winter can leave you feeling blah and out of sorts. For many, mood-lifting light therapy—which basically consists of sitting in front of a special light-emitting device called a light box each morning—will chase away the wintertime blues.

But there is research that shows that light therapy relieves not only wintertime seasonal affective disorder (SAD), but also nonseasonal depression.

In a study in *Archives of General Psychiatry*, one group of seniors (age 60 and up) with depression were exposed to the bright light of a light box for one hour daily for three weeks... the control group got a "sham" treatment with dim light. The bright-light group showed significantly greater improvement in mood and sleep quality (poor sleep often accompanies depression)...lower levels of the stress hormone cortisol...and more normal levels of melatonin, a hormone that helps regulate circadian rhythms and sleep-wake cycles by rising in the evening and falling in the morning. In fact, light therapy was as effective as antidepressant medication generally is—but did not carry the drugs' risk for side effects.

Bright-light therapy also can successfully treat a number of nonseasonal forms of depression, including chronic depression in women and men of various ages...bipolar disorder...and depression during pregnancy (offering a safe alternative to medications that might affect the fetus). There is also preliminary evidence of light therapy's positive effects for postpartum depression. Light therapy alone relieves mild, moderate or even severe depression in some cases...in other cases, light therapy is used along with psychotherapy, medication and/or other treatments.

Eyes must be open during light therapy because it works through the eyes, not the skin. A simple neural pathway connects the retina to the area of the brain that houses the body's internal clock. This clock is vulnerable to getting out of kilter with respect to the local time of day, which can cause mood and energy to plummet and make it hard to get to sleep or to wake up feeling alert. Bright-light therapy sends a signal that resets the internal clock, shifting the circadian rhythm so it is in sync with the local day/night cycle—and this in turn has positive effects on mood. In addition, if melatonin activity is high at the time of the light signal, a reaction is triggered that reduces melatonin secretion, thus reinforcing the corrective effects on the internal clock. Light therapy also may increase the availability of the mood-boosting neurotransmitter serotonin by reducing activity of a "transporter" molecule that removes serotonin from active sites in the nervous system.

Light therapy works surprisingly quickly. Effects may be seen within a week of daily use—and sometimes even faster.

HOW TO DO IT

You do not need a prescription to purchase a light box, and for people with mild depression, light therapy self-treatment generally is safe. However, certain people should use light therapy only under the supervision of a doctor. *This includes anyone who...*

- **Suffers from moderate-to-severe depression,** whether or not they are being treated with medication and/or psychotherapy—because if used incorrectly (such as at the wrong time of day), light therapy could potentially worsen depression symptoms.
- **Has bipolar disorder**—because if the condition is not being adequately treated with mood-stabilizing medication, light therapy could lead to mania...and because light therapy's timing may need to be adjusted to later in the day so as not to destabilize the circadian rhythm.
- **Takes medication that increases adverse reactions to sunlight, such as drugs used to control irregular heartbeat**—because bright light could damage the retina, which absorbs these drugs in its photoreceptors.
- **Has a degenerative eye problem, such as macular degeneration**—because bright white light could accelerate illness progression. (In such cases, a dimmer "dawn simulation" device, which also has an antidepressant effect, may be used instead.)

Using a light box at home: Buy a fluorescent light box that provides 10,000 lux of illumination, which is the type that has proven successful in clinical trials. (Lower lux levels can be effective, but require more exposure time to get the same effect.) The light box should filter out ultraviolet rays that can damage eyes and skin...and should give off white light, not colored light. Some insurance companies cover the cost if patients are using the light box under a physician's supervision.

Treatment typically involves sitting 12 inches from the light box for 30 minutes each day shortly after waking up. It's essentially a breakfast-time routine. You don't look directly into the light, but your eyes are open and bathed in light while you concentrate, for example, on your newspaper or laptop.

Important: The optimal time for and duration of treatment sessions varies among individuals.

People whose depression is not limited to winter can benefit from using a light box yearround. Most people experience no negative side effects from light therapy. A small number of users develop headaches, eyestrain, agitation and/or mild nausea. These symptoms tend to subside after a few days—but if symptoms persist, reducing the duration of light treatment sessions or sitting farther from the light box often takes care of the problem.

Music Therapy Helps Ease Anxiety and Depression

Suzanne B. Hanser, EdD, coauthor with Susan Mandel, PhD, of the book and CD *Manage Your Stress and Pain Through Music.* She is the founding chair of the music therapy department at Berklee College of Music in Boston and past president of the American Music Therapy Association and the World Federation of Music Therapy.

An increasing body of evidence shows that music therapy—whether it includes the listener's favorite Bach sonatas or Beach Boys' classics—can help improve symptoms associated with a wide variety of common health problems, including anxiety and depression.

ANXIETY

Anxiety can occur in response to a stressful situation such as public speaking or from chronic stress.

Important finding: A study in the journal *Heart* found that listening to relaxing music—such as sonatas by Bach or Mozart—reduced feelings of anxiety in patients about to undergo heart surgery even more than the antianxiety medication *midazolam*. Music therapy was found to help reduce patients' heart rates and their levels of the stress hormone cortisol.

What this means for you: Music can be used to reduce anxiety due to a stressful situation or chronic stressors. Prior to a speaking engagement or any other stressful event, listen to calming music or try singing your favorite song.

While Bach and Mozart were used in the study, look for music that you find soothing. Experiment with different types of music and test their impact on your mood. Then create your own playlist to elicit the desired feelings.

DEPRESSION

Americans who are depressed tend to rely mainly on prescription antidepressants. However, these drugs are notorious for side effects such as nausea, headaches and sexual dysfunction.

Recent finding: After reviewing 17 studies that tested whether listening to music could reduce depression symptoms in adults, a 2011 meta-analysis concluded that music can be used to help combat depression if listened to regularly for at least three weeks.

What this means for you: Using music to improve your mood can be a fun and cost-effective way to help ward off negative feelings caused by mild depression.

Important: Add music therapy to your daily life—not just when you are feeling blue. Play around with familiar songs and new pieces to find the music that makes you feel best.

Strong Relationships Between Grandparents and Adult Grandchildren Reduce Depression Risk for Both

Sara M. Moorman, PhD, assistant professor, department of sociology and the Institute on Aging, Boston College, Boston. Her study was presented at the annual meeting of the American Sociological Association in New York City.

It's sad but true that many seniors sink into depression in what could otherwise be very happy years...and that many young adults suffer from depression, too, as they struggle to establish themselves in their grown-up lives.

So let me jump straight to the happy news. There is a drug-free, cost-free way in which seniors and young adults alike can guard against depression—while bringing a great deal of enjoyment to themselves and to each other.

The secret lies in establishing strong relationships between grandparents and their adult grandchildren—and there are *two key factors* that make it work...

UNIQUE FAMILY DATABASE

With a life expectancy of 79 years, typical Americans now live long enough to really get to know their grandchildren—not just as adorable tots, but as full-fledged adults who are graduating from school, starting careers and finding life partners. At the same time, these grandchildren have a chance to interact with their grandparents from an adult perspective—to appreciate their wisdom and experiences, and perhaps even to repay their grandparents for all the help and support they received while growing up.

Yet there's a surprising lack of scientific research on such relationships. So it is unique data that comes from the Longitudinal Study of Generations, a survey of three- and four-generation American families that began back in 1971. Researchers drew on data collected at seven different points in time between 1985 and 2004 to see whether the risk for depression was affected by the relationships between 376 grandparents and 340 of their adult grandchildren. (In cases where a grandparent had multiple grandchildren, it was the researchers who selected the specific grandchild to include, thus removing bias that might occur if grandparents opted to report on a favorite grandchild.)

Depression was measured at each of the seven points in time by using a 20-item scale that asked the participants to report how frequently they felt certain symptoms, such as sadness, lack of appetite or insomnia. The scores for each item ranged from one (rarely or not at all) to four (most or all of the time).

Results: The researchers found correlations between the depression scores in both generations and the following two key factors...

- **How emotionally close the grandparents and grandchildren were.** Grandparents and grandchildren reported how emotionally close they were to each other by answering questions such as, "How close do you feel your relationship with your grandparent [or grandchild] is right now?" Answers ranged from one (not at all) to six (extremely).

Findings: The closer the grandparents and grandchildren felt to each other, the lower (better) the depression scores for *both generations* were likely to be over the course of the 19 years.

- **The amount of practical support they provided to each other.** Grandparent/grandchild pairs described how often they received help from each other in four specific "everyday" areas—household chores, information and advice, financial assistance and discussing important life decisions. There were four possible outcomes—neither party giving or receiving help...grandparent giving but not receiving help...grandchild giving but not receiving help...and both parties giving and receiving help.

Findings: Grandparents who both *gave* and *received* practical support had the lowest (best) depression scores. The next best scores were for grandparents who gave but did not receive support...followed by those who neither gave nor received support. It's noteworthy that grandparents who *received but did not give* practical support had the highest (worst) depression scores by far. The researchers suggested that this is because older adults want to be independent and productive, so it's depressing not to have the wherewithal to offer support to loved ones.

Somewhat surprisingly, for the grandchildren, there was no connection between depression symptoms and any exchange of practical support.

WHAT YOU CAN DO

Grandparents: Remember, just because your grandkids are grown doesn't mean they don't need you. However, what's important to their psychological well-being probably is not the goods and services you provide, but rather the emotional closeness. So even if you're on a tight budget or have health problems or are otherwise dependent on help from younger family members, you *do* have something to offer to your grandchildren—your unwavering love and affection. Having a close emotional bond with you can help them successfully navigate the life transitions of early adulthood, such as moving out of their parents' home, going to college, joining the full-time workforce, finding a life partner and having children of their own. This unique gift can be more valuable to your grandchildren than any material offering.

Grandkids: You may think that the best way to show respect is to take care of your elders' needs, and it's great to help with chores or drive them to appointments—but to be happy, your grandparents need to feel needed, too. So let Grandpa write you a birthday check (even if he's on a fixed income) or counsel you on a big career move...ask Grandma to share her secrets for baking perfect muffins or making a marriage last a lifetime. As a bonus, you might find amazing value in what they have to say!

Sandwich generation: If your parents and your grown children aren't close, encourage them to deepen their connection by nurturing a mutually supportive relationship. You'll be boosting the emotional health of both generations...and helping establish patterns for rewarding connections to your own future grandchildren.

If you don't have grandchildren/grandparents: Why not try forging a closer relationship with a neighbor who is two generations removed from you? Although this study did not look at such "honorary" grandchild/grandparent relationships, it seems reasonable that the mutual affection and support involved in such intergenerational friendships would be extremely rewarding for both you and your new friend.

"Movie Therapy" Cuts Divorce Rates in Half

Ronald Rogge, PhD, an associate professor in the department of clinical and social sciences in psychology at the University of Rochester, New York. His main research interests include the complexities of couplehood and the early years of marriage. Dr. Rogge is the lead author of a movie-relationships study that appeared in the *Journal of Consulting and Clinical Psychology.*

Let's face it. Many couples going through rough patches in their wedded bliss balk at turning to couples' therapy for help. But what if watching a handful of movies together in the comfort of one's own home could help prevent problems from getting to that point?

New approach: Having couples watch movies and then discuss the on-screen relationship issues afterward can sometimes be just as effective as more traditional relationship-strengthening interventions, according to research recently conducted at the University of Rochester.*

Even if your marriage isn't troubled: Watching films and answering targeted questions can help you identify ways that you can make a good relationship even better.

Here is how this fascinating research unfolded...

5 FILMS = A BETTER RELATIONSHIP

Even though couples' therapy can help when there's an emotional impasse, many people are uncomfortable discussing intimate problems with a stranger. On top of that, therapy sessions can sometimes go on for weeks or months, and it can cost an arm and a leg if it's not covered by your health insurance.

To find out whether there might be a way to head off relationship problems before they become too serious, researchers divided 174 couples who had been together for about three years (though not necessarily engaged or married for all that time) into four groups.

Two of the groups participated in one of two forms of relationship-strengthening programs for about a month (one type focusing on empathy and acceptance...the other type zeroing in on communication styles). Those in the third group watched and discussed five movies over the course of about a month. The fourth group was a control—the participants didn't watch movies or attend counseling.

Surprising result: Three years later, the movie watchers were half as likely to separate or divorce as those in the control group. In fact, their divorce and separation rates (11% over three years) were the same as those who

*This approach is not a substitute for formal couples' therapy but may obviate the need for it—especially if the partners use it as a way to help keep their relationships healthy.

participated in either the empathy or communication programs.

Important: Even though the couples in the study had not been together very long, researchers suspect that movie therapy also can help long-term relationships if the partners are willing to put in the work and communicate openly with one another.

HOW IT WORKS

Sometimes, relationships get torn apart by weighty conflicts over money, sex or how to raise the children. But other times, everyday interactions fuel the discontent. Maybe your partner interrupts your stories...leaves dishes in the sink...or nags about your driving. Any of this sound familiar?

The good thing about movie-watching is that it can jump-start conversations about virtually any issue that's tripping up your relationship. Plus, it's fun to do.

And if the thought of enduring hours of saccharine-sweet "chick flicks" makes you wince, relax.

Sure, *Love Story* and a few other sappy movies are on the researchers' suggested list of films to watch. But there also are films you might never expect—great old classics like *Gone With the Wind, Barefoot in the Park* and *The Out-of-Towners*. There are plenty of complex, critically acclaimed films, too—such as *American Beauty, Children of a Lesser God* and *On Golden Pond*. If you're looking for a little humor, there are even such choices as *Meet the Fockers, The Big Wedding* and *The Five-Year Engagement*.

To get started...

- **Pick your flicks.** You and your partner need to agree to watch a movie together once a week and choose ones that you both find interesting. Check the preselected list at *www.couples-research.com* for ideas.

When you watch, look at how the characters interact. Pay particular attention to the scenes that reflect your relationship—it might be flashes of temper, a condescending voice or frequent interruptions. These are the issues you'll want to talk about later.

- **Watch the films together.** It defeats the purpose if you watch a movie at separate times or in separate rooms—or don't even watch the same movie. Treat it like a date night. Watch the movie all the way through with a minimum of interruptions. Watch for the scenes that make you laugh (or groan or nod your head) when they hit close to home.

- **Talk it over.** After the movie's done, walk through some of the issues within its plot.

Some of the researchers' post-movie questions: What problems did the couple face? Are they similar to issues in your own life? Did the couples communicate well or poorly? Did they try to understand each other, or did they go on the attack? How did they handle conflicts or differences of opinion? For the complete list of discussion points to help you have your own conversations, go to *www.couples-research.com.*

- **Consider joining the study.** Couples in the study watched one movie each week followed up by a 45-minute discussion over a period of about a month. You can do this on your own, or you can use the above website to sign up for the online study. Couples who participate in the study will be asked to complete a short survey, watch five movies of their choosing in about a month's time and have 30- to 45-minute discussions after each movie they watch.

You'll be given individual feedback from the researchers conducting the survey on different parts of your relationship...and, at the end of the month, on changes that occurred within your relationship. There's no fee to participate.

The Root of Depression May Be in Your Stomach

Liz Lipski, PhD, CCN, professor of clinical nutrition and director of academic development, nutrition and integrative health at Maryland University of Integrative Health. She is author of several books, including *Digestive Wellness: Strengthen the Immune System and Prevent Disease Through Healthy Digestion. InnovativeHealing.com*

If you have a stomachache, nausea or some other digestive problem, you know that it stems from your gastrointestinal (GI) tract.

But very few people think of the GI system when they have a health problem such as arthritis, depression, asthma or recurring infections.

Surprising: Tens of millions of Americans are believed to have digestive problems that may not even be recognizable but can cause or complicate many other medical conditions.

There's now significant evidence showing just how crucial the digestive system is in maintaining your overall health. How could hidden GI problems be responsible for such a wide range of seemingly unrelated ills?

Here's how: If you can't digest and absorb food properly, your cells can't get the nourishment they need to function properly and you can fall prey to a wide variety of ailments.

Good news: A holistically trained clinician can advise you on natural remedies (available at health-food stores unless otherwise noted) and lifestyle changes that often can correct hidden digestive problems...*

LOW LEVELS OF STOMACH ACID

Stomach acid, which contains powerful, naturally occurring hydrochloric acid (HCl), can decrease due to age, stress and/or food sensitivities.

Adequate stomach acid is a must for killing bacteria, fungi and parasites and for the digestion of protein and minerals. Low levels can weaken immunity and, in turn, lead to problems that can cause or complicate many ailments, including diabetes, gallbladder disease, osteoporosis, rosacea, thyroid problems and autoimmune disorders.

If you suspect that you have low stomach acid: You can be tested by a physician—or simply try the following natural remedies (adding one at a time each week until symptoms improve)...

- **Use apple cider vinegar.** After meals, take one teaspoon in eight teaspoons of water.
- **Try bitters.** This traditional digestive remedy usually contains gentian and other herbs. Bitters, which also are used in mixed drinks, are believed to work by increasing saliva, HCl, pepsin, bile and digestive enzymes. Use as directed on the label in capsule or liquid form.
- **Eat umeboshi plums.** These salted, pickled plums relieve indigestion. Eat them whole as an appetizer or dessert, or use umeboshi vinegar to replace vinegar in salad dressings.
- **Take betaine HCl with pepsin with meals that contain protein.**

Typical dosage: 350 mg. You must be supervised by a health-care professional when using this supplement—it can damage the stomach if used inappropriately.

If you still have symptoms, ask your doctor about adding digestive enzymes such as bromelain and/or papain.

TOO MUCH BACTERIA

When HCl levels are low, it makes us vulnerable to small intestinal bacterial overgrowth (SIBO). This condition occurs when microbes are introduced into our bodies via our food and cause a low-grade infection or when bacteria from the large intestine migrate into the small intestine, where they don't belong. Left untreated, this bacterial overgrowth can lead to symptoms, such as bloating, gas and changes in bowel movements, characteristic of irritable bowel syndrome (IBS). In fact, some research shows that 78% of people with IBS may actually have SIBO.

SIBO is also a frequent (and usually overlooked) cause of many other health problems, including Crohn's disease, scleroderma (an autoimmune disease of the connective tissue) and fibromyalgia.

SIBO can have a variety of causes, including low stomach acid, overuse of heartburn drugs called proton pump inhibitors (PPIs) and low levels of pancreatic enzymes. Adults over age 65, who often produce less stomach acid, are at greatest risk for SIBO.

Important scientific finding: A study recently conducted by researchers at Washington University School of Medicine found that, for unknown reasons, people with restless legs syndrome are six times more likely to have SIBO than healthy people.

To diagnose: The best test for SIBO is a hydrogen breath test—you drink a sugary fluid,

*Consult your doctor before trying these remedies—especially if you have a chronic medical condition or take any medication.

and breath samples are then collected. If hydrogen is overproduced, you may have SIBO. The test, often covered by insurance, is offered by gastroenterologists and labs that specialize in digestive tests. A home test is available at *www.breathtests.com.*

How to treat: The probiotic VSL#3, available at VSL3.com, can be tried. However, antibiotics are usually needed. *Rifaximin* (Xifaxan) is the antibiotic of choice because it works locally in the small intestine.

LEAKY GUT SYNDROME

The acids and churning action of the stomach blend food into a soupy liquid (chyme) that flows into the small intestine. There, the intestinal lining performs two crucial functions—absorbing nutrients and blocking unwanted substances from entering the bloodstream.

But many factors, such as chronic stress, poor diet, too much alcohol, lack of sleep, and use of antibiotics, prednisone and certain other medications, can inflame and weaken the lining of the small intestine. This allows organisms, such as bacteria, fungi and parasites, and toxic chemicals we encounter in our day-to-day activities, to enter the blood. The problem, called increased intestinal permeability, or leaky gut syndrome, is bad news for the rest of your body.

What happens: The immune system reacts to the organisms and substances as "foreign," triggering inflammation that contributes to or causes a wide range of problems, such as allergies, skin problems, muscle and joint pain, poor memory and concentration, and chronic fatigue syndrome.

To diagnose: A stool test that indicates the presence of parasites, yeast infections or bacterial infection is a sign of leaky gut. So are clinical signs, such as food intolerances and allergies. However, the best test for leaky gut checks for urinary levels of the water-soluble sugars lactulose and mannitol—large amounts indicate a leaky gut.

How to treat: If you and your doctor believe that you have leaky gut, consider taking as many of the following steps as possible…

- **Chew your food slowly and completely to enhance digestion.**
- **Emphasize foods and beverages that can help heal the small intestine,** including foods in the cabbage family, such as kale, vegetable broths, fresh vegetable juices (such as cabbage juice), aloe vera juice and slippery elm tea.
- **Take glutamine.** This amino acid is the main fuel for the small intestine—and a glutamine supplement is one of the best ways to repair a leaky gut. Start with 1 g to 3 g daily, and gradually increase the dosage by a gram or two per week to up to 14 g daily. Becoming constipated is a sign that you're using too much.
- **Try the probiotic L. plantarum.** A supplement of this gut-friendly bacteria, such as Transformation Enzyme's Plantadophilus, can help heal the small intestine.
- **Add quercetin.** This antioxidant helps repair a leaky gut. In my practice, I've found that the product Perque Repair Guard works better than other quercetin products.

Typical dosage: 1,000 mg daily.

- **Use digestive enzymes with meals** to help ensure your food is completely digested.

Good brands: Enzymedica, Thorne and Now.

What Most People Don't Know About Heart Disease

Mimi Guarneri, MD, founder and medical director of Scripps Center for Integrative Medicine and attending physician in cardiovascular disease at Scripps Clinic, both in La Jolla, California. She is author of *The Heart Speaks: A Cardiologist Reveals the Secret Language of Healing.*

The physical risk factors for heart disease—smoking, elevated cholesterol, high blood pressure, diabetes, etc.—are well known. What very few people realize is that these factors contribute to only about half of the cases of coronary artery disease.

Surprising: Emotional factors, such as stress, anger and depression, may be even more predictive of heart disease than traditional risk factors, according to research. For example, a study reported in *The New England Journal of Medicine* found that heart attack survivors who were socially isolated and had a high degree of stress had more than four times the risk for death from heart attack and other causes over a three-year period than those with low levels of isolation and stress.

Each day, 2,600 Americans die of cardiovascular disease—one every 33 seconds. Many of these deaths are preventable through risk factor modification and lifestyle changes.

At Healing Hearts, a lifestyle change program at Scripps Center for Integrative Medicine in La Jolla, California, heart patients' physical and emotional risk factors are treated with a variety of personalized approaches, including medication, exercise and nutrition programs, group therapy, yoga and meditation. Research shows that patients who undergo these major lifestyle changes have half the number of hospital admissions for recurring cardiac events as those who receive only traditional cardiac care.*

STRESS

The chronic release of stress hormones is one of the most potent risk factors for the heart. Research has shown that chronic stress—from job pressures, financial worries, etc.—is comparable to hypertension as a risk factor for cardiovascular disease. Highly stressed individuals have elevated levels of cortisol and epinephrine, hormones that can raise cholesterol and/or blood pressure by 20% to 50%.

Helpful: Suppose you're late to work and have to stop at a railroad crossing to let a train pass. A "stress response" might be to get angry at the delay.

Better: Count yourself lucky to have a short break in the day. Take the time to relax and listen to the radio or talk to a companion… and remind yourself that the brief delay isn't likely to make much of a difference.

Also helpful: Take a few deep breaths whenever you feel yourself getting stressed. Breathe in deeply for about five seconds, then take another five seconds to exhale. Within a few seconds, your nervous system will begin to shift from an excited state to a relaxed state. Deep breathing helps lower stress hormones along with blood pressure and heart rate.

ANGER

Anger and hostility are the most toxic emotions for the heart. Studies have shown that men who are rated as "hostile" on personality tests are much more likely to experience angina (chest pain) and episodes of high blood pressure.

Feelings of hostility sharply increase blood pressure and heart rate and cause elevations in blood sugar, cholesterol and interleukin-6 (IL-6), a blood protein that acts as a marker for arterial inflammation. An outburst of anger more than doubles the risk for a heart attack in the next two hours.

Helpful: Biofeedback, in which a monitoring device and sensors record heartbeat, muscle tension and other bodily processes, is very effective. It helps you recognize and manage your anger triggers. To find a licensed biofeedback practitioner, consult the Biofeedback Certification Institute of America, 720-502-5829, *www.bcia.org*.

Also helpful: Anger management support groups, where people are encouraged to let down their emotional barriers, express feelings and listen compassionately to others. If you'd like to find a local group, ask your doctor for a referral to a psychologist, who can refer you to an anger management group.

DEPRESSION

Nearly one in 10 Americans suffers from a depressive disorder in a given year, and the incidence of depression is 10 times higher now than it was 50 years ago. Depression, which may be caused by social isolation as well as a chemical imbalance in the brain, is at least as serious as high cholesterol and hypertension as a risk factor for heart disease.

Patients with heart disease who also suffer from depression are up to four times more likely to die during the six months after a heart attack than those who aren't depressed. Studies have shown that depression, along with other emotional factors, such as anxiety, may

*To find a medical center near you that offers integrative heart care, go to the Academic Consortium for Integrative Medicine and Health, 703-556-9222, *www.imconsortium.org*.

be a better predictor of illness and death than the severity of coronary artery disease—even when arteries are blocked by as much as 70%.

Important: Antidepressant medications alone do not appear to reduce the risk for coronary artery disease, even when they significantly improve depressive symptoms. However, antidepressants help people change destructive behavior, such as not exercising or eating a poor diet, and allow them to make lifestyle choices that affect risk for heart disease.

Helpful: For some people, forming social connections is among the most effective ways to reduce depression as well as the risk for heart disease—and may explain why integrative approaches to heart disease are so effective. People who participate in such programs exercise together, join support groups and sometimes eat together.

Also helpful: Volunteer work. People who serve others have a stronger sense of purpose and self-worth. People often say that they'd like to volunteer, but aren't sure what to do.

Try this: What is your passion? It may be playing the piano, working with animals or taking care of children. Look around and find a volunteer program that includes the activities that you like best. To find volunteer activities in your area, go to VolunteerMatch, 415-241-6868, *www.volunteermatch.org*.

ISOLATION

Research shows that people who are socially isolated are two to three times more likely to die from heart disease and other causes over a nine-year period than those with strong social connections.

A long-running study that looked at residents of Roseto, Pennsylvania, found that over a 10-year period, people died of heart attack at a rate only half that of the surrounding communities—despite their high rates of smoking, a fatty diet and hazardous work in local slate quarries. Researchers concluded that their robust cardiac health was due, in part, to a tight civic community—extended families, frequent religious festivals, social clubs, etc.

Important: Stay socially engaged—attend church or synagogue services or engage in other community activities...do volunteer work...and encourage friends to visit.

Medical Disorders That Cause Mental Problems

Barbara Schildkrout, MD, psychiatrist and assistant clinical professor of psychiatry, Harvard Medical School and the Beth Israel Deaconess Medical Center, both in Boston. She is author of *Unmasking Psychological Symptoms: How Therapists Can Learn to Recognize the Psychological Presentation of Medical Disorders. BSchildkrout.WordPress.com*

If you develop anxiety or depression, your first thought might be to call a therapist.

What you should do instead: See your doctor. Many physical problems masquerade as mental health issues. For example, patients with a treatable thyroid disorder often experience intense anxiety. Some seizure disorders may cause intense emotional experiences. And manic behavior could be a medication side effect.

Frightening statistic: Up to 40% of patients in some nursing homes and mental health facilities have mental symptoms that are caused—or made worse—by underlying medical disorders.

According to Barbara Schildkrout, MD, a psychiatrist and leading expert on this subject, mental/physical issues are often intertwined. For example, a former football player suffering from midlife depression may have suffered multiple concussions in the past. Such head trauma may trigger depression...even years later.

Problem: Many primary care physicians don't spend enough time with patients to know their psychological histories, and mental health professionals may wrongly assume that a doctor has thoroughly considered a physical cause of mental symptoms. *Before you conclude that you have a mental health problem, ask yourself...*

- **Did it start quickly?** If you're fine one day and suffering from depression or another mental health symptom the next, you should suspect that there might be a physical cause.

• **Does your mood match your life?** It's understandable that someone who is recently divorced or having financial problems might be depressed. But if everything in your life is fine and you still feel lousy, you might have a physical disorder.

• **Are you experiencing any other symptoms, even if they seem unrelated?** Timing is important. A patient who is hallucinating might be psychotic. But hallucinations could also be symptoms of a seizure disorder or the sleep disorder narcolepsy.

CONFUSING CONDITIONS

More than 100 medical conditions cause symptoms (indicators of a disease or disorder that are detected by the patient) and signs (indicators detected by a physician) that may be misinterpreted to be the evidence of a mental illness. *Examples...*

• **Drug side effects versus mood disorder.** You would expect to experience mood changes when taking a sedating medication, such as codeine. But depression is a common side effect of many medications, including some of those used to treat asthma, elevated cholesterol and high blood pressure. Birth control pills also can cause depression.

Other drugs may trigger mania, a symptom of certain psychiatric conditions, such as bipolar disorder. Mania is marked by racing thoughts, euphoria and lack of sleep. Corticosteroids (such as hydrocortisone and prednisone) may cause mania. Some antidepressants, including selective serotonin reuptake inhibitors, such as *fluoxetine* (Prozac), and monoamine oxidase inhibitors, such as *phenelzine* (Nardil), may trigger an episode of mania.

What to look for: The timing of mood changes. If you've recently started a new medication and you're suddenly feeling depressed, talk to your doctor.

What to do: Make a list of all the medications that you take, and ask your doctor if they could be responsible for your mood changes. He/she may advise you to switch medications and/or take a lower dose.

• **Hyperthyroidism versus anxiety.** Patients who produce too much thyroid hormone (hyperthyroidism) may experience intense anxiety. Some spend months or even years in therapy before they discover that they have a physical problem. The diagnosis is easy to miss because, unlike many other psychological symptoms caused by physical ailments, the symptoms come on gradually, sometimes over a period of years.

What to look for: Feelings of anxiety that don't correspond with what's happening in your life. Patients who suffer from psychological anxiety will usually be worried or concerned about something in particular. One exception is patients with generalized anxiety disorder, who have excessive worry about everyday matters.

The anxiety caused by thyroid disorders will feel physical. Your heart might be pounding...you might sweat a lot...or have shaky hands. Patients interpret these sensations as anxiety even though they may just be physical symptoms.

What to do: If you experience these symptoms or you've been told that you have anxiety, make sure that your doctor has considered the possibility of thyroid disease. It's diagnosed with a blood test. Hyperthyroidism is treated with medication and sometimes surgery.

• **Seizures versus intense emotional episodes.** Emotional outbursts are a common symptom of mental illness, including psychotic disorders. But intense emotional experiences—feelings such as fear, a sense of impending doom, rage or déjà vu experiences—can sometimes be caused by seizures. In addition, seizures can disrupt sleep, which, in turn, may lead to irritability and more likely emotional outbursts.

What to look for: Intense emotional reactions when there's no clear reason. Patients with mental illness can usually describe what makes them angry, anxious, etc. With seizures, emotional outbursts "come out of the blue." Depending on the type of seizure, the episodes are usually brief, often only a minute or two. The short duration often indicates a physical rather than a psychological problem.

What to do: Ask your doctor/therapist if you should have an electroencephalogram, a test that measures electrical activity in the brain. A negative test doesn't mean that you don't have seizures—it just means that your brain activity was normal at the time of testing. If symptoms continue, a repeat test might be needed. If a seizure disorder is diagnosed, symptoms usually improve with medication.

Important: Certain types of seizures cause only subtle changes in consciousness—for example, a moment of unresponsiveness that may be misinterpreted as, say, a problem with attention. Some seizure disorders are also associated with various types of hallucinations, including auditory, visual and olfactory.

• **Normal pressure hydrocephalus (NPH) versus depression.** NPH is an enlargement of the fluid-filled ventricles of the brain that often causes symptoms such as apathy and depression along with cognitive and memory impairments. Some people who are diagnosed with Alzheimer's disease actually have NPH.

What to look for: NPH symptoms include apathy, depression and mental slowing, along with the development of an unsteady gait and urinary incontinence. With Alzheimer's, any trouble with walking or incontinence occurs only at very advanced stages of the disease.

What to do: If you or a loved one has any of these symptoms, there's a chance that the mental health problems have a physical origin. From a simple CT scan, a neurologist can tell whether a person might have NPH. The diagnosis must then be confirmed by further tests including a lumbar puncture in which a small amount of fluid is drained. Doctors then observe whether the patient's gait improves. If so, the diagnosis has been confirmed, and the condition is treated with the surgical insertion of a shunt to drain fluid from the brain.

Better Depression Treatment

In a recent finding, among people with both depression and insomnia, 87% of those whose insomnia was successfully treated with cognitive behavioral insomnia therapy also recovered from their depression, whether they were taking an antidepressant or not.

Possible explanation: Regular sleep-wake cycles are necessary to regulate neurotransmitters in the brain and stave off depression.

Colleen E. Carney, PhD, director, Sleep and Depression Laboratory, Ryerson University, Toronto, Ontario, Canada.

Salt Your Feet to Fall Asleep

Lindsey Duncan, ND, a naturopathic doctor and nutritionist in Austin, Texas. With more than 28 years of clinical experience, he uses a variety of natural therapies. He is also founder of Genesis Today, Inc., a supplement and natural-food product company.

A little-known secret to getting a good night's sleep is keeping the pH of your body alkaline rather than acidic.

Problem: A typical diet (too much processed food, red meat, dairy, fried food, sugar, salt, coffee and alcohol) and lifestyle (constant stress) acidify the body—a major reason why so many people don't get a good night's sleep. An acidic body chemistry creates tension, making it difficult to fall asleep. But an alkaline body chemistry creates a relaxed feeling.

Home remedy: Try a saltwater foot soak. Scientists haven't looked at this practice, but my clinical experience shows that it works.

What to do: Before bed, soak your feet for 20 minutes in hot water and sea salt, which is the best source of minerals to alkalinize and relax the body.

For an average-size-foot bath, add about one-half cup of sea salt to the water. If you're soaking your feet in a regular bathroom tub, use about one to two cups of salt. There are many types of sea salt, each with different beneficial minerals. I prefer Dead Sea salt, which has a high concentration of magnesium to relax the nervous system and other minerals (available online and in health-food stores).

Note: The water temperature for your foot soak should be as hot as your feet can bear—but not hot enough to break a sweat above your lip or to cause a burn. To keep the water hot for 20 minutes, add more hot water during the soak.

Caution: If you have diabetes, check with your doctor before doing this. Neuropathy, a complication of diabetes that can cause loss of feeling in the feet, could prevent you from noticing that the water is too hot.

Log On and Nod Off

Gregg Jacobs, PhD, insomnia specialist at the Sleep Disorders Center, University of Massachusetts Medical School, and author of *Say Good Night to Insomnia*.

Lee Ritterband, PhD, associate professor, Department of Psychiatry and Neurobehavioral Sciences at the University of Virginia Health System, in Charlottesville, Virginia. *SHUTi.net*

Maybe instead of Rx, your doctor's prescription pad should read Rzzz—because people who don't get enough sleep are more likely to get sick.

Newest research: Chronic insomnia has been linked to a higher risk for...

- **Anxiety**
- **Depression**
- **Diabetes**
- **High blood pressure**
- **Heart attack**
- **Stroke**
- **Substance abuse**
- **Suicide**

(And that's not to mention the fatigue and brain fog that often follow a poor night's sleep, hobbling daily performance.)

The official definition of chronic insomnia is having trouble falling asleep or staying asleep, or waking up too early, at least three times a week, for more than a month.

An estimated 30 to 45 million Americans fit that definition. Another 50 to 60 million have the symptoms of insomnia, but less frequently.

Yet out of those 100 million poor sleepers, only an estimated 7% receive treatment for insomnia, according to a survey from the National Sleep Foundation.

And most of them are treated with sleeping pills—which are only a short-term solution, don't treat the causes of insomnia and can have dangerous side effects, says Gregg Jacobs, PhD, an insomnia specialist at the Sleep Disorders Center at the University of Massachusetts Medical School, and author of *Say Good Night to Insomnia* (Holt).

What most people don't realize: There's a drug-free treatment for chronic insomnia that studies show is every bit as effective as sleeping pills—cognitive-behavioral therapy (CBT).

This psychological approach teaches you how to change two sleep-robbing factors: the everyday behaviors that can cause or complicate insomnia (example: an irregular sleep schedule) and the negative thoughts about sleep that are a setup for more sleeplessness (example: "This is going to be another night of insomnia").

"CBT treats the underlying issues that cause insomnia, while medication only treats the symptoms," says Lee Ritterband, PhD, associate professor in the Department of Psychiatry and Neurobehavioral Sciences at the University of Virginia Health System, in Charlottesville, Virginia. "And the beneficial effects of CBT—in contrast to those produced by sleeping pills—last long after the treatment ends."

Researchers in the US and Canada have figured out how to deliver CBT for insomnia via the Internet. And not just information about CBT. What they're offering is a self-help "Internet intervention" very similar to CBT, but without face-to-face contact with a therapist.

And after logging on, a lot of chronic insomniacs are sawing logs.

WWW.ZZZ

In the US, Dr. Ritterband and his colleagues studied 43 people who had chronic insomnia for ten years or longer, enrolling half of them in an Internet program and putting half on a waiting list.

Like face-to-face CBT for insomnia, the online program—Sleep Healthy Using the Internet, or SHUTi—offered weekly instruction in the behavioral and mental changes that can help a person overcome the problem.

The study participants learned and adopted a new set of skills and behaviors. *For example, they...*

- **Went to bed only when sleepy;**
- **Got out of bed when unable to sleep;**
- **Limited "sleep-incompatible" activities in the bedroom, such as watching TV and reading;**
- **Avoided daytime napping;**
- **Got up at the same hour every day;**
- **Increased exercise;**
- **Avoided nicotine, caffeine and alcohol before bedtime;**
- **Learned "cognitive restructuring" for unhelpful beliefs, thoughts and worries about sleep and**
- **Learned strategies to prevent relapse.**

Result: After nine weeks, those receiving therapy online had a 59% decrease in their "Insomnia Severity Index," a standard measurement for insomnia.

They also had improvements in two other measurements: a 55% decrease in the time spent awake during the night, and a 16% increase in "sleep efficiency" (the time spent sleeping while in bed).

Meanwhile, those on the waiting list didn't have significant changes in any of the measurements.

In all, 16 of the 22 participants in SHUTi, or 73%, were considered "in remission"—not insomniacs—after completing the program.

Six months later, 61% were still in remission.

That level of improvement, says Dr. Ritterband, is "almost identical" to typical improvements from face-to-face CBT and sleeping medications.

In Canada, researchers in the Department of Clinical Health Psychology at the University of Manitoba also designed an online treatment for insomnia using CBT. To test the program, they studied 79 people with chronic insomnia, assigning half to the program and half to a waiting list.

After five weeks, those enrolled in the program experienced "significant improvements in insomnia severity, daytime fatigue and sleep quality," compared with the waiting list group, says Norah Vincent, PhD, a clinical psychologist and the study leader, in the journal *Sleep.* Overall, four out of five participants said their sleep was improved.

"Our participants found the online program much more convenient than having to come into the therapist's office for treatment," she adds.

ONLINE RESOURCES FOR A GOOD NIGHT'S REST

For information on the SHUTi program and for future updates on research, visit *www.shuti.me.*

There are several other online CBT programs for insomnia, such as *www.cbtforinsomnia.com*, which uses techniques developed by Dr. Jacobs at Harvard Medical School.

There are also self-help books for insomnia using CBT methods, including *Relief from Insomnia* by Charles Morin, PhD (the techniques in this book were used by Dr. Ritterband to develop the Internet intervention for his study) and *Dr. Ritterband's Say Good Night to Insomnia.*

Beware Nighttime Exposure to Certain Colors of Light

Tracy Bedrosian, PhD, postdoctoral researcher, Salk Institute, La Jolla, California. Her study was conducted while she was a graduate student at The Ohio State University in Columbus and was published in *Journal of Neuroscience.*

What color is the light you sleep with? You may say that you don't sleep with any lights on. But if you take a closer look, you're likely to see some light coming from your alarm clock...cell-phone charger…computer…e-reader…night-light…and/or bedroom TV.

Problem: The color of the light you're exposed to at night, even while you're sleeping, may affect how you feel during the day—and not in a good way. In fact, certain colors are linked to signs of depression, a recent study reveals.

Good news: You can minimize your risk by making your room truly dark or, if you need a bit of illumination, by using the right kind of clock or night-light, a recent study suggests.

TESTING THE RED, WHITE AND BLUE

It's thought that exposure to light at night interferes with the release of hormones that affect mood and various physiological functions. Researchers wanted to explore whether certain colors of light would be better or worse than others in this regard. The experiments were conducted on hamsters, but these mammals share enough physiological similarities with humans that the findings might well apply to us, too.

For four weeks, all the hamsters were exposed to bright light (similar to normal daytime lighting) for 16 hours each day. However, their nighttime-light exposure differed. One group was exposed to no light at night, while three other groups were exposed to either dim white light…dim blue light…or dim red light. Then the hamsters were given various tests to assess depression-like symptoms. The tests were done during daytime, away from any immediate effects of nighttime light.

First the hamsters were placed in tanks filled with room-temperature water for 10 minutes. (From previous studies, the researchers knew that hamsters normally swim vigorously during this challenge—but those who demonstrate various depression-like behaviors are likely to just float passively.) In this study, hamsters that had slept in the dark spent almost all their time swimming (happy hamsters!)…while those that had been exposed to white or blue light at night spent the least time swimming (not so happy). Most interesting of all, those that had been exposed to red light at night spent significantly more time swimming than the other light-exposed hamsters—indicating that red light did not affect mood nearly as negatively as white or blue light did.

Another measure of depression is anhedonia, the inability to derive pleasure from normally enjoyable activities. For hamsters, drinking sugar water is very pleasurable.

Findings: Hamsters not exposed to any light at night consumed the most sugar water, followed closely by those exposed to red light…whereas those exposed to white or blue light consumed only about half as much. So again, red did best among the colors of light, coming in second only to darkness.

Finally, the researchers looked at the hamsters' brains, particularly the neurons in the hippocampus, an area known to be involved in mood regulation. The hamsters that had spent their nights in blue or white light had significantly reduced density of dendritic spines (hairlike growths on brain cells that are used to send chemical messages between cells), another sign that has been linked to depression. The dark-night hamsters showed the highest density of these dendritic spines…with the red-light hamsters again coming in a close second.

WAVELENGTH INTERFERENCE

What explains these results? Researchers suspect that specialized light-sensitive cells of the retina, called ipRGCs, are responsible. These cells, which detect the unique wavelengths emitted by various colors, are most sensitive to blue wavelengths and least sensitive to red wavelengths. The ipRGCs also send messages to the part of the brain that helps regulate circadian rhythm. When circadian rhythm is disrupted—by nighttime light or some other factor—the body feels the effects physically and psychologically. In addition, ipRGCs send messages to the brain's limbic system, which controls mood and emotion. All these factors help explain why red light at night had fewer detrimental effects on mood than other colors of light.

Good-mood lighting at night: It's best if you can keep your bedroom totally dark, and to do that, besides having light-blocking shades or curtains on your windows, you'll need to turn off, cover or remove all electronics and other light-emitting objects at night.

(The one exception is your smoke alarm/carbon monoxide detector, for obvious reasons.) If you want to have a clock immediately readable at all times or if you need a small night-light (for instance, to illuminate the way to the bathroom), use a clock that emits red light…or use a red bulb in your night-light. It's a simple enough thing to try…and you might just start feeling better because of it!

Low Moods at High Altitudes

The Western states have some of the highest altitudes—and also the highest suicide rates.

Theory: High altitudes can produce hypoxia, an inadequate oxygen intake that may worsen depression.

American Journal of Psychiatry.

Midlife Suicide Is on the Rise

Rates are increasing among both men and women ages 40 to 64. The current economic malaise could be a contributing factor.

Warning signs: Acting highly pessimistic, hopeless or angry…increasing alcohol or drug use…making impulsive, out-of-character decisions…getting rid of previously prized possessions…talking about wanting to die…withdrawing from friends, family and society…mood changes. If you notice any of these warning signs in someone you know, contact a mental health professional or call 800-273-TALK, a free 24-hour hotline sponsored by the Substance Abuse and Mental Health Services Administration.

Holly Wilcox, PhD, assistant professor of psychiatry and public health, Johns Hopkins School of Medicine, Baltimore, and coauthor of a study published in *American Journal of Preventive Medicine.*

Popular Drug Linked to Suicide

A popular asthma drug may be linked to suicide. The FDA recently investigated Singulair (*montelukast*) because anecdotal accounts suggest an association between the drug and suicidal thoughts and behavior. Clinical trials revealed an increased risk of insomnia only, but post-marketing surveys showed links to suicidal behavior and depression. The FDA has issued a black box warning.

What can you do: Be alert to changes in mood or behavior, and ask your doctor about switching to another drug. Do not stop any medication without first consulting with your doctor.

Martha V. White, MD, is director of research, Institute for Asthma and Allergy, Wheaton, Maryland.

Smoothing the Ride for Bipolar Disorder

Paul Anderson, ND, a core faculty member in the naturopathic medicine program of Bastyr University, teaching in the Clinical Science division. He has taught as adjunct or visiting professor at many US naturopathic medical schools, as well as many other universities and colleges.

Bipolar disorder is a common mood disorder that can tear families apart as the sufferer tries to cope with the roller coaster of his/her moods, swinging from high-highs and down into low-lows. Conventional medications for bipolar illness are incredibly complicated to "get right" and have such nasty side effects that many patients don't follow the regimen. The result? Lives ruined and sometimes lost. Since pharmaceuticals have not been completely successful for some, are there any natural treatments that could help sufferers with this debilitating illness gain balance from the inside out?

BIPOLAR BACKGROUND

"The best way to think about bipolar illness is as a group of disorders with a spectrum of symptoms," said Paul Anderson, ND, a faculty member at Bastyr University. Dr. Anderson explained that bipolar disorders can take two distinct forms, each of which gets its own "diagnosis." *Here are the basics...*

- **Bipolar I is what, in the old days, used to be called "manic depression."** It's the most serious of the two bipolar diagnoses. There can be long periods of sleeplessness and mania to the point of psychosis. "People suffering with mania don't sleep and frequently feel invincible," Dr. Anderson said. "In this phase they can be hospitalized because they can be a danger to themselves and those around them due to their distorted judgment." However, what goes up must come down. Bipolar I patients are usually depressed a much greater amount of time than they are manic and this depression is often so severe that it can lead to attempted suicide.

- **Bipolar II.** Though not quite as extreme as bipolar I, it's still severe and debilitating. The "up" episodes are known as hypomania, which might be described as a "mild" mania ('mild' when compared with the mania seen in bipolar I). Some of the symptoms are similar to mania, but they won't necessarily interfere with the person's ability to function. However, a diagnosis of bipolar ll requires at least one depressive episode, and it's often a very debilitating, major depression.

Both forms of bipolar disorder and their variants are associated with chronic or recurring depression. It has been speculated that long-term bouts of depression may wear down the nervous system's ability to continually compensate, which eventually allows for the manic episodes that characterize the disease state. If this is in fact at the root of bipolar disorders, treating the profound chronic recurring depression may successfully mediate the depression/mania swings and control the disease, says *Daily Health News* consulting medical editor Andrew L. Rubman, ND.

NATURAL SUPPORT

Though bipolar illness has not been found to be something that can be treated exclusively with "natural" remedies, there are things someone suffering from this illness can do to support his/her health and stability along with whatever medications he/she has been prescribed. That's because lifestyle choices can exacerbate the symptoms dramatically, or, conversely, can help modulate them. "Diet and regularity of eating are top on the list," explained Dr. Anderson. "When manic, people tend not to eat. So their blood sugar fluctuations exaggerate whatever tendencies they have." A similar helpful effect is seen with regular sleep patterns. Sleep regularity and dietary stability are incredible mood stabilizers in their own right. Unfortunately, most bipolar patients do neither when in the manic phase of their illness, Dr. Anderson explained.

In addition to diet and sleep, other factors can (more rarely) aggravate bipolar type symptoms. Alcohol, and many drugs, can elicit depressive or manic symptoms in many people. This can be directly due to neurological effects or indirectly due to depletion of nutrients at a quicker rate (such as alcohol causes with some B vitamins). Rarely, but significantly, prescribed steroids can cause significant neurological changes that can mimic mania or depression. And finally, some women who have a tendency toward the bipolar spectrum of disorders will have their first symptoms in the postpartum time period, Dr. Anderson explained.

Hormone fluctuations can do the same thing. For example, right before a woman's menstrual cycle her progesterone dips. "Progesterone is a natural anti-anxiety hormone," Dr. Anderson said. "So for a woman who has a tendency toward one of the bipolar illnesses the temporary disappearance of progesterone can make her either anxious or manic." Dr. Anderson suggests that a doctor who is keyed in to these kind of hormonal (and blood sugar) fluctuations would have a great advantage in effectively managing bipolar illness.

Dr. Anderson believes that hormones—endocrine balance—is an important factor in treating bipolar in both men and women in an integrative, holistic way. "Screening for abnormalities, checking adrenal function, checking progesterone, testing levels of the hormones cortisol, DHEA and testosterone all are very important," he said. "For example, low or high testosterone can be very aggravating for bipolar patients." A trained naturopathic physician can prescribe therapy that may include bioidentical hormones to help even out the hormone fluctuations for both men and women.

ENVIRONMENTAL SENSITIVITIES

Testing for environmental sensitivities is another important avenue to explore. "It's a good idea to have your physician test for heavy metals like mercury, lead and manganese," Dr. Anderson suggested. "Even clinically small amounts of toxic heavy metals in the body of someone with bipolar disorder may cause interference with the brain's processing of signals and neurotransmitter synthesis and receptor sensitivities," he said. Chelation therapy is the most direct method of dealing with toxic metals in the body. Since this is its own area of specialty in the medical field, patients should consult a physician (naturopathic or allopathic) with specific training and expertise in toxic metal detoxification, Dr. Anderson said.

SUPPLEMENTAL SUPPORT FOR BIPOLAR DISORDER

While people suffering from bipolar disorder should not try to manage their own treatment—there are some "natural" things that they can do to help matters considerably. In most people these recommendations can be employed with the common bipolar disorder medications as well. *Here are Dr. Anderson's top suggestions...*

- **Omega-3 fatty acids.** "These are important modulators of inflammation in both the peripheral and central nervous systems," Dr. Anderson said. He recommends at least 1 gram per day of the two important fatty acids found in fish, EPA (eicosapentaenoic acid) and DHA (docosahexaenoic acid), typically as 1 gram of the mixed EPA/DHA oil... and sometimes adds 200 mg to 400 mg of GLA (gamma-linolenic acid). "We sometimes prescribe as much as six grams of essential fatty acids a day before seeing clinical results," he said.

- **Exercise.** "Most bipolar patients—but especially those who are medicated—report feeling better when they exercise regularly," said Dr. Anderson.

  Recommended regimen: Any kind of moderate exercise, including brisk walking...three or four days a week for 30 minutes.

- **B-complex.** "Manic brain chemistry will use up B vitamins very quickly due to quicker brain metabolism and increased use," Dr. Anderson said. A high-potency B complex, in addition to the separate B-12, taken daily provide good support for the spotty diet many sufferers have.

- **Calcium and magnesium.** "Magnesium and calcium are especially helpful for people on lithium since it helps to alleviate the muscle cramping, twitching or weakness that can be a side effect of that drug."

While the above four recommendations are safe bets for just about anyone suffering from bipolar disorder, Dr. Anderson has also used two other supplements with good effect. One is molybdenum, which helps the brain and liver get rid of sulfite salts that can be toxic to those with bipolar disorder. The other is selenium, which helps support the excretion of heavy metals. Dr. Anderson recommends 50 mcg to 200 mcg of molybdenum once a day on an empty stomach... and between 200 to 400 mcg of selenium, which can be taken with food.

Dr. Anderson discussed a recent study conducted at the University of Calgary in which the mere addition of a nutritional supplement with high levels of chelated trace minerals and vitamins resulted in a more than 50% reduction in symptoms in bipolar patients. "Our brains are never static—and if you have a problem like bipolar and you compound it with poor nutrition, no exercise, stress and hormonal imbalances, you're going to exaggerate many symptoms," he observed.

Sadly, bipolar disorder is not an easily fixed condition. Rather it must be managed with love and respect. However, with careful attention it can become more manageable. *A number of good books that can help sufferers and caregivers through this experience...*

- *Too Good to Be True? Nutrients Quiet the Unquiet Brain: A Four Generation Bipolar Odyssey* by David Moyer
- *New Hope for People with Bipolar Disorder: Your Friendly, Authoritative Guide to the Latest in Traditional and Complementary Solutions* by Jan Fawcett, MD
- *The Bipolar Disorder Survival Guide: What You and Your Family Need to Know* by David Miklowitz
- *The Natural Medicine Guide to Bipolar Disorder* by Stephanie Marohn
- *Bipolar Disorder: Insights for Recovery* by Jane Mountain, MD
- *Overcoming Depression and Manic Depression (Bipolar Disorder): A Whole-Person Approach* by Paul Wider
- *Living Well with Depression and Bipolar Disorder: What Your Doctor Doesn't Tell You... That You Need to Know* by John McManamy
- *Loving Someone with Bipolar Disorder* by Julie A. Fast
- *Bipolar Disorder Demystified: Mastering the Tightrope of Manic Depression* by Lana R. Castle

---

New Help for an "Untreatable" Mental Illness

Joan Farrell, PhD, is director of the Schema Therapy Institute Midwest–Indianapolis Center, an adjunct professor of clinical psychology at Indiana University–Purdue University Indianapolis, and research and training director of the Center for BPD Treatment and Research at Indiana University School of Medicine/Midtown Community Mental Health Center.

Borderline personality disorder (BPD) is a mental illness marked by difficulty managing emotions, extreme fears of abandonment and self-destructive behaviors. The consensus of opinion among mental-health experts used to be, "There isn't much we can do for a patient like that. Therapy and drugs just don't help much."

That was numerous decades ago, and the disorder has continued to be notoriously difficult to treat—until now. BPD patients finally can get the help they need, thanks to a novel form of psychotherapy called schema therapy. (Unhealthy or early maladaptive "schemas" are self-defeating, core themes or patterns that we keep repeating throughout our lives.)

In one study, for instance, one group of BPD patients received the typical treatment consisting of weekly individual psychotherapy sessions—but after eight months, 84% of these patients still met the diagnostic criteria for the disorder. However, a second group received the typical treatment plus weekly sessions of schema therapy—and after eight months, only 6% still had BPD! According to study coauthor Joan Farrell, PhD, director of the Schema Therapy Institute Midwest–Indianapolis Center and coauthor of the new book *Group Schema Therapy for Borderline Personality Disorder*, the research is encouraging.

Who develops BPD? Though not as well-known as bipolar disorder or schizophrenia, BPD is actually more common, affecting from 2% to 6% of US adults. People who develop BDP tend to have sensitive, reactive temperaments. Dr. Farrell said that often their core emotional needs were not met during childhood. Perhaps they had an unstable home environment...did not form a secure attachment with a caregiver... and/or were physically, sexually or emotionally abused. Genetics also may play a role, as the disorder appears to run in families.

Although more US women than men are treated for BPD, Dr. Farrell noted that this could be due to a gender bias in diagnosis. For instance, men with certain BPD symptoms, such as intense anger and aggressiveness, often are diagnosed instead with antisocial personality disorder (a long-term pattern of manipulating and exploiting others). In many cases, for both women and men, BPD goes unrecognized.

Signs of the disorder: BPD symptoms often first appear in adolescence. The diagnosis generally is made if a person exhibits five or more of the typical symptoms. *For instance, he or she may...*

- **Make frantic efforts to avoid real or imagined abandonment.**

• **Have tumultuous, intense relationships in which he or she alternates between idealizing and disliking the other person.**

• **Have an unstable self-image** (signs include difficulty choosing friends or sticking to a career path).

• **Act impulsively and self-destructively** (overspending, binge eating, excessive drinking, risky sex).

• **Experience intense mood swings and excessive emotional reactions.**

• **Have chronic feelings of emptiness.**

• **Feel intense rage or have difficulty controlling anger.**

• **Experience brief episodes of being out of touch with reality.**

• **Engage in self-injury** (such as cutting) or make repeated suicide attempts.

The treatment that can help: Schema therapy combines cognitive behavioral and emotion-focused techniques. It centers on helping patients change longstanding, negative self-images and self-defeating behaviors, incorporating methods such as role-playing, letter writing, assertiveness training, anger management, guided imagery, relaxation, gradual exposure to anxiety-producing situations and challenges to negative thoughts and beliefs.

A unique key element of schema therapy is limited reparenting in which, within the bounds of a professional relationship, the patient establishes a secure attachment to the therapist. "Many patients with BPD missed some critical emotional learning as children. They were not adequately validated and encouraged to express their emotions and needs. In schema therapy, the therapist meets some of those core childhood needs—for example, by setting limits, expressing compassion and providing nurturance," Dr. Farrell said. The goal is for patients to become emotionally healthy and autonomous enough that eventually they no longer need the therapist to meet these core needs—because they learn to do so themselves.

Do you think that you or someone you love might benefit from schema therapy for BPD? Dr. Farrell recommended working with a therapist certified by the International Society of Schema Therapy. *www.schematherapysociety.org*.

Schema therapy usually is done in one-on-one sessions. However, research from Dr. Farrell and colleagues demonstrates a high level of effectiveness from a group-therapy version, and a large international trial is underway to further test this model. A combination of group and individual schema therapy may prove to be the optimal way, Dr. Farrell said, to go beyond the symptom control of other behavioral approaches to improve the quality of BPD patients' lives—and even lead to remission of the disorder. For more information, visit *http://bpd-home-base.org*.

You Don't Have to Be Young (or a Woman) to Have an Eating Disorder

Cynthia M. Bulik, PhD, director of The University of North Carolina (UNC) at Chapel Hill Eating Disorders Program. She is the author of *Crave: Why You Binge Eat and How to Stop* and *The Woman in the Mirror: How to Stop Confusing What You Look Like with Who You Are.*

Until recently, eating disorders have been primarily associated with adolescent girls who don't eat enough—or eat far too much.

Now: The landscape of these disorders has changed. More and more women (and men) in their 40s, 50s, 60s and beyond are struggling with these sometimes life-threatening conditions.

Most of the 11 million Americans—10 million women and one million men—who struggle with an eating disorder, such as anorexia nervosa, bulimia nervosa or binge-eating disorder (a condition that's only recently been recognized by health professionals), are under age 30.

However, in the last 10 years, there has been a substantial increase in the number of women over age 30 who seek treatment for an eating disorder. There are no up-to-date data to tell us whether eating disorders are increasing in men, but clinical experience suggests that they are.

WHAT IS AN EATING DISORDER?

Scientists aren't sure exactly what causes an eating disorder, but research shows that genetics play a role. People who have a first-degree relative, such as a parent or sibling, with an eating disorder are generally at greater risk themselves. When this genetic predisposition is combined with certain psychological and emotional triggers, an eating disorder may result.

Older adults battling an eating disorder fall into three categories—those who have struggled their entire lives…those who struggled as adolescents, recovered to some degree, then relapsed…and those who have recently developed the problem for the first time. Eating disorders can be divided into the following categories…

Anorexia nervosa is characterized by low weight (typically less than 85% of normal weight for one's age and height), fear of weight gain, denial of illness and distorted body image—typically, thinking you are overweight when you are not. Anorexia nervosa can lead to a number of complications, such as hair loss, osteoporosis, electrolyte imbalances, cardiac problems and organ failure.

Bulimia nervosa occurs in people at all weights and is marked by binge eating—uncontrolled consumption of unusually large amounts of food—accompanied by purging that seeks to "undo" the binge in the form of vomiting, unnecessary use of laxatives or excessive exercise. Bulimia causes many of the same health consequences as anorexia.

Binge-eating disorder (BED) is similar to bulimia but without the purging. BED differs from simple overeating in that sufferers feel a loss of control over what they eat. The condition can lead not only to obesity but also to problems such as insomnia and body aches.

AREN'T I TOO OLD FOR THIS?

Older women (and men) face a number of situations that can trigger an eating disorder…

- **Hormonal changes.** At menopause, most women are unprepared for the physical changes, including a hormonally driven redistribution of fat from other parts of the body to the abdomen. This can result in extreme weight-loss strategies to try to retain a youthful body. Hormonal changes also can lead to mood swings and sleep disturbances that often trigger cravings and increase appetite, setting the stage for binge eating. In men, decreases in testosterone and age-related changes in their bodies can trigger eating disorders.
- **Divorce.** Following a breakup, women may seek a new mate and want to appear as physically attractive as possible. This can prompt some women to take extreme measures to lose weight. If a man's wife initiates the divorce, he can feel lost and abandoned and turn to food for comfort.
- **Empty-nest syndrome.** A mother who has spent many years attending to her children can experience a sense of loneliness, uselessness and boredom when they leave home. This is a classic set-up for binge eating—often seen as a desperate attempt to find a sense of "fullness" in the pantry.
- **Depression.** Older women and men must contend with the deaths of friends and other life events that can trigger depression. Reduced appetite is a common symptom of depression and can lead to anorexia in some cases.
- **Overdoing fitness regimens.** Anorexia can develop in people who are overly zealous in diet and fitness regimens. Their good intentions can quickly cross the line from healthful to obsessive.

HOW TO GET HELP

One of the challenges of treating older adults is that, unlike a teenager, a 60-year-old woman or man cannot be compelled to enter treatment. It's crucial that women or men who experience thoughts and behaviors that characterize eating disorders (such as distorted body image, irrational fears of being overweight and an inability to control bingeing) realize that it may not be just a passing phase, and the earlier they seek help, the better.

In the case of anorexia, inpatient treatment is often necessary. With anorexia, the brain is unable to function properly because of malnutrition (decision-making can be impaired and brain shrinkage may occur). About 10%

of patients with anorexia die from medical complications of starvation, such as heart failure, or suicide.

Insurance companies often cover inpatient treatment for anorexia but tend to deny coverage for inpatient treatment of bulimia and BED.

For anyone struggling with bulimia or BED…

• **Find the right professional.** The most effective treatment includes a therapist (a psychiatrist, psychologist, social worker or other experienced health professional) with a background in treating eating disorders. To find a practitioner in your area, consult the National Eating Disorders Association, *www.nationaleatingdisorders.org*…or the Binge Eating Disorder Association, *www.bedaonline.com.* A registered dietitian should be consulted to offer advice on proper nutrition and healthful eating habits.

Also, be sure that the symptoms—mental and physical—are discussed with the patient's primary care physician. This is important to ensure that the doctor takes the patient's eating disorder into account when offering medical advice.

Caution: Some doctors are not educated about the growing prevalence of eating disorders among older patients. If you believe that you or a loved one has symptoms of one of these conditions but your doctor doesn't agree, get help from a therapist on your own and seek a second medical opinion.

• **Start therapy.** Cognitive behavioral therapy, a form of psychotherapy that teaches patients how to understand their own patterns of thinking and behavior, is the most effective treatment for eating disorders. With the help of a therapist, you will explore why you starve yourself and when you're more likely to binge so you can work to change these habits.

• **Consider medication.** The only FDA-approved medication for eating disorders is the anti-depressant *fluoxetine* (Prozac), which is approved for the treatment of bulimia. This drug can decrease the frequency of binge eating and purging but does not offer a permanent solution.

If you suspect that a loved one may have an eating disorder: Have a conversation that begins with a loving message such as "I care about you, and I care about your health. And I worry about how much you seem to be struggling with your eating."

Try to persuade your loved one to at least undergo a professional evaluation (with a dietitian or psychologist or psychiatrist) and to then think through the options. Point out that it's always better to have information and an expert's opinions than to make decisions in a vacuum.

Fish Oil May Lower Suicide Risk

Recent research showed that military service members with low levels of the omega-3 fatty acid DHA were 62% more likely to commit suicide. Some earlier research has shown that omega-3s in fish oil may relieve symptoms of certain forms of depression, but larger, more rigorous studies are needed.

Captain Joseph Hibbeln, MD, acting chief, section of nutritional neuroscience, National Institutes of Health, Bethesda, Maryland, and coauthor of a study published in *The Journal of Clinical Psychiatry.*

Touch Therapy Relieves PTSD

Shamini Jain, PhD, senior scientist, Brain, Mind, and Healing division, Samueli Institute, Corona Del Mar, California, and assistant professor of psychiatry, University of California, San Diego. Her study was published in *Military Medicine.*

Post-traumatic stress disorder (PTSD) can develop in anyone who suffers through a disaster…is a victim of violence or a crime…or experiences another traumatic event, such as a heart attack. Military personnel who are in combat are at particularly high risk for this anxiety disorder. Untreated PTSD can destroy lives, increasing the odds of substance abuse and even suicide—but many sufferers don't seek treatment due to the stigma attached to mental illness or concerns about medication side effects.

Good news: A special type of hands-on therapy can ease PTSD symptoms, according to a recent study conducted at Camp Pendleton, a military base in California.

Participants included 123 Marines returning from combat zones who were experiencing one or more of the hallmark symptoms of PTSD (flashbacks, nightmares, racing heart, jumpiness, concentration problems, anger, aggression, isolation, emotional numbness). At the start of the study, all were tested for symptom severity and rated on a numerical scale, with a score of 50 or higher meriting a PTSD diagnosis. Participants had an average pretreatment score in the mid-50s.

All participants continued to receive whatever standard treatment they were already getting (i.e., psychotherapy and/or medication). About half of the participants also received twice-weekly Healing Touch therapy, a biofield therapy in which trained practitioners use a gentle, noninvasive touch designed to work on the body's vital energy system to stimulate a healing response. (The concept of vital energy, often called chi or prana, is well-known in Eastern medical traditions. It is considered a subtle, nonmaterial field that interacts with and influences the functioning of the mind and body. During Healing Touch, practitioners enter a meditative state in which they act as conduits to sense and regulate patients' vital energy systems to promote mind-body healing.) In addition to the Healing Touch, this group of participants listened to a guided-imagery CD that used visualization techniques to induce deep relaxation and promote a sense of security.

Results: After three weeks, everyone was reevaluated. In the control group, the average PTSD score barely changed, dropping from the mid-50s to 52. In the Healing Touch/guided imagery group, however, the average score dropped to 41, which is a very significant improvement—in fact, these Marines no longer met the diagnostic criteria for PTSD.

More research is needed to determine whether Healing Touch therapy with guided imagery works for people whose PTSD stems from noncombat–related trauma (though it makes sense that it might)...how long the benefits last...and the optimal length of treatment.

In the meantime, if you are interested in trying Healing Touch therapy as a complement to conventional PTSD treatment, you can find a trained practitioner through the website of the Healing Touch Professional Association or Healing Touch International. Check with your insurance company to see whether the treatment is covered.

Take Advantage of Free Mental Health Screening

Screening for Mental Health Inc. offers free confidential screenings nationwide for depression, suicide risk, bipolar disorder, chronic anxiety and posttraumatic stress disorder, usually first week of October. *http://mentalhealthscreening.org*.

Jim Miller, an advocate for senior citizens, writes "Savvy Senior," a weekly information column syndicated in more than 400 newspapers nationwide. Based in Norman, Oklahoma, he offers a free senior newswire service. *SavvySenior.org*

Guide to Health Helplines and Crisis Hotlines

Gretchen Phillips, MD, a hospitalist (specialist in in-patient medicine) and family physician at Fairview Lakes Medical Center in Wyoming, Minnesota, with long-standing expertise in urgent care and women's health. She is the host of the regional radio programs Fairview On Call and WCCO Radio Check Up with Dr. Gretchen Phillips. *DoctorGretchen.com*

When someone is diagnosed with a serious disease or faces a personal or mental-health crisis, help can be as close as the nearest telephone. Health helplines provide information from national organizations on specific medical conditions…give referrals to treatment facilities…and suggest coping strategies. Crisis hotlines operate around the clock, providing emotional support and step-by-step guidelines on how to handle a crisis.

More hotlines: Check the government website *http://healthhotlines.nlm.nih.gov.*

CRISIS SITUATION

Domestic Violence: National Domestic Violence Hotline, 800-799-SAFE (800-799-7233), *www.ndvh.org.*

Sexual Assault: National Sexual Assault Hotline, 800-656-HOPE (800-656-4673), *www.rainn.org.*

Suicidal Intentions: National Suicide Prevention Lifeline, 800-273-TALK (800-273-8255), *www.suicidepreventionlifeline.org.*

MENTAL HEALTH

Alcoholism/Drug Addiction: National Council on Alcoholism and Drug Dependence, 800-NCA-CALL (800-622-2255), *www.ncadd.org.*

Alzheimer's Disease: Alzheimer's Foundation of America, 866-AFA-8484 (866-232-8484), *www.alzfdn.org.*

Depression/Bipolar Disorder: Depression and Bipolar Support Alliance, 800-826-3632, *www.dbsalliance.org.*

Grief/End of Life: Caring Connections, 800-658-8898, *www.caringinfo.org.*

CAREGIVING

Family Care Providers: Caregiver Action Network, 202-454-3970, *www.caregiveraction.org.*

Hospice: Hospice Education Institute, 800-331-1620, *www.hospiceworld.org.*

Senior Care: Department of Health and Human Services Eldercare Locator, 800-677-1116, *www.eldercare.gov.*

Are Cat Owners at High Risk for Suicide?

Teodor T. Postolache, MD, associate professor of psychiatry and director of the Mood and Anxiety Program at the University of Maryland School of Medicine, Baltimore.

Robert H. Yolken, MD, professor, pediatric infectious disease, The Johns Hopkins University School of Medicine, director, developmental neurovirology, Johns Hopkins Children's Center, Baltimore.

There were tabloid-like news reports out not too long ago about "cat ladies" being at higher risk for suicide because of exposure to a certain parasite that's carried in cat feces.

Was it all crazy hype? Maybe not.

The parasitic infection is called toxoplasmosis, and more than 60 million men and women in the US have it, according to the CDC.

Owning a cat can increase your risk for this infection because you can get it by handling cat feces, but lots of other stuff can also increase your risk, including eating or handling undercooked meat…accidentally ingesting contaminated soil, such as from not washing your hands after gardening…eating contaminated, unwashed fruits or vegetables…drinking contaminated water…or receiving an infected organ transplant. And pregnant women can pass the infection to their unborn children.

How could this infection be linked to a self-inflicted act such as suicide?

THE CONSEQUENCES OF INFECTION

The vast majority of infected people have no symptoms. But the parasite can cause brain and vision problems in those with weak immune systems, and it can be dangerous in fetuses—potentially causing mental disability, blindness or even death, which is why pregnant women are routinely advised to let someone else take over litter box duty.

But now two recent studies reveal a link with suicide.

In one study, researchers discovered that infected women were one and a half times as likely to attempt suicide as women who tested negative—even after controlling for mental illness. In another study, researchers discovered that men and women who had attempted suicide were seven times as likely to be infected with the parasite, compared with people who had never attempted suicide.

UNDERSTANDING THE CONNECTION

Remember, the research hasn't shown a causal relationship between the infection and suicide—only an association.

Why might the infection make you want to attempt suicide? We directed that question to the senior author of both studies, Teodor T. Postolache, MD. Since the infection rarely causes symptoms, it's unlikely that most people in the study felt so sick from the infection that they wanted to end their lives, he said. (He can't say for sure because this was an epidemiological study that analyzed a population retrospectively.) It could be that the infection causes alterations in brain functioning that leads to suicidal behaviors, Dr. Postolache said.

"But it's also possible that the reverse is true. Some behaviors associated with suicide—such as poor hygiene, including not washing hands after handling raw meat—may make a person more susceptible to infection," Dr. Postolache said.

TREATING THE PARASITE

In an otherwise healthy person who is not pregnant, treatment is usually not necessary because the immune system generally prevents the infection from causing symptoms. Those who are pregnant and/or have weak immune systems might be given antibiotics or antimalaria drugs to reduce or eliminate symptoms (at least temporarily) and/or to prevent a baby from becoming infected. But which drugs to use and how effective they will be are still being researched.

One problem is that this infection lives inside you forever—so symptoms may flare up and recede, but the infection can never be cured. Another problem is that the drugs listed above have serious potential side effects, including the suppression of bone marrow growth and liver toxicity.

"Unfortunately," said Dr. Postolache, "even if you know that you're infected, it's not always clear whether you should be treated—or how." But if you're experiencing cognitive issues, vision problems or suicidal thoughts—especially if you're pregnant or have a weak immune system—ask your doctor if you should be tested and/or treated.

PROTECT YOURSELF FROM INFECTION

The best thing to do, said Dr. Postolache, is take precautions to help prevent yourself from getting infected. Follow his tips…

- **Be cautious if you own a cat.** Keep your cat in the house as much as possible…feed it only canned or dried cat food or well-cooked meat rather than raw meat…and clean the litter box every day (or ask someone else to, if you're pregnant), because the parasite needs to sit in the litter box for more than a day to become infectious.
- **Peel or wash fruits and vegetables.** Wash them in hot, soapy water before eating or cooking them. Also, before using them, wash all cutting boards, utensils, dishes and counters with hot, soapy water.
- **Thoroughly cook meat.** Don't just "eyeball it"—use a food thermometer when cooking meat and follow the government's safety recommendations.
- **Wear gloves when gardening.** And wash your hands with hot, soapy water after working in soil.

No More Panic Attacks

Mark A. Stengler, NMD, is a naturopathic medical doctor and author of the *Health Revelations newsletter, The Natural Physician's Healing Therapies* and *Bottom Line's Prescription for Natural Cures.* He is also the founder and medical director of the Stengler Center for Integrative Medicine in Encinitas, California, and adjunct associate clinical professor at the National College of Natural Medicine in Portland, Oregon. *MarkStengler.com*

Your heart races, your head swims. You are suddenly in the grip of something quite frightful. The intense fear and heart attack-like symptoms of a panic attack come on without warning. Sometimes they are triggered by fatigue...anxiety...phobias (such as fear of heights)...stress...stimulants (such as caffeine)...low blood sugar...or medication withdrawal. But the good news is that natural therapies can help. I often recommend several natural therapies to my patients. *Here's my advice...*

DURING A PANIC ATTACK

• **Bach Flower Rescue Remedy.** This homeopathic blend of flower extracts, which comes in a spray or drop form, quickly and gently relaxes the nervous system. For panic, use the spray form—and spray once under the tongue every five minutes until anxiety subsides. Available at health-food stores, this product comes in a small, easy-to-carry bottle.

TO PREVENT PANIC ATTACKS

• **Take Alpha S1-casein hydrolysate.** This supplement, made of the milk protein casein, helps to calm the nervous system and has been shown to reduce stress-related symptoms. It is best used preventively for those with anxiety who are prone to regular bouts of panic attacks.

Brand to try: Nature's Plus Dreaminol (800-645-9500, *www.naturesplus.com* for a store locator).

• **Treat weak adrenal glands.** People who are prone to panic attacks often have weak adrenal glands, which keeps the body from effectively coping with stress. Several supplements can help, including the herb ashwagandha and a B-complex vitamin.

• **Avoid sugar.** Eliminating refined sugar from the diet helps to maintain natural blood sugar levels and makes it less likely that you will feel edgy due to a sugar-induced energy roller coaster. To keep your blood sugar on an even keel, eat small amounts of protein throughout the day, such as lean poultry, nuts, legumes and fish.

How to Truly Help Someone Who Is Depressed

Mitch Golant, PhD, a psychologist in private practice in Los Angeles and coauthor of seven books, including *What to Do When Someone You Love Is Depressed.* He is also a senior consultant for strategic initiatives at the Cancer Support Community. *CancerSupportCommunity.org*

Robin Williams's recent suicide started a national conversation about depression. And now, many people are still left wondering—*What would I do if a loved one were seriously depressed?*

We'll never know whether more could have been done to save Williams. But it is important for everyone to realize that there are practical and effective ways to help a loved one who is depressed—whether or not he/she is suicidal.

UNDERSTANDING DEPRESSION

Depression causes many well-known symptoms, such as lethargy, insomnia, loss of interest in work and hobbies, hopelessness and despair. But perhaps the most difficult behavior to cope with in a loved one who is depressed is the person's tendency to withdraw. Your loved one's depression is likely to leave him feeling deeply alone and misunderstood.

That's why it's crucial that you respond appropriately when your loved one shares *any* of his feelings—even if they sound angry, illogical or accusatory.

FINDING THE RIGHT WORDS

Here are the approaches that will allow you to help a loved one with depression...

• **Use the "observer's mind."** With this approach, you detach yourself from the situation so that you respond to the feelings *behind* your loved one's words rather than their literal content. This way, you don't take your loved one's comments personally—and you avoid being drawn into an argument neither of you wants. Instead, you simply look and listen without responding immediately to what the person with depression is saying—you are silently calm, receptive and empathetic—and *then* you respond with support and help, using the next step...

• **Validate your loved one's feelings.** Try a technique known as "mirroring." With this approach, you verbally reflect back what your loved one is saying on an *emotional* level, not necessarily on a content level—this process validates his emotions and helps him feel heard and understood (the experience that a person with depression wants the most). *Two examples...*

Example #1: Your loved one says: "I'm all alone."

Don't say: "No, you're not. I'm sitting here with you right now."

Do say: "I know that you're feeling alone right now. Is there anything I can do to help? Together, we'll get through this lonely feeling."

Example #2: Your loved one says: "Why bother? Life isn't worth living. There's no point in going on."

Don't say: "How can you think that? You have two beautiful children and a great job. I love you. You have everything to live for."

Do say: "I know it feels that way to you right now, but I want you to know that you matter to me and to the children. We'll get through this hopeless feeling together."

Very important: Notice that these "do say" examples all include statements that validate your loved one's feelings and a second statement that reminds him of your dependability—and of hope for the future.

GETTING HELP FOR YOUR LOVED ONE

Research shows that 80% of people with depression can be helped with psychotherapy and/or medication. You can play an active role in encouraging your loved one to get the care he needs. *What to do...*

• **Take charge.** Assisting your loved one in getting professional help is crucial—even if he protests.

• **Enlist support.** Call your family doctor, clergyman, therapist or another health-care professional, and ask for advice in creating a realistic plan of action to help the person with depression.

Schedule an appointment for your loved one to see his doctor, who may refer him to a psychiatrist or psychologist. (If you think your loved one would prefer scheduling this appointment himself, consider allowing him to do so.)

• **Call a meeting.** Include the person with depression and any other friends or family members whose support you can count on.

Tell your loved one: "Honey, we're all here because we're worried about you and don't want you to suffer. We've scheduled an appointment with the doctor. You and I can go together and figure this out." (As an alternative, you can simply give your loved one the doctor's phone number and offer to go with him to the appointment.) Most people who are suffering with depression are grateful that they are no longer emotionally invisible. When all of these elements are in place—especially your emotional resolve—there's a good chance your loved one will respond appropriately.

IF YOUR LOVED ONE IS SUICIDAL

If a loved one makes statements that suggest he/she may be thinking about suicide (for example, "You'd be better off without me"...or "I just want to check out"), this is an emergency. It's a myth that people who talk about suicide don't actually follow through. What you say and do in these situations can be vital to your loved one's survival.

What to say: "I know things look hopeless right now, and I'm taking this very seriously. We need to get help"...or "I'm here with you, and I'm not going to leave. You're not alone. We're going to the hospital right away." *For advice on assessing the problem...*

• **Call your local suicide-prevention center.** Or call the National Suicide Prevention Lifeline at 800-273-8255.

If the situation is dire...

• **Call 911 or the police.** Emergency workers and police are trained to deal with mental health emergencies. They will come and determine if your loved one should be hospitalized. The key is whether he is a danger to himself or others.

7

Diabetes

Fight Diabetes and Prediabetes Naturally with Three Proven Nondrug Remedies

Scientific research and the experience of doctors and other health professionals show that supplements and superfoods can be even more effective than drugs when it comes to preventing and treating diabetes. I reviewed thousands of scientific studies and talked to more than 60 health professionals about these glucose-controlling natural remedies. One is magnesium. Studies show that magnesium significantly reduces the risk for diabetes. *Here are three more standout natural remedies...*

Caution: If you are taking insulin or other medications to control diabetes, talk to your doctor before taking any supplement or changing your diet.

GYMNEMA

Gymnema has been the standard anti-diabetes recommendation for the past 2,000 years from practitioners of Ayurveda, the ancient system of natural healing from India. Derived from a vinelike plant found in the tropical forests of southern and central India, the herb also is called gurmar, or "sugar destroyer"—if you chew on the leaf of the plant, you temporarily will lose your ability to taste sweets.

Modern science has figured out the molecular interactions underlying this strange phenomenon. The gymnemic acids in the herb have a structure similar to glucose molecules, filling up glucose receptor sites on the taste buds. They also fill up sugar receptors in the intestine, blocking the absorption of glucose. And gymnemic acids stimulate (and even may

Bill Gottlieb, CHC, a health coach certified by the American Association of Drugless Practitioners. Based in northern California, he is author of *Defeat High Blood Sugar—Naturally! Super-Supplements and Super-Foods Selected by America's Best Alternative Doctors. BillGottliebHealth.com* regenerate) the cells of the pancreas that manufacture insulin, the hormone that ushers glucose out of the bloodstream and into cells.

Standout research: Studies published in *Journal of Ethnopharmacology* showed that three months of using a unique gymnema extract, formulated over several decades by two Indian scientists, reduced fasting blood glucose (a blood sample is taken after an overnight fast) by 23% in people with type 2 diabetes (defined as fasting blood sugar levels of 126 mg/dL or higher). People with prediabetes (defined as those with blood sugar levels of 100 mg/dL to 125 mg/dL) had a 30% reduction.

Important: The newest (and more powerful) version of this extract is called ProBeta, which is available at *www.pharmaterra.com.* A naturopathic physician who uses ProBeta with his patients told me that the supplement can lower fasting glucose in the 200s down to the 120s or 130s after five to six months of use.

Typical daily dose: ProBeta—two capsules, two to three times a day. Other types of gymnema—400 milligrams (mg), three times a day.

APPLE CIDER VINEGAR

Numerous studies have proved that apple cider vinegar works to control type 2 diabetes. Several of the studies were conducted by Carol Johnston, PhD, RD, a professor of nutrition at Arizona State University.

Standout scientific research: Dr. Johnston's studies showed that an intake of apple cider vinegar with a meal lowered insulin resistance (the inability of cells to use insulin) by an average of 64% in people with prediabetes and type 2 diabetes...improved insulin sensitivity (the ability of cells to use insulin) by up to 34%...and lowered postmeal spikes in blood sugar by an average of 20%. Research conducted in Greece, Sweden, Japan and the Middle East has confirmed many of Dr. Johnston's findings.

How it works: The acetic acid in vinegar—the compound that gives vinegar its tart flavor and pungent odor—blunts the activity of disaccharidase enzymes that help break down the type of carbohydrates found in starchy foods such as potatoes, rice, bread and pasta. As a result, those foods are digested and absorbed more slowly, lowering blood glucose and insulin levels.

Suggested daily intake: Two tablespoons right before or early in the meal. (More is not more effective.)

If you're using vinegar in a salad dressing, the ideal ratio for blood sugar control is two tablespoons of vinegar to one tablespoon of oil. Eat the salad early in the meal so that it disrupts the carb-digesting enzymes before they get a chance to work. Or dip premeal whole-grain bread in a vinaigrette dressing.

SOY FOODS

A new 10-year study published in *Journal of the American Society of Nephrology* found that the mortality rate for people with diabetes and kidney disease was more than 31%. Statistically, that makes kidney disease the number-one risk factor for death in people with diabetes.

Fortunately, researchers have found that there is a simple way to counter kidney disease in diabetes—eat more soy foods.

Standout scientific research: Dozens of scientific studies show that soy is a nutritional ally for diabetes patients with kidney disease. But the best and most recent of these studies, published in *Diabetes Care*, shows that eating lots of soy can help reverse signs of kidney disease, reduce risk factors for heart disease—and reduce blood sugar, too.

The study involved 41 diabetes patients with kidney disease, divided into two groups. One group ate a diet with protein from 70% animal and 30% vegetable sources. The other group ate a diet with protein from 35% animal sources, 35% textured soy protein and 30% vegetable proteins. After four years, those eating the soy-rich diet had lower levels of several biomarkers for kidney disease. (In another, smaller experiment, the same researchers found that soy improved biomarkers for kidney disease in just seven weeks.) In fact, the health of the participants' kidneys actually improved, a finding that surprised the researchers, since diabetic nephropathy (diabetes-caused kidney disease) is considered to be a progressive, irreversible disease.

Those eating soy also had lower fasting blood sugar, lower LDL cholesterol, lower total cholesterol, lower triglycerides and lower C-reactive protein, a biomarker for chronic inflammation.

How it works: Substituting soy for animal protein may ease stress on the delicate filters of the kidneys. Soy itself also stops the overproduction of cells in the kidney that clog the filters...boosts the production of nitric oxide, which improves blood flow in the kidneys...and normalizes the movement of minerals within the kidneys, thus improving filtration.

Suggested daily intake: The diabetes patients in the study ate 16 grams of soy protein daily.

Examples: Four ounces of tofu provide 13 grams of soy protein...one soy burger, 13 grams...one-quarter cup of soy nuts, 11 grams...one-half cup of shelled edamame (edible soybeans in the pod), 11 grams...one cup of soy milk, 6 grams.

WHAT'S WRONG WITH DIABETES DRUGS?

Doctors typically try to control high blood sugar with a glucose-lowering medication such as *metformin* (Glucophage), a drug most experts consider safe. But other diabetes drugs may not be safe.

Example #1: Recent studies show that *sitagliptin* (Januvia) and *exenatide* (Byetta) double the risk for hospitalization for pancreatitis (inflamed pancreas) and triple the risk for pancreatic cancer.

Example #2: *Pioglitazone* (Actos) can triple the risk for eye problems and vision loss, double the risk for bone fractures in women and double the risk for bladder cancer.

Secret Recipe for Fighting Diabetes

In a recent study, 24 herbs and spices were analyzed and found to contain high levels of polyphenols, antioxidant compounds that block the formation of inflammation-promoting substances that raise diabetes risk. Levels were highest in ground cloves...followed by cinnamon (shown in earlier research to help fight diabetes)...sage...marjoram...tarragon...and rosemary.

Instead of seasoning with salt: Consider trying the above herbs and spices.

James L. Hargrove, PhD, associate professor, department of foods and nutrition, University of Georgia, Athens.

Cinnamon—Cheap, Safe and Very Effective

Richard Anderson, PhD, lead researcher at the Beltsville Human Nutrition Research Center, US Department of Agriculture, Maryland.

Insulin is the hormone that controls blood sugar levels. Cinnamon is its twin.

"Cinnamon mimics the action of insulin," says Richard Anderson, PhD, a researcher at the Beltsville Human Nutrition Research Center in Maryland. "Cinnamon stimulates insulin receptors on fat and muscle cells the same way insulin does, allowing excess sugar to move out of the blood and into the cells."

Several recent studies provide new proof of cinnamon's effectiveness in preventing and controlling diabetes...

RECENT RESEARCH

- **Stopping diabetes before it starts.** In Britain, researchers studied healthy, young men, dividing them into two groups—one group received three grams of cinnamon a day and the other a placebo.

After two weeks, the men taking the cinnamon supplement had a much improved "glucose tolerance test"—the ability of the body to process and store glucose. They also had better "insulin sensitivity"—the ability of the insulin hormone to usher glucose out of the bloodstream and into cells.

- **Long-term management of diabetes.** The most accurate measurement of long-term blood sugar control is A1C, or glycated hemoglobin—

the percentage of red blood cells that have been frosted by blood sugar. Seven percent or less means diabetes is under control—and a decrease of 0.5 to 1.0% is considered a significant improvement in the disease.

In a study by a doctor in Nevada, 109 people with type 2 diabetes were divided into two groups, with one receiving 1 gram of cinnamon a day and one receiving a placebo. After three months, those taking the cinnamon had a 0.83% decrease in A1C. Those taking the placebo had a 0.37% decrease.

"We used standard, off-the-shelf cinnamon capsules that patients would find at their local stores or on the Internet," says Paul Crawford, MD, the study's author, in the *Journal of the American Board of Family Medicine*.

Important: He points out that the drop in A1C seen in his study would decrease the risk of many diabetic complications—heart disease and stroke by 16%; eye problems (diabetic retinopathy) by 17 to 21%, and kidney disease (nephropathy) by 24 to 33%.

- **After a bad night's sleep, include cinnamon in your breakfast.** Several recent studies show that sleep deprivation—a nearly universal problem of modern life—increases the risk of diabetes.

Solution: Writing in the *Journal of Medicinal Food*, researchers in the Human Performance Laboratory at Baylor University recommend the use of cinnamon to reverse insulin resistance and glucose intolerance after sleep loss.

- **Oxidation under control.** Oxidation—a kind of biochemical rust—is one of the processes behind the development of diabetes. In a study by French researchers of 22 people with prediabetes, three months of supplementation with a cinnamon extract dramatically reduced oxidation—and the lower the level of oxidation, the better the blood sugar control.

"The inclusion of cinnamon compounds in the diet could reduce risk factors associated with diabetes," conclude the researcher, in the *Journal of the American College of Nutrition*.

Bottom line: Cinnamon works. In a review study of the best research on cinnamon and diabetes to date, researchers in England concluded the spice has the power to fight high blood sugar. Their findings were in *Diabetes, Obesity and Metabolism*.

ONE TEASPOON DAILY

"Try to get ¼ to 1 teaspoon of cinnamon daily," says Dr. Anderson. Sprinkle it in hot cereals, yogurt or applesauce. Use it to accent sweet potatoes, winter squash or yams. Try it with lamb, beef stew or chilies. It even goes great with grains such as couscous and barley, and legumes such as lentils and split peas.

Or you can use a cinnamon supplement.

Consider taking 1 to 3 grams per day, says Dr. Anderson, which is the dosage range used in many studies.

Best: Cinnulin PF—a specially prepared water extract of cinnamon—is a supplement used in many studies showing the spice's effectiveness in supplement form. It is widely available in many brands, such as Swanson and Doctor's Best.

The dosage of Cinnulin PF used in studies is typically 250 mg, twice a day.

Testosterone Therapy Helps Men with Diabetes

Sandeep Dhindsa, MD, endocrinologist and associate professor, State University of New York at Buffalo. His research was presented at the 2013 meeting of the American Association of Clinical Endocrinologists.

Diminished energy, reduced lean muscle mass, decreased libido, erectile dysfunction...these symptoms are common in men with low levels of the hormone testosterone. Men with type 2 diabetes are particularly prone to this hormonal deficiency—it affects about one-third of them—and it can make their blood sugar problems even worse.

Good news: Testosterone replacement therapy has multiple benefits for such men, a recent study shows.

Participants included 81 men with diabetes. Some had normal levels of free testosterone (the amount of the hormone in the bloodstream)...some had low levels of less than five nanograms per deciliter (ng/dL). At the start of the study, all the men were given a battery of tests and, as expected, men with low testosterone had a bunch of problems. They had more body fat, less lean muscle and more inflammation, and they were more insulin-resistant—meaning their bodies were less able to recognize and respond to insulin.

Next, the men with low testosterone were divided into two groups. One group received injections of testosterone every two weeks for 24 weeks...the other group received placebo injections.

What the testosterone did: In the placebo group, nothing improved. However, among the men who received testosterone injections, insulin resistance improved by nearly 30%—and that was enough of an improvement to essentially get rid of their insulin resistance. What's more, these men lost an average of 4.5 pounds of fat and gained 4.5 pounds of lean muscle... their inflammation decreased...and they reported significant improvement in libido and increased satisfaction with their erections.

Men with diabetes: Doctors generally do not screen diabetes patients for testosterone deficiency, so ask to be tested—it is a simple and inexpensive blood test. If your free testosterone level is below five ng/dL, talk to your doctor about bringing it back up to normal with testosterone replacement therapy. There are four forms of testosterone therapy—injections, topical gel, topical custom-compounded cream and surgically inserted pellets. The treatment could make it easier for you to manage your diabetes by lessening your insulin resistance...and it could boost your energy, strength and sex life, as well.

Testosterone therapy is safe for most men.

Exceptions: Testosterone boosts red blood cell production, which is good for anemia, but too many red blood cells can raise heart attack risk. Men with high hematocrit (a measure of red blood cell concentration) should use testosterone cautiously, if at all. Men with advanced kidney or liver disease should avoid testosterone therapy—it could cause fluid retention, which already is a problem for such men.

Note: Testosterone therapy may cause some decrease in testicle size.

Reassuring: For decades, it was believed that increasing testosterone made prostate tumors grow, but there is now strong evidence that raising testosterone levels in men who have testosterone deficiency does not increase prostate cancer risk.

Weight-Loss Surgeries Beat Standard Treatments for Diabetes

Francesco Rubino, MD, chief, gastrointestinal metabolic surgery, and director, Metabolic and Diabetes Surgery Center at New York-Presbyterian/Weill Cornell, and associate professor, surgery, Weill Cornell Medical College, New York City.

Loren Wissner Greene, MD, endocrinologist, NYU Langone Medical Center, and clinical associate professor, New York University School of Medicine, New York City.

The New England Journal of Medicine, online.

A new international analysis comparing weight-loss procedures to standard diabetes treatments found that surgery is more effective at helping people combat type 2 diabetes.

The finding stems from two years of tracking 60 severely obese patients with type 2 diabetes who were between the ages of 30 and 60. One-third of the patients were treated with diabetes drugs and diet–lifestyle modifications, while the rest underwent one of two surgical procedures: Roux-en-Y gastric bypass or biliopancreatic diversion surgery.

The end result: All of the surgical patients were ultimately able to stop taking their diabetes medications, while the vast majority entered into full disease remission. Neither outcome occurred in the traditional treatment group.

"We have known for many years that bariatric surgery, and specifically certain types of operations like gastric bypass, are very effective in terms of helping to control diabetes," noted senior study author Francesco Rubino, MD, chief of gastrointestinal metabolic surgery and director of the Metabolic and Diabetes Surgery Center at New York-Presbyterian/ Weill Cornell in New York City.

"But what this new study shows is that even when you compare surgery against standard treatment, surgery performs far better in terms of the improvement that you can get in terms of diabetes," he continued. "Surgery dramatically reduces blood sugar levels, and very often surgical patients can stop taking the medications used for diabetes."

Dr. Rubino and his colleagues from Rome's Catholic University report their findings in the online edition of *The New England Journal of Medicine*. Cleveland Clinic researchers recently report similar findings in the same journal.

TWO STUDIES, SIMILAR RESULTS

In their study, the Cleveland Clinic doctors followed 150 patients with type 2 diabetes for a year, and found those who had undergone one of two types of weight-loss surgeries were much more likely than those on traditional therapies to get their blood sugar lowered to the desired level and reduce their use of diabetes medications.

The Italian study authors pointed out that standard medicinal therapies, while effective, could pose their own set of problems. For one, insulin therapy can cause patients to gain weight, which itself can have a negative impact on diabetes.

To explore the comparative benefit of surgical options, the team focused on 60 diabetic patients who had a body mass index (BMI) of 35 or more (BMI is a measurement that takes into account height and weight, and over 30 is considered obese). All had a minimal five-year history of struggling with diabetes.

Undergoing treatment in Rome, the patients were randomly divided into three groups. The first was treated with conventional insulin therapy and a range of other hypoglycemic drugs, alongside what was described as "rigorous" dietary and exercise counseling. The second and third group had one of the two types of bariatric surgery, and were placed on a daily regimen of vitamin and mineral supplementation.

The research team found that all of the surgical patients were able to stop taking all diabetes medications within just 15 days.

What's more, at the two-year mark, three-quarters of those who underwent Roux-en-Y gastric bypass surgery had entered diabetes remission, meaning that for a minimum of one year they had a fasting glucose level under 100 milligrams/deciliter and a hemoglobin A1c count of less than 6.5%.

The same was true among 95% of the biliopancreatic surgery group. By contrast, none of the patients in the standard treatment group had entered remission.

The team observed that BMI levels, diabetes history, postsurgical weight loss, age and gender did not appear to play a role in the likelihood that patients would enter into diabetes remission.

"Two years is a relatively short outcome," acknowledged Dr. Rubino. "And this was a small study. But the effect of surgery was almost immediate. And I think it's clear that while patients getting medicinal therapy did improve somewhat, the chance for patients to achieve robust improvement in diabetes is much greater for those who have surgery than those who are treated with standard medications."

EXPERT COMMENTARY

Loren Wissner Greene, MD, endocrinologist at NYU Langone Medical Center in New York City, expressed little surprise at the findings.

"That's been widely reported," she noted. "Of course, how one fares does depend on the individual. One can eat around any procedure, meaning that if a patient drinks high-caloric liquids following surgery, and manages not to lose weight, that can affect the result," Dr. Greene explained.

"At the same time, there is very good evidence for diabetic remission after surgery, particularly for diverting procedures, where there could be a beneficial impact on gut hormones like leptin and ghrelin," Dr. Greene added.

"There are some risks, however," she cautioned. "And people who have presurgical problems—those with high blood pressure or obesity-related sleep apnea—might be limited in terms of the type of obesity surgery they can get. But for those who can do it, it may really be the better way to go. And in the end, though surgery is extremely expensive, it might even be cheaper than having to take expensive diabetic medications for years to come."

Not to mention all the costs savings and relieved suffering of avoiding such diabetic complications as blindness, kidney failure and amputated limbs.

For more information on weight-loss surgery, visit the US National Library of Medicine at its website *www.nlm.nih.gov/medlineplus/weightlosssurgery.html.*

This Supplement Can Stop Diabetes

When researchers studied 4,497 healthy adults' diets for 20 years, those who consumed the most magnesium (about 200 mg per 1,000 calories) were 47% less likely to develop diabetes than those who consumed the least (about 100 mg per 1,000 calories).

Theory: Magnesium enhances enzymes that help the body process blood sugar.

Self-defense: Eat magnesium-rich foods, such as almonds (one-quarter cup roasted, 97 mg) and spinach (one-half cup cooked, 77 mg).

Ka He, MD, associate professor, departments of nutrition and epidemiology, University of North Carolina, Chapel Hill.

You Might Need Zinc

Zinc deficiency is linked to diabetes and cancer. Zinc absorption decreases with age, and that can cause decreased immunity, increased inflammation and greater susceptibility to such diseases as diabetes and cancer.

Foods rich in zinc: Oysters and other shellfish...nuts and seeds...fortified dry cereals. Supplements also may be recommended, but do not go over 40 milligrams a day.

Emily Ho, PhD, is associate professor at Oregon State University School of Biological and Population Health Sciences, Corvallis, and coauthor of a study published in *Journal of Nutritional Biochemistry.*

Hidden Diabetes—You Can Get a Clean Bill of Health...but Still Be at High Risk

Mark Hyman, MD, founder and medical director of The UltraWellness Center in Lenox, Massachusetts, *DrHyman.com.* Dr. Hyman is the author of several books, including *The Blood Sugar Solution: The UltraHealthy Program for Losing Weight, Preventing Disease, and Feeling Great Now!*

With all the devastating complications of diabetes, such as heart disease, stroke, dementia and blindness, you might assume that most doctors are doing everything possible to catch this disease in its earliest stages. Not so.

Problem: There are currently no national guidelines for screening and treating diabetes before it reaches a full-blown stage.

Research clearly shows that the damage caused by diabetes begins years—and sometimes decades—earlier, but standard medical practice has not yet caught up with the newest findings on this disease.

Fortunately, there are scientifically proven ways to identify and correct the root causes of diabetes so that you never develop the disease itself.

WHEN THE PROBLEM STARTS

Diabetes is diagnosed when blood sugar (glucose) levels reach 126 mg/dL and above. "Prediabetes" is defined as blood sugar levels that are higher than normal but not high enough to indicate diabetes. Normal levels are less than 100 mg/dL.

What most people don't know: Although most doctors routinely test blood sugar to detect diabetes, it's quite common to have a normal level and still have diabesity, a condition typically marked by obesity and other changes in the body that can lead to the same complications (such as heart disease, stroke and cancer) as full-fledged diabetes.

Important: Even if you're not diabetic, having "belly fat"—for example, a waist circumference of more than 35 inches in women and more than 40 inches in men—often has many of the same dangerous effects on the body as diabetes.

Important finding: In a landmark study in Europe, researchers looked at 22,000 people and found that those with blood sugar levels of just 95 mg/dL—a level that's generally considered healthy—already had significant risks for heart disease and other complications.

AN EARLIER CLUE

Even though we've all been told that high blood sugar is the telltale sign of diabetes, insulin levels are, in fact, a more important hallmark that a person is in the early stages of the "diabetes continuum."

High blood sugar is typically blamed on a lack of insulin—or insulin that doesn't work efficiently. However, too much insulin is actually the best marker of the stages leading up to prediabetes and diabetes.

Why is high insulin so important? In most cases, it means that you have insulin resistance, a condition in which your body's cells aren't responding to insulin's effects. As a result, your body churns out more insulin than it normally would.

Once you have insulin resistance, you've set the stage to develop abdominal obesity, artery-damaging inflammation and other conditions that increasingly raise your risk for prediabetes and diabetes.

A BETTER APPROACH

Because doctors focus on prediabetes and diabetes—conditions detected with a blood sugar test—they tend to miss the earlier signs of diabesity. A better approach...

Test insulin as well. The standard diabetes test is to measure blood sugar after fasting for eight or more hours. The problem with this method is that blood sugar is the last thing to rise. Insulin rises first when you have diabesity.

My advice: Ask your doctor for a two-hour glucose tolerance test. With this test, your glucose levels are measured before and after consuming a sugary drink—but ask your doctor to also measure your insulin levels before and after consuming the drink.

What to look for: Your fasting blood sugar should be less than 80 mg/dL...two hours later, it shouldn't be higher than 120 mg/dL. Your fasting insulin should be 2 IU/dL to 5 IU/dL—anything higher indicates that you might have diabesity. Two hours later, your insulin should be less than 30 IU/dL.

Cost: $50 to $100 (usually covered by insurance). I advise all patients to have this test every three to five years...and annually for a person who is trying to reverse diabetes.

STEPS TO BEAT DIABESITY

With the correct lifestyle changes, most people can naturally reduce insulin as well as risk for diabesity-related complications, such as heart disease.

Example: The well-respected Diabetes Prevention Program sponsored by the National Institutes of Health found that overweight people who improved their diets and walked just 20 to 30 minutes a day lost modest amounts of weight and were 58% less likely to develop diabetes. *You can reduce your risk even more by following these steps...*

- **Manage your glycemic load.** The glycemic index measures how quickly different foods elevate blood sugar and insulin. A high-glycemic slice of white bread, for example, triggers a very rapid insulin response, which in turn promotes abdominal weight gain and the risk for diabesity.

My advice: Look at your overall diet and try to balance higher-glycemic foods with lower-glycemic foods. In general, foods that are minimally processed—fresh vegetables, legumes, fish, etc.—are lower on the glycemic index. These foods are ideal because they cause only gradual rises in blood sugar and insulin.

- **Eat nonwheat grains.** Many people try to improve their diets by eating whole-wheat rather than processed white bread or pasta. It doesn't help.

Fact: Two slices of whole-wheat bread will raise blood sugar more than two tablespoons of white sugar. If you already have diabetes, two slices of white or whole-wheat bread will raise your blood sugar by 70 mg/dL to 120 mg/dL. Wheat also causes inflammation...

stimulates the storage of abdominal fat...and increases the risk for liver damage.

These ill effects occur because the wheat that's produced today is different from the natural grain. With selective breeding and hybridization, today's wheat is high in amylopectin A, which is naturally fattening. It also contains an inflammatory form of gluten along with short forms of protein, known as exorphins, which are literally addictive.

Best: Instead of white or whole-wheat bread and pasta, switch to nonwheat grains such as brown or black rice, quinoa, buckwheat or amaranth. They're easy to cook, taste good—and they don't have any of the negative effects. Small red russet potatoes also are acceptable.

• **Give up liquid calories.** The average American gets 175 calories a day from sugar-sweetened beverages. Because these calories are in addition to calories from solid food, they can potentially cause weight gain of 18 pounds a year. The Harvard Nurses' Health Study found that women who drank one sugar-sweetened soft drink a day had an 82% increased risk of developing diabetes within four years.

Moderation rarely works with soft drinks because sugar is addictive. It activates the same brain receptors that are stimulated by heroin.

My advice: Switch completely to water. A cup of unsweetened coffee or tea daily is acceptable, but water should be your main source of fluids.

Bonus: People who are trying to lose weight can lose 44% more in 12 weeks just by drinking a glass of water before meals.

Important: Diet soda isn't a good substitute for water—the artificial sweeteners that are used increase sugar cravings and slow metabolism. Studies have found a 67% increase in diabetes risk in people who use artificial sweeteners.

How to Beat the 3 Big Mistakes That Worsen Diabetes

Osama Hamdy, MD, PhD, medical director of the Joslin Diabetes Center's Obesity Clinical Program and an assistant professor of medicine at Harvard Medical School, both in Boston. He also is coauthor of *The Diabetes Breakthrough.*

Despite what you may have heard, type 2 diabetes doesn't have to be a lifelong condition. It can be controlled and even reversed in the early stages or stopped from progressing in the later stages—with none of the dire consequences of out-of-control blood sugar.

Sounds great, right? What person with diabetes wouldn't want to do everything possible to help prevent serious complications such as coronary heart disease, kidney disease, blindness or even amputation?

The problem is, even people who are following all the doctor's orders may still be sabotaging their efforts with seemingly minor missteps that can have big consequences. Among the most common mistakes that harm people with diabetes are oversights in the way they eat and exercise. *For example...*

Mistake #1: Skimping on protein. The majority of people with type 2 diabetes are overweight or obese. These individuals know that they need to lose weight but sometimes fail despite their best efforts.

Here's what often happens: We have had it drummed into our heads that the best way to lose weight is to go on a low-fat diet. However, these diets tend to be low in protein—and you need more protein, not less, if you have type 2 diabetes and are cutting calories to lose weight.

What's so special about protein? You need protein to maintain muscle mass. The average adult starts losing lean muscle mass every year after about age 40. If you have diabetes, you'll probably lose more muscle mass than someone without it. And the loss will be even greater if your diabetes is not well controlled.

Muscle is important because it burns more calories than other tissues in your body. Also, people with a higher and more active muscle mass find it easier to maintain healthy blood-glucose levels, since active muscle doesn't require insulin to clear high glucose from the blood.

My advice: Protein should provide 20% to 30% of total daily calories. If you're on an 1,800-calorie diet (a reasonable amount for an average man who wants to lose weight), that's about 90 g to 135 g of protein a day. If you're on a 1,200-to-1,500-calorie diet (a sensible amount for an average woman who is dieting), that's about 60 g to 113 g of protein a day.

Examples: Good protein sources include fish, skinless poultry, nonfat or low-fat dairy, legumes and nuts and seeds. A three-ounce chicken breast has about 30 g of protein...a three-ounce piece of haddock, 17 g...one-half cup of low-fat cottage cheese, 14 g...and one-quarter cup of whole almonds, 7 g of protein.

Note: If you have kidney problems, you may need to limit your protein intake. Check with your doctor.

Mistake #2: Not doing resistance training. It's widely known that aerobic exercise is good for weight loss and blood sugar control. What usually gets short shrift is resistance training, such as lifting weights and using stretch bands.

When you build muscle, you use more glucose, which helps reduce glucose levels in the blood. If you take insulin for your diabetes, toned muscles will also make your body more sensitive to it.

An added benefit: People who do resistance training can often reduce their doses of insulin or other medications within a few months.

My advice: Do a combination of resistance, aerobic and flexibility exercises. Start with 20 minutes total, four days a week—splitting the time equally among the three types of exercise. Try to work up to 60 minutes total, six days a week. An exercise physiologist or personal trainer certified in resistance training can help choose the best workout for you.

Mistake #3: Ignoring hunger cues. Many individuals are so conditioned to eat at certain times that they virtually ignore their body's hunger signals. Learning how to read these cues can be one of the best ways to achieve (and maintain) a healthy body weight.

The key is to recognize that there are different levels of hunger. It's easy to overeat when you do not acknowledge the difference between feeling satisfied and stuffing yourself.

My advice: Imagine a five-point hunger scale: 1 means you're feeling starved...2 is hungry...3 is comfortable...4 is full...and 5 is stuffed. Before you start eating, rate your hunger between 1 and 5. Halfway through the meal, rate it again.

Here's the secret: Stop eating when you rate your hunger somewhere between "comfortable" and "full." If you give your hunger a ranking of 4 and you still want to eat, get away from the table and do something else!

Note: It can take up to 20 minutes for the "satiety signal" to kick in, so eat slowly. If you eat too quickly, you may miss the signal and overeat.

After just a few weeks of eating this way, it usually becomes second nature.

IF YOU TAKE DIABETES MEDS

Sometimes, diet and exercise aren't enough to tame out-of-control blood sugar. *Traps to avoid...*

- **Drug-induced weight gain.**

Ironically, the drugs that are used to treat diabetes also can cause weight gain as a side effect. If you start taking insulin, you can expect to gain about 10 pounds within six months—with oral drugs, such as *glipizide* (Glucotrol), you'll probably gain from four to seven pounds.

My advice: Ask your doctor if you can switch to one of the newer "weight-friendly" medications.

Examples: A form of insulin called Levemir causes less weight gain than Lantus, Humulin N or Novolin N. Newer oral drugs called DPP-4 inhibitors, such as Januvia, Onglyza and Nesina, don't have weight gain as a side effect.

Important: The newer drugs are more expensive and may not be covered by insurance. But if they don't cause you to gain weight, you might get by with a lower dose—and reduced cost.

ERRATIC TESTING

You should test your blood sugar levels at least four to six times a day, particularly when you're making lifestyle changes that could affect the frequency and doses of medication. Your doctor has probably advised you to test before and after exercise—and before meals.

My advice: Be sure to also test after meals. This will help determine the effects of different types and amounts of foods.

Improved Diabetes Monitor

One group of type 1 diabetes patients did conventional blood tests several times daily. Another group used tiny sensors (which patients place under the skin every few days using an insertion device) to continuously monitor blood sugar. With constant feedback on when to eat or take insulin, sensor users had better blood sugar control—reducing risk for diabetes complications. Prescription sensor systems cost about $10 per day. Some insurance plans cover them.

Roy W. Beck, MD, PhD, executive director, Jaeb Center for Health Research, Tampa, and head of a study of 322 diabetes patients, published in *The New England Journal of Medicine.*

A Promising Treatment for Type 1 Diabetes

Eli Lewis, PhD, director of the Clinical Islet Laboratory and senior lecturer in the department of clinical biochemistry and pharmacology, Ben-Gurion University of the Negev, Beer Sheva, Israel. This research was published in *Journal of Clinical Endocrinology and Metabolism.*

For people with type 1 diabetes, each day means carefully monitoring blood sugar, planning every bite of food and bit of physical activity, and injecting the insulin they need to stay alive. Many hope for a miracle that will free them from this relentless challenge. *Now that miracle may be at hand, thanks to breakthrough research from Israel...*

WHY IT'S SO HARD

Type 1 diabetes (formerly called juvenile diabetes) most often appears during childhood or adolescence—but it can develop at any age, so none of us are free from the threat.

An autoimmune disease, it occurs when the immune system mistakenly attacks the beta cells in the pancreas. Normally, beta cells detect the amount of sugar in the blood and release insulin, the hormone that converts sugar to energy for our cells. When the beta cells are destroyed, the body produces little or no insulin...so sugar builds up in the bloodstream, where it can cause life-threatening complications. To prevent these, type 1 diabetes patients must take insulin injections or use an insulin pump every day—but these carry the risk of triggering an injection-related plummet in blood sugar levels, or "insulin shock," which can be fatal.

What sets off the mistaken immune response is still a mystery, but research suggests that inflammation plays a key role. For instance, studies in mice that are genetically engineered to develop type 1 diabetes have shown that treatment with alpha-1 antitrypsin (AAT), an anti-inflammatory protein normally made by the liver and specialized white blood cells, can actually reverse type 1 diabetes...at least in mice.

Of course, it's a huge leap to take a treatment from mice to humans—but that's what researchers from Israel, in collaboration with the University of Colorado Health Science Center, are trying to do. Eli Lewis, PhD, is director of the Clinical Islet Laboratory and senior lecturer in the department of clinical biochemistry and pharmacology at Ben-Gurion University of the Negev, one of the leaders of this promising research.

SAY GOODBYE TO INSULIN INJECTIONS?

Dr. Lewis and colleagues recently published an exciting phase I study (phase I studies are typically the first studies done on people after preclinical animal studies are completed). For this study, 12 people with type 1 diabetes were given intravenous infusions of AAT once per week for eight weeks. Participants ranged in age from 12 to 39 years old, and all had been diagnosed within the previous four years. Blood samples were taken before treatment began and periodically afterward, ending 18 months after treatment initiation. All participants reportedly tolerated the 30-minute infusions comfortably (typically playing video games or otherwise amusing themselves during the treatment), and no one dropped out—an excellent outcome relating to safety and compliance.

Very encouraging results: Five of the 12 participants had a stunning response—they are no longer dependent on insulin injections!

Participants who were the most recently diagnosed tended to have the best response. This makes sense. Newly diagnosed patients are still experiencing an ongoing immune attack, and they still have some functioning beta cells left, just not enough to control glucose. The active immune system and residual beta cells provide the AAT with an optimal platform to work on.

Is AAT safe? The only adverse event reported was temporary hyperglycemia (high blood sugar)—not surprising because AAT already has a proven track record for safety. This FDA-approved drug has been on the market for more than two decades and is used to treat people with a rare genetic disorder that renders them incapable of producing enough of their own AAT. These patients receive injections of the AAT drug once each week for their entire lives, and most experience no side effects (though occasionally some patients have mild side effects, such as headache or light-headedness, associated with a too-rapid infusion). The dosage used in this study was the same as that used for people with this genetic disorder.

The lack of adverse effects is one of AAT's significant advantages. There are dozens of other clinical trials for diabetes treatments in the works, and some are very extreme, including chemotherapy and other immunosuppressive treatments. With AAT, however, the worst that happens is that it doesn't work in some patients and they simply remain on insulin.

A PERMANENT SOLUTION?

It's too soon to say whether the diabetes patients who respond well to AAT therapy will remain in remission forever. However, in the study, none of the people who responded to AAT have yet experienced a relapse—and their treatment occurred more than two years ago. Also, some other type 1 diabetes patients for whom AAT was prescribed off-label as many as eight years ago are still free of the need for insulin injections, Dr. Lewis said.

Why it works: People with type 1 diabetes are not deficient in AAT, but the extra glucose in their blood ends up coating their own AAT molecules, making them unable to fight inflammation. In contrast, AAT molecules in the therapeutic infusion are "dry and clean," at least when they're first infused. After about a week, they do become coated with glucose and are too damaged to work...but before that happens, the AAT molecules stop inflammatory proteins from damaging the beta cells of the pancreas. Also, since the test-protocol treatment consists of weekly infusions, by the time one dose of molecules becomes coated with glucose, the next infusion arrives and provides a fresh supply of dry, clean molecules.

The dosage used in the study is very similar to the amount we naturally produce when our AAT production goes into high gear—for instance, when our bodies are in the midst of an inflammatory response due to the flu. Maintaining that level of AAT production for eight straight weeks was required in order to elicit a long-lasting response that sent type 1 diabetes into remission. We removed the inflammatory injury from the equation. This gave the beta cells a chance to survive and recover...and helped the immune system reeducate itself so it no longer sees the beta cells as targets for an immune attack. Unlike many other approaches, AAT treatment requires the presence of the immune system and does not attempt to get rid of it.

WHAT PATIENTS CAN DO NOW

Though this was a very small study, Dr. Lewis's team and collaborators have additional studies already under way, and so far the responses have been extremely encouraging. It will likely be a few years or so before AAT could receive FDA approval as an official ("on-label") treatment for type 1 diabetes.

In the meantime: Talk with your endocrinologist about using AAT off label at this current point in development. There's no guarantee of success...but for patients who do respond to AAT, the treatment may be truly life altering.

"We believe we will see similar results in a number of US patients who recently received this treatment outside the trials within several months of diagnosis and are still completely insulin free," Dr. Lewis said in a recent press release. "This is an excellent beginning in our mission to determine the exciting possibilities of a safe therapy for autoimmune diabetes."

Will the treatment ever work for people who were diagnosed years or even decades earlier? We still do not know. Our choice of adhering to recent-onset cases is to optimize the trial, but some success has also been evident in a few advanced patients. The closest AAT-related option for patients who appear too far down the road may be islet transplantation (transplantation of pancreas cells from a donor)—for this, we have evidence that AAT will provide profound protection with an extraordinary safety margin.

AAT is not cheap, costing several thousand dollars (depending on body weight) for the eight-session treatment. Because it is still experimental as a diabetes treatment, it is not covered by insurance. Still, compared to the price of a lifetime supply of insulin—plus the nonmonetary costs of needing to rely on an insulin pump or injections and constantly worrying about eating the wrong thing or injecting too much insulin—many patients may consider the cost of AAT to be a more-than-fair trade.

Recent Diabetes Diagnosis? Watch Out for This Cancer Risk

Babette S. Saltzman, PhD, is a research assistant at Seattle Children's Hospital and leader of a study conducted while at the Fred Hutchinson Cancer Research Center in Seattle.

If you recently learned that you have diabetes, the last thing you want to hear about is yet another potential health problem—in this case, an increased risk for cancer of the endometrium (uterine lining). But knowledge is power, so please take note of a study in the *American Journal of Epidemiology*.

Researchers analyzed data on 3,082 women ages 45 to 74. Compared with women who did not have diabetes, those who did have diabetes had a 30% higher risk for endometrial cancer if their diabetes had been diagnosed five or more years earlier...and a more than twofold higher risk for endometrial cancer if their diabetes had been diagnosed less than five years earlier.

Theory: Like other hormones (such as estrogen), insulin can influence endometrial cancer risk...and in the prediabetic or early diabetic stages, hyperinsulinemia (elevated blood level of insulin) often has not yet been adequately controlled.

Diabetes patients: The more recently your diabetes was diagnosed, the more important it is to speak with your doctor about strategies that can lower endometrial cancer risk—including many of the same strategies associated with good cardiovascular and overall health.

Helpful: Losing excess weight (obesity is a known risk factor for endometrial cancer)... exercising regularly...and eating a diet low in saturated fats and high in fruits and vegetables. If you are premenopausal, also ask your doctor about birth control pills—according to the National Cancer Institute, endometrial cancer risk decreases by about 50% after five years of oral contraceptive use.

Natural Help for the Diabetic Heart

Seth Baum, MD, medical director of Integrative Heart Care in Boca Raton, Florida, and author of *The Total Guide to a Healthy Heart. VitalRemedyMD.com*

Kenneth Madden, MD, assistant professor of geriatric medicine at the University of British Columbia.

Robb Wolf, owner of NorCal Strength and Conditioning, Chico, California, and author of *The Paleolithic Solution.*

If you have type 2 diabetes, you've already had a heart attack—whether you've had one or not!

"The guidelines for physicians from the American Heart Association are to treat a person with diabetes as if that individual has already had a heart attack," says cardiologist Seth Baum, MD, medical director of Integrative Heart Care in Boca Raton, Florida, and author of *The Total Guide to a Healthy Heart.*

HOW DOES DIABETES HURT YOUR HEART?

As excess sugar careens through the bloodstream, it roughs up the linings of the arteries.

Insulin resistance (the subpar performance of the hormone that moves glucose out of the bloodstream and into muscle and fat cells) raises blood pressure, damaging arteries.

Diabetes also injures tiny blood vessels called capillaries, which hurts your kidneys and nerves—damage that in turn stresses the heart.

The end result—an up to seven-fold increase in the risk of heart disease and stroke, the cardiovascular diseases (CVD) that kill four out of five people with diabetes.

But recent studies show there are several natural ways for people with diabetes to reverse the risk factors that cause heart disease...

RECENT RESEARCH

It's never too late to exercise—and a little goes a long way. Researchers at the University of British Columbia in Vancouver, Canada, studied 36 older people (average age 71) with type 2 diabetes, high blood pressure, and high cholesterol, dividing them into two groups.

One group walked on a treadmill or cycled on a stationary bicycle for 40 minutes, three days a week. The other group didn't.

To find out if the exercise was helping with CVD, the researchers measured the elasticity of the arteries—a fundamental indicator of arterial youth and health, with arterial stiffness increasing the risk of dying from CVD.

Results: After three months, the exercisers had a decrease in arterial stiffness of 15% to 20%.

"Aerobic exercise should be the first-line treatment to reduce arterial stiffness in older adults with type 2 diabetes, even if the patient has advanced cardiovascular risk factors" such as high blood pressure and high cholesterol, conclude the researchers, in *Diabetes Care.*

WHAT TO DO

Kenneth Madden, MD, the study leader, and assistant professor of geriatric medicine at the University of British Columbia, says, "You can improve every risk factor for diabetes and heart disease—and you can do it in a very short period of time."

Dr. Madden recommends that older people with diabetes and cardiovascular disease see a doctor for a checkup before starting an exercise program.

Once you get the okay from your physician, he says to purchase and use a heart monitor during exercise, so you're sure that you're exercising at the level used by the participants in his study—60% to 75% of maximum heart rate.

Example: An estimate of your maximum heart rate is 220, minus your age. If you're 60, that would be 220 – 60 = 160. Exercising at between 60% to 75% of your maximum heart rate means maintaining a heart rate of between 96 and 120 beats per minute.

Finally, Dr. Madden advises you exercise the amount proven to improve arterial elasticity—a minimum of three sessions of aerobic exercise a week, of 40 minutes each.

• **Maximize magnesium.** Researchers in Mexico studied 79 people with diabetes and high blood pressure, dividing them into two groups. One group received a daily 450 milligrams (mg) magnesium supplement; one didn't.

Results: After four months, those on magnesium had an average drop of 20 points systolic (the higher number in the blood pressure reading) and 9 points diastolic (the lower number). Those on the placebo had corresponding drops of 5 points and 1 point.

"Magnesium supplementation should be considered as an additional or alternative treatment for high blood pressure in people with diabetes," says Fernando Guerrero-Romero, MD, the study leader.

What to do: "Magnesium acts as a natural vasodilator, relaxing arteries and lowering blood pressure," says Dr. Baum. "People with diabetes should incorporate a magnesium supplement into their regimen."

He suggests a daily supplement of 400 mg, about the level used in the study.

"People with diabetes and high blood pressure should also be encouraged to increase their dietary intake of magnesium, through eating more whole grains, leafy green vegetables, legumes, nuts and fish," says Dr. Guerrero-Romero.

• **Eat like a Neanderthal.** Researchers in Sweden tested two diets in 13 people with type 2 diabetes—the diet recommended by the American Diabetes Association (ADA), a generally healthful diet limiting calories, fat and refined carbohydrates; and a "Paleolithic" diet, consisting of lean meat, fish, fruits, vegetables, root vegetables, eggs and nuts—and no dairy products, refined carbohydrates or highly processed foods, whatsoever.

In terms of lowering risk factors for heart disease, the Paleolithic diet clubbed the ADA diet.

Results: After three months, it had done a better job of decreasing...

• **High LDL "bad" cholesterol,**

• **High blood pressure,**

• **High triglycerides** (a blood fat linked to heart disease) and

• **Too-big waist size** (excess stomach fat is linked to heart disease).

The diet was also more effective at increasing HDL "good" cholesterol.

And it was superior in decreasing glycated hemoglobin (A1C), a measure of long-term blood sugar control.

"Foods that were regularly eaten during the Paleolithic, or 'Old Stone Age,' may be optimal for prevention and treatment of type 2 diabetes, cardiovascular disease and insulin resistance," concludes Tommy Jönsson, MD, in *Cardiovascular Diabetology*.

What to do: "Eating a Paleolithic Diet is far easier than most people think," says Robb Wolf, owner of NorCal Strength and Conditioning in Chico, California, and author of The *Paleolithic Solution*.

THE BASIC DIET

Eat more—lean meat, fish, shellfish, fruits, vegetables, eggs and nuts.

Eat less (or eliminate)—grains, dairy products, salt, refined fats and refined sugar.

Resource: For a collection of innovative Paleolithic snacks, visit *www.paleogrubs.com/healthy-snacks*.

• **Have a cup of hibiscus tea.** Researchers in Iran studied 53 people with type 2 diabetes, dividing them into two groups. One group drank a cup of hibiscus tea twice a day; the other drank two cups a day of black tea. (The hibiscus tea was made from Hibiscus sabdariffa, which is also known as red sorrel, Jamaican sorrel, Indian sorrel, roselle and Florida cranberry.)

Results: After one month, those drinking hibiscus had...

• **Higher HDL "good" cholesterol,**

• **Lower LDL "bad" cholesterol,**

• **Lower total cholesterol and**

• **Lower blood pressure.**

The black tea group didn't have any significant changes in blood fats or blood pressure.

The findings were in *The Journal of Alternative and Complementary Medicine* and the *Journal of Human Hypertension*.

What to do: Consider drinking a cup or two of hibiscus tea a day, says Hassan Mozaffari-Khosravi, PhD, an assistant professor of nutrition, Shahid Sadoughi University of Medical Sciences, Yazd, Iran, and the study leader.

Hospitalized for Heart Attack? Make Sure They Check You for Diabetes

Suzanne V. Arnold, MD, MHA, assistant professor at Saint Luke's Mid America Heart Institute and the University of Missouri at Kansas City. Her study was presented at the 2014 annual meeting of the American Heart Association.

It's well-known among health-conscious people that heart disease and diabetes are linked, so it seems a shame to be hearing news from the American Heart Association that 10% of Americans who've had a heart attack probably have undiagnosed diabetes. What's worse, though, is news that doctors are missing opportunities to detect and treat diabetes in people even when they are hospitalized for a heart attack.

ARE SO MANY DOCTORS THIS CLUELESS?

Although it might be a great challenge for health-care professionals to identify everyone with diabetes before complications, such as heart attack, occur, a basic precaution can at least help those who do land in the hospital because of heart attack. So if you've had a heart attack or have cardiovascular disease—or you want to be prepared to give yourself the best odds if you ever have a heart attack in the future—here's what you need to insist that your medical-care team does for you, especially if you land in the hospital...

A SIMPLE OVERLOOKED TEST

It comes down to getting a simple blood test. Doctors who order a hemoglobin A1c test when a patient is being treated for heart attack are making the right move to ensure that diabetes won't be missed and the heart attack can be treated correctly, said Suzanne V. Arnold, MD, MHA, an assistant professor at the University of Missouri in Kansas City. She led a study on undiagnosed diabetes in heart attack patients that was reported at this year's American Heart Association meeting. The hemoglobin A1c test shows average blood sugar levels for the preceding three months and is widely used to diagnose both type 1 and type 2 diabetes and monitor how well blood sugar is being controlled after diagnosis.

In her study, Dr. Arnold and her team took 2,854 patients who were hospitalized for heart attacks but had never received a diabetes diagnosis and arranged for them to have the hemoglobin A1c test. Both the hospitalized patients and the doctors treating them were kept in the dark ("blinded" in scientific speak) about the test results, and doctors were left to their business-as-usual patient care. Diabetes was considered "recognized" by the researchers if a patient either received diabetes education while hospitalized and/or diabetes medication when sent home.

The study results were a real eye-opener. Sure, Dr. Arnold's team discovered that 10% of these patients had diabetes and didn't know it, but the far bigger issue that patients and their families need to know about was that doctors failed to recognize diabetes in 69% of these previously undiagnosed patients.

That's a major fail—especially when all it took for the treating doctors themselves to discover diabetes was to order the same simple, inexpensive A1c test that Dr. Arnold's team had already ordered for their study.

Six months down the road, the researchers checked in on the patients they themselves knew had diabetes. They found that 71% of the patients whose diabetes had also been discovered by a doctor during their hospital stays were getting diabetes care. As for the patients whose diabetes had not been discovered by doctors treating them in the hospital, only 7% were getting diabetes care, meaning that the likelihood was strong that no one, except Dr. Arnold's team, had yet checked these folks for diabetes. This left them at high risk for more cardiovascular complications, including additional heart attacks.

KNOWLEDGE THAT CAN ALSO GUIDE HEART ATTACK TREATMENT

Knowing that a heart attack patient has type 2 diabetes is important in the moment because it determines treatment decisions, explained Dr. Arnold. For example, patients with multivessel coronary artery disease and diabetes may do better with bypass surgery (rather than stents) and particular blood pressure medications, such as ACE inhibitors.

Dr. Arnold's advice for people who have heart attacks and survive...but don't know whether they have diabetes...is that they insist on having a hemoglobin A1C test during their hospitalization. She does not advocate routine hemoglobin A1C screening for everyone, though, calling it "impractical," although it's certainly something you can bring up with your doctor if you know you have heart disease. And although you may be in-the-know about diabetes and heart disease prevention, this seems like a good place to include a refresher for you or a loved one. You can assess your risks and the warning signs of diabetes with these checklists from the American Diabetes Association...

Your chances of diabetes increase if you...

- Have a family history of type 2 diabetes
- Don't get much exercise and are otherwise physically inactive
- Are overweight
- Have high blood pressure
- Have low HDL cholesterol and high triglycerides
- Don't watch your diet and feast on high-calorie, fatty, sugary and low-fiber foods
- Smoke
- For women, had diabetes during pregnancy

These are warning signs of diabetes...

- Unquenchable thirst
- Excessive urination
- Increased appetite, despite eating
- Unexpected weight loss
- Tingling, pain and/or numbness in your hands and/or feet
- Blurred vision
- Cuts and bruises that take a long time to heal
- Extreme fatigue

It's not very challenging for health-conscious people to avoid type 2 diabetes and heart disease, but keeping this bit of information on a simple blood test in mind can protect you or a loved one even more.

Nighttime Heart Risk

Nighttime heart risk for people with diabetes.

Recent finding: Hypoglycemia (low blood sugar levels) at night can cause life-threatening changes in heart rate in people with type 2 diabetes. Risk for slow heart rate was eight times higher when blood sugar levels dropped at night. Low blood sugar also increased risk for arrhythmias and other heart-rate abnormalities.

Self-defense for people with diabetes: Check with your doctor to ensure that your glycemic goals are personalized for you. Consider using a glucose monitor that will alert you when blood sugar levels are low, especially if you also have or are at risk for heart disease.

Study of people with type 2 diabetes who had been on insulin for at least four years by researchers at University of Sheffield, England, published in *Diabetes.*

Diabetes Medications That Lower Cancer Risk

In a recent finding, women with type 2 diabetes taking insulin sensitizers, including the diabetes medication *metformin* (Glucophage), or thiazolidinediones, such as *pioglitazone* (Actos), had 21% lower risk for cancer than women taking insulin secretagogues. Insulin secretagogues include sulfonylureas, such as *glimepiride* (Amaryl), and meglitinides, such as *nateglinide* (Starlix).

Sangeeta Kashyap, MD, an endocrinologist and associate professor of medicine at the Cleveland Clinic's Endocrinology & Metabolism Institute. She is lead author of a study published in *Diabetes, Obesity and Metabolism.*

Curcumin Stops Diabetes from Progressing

When given a curcumin extract (1.5 grams daily) for nine months, study participants at risk for diabetes did not develop the disease. Among a similar group given a placebo, 16.4% developed the disease. Curcumin is the main compound in turmeric, a spice in curry powders and mustards.

Study of 240 people by researchers at Srinakharin wirot University, Bangkok, Thailand, published in *Tufts University Health & Nutrition Letter.*

Say Good-Bye to Your Diabetes Medication

Mark A. Stengler, NMD, licensed naturopathic medical doctor in private practice, Stengler Center for Integrative Medicine, Encinitas, California...adjunct associate clinical professor at the National College of Natural Medicine, Portland, Oregon...author of many books, including *The Natural Physician's Healing Therapies* and coauthor of *Prescription for Natural Cures.*

Some of my patients who have type 2 diabetes are able to keep the disease under control with diet, exercise and supplements. Lucky them! But for other diabetes patients, that's not enough and they must take pharmaceutical medications.

I'm happy to report that there is another natural treatment option for diabetes patients who currently take pharmaceutical medications. Research has found that a plant extract called berberine can control diabetes as well as, or better than, common medications such as *metformin* (Glucophage) and *rosiglitazone* (Avandia). And it does this with no side effects—and without damaging the liver, as some medications do. *Here's how berberine can help people with diabetes...*

A naturally occurring chemical compound, berberine is found in the roots and stems of several plants, including *Hydrastis canadensis* (goldenseal), *Coptis chinensis* (coptis or goldthread) and *Berberis aquifolium* (Oregon grape). Long used as a remedy in Chinese and Ayurvedic medicines, berberine is known for its antimicrobial properties and as a treatment for bacterial and fungal infections. Several decades ago, berberine was used to treat diarrhea in patients in China. That was when doctors noticed that the blood sugar levels of diabetes patients were lower after taking the herbal extract—and berberine began to be investigated for this purpose.

Over the past 20 years, there has been much research on berberine and its effectiveness in treating diabetes. In 2008, Chinese researchers published a study in *Metabolism* in which adults with newly diagnosed type 2 diabetes were given 500 milligrams (mg) of either berberine or the drug metformin three times a day for three months. Researchers found that berberine did as good a job as metformin at regulating glucose metabolism, as indicated by hemoglobin A1C (a measure of blood glucose over several weeks)...fasting blood glucose...blood sugar after eating...and level of insulin after eating. Berberine even reduced the amount of insulin needed to turn glucose into energy by 45%! In addition, those taking berberine had noticeably lower trigylceride and total cholesterol levels than those taking metformin.

In another 2008 study published in *Journal of Clinical Endocrinology and Metabolism*, researchers found that type 2 diabetes patients who were given berberine had significant reductions in fasting and postmeal blood glucose, hemoglobin A1C, triglycerides, total cholesterol and LDL (bad) cholesterol—and also lost an average of five pounds, to boot, during the three-month study period.

In a 2010 study in *Metabolism*, Chinese researchers compared people with type 2 diabetes who took either 1,000 mg daily of berberine or daily doses of metformin or rosiglitazone. After two months, berberine had lowered subjects' fasting blood glucose levels by an average of about 30%, an improvement over the rosiglitazone group and almost as much as people in the metformin group. Berberine also reduced subjects' hemoglobin A1C by 18%—equal to rosiglitazone and, again, almost as good as metformin. In addition, berberine lowered serum insulin levels by 28.2% (indicating increased insulin sensitivity)...lowered triglycerides by 17.5%...and actually improved liver enzyme levels. Pharmaceutical medications, on the other hand, have the potential to harm the liver.

These were remarkable findings. Here was a botanical that was holding up to scientific scrutiny—and performing as well as, or better than, some drugs that patients had been taking for diabetes for years.

HOW BERBERINE WORKS IN THE BODY

Berberine helps to lower blood glucose in several ways. One of its primary mechanisms involves stimulating the activity of the genes responsible for manufacturing and activating insulin receptors, which are critical for controlling blood glucose.

Berberine also has an effect on blood sugar regulation through activation of incretins, gastrointestinal hormones that affect the amount of insulin released by the body after eating.

HOW BERBERINE CAN HELP

I recommend berberine to my patients with newly diagnosed type 2 diabetes to reduce their blood sugar and prevent them from needing pharmaceutical drugs. When a diet, exercise and supplement program (including supplements such as chromium) is already helping a diabetes patient, I don't recommend that he/she switch to berberine.

Some patients are able to take berberine—and make dietary changes—and stop taking diabetes drugs altogether. People with severe diabetes can use berberine in conjunction with medication—and this combination treatment allows for fewer side effects and better blood sugar control. I don't recommend berberine for prediabetes unless diet and exercise are not effective. Berberine is sold in health-food stores and online in tablet and capsule form. The dosage I typically recommend for all diabetes patients is 500 mg twice daily.

For patients with diabetes who want to use berberine, I recommend talking to your doctor about taking this supplement. It's also important for every patient with diabetes to participate in a comprehensive diet and exercise program.

Note that berberine helps patients with type 2 diabetes, not type 1 diabetes (in which the body does not produce enough insulin).

Control Diabetes with Qigong

Guan-Cheng Sun, PhD, assistant research scientist at Bastyr University, Kenmore, Washington, qigong teacher, executive director and founder of the Institute of Qigong & Internal Alternative Medicine, Seattle.

Wouldn't it be great if you could just wave your arms to get better control over your blood sugar? A research scientist at Bastyr University in Washington has adapted the ancient Chinese practice of movement called qigong (pronounced chee-gong) to help people with type 2 diabetes achieve better blood sugar control...feel better...and even reduce their reliance on drugs.

Study author Guan-Chen Sun, PhD, assistant research scientist at Bastyr, qigong teacher and executive director and founder of the Institute of Qigong & Internal Alternative Medicine in Seattle, says there are many types of qigong. What makes his version unique is the way it explicitly incorporates an energy component.

Dr. Sun named his new system Yi Ren Qigong (Yi means "change" and Ren means "human") and says it works by teaching diabetic patients to calm the chi, or "life energy" of the liver (to slow production of glucose) and to enhance the chi of the pancreas (exhausted by overproducing insulin). The goal of this practice is to "improve the harmony between these organs and increase energy overall," he said, noting that his patients have achieved significant results—reduced blood glucose levels, lower stress and less insulin resistance. Some were even able to cut back the dosages of their medications.

HOW DO THEY KNOW IT WORKED?

Dr. Sun's research team studied 32 patients, all on medication for their diabetes.

They were divided into three groups: One group practiced qigong on their own at home twice a week for 30 minutes and also attended a one-hour weekly session led by an instructor. The second group engaged in a prescribed program of gentle exercise that included movements similar to the qigong practice but without the energy component for an equivalent period of time. And the third group continued their regular medication and medical care but did not engage in structured exercise.

The results: After 12 weeks, the qigong patients had lowered their fasting blood glucose, their levels of self-reported stress and improved their insulin resistance. The gentle exercise group also brought down blood glucose levels, though somewhat less...and lowered stress. It was worse yet for the third group—blood glucose levels climbed and so did insulin resistance, while there was no reported change in their stress levels. The study was published in *Diabetes Care.*

For more information on Yi Ren Qigong and training courses available, visit the Bastyr University website at *www.bastyr.edu/continuinged.*

Vitamin B-12—Better Than a Drug for Diabetic Neuropathy

Anne L. Peters, MD, professor of medicine and director of the USC Clinical Diabetes Program, author of *Conquering Diabetes.*

Mariejane Braza, MD, researcher, University of Texas Health Science Center and internist, Valley Baptist Medical Center, Harlingen, Texas.

Jacob Teitelbaum, MD, author of *Pain-Free 1-2-3!* and *From Fatigued to Fantastic!. EndFatigue.com*

Twenty-five percent of people with diabetes develop diabetic neuropathy—glucose-caused damage to nerves throughout the body, particularly in the hands, arms, feet and legs (peripheral neuropathy).

You experience tingling and prickling. Numbness. And pain—from annoying, to burning, to stabbing, to excruciating. Drugs hardly help.

"Many studies have been conducted on drugs for diabetic neuropathy, and no drug is really effective," says Anne L. Peters, MD, professor of medicine and director of the USC (University of Southern California) Clinical Diabetes Program and author of *Conquering Diabetes.*

But a new study says a vitamin can help...

LESS PAIN AND BURNING

Researchers in Iran studied 100 people with diabetic neuropathy, dividing them into two groups. One group received *nortriptyline* (Pamelor), an antidepressant medication that has been used to treat neuropathy. The other group received vitamin B-12, a nutrient known to nourish and protect nerves.

After several weeks of treatment, the B-12 group had...

- **78% greater reduction in pain,**
- **71% greater reduction in tingling and prickling and**
- **65% greater reduction in burning.**

"Vitamin B-12 is more effective than nortriptyline for the treatment of painful diabetic neuropathy," conclude the researchers, in the *International Journal of Food Science and Nutrition.*

Latest development: A few months after the Iranian doctors conducted their study, research in the US involving 76 people with diabetes showed that the widely prescribed diabetes drug metformin may cause vitamin B-12 deficiency—and that 77% of those with the deficiency also suffered from peripheral neuropathy!

Anyone already diagnosed with peripheral neuropathy who uses metformin should be tested for low blood levels of B-12, says Mariejane Braza, MD, of the University of Texas Health Science Center and the study leader. If B-12 levels are low, she recommends supplementing with the vitamin, to reduce the risk of nerve damage.

HEAL THE NERVES

"If you take metformin, definitely take at least 500 micrograms (mcg) a day of vitamin B-12, in either a multivitamin or B-complex supplement," advises Jacob Teitelbaum, MD, author of *Pain-Free 1-2-3!* "It's the single, most effective nutrient for helping prevent and reverse diabetic neuropathy.

"On a good day, the best that medications can do for neuropathy is mask the pain," he continues. "But vitamin B-12 gradually heals the nerves."

Best: If you already have neuropathy, Dr. Teitelbaum recommends finding a holistic physician and asking for 15 intramuscular injections of 3,000 to 5,000 mcg of methylcobalamin, the best form of B-12 to treat peripheral neuropathy. "Receive those shots daily to weekly—at whatever speed is convenient to quickly optimize levels of B-12," says Dr. Teitelbaum.

Resource: To find a holistic physician, Dr. Teitelbaum recommends visiting the website of the American Board of Integrative Holistic Medicine, *www.abihm.org*.

If you can't find a holistic physician near you, he suggests taking a daily sublingual (dissolving under the tongue) dose of 5,000 mcg for four weeks. (Daily, because you only absorb a small portion of the sublingual vitamin B-12, compared with intramuscular injections.)

At the same time that you take B-12, also take a high-dose B-complex supplement (B-50). "The body is happiest when it gets all the B-vitamins together," says Dr. Teitelbaum.

He points out that it can take three to twelve months for nerves to heal, but that the neuropathy should progressively improve during that time.

Also helpful: Other nutrients that Dr. Teitelbaum recommends to help ease peripheral neuropathy include:

- **Alpha-lipoic acid (300 mg, twice a day)**
- **Acetyl-l-carnitine (500 mg, three times a day)**

Sunshine for Diabetes Prevention

The late Frederic J. Vagnini, MD, a cardiovascular surgeon and director of the Heart, Diabetes & Weight Loss Centers of New York in Lake Success. His clinical interests included heart disease, diabetes, weight loss and nutrition. He was the author, with Lawrence D. Chilnick, of *The Weight Loss Plan for Beating Diabetes*.

Here's a simple preventative remedy that you might enjoy...

To prevent diabetes, be sure to get plenty of sunshine, which can provide most of the vitamin D that you need. The National Public Health Institute in Helsinki, Finland, recently reported that people with the highest vitamin D levels were 40% less likely to develop type 2 diabetes than those with lower levels. Studies indicate that adequate vitamin D also reduces insulin resistance, a hallmark of diabetes.

For a healthy vitamin D level, spend about 15 minutes in the sun a few times a week with your arms, hands and, if possible, legs exposed. Do this during the brightest part of the day (10 am to 3 pm). Wear sunscreen only on your face during timed sun exposure to prevent sun damage. If you have a history of skin cancer or you are at high risk for it, check with your doctor before practicing timed sun exposure.

If you live above 33° latitude—roughly north of Atlanta—you will not be able to produce significant amounts of vitamin D from sun exposure during the winter. Dark-skinned individuals are at increased risk for vitamin D deficiency.

To ensure adequate levels: Ask your doctor to test your vitamin D level. If you're deficient, you will be prescribed a therapeutic dose that is taken for about 12 weeks, followed by a regular daily dose to be determined by your physician.

What Your Doctor May Not Tell You About Your Diabetes

The late Frederic J. Vagnini, MD, a cardiovascular surgeon and director of the Heart, Diabetes & Weight Loss Centers of New York in Lake Success. His clinical interests included heart disease, diabetes, weight loss and nutrition. He was the author, with Lawrence D. Chilnick, of *The Weight Loss Plan for Beating Diabetes.*

For most of the 19 million Americans diagnosed with type 2 diabetes, the main goal of treatment is simply to control their glucose (blood sugar) levels with diet, exercise and sometimes medication.

But there's much more that should be done to help prevent serious complications, which can shorten the life expectancy of a person with diabetes—by about 7.5 years in men and 8.2 years in women.

Sobering statistics: About 80% of people with diabetes die from cardiovascular complications, such as a heart attack. About half the patients with poor glucose control will eventually suffer from nerve damage (neuropathy). Another 20% to 30% may experience retinopathy or other eye disorders.

Whether or not you're taking medication for diabetes, virtually all of these complications can be avoided—and, in some cases, reversed—with natural approaches.

Important: Be sure to speak to your doctor before following any of the steps in this article—some may affect diabetes drugs and other types of medication.

Best ways for people with diabetes to avoid complications...

CONTROLLING INFLAMMATION

People with diabetes typically have elevated levels of C-reactive protein, a blood protein that indicates chronic low-level inflammation, the underlying cause of most cardiovascular, eye and nerve disorders. Inflammation also exacerbates arthritis, which is more common in diabetics than in those without the disease. *Effective options...*

• **Stop eating wheat.** Many people with diabetes are allergic or sensitive to gluten, a protein found naturally in wheat, barley and rye—and sometimes in other grains, such as oats, because they become "cross-contaminated" during processing. Even trace amounts of gluten can stimulate the production of cytokines, substances that increase inflammation. (See self-test below to determine whether you are sensitive to gluten.)

Besides increasing inflammation in these patients, exposure to gluten may lead to fatigue and joint problems. Gluten may also impair digestion in these people, making it harder to lose weight—a serious problem because excess body fat increases inflammation even more.

Important: Read food labels. Besides avoiding obvious sources of gluten such as wheat bread and wheat pasta, look for terms such as "amino peptide complex," "filler flour," "hydrolyzed protein" and "vegetable starch"—these indicate that gluten is or may be found in the product. Gluten is also present in unexpected sources, such as soy sauce, malt and graham flour, as well as thousands of nonfood products, including some medications. To determine if a medication contains gluten, call the drug manufacturer. For a list of foods and products that contain gluten, consult the Gluten Intolerance Group's website, *www.gluten.org.*

• **Give up dairy.** Oftentimes people who are sensitive to gluten also have problems digesting casein, a dairy protein.

To test for a gluten or dairy sensitivity: Eliminate each food type one at a time for several weeks. If you notice an improvement in energy, or a reduction in joint pain or digestion problems, you're probably sensitive to one or both. To make sure, reintroduce dairy and/or gluten foods one at a time to see if your symptoms return.

Important: Foods that are labeled "lactose-free" or "dairy-free" are not necessarily casein-free. Foods that are both gluten-free and casein-free can be found online at *www.traderjoes.com* or *www.wholefoods.com.*

To keep it simple: Remember that all unprocessed meats, vegetables and fruits are gluten-free and dairy-free.

• **Supplement with omega-3 fatty acids.** The American Diabetes Association recommends a diet high in these fatty acids because of their ability to reduce inflammation and other diabetes complications. Unfortunately, many people find it difficult to eat enough omega-3–rich foods, such as salmon, mackerel and herring—two six-ounce servings a week are recommended—so supplements often are a good choice.

My advice: Take a daily supplement with at least 1,500 mg of eicosapentaenoic acid (EPA), the component in fish oil that helps reduce the inflammation that contributes to diabetes-related complications. If you're allergic to fish, you can use an omega-3 supplement derived from algae.

Omega-3 fatty acids, also found in flaxseed and walnuts, have the additional benefit of helping to lower triglycerides, blood fats that have been linked to atherosclerosis and cardiovascular disease.

FIGHT ARTERIAL CALCIFICATION

The Rotterdam Heart Study, which looked at the dietary histories of more than 4,800 patients, found that those with low blood levels of vitamin K2 were 57% more likely to develop heart disease, due in part to an increase in calcium in the arteries. Paradoxically, these patients had lower bone levels of calcium, which increases the risk for fractures.

Because diabetic patients have an extremely high risk for heart disease, I routinely recommend a daily supplement (45 mcg) of vitamin K2. You can also get more of this nutrient by eating such foods as liver, eggs and certain cheeses.

Caution: Because there are different forms of vitamin K—some of which interfere with the effects of *warfarin* (Coumadin) and other blood thinners—always speak to your doctor before taking any vitamin K supplement.

OVERCOME FATIGUE

Both inflammation and elevated blood sugar increase fatigue, making it one of the most common symptoms of diabetes. Helpful…

• **Coenzyme Q10** (CoQ10) increases the body's production of adenosine triphosphate (ATP), a molecule that enhances the performance of mitochondria, the energy-producing components of cells. CoQ10 is also an antioxidant that reduces inflammation. Typical dose: 100 mg to 200 mg, twice daily.

• **Magnesium** is involved in glucose and insulin reactions and is typically lower than normal in people with diabetes who experience fatigue. Patients who eat a healthy diet, including magnesium-rich foods such as nuts and oatmeal, and supplement with magnesium often report an increase in energy. They also show improvements in blood pressure and cardiac performance. Talk to your doctor about the appropriate dosage of a magnesium supplement—especially if you have kidney disease or heart disease, both of which can be worsened by too much magnesium.

All forms of supplemental magnesium can be used, but magnesium citrate causes diarrhea in some people. If this happens to you, take a different form, such as magnesium taurate or magnesium glycinate.

AVOID DIABETIC NEUROPATHY

Excess blood sugar can damage the tiny blood vessels that carry blood and nutrients to nerves in the fingers, legs and/or feet, causing neuropathy. Neuropathy can eventually lead to tissue damage that requires amputation. *What to try…*

• **Alpha-lipoic acid** makes the cells more sensitive to insulin and can relieve symptoms of diabetic neuropathy.

Typical dose: 600 mg to 1,200 mg daily for people with diabetes who have neuropathy. To help prevent neuropathy, 100 mg to 300 mg daily is the typical dose.

• **B-complex supplement** may help prevent neuropathy or reduce symptoms in patients who already have it.

Typical dose: Two B-100 complex supplements daily for people with diabetes who have neuropathy…one B-100 complex daily to help prevent neuropathy.

PREVENT EYE DAMAGE

High blood sugar can cause diabetic retinopathy, which can lead to blindness. It can also increase eye pressure and lead to glaucoma.

Self-defense: Eat more fresh fruits and vegetables. These foods contain antioxidants such as lutein, zeaxanthin and vitamin C, which strengthen eye capillaries, fight free radicals and reduce the risk for blindness. Frozen fruits and vegetables also can be used.

Best choice: Blueberries or bilberries—both contain anthocyanins, antioxidants that help prevent eye damage and appear to improve glucose levels.

New Help for Diabetes

Sometimes the constant delivery of insulin causes blood sugar to drop too low—a potentially fatal condition called hypoglycemia. Medtronic's MiniMed 530G has a sensor that alerts patients to this danger and, if the person is asleep or unconscious, shuts off automatically for two hours. The pump has been used in Europe for over two years and was approved in the US in September 2013.

Joel Zonszein, MD, FACE, FACP, director of the Clinical Diabetes Center, Montefiore Medical Center, the Bronx, New York.

Got Diabetes? The Extra Help You Need

Joel Zonszein, MD, CDE, FACE, FACP, professor of clinical medicine, Albert Einstein College of Medicine, director, Clinical Diabetes Center, Montefiore Medical Center, New York City.

If you've been diagnosed with type 2 diabetes, you might think that you have a good handle on keeping your blood sugar under control...and maybe you do...but there's a good chance you don't. Research has shown that only 16% of people with type 2 diabetes properly carry out the recommended "self-care behaviors," such as eating healthy foods, staying active, taking medications and monitoring blood sugar. But help is available. A recent study has found that diabetics who get regular individual instruction from a nurse or dietitian do much better and feel much better.

GETTING FACE TIME

Study participants included 623 patients (men and women, average age 62) who had had type 2 diabetes for 12 years, on average. Researchers considered only patients who had taken a type of blood test called the A1C, which measures the average blood sugar levels within the previous two to three months, and selected only those whose A1C scores were above 7%—that's higher than what is considered healthy, so it indicated that, like the vast majority of diabetics, these people were poorly managing their condition. These patients were then split into three groups—one group received individual education, another received group education and another received no education.

After seven months, the researchers asked participants to take the A1C test again. *And here's what they discovered...*

It was basically "no contest" when comparing the results from group to group. The no-education group lowered its A1C score by 24% (perhaps because they knew that they were being studied)...those who received group education by 27%...and individual-education participants lowered their A1C scores by a whopping 51%.

The proportion of participants who got their scores into a healthy range (under 7%) was highest among those who were individually educated—21% of those participants achieved this fantastic result. Meanwhile, only 13% of the no-education group and 14% of the group-education group got into the healthy range.

What's even better is that the individual education didn't take up much time at all—it consisted of exactly three one-hour sessions with a certified diabetes educator (either a nurse or a dietitian) about one month apart. Three short visits! The educators focused on topics that included all the healthy behaviors mentioned above (eating right, staying active, taking medications and monitoring) along with problem solving (for instance, if a patient doesn't take a pill, maybe it's because he doesn't understand why he needs it and what it does)...healthy coping (such as if a patient is frustrated, instead of grabbing a bag of chips, he's taught to go for a walk or listen to calming music)...and setting personalized, action-oriented goals (for example, scheduling an eye exam once a year to prevent diabetic complications such as retinal detachment or blindness).

WHY IT WORKS SO WELL

The reason this little bit of attention might work so well can be summed up in one word—accountability. Having to face someone regularly and acknowledge mistakes that you may be making is a powerful motivator—apparently more powerful than just the idea of being healthy. It's also about empowerment—teaching diabetics to be in charge of the disease rather than letting the disease control them. And there's another, slightly darker side to all this—doctors aren't typically trained to give appropriate diabetes education, and they aren't reimbursed for the time they spend educating patients about it. So in too many cases, after an initial diagnosis and a hastily written prescription, patients are essentially sent out into the cold to muddle through on their own—not a shining example of great health care.

So, what can you do for you? The best diabetes education programs are hospital-based with certification from the American Diabetes Association (ADA), since these are regularly evaluated to ensure that they meet high standards. To find one in your area, check the ADA's site, *www.diabetes.org*. Call the programs in your area and ask them specifically if they offer one-on-one instruction, what it costs and whether it is covered by insurance. Try one-on-one counseling for at least three months. If possible, you might want to keep at it indefinitely.

At the very least, don't assume that you already know all that you need to know about managing your diabetes—ask your doctor for diabetes brochures and visit reputable websites such as *www.diabetes.org* for the latest information and advice. And then make a point to discuss the info with your doctor at your next appointment. (Don't expect him or her to bring it up.)

Though one-on-one counseling might make you feel embarrassed or might seem like a nuisance, it's clear that the more you know about your disease and the more accountable you are about taking care of yourself, the better you will manage it...it's just human nature...so get the help!

---

5 DIY Tests That Could Save Your Life

David L. Katz, MD, MPH, an internist and preventive medicine specialist. He is cofounder and director of the Yale-Griffin Prevention Research Center in Derby, Connecticut, and clinical instructor at the Yale School of Medicine in New Haven, Connecticut. Dr. Katz is also president of the American College of Lifestyle Medicine and the author of *Disease-Proof: The Remarkable Truth About What Makes Us Well.*

If you're conscientious about your health, you probably see your doctor for an annual physical...or perhaps even more often if you have a chronic condition or get sick.

But if you'd like to keep tabs on your health between your doctor visits, there are some easy, do-it-yourself tests that can give you valuable information about your body. These tests can sometimes tip you off that you may have a serious medical condition even though you don't have any symptoms.

Here are self-tests that you can do at home—repeat them once every few months, and keep track of results. *See your doctor if you don't "pass" one or more of the tests...**

TEST #1: STAIRS TEST

Why this test? It helps assess basic lung and heart function.

The prop you'll need: A single flight of stairs (about eight to 12 steps).

*These self-tests are not a substitute for a thorough physical exam from your doctor. Use them only as a way to identify potential problem areas to discuss with your physician.

What to do: Walk up the steps at a normal pace while continuously reciting "Mary had a little lamb" or some other simple verse.

Watch out: You should be able to talk easily while climbing the stairs and when at the top—without feeling winded. If you cannot continue to talk, or if you feel discomfort or tightness in your chest at any time during this test, see your doctor as soon as possible.

Beware: If the small stress of climbing one flight of stairs causes physical problems, it could be a sign of hardening of the arteries (arteriosclerosis) or heart disease.

For some individuals, being out of breath could mean that they have asthma or bronchitis...chronic obstructive pulmonary disease (COPD), including emphysema...or even lung cancer.

TEST #2: GRAVITY TEST

Why this test? It measures how well your body adapts to changes in position, which can signal a variety of health problems, ranging from anemia to medication side effects.

The prop you'll need: Either a stopwatch or clock that measures seconds.

What to do: Lie down on a bed or the floor, and rest there for a minute or two. Then, start the stopwatch and stand up at a normal pace with no pauses (it's OK to use your hands).

Watch out: If you feel dizzy, make note of this. Most people can go from lying down to standing up within five seconds—and feel perfectly normal. In a healthy person, the body responds to the change in posture by pumping blood more strongly to the head.

Beware: Dizziness can signal any of the following...

- **Low blood pressure.** With orthostatic hypotension, your body doesn't pump enough blood to counteract the effects of gravity when you stand up.
- **Medication side effects,** especially from diuretics, such as *furosemide* (Lasix)...beta-blockers, such as *atenolol* (Tenormin) or *propranolol* (Inderal)...drugs for Parkinson's disease, such as *pramipexole* (Mirapex) or *levodopa* (Sinemet)...tricyclic antidepressants, such as *imipramine* (Tofranil) or *amitriptyline*...or drugs to treat erectile dysfunction, such as *sildenafil* (Viagra) or *tadalafil* (Cialis).
- **Dehydration.**
- **Anemia.**
- **Atherosclerosis,** in which blood flow is partially blocked by fatty deposits in blood vessels, or other vascular problems.

TEST #3: PENCIL TEST

Why this test? It checks the nerve function in your feet—if abnormal, this could indicate diabetes, certain types of infections or autoimmune disease.

The prop you'll need: A pencil that is freshly sharpened at one end with a flat eraser on the other end...and a friend to help.

What to do: Sit down so that all sides of your bare feet are accessible. Close your eyes, and keep them closed throughout the test.

Have your friend lightly touch your foot with either the sharp end or the eraser end of the pencil. With each touch, say which end of the pencil you think was used.

Ask your friend to repeat the test in at least three different locations on the tops and bottoms of both feet (12 locations total). Have your friend keep track of your right and wrong answers.

Watch out: Most people can easily tell the difference between "sharp" and "dull" sensations on their sensitive feet. If you give the wrong answer for more than two or three locations on your feet, have your doctor repeat the test to determine whether you have nerve damage (neuropathy).

Beware: Neuropathy is a common sign of diabetes...certain autoimmune disorders, including lupus and Sjögren's syndrome...infection, such as Lyme disease, shingles or hepatitis C...or excessive exposure to toxins, such as pesticides or heavy metals (mercury or lead).

TEST #4: URINE TEST

Why this test? It helps evaluate the functioning of your kidneys.

The prop you'll need: A clear plastic cup or clean, disposable clear jar.

What to do: In the middle of the day (urine will be too concentrated if you do this first thing in the morning), urinate into the cup or jar until you have caught at least an inch of urine. Throughout the day, note how often you urinate (about once every three waking hours is typical).

Watch out: The urine should be a pale, straw color—not deep yellow, brown or pinkish. Urine that's discolored could indicate dehydration, abnormal kidney function or another health problem.

Next, smell the urine. It should have nothing more than a very faint urine odor (unless you recently ate asparagus).

Beware: While dark-colored or smelly urine could simply mean that you are dehydrated, there are too many other potentially serious causes to ignore the signs.

Some of the disorders that can affect urine include...

- **Kidney or bladder infection,** which can cause discolored urine and frequent urination.
- **Kidney disease,** which can cause smelly, discolored urine. Interestingly, both too frequent urination and infrequent urination are signs of kidney disease.
- **Diabetes or enlarged prostate,** which can cause frequent urination.

TEST #5: "RULE OF THUMB" TEST

Why this test? It can help identify hearing loss.

The prop you'll need: A perfectly quiet room.

What to do: Rub your right thumb and index finger together continuously to create a kind of "whisper" sound. Raise your right arm so that it's level with your ear and your arm is roughly forming a right angle. Continue rubbing your thumb and index finger together. Can you still hear the sound? If not, move your hand toward your right ear, stopping when you can just hear the sound. Repeat on the left side.

Watch out: You should be able to hear this "finger rub" when your hand is six inches or more away from your ear.

Beware: If you need to be closer than six inches to hear the sound in either ear, you may have hearing loss. See an audiologist or otolaryngologist (ear, nose and throat specialist) for an evaluation.

While many people dismiss hearing loss as a mere inconvenience, it can have serious repercussions, such as getting into a car wreck because you can't hear the sound of a car approaching from the side.

Mysterious Pain or Numbness in Your Arms or Legs?—It Could Be a Sign of Peripheral Neuropathy

Michael Costigan, PhD, an assistant professor of neurology at Boston Children's Hospital and Harvard Medical School and a specialist in neuropathic pain medicine. His research on the peripheral nervous system led to the discovery of GCH1, a gene that activates enzymes involved in neuropathic pain and that could be a target for more effective treatments.

Have you ever felt pain or numbness in your hands, legs or feet? This can be caused by a condition called peripheral neuropathy (PN), a form of nerve damage.

PN is relatively common—about 20 million Americans have it—and most people associate it with diabetes. But there are literally hundreds of forms of PN.

The condition can be caused by athletic injuries, repetitive motions and autoimmune diseases. Continual pressure on one part of the body (from using crutches, for example) or a ligament compression (such as carpal tunnel syndrome) also can cause PN, as can exposure to toxic chemicals. Even hormonal changes in women could be the cause.

What you need to know...

HUNDREDS OF CAUSES

About one-third of neuropathy patients also have diabetes. And up to 70% of people with diabetes will eventually develop PN. Elevated blood sugar damages vessels carrying blood to the extremities, causing PN. The highest risk for PN is in people who have had diabetes for at least 25 years.

Other causes of PN...

• **Nerve entrapment injuries.** Activities involving repetitive motions—for example, typing, working a cash register or riding a bike—are a common cause of nerve inflammation and damage. You should suspect a local injury if you have symptoms in just one area (mononeuropathy). Patients who have diabetes or other systemic diseases are more likely to have damage to multiple nerves (polyneuropathy).

• **Vitamin B-12 deficiency** damages the coating that surrounds and protects nerves (the myelin sheath), which can lead to PN. Between 10% and 25% of older adults are deficient in B-12 because of an age-related decline in intrinsic factor, a protein that's needed for absorption of the vitamin.

• **Autoimmune diseases** (such as lupus and rheumatoid arthritis) can cause the immune system to attack and damage the myelin sheath. Nerve damage also can be caused by conditions such as kidney disease, hypothyroidism, hepatitis C and Lyme disease.

• **Toxic neuropathy,** usually caused by chemotherapy during cancer treatments, can result in severe nerve damage. Additionally, exposure to environmental chemicals, such as heavy metals or agricultural pesticides, can cause PN.

LITTLE-KNOWN SYMPTOMS

Although pain is often a symptom of PN, many patients with the condition experience uncomfortable but painless sensations, including tingling, itching and/or numbness. For example, most patients who have diabetic neuropathy experience foot numbness rather than pain—in fact, some cannot feel their feet at all.

Warning: Pain, tingling, numbness or burning sensations in the feet may be the first sign of diabetes.

DIFFICULT TO DETECT ROOT CAUSE

Most cases of PN can be diagnosed in a doctor's office with simple tests, including reflex and manual muscle testing, along with "touch tests" that can identify a loss of sensation in a particular location.

You also might need nerve conduction studies, which determine how fast the nerves can carry the signal and how well the muscles can respond to it, or electromyography, which helps distinguish nerve damage from muscle-related disease. In addition, your doctor might order blood tests to check for infection, hormone deficiencies or nutritional status.

The catch: Even though it's usually easy to identify PN, it can be a challenge to find the underlying cause. In nearly one-third of cases, the cause is never determined. In these patients, treatments can only relieve symptoms, and damage to the nerve or nerves will probably continue because the mechanism can't be identified. Research is under way to try to find solutions.

RECOVERY IS POSSIBLE

The good news is that the majority of patients with PN will gradually heal once the underlying cause is identified and treated—although it could take years before the nerves fully recover.

Example: Patients with diabetes who improve their glucose control will frequently experience a reduction in neuropathy symptoms over a period of months, but it might take a year or longer before their symptoms are mainly or completely gone.

The odds for making a complete recovery improve when the nerve damage is recent and treatment is started quickly.

Example: The nerve will completely regenerate in most patients with carpal tunnel syndrome if they're diagnosed and surgically treated within six months.

Important: Go to a doctor right away if you suspect that you have PN. The longer you wait, the higher the risk that you'll have permanent nerve damage—and a lifetime of pain and/or other undesirable symptoms.

BEST TREATMENTS NOW

The current treatments available for PN only relieve discomfort—they do not affect the ability of nerves to regenerate. Scientists are developing medications that specifically target nerve pain and improve the ability of nerves to heal, but these drugs are still in the experimental stage. *For now...**

*Tell your doctor if you take other medications to avoid possible interactions.

• **Don't depend on aspirin, ibuprofen or related medications.** They are not very effective for PN—and the potential side effects (such as gastrointestinal bleeding and kidney or liver damage) make them a poor choice for most patients.

• **Tricyclic antidepressants,** such as *nortriptyline* (Pamelor) or *desipramine* (Norpramin), are an effective treatment for PN, particularly when the nerve discomfort is caused by diabetes. Taken at low doses, they reduce pain even in patients who don't suffer from depression. Side effects, which may include a dry mouth and constipation, are somewhat rare.

Also helpful: Selective serotonin and norepinephrine reuptake inhibitors (SSNRIs), such as *duloxetine* (Cymbalta). Side effects may include nausea.

• *Gabapentin* (Neurontin) and *pregabalin* (Lyrica). First developed for seizures, they change electrical activity in the brain and reduce pain caused by many types of PN, including the pain caused by cancer and cancer treatments.

Bonus: Pregabalin reduces anxiety in some patients—helpful because stress and anxiety often increase due to chronic pain. Possible side effects include dizziness, sedation and sometimes cognitive impairment in older adults. Side effects can be reduced, however, by starting patients on a low dose that's increased over a period of weeks.

• **Topical lidocaine** (such as Lidoderm and Topicaine) used in patch or gel form is a good choice for patients whose painful neuropathy is limited to specific, localized areas. Even at high doses (three patches daily, applied for a total of 12 hours), little of the drug enters the bloodstream, which reduces risk for side effects. A local rash where the gel/patch is applied may occur in some patients.

• **Opioid painkillers,** such as *oxycodone* (OxyContin) and *levorphanol*, can be effective for reducing neuropathic pain. However, many doctors avoid them because they cause sedation and could lead to addiction. These drugs are mainly used for patients with severe pain who do not respond to other treatments. In addition to sedation and dependency, side effects may include nausea and constipation.

For more information, including clinical trials and the latest research: Contact the Foundation for Peripheral Neuropathy at 877-883-9942 or *www.foundationforpn.org.*

8

Eyes, Ears, Nose and Mouth Conditions

Natural Ways to Protect Your Vision

Millions of Americans have lost some or all of their sight to cataracts, glaucoma, macular degeneration and other eye diseases. Medications and surgical procedures can help, but the results are rarely optimal.

Fact: Up to 80% of all diseases can be prevented with natural approaches*—and there is evidence that nutritional treatments can halt or even reverse underlying vision problems.

Sun exposure is one of the main causes of vision loss. Everyone should wear sunglasses that block the sun's damaging ultraviolet (UV) rays.

Other measures to combat vision loss include eating certain foods and taking supplements. The antioxidants described below (lutein, zeaxanthin and the recommended vitamin supplements) help prevent and treat most eye conditions. The other remedies described can help specific problems. You can take all the supplements listed here (available at health-food stores), but it is always wise to consult with your physician before taking any supplement.

LUTEIN

Spinach, kale and other leafy greens contain an antioxidant called lutein, which reduces damage caused by unstable molecules known as free radicals. Smoking and exposure to UV light are two common sources of free radicals. Decreasing damage from free

---

Jamison Starbuck, ND, naturopathic physician in family practice in Missoula, Montana. She is past president of the American Association of Naturopathic Physicians and a contributing editor to *The Alternative Advisor: The Complete Guide to Natural Therapies and Alternative Treatment.*

Mark A. Stengler, NMD, licensed naturopathic medical doctor in private practice, Stengler Center for Integrative Medicine, Encinitas, California...adjunct associate clinical professor at the National College of Natural Medicine, Portland, Oregon...author of many books including *The Natural Physician's Healing Therapies. MarkStengler.com*

radicals can reduce the risk of cataracts and macular degeneration.

Recommended: One to two servings of leafy greens daily, or supplement with 15 mg of lutein daily. I usually have my patients take a daily supplement that combines *lutein* (15 mg) with *zeaxanthin* (3 mg), another antioxidant.

VITAMINS C & E

Individually, these vitamins are among the most potent antioxidants. Taken together, they're very effective at preventing vision loss. Vitamin E blocks free radicals in the fatty parts of cells, such as in the macula of the eye, while vitamin C fortifies the watery portions in the cornea and retina.

For optimal protection, I recommend to my patients supplements of vitamins C and E, along with zinc and beta-carotene. Patients who take this combination daily can reduce their risk of vision loss. In patients who have age-related macular degeneration, these supplements can slow the disease's progression.

Recommended: Daily supplements with 400 IU of mixed natural vitamin E (a mixture of tocopherols and tocotrienols), 500 mg of vitamin C, 80 mg of zinc and 15 mg of beta-carotene.

GINKGO BILOBA

The herb ginkgo biloba blocks free radicals and dilates blood vessels, increasing circulation to the optic nerve. There is some evidence that it can improve peripheral vision in patients with glaucoma.

Recommended: 120 mg of ginkgo daily. Choose an extract that is standardized to 24% flavone glycosides.

Caution: Do not take a supplement with ginkgo if you are taking a prescription blood-thinning medication, such as *warfarin* (Coumadin).

N-ACETYL CARNOSINE

This naturally occurring molecule is composed of two amino acids. Unlike most supplements, N-acetyl carnosine (NAC) can be used topically in drop form or taken orally. When taken orally, it substantially boosts levels of glutathione—important because the lens of the eye in a patient with cataracts has reduced amounts of glutathione.

A recent study found that NAC eyedrops improved visual acuity and glare sensitivity in patients with cataracts. During the two-year study, 90% of the eyes treated with NAC had significant improvements in vision.

Recommended: An oral supplement of 500 mg of NAC daily. Patients with cataracts should ask their doctors about also using topical drops.

FISH OIL

About half of the retina consists of *docosahexaenoic acid* (DHA), a component in fish oil that provides the main structural support in cell membranes. DHA causes a significant drop in intraocular pressure—important for patients with glaucoma. Another component in fish oil, *eicosapentaenoic acid* (EPA), has anti-inflammatory effects and is thought to play an important role in maintaining visual acuity.

Recommended: Eat fish twice a week. Avoid fish high in mercury, including shark, swordfish, tilefish, king mackerel and large tuna, such as albacore, yellowfin, bigeye and bluefin. Or take a fish-oil formula daily that includes 600 mg of EPA and 400 mg of DHA. Check with your doctor if you are on a blood thinner, such as warfarin.

MAGNESIUM AND CHROMIUM

Each of these minerals dilates blood vessels in the eye and reduces pressure from glaucoma. Chromium is particularly important for patients with diabetes, a common cause of vision loss. Chromium supplements help maintain an optimal blood-sugar balance and reduce the risk of glaucoma.

Recommended: Take 250 mg of magnesium (citrate or chelate) and 200 mg of chromium (polynicotinate or picolinate) twice daily.

DIGESTIVE ENZYMES

Cells in the retina have an extremely high rate of metabolism. They require high levels of nutrients (along with blood and oxygen) for optimal function and to repair normal damage. Older adults often get insufficient nutrients, in part because levels of stomach acid decline with age and impair normal digestion.

Supplements that contain betaine hydrochloride mimic the hydrochloric acid normally produced by the stomach and can improve the digestion/absorption of eye-protecting nutrients, which are particularly helpful in the prevention and treatment of macular degeneration.

Recommended: One or two capsules of betaine hydrochloride with each meal.

Also helpful: One or two capsules of a full-spectrum plant-based enzyme (such as Longevity Science Total Gest) during or at the end of meals.

Caution: Patients who have active ulcers should not take digestive enzymes.

- **Make an herbal eye compress.** The herb eyebright has been widely used to treat eye ailments, particularly the itchy, watery, red eyes that accompany allergies, colds and sinusitis. For relief from these symptoms, make a cold compress (to be used externally on your eyes) with eyebright tea. Use two teaspoons of dried eyebright leaf (available at health-food stores) per eight ounces of boiling water. Steep covered for five minutes, strain and refrigerate in a closed jar. When cool, pour the tea over a clean cotton cloth and place it over your closed eyes for 10 minutes. For additional relief from symptoms, drink a mixture of 60 drops of eyebright tincture in one ounce of water, three times a day.

Warning: Do not put eyebright tea or extract directly into your eyes.

*If you have a serious eye symptoms such as floaters, chronic redness, blurred vision or pain, see an ophthalmologist. Annual eye exams are also recommended.

Prevent Glaucoma with a Folate Supplement

Study titled "A Prospective Study of Folate, Vitamin B-6, and Vitamin B-12 Intake in Relation to Exfoliation Glaucoma or Suspected Exfoliation Glaucoma," published in *JAMA Ophthalmology*.

Glaucoma is an insidious disease—literally happening before your very eyes undetected, having virtually no symptoms until, in a blink, you've got eye surgery on your plate and you may even be going blind. You may think that, nowadays, glaucoma is easily treatable, but one form of glaucoma, *pseudoexfoliation glaucoma* (called "PEX" or sometimes just exfoliation glaucoma) is much harder to fix than others. Research from Harvard Medical School, though, is showing that the more folate you get each day, the less likely PEX will develop.

ARE YOU AT RISK?

PEX is caused by pressurized buildup of debris that clogs the eye's ability to drain, and it can lead to cataract formation, destruction of the optic nerve and blindness. PEX can happen because it's in your genes or because your eyes have been exposed to too much of the sun's ultraviolet (UV) light. People who live in some northern parts of the world, such as Scandinavia (possibly because of genes) and higher altitudes (where the thin air encourages more UV-radiation exposure) are also more at risk for this eye disease. People with PEX also have high levels of an amino acid called homocysteine in their blood, tears and eye fluid. Because B vitamins can help keep homocysteine levels in check, some researchers thought that getting enough B vitamins was the key, but the team from Harvard Medical School discovered that it's not quite that simple—it appears that you must get a certain B vitamin in a certain specific way.

UNCOVERING THE PRECISE NUTRITIONAL LINK

To get a clearer picture, the Harvard researchers analyzed information from about 120,000 people from two very large, long-term health study databases, the Nurses' Health Study and the Health Professionals Follow-up Study, with a specific focus on people who were 40 years old or older, were free of glaucoma at the start of the study, had had eye exams within a certain two-year period and had provided information about their dietary habits. They discovered that people who ultimately got PEX were deficient in one particular B vitamin, folate. They also found that, although the amount of folate gotten only from food had little impact on prevention of

PEX, getting enough from a supplement made a big difference.

FOLATE IS AN EYE-SAVER

People with the highest intake of folate—at least 335 micrograms (mcg) per day for women and 434 mcg for men—from vitamin supplements had an 83% reduced risk of PEX compared with people who did not take such supplements. The good news is that any high-quality B complex vitamin supplement, which will generally contain 400 mcg of folate, together with a diet rich in green leafy vegetables, fortified whole grains, beans and peas and especially beef liver (if you have a taste for it) will supply you with enough folate to protect you from PEX. You can even find folate supplements that contain 800 mcg or more, but be aware that the daily tolerable upper limit of supplemental folate for adults, according to the Institute of Medicine, is 1,000 mcg. Also, be aware that folate supplements can interfere with the anticancer effectiveness of the drug methotrexate. Speak with your doctor if you take that drug. Folate supplements also aren't well absorbed in people taking antiepileptic drugs or *sulfasalazine* (Azulfidine, used to treat ulcerative colitis), so guidance about folate supplement dosage, in these instances, also should be discussed with a doctor.

We're increasingly being told by medical experts to ditch vitamin supplements and get our nutrients from whole foods. Although I think this is generally sound advice over pill-popping, even if those pills are vitamins, I also think it's important to pay heed to studies like this one that show that a supplement is exactly what's needed to stave off a serious condition. And sight-robbing glaucoma is serious enough in anyone's book!

Vision Loss Can Be Deadly

In a study of 2,520 adults (ages 65 to 84), vision decline—as measured by the mistaken identification of one additional letter per year on a visual acuity chart—was associated with a 16% increased risk for death from any cause over eight years.

Possible reason: Visual acuity is closely associated with a person's ability to perform daily activities such as shopping and doing housework—and risk for death increases with the inability to perform daily tasks.

What to do: As you age, be sure to get an eye exam every year or two and corrective lenses if needed.

Sharon Christ, PhD, assistant professor of human development & family studies, Purdue University, West Lafayette, Indiana.

Help for Watery Eyes

Common causes of watery eyes—and what to do...

- **Age-related changes of the surface of the eye can cause tears to pool in the corners of your eyes.** Artificial tears or resurfacing surgery may help—see an ophthalmologist.
- **A blocked tear duct can cause eyes to water.** An in-office procedure or topical steroid drugs can often relieve the problem.
- **Eye irritation or infection can cause constant watering,** which will clear up when the irritation or infection goes away.
- **Excessively dry eyes,** caused by allergies or other factors, can cause reflex tearing—the underlying cause needs to be treated.
- **Some medical conditions, such as a thyroid disorder,** can cause eyes to water—ask your doctor.

Steven L. Maskin, MD, Dry Eye and Cornea Treatment Center, Tampa, *DrMaskin.com.*

Contacts with Built-In Sun Protection

New contact lenses protect eyes from the sun's harmful rays.

Recent finding: Hats and sunglasses don't provide enough protection from the sun's ultraviolet (UV) radiation, which can damage the corneas and lenses of the eyes and eventually lead to cataracts.

Self-defense: UV-absorbing contact lenses, even for adults and children who don't need contact lenses to improve vision.

But: Absorption levels vary among brands of lenses. Talk to your doctor about contact lenses that will protect your eyes from the sun.

Heather Chandler, PhD, assistant professor, College of Optometry, The Ohio State University, Columbus, Ohio, and leader of an animal study published in *Investigative Ophthalmology and Visual Science.*

Protocols for Cataracts and AMD

Here is a summary of my recommendations for people diagnosed with eye disease. Preventive doses appear in parentheses.

CATARACTS

Lutein: 15 mg daily (2 mg to 5 mg daily in a high-potency multivitamin or eye formula).

Vitamin C: 2,000 mg to 3,000 mg daily (500 mg daily).

Bilberry: 160 mg two to three times daily of a 25% anthocyanoside extract (same dose).

Vitamin E complex: 400 IU daily (200 IU daily).

Zinc: 45 mg to 80 mg daily with 1 mg to 2 mg of copper (15 mg to 30 mg daily with 1 to 2 mg of copper).

Betaine hydrochloride: One to two 500- to 600-mg capsules with each meal (same dose).

Vitamin B complex: 50 mg daily plus a high-potency multivitamin (high-potency multivitamin).

N-acetylcarnosine eyedrops: Two drops twice daily of a 1% aqueous solution, used under a doctor's supervision.

MACULAR DEGENERATION

Take the first six supplements listed above, plus...

Zeaxanthin: 3 mg daily (500 mcg to 1 mg daily).

Beta-carotene: 15 mg daily (same dose).

Mark A. Stengler, NMD, licensed naturopathic medical doctor in private practice, Stengler Center for Integrative Medicine, Encinitas, California...adjunct associate clinical professor at the National College of Natural Medicine, Portland, Oregon...author of many books including *The Natural Physician's Healing Therapies. MarkStengler.com*

Cheap Sunglasses

Wearing cheap sunglasses is worse than not wearing any shades at all. Most low-quality sunglasses have little ultraviolet protection. And the darkened lenses trick your pupils into dilating, letting in more damaging rays.

Best: Choose sunglasses with UV 400 protection—that is the equivalent of 100% UV protection.

Lauren B. Yeager, MD, ophthalmologist, New York-Presbyterian Hospital/Columbia University Medical Center, New York City, writing in *Self.*

Simple Solutions for Computer Vision Syndrome

Gary Heiting, OD, who worked as a clinical optometrist and optical-industry consultant for more than 25 years. He is senior editor at *AllAboutVision.com.*

Are you prone to headaches or a stiff neck—and you can't figure out why? The surprising cause may be computer vision syndrome. *Here's what you need to know...*

DISTANCE IS EVERYTHING

Computer monitors usually are positioned between 20 and 26 inches from the eyes. Eye-care professionals call this the intermediate zone of vision.

Generally, children and young adults can see clearly and comfortably at this distance without glasses (if they have perfect vision) or with their general-purpose glasses or contacts (if they need prescription eyewear for nearsightedness, farsightedness and/or astigmatism).

Seeing clearly at the intermediate zone becomes more difficult once we reach our 40s, due to a normal age-related loss of focusing power and flexibility called presbyopia. This is especially true once it becomes apparent that you need multifocal lenses—bifocals, trifocals or progressive lenses—or reading glasses.

Multifocal lenses for general-purpose use may not have a large enough intermediate-viewing zone for computer use, or the zone might be positioned too high or too low in the lens.

And reading glasses that may be perfect for reading a book or magazine may be too powerful for comfortable computer vision.

The end result: You may find yourself with less-than-clear vision while using a computer that leads to squinting, eyestrain and headaches, or adopting bad postures—leaning forward in your chair, craning your neck or hunching your shoulders—causing neck, shoulder and back pain. This combination of stress-related symptoms is called computer vision syndrome.

WHICH GLASSES?

How can you avoid the discomfort, fatigue and lost productivity associated with computer vision syndrome? For many people, the answer is specially prescribed computer glasses.

Though computer vision syndrome can affect people of any age, computer glasses tend to be most helpful for adults with presbyopia and younger adults who may not yet need multifocal glasses or reading glasses but have symptoms of eyestrain during and after computer use.

To help your eye doctor determine the best prescription for your computer glasses, measure the distance from your eyes to your computer screen. Measure from the bridge of your nose to the middle of the screen—whether the screen is on your desk or balanced on your lap. Write down the measurement, and bring it with you to your eye exam.

Best choices...

• **Single-vision computer lenses** work well for people who keep the monitor or laptop screen at a consistent distance—on a desk, balanced on the lap, etc.

Your eye doctor will prescribe lenses that match that distance. It doesn't matter if you also use reading/distance glasses, since you will use the computer glasses only when you're working on the computer. Single-vision lenses provide a larger field of view (the total area that you can see clearly through the glasses) than other designs. They also are less expensive than multifocal computer lenses.

• **Multifocal computer lenses.** Multifocal is the general term for bifocals, trifocals and progressive lenses (which don't have the lines that you can see on bifocals and trifocals).

Because they have different viewing zones for intermediate and near vision, multifocal computer lenses allow you to use one pair of glasses for computer work, reading small print and using your phone and other handheld devices.

You might prefer a multifocal lens if you frequently move your eyes back and forth from your computer screen to documents on your desk. Someone who does data entry, for example, might find multifocal computer glasses more comfortable than single-vision lenses. Multifocal lenses also might enable you to see both your computer screen and your keyboard more clearly than single-vision lenses.

Some computer lenses are for intermediate and near vision only, while others include a small "distance" zone in the top portion of the lens for looking at objects or people several feet away or even across the room. The distance zone of a computer multifocal (if one is present) is limited in size, so never wear multifocal computer glasses for driving or other tasks that require a clear, wide field of view in the distance.

Important: If you decide to get multifocal lenses, take measurements of the distance from your eyes to your desk surface, as well as from your eyes to your computer screen. The main portion of the lenses will be adjusted for the computer, and the bottom portion will have added magnification for closer objects.

• **Antireflective (AR) coating.** This coating eliminates most of the reflections of overhead lighting that appear on both the front and back surfaces of eyeglass lenses. This improves the brightness and clarity of the computer screen and reduces eye fatigue.

Also helpful: A slight tint on the lenses to block the "blue" light emitted from computer screens and overhead lighting that increases glare and eyestrain.

EYE CARE

Wearing glasses might not eliminate all discomfort if you spend long hours in front of the screen. *Also important...*

• **The 20-20-20 rule.** Take at least a 20-second break for every 20 minutes that you're in front of the computer...and let your eyes completely relax by looking at something that's at least 20 feet away—this relaxes the focusing muscle inside the eye, reducing the risk of eyestrain and fatigue.

• **Blink.** Research has shown that during normal, face-to-face conversations, people tend to blink an average of 15 to 16 times per minute. During computer use, this drops to an average of just over five blinks per minute. This greatly increases the risk for eye dryness and irritation.

Blinking spreads a fresh lubricating layer of tears across the surface of your eyes to improve comfort and the clarity of your vision. Remind yourself to blink normally—or take a "blink" break every minute or two. And blink fully. Some people blink only partially when they work on a computer.

• **Remove your contacts.** Because prolonged computer use increases your risk for dry eyes, it also frequently causes contact lens discomfort. And when your contacts dry out, you're more likely to experience blurred vision, eyestrain and headaches. Contacts are fine for brief periods of computer use, but if you know you're going to be staring at a screen for hours, remove your contacts and wear glasses or computer glasses instead.

Also helpful: Keep artificial tears at your desk, and apply a drop in each eye when you first notice dryness, fatigue or irritation. Use preservative-free artificial tears—preservatives can cause increased eye sensitivity and irritation with prolonged use.

The Dry-Eye Epidemic—Remedies That Really Work

Robert Latkany, MD, ophthalmologist and founder and director of the Dry Eye Clinic at The New York Eye and Ear Infirmary and the Dry Eye Center at Physician Eyecare of NY, both in New York City. He is actively involved in dry-eye research and author of *The Dry Eye Remedy: The Complete Guide to Restoring the Health and Beauty of Your Eyes. DryEyeDoctor.com*

It's an epidemic—as many as 25 million Americans are suffering from dry-eye syndrome. They're complaining to their doctors of irritated and burning eyes. In fact, it's the second-most-common eye complaint after vision problems.

One reason dry eyes are so common is that the mucous membranes that produce a key component of tears get drier as we age. About one-third of adults ages 65 and older suffer from dry eyes.

Another key factor is that electronics aren't kind to eyes. If you spend a good part of your day in front of a computer or squinting at your smartphone or watching TV, you "forget" to blink. Your blink rate, as well as how completely you blink, affects eye moisture.

That's because tears consist of oil as well as water. The oil is squeezed from the meibomian glands in the upper and lower eyelids when you blink. It allows tears to cling to the surfaces of the eyes and also slows their evaporation. If you aren't blinking enough and, as a result, secreting little or no oil, the tears evaporate quickly. This condition, known as evaporative dry eye, is the most common cause of dryness.

Other conditions that can lead to eye dryness include medication side effects (from some antihistamines and antidepressants, for example)...autoimmune diseases, such as Sjögren's syndrome, lupus and rheumatoid arthritis...and vision-correcting surgery (such as LASIK). Diabetes, too, can contribute to eye dryness by causing a decreased sensation of dryness, thus reducing your blink rate.

Before recommending a treatment, your doctor will want to know why your eyes are dry. Once the underlying cause—for example, medication use, autoimmune disease or diabetes—is identified and treated, the dryness may start to improve.

But even if medication use or a chronic illness is not to blame, you don't have to suffer from dry eye. *There are steps you can take to relieve the discomfort...*

WHAT YOU CAN DO

If your symptoms are mild, the following steps that you can take on your own may be enough to relieve dry eye. *If your symptoms are more severe, these steps can augment other treatments (see below) that your doctor may suggest...*

• **Blink better.** People normally blink between six and 15 times a minute. (You blink less when you're reading or concentrating and more when your eyes are relaxed.)

If you watch a lot of TV or use a computer for more than an hour at a time, your eyes probably are drier than they should be. This also happens to long-distance drivers (such as truckers) or people who stare at anything for long periods of time.

Important: Remind yourself to blink even when you don't feel that you need to.

Also helpful: Take a "blink break" at least twice an hour. Shut your eyes for 10 seconds, and move your eyeballs under the closed lids to bathe and lubricate them.

• **Try omega-3 fatty acids.** These healthful fats, found in walnuts, flaxseed oil and fish, can help reduce gland inflammation and improve the quality of your tears. Fish-oil supplements—a typical dose is 1,000 milligrams (mg) daily—aren't a replacement for other treatments, but they can slightly improve dryness.

Oily, cold-water fish, such as tuna and salmon, may be even better. A study at Harvard's Brigham and Women's Hospital found that patients who ate tuna five to six times a week had a 68% reduced risk of developing dry eye, compared with those who had only one serving a week.

• **Use warm compresses to unclog tear glands.** Use them two to four times a day for five minutes at a time.

• **Try artificial tears.** Sold over the counter, products such as Blink and TheraTears are very helpful for short-term relief. They work quickly and are soothing, particularly if you keep them chilled in the refrigerator. The liquid drops are mainly used for mild cases of dryness. Gel-containing drops are recommended for more severe dryness. If you use drops more than three or four times a day, get a product without preservatives, which can cause some discomfort.

• **Avoid foods high in omega-6 fatty acids, such as margarine, mayonnaise and oils made from corn and soybeans.** Also, reduce the salt in your diet and avoid alcohol.

DOCTOR HELP

If the steps above don't help you, see your ophthalmologist. *He/she may recommend the following...*

• **Restasis** (cyclosporine ophthalmic emulsion) is the only FDA-approved medication for increasing tear production. This prescription eyedrop reduces inflammation and helps prevent blockages in the tear-secreting ducts. It's a good choice for dryness that's caused by vision-correcting surgery, cataract surgery or postmenopausal declines in estrogen, among other conditions.

• **Punctal plugs.** After tears wash across the eyeballs, they drain into small openings. These tear duct openings, or puncta, are located on the inner corners of the eyelids. Their job is to divert "used" tears into nasal cavities and from there to the back of the throat. Your doctor might recommend that you block these openings to keep more of your tears in your eyes.

It's a simple office procedure that takes less than an hour. Your doctor might recommend that you start with temporary plugs. Made from collagen, they last about three months and then dissolve. If you're satisfied with the improvement, you can get another set of temporary plugs.

Another option: Permanent punctal plugs. If you get nondissolvable, silicone plugs, you won't have to replace them. However, they stick out a little more than temporary plugs. You might not see them, but you will feel them with your finger when you touch the eye.

• **Gland expression.** Blockages in the oil-producing meibomian glands will decrease the quality of your tears and lead to dryness. You can express (empty) the glands by using a cotton-tipped swab to push the lower edges of the eyelids against the eyeballs. It's like popping a pimple. The pressure pushes the oil out. Don't try this unless your doctor shows you how—you don't want to injure your eye.

You might have to do this every day—preferably after a shower, when heat and steam have softened the accumulated oil.

If you are considering vision-correcting surgery: Millions of Americans have had LASIK, one of the less expensive forms of vision-correcting surgery. It is a generally safe procedure, but it can reduce the frequency of your blinks for several years. In the meantime, many patients will have dry eyes as a side effect.

Ask your doctor about other forms of corrective surgery, such as PRK or LASEK. They are less likely to cause blink problems, so you have less chance of developing dry eye.

Device for Macular Degeneration

People with macular degeneration may be able to see objects better with an implanted mini-telescope. The device is smaller than a pencil eraser and magnifies images to twice or almost three times their size. It can be implanted inside the eye in an outpatient procedure. It was approved for use in the US in October 2014. Macular degeneration is the leading cause of visual impairment in the US.

Lylas Mogk, MD, director, Center for Visual Rehabilitation and Research, Henry Ford Health System, Grosse Pointe and Livonia, Michigan.

Ways to Slow, Stop and Even Reverse Macular Degeneration

Stephen Rose, PhD, chief research officer of the Foundation Fighting Blindness. He has received the US Secretary of Health's Distinguished Service Award, the NIH Director's Award and the NIH Merit Award. *Blindness.org*

Age-related macular degeneration (AMD), the most common cause of vision loss in people over age 55, has always been considered a difficult—if not impossible—condition to treat.

Now: There is more reason than ever before to be hopeful that this dreaded eye disease, which affects about 10 million Americans, can be slowed, stopped or even reversed.

WHAT IS MACULAR DEGENERATION?

Age-related macular degeneration (AMD) causes progressive damage to the macula, the part of the eye that allows us to see objects clearly. With "dry" AMD, there is a thinning of the macula, which gradually blurs central vision but generally does not cause a total loss of sight. With "wet" AMD, a more severe form of the disease, abnormal blood vessels grow beneath the macula, leaking fluid and blood. Wet AMD often progresses rapidly, leading to significant vision loss or even blindness.

Exciting new scientific findings...

BREAKTHROUGHS FOR DRY AMD

Dry AMD, which affects about 90% of people with AMD, occurs when the light-sensitive cells in the macula slowly break down, gradually blurring central vision—which is necessary for reading and driving.

There is no treatment for dry AMD, though many drugs are in clinical trials. In the meantime, we now have evidence that certain nutrients can help control the disease, and exciting advances are taking place in stem cell therapy.

• **Nutrients that can help.** The Age-Related Eye Disease Study (AREDS), landmark research conducted by the National Eye Institute, found that a supplement containing high levels of antioxidants and zinc reduced the risk for advanced dry and wet AMD (the latest stages of AMD) in people with vision loss in one or both eyes.

The daily regimen: 500 mg of vitamin C...400 international units (IU) of vitamin E...15 mg of beta-carotene...80 mg of zinc... and 2 mg of copper. People with all stages of AMD were studied. With early-stage AMD, there may be no symptoms or vision loss. The condition is detected when an eye-care professional can see drusen (yellow deposits under the retina) during a dilated eye exam.

Scientists also are studying other nutrients for dry AMD, and there have been several positive reports. *For example...*

• **Zeaxanthin and lutein.** When 60 people with mild-to-moderate dry AMD took 8 mg a day of zeaxanthin for one year, they reported a marked improvement in vision (more "visual acuity" and a "sharpening of detailed high-contrast discrimination") along with visual restoration of some blind spots, researchers reported in the November 2011 issue of *Optometry*. A group receiving 9 mg of lutein daily along with zeaxanthin also had improvements in vision.

Many supplements that contain all of the nutrients mentioned earlier are available over-the-counter (OTC). But these should not be taken without a diagnosis of large drusen and monitoring by a doctor—some of these nutrients could be harmful for certain individuals, such as current and former smokers.

• **Stem cell therapy.** Perhaps one of the most remarkable findings ever reported in the literature of AMD treatment occurred earlier this year when new retinal cells grown from stem cells were used to restore some of the eyesight of a 78-year-old woman who was nearly blind due to a very advanced form of dry AMD.

The breakthrough therapy involved the use of human embryonic stem cells, which are capable of producing any of the more than 200 types of specialized cells in the body. New retinal cells grown from stem cells were injected into the patient's retina. Four months later, the patient had not lost any additional vision and, in fact, her vision seemed to improve slightly.

For more information: Go to *www.clinicaltrials.gov* and search "advanced dry age-related macular degeneration and stem cells."

BREAKTHROUGHS FOR WET AMD

Wet AMD, which affects about 10% of people with AMD, is more severe than the early and intermediate stages of the dry form. It occurs when abnormal blood vessels behind the retina start to grow. This causes blood and fluid to leak from the vessels and the macula to swell. Because the condition progresses quickly, it requires prompt treatment for the best chance of saving your vision. You are at an increased risk for wet AMD if you have dry AMD in one or both eyes...or you have wet AMD in one eye (the other eye is at risk).

The two standard treatments for wet AMD are the injection of a medication directly into the eye to block the growth of the abnormal blood vessels...and photodynamic therapy, in which a drug that's injected into the arm flows to the abnormal blood vessels in the eye and is activated there by a laser beam that destroys the vessels.

What's new...

• **More affordable drug choice.** The drugs *ranibizumab* (Lucentis) and *bevacizumab* (Avastin), which are injected into the eye, halt or reverse vision loss. However, these drugs have a huge price disparity. Lucentis, which is FDA-approved as a treatment for wet AMD, costs $2,000 per injection, while Avastin, a cancer drug that is used "off-label" to treat AMD, costs $50.

New finding: In a two-year study, both drugs worked equally well, with two-thirds of patients having "driving vision" (20/40 or better).

Another option: *Aflibercept* (Eylea), also injected into the eye, was approved by the FDA for wet AMD in November 2011. Research shows that every-other-month injections of Eylea (about $1,800 per injection) can be as effective as monthly injections of Lucentis.

Bottom line: You now have three safe and effective AMD treatment options to discuss with your doctor.

• **At-home monitoring.** Monthly monitoring by an ophthalmologist or optometrist for the subtle visual changes that herald wet AMD (or indicate a diagnosed case is worsening) is impractical for many.

New: An at-home system, the ForeseeHome AMD Monitoring Program, was recently approved by the FDA. You look into this lightweight and portable monitor for a few minutes daily. If results indicate a problem, you and your doctor are alerted to schedule an eye appointment.

Food for Your Ears

Eating fish helps hearing. *Recent finding:* Women who consume at least two servings of fish a week had a 20% lower risk for hearing loss.

Reason: Blood-supply problems to the ears can cause hearing loss, and a higher intake of fish—rich in omega-3 fatty acids—may help to maintain blood flow.

Other ways to protect hearing: Exercise regularly, manage your weight, and avoid excessively loud noises—or wear protection if you can't.

Sharon E. Curhan, MD, is an instructor in medicine and a clinical researcher in epidemiology at Brigham and Women's Hospital, Boston, and leader of a study of 65,215 women, published in *American Journal of Clinical Nutrition.*

Everyday Vitamins May Prevent Common Hearing Loss

Colleen Le Prell, PhD, department of communicative disorders, University of Florida, Gainesville.

How about a "morning after" pill for loud concerts? Researchers recently identified supplements so helpful at preventing and healing noise-induced hearing loss that we may very well see pills and snack foods marketed with that premise in the not-too-distant future. Long viewed as a hazard for people exposed to prolonged high-decibel sound (such as workers around jet engines or jackhammers, battlefield soldiers and rock stars), excess noise contributes to more than one-third of the 28 million Americans suffering from some degree of hearing loss.

RESEARCH RESULTS SOUND PROMISING

According to Colleen Le Prell, PhD, associate professor, department of communicative disorders, University of Florida in Gainesville, her research showed that a simple blend of common nutrients may help reduce hearing loss. In the study, four groups of guinea pigs were exposed to five hours of 120-decibel sound, which is as loud as a jet engine at takeoff. One hour before exposure, each group received either a nutrient blend or placebo. Thereafter, each group continued receiving the treatment regimen once daily for five days. One group was fed the synergistic blend of vitamins A, C and E with magnesium...a second group received magnesium alone...a third group was given A, C and E without magnesium...and a fourth group received a placebo.

The result: Using electrodes to test the animals' threshold hearing sensitivity before and after noise exposure, the group receiving the blend of vitamins A, C and E with magnesium had significantly less hearing loss than any of the three other groups.

Why should these extremely common supplements make such a big difference in hearing protection? Loud noise causes the overstimulation of inner ear sensory cells, which drives the production of free radicals even after noise exposure. The free radicals and a resulting constriction of blood flow ultimately damages the outer hair cells. The blend of vitamins A, C and E with magnesium binds with the free radicals in the inner ear, helping to prevent this damage.

YOU HEARD IT HERE FIRST

According to Dr. Le Prell, the upper limit for intake of vitamins A, C and E and magnesium has been well defined by the US Institute of Medicine (IOM), and should not be exceeded. As with any dietary supplement, moderation and supervision by a physician trained in natural medicine is important. Clinical trials to confirm safety and efficacy of this micronutrient blend for humans, at levels that adhere to IOM limits are underway and soon, says Dr. Le Prell, we may see products marketed to be taken around the time of noise exposure or daily as a preventive measure. For now though, Dr. Le Prell suggests checking with your physician to maintain (but do not exceed) recommended daily doses of vitamins A, C, E and magnesium—and turning down the volume.

Surprising Ways to Improve Your Hearing

Michael Seidman, MD, director of the Otolaryngology Research Laboratory and the Division of Otologic/Neurotologic Surgery and chair of the Center for Integrative Medicine at the Henry Ford Health System in Detroit. Dr. Seidman is coauthor, with Marie Moneysmith, of *Save Your Hearing Now.* His formulations for preventing and treating hearing loss are available at *BodyLanguageVitamins.com.*

Aside from protecting your ears from blasting stereos and jackhammers, there's not much you can do to control what happens to your hearing, right? Wrong!

It's true that genetic and environmental factors (such as loud noises) are usually what cause hearing loss. But most people have far more ability to prevent hearing loss—or even improve their hearing—than they realize.

Here's why: Most problems with hearing begin when the hair cells located in the cochlea, or inner ear, don't work well or stop functioning and die. Improving blood supply to the inner ear and tamping down inflammation within the body are among the strategies that may help keep your hearing sharp.

At first glance, you wouldn't think that the steps below would have anything to do with your hearing. But they have a lot to do with it.

Here's my advice for improving your hearing or keeping it intact...

CHECK YOUR MEDS

If you're having trouble hearing, see an otolaryngologist (ear, nose and throat specialist) or audiologist for an evaluation—and ask your doctor about the medications you take. *Among the many medications that are "ototoxic"—that is, they can lead to hearing loss...*

- **Antidepressants** such as *fluoxetine* (Prozac) and *amitriptyline.*
- **Antibiotics,** such as erythromycin, gentamicin and tetracycline.
- **Nonsteroidal anti-inflammatory drugs (NSAIDs),** such as aspirin and *ibuprofen* (Motrin).

If medication is causing your hearing loss, stopping the drug or switching to a new one, under your doctor's supervision, may improve your hearing.

For a list of drugs that can cause hearing loss: Go to the American Tinnitus Association's website, *www.ata.org,* and click on "Causes."

GET THE RIGHT NUTRIENTS

Certain nutrients are known to promote blood flow and help fight inflammation throughout the body—including in the ears.

To ensure that you have adequate levels of such nutrients, consider taking targeted supplements to protect your hearing. Among those that are beneficial are alpha lipoic acid, acetyl-L-carnitine, L-glutathione and CoQ10. Taking these supplements may help slow hearing loss and protect against damage from loud noises.

What to do: To determine which supplements (including doses) are best for you, consult an integrative physician. To find one near you, contact the Academy of Integrative Health & Medicine at *www.aihm.org.*

LOOK AT YOUR LIFESTYLE

Other ways to increase your odds of keeping your hearing sharp as long as possible...

- **Chill out.** If you're late for a meeting and stuck in traffic, your stress levels will probably climb. But what's that got to do with your hearing? Quite a lot, actually.

Research has now shown that brain chemicals called dynorphins respond to stress by triggering inflammation in the brain—and in the inner ear. Inflammation not only exacerbates hearing loss but also hearing-related problems such as tinnitus.

What to do: Setting aside time each day for anything that alleviates tension—be it daily meditation, yoga or listening to restful music—may reduce your stress levels...and improve your hearing or help prevent hearing loss.

Surprising new research: Chewing gum may curb hearing loss in some cases—perhaps by distracting the brain from stress that may be interfering with the brain's processing of sound.

• **Keep off the pounds.** Evidence is continuing to mount that the more a person is overweight, the greater his/her risk for hearing loss. What's the link? Factors closely related to obesity, such as high blood pressure, are believed to restrict blood flow to the inner ear.

What to do: Both men and women should aim for a body mass index (BMI) of 18.5 to 24.9.

• **Get enough exercise.** In recent research, women who walked at least two hours a week had a 15% lower risk for hearing loss, compared with those who walked less than one hour a week. The hearing protection conferred by exercise is also believed to apply to men.

What to do: To protect your hearing—and perhaps even improve it—spend at least two hours a week doing exercise, such as brisk walking.

• **Avoid cigarette smoke.** Smoking is bad for the lungs, the heart and many other parts of the body. But the ears? Absolutely! In a study of adults ages 48 to 92, smokers were more likely than nonsmokers to have hearing impairment. And though it's not well known, even nonsmokers who live with smokers (this includes cigar and pipe smokers, too) are more likely to have hearing loss, suggesting that secondhand smoke can cause damage that impairs hearing.

What to do: Kick the tobacco habit—and encourage family members to do the same.

GET ENOUGH Zs

Sleep apnea, a disorder marked by chronic breathing pauses during sleep, has been recently linked to a 90% increased risk for low-frequency hearing loss (difficulty hearing conversation on the phone is a hallmark) and a 31% increased risk for high-frequency hearing loss (this often makes it hard to understand higher-pitched sounds, such as a woman's voice).

The results are preliminary, but some researchers believe that sleep apnea may trigger hearing loss due to poor blood flow to the cochlea, or inner ear.

What to do: If you snore (a common symptom of sleep apnea), see a doctor to determine whether you have sleep apnea and ask whether you should also have your hearing tested. If you have sleep apnea, it's possible that treating it will improve your hearing.

Don't Feel Ready for a Hearing Aid?

Barbara E. Weinstein, PhD, a professor of audiology and head of the Audiology Program at The City University of New York Graduate Center, where she specializes in hearing loss in older adults, hearing screening, disability assessment and evidence-based practice. She is the author of the textbook *Geriatric Audiology.*

If you are reluctant (or can't afford) to use a hearing aid, there are dozens of personal sound amplification products (PSAPs), over-the-counter devices that can help you hear a little better but don't cost as much as hearing aids, which run up to $3,000 each.

NOT QUITE A HEARING AID

Hearing aids are recommended for those who have been diagnosed with hearing loss by an audiologist. PSAPs, which come in many shapes and sizes, often resembling a Bluetooth headset, are meant to amplify sounds in situations where hearing is difficult, such as large gatherings or noisy restaurants.

In reality, it's not an either-or choice. Only 20% to 25% of people who could benefit from a hearing aid actually use one. PSAPs, with their lower price and availability on the Internet, in pharmacies and in stores such as RadioShack, can serve as "training wheels" for people who want to hear better but hesitate to shell out big bucks for a hearing aid.

Important: The hearing aids sold by audiologists are approved by the FDA as medical devices and must meet certain standards related, for example, to frequency ranges and distortion. PSAPs, on the other hand, are classified as electronic products. They aren't subject to FDA review, so you can't assume that they'll work for you. However, some PSAPs already rival the quality of "official" hearing aids and will keep getting better as technology improves.

KNOW WHAT YOU NEED

Before you look into PSAPs, get tested by an audiologist. About 14% of adults in their 50s, one-quarter in their 60s and more than one-third of those age 65 and older have some degree of age-related hearing loss. But do not assume that your hearing is normal—or that hearing loss is inevitable.

You may think that your hearing is becoming impaired because of your age when, in fact, it may be due to a medical issue, such as infection, abnormal bone growth, an inner-ear tumor or even earwax—all of which can be treated and sometimes reversed.

If your hearing loss is not related to a medical issue, a PSAP may be appropriate in the following situations...

- **You have trouble hearing the TV.** It is a common complaint but fairly easy to overcome. Inexpensive earbuds or a headset that merely amplifies the sound may be all that you need. Some products are wireless or have long cords that plug directly into the TV.

- **You have trouble hearing in quiet environments.** Speech can sound muffled or be entirely unintelligible if you have age-related hearing loss. Even if you can easily hear background sounds (such as music), you might struggle with the high-frequency sounds that are characteristic of speech.

If you plan to use a PSAP mainly at home or in other quiet settings (such as a museum or a hushed restaurant), look for a device that amplifies high frequencies more than low ones. You'll hear voices more clearly without being overwhelmed by the volume of sounds.

Warning: Some inexpensive products boost both high and low frequencies indiscriminately—avoid them. Your best choice will be a product that allows you to make adjustments and fine-tune it in different settings.

- **You have trouble hearing in noisy environments.** Even mild hearing loss can make it hard to hear voices over the din of clattering plates, a chattering crowd and background music. A simple amplifier won't work because it will make all of the sounds louder.

Better: A device that amplifies the sounds you want to hear while filtering out the rest. Look for a PSAP that has a directional microphone that will pick up speech while muting noise...noise cancellation to filter out low-frequency background sounds...volume control...and multiple channels that are suitable for different sound environments.

- **You're on the fence.** It's common for people to put off getting a hearing aid because of embarrassment or cost. (Hearing aids aren't covered by Medicare or most insurance plans.) You might be telling yourself, "Maybe I'll get one when I'm a lot older."

Important: Don't wait too long. The parts of the brain associated with hearing become less active when they aren't used. You need to hear sounds to keep this brain circuitry working and actively processing speech.

You might want to use a PSAP while you're making up your mind about hearing aids. Even if you get a PSAP that just boosts volume, it will keep the brain signals firing. In my opinion, it's reasonable to use one of these devices for a few months or even a few years. You can always buy a hearing aid later.

GREAT PSAP MODELS

Personal sound-amplification products you may want to consider...

• **For TV listening.** Sennheiser Wireless RS Headphones look like old-fashioned stereo headsets, but they let you turn up the sound. $220 to $450, *www.sennheiser.com.*

• **For more volume in loud environments.** Able Planet Personal Sound 2500 AMP is packed with high-end electronics to reduce background noise while amplifying sounds you want to hear (such as voices). $900 a pair, $500 for one. Available at various outlets online.

• **For more volume in both loud and quiet places.** The Bean Quiet Sound Amplifier by Etymotic provides amplification of soft speech without distorting sounds. $550 a pair, $300 for one, *www.etymotic.com.*

• **For more volume at a low cost.** Dozens of affordable products mainly increase volume without other features.

Example: Sonic SE4000X SuperEar Personal Sound Amplifier, a handheld amplifier you can attach to a pocket, belt, hat or purse strap. Costs $50, *www.sonictechnology.com.*

All of the PSAP manufacturers listed here offer a money-back guarantee if the product is returned within 30 days.

Ignoring Hearing Loss Is Dangerous

Virginia Ramachandran, AuD, audiologist at Henry Ford Hospital in Detroit. She is coauthor of *Basic Audiometry Learning Manual* and an adjunct professor and clinical education coordinator at the audiology program in the department of communication sciences and disorders at Wayne State University, also in Detroit.

For most people, age-related hearing loss, also known as presbycusis, happens so slowly that they don't notice it at first.

In fact, hearing loss actually begins in our late 20s and early 30s, when we lose the ability to hear high pitches, such as that of a buzzing mosquito. And by the time we reach our 70s, about half of us have diagnosable hearing loss.

What you may not know: Despite the high incidence of hearing loss, only about two in every five adults over age 65 with hearing loss use hearing aids. Plenty of people resist getting a hearing aid because they fear that it will make them look old, be too complicated to use and/or cost too much money.

Now: Based on recent research, people with untreated hearing loss have more reason than ever before to consider getting a hearing aid.

HEALTH HAZARDS

While most people consider hearing loss a mere annoyance, researchers are now discovering that it may increase one's risk for...

• **Dementia.** In a study of 639 men and women (ages 36 to 90) published in the *Archives of Neurology,* the risk of developing dementia was two, three and five times higher in those with mild, moderate and severe hearing loss, respectively, than in those with normal hearing.

Researchers do not have an explanation for the association between hearing loss and dementia—and they point out that the link does not prove cause and effect.

However, it's possible that damage to the cells involved in hearing may be a sign that damage has also occurred to nerve cells that are responsible for cognitive functions, including memory. Hearing loss also can cause social isolation, which contributes to the risk for dementia.

• **Depression.** Significantly more older adults with hearing loss who did not wear hearing aids reported feelings of sadness and depression for two or more weeks during a one-year period than their peers who wore hearing aids, according to a study from the National Council on Aging.

Possible reason: Depression may be caused or worsen in people with hearing loss who withdraw from social interactions.

• **Injury.** Hearing loss is a safety hazard, especially for pedestrians who may have trouble hearing oncoming traffic and for drivers who rely on their ability to hear to prevent collisions. It also affects a person's ability to hear a phone, doorbell and smoke detector alarm.

DO YOU NEED A HEARING AID?

If you have hearing loss, a loved one may be the first to notice it. *In addition, if any of the statements below applies to you, it may mean that you have hearing loss...*

• **You frequently ask, "What?" in conversations.**

• **You have trouble following conversations.**

• **Everyone around you seems to mumble.**

• **You're always turning up the volume on the TV.**

• **You can hear someone talking,** but not what the person is saying.

• **It's especially difficult for you to hear women and children,** both of whom have higher-pitched voices and generally speak with a lower volume than men. Higher-pitched voices are the most difficult to hear.

BEST HEARING AID OPTIONS

Many of today's hearing aids are highly sophisticated. *For example...*

Cutting-edge product: One of the newest hearing aids available is the SoundBite Hearing System, which allows sound to travel via the teeth to the inner ear. A small microphone in the ear canal transmits sounds to a wireless unit behind the ear, which sends a signal to a device that fits over the back teeth. The device converts the signals into vibrations, rerouting sound to the inner ear. SoundBite is especially helpful for people with hearing loss in one ear or who have conductive hearing loss—a problem in the middle or outer ear.

Main types of hearing aids...

• **Behind-the-ear (BTE) hearing aids,** which are generally larger than other types of hearing aids, are the traditional kind that hooks over the top of your ear and sits behind it. The hearing aid picks up sound, amplifies it and carries the amplified sound to an ear mold that fits inside your ear canal. The large size allows for directional microphones and easier adjustment of volume and battery changing.

The BTE hearing aid is appropriate for almost all types of hearing loss and does the best job of amplifying sound for people with severe hearing loss. Siemens offers a couple of rechargeable BTE hearing aids for mild-to-moderately severe hearing loss.

Typical cost: $500 to $2,000 per ear.

• **Open-fit models are among the newer aids available today.** They are smaller than BTE aids and suitable for mild-to-moderate hearing loss. Generally placed behind the ear, these aids leave the ear canal mostly open and are less visible than BTE models. Sound travels from the open-fit hearing aid through a small tube or wire to a tiny dome or speaker in the ear canal.

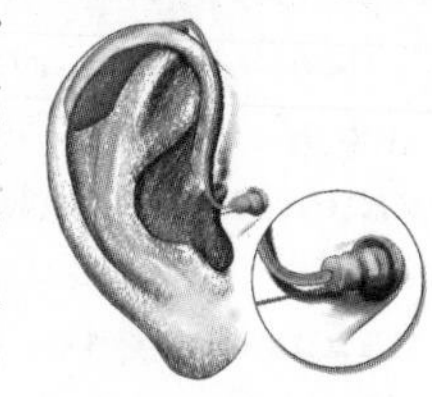

Typical cost: $1,000 to $2,500 per ear.

• **In-the-ear (ITE) hearing aids are custom-made to fit in the outer ear.** ITE devices may pick up background sounds such as wind, since the microphone sits at the outermost portion of the ear. But the batteries tend to last longer than other types of hearing aids and are easier to change, especially if you have arthritis in your fingers.

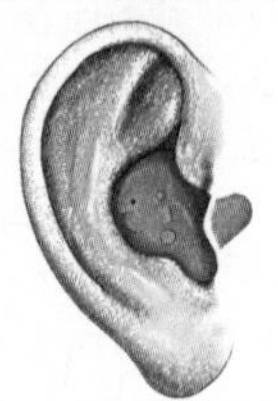

Typical cost: $1,200 to $2,500 per ear.

• **In-the-canal (ITC) hearing aids fit farther into the ear canal than ITE aids.** This style is best for mild-to-moderate hearing loss. It is hardly visible and is easy to use with the telephone. The small size makes adjustments, including battery changes and volume control, difficult for some people. The device may not fit well in smaller ears.

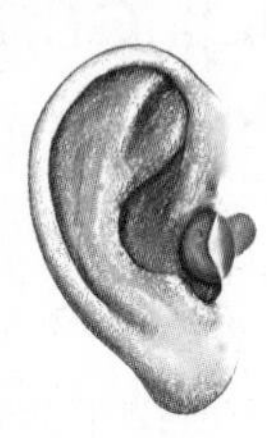

Typical cost: $1,300 to $2,500 per ear.

• **Completely-in-the-canal hearing aids are custom-molded and best for mild-to-moderate hearing loss.** This is the least noticeable type of hearing aid and the least likely to pick up background noises such as wind. It also works well with telephones. But the small batteries require frequent replacement.

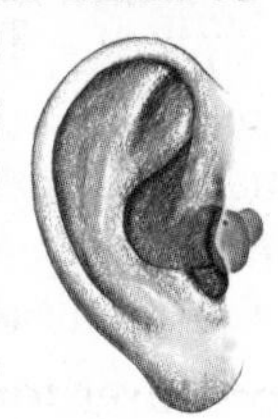

Typical cost: $1,300 to $3,000 per ear.

Main hearing aid manufacturers: Oticon, Phonak, Starkey, ReSound, Widex and Siemens.

Important: There are many over-the-counter devices that simply amplify sound. However, hearing aids are usually preferable because they are customized for an individual's specific degree and type of hearing loss, allowing them to be programmed for optimal hearing improvement.

If you are having difficulty hearing: See an audiologist. You can find one at the American Academy of Audiology consumer website at *www.howsyourhearing.org.* An audiologist can help you select the best hearing aid for you and explain how to properly use and maintain it. If the audiologist suspects that you may have an undetected medical condition that is causing your hearing loss, you will be referred to a physician.

WHAT ABOUT COST?

Some people don't get hearing aids because of their high cost—about $500 to $3,000 per ear.

New research finding: People who have insurance plans that cover the entire cost of hearing aids purchased them seven years earlier, on average, than those who had partial or no insurance, according to a study conducted at Henry Ford Hospital in Detroit.

But only about one-third of health insurance policies cover the cost of hearing aids. Medicare does not. Health insurance from the Veterans Administration does cover the cost, and the Lions Club has a program that provides hearing aids to people who can't afford them.

You can use a health savings account or flexible spending account to pay for hearing aids with pretax funds, or you can deduct the cost on your tax return (check with your tax preparer for details).

Illustrations: Courtesy of NIH Medical Arts.

Natural Way to Beat Ringing in the Ears

Kathleen Yaremchuk, MD, chair, department of otolaryngology/head and neck surgery, senior staff, division of sleep medicine, Henry Ford Hospital, Detroit.

You're trying to fall asleep, but that annoying ringing in your ears just won't quit. You toss and turn, but you just can't nod off—and the distracting noise is starting to drive you nuts.

How can any of the 50 million people who are coping with this problem (which is technically called tinnitus) get their ZZZs through all that racket?

In an unfortunate twist, a new study found that getting poor sleep might actually make tinnitus symptoms even worse.

The good news is that there are tricks that you can use to fall asleep faster when you have tinnitus—and snoozing more at night may lessen your symptoms.

SLEEPLESS WOES

Scientists from Henry Ford Hospital in Detroit found that tinnitus patients with insomnia (defined as poor sleep quality stemming from difficulty falling and/or staying asleep) were more likely to rate their tinnitus symptoms worse, compared with tinnitus patients who did not have insomnia.

What the study suggests, according to lead researcher Kathleen Yaremchuk, MD, the hospital's chair of otolaryngology/head and neck surgery, is that if you suffer from tinnitus and insomnia and you find a way to get more sleep, then your tinnitus symptoms are likely to become less severe. But how do you get your ZZZs when you have tinnitus?

SNOOZE-WORTHY TACTICS

Dr. Yaremchuk suggested several proven methods that help tinnitus sufferers achieve sweet slumber...

1. Put on a fan or white noise machine while you're trying to fall asleep. Adding background noise can help mask the ringing, buzzing or rushing in your ears. Or fall asleep to soft music.

2. Avoid taking the occasional aspirin, which can make tinnitus symptoms worse, and lay off caffeine (a stimulant that can keep you awake).

3. Ask your doctor whether one of your regular medications might be worsening your tinnitus. More than 200 prescription and nonprescription drugs, including some antibiotics and antidepressants, can make tinnitus worse. If tinnitus is one of your drug's side effects, then consider switching drugs or using a natural treatment instead.

4. Talk to your doctor about taking a sleep aid, such as melatonin or a prescription medication that will treat the insomnia and lessen the effects of tinnitus.

5. Try cognitive behavioral therapy for the treatment of insomnia.

6. Learn hypnotherapy or other relaxation exercises from a website, DVD or trained counselor.

7. Consider trying Arches Tinnitus Formula (available at *www.tinnitusformula.com* or 800-486-1237; $35 for a 100-capsule bottle, a 25-day supply), a supplement incorporating gingko biloba, zinc and garlic. Dr. Yaremchuk recommends it to many of her patients. Some research indicates that this product may ease tinnitus symptoms. Before taking this supplement, check with your doctor to make sure that it's right for you.

Urgent: How Good Is Your Sense of Smell?

Jayant Pinto, MD, associate professor of otolaryngology–head and neck surgery in the department of surgery at The University of Chicago Medicine, where he specializes in sinus and nasal diseases and olfactory dysfunction. He is the lead author of "Olfactory Dysfunction Predicts 5-Year Mortality in Older Adults," a study published in the online journal *PLOS ONE.*

Can you smell the rose that's under your nose? What about the odor of burning toast? Or the foul smell of spoiled food?

Just as it's common to have fading vision or diminished hearing as you age, many people lose at least some of their ability to smell. In fact, about 25% of adults over the age of 53 have a reduced sense of smell, and the percentage rises to more than 60% in those age 80 and older.

AN EARLY ALERT

You're probably well aware that a decreased sense of smell can affect appetite. People who can't smell and/or taste their food tend to eat less and may suffer from weight loss or nutritional deficiencies. *But you might not know that a diminished sense of smell could also be an early indicator of a serious health problem…*

Surprising finding: In a recent study, people ranging from ages 57 to 85 who lost their ability to smell were more than three times more likely to die within five years than those with a normal sense of smell—the risk of dying was even higher than for individuals diagnosed with lung disease, heart failure or cancer.

This study didn't uncover the exact link between smelling loss and earlier-than-expected deaths. But the risk for neurodegenerative diseases could be a factor. For example, people who eventually develop Parkinson's or Alzheimer's disease may notice a diminished sense of smell long before they have neurological symptoms.

It's also possible that cellular senescence, the age-related reduction in cell regeneration, affects the olfactory bulb or other parts of the olfactory system before it becomes apparent in other parts of the body.

TEST YOURSELF

Even if you think your sense of smell is fine, some basic testing might show otherwise. In the study mentioned earlier, some individuals who thought they had a good sense of smell actually didn't, while some people who thought they had a problem with their sense of smell actually did well on the smell tests.

How to test yourself…

• **The alcohol test.** Hold an alcohol-swab packet near your belly button and open it up.

If your sense of smell is perfect, you will detect the odor. If you can't smell it, raise it higher until you can. Some people won't detect the odor until it's just a few inches from the nose—or not even then. You can do the same test with anything that's strongly scented. The closer the item needs to be for you to smell it, the worse your sense of smell is.

• **Compare yourself to others.** Suspect that you have a problem if you're the only one in the family who doesn't notice the wonderful smell of brownies in the oven. Or if you say "Huh?" when your spouse mentions that the fireplace is smoking or that there's a nasty smell in the refrigerator.

If you think you have a diminished sense of smell: Get evaluated by an otolaryngologist or a neurologist. He/she can determine if your impairment is due to aging or a more serious problem that may have a better outcome if it is detected early.

WHAT YOU CAN DO

So far, a reduced sense of smell can't be restored.* *What can help...*

• **Practice smelling.** German scientists report that it may be possible to improve your sense of smell by smelling more. Spend a few minutes every day sniffing a variety of scents—spices, perfumes, aromatic foods, etc. This approach hasn't been proven, but it could be helpful for some people.

• **Eat a well-balanced diet and take a multivitamin,** which will provide the necessary micronutrients that help slow aging of the olfactory system and promote regeneration.

If you have appetite loss due to a reduced sense of smell...

• **Kick up the seasoning.** Food will not be very appealing if you can't smell or taste it. To make your dishes as flavorful and aromatic as possible, use plenty of strong spices, such as pepper, garlic, cilantro, ginger, etc., in your cooking.

• **Focus on preparation and presentation.** Chefs have a saying: "The eyes eat first." Use brightly colored fruits and vegetables and other colorful ingredients, and add garnishes to your plate. Also, vary the textures of the foods you eat.

**Exception*: If your loss of smell is due to nasal inflammation—from allergies, chronic sinusitis, etc.—intranasal steroid sprays and antihistamines may restore it.

Keep Your Nose Happy

Murray Grossan, MD, an otolaryngologist and head and neck surgeon with the Tower Ear, Nose and Throat Clinic at Cedars-Sinai Medical Center in Los Angeles. He is the author of *Free Yourself from Sinus and Allergy Problems—Permanently.*

If you suffer from hay fever (allergic rhinitis), you may dread the arrival of spring. As billions of pollen spores are released into the air, it's likely that your nose will start running or become stuffy, your eyes will itch, you won't be able to stop coughing and your head will ache.

At least 30% of people who suffer from hay fever go on to develop a related condition known as sinusitis (inflammation of the sinus cavities, usually due to a bacterial or viral infection). But airborne allergens aren't the only culprit.

If you're exposed to air pollution, smoke or dry or cold air, or even if you have a common cold, you also are at increased risk for sinusitis. In all of these instances, the mucous glands secrete more mucus to dilute the offending material. Unless the cilia (tiny hairs on the cells of the mucous membrane) move the mucus out, this creates an ideal breeding ground for infection.

When you have coldlike symptoms that last for at least 12 consecutive weeks, you are likely to have chronic sinusitis, the most commonly diagnosed chronic illness in the US. Most of the 37 million Americans who suffer from sinusitis each year turn to decongestants, antihistamines and antibiotics.

What most sinusitis sufferers don't know: You will have the best chance of preventing sinus problems in the first place if you take care of the cilia. *My secrets to improving the health of your cilia...*

CILIA: THE MISSING LINK

The cilia play a crucial—though under-recognized—role in keeping the respiratory tract healthy. These tiny hairs wave rhythmically to carry tiny airborne particles and bacteria out of the nasal passages. When allergy symptoms persist for many days or even weeks, however, the cilia become overworked and quit moving.

Cilia also can be damaged if you regularly take antihistamines or breathe dry air—both of which decrease the liquid component of mucus that traps bacteria and is needed for good cilia movement. When the cilia no longer do their job, bacteria multiply, setting the stage for infection.

To test the health of your cilia: Many ear, nose and throat specialists (otolaryngologists) use the so-called saccharin test. With this test, the doctor places a particle of saccharin in your nose and times how long it takes you to taste it.

Normally, the patient tastes the saccharin in five to eight minutes. If the cilia are damaged, however, it may take 25 minutes or longer for the patient to taste it. If the damage is severe, special treatment, such as breathing exercises, may be required.

KEEP YOUR CILIA HEALTHY

When allergy or cold symptoms persist or when nasal discharge becomes colored (usually yellow or green)—a symptom of sinusitis—there are some surprisingly simple steps you can take to ensure the health of your cilia. *Favorite methods...*

- **Drink hot tea with lemon and honey.** Compounds found in black and green tea help block the body's allergic response to pollen by inhibiting the production of histamine, the substance that causes nasal stuffiness and dripping due to a cold or hay fever.

Drinking five cups of hot tea a day helps the body mount its natural defenses against infection, scientific studies have shown. The moist heat stimulates the cilia, while lemon and honey thin mucus, allowing for better cilia movement.

- **Sing "oooommmmm" in a low tone.** You might feel a little silly at first, but singing the "oooommmmm" sound, which was used by the ancient yogis as a form of meditation, causes a vibration of air that stimulates the cilia. Make this sound often throughout the day. As an alternative, buy a toy kazoo and hum into it for 10 minutes daily.

- **Use pulsatile irrigation.** This highly effective strategy involves rapidly but gently rinsing your nose with a stream of saltwater (saline solution) that pulses at a rate matching the normal pulse rate of healthy cilia—hence the name pulsatile irrigation.

Clinical trials involving thousands of patients have shown that pulsatile irrigation increases blood flow to the nasal passages and helps restore function to damaged cilia.

Several pulsatile irrigation devices are available from websites specializing in allergy or medical products, such as National Allergy (*www.natlallergy.com*, 800-522-1448) or Health Solutions Medical Products (*www.pharmacy-solutions.com*, 800-305-4095). The typical cost is around $80 to $140. For best results, use this form of irrigation twice daily, as needed.

Stop a Nosebleed Now

To stop a nosebleed, sit upright, lean forward and pinch the soft part of your nose with your thumb and forefinger for five to 15 minutes.

To prevent recurrent nosebleeds: Humidify your living space...lubricate your nose with saline spray or a thin film of petroleum jelly. Also, talk to your doctor—the blood vessel causing nosebleeds may need to be cauterized.

Caution: If a nosebleed doesn't stop after 30 minutes, go to the hospital. A doctor may have to insert packing material into the nostril or surgery may be needed.

Mayo Clinic Health Letter, 200 First St. SW, Rochester, Minnesota 55905, *HealthLetter.MayoClinic.com.*

Is Your Nose Getting Bigger?

With age, your nose can thicken, getting wider and bulkier as nasal pores plug with oil that solidifies. To prevent this, cleanse oily skin on the nose twice daily. Cleansing facials also help.

Also: Fatty tissue under the skin of the nose thins with age and can no longer support the nose's heavy tip. The tip then starts to droop, moving closer to the upper lip and possibly blocking breathing at night. If you experience this, use one-half-inch-wide medical tape to hold the tip up while you sleep. Start the tape between the nostrils, then gently lift the tip by pulling the tape up along the main nasal bridge, stopping between the eyes.

Murray Grossan, MD, Los Angeles–based otolaryngologist in private practice and author of *Free Yourself from Sinus and Allergy Problems Permanently. GrossanInstitute.com*

What's Up with Nosebleeds and Menopause?

After menopause, lower hormone levels can cause tissues in the nose to become drier, which can trigger bleeding.

Dry indoor air also can irritate and dry out the nasal tissues. A dab of a water-soluble gel, such as Breathe-ease XL Nasal Moisturizer Gel, twice a day will help heal nasal passages and keep them from getting dry.

In some instances, nosebleeds can be a sign that the nasal membranes have become too thin, which can happen when taking nonsteroidal anti-inflammatory drugs and other anticoagulant medications and/or blood-thinning supplements such as ginkgo biloba.

Murray Grossan, MD, Los Angeles–based otolaryngologist in private practice and author of *Free Yourself from Sinus and Allergy Problems Permanently. GrossanInstitute.com*

Help for a Bad Nose Job

If you get a nose job that leaves you with a bump, microdroplets of liquid silicone can be injected into low areas to plump them up and disguise the bump. Most patients require three or four short treatments at six-week intervals.

Advantages over a second surgery: No anesthesia...no swelling or bruising...less downtime...and it is significantly less expensive—a nose job can cost from $7,000 to $12,000. The full round of silicone treatments typically costs about $2,000 to $4,000. Silicone filler is permanent, unlike such temporary fillers as Juvederm and Restylane.

Note: Silicone has gotten a bad reputation because of breast implant risks, but this product and technique are different—and safe.

Robert Kotler, MD, rhinoplastic surgeon in Beverly Hills, California, clinical instructor at the David Geffen School of Medicine, University of California-Los Angeles, and author of *The Essential Cosmetic Surgery Companion* and *Secrets of a Beverly Hills Cosmetic Surgeon. RobertKotlermd.com*

What to Do with Nose Whistles

Sometimes it seems like your nose will not stop whistling.

What it means: You have a too-narrow nasal opening. This usually is due to congestion from allergies and colds.

Simply blowing your nose may eliminate the whistle. If this doesn't help, try using an over-the-counter saline nasal spray (such as Ocean) twice a day as directed on the label. This nasal moisturizer offers natural, nonmedicating dryness relief, shrinking nasal membranes and thus opening up the "whistling" passage. Nasal decongestant sprays that contain *oxymetazoline* (such as Afrin) work, but use them only for a day or two—they can cause increased, "rebound" congestion if you use them regularly for more than three days.

Richard O'Brien, MD, associate professor of the clinical sciences at The Commonwealth Medical College, Scranton, Pennsylvania. He is an emergency physician and a spokesperson for the American College of Emergency Physicians (*ACEP.org*).

The Longevity Secret That Most Doctors Forget to Talk About

Victor Zeines, DDS, a holistic dentist with practices in New York City and Woodstock, New York. He is a founder of the Institute for Nutritional Dentistry in Woodstock, New York, and author of *Healthy Mouth, Healthy Body: The Natural Dental Program for Total Wellness. NatDent.com*

Would you believe that you can add years to your life just by taking care of your mouth? Many people can. That's because the disease processes that lead to heart problems, stroke and even lung disease often first present themselves in the gums, teeth and tongue.

What few people realize: To avoid gum disease and tooth decay, you need to do more than brush your teeth and floss. These practices may keep your mouth clean, but they do not address one of the underlying causes of oral health problems—nutritional deficiencies.

Good news: Easy, natural treatments, as well as a type of laser therapy that is becoming more popular, can treat severe gum disease and help ward off medical conditions that may shorten your life. These treatments can help not only people who want to prevent gum disease but also those who already have it.

DEFEATING GUM DISEASE

Why is poor oral health so dangerous? Harmful bacteria from the mouth enter the bloodstream via blood vessels in the mouth and then travel throughout the body, wreaking havoc. Infected gums quadruple your heart attack risk and triple your stroke risk.

Frighteningly, about 75% of adults have some form of gum disease, including gingivitis, which occurs when a bacteria-laden film accumulates on and irritates the gums at the base of the teeth.

The more advanced form, periodontitis, occurs when infection and/or inflammation of gum tissues is accompanied by tissue destruction. Warning signs include persistent bad breath, gums that bleed while brushing and/or tender or receding gums. Here are several natural treatments that can help...

- **Coenzyme Q10 (CoQ10).** Found naturally in the body, though not always at a high enough level, CoQ10 is linked to reduced risk for heart disease. However, CoQ10 also strengthens gum tissue and promotes faster tissue repair and healing. It is available as a supplement.

Typical dose for oral health: 200 mg daily. If you take a blood-thinning drug, such as *warfarin* (Coumadin), consult a doctor before taking CoQ10—it can reduce the drug's blood-thinning effect.

- **Calcium.** This mineral helps rebuild bone, which can be destroyed by gum disease. Strive for 1,000 mg daily if you are age 19 to 50 and 1,200 mg daily if you are age 51 or older by eating calcium-rich foods, such as green leafy vegetables and canned sardines with their bones, and/or taking a calcium supplement. To enhance calcium absorption, look for a formula with vitamin D.

- **Goldenseal, myrrh and calendula.** These herbs work together to inhibit bacteria, stimulate immunity and reduce inflammation. Combine equal amounts of each herb in tincture form. After brushing your teeth, rinse your mouth with one teaspoon of the liquid and spit it out. Store the mixture in a brown bottle in a dark place.

- **Massage your gums.** To increase blood supply and bring more oxygen and nutrients to the area (as well as infection-fighting white blood cells), gently rub your gums a few times a day with clean fingers.

- **Laser therapy.** Lasers are used in dentistry to treat gum disease. This type of therapy targets the infected area to get rid of bacteria. Since gum disease can promote bone loss, the lasers also can stimulate the body to regrow bone. Laser treatment, which often is accompanied by nutritional therapy, can last for six months to a year, depending on severity. Check with your insurer to see if laser therapy is covered.

BATTLING TOOTH DECAY

Cavities are a consequence of acid and bacteria eroding the enamel or outer coating of the tooth. This creates openings and holes that can penetrate to the inner layers of the tooth and eventually kill the nerves. Cavities aren't just the result of poor brushing skills, but rather a signal that the body is overwhelmed by acid-producing bacteria (often from excess sweets, dairy and most fats).

Important: Many people are allergic to dairy, which, when consumed, can weaken their immune system and produce even more acid-producing bacteria. *Best remedies to prevent tooth decay...*

- **Natural toothpastes that contain herbs are just as effective as mainstream toothpastes at cleaning the teeth but are more gentle.** In fact, most mainstream toothpastes have a warning on the label telling users to seek medical attention if more than a pea-sized amount is swallowed.

Remember: The main purpose of using toothpaste is to keep your teeth and mouth clean.

Natural toothpastes to try: Nature's Gate, Homeodent and Vicco. In addition to regular flossing, brush after every meal. If you're at a restaurant and can't brush, simply rinse your mouth with water after eating.

- **Alfalfa, dandelion and horsetail.** These herbs have minerals that are absorbed by the teeth, making them stronger and more decay resistant.

To help strengthen enamel: Open 200-mg capsules of each herb and mix the contents with water, making a sludgy paste. Place a small amount of the paste at the gumline and rub it around your teeth. Repeat after brushing, twice daily. You can make a few days' supply and refrigerate.

All natural remedies in this article are available at health-food stores. Always talk with your doctor before using any herbs or supplements. For more advice on natural remedies for oral health, contact the International Academy of Biological Dentistry and Medicine (281-651-1745, *www.iabdm.org*) to find a holistic dentist near you.

A Toothache Can Turn Deadly

Samuel O. Dorn, DDS, chair of the department of endodontics and program director at The University of Texas Health Science Center at Houston, where he holds the Frank B. Trice, DDS, Professorship in Endodontics.

It's hard to imagine how a toothache could turn deadly—but it can. Even mild or moderate discomfort (for example, pain while chewing...sensitivity to hot and cold...and/or redness and swelling of the gums) can quickly turn into a potentially serious condition, known as an abscess, a pus-filled infection inside the tooth or between a tooth and the gum. Though the pain may be merely annoying in the beginning, within a day or so, it can turn into the intense, throbbing pain or sharp, shooting pain that is the telltale sign of an abscess.

Dangerous trend: The number of Americans hospitalized for dental abscesses is on the rise. Over a recent eight-year period, hospitalizations for periapical abscesses (infections at the tip of the tooth root) increased by more than 40%.

No one has a precise explanation for the trend, but some experts speculate that the high cost of dental insurance is preventing many people from seeking routine dental care and perhaps delaying treatment when a problem occurs. Medicare does not cover routine dental care, and many private health insurance plans offer very limited coverage.

WHAT GOES WRONG

If there's a breach in a tooth's protective enamel—from tooth decay, a chip or even gum disease, for example—you're at risk for an abscess. Some cracks can be taken care of with bonding or a crown (see below). Some don't need treatment at all because they don't go through to the tooth pulp (the soft tissue inside the tooth). But if bacteria get inside the tooth, an abscess can form.

Other signs to watch for: In addition to the symptoms described earlier, other red flags of a dental abscess may include persistent foul breath, a swollen face, jaw and/or neck glands and a fever.

Once the pain kicks in, people who have dental abscesses will often describe it as the worst they've ever experienced. If you've ever had a root canal (see below), you might have had an abscess.

- **Get help immediately.** An abscess will not go away on its own. Worse, the infection can spread as quickly as overnight (in some cases, however, it can take years to spread). An abscess can cause death when the infection spreads to the brain or heart or when swelling cuts off the airway.

When to be especially suspicious: If you have pain in one of your back teeth. They're the ones that do most of the chewing, and they're also the ones that are harder to reach with dental floss and a toothbrush. If you crunch something hard, such as a popcorn kernel, piece of ice or even an almond, a back tooth is the one most likely to be cracked.

GETTING PROMPT TREATMENT

Your dentist can diagnose an abscess in just a few minutes. All he/she has to do is gently tap on the suspected tooth with a small metal device and see if you wince. A tooth abscess will be very sensitive to pressure. An X-ray will confirm if there's a pus-filled pocket near the tooth root.

You might be given penicillin or another antibiotic if the infection has spread beyond the tooth. *In addition, your dentist will treat the abscess in one of three ways…*

- **Incision and draining.** If the abscess is between the tooth and the gum, your dentist will make a small incision, drain out the pus and clean the area with saline. The pain will start to diminish almost immediately. Your dentist also can drain an abscess that occurs inside a tooth, but this won't cure it—the infection will probably come back.

- **Root canal.** This is the most widely used treatment for an abscess near the tooth root. Your dentist will drill into the infected area, scrape away damaged tissue and drain the pus. After that, the canal will be filled with sealant, and the tooth will be crowned (a porcelain or metal cap is put over the tooth).

If you get a root canal, there's a good chance that the tooth will survive. The drawback is cost. Root canals usually are done by an endodontist (a dentist with advanced training). Expect to pay from $300 (for a front tooth) to $2,000 for a molar. The crown is an additional $500 to $3,000 (prices depend on where you live and whether you go to a specialist or your regular dentist).

- **Extraction.** This is the most permanent treatment for a deep abscess. It costs about $75 to $300 to remove a tooth—and once the tooth is gone, the abscess goes away with it.

Some patients save money by choosing not to replace an extracted tooth. But there are health risks associated with not replacing a tooth, such as increased chance of additional decay and infection, bone loss, poor chewing function and speech disturbances.

Better: Replace the tooth with an implant (at least $2,400) or a bridge (at least $1,100).

If you can't see a dentist immediately: Consider going to an ER if you have severe pain and/or swelling. If you are having trouble breathing, go to an ER right away.

PREVENTING AN ABSCESS

If you take care of your teeth, there's a good chance that you'll never have an abscess.

In addition to regular brushing and flossing and avoiding a lot of sugar-filled foods and drinks…

- **Use fluoride toothpaste.** It remineralizes tooth enamel and makes it stronger. This is particularly important for older adults, whose receding gums can expose parts of the tooth and leave it vulnerable to decay.

Also helpful: A fluoride mouth rinse. There are many brands in drugstores. They strengthen the enamel and reduce tooth decay.

• **Don't slack off on dental visits.** Most people should have dental checkups and cleanings every six months. If you smoke or have gum disease, diabetes or any other condition that increases your risk for dental problems, it's usually a good idea to schedule even more frequent dental visits.

How to Get Yourself to Floss Daily

Victor Zeines, DDS, a holistic dentist with practices in New York City and Woodstock, New York. He is a founder of The Institute for Holistic Dentistry and the author of several books, including *Healthy Mouth, Healthy Body: The Natural Dental Program for Total Wellness*. *NatDent.com*

Just can't get in the habit of flossing every day? You know it's good for your gums and teeth and can help prevent bad breath, but consider this: Scientists recently discovered bacteria linked to gum disease in the brains of Alzheimer's patients...and research shows that people with gum disease are more likely to get heart disease and diabetes. *If this doesn't have you reaching for the dental floss right now, here are some other tricks to get you on track...*

• **Get gross.** The following advice may seem extreme, but it works—tape a photo showing the ravages of periodontal disease (search for one online) in a prominent place in your bathroom. After your first month of daily flossing, replace it with an image of a healthy white smile as positive reinforcement.

• **Try different flosses**—one type isn't more effective than another. The point is to find a floss that you're comfortable with so that you'll be more likely to use it regularly. In general, there are two types—multifilament (nylon) and single filament (plastic/rubber). Multifilament floss has been around for a long time and is cheaper. It comes unwaxed or waxed. Single filament uses newer technology—it doesn't rip, tear or fray and glides very easily between the teeth even though it isn't waxed. These products are available in a wide variety of flavors. Try a bunch!

• **Floss while doing something else**—while in the shower, watching TV or reading the newspaper.

• **Master your technique.** I recommend flossing after eating and when you brush. It really doesn't matter if you floss before or after brushing, as long as you do a thorough job.

To floss correctly: Bring the string down gently along the side of one tooth, then back up. Do the same on the adjacent tooth, and work your way around the entire mouth. If you have restorative work, like crowns, pull the floss out sideways instead.

You Can Get Relief for Hard-to-Treat TMD

Noshir R. Mehta, DMD, a professor and chair of the department of general dentistry, and director of the Craniofacial Pain Center at Tufts University School of Dental Medicine in Boston. He is the chief editor of *Head, Face and Neck Pain Science, Evaluation and Management: An Interdisciplinary Approach*.

Some dentists are quick to recommend surgery for people who suffer from the often painful conditions known as temporomandibular disorders (TMD).

But that's a mistake. Surgery should be the last resort for the vast majority of patients who suffer from these disorders, which affect the jaw joint and/or facial muscles that allow us to chew, speak and swallow.

Good news: Roughly 95% of the 10 million Americans who have TMD can get relief without surgery—if they use the right treatments. *What you need to know...*

RED FLAGS TO WATCH FOR

Contrary to popular belief, people with TMD do not always suffer jaw pain. In fact, these disorders often go undiagnosed because they can cause symptoms in other areas of the body, including in the neck, head, face or ears.

When jaw pain does occur, it's usually related to the temporomandibular joint (TMJ)—there's one on each side of the head, and it acts as a hinge connecting the lower jaw to the skull. These joints are almost constantly in motion—when we chew, yawn, speak or tighten or relax our facial muscles.

This constant movement means that even slight misalignments of the jaw (the bite) or other problems can produce painful inflammation that can persist for years or even indefinitely without treatment.

Many TMD patients—with or without jaw pain—first complain to their doctors about headaches, earaches or sinus pain. About 75% of my TMD patients also have neck pain. Most people with TMD eventually experience pain in the jaw. *Common TMD symptoms...*

• **Headaches, particularly tensionlike pain on the sides or the back of the head.** Headaches in the morning indicate that the TMD might be related to bruxism, nighttime tooth-grinding, gnashing or clenching. Headaches during or after meals indicate a problem with bite alignment.

• **Aching facial pain or face fatigue, especially after meals.** This can be due to an uneven bite or teeth making premature contact, which stresses the jaw and causes fatigue.

• **Ear pain and stuffiness** (meaning the ears feel clogged) are common symptoms because the same nerves that carry signals to the chewing muscles also connect to muscles in the middle ear. People who clench their teeth often report ear discomfort as well as jaw pain.

• **Clicking or popping sound in the jaw, with or without pain.** Clicking means that something within the joint is binding (so that the cartilage is slipping back and forth).

DIAGNOSIS AND TREATMENT

Most cases of TMD can be diagnosed by a dentist who takes the patient's medical history, followed by a hands-on evaluation of the movement of the joints and/or jaw muscles, listening for clicking, popping or grating, looking for limited jaw motion and examining the bite. *Main causes...*

• **Disk displacement.** Each temporomandibular joint has a ball-and-socket that is held together with a shock-absorbing disk. When this disk slips out of place, the cushioning between the joints is gone, causing clicking.

Two possible treatments...

• Disk manipulation. During this in-office procedure, the dentist will inject a local anesthetic, then manipulate the jaw to push the disk back into the normal position. This can eliminate pain and/or unlock the jaw, but it's a temporary solution because the disk will still have a tendency to move out of position.

• Bite plate appliances, such as bite guards or mouth guards, are usually custom-made for each patient and fit over the teeth and keep the jaw stable. This prevents the disk from slipping. Most patients will need to wear the plate continuously for the first few days. This allows inflammation and muscle tightness to subside. After that, they need to wear the guard only while sleeping to prevent tooth grinding, a common cause of displacement.

Important: A custom-made dental guard from your dentist, which typically costs $250 to $1,000, is more durable than an over-the-counter mouth guard.

• **Bruxism** is a common cause of TMD because the jaw is in continuous—and forceful—motion when a person grinds his/her teeth during sleep. Most patients with this condition have only minor, occasional pain, but it can cause long-term damage to the teeth and, secondarily, the gums unless it's treated.

Stress management is critical because stress can exacerbate the grinding or trigger it. Relaxation techniques such as massage therapy and biofeedback can be helpful. These patients should also wear a dental guard at night.

• **Teeth alignment.** Patients with missing teeth, or changes in how the upper and lower teeth come together, will often experience neck pain and other symptoms of TMD.

Self-test: When you bring your teeth together, the bite should close without any shifting of the jaw. If your lower teeth slide against the upper teeth to achieve a "normal" bite, there's a misalignment that may be causing excessive pressure.

A dentist can evaluate your bite height and tooth positions and make the necessary adjustments—by removing tooth material in some places, for example, or by adding height with a crown.

Herbal Relief for Painful Mouth Sores

Eric Yarnell, ND, is an associate professor in the department of botanical medicine at Bastyr University in Kenmore, Washington, and a private practitioner at Medella Optimal Health in Seattle. He is the author or coauthor of 10 books on natural medicine, including *Nature's Cures: What You Should Know. MedellaOptimalHealth.com*

The inside of your mouth hurts like crazy, so you stand in front of a mirror and open wide. Do you see white, lacy, raised patches…red, swollen, tender spots…and/or open sores? If so, you may have oral lichen planus (LIE-kun PLAY-nus), an inflammatory disease that affects more women than men and often arises in middle age. Lesions usually appear on the inside of the cheeks but also may develop on the tongue, gums, inner lips and throat. The disorder causes burning pain…a metallic taste in the mouth…sensitivity to spicy foods…dry mouth…and/or bleeding gums.

Oral lichen planus is not contagious. It occurs when the immune system attacks the cells of the mucous membranes in the mouth. The exact reason for this attack is unknown, but outbreaks can be triggered by allergies (for instance, to a food or dental product)…a viral infection (such as hepatitis C)…certain vaccines and medications (including nonsteroidal anti-inflammatory drugs)…or stress.

When outbreaks are linked to an allergy or drug, identifying and avoiding the offending substance can resolve the problem. However, in many cases, oral lichen planus is a chronic condition in which flare-ups continue to come and go indefinitely, with lesions lasting for days, weeks or even months. Since there is no known cure, treatment focuses on alleviating discomfort and promoting the healing of lesions.

Problem: Steroid medication helps but has potentially serious side effects. Topical steroids can lead to thrush (a fungal infection of the mouth) and suppress adrenal gland function, while oral and injected steroids increase the risk for osteoporosis, diabetes, high blood pressure and high cholesterol. And once steroid treatment is halted, lesions may return.

Intriguing alternative: Herbs. Eric Yarnell, ND, an associate professor in the department of botanical medicine at Bastyr University, explained that while the herbs below have not been proven to cure oral lichen planus, they can ease discomfort…and some patients who use herbal treatments experience quick resolution of symptoms and remain free of recurrences for long periods of time, Dr. Yarnell said.

Important: Certain herbs can have side effects, so work with a health-care provider knowledgeable about herbal medicines, such as a naturopathic doctor, who can devise a safe and effective protocol for you and determine appropriate dosages. Dr. Yarnell generally prescribes a swish-and-swallow approach (taking a mouthful of a diluted herbal extract and swishing it in the mouth before swallowing it) so the herb acts topically as well as systemically—your own practitioner can advise you on this. Typically, Dr. Yarnell has his oral lichen planus patients use one or more of the following herbs, depending on the specific symptom (or symptoms) that bothers them most. *Ask your health-care provider about using the following…*

- **For pain—aloe vera** (*Aloe barbadensis*). The gel found inside the leaves of the aloe plant contain complex carbohydrates, including glucomannan, that soothe painful tissues and modulate the immune response.
- **For inflammation—turmeric** (*Curcuma longa*). This spice contains substances called curcuminoids that reduce inflammation via multiple pathways. It doesn't dissolve well in water, so Dr. Yarnell has patients dissolve turmeric in soy milk, nut milk or animal milk.

Caution: People who are prone to kidney stones should not use turmeric (which is high in oxalic acid)—for them, curcumin extract is better.

• **For easily irritated tissues—tormentil** (*Potentilla tormentilla*). Used in the form of a tincture (a medicinal extract in a solution of alcohol), this herbal preparation coats lesions, protecting them from irritation by food or compounds in saliva, Dr. Yarnell said. This remedy should not be used within 30 minutes of taking any other medications, as the herb may block absorption of other drugs.

Caution: People who want to avoid alcohol should not use tormentil tincture.

• **For stress—licorice root** (*Glycyrrhiza glabra*) or deglycyrrhizinated licorice (DGL). This is an adaptogen that helps patients handle the anxiety and stress that can contribute to oral lichen planus...it also modulates the immune system. It often is used in tincture form, though patients who want to avoid alcohol should use chewable DGL tablets instead.

Caution: Licorice root remedies should not be used by patients who have uncontrolled hypertension or who are taking corticosteroids or other drugs that can deplete potassium, Dr. Yarnell said.

Note: Oral lichen planus may increase the risk for oral cancers, so it is important for patients to get regular oral cancer screenings from a doctor or dentist.

9

Falls and Aging Bones

Catch Your Balance Problem Before It's Too Late

No one expects to get seriously injured—or even die—from a fall. But it happens all the time. And while older adults are at greatest risk for falls, there are no age requirements for taking a tumble.

Surprising statistic: Even among adults in their 30s, 40s and 50s, falls are the leading cause of nonfatal injuries (more than 3 million each year) that are treated in US hospital emergency departments. For adults age 65 and older, falls are the leading cause of fatal injuries.

Certain "fall hazards" are well known—electrical cords and area rugs...slippery floors... medications such as sleeping pills and blood pressure drugs...vision problems...and even poorly fitting shoes.

What often gets overlooked: Subtle changes in the neuromuscular system (the nervous system and muscles working together), which helps keep us upright. Regardless of your age, exercising and strengthening this system before you get unsteady (or fall) is one of the best steps you can take to protect your health. *Here's how...*

WHY OUR BALANCE SLIPS

Does your foot or ankle feel a little wobbly when you stand on one leg? Some of that is probably due to diminished strength and flexibility. After about age 40, we begin to lose roughly 1% of our muscle mass every year (see page 294). As we age, we also become more sedentary and less flexible. These factors make the body less able to adapt to and correct a loss of balance.

Jason Jackson, MSPT, a physical therapist in the outpatient rehabilitation department at Mount Sinai Hospital in New York City, where he specializes in balance training, along with prosthetic training, manual therapy and neuromuscular disease.

The nervous system also gets less sensitive with age.

Example: Sensory receptors known as proprioceptors are found in the nerve endings of muscles, tendons, joints and the inner ear. These receptors make us aware of our bodies in space (proprioception) and can detect even the slightest variations in body positions and movements. But they don't work well in people who don't exercise them (see suggestions on next page)—and these people find it harder to keep their balance.

The other danger: Muscle weakness, even when it's slight, can lead to apprehension about losing your balance. You might then start to avoid physical activities that you feel are risky—walking on uneven pavement, for example. But avoiding such challenges to your balance actually accelerates both muscle and nervous system declines.

ARE YOU STEADY?

If you're afraid of falling or have a history of falls, a professional balance assessment, done by your doctor or a physical therapist, is the best way to find out how steady you are on your feet. *The assessment usually includes tests such as the following (don't try these tests on your own if you feel unsteady)...*

- **Sit-to-stand.** Sit in a straight-backed chair. If your balance and leg strength are good, you'll be able to stand up without pushing off with your hands.
- **Stand with your feet touching.** You should be able to hold this position for 15 seconds without any wobbling.
- **The nudge test.** Ask someone to gently push on your hip while you're in a normal stance. If you stagger or throw out your hands to catch yourself, your balance is questionable. If you start to fall, your balance needs improvement.

BOOST YOUR BALANCE

Balance, like strength and endurance, can be improved with simple workouts. Incorporate the exercises below into your daily routine—while at the grocery store, in the office, while watching TV, etc. Do them for about 15 minutes to 30 minutes a day, three to four days a week (daily if you have the time). What to do...*

- **One-legged stands.** You don't have to set aside time to do this exercise. You simply stand on one leg as you go about your daily activities—while waiting in line, for example. Lift your foot about six inches to 12 inches off the floor to the front, side and back. Try to hold each position for about 15 seconds, then switch legs. This strengthens the muscles in the ankles, hips and knees—all of which play a key role in one's balance.
- **Heel raises.** This move is good for balance and strength. While standing, rise up on your toes as far as you can. Drop back to the starting position, then do it again. Try for 10 repetitions. You can make this exercise more difficult by holding weights. Start with three-pound weights, gradually increasing weight as you build tolerance.

FOR MORE BENEFITS

Once you have become comfortable with the exercises described earlier, you can up your game with the following to keep you even safer from falling...

- **Balance on a Bosu ball.** It's a rubberlike half-ball (about two feet in diameter) that you can use for dozens of at-home workouts, including balance and abdominal exercises.

Cost: About $100, on *www.amazon.com* and in some sporting-goods stores.

Example: With the flat side on the floor, start by standing with both feet on the ball. Your muscles and joints will make hundreds of small adjustments to keep you balanced. When you get better at it, try to stand on one leg on the ball. When you're really comfortable, have someone toss you a basketball or tennis ball while you maintain your balance.

JUST FOR FUN

You don't always need formal balance exercises. *Try this...*

- **Walk barefoot.** Most of us spend our days in well-padded shoes that minimize the "feed-

*Do these exercises next to a stable object, such as a countertop, if you feel unsteady. Also, they are more easily done while wearing shoes. When you feel comfortable doing these moves, you can perform them barefoot to add difficulty.

back" between our feet and the ground. Walking without shoes for at least a few minutes each day strengthens the intrinsic muscles in the feet and improves stability. If you prefer to wear socks, be sure to use nonslip varieties that have treads to avoid slipping on wood or tiled floors.

Also helpful: Minimalist walking/running shoes. They're made by most major footwear companies, such as New Balance, Adidas and Nike, as well as by Vivobarefoot. Because they have a minimal amount of heel cushioning and arch support, they give the same benefits as barefoot walking but with a little extra protection.

More Exercises for Better Balance...

Juan Carlos Santana, MEd, CSCS, director and CEO of the Institute of Human Performance in Boca Raton, Florida. *IHPfit.com*

Every day is a balancing act...how true, especially as we age, since losing balance is often what causes dangerous falls. The simplest motions, such as walking, standing, reaching and lifting, require balance skills that many of us take for granted until we are challenged by injury, illness or simply the aches and pains of aging. Surprisingly, even those who exercise regularly may have muscle development that is out of balance. Exercise specialists recommend balance training, along with aerobic exercise and strength training, as an integral part of a regular fitness routine at every age.

Balance training teaches you how to stabilize your body by engaging your muscles and joints. Even those who exercise regularly can still have muscles that are "out of balance" and unable to support you from all angles. Balance exercises are easy to incorporate into your life, no matter what your age. I've taught these exercises to my mother. She always eats her lunch standing at her kitchen counter. About a year ago, I taught her to do balance exercises while she eats her lunch. Now, in between bites, she holds on to the kitchen counter and does single-leg balance exercises and mini pumps.

USE IT OR LOSE IT

Balance exercise is important for everyone at every level of fitness, including elite athletes, patients recovering from illness, and, of course, seniors. As with all forms of exercise, how much you need depends on your fitness level. For people in good shape, daily life likely provides a lot of balance movement. Those who are less fit need to do more. In other words—use it or lose it.

In order to be effective, each balance repetition should be done in a slow and fluid motion, at a rate of about four to five seconds per repetition. Begin by holding onto something or use your arms in the exercises for security and added balance—but eventually try to perform balance exercises without support. Fix your eyes on a point straight ahead (e.g., a painting or light switch on a wall). Maintain good posture, keep your core tight and bend knees slightly while doing the exercises. When you can successfully perform them in a slow and controlled fashion, start to speed up the movement. This will help develop a quick reaction when you need to move fast to maintain balance, for instance when you start to slip on a wet floor.

WHAT TO DO

Here are some exercises: Begin with both feet on the floor, hip-width apart and do five squats, trying to get a little lower each time. Once you master the squats, which may take about a week, progress to balancing on a single leg. To progressively master the single-leg balance, gradually go from being assisted (holding onto something) to unassisted (letting go and balancing on your own). After mastering the single-leg balance, progress to single-leg pumps (i.e., mini squats on a single leg, with upper body upright). Start with five repetitions of each exercise and work up to 20 repetitions. This type of balance training can eventually be performed every day. Cut back on the frequency if you feel pain or see swelling. *Here are* *some additional suggestions and variations for balance training...*

• **Stand upright on one leg for 15 to 30 seconds** (most people find this is a challenge). Now do it on the other leg.

• **Stand upright on the ball of one foot for 15 to 30 seconds,** then the other.

• **Stand upright on your right leg while slowly "writing" your initials on the ground with the left foot in front,** to the left and behind you. Do not put any weight on the left foot while you are moving it over the surface of the ground. Now switch legs and do this with your right foot.

• **This next exercise can be performed on any 12- to 14-inch grid,** such as floor tiles, or you can draw the grid on a sidewalk or driveway with chalk, as you used to do with hopscotch. Stand with your right foot on the line where four tiles intersect under your arch. It does not matter which direction you face. Now, touch the center of each of the four tiles that meet under your right foot with the first toe of your left foot. Take four to five seconds to move from target to target to ensure you are moving slowly and maintaining control of your body. Feel free to bend your right knee and rotate your hips as necessary to accomplish the task. Do this clockwise and counterclockwise, with each foot, until you reach the point where you don't need to plant your moving foot for balance—then proceed to the next level.

• **Set yourself up the same way and then try to touch the outside corners of the same tiles you've just touched at the center.** When you succeed at this, try touching the center of each of the tiles surrounding the previous four tiles. For those of you who still need to be challenged further, try touching the outside corners of those tiles.

BALANCED WORKOUT SCHEDULE

Try to practice balancing about five to 10 minutes per day, three to five days per week. You can use this type of exercise as a prelude or conclusion to recreational activities such as golf or tennis. This light protocol also makes a great warm-up for walking or running. After mastering this simple progression, you will be ready to partake in even more difficult balancing exercises.

Equipment like rockerboards, foam rollers, balance disks and large stability balls can add challenges and interest by providing an unstable environment on which to practice balance. But, don't experiment with these devices when you're home alone...and also, make sure you have ample space so you won't hit your head in the event you take a tumble. When using apparatus, always start supported, by holding onto a wall or a rail with your hands. Then let go with one hand before trying no hands—keep in mind that these balance toys are not as easy to use as they may seem.

As with any exercise, begin balance training slowly and carefully to avoid injury. It's risky to go too fast, too soon. If you don't know how to do an exercise, ask a fitness professional. For more information, visit the Institute of Human Performance website at *www.ihpfit.com.*

• **Balance training is a lifelong exercise.** Once you're good at balance, it's yours for life, and you need only a minimal amount of balance training every day to maintain it.

The Secret Thief of Good Health

Michael J. Grossman, MD, a specialist in antiaging and regenerative medicine. He is medical director of BodyLogicMD of Irvine, California, which focuses on bioidentical hormones, nutritional support and stress reduction. He is author of *The Vitality Connection: Ten Practical Ways to Optimize Health and Reverse the Aging Process.*

You probably know all about osteoporosis, the gradual, age-related loss of bone.

What you may not know: There also is an age-related loss of muscle mass, strength and function—a condition called sarcopenia. And it is a problem for all of us as we age.

Sarcopenia generally starts at age 40. By the time you're 50, you're losing 1% to 2% of your muscle mass every year. And as you lose muscle, you lose strength.

Example: Starting in your 40s, leg strength typically drops by 10% to 15% per decade until you're 70, after which it declines by 25% to 40% per decade.

But you don't have to become physically debilitated to suffer the devastating effects of muscle loss. When you have less muscle, you have more fat—and fat cells produce inflammatory compounds that drive many deadly chronic diseases, such as heart disease and cancer.

The good news: Starting today, there are many actions you can take to slow, stop and even reverse sarcopenia...

WHAT YOU NEED TO KNOW

When sarcopenia is at its worst—what some experts call pathological sarcopenia—you become weak, walk slowly, fall easily, are less likely to recover from an illness and are more likely to die from any cause. That degree of sarcopenia afflicts 14% of people ages 65 to 75 and 45% of those 85 and older.

Sarcopenia is linked to a 77% increased risk for cardiovascular disease. It's also linked to higher death rates in breast cancer survivors and older people with lymphoma.

With less muscle, you burn less glucose (blood sugar), so it becomes harder to prevent, control or reverse type 2 diabetes, a disease of chronically high blood sugar that can plague your life with complications such as vision loss, nerve pain and kidney failure. Diabetes also doubles your risk for heart attack, stroke and Alzheimer's disease.

Studies also link sarcopenia to triple the risk for osteoporosis, a fourfold increase in postoperative infections and severe menopausal symptoms.

NUTRITION

The right diet and supplements can fight muscle loss...

- **Eat protein-rich food daily.** Increasing the amount of protein in your diet not only can help stop the breakdown of muscle, but it also helps build new muscle.

Scientific evidence: In a three-year study, published in *The American Journal of Clinical Nutrition*, older people who ate the most protein lost 40% less muscle compared with people who ate the least.

My advice: Every day, eat at least four ounces of protein-rich food, such as lean beef, fish, chicken or turkey. A four-ounce serving is about the size of a deck of cards.

Helpful: Whey protein, from milk, is rich in branched-chain amino acids. These three amino acids (leucine, isoleucine and valine) comprise 35% of muscle protein and are uniquely effective in building muscle. Look for a protein powder derived from whey protein, and use at least one scoop daily in a smoothie or shake. You also can get some of these amino acids by eating Greek yogurt, nuts, seeds, cheese and hard-boiled eggs.

- **Take vitamin D.** Vitamin D is widely known to stop bone loss, but it also stops muscle loss.

Scientific evidence: A study published in *Journal of Internal Medicine* linked low blood levels of vitamin D to a fourfold increase in the risk for frailty, a problem of old age that includes pathological sarcopenia.

Vitamin D works to protect muscle by decreasing chronic, low-grade inflammation, which contributes to the breakdown and loss of muscle protein.

Unfortunately, an estimated nine out of 10 Americans have suboptimal blood levels of vitamin D, below 30 nanograms per milliliter (ng/ml). A simple blood test can reveal your vitamin D level. Research shows that people with a blood level of 55 ng/ml or higher of vitamin D have 50% less heart disease and cancer than people with a blood level of 20 ng/ml or below. It also reduces the risk of falling by 19%.

My advice: I recommend the same 55 ng/ml level to control muscle loss. To achieve that level, most people need to take a daily vitamin D supplement that supplies 3,000 international units (IU) to 5,000 IU.

- **Take fish oil.** Like vitamin D, fish oil works to protect muscle by reducing the chronic inflammation that damages muscle cells.

Scientific evidence: In a study in *The American Journal of Clinical Nutrition*, women who participated in strength-training and also took fish oil had much stronger muscles after three months than women who did only strength-training.

My advice: To protect and build muscle, I recommend a supplement containing 1,000 milligrams (mg) of omega-3 fatty acids, with 400 mg of EPA and 300 mg of DHA. Take it twice daily.

- **Consider creatine.** Creatine is an amino acid–like compound found mostly in red meat, pork and fish, such as salmon, tuna and herring. More than 70 clinical studies show that regularly taking a creatine supplement can help build muscle and increase strength.

However: The nutrient works to build muscle only if you are exercising—without that regular challenge to the muscles, supplemental creatine has no effect.

My advice: If you're exercising regularly, take three grams of creatine daily.

EXERCISE

Regular exercise is one of the best ways to stop or reverse muscle loss. You need both aerobic exercise and resistance exercise (which stresses the muscles, causing them to get stronger). *My advice...*

- **For aerobics, use your lower and upper body.** Walking is a good exercise, but it builds only lower-body strength. Also include aerobic exercise that uses the lower and upper body, such as tennis, ballroom dancing or working out on an elliptical machine. Try to participate in 30 to 60 minutes of aerobic exercise five or more days a week.

- **For resistance training, work all your muscles.** I recommend resistance exercise three times a week, concentrating on the different muscle groups at each session—chest and triceps...back and biceps...and legs and shoulders. If you don't like weight-lifting, try another form of resistance exercise, such as resistance bands.

HORMONES

As you age, you lose bone, muscle—and hormones. And many of those hormones, particularly testosterone, are crucial for building muscle in both men and women. (Women manufacture testosterone in the ovaries and adrenal glands.) Estrogen and dehydroepiandrosterone (DHEA) also play a role in creating and maintaining muscle.

My advice: Find a doctor trained in anti-aging medicine and bioidentical hormone replacement therapy (BHRT), which uses compounds that are identical to the hormones that your body manufactures rather than synthetics. Ask the doctor to test your hormone levels and determine if BHRT is right for you.

Is Your Head Where It Should Be?

Steven Weiniger, DC, member, postgraduate faculty, Logan University, Chesterfield, Missouri, and managing partner, *BodyZone.com*, a national online health information resource and referral directory for posture-exercise professionals. He is author of *Stand Taller, Live Longer: An Anti-Aging Strategy*.

Are you part of the poor-posture epidemic? It's estimated that two out of every three American adults now have forward head posture (FHP), an increasingly common condition in which the head juts out past the shoulders, placing excessive stress on the neck and back.

FHP can be caused by such simple things as texting, driving or even the type of glasses you wear, but it can trigger a surprisingly wide variety of troubling health conditions—from neck, back and shoulder pain...to headaches, digestive issues, breathing difficulties and even arthritis.

Good news: FHP can often be corrected with simple exercises and lifestyle changes.

WHAT CAUSES FHP

A main culprit of FHP is frequent computer use—people tend to lean forward in an effort to see their computer screens. Texting is another common cause, as most people hunch over their smartphones.

Other triggers include: Bucket seats in cars—they encourage an unnatural bend in the body...reading or watching TV while on an exercise machine at the gym—straining to see the page or screen forces the head out of alignment...bifocals—these glasses force you to tilt your head backward and stick your chin out in order to see through the lower portion of the lenses...carrying a heavy backpack—the load causes your head to protrude forward... and the natural process of aging—as the neck muscles weaken, the head drifts forward.

Startling fact: Every inch that your head moves forward past your spine adds 10 pounds of pressure to the neck and back, which often leads to muscle and joint pain and headaches. A forward-hanging head also compresses the rib cage, compromising the lungs' ability to expand by as much as 30% and slowing down digestion. What's more, over time, FHP can cause the spine to stiffen, limiting range of motion and contributing to osteoarthritis.

Recent study: When more than 800 adults over age 65 were followed for about five years, those who began leaning forward at an earlier age were 3.5 times more likely to require assistance bathing, dressing, eating and getting in and out of chairs than those who started leaning forward later.

EASY TO SELF-DIAGNOSE

A simple photo is often all you need to determine whether you have FHP. Put on some gym clothes and stand as you normally would in a straight but not stiff position. Then have a spouse or friend snap a full-length photo of you from the side. Look at the photo—the middle of your ear should be lined up with your shoulder, hipbone and ankle. If your head is forward, the alignment of your body is off. Save the photo as a baseline, and have a photo taken monthly to monitor your progress once you begin using the strategies below.

HOW TO HELP YOURSELF

- **Become more aware of your head position.** Lying down on the floor, flat on your back, take a moment to notice where your gaze naturally falls—if you have FHP, you will likely be looking slightly back and away from your feet (those who have healthy posture will be looking straight up at the ceiling).

To recognize the proper head position: While still lying on your back, gently lift your head just off the floor and tuck in your chin to give yourself a slight double chin. Then, keeping your chin tucked, put your head back down. If you're looking straight up at the ceiling, your head is now in the proper "level-head" position.

Take five slow breaths here, then relax on the floor for two to three minutes to let your head align with your torso and pelvis. Do this two to three times a day to help retrain your body. If you have discomfort in your low back, put a small pillow under your knees.

- **Perform chin tucks every day.** Initially, do these exercises on the floor. Lying down in the level-head position, take a deep breath in...while exhaling, press your chin into a tuck. Release and repeat for five cycles, two to three times a day.

If the stretch in the back of your neck feels too intense or you can't keep your head level, try propping your head up on an inch-thick book wrapped in a thin towel. (Use a book you don't want, since you're going to be removing pages.) After doing this exercise a few times a day for three or four days, remove about an eighth of the pages. Repeat for a few more days and remove another small section of pages, continuing this cycle until the book is empty and your head is flat on the ground.

As chin tucks become easier, you don't have to do them lying down and can do them regularly throughout the day—at your computer or even walking down the street.

- **Make other changes to your daily routine.** The average American logs about 11 hours of screen time per day—including time spent on computers, using smartphones and watching TV. At work and at home, make sure your computer screen is at eye level. If you use a laptop, use a laptop stand and purchase a separate keyboard. When using a smartphone for texting or e-mail, try to hold it at eye level. When wearing bifocals for reading, adjust the glasses on your nose rather than changing your head position. These strategies will help keep your ears in line with your shoulders and may even help prevent wrinkles caused by squinting.

And before driving, be sure the seat is not tilted excessively backward—this forces you to hold your head at an angle that contributes to FHP.

• **Use a cervical pillow for sleeping.** Cervical pillows improve spinal alignment by cradling the head and supporting the neck, usually with an indentation or cutout in the middle of the pillow. You may need to try several pillows before finding the one that's most comfortable for you. I like the cervical pillows by Therapeutica (*www.therapeuticainc.com*) and Tempur-Pedic (*www.tempurpedic.com*) and the Chiroflow Water Pillow (*www.chiroflow.com*).

If after two to four weeks of trying these strategies you're still experiencing health problems related to FHP, be sure to see a chiropractor or physical therapist.

Is the Way You Walk Giving You a Warning?

Mary Harward, MD, a geriatrician in private practice in Orange, California. She specializes in the diagnosis and treatment of gait disorders and other diseases affecting older adults. She is editor of *Medical Secrets.*

Have you surprised yourself recently with a stumble or a fall? If you blamed it on your shoes...your eyesight...or an obstacle, such as a throw rug, you may not be getting at the root cause of why you stumbled or fell. The fact is, the real reason many people fall (and sometimes die from it) is the way that they walk.

A problem that goes undetected: Most people who have treatable abnormalities in their gait (the way in which a person walks) never even discuss it with their doctors.

Here's why: When you go to the doctor, odds are that you are taken to an exam room and asked to "have a seat" until the doctor arrives. The problem is, you'll probably stay seated during the entire visit, and your doctor may miss a symptom—a dangerous gait—that's just as important as abnormal X-rays or blood tests.

TAKE IT SERIOUSLY

It's never normal to shuffle, be off-balance or have an unusual posture. A gait disorder always means that something—or, in most cases, a combination of factors—is awry.

Problems with gait affect about 15% of adults age 60 and older and more than 80% of those age 85 and older. Gait disorders, which interfere with stability and balance, are not only among the most common causes of falls and subsequent hospitalizations, but also can be one of the first health problems that eventually leads to nursing home care.

My advice: Doctors should ask every patient if he/she has fallen in the last year. In addition, if you're age 65 or older, you should ask your doctor to check your gait at least once a year.

WHAT'S BEHIND IT?

Patients often assume that problems with one's gait are due to neurological disorders, such as Parkinson's disease or multiple sclerosis (MS). With Parkinson's disease, patients also experience a resting tremor or shaking of one hand, muscle rigidity and slow movements, while MS typically is accompanied by vision problems, dizziness and trouble speaking. *But there are other possible causes of gait problems...*

• **Arthritis.** Gait problems are common in patients with arthritis, particularly osteoarthritis of the knee or hip. If you have knee or hip pain, you may favor that side and use other muscles to compensate. This throws off your posture and body mechanics, which may cause you to limp or take tentative steps.

Helpful: Ask your doctor if it's appropriate to see a physical therapist for advice on exercises to strengthen the muscles around the arthritic joint—this will help you walk normally and with less pain.

Pain control is also very important. Apart from making you more comfortable, it will help you do the exercises that you need for a better gait. If you don't get adequate relief from over-the-counter pain relievers, talk to your doctor about stronger forms of pain control. Stretching, massage, heating pads, cold packs and/or acupuncture are helpful to some people.

• **Back problems.** A gait problem often is due to a painful back. Patients with lumbar stenosis, for example, will frequently experience nerve pressure from damaged vertebrae in the spine, affecting their ability to walk. Patients with sciatica (nerve pain that often accompanies lower-back problems) will have difficulty walking or standing. Suspect nerve problems if you have back or leg pain that gets worse when you walk or stand for more than a few minutes and gets better when you're off your feet. See your doctor for treatment advice.

• **Balance disorders.** If you sometimes feel as though you're about to fall (even when you're not), see a doctor right away. Problems with balance—often accompanied by dizziness, spinning sensations, etc.—are a major cause of falls. Potential causes include ear infections, inner-ear disorders, neuropathy (nerve damage) and circulatory problems.

Also: Ask your doctor to test your vitamin B-12 level. Older adults often have low levels of intrinsic factor, a protein that's needed for B-12 absorption. It's also common for vegetarians to be deficient in this vitamin because meat is a major source of B-12. Low B-12 can make you feel light-headed, cause numbness and/or tingling in the feet and make it difficult to walk.

Similar foot and leg symptoms are caused by diabetic neuropathy, nerve damage that may occur in patients with poorly managed (or undiagnosed) diabetes. Bunions and other foot conditions also can contribute to gait disorders.

• **Drug side effects.** It's not surprising that sedating medications such as *diazepam* (Valium) can increase fall risk. What many people don't realize is that nonsedating medications also can be an issue.

Example: Medications that lower blood pressure, such as diuretics, can cause orthostatic hypotension, a sudden drop in blood pressure that can make you dizzy or lightheaded. Some blood pressure drugs also decrease magnesium, which can cause leg weakness or cramps. Your doctor might advise changing medications. Alcohol or drugs that lower blood sugar or affect mood or sleep also can change one's gait.

Important: Be especially careful after eating. Studies have shown that dizziness and gait problems tend to get worse about 30 minutes after meals—blood travels to the digestive tract after meals, sometimes lowering blood pressure.

• **Reduced brain circulation.** Gait disorders are often the first sign of infarcts, areas of brain damage caused by impaired circulation. Infarcts occur in patients who have had a stroke or other problems that affect blood vessels in the brain, such as hypertension or high cholesterol.

A patient who has multiple infarcts might walk very slowly...take short steps...stand with his feet wider apart than usual...and/or hesitate when starting to walk or have trouble slowing momentum when stopping.

HOW'S YOUR GAIT?

If you've noticed changes in the ways in which you move, see your doctor for an evaluation. *He/she will give you tests that may include...*

• **The timed get-up-and-go test.** This measures the time it takes you to get up from a chair (without using your hands to push off from the armrests), walk 10 feet, turn around and walk back to the chair. You should be able to complete the sequence safely in 14 seconds or less. If it takes longer than 20 seconds, your gait is seriously impaired.

Prevent Falls...Take Care of Your Feet!

Hylton Menz, PhD, deputy director of the Musculoskeletal Research Center at La Trobe University in Victoria, Australia. He is the author of the textbook *Foot Problems in Older People: Assessment and Management* and a coauthor of *Falls in Older People: Risk Factors and Strategies for Prevention.*

Each year, about one in every three people over age 65 suffers a fall, a mishap that is far more dangerous than most people realize.

Important new research: In a 20-year study of nearly 5,600 women ages 70 and older, breaking a hip doubled the risk for death in the following year. Men who suffer a broken hip after a fall are also at increased risk for an untimely death.

Most people know the standard recommendations to reduce their risk for falls—get medical attention for balance and vision problems…improve the lighting in and around their homes…and eliminate loose carpets, cords and other obstacles.

What often gets overlooked: Painful feet…foot deformities such as bunions…weak foot and ankle muscles…and improper footwear also can significantly increase one's risk for falls.

Recent scientific evidence: In a 2011 study in the *British Medical Journal*, a comprehensive program of foot care reduced falls by one-third among a group of older people with assorted foot problems.

GET A FIRM FOUNDATION

With age, the muscles that support our ankles and feet often become weak—a common problem that contributes to foot pain and reduced activity levels. Structural abnormalities in the feet, such as bunions and hammertoes, undermine stability. And conditions that blunt sensations in the feet, such as nerve damage commonly caused by diabetes, may impair the ability of one's feet to react quickly and adjust to potentially hazardous conditions.

BASIC FALL-PREVENTION WORKOUT

Stretching and strengthening exercises can reduce foot pain—and lower your risk for falls. Basic exercises to perform daily…

To increase your ankles' range of motion: Sit in a chair with one knee extended. Rotate your foot in a clockwise, then counterclockwise direction. Repeat 10 times with each foot, in each direction.

To strengthen your toe muscles: Place small stones or marbles on the floor in front of you. While seated, pick up the stones with your bare toes and place them in a box, one by one. Pick up 20 stones with each foot, then repeat.

To stretch your calf muscles: Stand about two feet from a wall, then lean into it with one leg slightly bent at the knee about three inches in front of the other. Then reverse the position of your feet and lean forward to stretch the muscles of the other calf. Hold the stretch for 20 seconds, three times for each leg.

PROPER FOOTWEAR

The right shoes are essential for everyone, but especially those with problem feet.

Most women know to avoid high heels, which make it more difficult to maintain balance. But many people opt for flimsy slip-on footwear, such as flip-flops, which may be comfortable but often become loose or come off the foot altogether, creating a balance hazard. It's far better to wear shoes that fasten to your feet with laces, Velcro or buckled straps.

Surprising fact: Most people assume that thick, cushiony soles, such as those found on most sneakers, help prevent falls because they tend to provide good support for your feet. But thinner, harder soles, such as those on some walking shoes, are safer because thin-soled shoes allow your feet to feel the sensations that help you maintain balance. A trade-off between comfort and safety may be necessary—you may have to wear less cushiony shoes that optimize balance.

Also, be sure that your shoes are the right size. Your feet may slide around in shoes that are too loose, while tight footwear won't allow your toes to respond to variations in the ground to help maintain stability while walking.

Remember: Shoe size often changes with age, as feet swell and spread. So have your feet measured every time you buy shoes.

Slightly more falls occur indoors than outdoors, and the proportion increases with age. Therefore, even when you're at home, proper footwear is crucial.

Important recent finding: When researchers at Harvard's Institute for Aging Research followed a group of older adults for more than two years, they found that more than half of those who fell indoors were barefoot, in their stocking feet or wearing slippers. These injuries tended to be more serious than those of people who were wearing shoes when they fell.

Best to wear at home: Sturdy, thin-soled shoes that have more structural integrity than the average slipper.

DO YOU NEED ORTHOTICS?

Many adults over age 65 could benefit from wearing orthotics—inserts that fit inside the shoe—to help prevent falls by providing additional support.

Properly made orthotics may improve the way your feet move as you walk, distribute your weight more broadly to reduce pressure on sensitive spots and help convey sensory information to your feet, all of which may lessen the risk for falls.

If you have structural foot problems due to diabetes or rheumatoid arthritis, you may need customized orthotics from a podiatrist.

Typical cost: About $400. Insurance coverage varies.

Over-the-counter versions (made with firm material, not just a soft cushion) may work as well if your feet are relatively normal and your foot pain is fairly mild. Good brands include Vasyli and Langer. Usually, you will be able to transfer orthotics between shoes.

Most people find that full-length orthotics are less likely to slip inside the shoe than the half-length variety. Full-length orthotics also may feel more comfortable, especially if you have corns or calluses under the toes or on the ball of your foot.

GETTING HELP

If you have foot problems, seek care from a podiatrist or other health professional—and be sure to mention any concerns about falling. Also ask for exercises, in addition to the ones described here, to address your specific foot issues.

10 Low-Cost Ways to Make Your Home Easier and Safer to Live In

Tom Kraeutler, a former professional home inspector and contractor in New York City. He is host of *The Money Pit*, a nationally syndicated radio show on home improvement broadcast to more than three million listeners. He is also the home improvement editor for AOL. *MoneyPit.com*

Remodeling a house to make it safer and more user-friendly can run to tens of thousands of dollars. *But I've found clever ways to improve and update your home without spending much...*

THROUGHOUT THE HOME

- **Replace round doorknobs,** which are difficult to grasp and turn, with lever-style handles that you push down to open. Most of the time, the lever handles can be attached to the existing latch mechanism already on the door. You can do the job yourself with just a screwdriver. Also, consider replacing cabinet door and drawer knobs with easy-to-grasp C- or D-shaped handles.

Cost: About $25/lever and $5/handle. Available at home-improvement centers.

- **Switch to rocker light switches.** They are on/off switches that rock back and forth when pressed. They are larger and easier to operate, and many people find them more attractive than the standard, small flip switches used in most homes. Rocker switches let you turn on a light with your elbow or fist if you're entering a room when your hands are full, and they're easier to find in the dark.

Cost: About $3 per light switch. Available at home-improvement centers.

- **Raise the position of some electrical outlets.** Wall outlets that are close to the floor can be hard to reach and inconvenient for plugging in appliances that you use intermittently, such as vacuums, heating pads and chargers for phones and laptops. Use those low outlets for lamps and other devices that you rarely unplug. Hire an electrician to raise other outlets at least 27 inches off the floor. They'll still be inconspicuous but much more accessible.

Cost: Typically $250 and up to move half a dozen outlets.

• **Use remote controls for more than TVs.** They can operate window coverings, such as drapes and blinds, so you avoid stretching and straining, and let you control interior and exterior lights from your car or from within the home to prevent you from tripping in the dark.

My favorite: INSTEON at SmartHome.com (800-762-7846, *www.smarthome.com*).

Cost: The AuroRa entry system starts at around $800 and provides wireless house-lighting control for up to five dimmers that can be operated from the car or the bedside. Online retailers, such as Home Depot and Amazon, offer it at a significant discount.

• **Create "wider" doorways.** Residential building codes and home builders don't consider the needs of older people who may need more than the standard 32-inch doorway, especially if they use a wheelchair or walker. Actually widening a doorway can be expensive and impractical, especially if it's along a weight-bearing wall.

Instead: Replace your standard door hinges with expandable "offset" hinges. These special hinges allow the door to close normally. But upon opening, they swing the door clear of the door frame by an extra two inches. This lets you use the entire width of the doorway when you enter or exit.

Cost: About $20 for a set of two door hinges. Available at home-improvement stores. A handy person can install these hinges because they fit in the existing holes in your door frame. Otherwise, a carpenter will charge about $100/hour.

• **Add a second handrail to staircases.** It's easier and safer to climb and descend when you can use both hands. Adding an extra handrail is an inexpensive and easy way to increase safety. Make sure both handrails are at the same height and between 30 and 34 inches above the front edge of the step. Also, for maximum safety, handrails should extend about six inches beyond the top and bottom steps if possible.

Cost: About $85 to $250 for each new handrail plus carpenter installation. Available at home-improvement stores.

KITCHEN

• **Lower your microwave.** Many home builders, contractors and home owners like to save space by mounting microwave ovens above the stove or high on a wall. This position is hazardous because it requires you to reach above your head to get hot foods or forces you to balance on a stool.

Better: If your existing microwave is on the wall, build a shelf under it where you can rest hot foods after they finish cooking. Or choose a new model with a tray feature that slides out and is easier to reach.

Example: The Sharp Insight Pro Microwave Drawer Oven installs just beneath your countertop. The entire oven slides open, drawer-style, giving you access to the cooking compartment from above.

Cost: About $650 to $850 for the microwave and $150 and up for carpenter installation.

• **Install a pullout kitchen faucet.** Lugging heavy pots of water to the stove can be difficult and even dangerous. Many plumbing manufacturers now offer kitchen faucets featuring high-arc, pullout spouts. You can remove the spout and use it as a sprayer hose to fill pots within three to five feet of the stove.

Cost: About $150 plus plumber installation. Available at home-improvement stores.

• **Install a pull-down shelving system inside your kitchen wall cabinets.** Top shelves in cabinets are difficult to reach. This simple device rests in your upper cabinet until you grab a handle on the shelf frame. A set of three or four shelves swings out of the cabinet and down toward you. The shelves lock in place so you can get the item you need. Afterward, the whole unit swings back into place.

My favorite: Rev-A-Shelf's chrome pull-down shelving system for 24- and 36-inch cabinets. You can do the installation yourself.

Cost: About $300 (800-626-1126, *www.rev-a-shelf.com*).

BATHROOM

Add upscale grab bars near toilets and tubs. Some people have avoided installing grab bars in their bathrooms because they look too institutional. Now, there are much more attractive versions. Brushed nickel or oil-rubbed bronze grab bars by Moen are designed to match other Moen bath accessories and faucets for a coordinated look. The grab bars meet all federal government guidelines. They have a stainless steel core and are 1¼ inches in diameter, making them easy to hold.

Cost: About $25 to $70 for the bar. Available at home-improvement stores. You can install them yourself, but it requires drilling holes in the wall.

How to Fall Down Without Getting Hurt: Tricks from an Oscar-Winning Stuntman

Hal Needham, who appeared as a stuntman in more than 4,000 television episodes and more than 300 feature films. He is author of *Stuntman! My Car-Crashing, Plane-Jumping, Bone-Breaking, Death-Defying Hollywood Life.*

When we fall, our natural instinct is to reach out for the ground with our hands. Unfortunately, that only increases our odds of injury—our hands, wrists and arms are full of small bones that are easily broken. *Instead, when you realize you are falling...*

1. Buckle your knees. This can in essence lower the height that your upper body falls by as much as a foot or two, significantly reducing the impact when you hit the ground. In a forward fall, it might result in bruised knees, but that's better than a broken bone in the upper body.

Helpful: In a backward fall, tuck your head into your chest as you buckle your knees—try to turn yourself into a ball.

2. Throw one arm across your chest whether you're falling forward or backward. Do this with enough force that it turns your body to one side. It doesn't matter which arm you use.

3. Rotate the rest of your body in the direction that you threw your arm, increasing your spin. If you can rotate enough, you can come down mainly on your backside, a well-padded part of the body unlikely to experience a serious injury.

Trouble is, while stuntmen know exactly when and where they're going to fall, real-world falls usually take people by surprise. It can be difficult to overcome instinct and put this falling strategy into action in the split second before hitting the ground.

Practice can help. If you have access to a thick gym mat and you don't have health issues that make it risky, try out this falling technique until it feels natural.

Can Yoga Cure the Fear of Falling?

Arlene A. Schmid, PhD, occupational therapist registered (OTR), Roudebush Veterans Administration Medical Center and assistant professor of occupational therapy, School of Health and Rehabilitation Sciences, Indiana University-Purdue University, Indianapolis.

There's a well-known TV commercial in which an elderly woman who is lying on the floor in her home calls out, "I've fallen and I can't get up!" That old spot from 1987 has been quoted jokingly and parodied umpteen times—but it isn't funny at all. In fact, it touches a universal chord of real fear—especially if you know that falls are the leading cause of death by injury in those over age 65.

Falling is certainly a gigantic fear for people who have suffered a stroke as well as for their families—an estimated 80% of stroke patients suffer impaired balance.

There's a "new" approach that is being tried to keep people with stroke steady on their feet...and that is the ancient practice of yoga.

This doesn't mean the pretzel-positions that traditional yogis can twist themselves into, but rather yoga postures greatly modified to meet the needs of people with stroke. Arlene A. Schmid, PhD, a registered occupational therapist and a rehabilitation research scientist at the Richard L. Roudebush VA Medical Center in Indianapolis, was the head of the project. Her study participants, all of whom were veterans, included 19 men and one woman with an average age of 66. She said that the special yoga poses provided significant improvement in study participants' ability to maintain balance—and also in their confidence. After eight weeks of instruction, the participants demonstrated impressive physical progress and came to embrace the practice of yoga—many also told Dr. Schmid that they did not want the sessions to end.

A GRADUAL APPROACH

Dr. Schmid explained that the group met twice a week, starting their yoga practice while sitting in chairs where they would feel safe and comfortable. Initially they learned the very simplest aspects of yoga, such as breathing properly while sitting still. Next they learned simple poses that emphasized improving strength and range of motion in the ankles and hips, the better to protect themselves from falls. Eight weeks in, the vets had progressed from doing eight poses in chairs to performing 15 to 20 poses while sitting in chairs, standing at the wall and lying on the floor. The fact that the participants became willing to do floor work was especially impressive, says Dr. Schmid. Many older adults—even those who have never had a stroke—find being on the floor frightening, as their limitations make it all the more difficult to get back up. (Sessions included practice in getting back up and assistance as needed.)

WALKING TALL

To evaluate the main goal of the study—to improve one's balance, as well as one's confidence in the ability to maintain balance and avoid falling—Dr. Schmid used the Berg Balance Scale. This is a tool that rehab professionals often use to determine an individual's risk of falling. If you have a score under 46, you are considered to be at risk. Although the study participants had been through standard rehab after their strokes, when they started the yoga, their average Berg Balance score was a dismaying 40. Just eight weeks and 16 yoga sessions later, they had increased their scores to an impressive 47, on average—this meant that as a group, they were now into the low risk for falling category. They also improved their balance confidence by 17%. Equally important, says Dr. Schmid, the vets made great strides in their walking capacity, or endurance, showing significant improvement in distance walked during a six-minute walk test. At the start of the study, participants walked an average of 898 feet in six minutes. At eight weeks, they improved to an average of 985 feet in six minutes.

THERAPEUTIC YOGA FOR US

At this time, this type of therapeutic yoga is not widely available, says Dr. Schmid. However, there is certainly an encouraging trend toward its development as yoga teachers and occupational and physical therapists are more frequently cross training in each other's area of expertise. The Rocky Mountain Stroke Center, for instance, continues to offer a "Yoga for Stroke" class (*www.strokecolorado.org*, 303-730-8800).

If you are interested in exploring therapeutic yoga for disability such as from a stroke or injury, ask around your community to find a yoga therapist or see if modified yoga is being offered at a local hospital, yoga studio or in physical rehab programs. At the very least, Dr. Schmid says, the DVDs with seated yoga postures that are on the market might be good for you. By all means, though, discuss any yoga offerings you are considering with your doctor before you start any sort of program. You'll want to be sure your choice is appropriate for your current needs.

Treat Osteoporosis to Stop Accidents

People with osteoporosis are more likely to fall and have a greater risk for fractures when they do. People with the bone-thinning disorder osteoporosis are three times more likely to have vertigo—characterized by a feeling of spinning, whirling and/or dizziness—than people with normal bone density. This increases the chance of falls. Vertigo is common in older women, which could mean that changes in calcium metabolism after menopause lead to dizziness and osteoporosis. In men, age-related bone thinning may be linked to vertigo.

Self-defense: Ask your doctor how to build bone strength and reduce falls.

Ji Soo Kim, MD, PhD, department of neurology, Seoul National University College of Medicine, Seoul, South Korea, and leader of a study of 411 people, published in *Neurology.*

Drug-Free Bone Builders

Ray Hinish, PharmD, CN, a certified nutritionist and author of *The Osteoporosis Diet: The Natural Approach to Osteoporosis Treatment.* He is owner of The Expert Nutrition Center, Owings Mills, Maryland. *ExpertNutrition.com*

Bone is constantly breaking down and rebuilding, a process called remodeling. If you have osteoporosis or osteopenia (an earlier stage of bone thinning), the rate of breakdown exceeds that of reconstruction.

Result: Porous bones that are brittle and prone to fractures.

A broken bone means pain, tests, repeated doctor visits and maybe even surgery—and that could be just the beginning.

About half of women with osteoporosis (and one in eight men) eventually will have a bone fracture, and many will have more than one.

DRUGS ARE NOT THE SOLUTION

The main class of drugs for treating osteoporosis, the bisphosphonates, have been linked to rare but serious side effects, including severe bone, muscle and joint pain and possibly an increased risk for esophageal cancer (due to inflammation of the esophagus). Other rare side effects include atypical femoral fracture, in which the thighbone cracks, and osteonecrosis of the jaw, in which a section of the jawbone dies and deteriorates.

The risks might be justified if the drugs worked—but often they don't. One study published in *The Journal of the American Medical Association* found that 99.8% of patients who took *alendronate* (Fosamax) did not suffer a subsequent fracture. That sounds impressive, but it turns out that people in the study who took placebos had nearly the same result.

It's estimated that 81 women would have to take alendronate to prevent just one fracture. Put another way, 80 out of 81 patients who take the drug won't benefit at all. *Here are effective, safer treatments...*

CALCIUM-PLUS

Everyone knows that calcium is important for strong bones. But calcium alone isn't enough. Bones are made up of a variety of minerals. You need all of them to increase—or just maintain—bone strength. *Examples...*

- **Magnesium.** Up to 80% of Americans don't get enough magnesium. There is some evidence that people who are low in magnesium are more likely to develop osteoporosis.

My advice: Eat magnesium-rich foods, including dark leafy greens, nuts, fish and whole grains. Because most people don't get enough magnesium from food, I also recommend a daily supplement that contains 500 milligrams (mg).

- **Phosphorus.** It's the second-most-abundant mineral in the body after calcium, and 80% to 90% is found in the bones and teeth.

My advice: Eat phosphorus-rich foods, which include meats, fish, nuts, beans and dairy. Aim for 700 mg of phosphorous a day.

Examples: Salmon (three ounces) has 315 mg...beef (three ounces), 243 mg...yogurt (one cup), 386 mg.

• **Calcium.** You can't have strong bones without calcium—but despite what you've heard, you do not have to consume dairy to get sufficient calcium. Leafy green vegetables—such as kale, spinach and collard greens—are rich in calcium. A four-ounce serving of steamed collard greens or kale has about the same amount of calcium as one cup of milk.

My advice: Since many people don't get enough calcium from their diets, a supplement is helpful. Take 600 mg to 800 mg daily. I recommend any calcium supplement other than calcium carbonate, which is poorly absorbed. Combined with the calcium that you get from foods, it will get you into the recommended daily range of 1,200 mg to 1,500 mg.

Some studies have shown a link between calcium supplements and heart attacks, but a recent study by researchers at Brigham and Women's Hospital found no correlation between calcium supplementation and coronary artery disease, and previous research failed to show a link when calcium was taken with other supplements such as vitamin D and magnesium.

VITAMIN D

Vitamin D increases the body's ability to absorb calcium from foods and supplements. It also appears to inhibit both the production and activity of osteoclasts, cells that break down bone.

One study found that people who took a daily vitamin-D supplement had a 23% decrease in nonvertebral fractures and a 26% decrease in hip fractures.

Vitamin D is called the "sunshine vitamin" because it is produced in the skin when you're exposed to sun. But most people don't get enough sun to produce adequate amounts.

My advice: Take 2,000 international units (IU) to 4,000 IU of vitamin D daily. And take it with meals for up to 50% better absorption. I recommend the natural D-3 form. It raises blood levels 1.7 times more than the synthetic D-2 form.

LEAFY GREENS

Leafy greens are not only high in calcium but also rich in vitamin K. Vitamin K works with vitamin D to increase the activity of bone-building osteoblasts.

The Harvard Nurses' Health Study found that women who ate a daily serving of leafy green vegetables, such as spinach, dark green lettuce or kale, were 50% less likely to suffer a fracture than those who had only one serving a week.

My advice: Eat a salad every day. Make side dishes that include spinach, kale or beet greens. Other green vegetables, such as broccoli, cabbage, asparagus and Brussels sprouts, also are high in vitamin K.

ONE PART PROTEIN TO FOUR PARTS VEGETABLES

This ratio seems to be ideal for bone health. You need protein to decrease calcium loss from the body and to increase levels of bone growth factors. But too much protein (particularly from animal sources) increases acidity, which depletes bone minerals.

It's a delicate balancing act. The Framingham Osteoporosis Study found that people who ate the least protein were more likely to have a bone fracture than those who ate the most. But a Harvard study found that people who ate the most protein (from animal sources) had a higher risk for forearm fractures. (Those who got their protein from soy or other nonmeat sources didn't have the same risk.)

My advice: For every serving of a meat-based protein, consume three to four servings of vegetables to alkalinize your body. An alkaline (low-acid) environment helps prevent bone loss.

EXERCISE WITH WEIGHTS

You need to stress the bones to promote new growth. Lifting weights is the best way to do this, particularly when it's combined with aerobic workouts. A University of Washington study found that women who did both during a 50-to-60-minute session, three times a week, gained 5.2% in spinal mineral density in just nine months.

Don't make it easy. If you can lift a weight more than 10 times, you're not stressing the bones enough. Pick a weight that you can lift only between six and 10 times. You want the last few lifts to be a struggle. When that gets too easy, move up to a heavier weight.

Walking is another good way to build bone. One study found that people who were sedentary lost an average of 7% of bone mass in the spine, while those in a walking program gained 0.5%.

My advice: Wear a weighted vest when you walk. You can build more bone by adding to your body weight. You can buy weighted vests at sporting-goods stores and discount stores such as Target and Walmart. Most are adjustable—you can start with five pounds and work your way up to about 10% of your body weight.

Hip Fractures and Bone Health

Hip fractures from osteoporosis are unusual before age 70. A 70-year-old woman suffering some bone loss has only a 5% risk for fracturing a hip within the next decade...and an 80-year-old woman with average bone density has a 9.7% risk.

Susan Ott, MD, associate professor of medicine, University of Washington, Seattle.

Fats That Fight Hip Fractures

Study titled "The Association of Red Blood Cell n-3 and n-6 Fatty Acids with Bone Mineral Density and Hip Fracture Risk in the Women's Health Initiative," published in *Journal of Bone and Mineral Research.*

Sandra was nimble for her 70 years, but one day she tripped over a rug and fell, breaking her hip. In the hospital after she had surgery to fix the hip, she laughed at her own clumsiness and vowed that she'd soon be up and about, participating in her usual activities.

She wasn't. Her pain was severe and she had to rest a lot...then she developed pneumonia...and then she died. All from one simple fall in her own home.

Unfortunately, it's not an unusual scenario. Every year, 220,000 women in the US break their hips—and in so doing, they double their risk of dying within the year. As for men, they're less likely than women to fracture their hips...but their odds of dying soon afterward are even higher.

There's something very simple you can do to reduce your chances of becoming such a sad statistic yourself, a recent study shows. Just eat more of a certain kind of fat...and less of another kind fat.

FATS VS. FRACTURES

Researchers (along with many health-concious individuals) already knew that certain dietary fats are good for cardiovascular and brain health. But they wanted to see whether fats also affected bone health—and fracture risk. To do so, they drew on data from the Women's Health Initiative, a huge study that started in 1993. Participants periodically provided information about their health, diet, lifestyle and family medical history...gave blood samples...and/or underwent various tests, such as scans to measure bone mineral density.

Combing through this mountain of records, the researchers found 324 women who had fractured a hip at some point between 1993 and 2008. Then they selected an equal number of women who had not suffered a broken hip, matching the groups by various factors that influence fracture risk, such as age, ethnicity, geographic location (to account for vitamin D exposure) and use of hormone therapy.

To determine dietary fat consumption, the researchers didn't use the participants' own reports of what they ate, because such self-reporting can be notoriously inaccurate. Instead, they thawed the participants' frozen blood samples and measured the various fatty acids in them, looking specifically at the red blood cells because these cells reflect dietary intake over the course of several months (not just days).

Next, the women were grouped into three categories (low, medium and high) based on their red blood cell levels of omega-3 fatty acids…omega-6 fatty acids…and the ratio between the two. Finally, after adjusting for other factors that influence bone health (smoking, exercise, weight, diabetes, etc.), the researchers calculated the hip fracture risk as it related to dietary fats. *What they found…*

- **Omega-3 fats.** More was definitely better. Compared with women who had the lowest omega-3 levels, women with the highest omega-3 levels had a 45% lower hip fracture risk…and women with mid-level omega-3s had a 15% lower hip fracture risk. Particularly beneficial types of omega-3s included alpha-linolenic acid (ALA), found in flaxseed and walnuts…and eicosapentaenoic acid (EPA), found in fatty fish.
- **Omega-6 fats.** With these fatty acids, less was better—particularly in terms of the ratio between omega-6s and omega-3s. Women with the lowest ratios of omega-6 to omega-3 had about half the hip fracture risk of women with the highest ratios of omega-6 to omega-3. Omega-6 fats are found in abundance in many margarines, corn oil, safflower oil, sunflower oil, fatty red meats and various processed foods.

What's behind the findings? As with so many health problems, it mostly comes down to inflammation. Chronic inflammation may disrupt the normal ongoing process of bone formation. Omega-3s are anti-inflammatory, decreasing the activity of inflammatory proteins called cytokines. In addition, omega-3s may directly and positively affect calcium absorption, further benefiting bones.

Omega-6s, in contrast, tend to promote inflammation. You can't entirely eliminate omega-6s from your diet—and you wouldn't want to, because they do play a crucial role in brain function as well as normal growth and development. However, problems arise when an overabundance of omega-6s overwhelm the omega-3s.

This study, because it used fatty acid content of the blood, cannot reveal the magic number of grams of omega-3 to shoot for each day, but it does highlight the importance of a healthful ratio of omega-6 to omega-3. Many experts suggest that an appropriate ratio is less than 4-to-1 or even 2-to-1. Don't assume that you already meet this goal—the ratio of the typical American diet is about 16-to-1!

Bottom line: To protect your bones and reduce your fracture risk, reduce your consumption of omega-6 fats and increase consumption of foods rich in healthful omega-3s.

Best Osteoporosis Formulas

Mark A. Stengler, NMD, licensed naturopathic medical doctor in private practice, Stengler Center for Integrative Medicine, Encinitas, California…adjunct associate clinical professor at the National College of Natural Medicine, Portland, Oregon…author of many books, including *The Natural Physician's Healing Therapies. MarkStengler.com.*

These products contain all the vitamins and minerals in the therapeutic doses used for osteoporosis treatment…

- **Bone-Up by Jarrow.** To find an online retailer, call 310-204-6936 or go to *www.jarrow.com.*
- **OsteoPrime by Enzymatic Therapy.** To find a retailer, call 800-783-2286 or go to *www.enzymatictherapy.com.*
- **Pro Bone by Ortho Molecular Products** is available from health-care professionals, including naturopaths, holistic MDs, chiropractors, nutritionists and acupuncturists. If you cannot locate a health-care professional in your area who sells the formula, it is available from my clinic at 855-362-6275, *http://www.markstengler.com/product-category/bone-support/.*

Hidden Bone Loss Danger

Low bone density is known to boost fracture risk, but a new study shows that it also impairs balance and hearing. Participants age 65 and older with low bone density were almost four times more likely (and those 40 and older twice as likely) to fail a balance test than those with normal density.

Explanation: Bone loss affects the entire body, including bones in the skull that house the organs for balance and hearing.

Angelico Mendy, MD, MPH, researcher in epidemiology, The University of Iowa College of Public Health, Iowa City.

Prunes Help Prevent Osteoporosis

As we age, our bones break down faster than they are built. Prunes suppress the rate at which people's bones break down.

Recent finding: Women who ate about 10 prunes per day for 12 months had higher bone mineral density than women who ate dried apples. These women also took 500 milligrams of calcium and 400 international units of vitamin D daily.

Bahram H. Arjmandi, PhD, RD, chair, department of nutrition, food and exercise sciences, The Florida State University, Tallahassee, and leader of a study published in *British Journal of Nutrition*.

Breakthrough in Bone Health

Omega-3 supplements do it again! A team of US-Iranian researchers have found that omega-3 supplements, in conjunction with exercise, actually increase bone density in postmenopausal women. This is a finding that could help millions of Americans who have osteoporosis, including younger women and men.

Findings: Researchers found that women who took daily omega-3 supplements (180 mg of EPA and 120 mg of DHA) and exercised (walking or jogging three times weekly at up to 65% of maximum heart rate) had bone mineral density increases of 15% in the lower back and 19% at the top of the thighbone at the hip. The exercise-only group had no increases in bone mineral density at all. The omega-3/exercise group also had decreased blood levels of inflammatory compounds—a key finding because omega-3 fatty acids are powerful agents in the body's fight against inflammation, and inflammation is related to bone breakdown. These increases are even better than what you would get with drugs—so you can see why this is my prescription for bone health.

Mark A. Stengler, NMD, licensed naturopathic medical doctor in private practice, Stengler Center for Integrative Medicine, Encinitas, California...adjunct associate clinical professor at the National College of Natural Medicine, Portland, Oregon...author of many books, including *The Natural Physician's Healing Therapies. MarkStengler.com*

The Real Secret to Strong Bones...It Is Not What You Think

Susan E. Brown, PhD, medical anthropologist, certified nutritionist and director, The Center for Better Bones and Better Bones Foundation, both in Syracuse, New York. She is author of *Better Bones, Better Body* and *The Acid-Alkaline Food Guide. BetterBones.com*

Contrary to popular belief, the degenerative bone disease osteoporosis is not an inevitable result of aging.

Recent research: An important but overlooked cause of osteoporosis is an acid-forming diet.

Susan E. Brown, PhD, author of *Better Bones, Better Body*, discusses her insights...

THE ACID/ALKALI BALANCE

For survival, the body must maintain a balance between acids and alkalis, with good health depending on slight alkalinity. If the body's alkali reserves run low—a condition called chronic low-grade metabolic acidosis—alkaline mineral compounds are drawn from bones to buffer excess acids in the blood. The immediate benefit is that the body's pH (a measure of acidity or alkalinity) is balanced. But over time, if bone mineral compounds are not replenished, osteoporosis develops.

Bone-depleting metabolic acidosis is easily reversible through diet. Yet the average American diet is woefully deficient in many of the nutrients needed to balance pH.

To protect bones: Follow the dietary suggestions below. It's generally best to get nutrients from food. However, to help ensure adequate intake, take a daily multi-vitamin/mineral plus the other supplements noted...and consider additional supplements as well.

Before you start: Gauge your pH with a urine test kit, such as those sold in some pharmacies...or use the Better Bones Alkaline for Life pH Test Kit.

Cost: $29.95 (*www.betterbones.com*, click on "Shop," or call 877-207-0232). An ideal first morning urine pH is 6.5 to 7.5. The lower your pH is, the more helpful supplements may be. As with any supplement regimen, talk to your doctor before beginning.

BONE-SUPPORTIVE DIET

For a diet that builds bones...

- **Emphasize vegetables (particularly dark,** leafy greens and root vegetables), fruits, nuts, seeds and spices—these are alkalizing.

Daily targets: Eight servings of vegetables...three to four servings of fruit...two servings of nuts or seeds...and plentiful spices.

- **Consume meat, poultry, fish, dairy, eggs, legumes and whole grains in moderation—** they are acidifying.

Daily targets: One serving of meat, poultry or fish...one serving of eggs or legumes... one to two servings each of dairy and whole grains.

- **Minimize sugar, refined grains and processed foods...**limit coffee to two servings daily...limit alcohol to one serving daily. All these are very acidifying.

- **Fats neither increase nor decrease blood acidity—**but for overall health, keep fat intake moderate and opt for those that protect the heart, such as olive oil.

Important: It's not the acidity of a food itself that matters, but rather its metabolic effects. For instance, citrus fruits taste acidic, yet once metabolized, they are alkalizing.

MINERALS THAT BONES NEED MOST

Bone is composed of a living protein matrix of collagen upon which mineral crystals are deposited in a process called mineralization. *Key minerals, in order of importance...*

- **Potassium neutralizes metabolic acids and reduces calcium loss.**

Daily goal: 4,000 milligrams (mg) to 6,000 mg.

Sources: Avocados, baked potatoes, bananas, beet greens, cantaloupe, lima beans, sweet potatoes.

- **Magnesium** boosts absorption of calcium and production of the bone-preserving hormone calcitonin.

Daily goal: 400 mg to 800 mg.

Sources: Almonds, Brazil nuts, kelp, lentils, pumpkin seeds, soy, split peas, whole wheat, wild rice.

- **Calcium gives bones strength.**

Daily goal: 1,000 mg to 1,500 mg.

Sources: Amaranth flour, broccoli, canned sardines with bones, collards, dairy, kale, mustard greens, sesame seeds, spinach.

Also: Supplement daily, at a two-to-one ratio, with calcium citrate or calcium citrate malate plus magnesium—increasing calcium intake without also increasing magnesium can exacerbate asthma, arthritis and kidney stones.

- **Zinc aids collagen production and calcium absorption.**

Daily goal: 20 mg to 30 mg.

Sources: Alaskan king crab, cashews, kidney beans, meat, oysters, sesame seeds, wheat germ.

- **Manganese helps form bone cartilage and collagen.**

Daily goal: 10 mg to 15 mg.

Sources: Beets, blackberries, brown rice, loganberries, oats, peanuts, pineapple, rye, soy.

• **Copper blocks bone breakdown and increases collagen formation.**

Daily goal: 1 mg to 3 mg.

Sources: Barley, beans, chickpeas, eggplant, liver, molasses, summer squash.

• **Silica increases collagen strength and bone calcification.**

Daily goal: 30 mg to 50 mg.

Sources: Bananas, carrots, green beans, whole grains.

• **Boron helps the body use calcium, magnesium and vitamin D.**

Daily goal: 3 mg to 5 mg.

Sources: Almonds, avocados, black-eyed peas, cherries, grapes, tomatoes.

• **Strontium promotes mineralization.**

Daily goal: 3 mg to 20 mg.

Sources: Brazil nuts, legumes, root vegetables, whole grains.

• **Vital vitamins**

The following vitamins enhance bones' self-repair abilities...

• **Vitamin D** is essential because, without adequate amounts, you cannot absorb enough calcium. Many people do not get adequate vitamin D from sunlight. Vitamin D deficiency accounts for up to 50% of osteoporotic fractures.

Daily goal: 1,000 international units (IU) to 2,000 IU.

Best source: A daily supplement of cholecalciferol (vitamin D-3)—foods that contain vitamin D (fatty fish, fortified milk) do not provide enough and are acidifying.

• **Vitamins K-1 and K-2** boost bone matrix synthesis and bind calcium and phosphorous to bone.

Daily goal: 1,000 micrograms (mcg) of K-1...and 90 mg to 180 mg of K-2.

Sources: Aged cheese, broccoli, Brussels sprouts, collard greens, kale, spinach, green tea.

If you supplement: For vitamin K-2, choose the MK-7 form.

Caution: Vitamin K can interfere with blood thinners, such as *warfarin* (Coumadin)—so talk to your doctor before altering vitamin K intake.

• **Vitamin C aids collagen formation,** stimulates bone-building cells and helps synthesize the adrenal hormones vital to postmenopausal bone health.

Daily goal: 500 mg to 2,000 mg.

Sources: Cantaloupe, kiwifruit, oranges, papaya, pink grapefruit, red peppers, strawberries.

• **Vitamins B-6, B-12 and folate** help eliminate homocysteine, an amino acid linked to fracture risk.

Daily goal: 25 mg to 50 mg of B-6...200 mcg to 800 mcg of B-12...800 mcg to 1,000 mcg of folate.

Sources: For B-6—avocados, bananas, brown rice, oats, turkey, walnuts. For B-12—beef, salmon, trout. For folate—asparagus, okra, peanuts, pinto beans.

• **Vitamin A** helps develop bone-building osteoblast cells.

Daily goal: 5,000 IU.

Sources: Carrots, collard greens, pumpkin, sweet potatoes.

If you supplement: Choose the beta-carotene form.

Secrets to Better Bone Health

Jamison Starbuck, ND, is a naturopathic physician in family practice in Missoula, Montana. She is past president of the American Association of Naturopathic Physicians and a contributing editor to *The Alternative Advisor: The Complete Guide to Natural Therapies and Alternative Treatments.*

If you are among the 44 million American women and men over age 50 who have or are at risk for osteoporosis, you've no doubt heard that it's important to boost your intake of calcium-rich foods. What most people do not realize is that other factors can have a significant impact on whether the nutrients in bone-building foods are actually absorbed so that they can provide the maximum benefit. Our bones are living parts of our anatomy, as vital and alive as the heart or the brain. What you eat—and how you assimilate what you eat—helps determine your bone health and whether or not you develop osteoporosis.

A recent study published in the *Journal of the American Medical Association* illustrates this point. Researchers examined data linking long-term use (more than one year) of heartburn and ulcer medications known as proton pump inhibitors (PPIs) and the risk for hip fracture in people over age 50.

The unequivocal results: Hip fracture risk increases with long-term PPI use. PPIs, such as *omeprazole* (Prilosec), *lansoprazole* (Prevacid) and *esomeprazole* (Nexium), reduce stomach acid. However, I've never recommended a PPI for a patient of mine, because I believe that a good supply of acid in the stomach improves the absorption of bone-building minerals, such as calcium and magnesium, and fat-soluble vitamins D and K, all of which are necessary for bone growth and maintenance.

For bone health, eat calcium-rich foods and/or take 600 mg of calcium citrate daily, which is readily absorbed, and perform weight-bearing exercise, such as walking, hiking, gardening or dancing. *Also...*

- **Limit mineral-robbing foods.** Eat plenty of mineral-rich whole foods, including whole grains, vegetables, fruits and nuts, but consume only small amounts of foods that steal minerals from your body. These include coffee, hard liquor and carbonated beverages.

- **Use vinegar or fresh lemon.** Add one teaspoon of vinegar or fresh lemon juice to your vegetables or salad at lunch and dinner. Substituting vinegar or lemon juice for fat-laden butter, ranch dressing or sour cream will enhance your body's absorption of essential nutrients.

Caution: Vinegar and lemon juice are not recommended for people with ulcers or gastritis.

- **Don't forget to take vitamin D.** Vitamin D, known as the sunshine vitamin, increases the absorption of calcium from the intestines, eventually increasing calcium deposition in bones. Get 800 international units (IU) of vitamin D through diet and supplementation.

- **Eat foods rich in vitamin K.** Good choices include broccoli, cabbage and spinach—and green tea. Recent studies show that vitamin K is very effective in maintaining and building bone.

Caution: If you take *warfarin* (Coumadin), consult your doctor before eating vitamin K–rich foods and do not take a vitamin K supplement. Vitamin K can interfere with blood-thinning medication.

The Best Bone-Building Exercises

Raymond E. Cole, DO, clinical assistant professor, Department of Internal Medicine, Michigan State University College of Osteopathic Medicine, East Lansing. He is author of *Best Body, Best Bones: Your Doctor's Exercise Rx for Lifelong Fitness. DrRaymondCole.com*

Women whose bones are fragile and porous—due to the severe loss of bone density that characterizes osteoporosis—often avoid exercise for fear that jarring or twisting motions could cause fractures.

Done properly, however, exercise is not only safe for people with osteoporosis or its milder form, osteopenia, it actually can reduce or even reverse bone loss. For people whose bones are still healthy, exercise helps ensure that osteoporosis never develops.

Reason: When a muscle exerts tension on a bone, it stimulates specialized cells that increase new bone formation. Also, when muscles that contribute to balance are strengthened, falls (and resulting fractures) are less likely.

Keys: Doing the types of workouts that build bone most effectively...and modifying techniques as necessary to avoid overstressing already weakened bones.

What to do: Start by exercising for 10 to 20 minutes several times a week, gradually building up to 30 minutes a day six days per week.

Alternate between a strength-training workout one day and an aerobic activity the next.

Important: Before beginning the exercise program below, ask your doctor which instructions you should follow—the ones labeled "If you have healthy bones" or the ones labeled "If you already have bone loss."

STRENGTH TRAINING FOR BONES

The only equipment you need are hand weights (dumbbells) and ankle weights (pads that strap around the ankles), $20 and up per pair at sports equipment stores.

For each exercise, begin with one set of eight repetitions ("reps"). If you cannot do eight reps using the suggested starting weights, use lighter weights. Over several weeks, gradually increase to 10, then 12, then 15 reps. Then try two sets of eight reps, resting for one minute between sets...and again gradually increase the reps. When you can do two sets of 15 reps, increase the weight by one to two pounds and start again with one set of eight reps.

Keep your shoulders back and abdominal muscles pulled in. With each rep, exhale during the initial move...hold the position for two seconds...inhale as you return to the starting position. Move slowly, using muscles rather than momentum. Do not lock elbow or knee joints.

• **Upper body.** These exercises build bone density in the shoulders, arms and spine.

If you have healthy bones: Stand during the exercises. Start by holding a five-pound weight in each hand...over time, try to work up to eight, then 10, then 12 pounds.

If you already have bone loss: To guard against falls, sit in a straight-backed chair while exercising. At first, use no weights or use one- or two-pound weights...gradually work up to three-, then five-, then a maximum of eight-pound weights if you can. Avoid heavier weights—they could increase the risk for vertebral compression fractures.

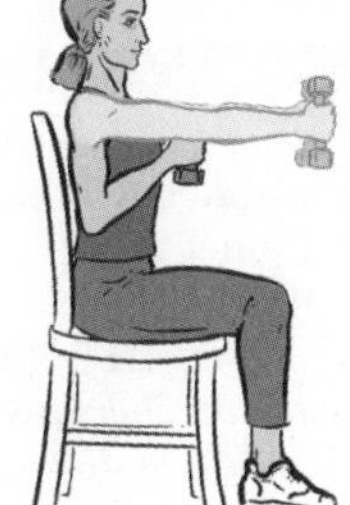

• **Arms forward.**

To start: Bend elbows, arms close to your body, hands at chest-height, palms facing each other. One rep: Straighten elbows until both arms are extended in front of you, parallel to the floor...hold...return to starting position.

• **Arm overhead.**

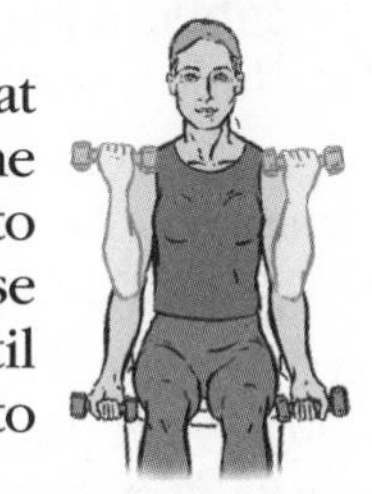

To start: Raise right arm straight overhead, palm facing forward. One rep: Bend right elbow, bringing right hand down behind your head...hold...return to starting position. Do a set with the right arm, then with the left.

• **Arms up-and-down.**

To start: Have arms down at your sides, palms forward. One rep: Keeping elbows close to your sides, bend arms to raise hands toward shoulders until palms face you...hold...lower to starting position.

• **Midbody.** This strengthens and stabilizes "core" muscles (abdomen, back, pelvic area). By improving body alignment, it helps prevent falls and reduces pressure on the vertebrae, protecting against compression fractures of the spine. No weights are used.

If you have healthy bones: Do this exercise while standing...or try it while lying on your back, with knees bent and feet flat on the floor.

If you already have bone loss: Done while standing, this is a good option for osteoporosis patients who are uncomfortable exercising on the floor. If you have balance problems, hold onto a counter...or sit in a chair.

• **Tummy tuck/pelvic tilt.**

To start: Have arms at sides, feet hip-width apart. One rep: Simultaneously contract abdominal muscles to draw your tummy toward your spine, tighten buttocks muscles, and tilt the bottom of your pelvis forward to flatten the arch of your back...hold...return to starting position.

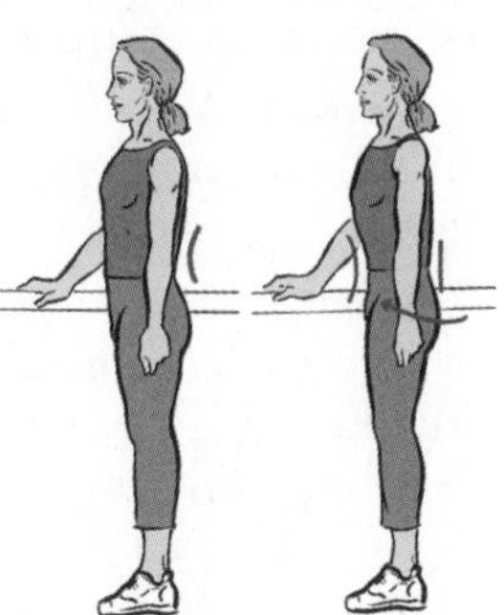

• **Lower body.** These moves increase bone density in the legs and feet. For each rep, raise the leg as high as possible without leaning... hold for two seconds...return to starting position.

Advanced option: Try not to touch your foot to the ground between reps.

If you have healthy bones: Start by wearing a two-pound ankle weight on each leg... gradually increase to 10 pounds per ankle.

If you already have bone loss: Hold onto a counter for balance. To begin, use no weights...build up, one pound at a time, to five pounds per ankle.

• **Leg forward-and-back.**

To start: Stand on your right foot. One rep: Keeping both legs straight, slowly swing left leg forward and up...hold...swing leg down through the starting position and up behind you...hold... return to starting position. After one set, repeat with the other leg.

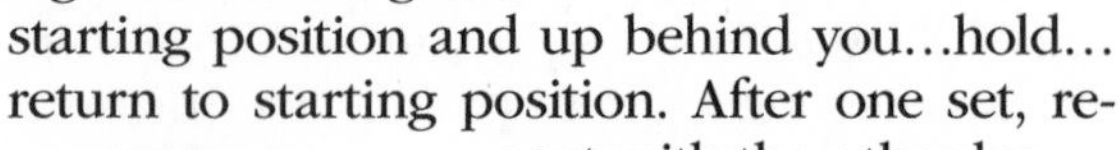

• **Leg out.**

To start: Stand on your right foot. One rep: Keeping both legs straight, slowly lift left leg out to the side...hold...return to starting position. After one set, repeat with the other leg.

BONE-BENEFITING AEROBICS

Biking, stationary cycling, swimming and rowing are good for heart health—but they do not protect against osteoporosis.

Better: Weight-bearing aerobic activities in which you're on your feet, bones working against gravity, build bone mass in the hips and legs.

If you have healthy bones: Good choices include jogging, dancing, stair climbing, step aerobics, jumping rope, racket sports and interactive video games, such as Wii Fit and Dance Dance Revolution. If you enjoy walking, you can boost intensity by wearing a two- to 20-pound weighted vest ($50 and up at sports equipment stores).

Warning: Do not wear ankle weights during aerobic workouts—this could stress your joints.

If you already have bone loss: Refrain from high-impact activities (running, jumping) and those that require twisting or bending (racket sports, golf). Do not wear a weighted vest.

Safe low-impact options: Walking, using an elliptical machine (available at most gyms), qigong and tai chi.

Photos: Illustrations by Shawn Banner.

Osteoporosis Screening for Men

Osteoporosis in men is substantially underdiagnosed, undertreated and inadequately researched. Rates are expected to increase by nearly 50% in the next 15 years as the population ages. Sufferers are vulnerable to hip fractures, which are projected to double or triple by 2040.

New guidelines: Men over age 50 should be assessed for osteoporosis risk factors, according to the American College of Physicians.

In my view, low body weight, inactivity and weight loss are strong predictors of increased risk for osteoporosis. Most vulnerable are smokers, heavy alcohol drinkers, men with testosterone deficiency and those who have been on steroid therapy. I agree that it is smart for men to join women in being screened for osteoporosis beginning at age 50.

Mark A. Stengler, ND, naturopathic physician in private practice, Encinitas, California...adjunct associate clinical professor at the National College of Natural Medicine, Portland, Oregon...author of many books, including *The Natural Physician's Healing Therapies* and coauthor of *Prescription for Natural Cures.*

Vitamin D Helps You Stand Tall and Not Fall

Richard L. Prince, MD, associate professor, School of Medicine and Pharmacology, University of Western Australia, Perth, Australia.

Vitamin D, long known as the "sunshine vitamin," is rapidly turning into the "must-have" vitamin. It is well established that vitamin D is crucial for maintaining strong bones, but more recent research shows that vitamin D may help prevent or reduce the risk of colon cancer and other diseases, and maybe even improve cognitive health. You can now add yet another benefit to the list of vitamin D's virtues—it may help prevent falls in older adults.

A one-year study at the School of Medicine and Pharmacology, University of Western Australia (Perth) tracked 302 women ages 70 to 90 who had vitamin D levels lower than the median for women their age in their region, and who had also experienced a fall in the past year. Study researchers randomly assigned the women to one of two groups—one took 1,000 IU of vitamin D-2 (ergocalciferol) daily while the other took an identical placebo. All women in both groups also took 1,000 mg of calcium citrate per day. After adjusting for the differences in height, since it was previously shown that taller people generally have stronger muscles and therefore fall less often, statistics showed that the women taking vitamin D had a 19% lower rate of falls. Surprisingly, though, taking vitamin D supplements did not reduce the risk of multiple falls for those who fell at least once.

HOW DOES "D" PREVENT FALLS?

Vitamin D contributes to stronger muscles, which of course would help prevent falling. Vitamin D and calcium work synergistically to improve muscle function and strengthen bones, thereby making falls and fractures even less likely. But Dr. Prince admits they were taken aback by the finding that vitamin D plus calcium didn't help prevent multiple falls. The researchers concluded that this was likely because women who fell more often were frailer and had other contributory problems.

Many people get enough vitamin D from outdoor exposure. Depending on sunlight intensity where you live, direct sunlight may be enough, but most experts recommend supplementing in the winter months at least. If you are not sure, ask your doctor to check vitamin D levels in your blood.

Foods fortified with vitamin D are a good place to start. Besides those, however, dietary sources of vitamin D are limited. Cod liver oil is one good source, but don't exceed recommended levels/dosage, as high levels can be toxic. Salmon and mackerel also have vitamin D, though in lesser amounts.

If you choose to supplement, as many people do, be careful—excess supplemental vitamin D can cause nausea, vomiting and constipation, and sometimes even more serious problems, including confusion and neurological and heart problems. One thousand IU per day is generally considered safe and effective.

Natural Ways to Feel Much Better After a Fall...

Jamison Starbuck, ND, is a naturopathic physician in family practice and a guest lecturer at the University of Montana, both in Missoula. She is past president of the American Association of Naturopathic Physicians and a contributing editor to *The Alternative Advisor: The Complete Guide to Natural Therapies and Alternative Treatments.*

Ever since I took that fall, I haven't felt quite right." This is a refrain that I hear from a surprising number of my patients. We tend to think of falls as affecting only older adults and causing primarily physical injuries. But neither is true. People of all ages fall, and the aftereffects can be harmful in a variety of ways.

My theory is that unexpected falls destabilize the nervous system. Even if you aren't badly hurt, these falls are scary. Our inner protective mechanisms become hypervigilant—our muscles become tense and we hold ourselves more rigidly. We also struggle with a lingering sense of unease and begin to mistrust our ability to safely do everyday activities. When a patient falls, I perform a thorough exam to rule out a concussion and possibly order an X-ray to check for fractures. I also treat the patient's nervous system. In addition to the use of ice to treat an injury for the first 48 hours, followed by heat and painkillers, if needed, I've found that natural medicine can help people avoid lasting problems from falls. *My favorite approaches...**

• **Use natural remedies.** Arnica is a well-known homeopathic remedy that is used topically for physical trauma. Arnica lotion, for example, can be applied to bruises or sprains several times a day until they are healed. Along with arnica, I recommend using homeopathic Aconite, a remedy that is excellent in treating the fright that follows sudden, violent accidents. Aconite is best taken within 48 hours of a fall. I typically recommend one dose (two pellets of Aconite 30C) taken under the tongue. If 24 hours after taking Aconite you remain anxious or scared about your fall, repeat the same dose once a day for up to a week.

• **Try nervine herbs.** Chamomile, valerian and hops are plant medicines that calm the nervous system and help the body recover from a fall by promoting rest and muscle relaxation. Take these herbs alone or in combination in tea or tincture form.

Typical dose for a single herb or mixture: Drink 10 ounces of tea three times a day or take 60 drops of tincture in one ounce of water three times a day for up to two weeks.

• **Get plenty of rest.** Soaking in a warm bath with Epsom salts relaxes muscles and helps you get a good night's sleep. Until you have fully recovered from the fall, it also helps to take 150 mg of magnesium citrate (the form most easily absorbed) twice daily. This mineral promotes relaxation.

• **Consider bodywork.** Soon after a fall, consider getting full-body massage or acupressure treatment several times. These therapies not only promote circulation and healing, but also help people regain trust in their bodies after a scary event.

Caution: If you hit your head, are bleeding significantly or suspect a fracture from a fall, get to a hospital emergency department. If you experience headache, vision changes, dizziness, confusion, nausea, vomiting or a balance problem (even days after the fall), you may have a head injury and must seek immediate medical help.

*Check with your doctor first if you have a chronic condition or take medication.

10

Heart Disease

Do You Have a Heart Attack Gene? Finding Out Could Save Your Life

Even if you do everything right—you don't smoke, you keep an eye on your stress levels, you're not overweight and you manage your cholesterol and blood pressure—your odds of having a heart attack might be higher than you think.

An eye-opening case: One of our patients, a 44-year-old executive whom we nicknamed "Superman," looked very healthy. His Framingham Risk Score—a standard measure of heart disease risk—predicted that he had only a 1% risk of having a heart attack over the next 10 years. That should have been good news—except that other tests we did, which most doctors do not routinely give, showed that his real risk was about 40 times higher.

THE GENETIC TESTS YOU NEED

Many of the tests that are used to detect heart disease are decades old. Some look for risk factors (such as arterial narrowing) that have less to do with the actual risk of having a heart attack than most people think. Many of the tests that can make a difference still aren't used by most doctors.

Most cardiologists routinely recommend angiography, an imaging test that looks for large blockages in the coronary arteries. If a blockage of 70% or more is found, a patient might be advised to receive a stent or undergo a bypass, surgical procedures that don't always help and can have a high rate of complications.

Severely blocked arteries can be a problem, but a more common, and typically overlooked, threat is from small deposits inside

---

Bradley F. Bale, MD, cofounder of the Heart Attack & Stroke Prevention Center, Nashville, and medical director of the Grace Clinic Heart Health Center, Lubbock, Texas. He is coauthor, with Amy Doneen, ARNP, and Lisa Collier Cool, of *Beat the Heart Attack Gene: The Revolutionary Plan to Prevent Heart Disease, Stroke, and Diabetes*.

artery walls. A patient might have dozens or even hundreds of deposits that are too small to be detected with angiography.

The risk: When these "hidden" deposits are exposed to inflammation—triggered by insulin resistance, smoking, a poor diet or stress, for example—they can rupture, tear the blood vessel lining and trigger a clot, the cause of most heart attacks.

New approaches: Doctors can now predict the risk for a heart attack with far more accuracy than in the past—if you know which tests to ask for. *Tests I recommend...*

• **Carotid intima-media thickness (CIMT).** This is an effective way to measure atherosclerosis inside an artery wall (between the intima and media layers). The FDA-approved test uses an ultrasound wand to look for the thickening of the carotid arteries that occurs when plaque between the two layers accumulates and pushes outward.

An isolated area of thickness measuring 1.3 mm or greater indicates plaque—and an increased risk for a heart attack or stroke.

Most patients who have excessive arterial thickening will be advised to exercise more, eat a healthier diet and take a daily baby aspirin to reduce the risk for clots. A cholesterol-lowering statin drug also may be prescribed.

• **Genetic tests.** More than half of all Americans have one or more gene variations that increase the risk for a heart attack and a stroke. According to research published in *Circulation*, up to 70% of patients who are given the genetic tests described below will be reclassified as having a higher heart attack risk than their doctors originally thought. The cost of testing has dropped to about $100 per gene. Your insurance may cover the cost. *Important gene tests...*

• 9P21. If you inherit two copies of this "heart attack gene" (one from each parent), your risk of developing heart disease or having a heart attack at an early age (in men, under age 45...in women, under age 55) is 102% higher than that of someone without the gene. And increased risk continues if you are already past these ages.

You'll also have a 74% increased risk for an abdominal aortic aneurysm, a dangerous weakening in the heart's largest blood vessel. If you test positive, your doctor will advise earlier and more frequent abdominal aortic scans. If you smoke, stop now. Most aortic aneurysms occur in smokers.

You should also exercise for at least 22 minutes daily (the amount found in research to be protective) and maintain healthy cholesterol and blood pressure levels.

Important: Patients with the 9P21 gene often are advised to have an ankle-brachial index test, which involves measuring blood pressure in the arms and ankles. It's used to diagnose peripheral artery disease (PAD), plaque buildups in the legs that quadruple or even quintuple the risk for a heart attack or stroke.

• Apo E. This gene affects how your body metabolizes nutrients. There are different types of Apo E. The 3/3 genotype—64% of Americans have it—increases cardiovascular disease, but not as much as the 3/4 or 4/4 types. Those with 3/4 or 4/4 need to eat a very low-fat diet (with no more than 20% of calories from fat). Those with the 3/3 genotype are advised to eat a Mediterranean-style diet—focusing mainly on plant foods...fish...and olive oil.

• KIF6. Patients with the so-called arginine gene variant have up to a 55% increased risk for cardiovascular disease. There are no particular lifestyle changes known to be especially helpful for these patients. It's also useful to know if you're a noncarrier of KIF6—as such, you won't receive significant risk reduction if you are prescribed either *atorvastatin* (Lipitor) or *pravastatin* (Pravachol), two of the most popular statin drugs. Instead, you'll need a different statin, such as *lovastatin*.

ANOTHER CRUCIAL TEST

An oral glucose tolerance test can detect insulin resistance years or even decades before it progresses to diabetes. But many doctors still use the simpler A1C test. It's more convenient—it doesn't require fasting—but it often fails to detect insulin resistance, one of the main causes of heart attacks and strokes. Insulin resistance leads to inflammation that can trigger plaques to rupture and form clots.

With an oral glucose tolerance test, your blood sugar is measured. Then you drink a sweet solution, and your blood sugar is measured again two hours later. A level of 100 mg/dL to 139 mg/dL could indicate insulin resistance. Higher levels may indicate prediabetes—or, if they're high enough, full-blown diabetes.

Next steps: Regular exercise is critical if you have insulin resistance or diabetes.

Also helpful: Weight loss, if needed, reduced intake of sugary beverages and foods, and a diet rich in fruits, vegetables and grains.

Think You Know Your True Risk for Heart Attack and Stroke? More Tests You Need

James Ehrlich, MD, a clinical associate professor of endocrinology at the University of Colorado, Denver. The chief medical officer of United Cardio Systems, based in Castle Rock, Colorado.

You may think that you are at low risk for a heart attack because the heart tests that your doctor has ordered had "negative" results. The standard blood test that you received may show that your cholesterol and triglyceride levels are fine. And you may have even received a clean bill of health after taking a cardiac stress test (exercising on a treadmill while heart rhythms are electronically monitored).

Surprising fact: Those two standard heart tests miss many high-risk individuals with early heart disease. For example, a study published in the *Journal of the American College of Cardiology* found that 95% of women who had heart attacks at age 65 or younger were considered low risk.

For the greatest protection: In addition to the standard heart tests, all adults should consider receiving the highly accurate heart tests described in this article, which are not regularly ordered by most physicians but serve as stronger predictors of cardiovascular disease.

Why don't more doctors have conversations with their patients about these important tests? Many physicians closely adhere to the guidelines of the government's Preventive Services Task Force, whose evidence-based recommendations tend to include tests that are less sophisticated and less expensive.

But if your primary care physician or cardiologist does not mention these tests, ask him/her which ones might be right for you. The results will provide the best possible information for your doctor to create a customized medical and lifestyle regimen that can help prevent heart attacks and strokes.

CORONARY CALCIUM CT SCAN

This radiological imaging test—also called a CT heart scan—detects and quantifies calcified plaque, a marker for atherosclerosis (fatty buildup in the arteries). This test is up to 10 times more predictive of future heart problems than a cholesterol test and can detect early heart disease that often goes undetected by a stress test.

My advice: Men over age 35 and women over age 40 with one to two risk factors for cardiovascular disease are good candidates for screening with a heart scan. Risk factors include being overweight...having hypertension, diabetes (or prediabetes), high LDL "bad" cholesterol, low HDL "good" cholesterol, elevated triglycerides, a family history of heart disease...and/or smoking.

Risks: Cardiac CT tests expose patients to ionizing radiation (the same type used in X-rays), which has been linked to an increased risk for cancer. Heart scans, such as electron-beam CT scans and late-generation spiral CT scans, now are performed at lower radiation doses—the equivalent of 10 to 25 chest X-rays is typical. These CT scans use faster speeds than standard CT scans to produce the image, are accurate and expose you to less radiation.

Cost and coverage: $150 to $500 and may be covered by insurance.

CAROTID TEST

An ultrasound test of the carotid (neck) arteries leading to the brain does not involve radiation and measures two important conditions that help predict cardiovascular disease—the dangerous presence of plaque and the thickness of the two inner layers of each artery (the intima and media).

The carotid test is a stronger predictor of a future stroke than coronary calcium and a moderate predictor of heart attack risk.

My advice: I recommend this test for men over age 35 and women over age 40 with one to two risk factors such as hypertension and/or a family history of heart disease or stroke. People with such risk factors as high cholesterol and type 2 diabetes also may benefit from the test.

Results: If there is any noticeable plaque or the thickness of the intima/media is in the top 25% for people of your age, sex and ethnicity, you are at a higher than desirable cardiovascular risk and should pay close attention to all risk factors—especially hypertension.

Cost and coverage: $100 to $500 and often is covered by insurance.

ADVANCED LIPOPROTEIN ANALYSIS

Advanced lipoprotein analysis includes blood tests that measure hidden risk factors such as…

- **Lp(a),** a dangerous particle that often is elevated in families with a history of premature heart attacks.
- **ApoB/ApoAI,** a ratio of dangerous particles to protective particles.

My advice: This analysis is especially useful for people with heart disease that occurs in the absence of risk factors or who have a family history of premature heart disease (heart attack before age 55 in a father or brother and before age 65 in a mother or sister, for example). Those with type 2 diabetes (or prediabetes) or "metabolic syndrome"—often with a bulging waistline, hypertension, low HDL, elevated triglycerides and/or elevated blood sugar—also are good candidates.

Cost and coverage: Varies widely from as little as $40 to as much as $400—often covered by insurance.

However, not all labs perform these tests. Labs that perform advanced lipoprotein analysis: Atherotech (*www.atherotech.com*)…Boston Heart Diagnostics (*www.bostonheartdiagnostics.com*)…Health Diagnostic Laboratory (*www.hdlabinc.com*)…LipoScience (*www.liposcience.com*)…Quest Diagnostics (*www.questdiagnostics.com*) and SpectraCell (*www.spectracell.com*).

OTHER BIOMARKERS

- **Lp-PLA2** (PLAC test). This blood test, which measures inflammation in blood vessels themselves, is a powerful predictor of the most common type of stroke (ischemic stroke). The test is more specific for vascular disease than the commonly ordered test for C-reactive protein (which is elevated with any type of inflammation in the body).

Cost and coverage: About $50 to $200 and may be covered by insurance.

- **BNP or NT-proBNP** (B-type natriuretic peptide). This is an early indicator of a weakening heart muscle (even before overt heart failure) and an excellent test for managing patients with heart failure. The test can also be used to help predict risk for heart attack.

Cost and coverage: About $50 to $250 and may be covered by insurance.

ASPIRIN RESISTANCE TESTING

Aspirin helps stop blood components called platelets from sticking together, which reduces the risk for an artery-plugging blood clot. A daily "baby" aspirin (81 mg) or higher doses usually are prescribed for anyone who has had a heart attack or stroke…or for someone who is at risk for either condition.

However, 25% of people are aspirin resistant—the drug doesn't effectively prevent platelet "stickiness."

Aspirin resistance testing measures a urinary metabolite (11-dehydrothromboxane B2), which is high if you are aspirin resistant.

Who should be tested: Anyone taking aspirin to treat or prevent cardiovascular disease.

Cost and coverage: $30 to $150 and often covered by insurance.

Good news: Recent research published in the *Journal of the American College of Cardiology* shows that supplementing the diet with omega-3 fatty acids can overcome aspirin resistance.

The 15-Minute Test That Could Save Your Life

Rebecca Shannonhouse, editor of *Bottom Line/ Health*, Boardroom Inc., 281 Tresser Blvd., Stamford, Connecticut 06901.

The standard risk factors used to predict cardiovascular disease, such as age, sex, low HDL ("good") cholesterol, smoking and high blood pressure, don't tell the whole story.

You can appear to be relatively healthy and at low risk for coronary artery disease but actually have a higher risk than you realize—and an increased risk for such conditions as heart attack and stroke.

Underrecognized marker for coronary artery disease: The thickness of the carotid (neck) arteries, which carry blood from the heart to the brain.

Important new finding: When ultrasound was used to measure the thickness of the carotid artery wall and to detect the presence of plaque in 13,145 patients, about 12% who would have been classified as having a low or intermediate risk of developing heart disease were found to actually belong in a higher-risk group—and may require treatment, such as medication.

There should be no plaque in the carotid artery, says cardiologist Vijay Nambi, MD, lead author of the study, which recently appeared in the *Journal of the American College of Cardiology*. Patients with plaque have a significantly higher risk of developing cardiovascular disease, regardless of their other risk factors.

Used in combination with other tests (such as those for blood pressure and cholesterol), carotid imaging with ultrasound allows doctors to more accurately determine who is at higher risk for heart disease. This 15-minute test is noninvasive, painless and usually costs $150 to $200. Patients should ask if the test is covered by their insurance.

6 Secrets to Holistic Heart Care

Joel K. Kahn, MD, clinical professor of medicine at Wayne State University School of Medicine in Detroit and director of Cardiac Wellness at Michigan Healthcare Professionals. He is a founding member of the International Society of Integrative, Metabolic and Functional Cardiovascular Medicine and the author of *The Whole Heart Solution. DrJoelKahn.com*

You don't smoke, your cholesterol levels look good and your blood pressure is under control.

This means that you're off the hook when it comes to having a heart attack or developing heart disease, right? Maybe not.

Surprising statistic: About 20% of people with heart disease do not have any of the classic risk factors, such as those described above.

The missing link: While most conventional medical doctors prescribe medications and other treatments to help patients control the "big" risk factors for heart disease, holistic cardiologists also suggest small lifestyle changes that over time make a significant difference in heart disease risk.* *My secrets for preventing heart disease...*

SECRET #1: Stand up! You may not think of standing as a form of exercise. **However, it's more effective than most people realize.**

Think about what you're doing when you're not standing. Unless you're asleep, you're probably sitting. While sitting, your body's metabolism slows...your insulin becomes less effective...and you're likely to experience a gradual drop in HDL "good" cholesterol.

A study that tracked the long-term health of more than 123,000 Americans found that those who sat for six hours or more a day had an overall death rate that was higher—18% higher for men and 37% for women—than those who sat for less than three hours.

*To find a holistic cardiologist, go to the website of the American Board of Integrative Holistic Medicine, *www.abihm.org*, and search the database of certified integrative physicians.

What's so great about standing? When you're on your feet, you move more. You pace...fidget...move your arms...and walk from room to room. This type of activity improves metabolism and can easily burn hundreds of extra calories a day. Standing also increases your insulin sensitivity to help prevent diabetes. So stand up and move around when talking on the phone, checking e-mail and watching television.

SECRET #2: Count your breaths. Slow, deep breathing is an effective way to help prevent high blood pressure—one of the leading causes of heart disease. For people who already have high blood pressure, doing this technique a few times a day has been shown to lower blood pressure by five to 10 points within five minutes. And the pressure may stay lower for up to 24 hours.

During a breathing exercise, you want to slow your breathing down from the usual 12 to 16 breaths a minute that most people take to about three breaths. I use the "4-7-8 sequence" whenever I feel stressed.

What to do: Inhale through your nose for four seconds...hold the breath in for seven seconds...then exhale through the mouth for eight seconds.

Also helpful: A HeartMath software package, which you can load on your computer or smartphone, includes breathing exercises to help lower your heart rate and levels of stress hormones.

Cost: $129 and up, at *www.heartmath.org*. You can also sign up for some free tools on this website.

SECRET #3: Practice "loving kindness." This is an easy form of meditation that reduces stress, thus allowing you to keep your heart rate and blood pressure at healthy levels.

Research has shown that people who meditate regularly are 48% less likely to have a heart attack or stroke than those who don't meditate. "Loving kindness" meditation is particularly effective at promoting relaxation—it lowers levels of the stress hormones adrenaline and cortisol while raising levels of the healing hormone oxytocin.

What to do: Sit quietly, with your eyes closed. For a few minutes, focus on just your breathing. Then imagine one person in your life whom you find exceptionally easy to love. Imagine this person in front of you. Fill your heart with a warm, loving feeling...think about how you both want to be happy and avoid suffering...and imagine that a feeling of peace travels from your heart to that person's heart in the form of white light. Dwell on the image for a few minutes. This meditation will also help you practice small acts of kindness in your daily life—for example, giving a hand to someone who needs help crossing the street.

SECRET #4: Don't neglect sex. Men who have sex at least two times a week have a 50% lower risk for a heart attack than those who abstain. Similar research hasn't been done on women, but it's likely that they get a comparable benefit.

Why does sex help keep your heart healthy? It probably has more to do with intimacy than the physical activity itself. Couples who continue to have sex tend to be the ones with more intimacy in their marriages. Happy people who bond with others have fewer heart attacks—and recover more quickly if they've had one—than those without close relationships. (But see page 326 to find out when sex is dangerous for your heart.)

SECRET #5: Be happy! People who are happy and who feel a sense of purpose and connection with others tend to have lower blood pressure and live longer than those who are isolated. **Research shows that two keys to happiness are to help others be happy—for example, by being a volunteer—and to reach out to friends and neighbors.** Actually, any shared activity, such as going to church or doing group hobbies, can increase survival among heart patients by about 50%.

SECRET #6: Try Waon (pronounced Waown) therapy. With this Japanese form of "warmth therapy," you sit in an infrared (dry) sauna for 15 minutes, then retreat to a resting area for half an hour, where you wrap yourself in towels and drink plenty of water. Studies show that vascular function improves after such therapy due to the extra release of nitric oxide, the master molecule in blood vessels that helps them relax.

Some health clubs offer Waon treatments, but the dry saunas at many gyms should offer similar benefits. I do not recommend steam rooms—moist heat places extra demands on the heart and can be dangerous for some people (see page 328 for more information about the health benefits of saunas).

Heart Attack: All About The Hidden Risk Factors

Robert M. Stark, MD, a preventive cardiologist in private practice in Greenwich, Connecticut. He is also a clinical assistant professor of medicine at the Yale University School of Medicine in New Haven, Connecticut, and medical director of the Cardiovascular Prevention Program at Greenwich Hospital (affiliated with the Yale New Haven Heart Institute). Dr. Stark is a Fellow of the American College of Cardiology.

We've all been told how important it is to control major risk factors for heart attack and coronary artery disease. We know, for example, not to smoke...to maintain LDL (bad) cholesterol at safe levels...raise HDL (good) cholesterol as high as possible...keep blood pressure below 120/80...and monitor our blood levels of C-reactive protein and homocysteine—a protein and amino acid that, when elevated, indicate increased heart attack risk.

What you may not know: Cardiovascular risk factors are synergistic, so any one of the risk factors mentioned above increases the effect of other risk factors.

Example: Even slightly elevated cholesterol or blood pressure becomes more dangerous in the presence of smaller, lesser-known risk factors such as...

- **Steroid medications.** Most people now know that nonsteroidal anti-inflammatory drugs, including the prescription medication *celecoxib* (Celebrex) and over-the-counter products such as *ibuprofen* (Advil) and *naproxen* (Aleve), increase heart attack and stroke risk by making blood platelets sticky. However, steroid drugs are perhaps the most dangerous of the "stealth" risk factors for heart attack.

Steroids, which include cortisone, prednisone and *prednisolone* (Orapred), are prescribed for inflammatory conditions such as colitis, inflammatory bowel disease, psoriasis, asthma and rheumatoid arthritis.

Besides raising cholesterol levels and blood pressure slightly, steroids also tend to promote the entry of cholesterol into the artery wall to form atherosclerotic plaque deposits.

Important: Only oral and injectable forms of steroid medications carry these risks—the inhaled form used to treat asthma does not.

Taking steroid medications also raises risk for atrial fibrillation, an irregular heartbeat associated with increased risk for stroke.

Self-defense: Avoid using oral and injectable steroids if at all possible. If you must use them, make sure your cholesterol levels and blood pressure are well-managed...take the lowest possible dose...and, whenever possible, avoid using them for more than a week or two.

Important: Abrupt discontinuation of steroids, without gradually tapering off, may cause serious side effects. Always consult your physician before stopping a steroid medication.

- **Stress.** Both chronic and acute stress can be hard on the heart—but in slightly different ways.

Chronic stress, such as from ongoing financial pressures or a strained relationship, raises blood levels of the stress hormones epinephrine (adrenaline), norepinephrine and cortisol, accelerating buildup of dangerous plaque in the coronary arteries much as steroid drugs do.

Self-defense: Address the underlying cause of the chronic stress...engage in daily aerobic exercise, which burns off excess epinephrine in the bloodstream and reduces anxiety...and practice stress-reduction techniques, such as biofeedback and meditation, which have been shown to lower epinephrine and norepinephrine levels.

Acute stress, such as from the sudden death of a spouse, not only increases stress hormones but also causes the coronary arteries to constrict. In addition, acute stress increases the heart's need for, and consumption of, oxygen. If you already have a partially blocked coronary artery due to plaque buildup, this constriction and increased oxygen consumption can contribute to a dangerous shortage of blood flow to the heart.

Self-defense: If you are confronted with acute or chronic stress, ask your doctor to consider prescribing a beta-blocker, such as *propranolol* (Inderal), *atenolol* (Tenormin) or *metoprolol* (Lopressor). These drugs are typically used to treat heart conditions and high blood pressure. However, beta-blockers also protect against the harmful arterial effect that occurs with stress and can be taken as long as stress-related symptoms occur. These drugs are not recommended for those with low blood pressure, asthma or abnormally low heart rate.

• **Sleep apnea.** People who suffer from this condition stop breathing during their sleep for a few seconds at a time many times per night. Sleep apnea not only disrupts sleep but also is associated with an increased risk for heart attack and heart disease.

Self-defense: Half of people with mild sleep apnea (those who stop breathing five to 15 times per hour) and 20% of those with moderate apnea (15 to 30 breathing stoppages per hour) have so-called positional sleep apnea—that is, the disturbed breathing occurs only when the person is sleeping on his/her back.

Good solution: A relatively new strap-on foam device called Zzoma, which forces you to lie on your side, appears to help prevent positional sleep apnea (available for $189.95 from the manufacturer at 877-799-9662 or *www.zzomasleep.com*).

For more serious cases, continuous positive airway pressure (CPAP), a type of therapy in which the sleeper wears a mask that blows air into his nostrils, helps reduce apnea symptoms. For those who find the CPAP mask uncomfortable, oral appliances, prescribed by dentists, also help reduce apnea symptoms.

• **Anemia.** With this condition, the blood's ability to carry oxygen is impaired. This can trigger chest pain (angina) or even a heart attack in people whose coronary arteries are partially blocked. Always seek immediate medical attention if you have chest pain.

Self-defense: Anemia often can be treated with iron, vitamin B-12 or folic acid supplements or medications. After you've sought medical attention for chest pain, be sure that your physician tests you for anemia.

• **Chlamydia infection.** Chlamydia pneumoniae is a bacterium found in the respiratory tract of more than two million Americans. Different from the germ that causes the sexually transmitted disease chlamydia, C. pneumoniae is associated with increased risk for coronary artery disease, possibly because it contributes to arterial inflammation.

Self-defense: If you have signs of a respiratory infection, your doctor may want to order a blood test for C. pneumoniae. Antibiotics can effectively treat an infection caused by this bacterium.

• **Vitamin K deficiency.** Vitamin K (found mostly in meats, cheeses and leafy green vegetables) has been shown to reduce cardiovascular risk in people by more than 50% and also has prevented hardening of the arteries in animal studies. Vitamin K is also produced by the bacteria naturally residing in the intestine. Researchers have found, however, that most people don't get enough vitamin K in their diets.

Self-defense: To ensure that you get enough of this crucial vitamin, ask your doctor about taking a high-dose vitamin K supplement (100 mcg daily for adults). Because vitamin K can reduce the effects of blood-thinning medication, it is never recommended for people taking *warfarin* (Coumadin) or other blood thinners.

• **Horizontal earlobe creases.** Though no one knows why, some research has shown that people who have a horizontal crease in one or both of their earlobes may be at increased risk for coronary artery disease.

Self-defense: While there's nothing that can be done to change this risk factor, anyone with such creases should be especially careful about monitoring other cardiovascular risk factors.

Sex Can Cause a Heart Attack—and Four More Important Triggers

Barry A. Franklin, PhD, director of preventive cardiology and cardiac rehabilitation at William Beaumont Hospital in Royal Oak, Michigan. He is coauthor, with Joseph C. Piscatella, of *Prevent, Halt & Reverse Heart Disease* and coauthor, with Robert Sweetgall, of *One Heart, Two Feet.*

We've all seen dramatic scenes in movies in which a person suffers a heart attack following an angry outburst... after hearing of the death of a loved one...or while having sex.

But that's just Hollywood melodrama, right? Well, actually, no.

An ever-increasing body of scientific evidence shows that some emotional and physical "stressors" can temporarily increase the risk for a heart attack, stroke or sudden cardiac death.

While these dangers are highest in people with heart disease, elevated cholesterol, high blood pressure or cardiovascular risk factors, such as smoking, obesity and/or a lack of exercise, even seemingly healthy people can be affected.

How to protect yourself: If you do aerobic or endurance exercise, such as brisk walking, jogging or walking up a treadmill incline, for 45 to 60 minutes, five days a week, you'll be much less susceptible to cardiovascular triggers than people who get less exercise or are mainly sedentary, according to research. It's believed that moderate-to-vigorous exercise increases the body's ability to adapt or safely respond to periodic bursts of sympathetic stimulation (the body's reaction to stress, such as a faster heartbeat or a spike in blood pressure), which can trigger cardiac events. *Cardiac dangers you should know about...*

DANGER #1: Getting angry. When you get really angry, your risk for a heart attack in the next two hours is two to nine times higher than it was before. Extreme anger can trigger arrhythmias (heartbeat irregularities), constriction of the arteries and an increase in blood clots.

Important: Mere annoyance does not have the same effect—the risks are associated with physiological changes that can occur when a person is enraged.

Self-defense: Consider therapy if you're prone to extreme anger—for example, during arguments or when someone cuts you off in traffic. In therapy, you'll learn to respond appropriately to stressful situations and not to overreact.

Also helpful: If you're unable (or unwilling) to get your emotions under control, ask your doctor if he/she recommends taking a daily aspirin to help prevent blood clots and/or a beta-blocker such as *atenolol* (Tenormin) to slow heart rate. The risk for an emotionally triggered heart attack may be lower in patients who use these medications.

DANGER #2: Receiving very bad news. Suppose you've just learned that a loved one has died or that you have cancer. Your immediate risk for a heart attack is six to 21 times higher than it was before you heard the bad news.

Two new studies reported in *Circulation* and *The New England Journal of Medicine* discovered that the risk of having a heart attack is highest on the day that you receive bad news, but the risk remains higher than normal for at least the next four weeks.

Self-defense: Regular exercise and some medications (such as a beta-blocker or aspirin) may reduce this cardiovascular risk. I also advise patients who have experienced emotional trauma to spend more time with family and friends. Staying socially active and maintaining close emotional ties have been shown to lower cardiovascular risks.

DANGER #3: Having sex. Some people may find it hard to believe that having sex could trigger a heart attack in a man.

What's risky: Sex with an extramarital lover. According to one widely cited report, about 80% of heart attack deaths during or after sex take place in hotel rooms when people are not with their spouses.

Extramarital sex can cause higher-than-normal levels of arousal, which can produce an abrupt and sustained rise in heart rate and tax the heart. Also, these encounters are more often accompanied by increases in smoking or excessive alcohol use—both of which increase heart attack risk—than sexual relations with a spouse or steady partner.

Self-defense: Sex is safer if you exercise regularly. In general, sexual activity increases the heart rate by about 20 to 30 beats per minute. Extramarital sex may produce a considerably higher increase in heart rate. If you are not in good physical shape, start walking. Regular walking appears to prevent the triggering of a heart attack during or immediately after sex. Sex with a regular partner or spouse isn't risky for people who are physically active.

DANGER #4: Watching sporting events. If you're passionate about sports—and really care who wins—your heart could pay the price.

For example, during the World Cup soccer matches in Germany in 2006, there were 2.7 times more cardiac emergencies on the days when the German team played. When sports fans get excited, the heart rate can increase from about 70 beats a minute to 170 beats in some cases. In people with existing (sometimes undiagnosed) heart disease, this can trigger life-threatening clots or arrhythmias.

Self-defense: Don't get carried away at sporting events...and don't let the excitement of big games lead you into unhealthy practices—for example, forgetting to take your heart medications...drinking excessively...and/or smoking.

DANGER #5: Shoveling snow and other strenuous activities. Every winter, we read about people who die from a heart attack while shoveling snow. Even though cold temperatures usually are blamed, the main reason is overexertion of a diseased or susceptible heart.

When habitually sedentary people engage in unaccustomed, vigorous physical activity, they may be 50 to 100 times more likely to have a cardiovascular event, such as a heart attack, than those who don't exert themselves.

Shoveling snow can cause increases in heart rate and blood pressure that are comparable to maximal exertion on a treadmill. The upper-body movements involved in shoveling are more taxing on the heart than movements involving only the legs. And breathing cold air can constrict the arteries that supply the heart. Holding one's breath, muscle straining and mainly standing still while shoveling, all of which impair blood flow to the heart, also can create excessive cardiac demands.

Skiing, especially cross-country (and downhill, to a lesser extent), can tax the heart, too. At higher altitudes, the relatively low pressure of oxygen in the air makes the heart work harder.

Self-defense: Don't shovel snow if you're generally sedentary or have been diagnosed with cardiovascular disease or have risk factors (such as high blood pressure or a family history of heart disease). Hire someone to do it for you. If you must shovel, work slowly and for only a few minutes at a time. If possible, push the snow or sweep it rather than lifting it or throwing it. Consider buying an automated snowblower, which decreases demands on the heart.

If you are an amateur skier and mostly sedentary, gradually increase your activity levels for at least four weeks before a ski trip.

When outdoors in cold weather, wear layers of clothing, a hat, gloves and a scarf to cover your mouth and nose. This helps prevent constriction of the arteries.

You Can Exercise Less and Be Just as Healthy

Barry A. Franklin, PhD, director of Preventive Cardiology and Cardiac Rehabilitation at William Beaumont Hospital in Royal Oak, Michigan. He is coauthor, with Joseph C. Piscatella, of *109 Things You Can Do to Prevent, Halt & Reverse Heart Disease.*

Do you struggle to fit the recommended amount of exercise into your busy schedule?

Well, what if we told you that the amount of exercise needed to reap health benefits might be less than you think? Maybe you could free up some of your workout time for other activities that are important to you and beneficial to your health—like playing with your kids or grandkids, volunteering for a favorite charity or cooking healthful meals.

THE LATEST IN EXERCISE RESEARCH

A recent study published in the *Journal of the American College of Cardiology* found that people lived longest when they ran, on average, for 30 minutes or more, five days a week. Surprisingly, that research also showed that people who jogged at an easy pace for as little as five to 10 minutes a day had virtually the same survival benefits as those who pushed themselves harder or longer.

Also surprising: A study recently done at Oregon State University found that one- and two-minute bouts of activity that add up to 30 minutes or more per day, such as pacing while talking on the telephone, doing housework or doing sit-ups during TV commercials, may reduce blood pressure and cholesterol and improve health as effectively as a structured exercise program.

HOW TO EXERCISE SMARTER, NOT HARDER

Here are four strategies to help you exercise more efficiently...

- **Recognize that some exercise is always better than none.** Even though exercise guidelines from the Centers for Disease Control and Prevention (CDC) call for at least 150 minutes of moderate exercise each week, you'll do well even at lower levels.

A *Lancet* study found that people who walked for just 15 minutes a day had a 14% reduction in death over an average of eight years. Good daily exercises include not only walking but working in the yard, swimming, riding a bike, etc.

If you're among the multitudes of Americans who have been sedentary in recent years, you'll actually gain the most. Simply making the transition from horrible fitness to below average can reduce your overall risk for premature death by 20% to 40%.

- **Go for a run instead of a walk.** The intensity, or associated energy cost, of running is greater than walking. Therefore, running (or walking up a grade or incline) is better for the heart than walking—and it's easier to work into a busy day because you can get equal benefits in less time.

For cardiovascular health, a five-minute run (5.5 mph to 8 mph) is equal to a 15-minute walk (2 mph to 3.5 mph)...and a 25-minute run equals a 105-minute walk.

A 2014 study of runners found that their risk of dying from heart disease was 45% lower than nonrunners over a 15-year follow-up. In fact, running can add, on average, three extra years to your life.

Caution: If you take running seriously, you still should limit your daily workouts to 60 minutes or less, no more than five days a week. (See below for the dangers of overdoing it.) People with heart symptoms or severely compromised heart function should avoid running. If you have joint problems, check with your doctor.

- **Ease into running.** Don't launch into a running program until you're used to exercise. Make it progressive. Start by walking slowly—say, at about 2 mph. Gradually increase it to 3 mph...then to 3.5 mph, etc. After two or three months, if you are symptom-free during fast walking, you can start to run (slowly at first).

- **Aim for the "upper-middle."** I do not recommend high-intensity workouts for most adults. Strive to exercise at a level you would rate between "fairly light" and "somewhat hard."

How to tell: Check your breathing. It will be slightly labored when you're at a good level of exertion. Nevertheless, you should still be able to carry on a conversation.

Important: Get your doctor's OK before starting vigorous exercise—and don't ignore potential warning symptoms. It's normal to be somewhat winded or to have a little leg discomfort. However, you should never feel dizzy, experience chest pain or have extreme shortness of breath. If you have any of these symptoms, stop exercise immediately, and see your doctor before resuming activity.

TOO MUCH OF A GOOD THING?

Most people who run for more than an hour a day, five days a week, are in very good shape. Would they be healthier if they doubled the distance—or pushed themselves even harder? Not necessarily. *Risks linked to distance running include...*

- **Acute right-heart overload.** Researchers at William Beaumont Hospital who looked at distance runners before and immediately after marathon running found that they often had transient decreases in the pumping ability of the right ventricle and elevations of the same enzymes (such as troponin) that increase during a heart attack.
- **Atrial fibrillation.** People who exercise intensely for more than five hours a week may be more likely to develop atrial fibrillation, a heart-rhythm disturbance that can trigger a stroke.
- **Coronary plaque.** Despite their favorable coronary risk factor profiles, distance runners can have increased amounts of coronary artery calcium and plaque as compared with their less active counterparts.

Watch out: Many hard-core runners love marathons, triathlons and other competitive events. Be careful. The emotional rush from competition increases levels of epinephrine and other "stress" hormones. These hormones, combined with hard exertion, can transiently increase heart risks.

Of course, all this doesn't mean that you shouldn't enjoy a daily run...or a few long ones—just don't overdo it!

Sauna Health Benefits Equal to Exercise

Walter J. Crinnion, ND, professor and director of the environmental medicine department at Southwest College of Naturopathic Medicine, Tempe, Arizona.

We know that "working up a sweat" is healthy when it involves being physically active—but what about the more relaxing ways to achieve that damp, rosy glow? I'm talking about saunas and steam rooms, both common in spas, gyms and hotels—and, increasingly, in private homes. They certainly feel good, but many people, including health practitioners, believe that steam rooms and saunas also have unique therapeutic benefits, including relaxing and soothing tired muscles...reducing chronic pain...detoxifying skin and bodily tissue...clearing out sinuses...even improving cardiovascular health.

Is there any merit to the claims—all of them or just some? Which is better, the dry heat of a sauna or the moist heat of a steam room? Walter J. Crinnion, ND, director of the environmental medicine department at Southwest College of Naturopathic Medicine in Tempe, Arizona, and author of the book *Clean, Green & Lean* shared his views on these hot health topics.

WET OR DRY—WHICH IS BEST?

First, let's understand how steam rooms and saunas differ. The primary difference between the two relates to humidity. Steam rooms use moist heat, pumping water vapor through vents into enclosed rooms to create temperatures of about 110°F, with 80% to 100% humidity. Saunas, on the other hand, essentially cook rocks so that they emanate dry heat to an ambient temperature as high as 160°F to 200°F, with humidity that is only from 15% to about 20%. The dry heat allows for the higher temperature—moist air at that temperature would burn the skin, nostrils and lungs, and potentially cause the body to overheat.

According to Dr. Crinnion, both steam and sauna can claim many of the same health benefits, including improving blood circulation and strengthening the immune system by inducing a mild and temporary "fever" that stimulates antibodies and other disease fighters in the body. For most people, the difference is a matter of personal preference—some people say that the moist air feels restorative, while others find it oppressive. Some relish the dry heat in a sauna, but others say the aridity is uncomfortable.

Though the scientific evidence is lacking, there is lots of anecdotal evidence that the moistness of steam rooms provides at least temporary relief for people with respiratory problems, whether from a cold or flu, bronchitis, allergies or asthma. The high humidity seems to help thin and clear mucus, thereby reducing congestion in the lungs and sinuses. Some people also find that the wet heat in steam rooms soothes joint pain and makes their skin look better.

SAUNA HEALTH BENEFITS—A HOT RESEARCH TOPIC

In contrast, there's quite a bit of research supporting the health benefits of saunas, so much so that Dr. Crinnion calls their dry heat a "wonderful therapeutic modality." *Here is some of the research...*

A number of studies show that sauna therapy is helpful for people with congestive heart failure and ventricular arrhythmias. Sauna sessions are the cardiovascular equivalent to a moderate workout, increasing cardiac rate and respiration.

Among men who'd had a mild heart attack, studies showed that spending 15 to 30 minutes in a sauna several times a week reduced the incidence of angina and hypertension.

A new study found that young women who spent 30 minutes in a sauna every other day over two weeks increased HDL "good" cholesterol and slightly decreased LDL "bad" cholesterol, pointing to its value in supporting heart health for other populations as well.

Dr. Crinnion said that he believes saunas also are helpful as an ancillary therapy in eliminating toxins for people with a range of conditions, including toxin-associated cancers...heavy metal toxicity (lead or mercury poisoning)...chronic neurological disorders such as Parkinson's disease or ALS...and autoimmune diseases. For such patients, he often prescribes intense sauna therapy, typically a half-hour to an hour twice weekly for multiple weeks.

SAFE USE GUIDELINES

Whichever you prefer, steam or sauna, Dr. Crinnion said it's smart to check with your doctor before using either—and that's imperative if you have any type of medical condition.

Note: Pregnant women and people with aortic valve stenosis should avoid both steam and sauna.

Because they increase sweating, both steam and sauna can be dehydrating. Avoid alcohol for at least a few hours before and afterward, and drink plenty of fluids—eight ounces for every 15 minutes of time spent in the heat. This is especially important for people taking antibiotics or blood pressure medications, both of which are dehydrating.

The maximum amount of time advised for steam rooms is no more than 20 minutes, while sauna sessions routinely run up to 30 minutes (the dry heat doesn't raise the body temperature so quickly).

And one more caveat—any public place can harbor pathogens, but steam rooms in particular can breed an abundance of microbes and fungi. Protect yourself by wearing flip-flops or shower shoes and, whether you are heading into a steam room or sauna, remember the towel to sit on—for your own protection and as a courtesy to other users.

Can You Survive When Your Heart Just Stops?

Norman S. Abramson, MD, chair of the board of directors of the Sudden Cardiac Arrest Foundation, *SCA-Aware.org*, based in Pittsburgh and a former professor of emergency medicine at the University of Pittsburgh. His research focuses on improving neurological outcomes among survivors of cardiac arrest.

Sudden chest pain isn't something you're likely to ignore. This symptom—along with breathlessness, cold sweats and other classic heart attack symptoms—is a clear sign that you need to call 911.

While a possible heart attack is scary enough, the reality actually could be even worse. With sudden cardiac arrest (SCA), brain damage is almost certain unless you are treated within just a few minutes. And unlike a heart attack, which many people survive, SCA is almost always fatal. But what if that grim picture could be improved?

A chance of survival: New research suggests that paying close attention to early signs that may precede SCA—as well as being prepared in your home, where this killer condition most often strikes—could mean the difference between life and death.

What you need to know…

WHEN THE HEART JUST STOPS

A heart attack occurs when a blood clot interrupts blood flow to a section of the heart. In contrast, with SCA, an electrical malfunction in the heart triggers a dangerous abnormality in the heart rhythm (arrhythmia) that disrupts blood flow to the brain and other organs.

Only about 10% of people who suffer SCA live long enough to get to a hospital. Most—such as newsman Tim Russert who succumbed to SCA in 2008—collapse and then die within minutes.

ARE YOU AT RISK?

More than 400,000 Americans (not including hospitalized patients) suffer SCA each year. If your doctor has warned you about elevated cholesterol, high blood pressure or other cardiovascular risk factors, you know that you could be setting yourself up for a heart attack. But the same conditions also mean that you're at risk for SCA.

For certain other people, SCA is truly a stealth killer. It sometimes occurs in those who have "silent" (often congenital) cardiovascular disease. Abusing drugs or alcohol also increases risk for SCA.

KNOW THE SIGNS

When someone suffers cardiac arrest, the only symptoms that occur simultaneously tend to be sudden collapse and a loss of consciousness. The victim also will have stopped breathing and won't have a detectable pulse.

What's new: Many individuals do have advance warning of SCA—even if they choose to ignore it.

In fact, when researchers recently looked into this, they found that 53% of SCA patients had prior symptoms, including chest pain, shortness of breath, heart palpitations and/or fainting. The symptoms—identical to those that often accompany heart attacks—occurred anywhere from one hour to four weeks before the SCA. Since SCA is so closely tied to heart disease, it makes sense that many victims will have heart disease symptoms before they suffer from SCA. If you have any of these symptoms, consult a doctor!

PROTECT YOURSELF

Most of the same approaches that will protect you from a heart attack—such as maintaining a healthy weight and not smoking—will help you avoid SCA. *Also useful for people concerned about SCA…*

- **Consider buying an automated external defibrillator (AED).** It can triple the likelihood of survival when used within the first minute or two of SCA. An AED is about the size of a laptop computer. The cost ranges from $1,200 to $2,500 but might be covered by insurance or Medicare if you have a high-risk arrhythmia or another heart condition. The device is easy to operate. Once it's turned on, a voice and screen explain where to attach the electrodes and when to push the buttons.

Be sure to act quickly: If someone collapses, use the device immediately. It won't prompt you to deliver a shock unless the person is experiencing SCA. For each one-minute delay, the chance of survival from SCA drops about 10%.

Important: I advise everyone who has heart disease or heart disease risk factors to talk to his/her doctor about owning one of these devices (or sharing one with close neighbors)—and to watch an online video or take an in-person class on how to use it. AEDs are available online.

- **Chest compressions.** Even if an AED is available, give chest compressions until it is ready to be placed on the victim's chest. If the heartbeat hasn't started after following

AED voice prompts, do chest compressions for two minutes and use the AED again. Or if there's no AED, do chest compressions alone. Don't waste time checking for a pulse or giving mouth-to-mouth breathing—it's the chest compressions that are needed to restart the victim's heart. If someone collapses and is unresponsive and you suspect it's SCA, call 911 first. Then give the compressions, and don't stop (it's hard work, so you may need help from a bystander) until the emergency medical service arrives.

How to do compressions: Put the heel of one hand on the center of the chest (between the nipples)...place the heel of your other hand on top of the first hand for strength...position your body over your hands...and press hard about two inches into the chest. Try to give at least 100 compressions per minute (almost two per second).

For a hands-only CPR video: Go to *www.heart.org/handsonlycpr*. For more detailed instruction, sign up for in-person training at your local hospital or fire department.

HOSPITAL CARE

If you suffer SCA in the hospital (or if you get to an ER in time), you'll be given treatments to restart the heart and reestablish heart, brain and lung functions.

Induced hypothermia, a promising therapy to reduce the damage from SCA, is available at many hospitals. This therapy involves rapid cooling of the body to about 89°F for about 24 hours. Cooling the body as soon as the heart has been restarted lowers the metabolic requirements of the brain and reduces the risk for long-term neurological problems, such as coma.

People who survive SCA may need additional treatments to prevent a second cardiac arrest.

Examples: Some are given an implantable cardioverter defibrillator (ICD), a surgically implanted device that analyzes the heartbeat and administers shocks to treat ventricular fibrillation. Another approach, radio-frequency ablation, uses radio-frequency energy to destroy abnormal heart cells that can cause irregular rhythms.

You Can Cure Heart Disease—With Plant-Based Nutrition

Caldwell B. Esselstyn, Jr., MD, surgeon, clinician and researcher at The Cleveland Clinic for more than 35 years. He is author of *Prevent and Reverse Heart Disease: The Revolutionary, Scientifically Proven, Nutrition-Based Cure. DrEsselstyn.com*

In the mid-1980s, 17 people with severe heart disease had just about given up hope. They had undergone every available treatment, including drugs and surgery—all had failed. The group had experienced 49 cardiovascular events, including four heart attacks, three strokes, 15 cases of increased angina and seven bypass surgeries. Five of the patients were expected to die within a year.

Twelve years later, every one of the 17 was alive. They had had no cardiovascular events. The progression of their heart disease had been stopped—and, in many cases, reversed. Their angina went away—for some, within three weeks. In fact, they became virtually heart-attack proof. And there are hundreds of other patients with heart disease who have achieved the same remarkable results. *What you need to know...*

HOW THE DAMAGE IS DONE

Every year, more than half a million Americans die of coronary artery disease (CAD). Three times that number suffer heart attacks. In total, half of American men and one-third of women will have some form of heart disease during their lifetimes.

Heart disease develops in the endothelium, the lining of the arteries. There, endothelial cells manufacture a compound called nitric oxide that accomplishes four tasks crucial for healthy circulation...

- **Keeps blood smoothly flowing,** rather than becoming sticky and clotted.
- **Allows arteries to widen when the heart needs more blood,** such as when you run up a flight of stairs.

• **Stops muscle cells in arteries from growing into plaque**—the fatty gunk that blocks blood vessels.

• **Decreases inflammation in the plaque**—the process that can trigger a rupture in the cap or surface of a plaque, starting the clot-forming, artery-clogging cascade that causes a heart attack.

The type and amount of fat in the typical Western diet—from animal products, dairy foods and concentrated oils—assaults endothelial cells, cutting their production of nitric oxide.

Study: A researcher at University of Maryland School of Medicine fed a 900-calorie fast-food breakfast containing 50 grams of fat (mostly from sausages and hash browns) to a group of students and then measured their endothelial function. For six hours, the students had severely compromised endothelial function and decreased nitric oxide production. Another group of students ate a 900-calorie, no-fat breakfast—and had no significant change in endothelial function.

If a single meal can do that kind of damage, imagine the damage done by three fatty meals a day, seven days a week, 52 weeks a year.

PLANT-BASED NUTRITION

You can prevent, stop or reverse heart disease with a plant-based diet. *Here's what you can't eat—and what you can...*

• **What you cannot eat...**

• No meat, poultry, fish or eggs. You will get plenty of protein from plant-based sources.

• No dairy products. That means no butter, cheese, cream, ice cream, yogurt or milk—even skim milk, which, though lower in fat, still contains animal protein.

• No oil of any kind—not a drop. That includes all oils, even virgin olive oil and canola.

What you may not know: At least 14% of olive oil is saturated fat—every bit as aggressive in promoting heart disease as the saturated fat in roast beef. A diet that includes oils—including monounsaturated oils from olive oil and canola oil—may slow the progression of heart disease, but it will not stop or reverse the disease.

• Generally, no nuts or avocados. If you are eating a plant-based diet to prevent heart disease, you can have moderate amounts of nuts and avocados as long as your total cholesterol remains below 150 milligrams per deciliter (mg/dL). If you have heart disease and want to stop or reverse it, you should not eat these foods.

• **What you can eat...**

• All vegetables.

• Legumes—beans, peas, lentils.

• Whole grains and products that are made from them, such as bread and pasta—as long as they do not contain added fats. Do not eat refined grains, which have been stripped of much of their fiber and nutrients. Avoid white rice and "enriched" flour products, which are found in many pastas, breads, bagels and baked goods.

• Fruits—but heart patients should limit consumption to three pieces a day and avoid drinking pure fruit juices. Too much fruit rapidly raises blood sugar, triggering a surge of insulin from the pancreas—which stimulates the liver to manufacture more cholesterol.

• Certain beverages, including water, seltzer water, oat milk, hazelnut milk, almond milk, no-fat soy milk, coffee and tea. Alcohol is fine in moderation (no more than two servings a day for men and one for women).

• **Supplements**

For maximum health, take five supplements daily...

• Multivitamin/mineral supplement.

• Vitamin B-12—1,000 micrograms (mcg).

• Calcium—1,000 milligrams (mg) (1,200 mg if you're over 60).

• Vitamin D-3—1,000 international units (IU).

• Flaxseed meal (ground flaxseed)—one tablespoon for the omega-3 fatty acids it provides. Sprinkle it on cereal.

THE CHOLESTEROL CONNECTION

If you eat the typical, high-fat Western diet, even if you also take a cholesterol-lowering statin drug, you will not protect yourself from heart disease—because the fat in the diet will damage the endothelium cells that produce nitric oxide.

In a study in *The New England Journal of Medicine*, patients took huge doses of statin drugs to lower total cholesterol below 150 but didn't change their diets—and 25% experienced a new cardiovascular event or died within the next 30 months.

Recommended: Eat a plant-based diet, and ask your doctor if you should also take a cholesterol-lowering medication. Strive to maintain a total cholesterol of less than 150 and LDL ("bad" cholesterol) below 85.

MODERATION DOESN'T WORK

The most common objection physicians have to this diet is that their patients will not follow it. But many patients with heart disease who find out that they have a choice—between invasive surgery and nutritional changes that will stop and reverse the disease—willingly adopt the diet.

Why not eat a less demanding diet, such as the low-fat diet recommended by the American Heart Association or the Mediterranean Diet?

Surprising: Research shows that people who maintain a so-called low-fat diet of 29% of calories from fat have the same rate of heart attacks and strokes as people who don't.

Plant-based nutrition is the only diet that can effectively prevent, stop and reverse heart disease. It also offers protection against stroke...high blood pressure...osteoporosis... diabetes...senile mental impairment...erectile dysfunction...and cancers of the breast, prostate, colon, rectum, uterus and ovaries.

How a Firefighter Lowered His Cholesterol 148 Points—Without Drugs

Rip Esselstyn, a world-class athlete who has competed professionally in triathalons, winning or placing in major competitions. In 1997, at the age of 34, Rip became a firefighter at the Engine 2 firehouse in Austin, Texas. He is author of *The Engine 2 Diet. Engine2.com*

Like my Dad, I have long been a proponent of a plant-based diet—or what I like to call "plant-strong nutrition." (My father is Caldwell Esselstyn, MD, who was interviewed for the previous article.) I find that plant-strong nutrition gives me the energy I need for my active lifestyle, which includes working as a firefighter at the Engine 2 firehouse in Austin, Texas.

At the firehouse, in a spirit of camaraderie, firefighters compete about everything—from Ping-Pong to who can climb the fire pole hand over hand without using his feet. One day, some of my Engine 2 colleagues and I had a competition to find out who had the lowest cholesterol. The competition was lost by JR—who had a total cholesterol of 344.

I asked JR if he would be willing to try out plant-strong nutrition for three weeks. He knew that I ate this way and that my cholesterol fluctuates between 130 and 150. JR was so shocked by his 344 that he decided to try my eating plan. His cholesterol dropped a whopping 148 points—to 196.

The results were so dramatic that I decided to develop "The Engine 2 Diet"—a four-week, plant-strong regimen that isn't as strict as my father's diet. It allows a little more fat. I tested the diet on 80 people, including many firefighters. In one group, total cholesterol dropped from an average of 197 to 135...average LDL ("bad" cholesterol) dropped from 124 to 74...and the average weight loss was 14 pounds.

I know that it can be hard to radically change how you eat, so I came up with a gradual program to get started...

Week One. No dairy of any kind—no milk, cheese, cream, yogurt, butter, ice cream or sour cream. No processed or refined foods—no white rice, white flour, white pasta, white bread or anything else that is processed, including cakes, cookies, chips and sodas.

Week Two. Stop eating meat, chicken, eggs and fish, while continuing to avoid dairy and refined foods.

Week Three. Eliminate oil, including olive, canola, coconut and any other oils. No baked goods, salad dressings or cooking with added oils.

Week Four. Continue with the total Engine 2 diet—fruits, vegetables, whole grains, legumes, nuts and seeds.

I find that after four weeks on the diet, you look better, sleep better, have more energy and can eat as much food as desired without gaining weight. You feel so good that the diet becomes a natural way of life.

If You Don't Want to Take a Statin...Natural Ways to Effectively Reduce Your Heart Attack Risk

Allan Magaziner, DO, an osteopathic physician and the founder and director of the Magaziner Center for Wellness in Cherry Hill, New Jersey. One of the country's top specialists in nutritional and preventive medicine, Dr. Magaziner is coauthor of *The All-Natural Cardio Cure: A Drug-Free Cholesterol and Cardiac Inflammation Reduction Program. DrMagaziner.com*

As the controversial new guidelines on statins begin to kick into use in doctors' offices around the country, the number of Americans for whom these drugs will be recommended is expected to double. But plenty of people don't like to take any type of prescription medication if they can avoid it.

Most integrative physicians, who prescribe natural therapies (and drugs when needed), agree that the majority of people who take statins—and most of those who will be recommended to do so under the new guidelines—could get many of the same benefits, such as lower cholesterol and inflammation levels, with fewer risks, by relying on targeted food choices (see examples on the next page) and supplements. Exercise—ideally, about 30 minutes at least five days a week—should also be part of a healthy-heart regimen.*

The natural regimen that I've fine-tuned over the past 25 years for my patients...

*Talk to your doctor before taking any of these supplements—they may interact with medications or affect certain chronic health conditions.

THE BEST CHOLESTEROL-LOWERING SUPPLEMENTS

- **Fish oil.**

Typical daily dose: 1,000 mg total of EPA and DHA) fights inflammation, lowers LDL "bad" cholesterol and is part of most good heart-protective regimens.** *In addition, I recommend using the first supplement below and adding the other three supplements if total cholesterol levels don't drop below 200 mg/dL...*

- **Red yeast rice.** You have probably heard of this rice, which is fermented to produce monacolins, chemical compounds with statin-like effects. It can lower LDL cholesterol by roughly 30%.

Red yeast rice can be a good alternative for people who can't tolerate statins due to side effects such as muscle aches and increased risk for diabetes. Red yeast rice also has other natural protective substances, such as isoflavones, fatty acids and sterols, not found in statins.

Typical dosage: 1.2 g to 2.4 g daily. I advise starting with 1.2 g daily. The dose can be increased as needed, based on your physician's advice.

What I tell my patients: Unfortunately, red yeast rice has gotten a bad rap because of the way some products were labeled. The supplements that I recommend are manufactured with high standards of quality control and contain therapeutic levels of active ingredients.

Good products: Choleast by Thorne Research, *www.thorne.com*...and High Performance Formulas' Cholestene, *www.hpfonline.com.*

When taking red yeast rice, some people have heartburn, gastrointestinal (GI) upset or mild headache—these effects usually are eliminated by taking the supplement with food.

- **Niacin.** Few doctors recommend niacin routinely even though it's one of the most effective cholesterol remedies. Although a recent study questioned the effectiveness of niacin, most research finds it beneficial. It may lower LDL by about 10% and increase HDL "good"

**A recent study linking fish oil to increased risk for prostate cancer is not supported by other medical research, so most men can take fish oil supplements under a doctor's supervision.

cholesterol by 15% to 35%. It can lower levels of triglycerides and Lp(a), a sticky cholesterol particle that causes atherosclerosis.

Typical dosage: 1 g to 3 g of time-released niacin daily, divided into two doses and taken with food.

What I tell my patients: Start with 250 mg daily, and increase the dose by 250 mg every two weeks until you are taking the amount recommended by your doctor. People who take high doses of niacin too quickly often have uncomfortable facial flushing and sometimes stomach upset or other GI disturbances. "Flush-free" niacin is available, but it doesn't lower cholesterol as effectively as the regular version.

- **Pantethine.** You may not be familiar with this supplement, a form of pantothenic acid (vitamin B-5). Recent studies show that it raises HDL cholesterol—and it prevents LDL from oxidizing, the process that causes it to cling to arteries.

Typical dosage: 900 mg, divided into two or three doses daily. Good pantethine products are made by Jarrow, *www.jarrow.com*... and NOW Foods, *www.nowfoods.com*.

What I tell my patients: Take pantethine with meals to reduce the risk for indigestion and to aid absorption.

- **Sterols and stanols.** These cholesterol-lowering plant compounds are found in small amounts in many fruits, vegetables and grains. But sterol and stanol supplements are much more powerful. In supplement form, the plant compounds reduce LDL by about 14% and cause no side effects.

Typical dosage: Take 3 g of a sterol/stanol supplement daily. Pure Encapsulations makes a good product, *www.pureencapsulations.com*.

Most integrative physicians are very knowledgeable about natural remedies. To find one in your area, consult the American College for Advancement in Medicine at *www.acam.org*.

YUMMY CHOLESTEROL FIGHTERS

For years, oat bran and oatmeal were touted as the best foods for high cholesterol. Rich in soluble fiber, these foods help prevent cholesterol from getting into the bloodstream. A daily serving of oats, for example, can lower LDL by 20%. Other good foods rich in soluble fiber include barley, beans, pears and prunes. But research has now gone beyond these old standby food choices. *Here are some other fiber-rich foods that fight cholesterol...*

- **All nuts.** Walnuts and almonds are great cholesterol fighters, but so are pistachios, peanuts, pecans, hazelnuts and other nuts, according to recent research. Eat a handful (1.5 ounces) of nuts daily.
- **Popcorn** actually contains more fiber per ounce than whole-wheat bread. Just go easy on the salt and butter, and stay away from store-bought microwave popcorn (it can contain harmful chemicals).

Smart idea: Put one-quarter cup of organic plain popcorn in a lunch-size brown paper bag, and pop in the microwave. It's delicious—and there's no cleanup.

Better Heart Attack Care

In a review of 13 studies of 3,629 patients who had suffered heart attacks up to 24 years earlier, those who took the amino acid L-carnitine experienced significantly improved cardiac health—deaths from all causes were reduced by 27%, ventricular arrhythmias by 65% and angina by 40%—compared with those who took a placebo.

Theory: During a heart attack, blood levels of L-carnitine are depleted.

If you've had a heart attack: Talk to your cardiologist about starting on 2 g daily of L-carnitine and increasing the dose as needed.

Caution: It may interact with thyroid medication and increase risk for seizure in people with a history of seizures.

James J. DiNicolantonio, PharmD, medication therapy management specialist, Wegmans Pharmacy, Ithaca, New York.

Artery Inflammation: Six Simple, Lifesaving Tests

Bradley Bale, MD, medical director, Grace Clinic Heart Health Program, Lubbock, Texas, and cofounder, Heart Attack & Stroke Prevention Center, Spokane. He is coauthor, with Amy Doneen, ARNP, and Lisa Collier Cool, of *Beat the Heart Attack Gene: The Revolutionary Plan to Prevent Heart Disease, Stroke and Diabetes.*

A fire could be smoldering inside your arteries...a type of fire that could erupt at any moment, triggering a heart attack or stroke. In fact, the fire could be building right this minute and you wouldn't even know it. That's because the usual things doctors look at when gauging cardiovascular risk—cholesterol, blood pressure, blood sugar, weight—can all appear to be fine even when your arteries are dangerously hot.

What does work to detect hot arteries? A set of six simple, inexpensive and readily available blood and urine tests.

Problem: Few doctors order these tests, and few patients know enough to ask for them. *Here's how to protect yourself...*

THE BODY'S ARMY ON ATTACK

Hot arteries are not actually hot (as in very warm)—instead, in this case "hot" refers to the effects of chronic inflammation. Why call them hot, then? Chronic arterial inflammation can put you on the fast track to developing vascular disease by speeding up the aging of your arteries. It's so dangerous to the arterial lining that it's worse than having high LDL cholesterol. And if your arteries are already clogged with plaque—which acts as kindling for a heart attack or stroke—inflammation is what lights the match.

Inflammation in the body isn't always bad, of course. In fact, it's an important aspect of healing. When something in your body is under attack, the immune system sends in troops of white blood cells to repair and fight off the attacker, and temporary inflammation results. That's why when you cut yourself, for example, you'll see swelling at the site of the injury—it's a sign that your white blood cells are at work for your benefit.

But: When an attack against your body persists (for instance, as occurs when you have an ongoing infection of the gums), your white blood cells continue to drive inflammation. When it turns chronic, inflammation becomes highly damaging to many tissues, including the arteries.

Normally, the endothelium (lining of the arteries) serves as a protective barrier between blood and the deeper layers of the arterial wall. However, when that lining is inflamed, it can't function well and it gets sticky, almost like flypaper, trapping white blood cells on their way through the body. The inflamed endothelium becomes leaky, too, allowing LDL "bad" cholesterol to penetrate into the wall of the artery. The white blood cells then gobble up the cholesterol, forming fatty streaks that ultimately turn into plaque, a condition called atherosclerosis. Then when the plaque itself becomes inflamed, it can rupture, tearing through the endothelium into the channel of the artery where blood flows. This material triggers the formation of a blood clot—a clot that could end up blocking blood flow to the heart or brain.

THE 6-PART FIRE PANEL

Just as firefighters have ways of determining whether a blaze is hiding within the walls of a building, certain tests can reveal whether inflammation is lurking within the walls of your arteries. I use a set of six tests that I call the "fire panel." Each reveals different risk factors and, for several of the tests, too-high scores can have more than one cause—so it's important to get all six tests, not just one or two.

The fire panel can identify people at risk for developing atherosclerosis...reveal whether patients who already have atherosclerosis have dangerously hot arteries that could lead to a heart attack or stroke...and evaluate patients who have survived a heart attack or stroke to see whether their current treatments are working to reduce the inflammation that threatens their lives. Your individual test results will help determine your most appropriate course of treatment.

I recommend that all adults have this panel of tests done at least every 12 months—or every three to six months for patients at high risk for heart attack or stroke. All of these tests are readily available...are inexpensive and usually covered by insurance...and can be ordered by your regular doctor. *Here are the six tests...*

• **F2 Isoprostanes.** My nickname for this blood test is the "lifestyle lie detector" because it reveals whether or not patients are practicing heart-healthy habits. The test, which measures a biomarker of oxidative stress, helps determine how fast your body's cells are oxidizing, or breaking down. According to one study, people who have the highest levels of F2 isoprostanes are nine times more likely to have blockages in their coronary arteries than people with the lowest levels.

The score you want: A normal score is less than 0.86 ng/L...an optimal score is less than 0.25 ng/L.

• **Fibrinogen.** An abnormally high level of this sticky, fibrous protein in your blood can contribute to the formation of clots...it's also a marker of inflammation. One study divided people into four groups (quartiles) based on their fibrinogen levels and found that stroke risk rose by nearly 50% for each quartile. High fibrinogen is particularly dangerous for people who also have high blood pressure because both conditions damage the blood vessel lining and make it easier for plaque to burrow inside.

Normal range: 440 mg/dL or lower.

• **High-Sensitivity C-Reactive Protein (hs-CRP).** Your liver produces C-reactive protein, and the amount of it in your blood rises when there is inflammation in your body—so an elevated hs-CRP level generally is considered a precursor to cardiovascular disease. The large-scale Harvard Women's Health Study cited this test as being more accurate than cholesterol in predicting risk for cardiovascular disease...while another study of women found that those with high scores were up to four times more likely to have a heart attack or stroke than women with lower scores. A high hs-CRP score is especially worrisome for a person with a large waist. Excess belly fat often is a sign of insulin resistance (in which cells don't readily accept insulin), a condition that further magnifies heart attack and stroke risk.

The score you're aiming for: Under 1.0 mg/L is normal...0.5 mg/L is optimal.

• **Microalbumin/Creatinine Urine Ratio (MACR).** This test looks for albumin in the urine. Albumin is a large protein molecule that circulates in the blood and shouldn't spill from capillaries in the kidneys into the urine, so its presence suggests dysfunction of the endothelium. Though this test provides valuable information about arterial wall health, doctors rarely use it for this purpose.

Important: New evidence shows that MACR levels that have traditionally been considered "normal" can signal increased risk for cardiovascular events.

Optimal ratios, according to the latest research: 7.5 or lower for women and 4.0 or lower for men.

• **Lipoprotein-Associated Phospholipase A-2 (Lp-PLA2).** This enzyme in the blood is attached to LDL cholesterol and rises when artery walls become inflamed. Recent research suggests that it plays a key role in the atherosclerosis disease process, contributing to the formation of plaque as well as to the plaque's vulnerability to rupture. People with periodontal (gum) disease are especially likely to have elevated Lp-PLA2 scores—chronic inflammation can start in unhealthy gums and, from there, spread to the arteries.

Normal range: Less than 200 ng/mL.

• **Myeloperoxidase (MPO).** This immune system enzyme normally is found at elevated levels only at the site of an infection. When it is elevated in the bloodstream, it must be assumed that it's due to significant inflammation in the artery walls and leaking through the endothelium. This is a very bad sign. MPO produces numerous oxidants that make all cholesterol compounds, including HDL "good" cholesterol, more inflammatory. If your blood levels of MPO are high, HDL goes rogue and joins the gang of inflammatory thugs. It also interacts with another substance in the bloodstream to produce an acid that can eat holes in blood vessel walls. Smokers are particularly prone to high MPO levels.

Normal range: Less than 420 pmol/L.

HOW TO PUT OUT THE FIRES

While the "fire panel" tests above may seem exotic, the solution to the hot artery problem, for most of us, is not. That's because the best way to combat chronic inflammation is simply to maintain a healthful lifestyle. You just have to do it! Key factors include...

- **Following a heart-healthy Mediterranean-style diet.**
- **Managing stress.**
- **Getting plenty of exercise.**
- **Guarding against insulin resistance.**
- **Taking good care of your teeth and gums.**
- **Not smoking.**

In some cases, lifestyle changes alone are enough to quell the flames of chronic inflammation and to put your arteries on the road to recovery. In other cases, patients also need medication such as statins and/or dietary supplements such as niacin and fish oil. Either way, the good news is that once you shut the inflammation off, the body has a chance to heal whatever disease and damage has occurred—so you're no longer on the fast track to a heart attack or stroke.

Do You Have a Faulty Heart Valve?

Robert O. Bonow, MD, the Goldberg Distinguished Professor of Cardiology at Northwestern University Feinberg School of Medicine and chief of the division of cardiology at Northwestern Memorial Hospital, both in Chicago. Dr. Bonow is the lead author of the American College of Cardiology/American Heart Association *2006 Guidelines for the Management of Patients with Valvular Heart Disease.*

About 20 million Americans have at least one dysfunctional heart valve, caused by either a congenital defect or other factors, such as age, high blood pressure (hypertension), coronary artery disease or a previous heart attack.

Until recently, treatment for a person with valvular heart disease depended largely on his/her cardiologist's personal preferences. This lack of standardized care increased a patient's odds of undergoing an operation either earlier or later than necessary or even suffering a preventable death.

Now: Consistent clinical evidence and a consensus among medical experts regarding valvular heart disease have resulted in new treatment guidelines from the American College of Cardiology (ACC) and the American Heart Association (AHA).

WHAT IS VALVULAR HEART DISEASE?

Blood flow through the heart is regulated by four heart valves (mitral, aortic, tricuspid and pulmonic). Mitral valve prolapse (MVP), in which the two leaflets (flaps) of the mitral valve don't close properly, affects about 2% to 5% of adults. MVP typically requires no treatment, except for the use of antibiotics to prevent a potentially fatal valve infection (endocarditis) before certain dental procedures and surgeries.

Many Americans are affected by a complication of valvular disease, known as regurgitation, in which the valves fail to close completely, allowing blood to leak backward through the valve.

In many other people with valvular heart disease, one of the valves stiffens and narrows, compromising blood flow. This condition is called stenosis and has several possible causes. Among people age 60 or older, a common cause is the accumulation of calcium deposits in the aortic valve.

To diagnose valvular heart disease, a doctor will perform a physical exam and review the patient's medical history. He may order one or more tests, such as an ultrasound of the heart, also known as an echocardiogram...a chest X-ray...or an electrocardiogram (ECG), which records the electrical activity of the heart.

Both valvular regurgitation and stenosis force the heart to work harder to pump blood. Medication can't correct valve function. If a valve is severely diseased or damaged, surgery to repair or replace it may be necessary.

Key recommendations from the new ACC/AHA guidelines...

• **Make sure that you receive an echocardiogram.** Doctors typically use a stethoscope to detect valvular heart disease—the abnormal blood flow causes a murmur. However, it's often difficult to distinguish between benign and disease-related murmurs with a stethoscope alone. Without an echocardiogram, it's impossible to gauge the severity of any valve dysfunction.

• **Get a precise diagnosis.** An echocardiogram and other quantifiable data, such as a chest X-ray or ECG, should be used in the diagnosis of valvular heart disease to identify its severity. The diagnosis should characterize the valve problem as mild, moderate or severe.

• **Consider surgery.** Valve disease can be fairly advanced before a patient notices any symptoms...and with today's minimally invasive repair/replacement techniques, surgery is often less risky than waiting for heart damage or heart failure to develop.

Important: Unless you're facing emergency surgery (which rarely occurs in patients with valvular disease), always get a second opinion before undergoing valve repair or replacement.

• **Ask your doctor whether mitral valve repair rather than valve replacement is an option.** Evidence shows that repair leads to better heart function and a greater chance of survival.

Important: Before consenting to mitral valve replacement, consult a cardiologist who specializes in valve repair. Ask your doctor to refer you to a hospital or surgical center where doctors are known to have a successful record of performing the procedure.

It's well established that people who undergo valve repair instead of replacement have a much lower risk of dying within 30 days of the surgery, have a much better quality of life and don't have to worry about the long-term risks of an artificial valve.

• **Talk to your doctor about mechanical and biological replacement valves.** Most mitral valves can be repaired, but diseased aortic valves typically need to be replaced. Patients have two options—a biological valve (from a human cadaver or pig or cow tissue) or a mechanical valve.

Mechanical valves can last a lifetime, but they also heighten the risk for blood clots. That's why anyone who receives a mechanical valve must take an anticoagulant, such as *warfarin* (Coumadin), for the rest of his life.

Biological valves don't pose a clot risk, but they do degrade over time and may eventually need replacing. For this reason, patients younger than age 65 requiring an aortic valve or younger than age 70 requiring a mitral valve were automatically given a mechanical replacement in the past to avoid a second surgery.

Now clinical evidence has shown that the newer biological valves can last much longer than the previous generation of biological valves. If a biological valve is inserted into a 55-year-old, there's a 75% chance that the valve will still be functioning well in 20 years.

In addition, improved surgical techniques have made the possibility of a second operation in 20 years less risky, in many cases, than daily anticoagulant therapy, which poses the constant danger of bleeding. Therefore, a biological valve may be the better choice, especially if you're age 55 or older.

New Heart-Valve Treatment

Mitral valve regurgitation is a condition in which a heart valve doesn't close all the way—it can cause fatigue, difficulty breathing and heart damage. Until now, the only treatment was open-heart surgery. Now the MitraClip—recently approved by the FDA—can be used to fasten together the loose flaps of the valve. The device is implanted through a catheter, a minimally invasive procedure. It currently is available at the 52 medical centers that participated in the clinical trials. Other hospitals will use the therapy soon.

Ted Feldman, MD, is director of the Cardiac Catheterization Laboratory at NorthShore University HealthSystem in Evanston, Illinois.

A Top Cardiologist Reveals the Best Supplements for Your Heart

Patrick M. Fratellone, MD, is an integrative cardiologist and executive medical director of Fratellone Medical Associates, and an attending physician at St. Luke's Hospital, Roosevelt Hospital and Beth Israel Hospital, all in New York City. *FratelloneMedical.com*

Put your hand on your heart. How's it doing in there? For too many women, the answer is, "Not so good." Despite the fact that we try to eat right, exercise and watch our weight, heart disease is still the number-one killer of women in America.

What are we doing wrong? For one thing, we're not getting enough of the nutrients that our hearts need to stay healthy. "Much of our food is depleted of life-sustaining vitamins and minerals," explained integrative cardiologist Patrick M. Fratellone, MD. "That's why many people can benefit from specific supplements—whether their goal is to prevent heart disease or to minimize harm from the particular cardiovascular risk factors they already have."

Here's how the various heart-healthy supplements work...and the protocols Dr. Fratellone typically recommends based on patients' particular risk factors.

Important: Check with your doctor before beginning any supplement regimen. Some supplements can interact with other supplements or medications and/or cause side effects for people with certain medical conditions.

HOW THE HEART HELPERS WORK

• **Coenzyme Q10 (CoQ10),** the energy generator of all cells, enhances the heart's pumping ability.

Caution: CoQ10 may decrease the effectiveness of blood-thinning medication, such as warfarin.

• **Folic acid,** a B vitamin, helps prevent the formation of homocysteine, an amino acid that damages artery linings.

Caution: Avoid folic acid supplementation if you have a history of cancer.

• **Hawthorn,** an herb, may strengthen heart contractions and reduce blood pressure by relaxing blood vessels.

Caution: Don't use hawthorn if you have low blood pressure or take a beta-blocker or calcium channel blocker medication.

• **L-carnitine,** an amino acid, increases the heart's pumping action...and may facilitate weight loss by increasing metabolism.

Caution: Don't use L-carnitine if you have kidney disease.

• **L-taurine,** another amino acid, dilates blood vessels, improves blood flow and helps reduce blood pressure.

Caution: L-taurine may not be appropriate if you take diuretic medication or have stomach ulcers.

• **Magnesium regulates blood pressure and heart rate.**

Caution: Don't take magnesium if your blood pressure is already low.

• **Omega-3 fatty acids,** found in fish oil, increase HDL (good) cholesterol...decrease LDL (bad) cholesterol and triglycerides...slow plaque buildup in arteries...reduce the risk for arrhythmia (abnormal heartbeat)...and reduce blood pressure.

• **Vitamin B-12 inhibits harmful homocysteine formation.**

• **Vitamin D-3 helps prevent inflammation...**reduces heart attack and stroke risk in people with high blood pressure...and may protect against heart failure.

Next step: To make use of the information above, you need to know which specific nutrients are most beneficial for you—and that depends on your personal health status.

TO PREVENT HEART PROBLEMS

Below is Dr. Fratellone's heart-protecting supplement protocol (to be taken daily, continuing indefinitely) for the typical perimenopausal or postmenopausal woman who has not been diagnosed with any condition that increases cardiovascular risk. Ask your doctor if you should take any or all of these five supplements. If you take a multivitamin, check which of the nutrients below your multi already provides.

Preventive protocol...

- **CoQ10**—100 mg daily.
- **Magnesium**—350 mg daily.
- **Omega-3s (in the form of fish oil)**—1,000 mg to 2,000 mg daily of combined EPA and DHA, the most beneficial components.
- **Vitamin B-12**—1,000 micrograms (mcg) daily.
- **Vitamin D-3**—1,000 international units (IU) daily.

IF YOU ARE ALREADY AT RISK

You may benefit from additional protection if you have a condition that increases cardiovascular risk. Dr. Fratellone said that it is generally advisable to continue taking the five supplements above, though in some cases, a higher dosage is appropriate (as detailed below)...and to consider additional supplements (observing the aforementioned cautions), depending on an individual's particular health problem.

Ask your doctor about modifying your regimen as follows if you have...

- **Atrial fibrillation or other arrhythmia**
  - Hawthorn (extract ratio 1:2)—20 drops mixed with water three times daily.
  - Magnesium—increase to 500 mg daily.
  - Omega-3s—increase to 1,000 mg three times daily.
- **Congestive heart failure**
  - Hawthorn (extract ratio 1:2)—20 drops mixed with water three times daily.
  - Vitamin D-3—increase to 2,000 IU daily.
- **Coronary artery disease**
  - Folic acid—1,000 mcg daily.
  - L-carnitine—1,000 mg three times daily.
  - L-taurine—500 mg three times daily.
  - Omega-3s—increase to 1,000 mg three times daily.
- **Diabetes**
  - CoQ10—increase to 100 mg three times daily.
  - L-carnitine—1,000 mg three times daily.
  - Magnesium—increase to 500 mg daily.
- **Excess weight** *(body mass index of 25 or higher)*
  - L-carnitine—1,000 mg three times daily.
- **High blood pressure**
  - L-taurine—500 mg three times daily.
  - Magnesium—increase to 500 mg daily.
  - Omega-3s—increase to 1,000 mg three times daily.
  - Vitamin D-3—increase to 2,000 IU daily.
- **High cholesterol**
  - CoQ10—increase to 100 mg three times daily.
  - L-taurine—500 mg three times daily.
  - Omega-3s—increase to 1,000 mg three times daily.
- **High homocysteine**
  - Folic acid—1,000 mcg daily.
- **High triglycerides**
  - CoQ10—increase to 100 mg twice daily.
  - Omega-3s—increase to 1,000 mg three times daily.

Anticlotting Drug Saves Lives

Heart attack patients live longer with a new anticlotting drug, says C. Michael Gibson, MD. Patients hospitalized for heart attack or severe angina who were given the drug Xarelto (*rivaroxaban*) for an average of 13 months, along with standard anticlotting medicines, were 34% less likely to die from a heart-related problem during that time. Xarelto has not yet been approved by the FDA for patients with heart attacks—but the FDA currently allows its use to prevent strokes in people with abnormal heart rhythms.

C. Michael Gibson, MD, is an interventional cardiologist and chief of clinical research, division of cardiology, Beth Israel Deaconess Medical Center, Harvard Medical School, Boston. He led a study of 15,526 people, published online in *The New England Journal of Medicine.*

The Hidden Heart Disease Even Doctors Miss

Holly S. Andersen, MD, attending cardiologist and director of Education and Outreach at the Ronald O. Perelman Heart Institute of New York-Presbyterian Hospital in New York City and medical adviser to the Women's Heart Alliance. She is an expert in the field of heart disease in women.

It's hard to imagine that, with all the technology available today, heart disease could be completely missed. But that's exactly what's frequently occurring with a tricky heart condition known as small vessel disease or coronary microvascular disease (MVD).

Here's what happens: Patients, most often women, have chest pain, other symptoms that suggest heart disease or even heart attacks. But when doctors examine their coronary arteries, they find no evidence of blockage and often rule out heart disease.

Result: Patients go without the vital treatment they need.

Mystery solved: The problem in these cases, researchers have recently discovered, often lies in the tiny blood vessels—which can't be seen with the naked eye or conventional heart disease testing—that branch off the larger coronary arteries in the heart.

Researchers still have much to learn about MVD, but here's what's known now and what you can do to protect yourself...

A DIFFERENT KIND OF HEART DISEASE

The most common variety of coronary heart disease (CHD) is caused by atherosclerotic plaques—cholesterol-containing deposits that pile up and narrow one or more of the large arteries that carry blood to the heart, restricting flow. When the heart gets too little blood to meet its needs—during exertion, for example—people with CHD have chest pain (angina). And if blood flow is restricted even further—usually due to a clot lodged in the narrowed artery—a heart attack and death may occur.

Plaque is often involved in MVD, too. But instead of accumulating in clumps that block off segments of specific coronary arteries, cholesterol is deposited more evenly inside whole areas of microscopic circulation. Additionally, in MVD the walls of the tiny arteries are injured or diseased—instead of opening wider to allow more blood to reach the heart during exercise or at times of emotional stress, they tighten up, constricting blood flow when it's needed most.

The reason for this is unclear, but it seems that at least some of the time, it's due to malfunction of the endothelial cells that line the blood vessels. The resulting symptoms can be indistinguishable from garden-variety CHD—and the risk for heart attack may be just as real.

DO YOU HAVE MICROVASCULAR DISEASE?

Diabetes and high blood pressure raise one's risk for MVD, as does CHD. High cholesterol, obesity, smoking and a lack of physical activity are risk factors, too, and like CHD, MVD becomes more common with advancing age.

Symptoms of MVD can be identical to the classic signs of CHD—pain, a squeezing sensation or pressure in the chest, usually during activity or emotional stress. The discomfort can also occur in the shoulders, arms, neck or jaw.

MVD tip-off: Painful episodes of MVD usually last longer—more than 10 minutes, and sometimes longer than 30 minutes—than those of classic CHD.

Other symptoms of MVD: Fatigue or lack of energy, trouble sleeping and shortness of breath. Women are particularly likely to have these vague manifestations rather than the kind of distinct chest pain that we usually associate with heart disease. Forty percent of women don't have chest pain even while having a heart attack, whether it's caused by CHD or MVD.

Another clue: With MVD, patients often notice symptoms during daily activities and/or during times of mental stress rather than during times of physical exertion as is more often the case with CHD.

GETTING A DIAGNOSIS

The standard tests for heart disease may not uncover MVD. If you suspect you have the condition, be sure to see a cardiologist with significant experience in treating MVD.

An academic medical center is the best place to find such a doctor. *He/she may be able to diagnose it from your symptoms, medical history and earlier test results, or he may order additional tests...*

• **Nuclear imaging,** which uses a radioactive compound injected into the bloodstream to reveal a detailed image of the heart and blood flow through the arteries, including microcirculation.

• **Magnetic resonance imaging (MRI)** to produce a picture of the heart and its circulation without subjecting the patient to dye or radiation.

• **Positron emission tomography (PET),** which provides information on metabolism in the heart. This can uncover certain areas that aren't getting enough fuel and oxygen, suggesting MVD.

IF YOU HAVE MVD

If MVD is diagnosed, the goal is to keep it from progressing and to prevent heart attack and stroke. *Key strategies...*

• **Tweak your diet, and punch up your exercise routine.** A healthy eating plan, such as the Mediterranean diet, emphasizes fruits, vegetables, legumes, whole grains and nuts and fish, which contain healthy fats. Weight control and exercise reduce heart disease risk overall and also reduce blood pressure and help prevent diabetes, which are additional MVD risk factors. Beyond its general cardiovascular benefits, regular exercise appears to improve the function of the endothelial cells that line blood vessels and function poorly in MVD.

• **Get help from medication.** Doctors prescribe the same medications to treat MVD as for CHD—to reduce blood pressure and cholesterol. Aspirin or other drugs to reduce clotting risk are recommended as well.

Some evidence suggests that statins may be particularly useful because they not only reduce cholesterol but also improve endothelial function and relax the muscles around tiny blood vessels.

Similarly, calcium channel blockers, such as *amlodipine* (Norvasc), and ACE inhibitors, like *enalapril* (Vasotec), may be good choices for lowering blood pressure because they too help keep arteries open.

• **Get treated for anemia if you have it.** Anemia (low red blood cell count) may slow the growth of cells that help repair artery walls. This condition is treated with iron or B-12 supplements.

Note: If you have CHD and MVD (it's possible to have both) and have had angioplasty, a stent or bypass surgery, be aware that these procedures do not help MVD.

Cardiac Rehab Saves Lives—But Women Don't Get It

Jillian Colbert, MD, cardiology fellow in training, University of Calgary, and James A. Stone, MD, PhD, cardiologist, Cardiac Wellness Institute of Calgary, both in Alberta, Canada. Their study was presented at the 2013 annual meeting of the American College of Cardiology.

There's a proven way for men and women to slash their risk of dying from heart disease, yet few women take advantage of the opportunity—often because their doctors don't tell them about it. Called cardiac rehabilitation, it's a simple program that's widely available and hugely helpful, yet vastly underused. A recent study shines a spotlight on the dark facts.

Study participants included nearly 26,000 patients with coronary artery disease (CAD), a buildup of waxy plaque in the arteries that deliver blood and oxygen to the heart. CAD affects about 20% of people age 65 and older and is the leading cause of death for both women and men. Cardiac rehab typically is a 12-week outpatient program appropriate for people who have been diagnosed with CAD, have suffered a heart attack or have some other heart problem. It is an individualized program that includes supervised exercise sessions, nutrition counseling, stress-management training, smoking-cessation assistance and encouragement to make permanent lifestyle changes. For the study, researchers reviewed medical records spanning up to 15 years to see who attended cardiac rehab and how much it helped boost patients' survival.

Findings: The good news was that women with CAD who attended rehab were 66% less likely to die than women who did not attend. Rehab also benefited men with CAD, but not to as great a degree. However, only 31% of the women in the study were ever even referred to a cardiac rehab program by their doctors, compared with 42% of men. Physicians don't deserve all the blame, though—because among the patients who did get a rehab referral, only 50% of women (versus 60% of men) bothered to go.

Though the study didn't look at why so few women were referred to cardiac rehab, it could be that many doctors as well as patients still mistakenly think of heart disease as "mostly a man's problem"...or that some doctors refer only their healthier female heart patients to rehab, assuming that sicker ones are too ill to be helped.

As for why women who were referred declined to go? Researchers speculate that women may feel that they have too many family obligations and other responsibilities to make time for rehab...and that women tend to put their own health needs on the back burner. That's ironic, though—because if women with CAD don't take care of themselves, they won't be around to take care of their families.

Though this new research was conducted in Canada, smaller studies have shown that the same problem occurs in the US.

Self-defense: Male or female, if you have CAD or some other cardiovascular problem (for instance, a history of heart attack, bypass, angioplasty, stenting, angina, valve surgery or heart transplant), don't wait for your doctor to bring up the subject of cardiac rehab—come right out and ask whether it's appropriate for you. If the doctor says you don't need it, request a detailed explanation...and consider getting a second opinion, too. And if you are referred for cardiac rehab, go! Programs are offered at many hospitals and medical centers and typically are covered by Medicare and other health insurance.

How the Right Heart Surgeon Can Save Your Life

Albert J. Miller, MD, recently retired professor of clinical medicine (cardiology) at Feinberg School of Medicine of Northwestern University, and a clinical cardiologist at Northwestern Memorial Hospital, both in Chicago. He is author of *Chest Pain—When & When Not to Worry.*

Sometimes research affirms what makes sense anyway—but the discovery still is compelling and important.

Case in point: Recent research published in *Journal of the American Medical Association* concluded that patients who need an implantable cardioverter defibrillator (ICD)—an implanted electronic device to correct heart rhythm problems—do better when a board-certified electrophysiologist performs the procedure.

WIRING EXPERTS

An electrophysiologist is basically a cardiologist who specializes in the electrical behavior of the heart and who has undertaken specialized training (usually two years) in this field. In this study of patients at risk of life-threatening arrhythmias, the overall complication rate (meaning any complication from the surgery) with electrophysiologists was 3.5%, and the major complication rate (meaning serious medical events, ranging from cardiac arrest and cardiac-valve injury to death) was 1.3%. This is notably better than the complication rates when the devices are implanted by other types of doctors, such as non-electrophysiologist cardiologists, thoracic surgeons or other specialists, which average 5.8% (any complication) and 2.5% (major complication).

Another advantage—the electrophysiologists were more likely to also use cardiac resynchronization therapy (CRT-D) in heart failure patients who could benefit from this treatment. CRT-D uses a special pacemaker to synchronize the action of the left and right ventricles of the heart. Though the reasons for the difference in application rates of this therapy weren't explored in the study, it's a good guess to assume that the electrophysiologists are more up-to-date on the latest technology.

So what does this mean for you? If you're a candidate for a cardiac implant of any kind—whether it's a pacemaker, ICD or CRT-D, consider a board-certified electrophysiologist. There are about 1,000 in the US. To find the one nearest you, contact the Heart Rhythm Society at 202-464-3400 or visit www.hrsonline.org. When it's your heart, any edge you can get is worth the trouble.

Better Treatment for Arrhythmia

Doctors administered either anti-arrhythmic drugs or a procedure called radiofrequency catheter pulmonary vein isolation (PVI) to patients with intermittent atrial fibrillation.

Result: Those who received PVI were 44% less likely to experience further arrhythmia than those who took anti-arrhythmic drugs.

Theory: PVI eliminated tissue surrounding the pulmonary veins that generate erratic electrical currents and trigger atrial fibrillation, reducing the recurrence of this abnormal heart rhythm.

If you have atrial fibrillation: Ask your cardiologist if you're a candidate for PVI.

Carlos Morillo, MD, professor of cardiology, McMaster University, Hamilton, Ontario, Canada.

After a Heart Attack—Nutrients That Can Help

Mark A. Stengler, NMD, naturopathic medical doctor and founder and director of the Stengler Center for Integrative Medicine Encinitas, California...adjunct associate clinical professor at the National College of Natural Medicine, Portland, Oregon...author of many books, including *The Natural Physician's Healing Therapies*.

An elderly patient recently came to my clinic for a routine visit. He had been experiencing indigestion, chest pain and shortness of breath since the previous night. His blood pressure and pulse were mildly elevated, and his heartbeat was erratic. I suspected that he was having a heart attack. I had him lie back in a reclining chair (to reduce stress on his heart)...put an oxygen mask on him...and called paramedics to transport him to the hospital. Later, his wife called to tell me she was grateful that I had sent him to the hospital so quickly.

I immediately prescribed several nutrients to my patient and suggested that he start taking them while still in the hospital. These nutrients limit heart damage...promote recovery...and help to prevent a second heart attack. Other nutrients can be used several months later as patients make the transition from pharmaceutical medications.

FIRST STEPS

Several nutrients help patients immediately after a heart attack. The four nutrients below can help anyone who has had a heart attack or is at risk for one. People who are not at risk but who want to prevent a heart attack can take the first two supplements. Except as noted, most of these nutrients are safe to take with other medications and there are no side effects. They all are available at health-food stores.

- **Coenzyme Q10 (CoQ10).** Heart cells cannot produce energy without CoQ10. This nutrient has been found to reduce the risk for subsequent cardiac events, which usually are increased in people who have had a heart attack. I recommend that patients take 100 milligrams (mg)—and optimally 300 mg—daily of CoQ10 with food.

Caution: CoQ10 may interfere with some blood-thinning and blood pressure medications (and heart attack patients often are on both), so take CoQ10 only while supervised by a physician.

- **Magnesium.** This mineral enables the heart to manufacture enough energy to beat properly. It also contributes to blood-clot prevention. I usually suggest 200 mg of supplemental magnesium glycinate twice daily for long-term heart protection.

• **L-carnitine.** This supplement helps to fuel heart cells. Studies have found that L-carnitine minimizes damage to heart cells after a heart attack by strengthening the heart muscle and can reduce the likelihood of a repeat heart attack. I recommend L-carnitine in combination with CoQ10. Together, these supplements can maintain normal heart energy levels. For most people, taking 2,000 mg of L-carnitine daily helps strengthen the heart.

• **D-ribose.** During a heart attack, heart muscle cells are deprived of oxygen, and afterward they require large amounts of energy to repair damaged tissue and restore blood flow.

D-ribose helps to generate energy in heart cells. I often recommend that heart attack patients take 5 grams two to three times daily.

TRANSITIONING FROM DRUGS

I often help patients switch from the drugs that they were given after a heart attack to natural treatments that work as effectively. Depending on the patient's health, we begin the transition about four months to a year after a heart attack.

Important: Work with your cardiologist and a holistic doctor to make this transition. Do not do it on your own.

Drugs to transition from...

• **Statins.** Statin drugs often are prescribed to protect against vascular inflammation immediately following a heart attack. If you use statins, you should take CoQ10 (see doses on page 345), because statins deplete CoQ10. They also can have dangerous side effects, such as muscle pain and damage. After carefully assessing the health of a heart attack patient, I begin to help him/her switch to natural remedies that can reduce inflammation.

• **Blood-thinning therapies.** Anticoagulants such as *warfarin* (Coumadin) often are prescribed after a heart attack to prevent blood clots. But these medications have dangerous side effects, including hemorrhage, that natural anticoagulants do not have. About six months after a heart attack, patients often are able to switch to a natural blood thinner.

I generally have patients take both of the following natural anticoagulants indefinitely...

• **Omega-3s.** Fish oils are rich in the two key omega-3 fats, specifically eicosapentaenoic acid (EPA) and docosahexaenoic acid (DHA). The omega-3s are mild blood thinners, and they reduce inflammation—now considered a fundamental cause of heart disease. I recommend up to 3,000 mg daily of combined DHA and EPA for people who have had a heart attack. If you continue to take blood-thinning medication, you can take low-dose fish oil (1,000 mg daily of combined DHA and EPA).

• **Nattokinase.** This enzyme, found in a fermented Japanese soy food called natto, has impressive clot-busting benefits. In a study published in *Nutrition Research*, doctors reported that taking 4,000 fibrin units (FU) daily of nattokinase for two months significantly reduced blood levels of several clotting factors. Don't take nattokinase if you are taking blood-thinning medication.

Transitioning from drugs has helped many of my patients who have had heart attacks resume normal lives. If you have had a heart attack, talk to a holistic doctor.

Surprising Benefits of the Flu Vaccine

A review of six studies of more than 6,700 adults found that the flu vaccine lowered risk for heart attack, stroke, heart failure or death from any cardiac cause by 36%.

Theory: The vaccine may reduce flu-related inflammation that can make plaque in the arteries unstable and trigger a heart attack or other cardiac event. Violent coughing, elevated heart rate, pneumonia and other flu symptoms also may stress the heart.

Jacob A. Udell, MD, MPH, cardiologist, Women's College Hospital, University of Toronto, Canada.

The 15-Minute Heart Cure

John M. Kennedy, MD, medical director of preventive cardiology and wellness at Marina Del Rey Hospital, California. He is a clinical associate professor at Harbor-UCLA Medical Center and is on the board of directors for the American Heart Association. He is author, with Jason Jennings, of *The 15 Minute Heart Cure: The Natural Way to Release Stress and Heal Your Heart in Just Minutes a Day*. *JohnMKennedyMD.com*

Most people know that smoking, high cholesterol and high blood pressure are among the main risk factors for heart disease. Few of us realize that daily stress is another key risk factor. It can damage the heart and arteries even in people who are otherwise healthy.

Recent finding: A University of Southern California study that looked at 735 patients for more than 12 years found that chronic stress and anxiety were better predictors of future cardiovascular events (such as a heart attack) than other risk factors. The researchers estimate that those who reduce or stabilize their stress levels are 50% to 60% less likely to have a heart attack than those who experience increasing stress.

TOXIC OVER TIME

Researchers have known for a long time that sudden traumatic events can trigger heart problems. Three years after the 9/11 terrorist attacks, for example, study participants—most of whom watched the attacks on live television—were questioned about their stress levels. Those who still were severely stressed were 53% more likely to have heart problems, and twice as likely to develop high blood pressure, as those with lower stress levels.

It appears that even "normal" stress—financial pressures or an unhappy job situation—is dangerous when it continues for a long time. It's estimated that more than 75% of visits to primary care physicians are linked to stress-related disorders.

What happens: Chronic stress increases vascular resistance, the main cause of high blood pressure. It increases the activity of platelets, cell-like structures in blood that clump together and trigger most heart attacks. It increases levels of cortisol, adrenaline and other stress hormones that promote arterial inflammation.

Doctors have been slow to acknowledge stress as a major cardiovascular risk factor. This is partly because stress (like pain) is subjective and highly individual—it's difficult to quantify, because everyone has different stress triggers and experiences stress differently. One lawyer might thrive on hectic 16-hour days, while another might react with high anxiety.

Stress can't be directly measured, but tests show its toxic effects. When laboratory subjects who are asked to count backward from 100 by eights get increasingly frustrated, there is a corresponding increase in their heart rate, adrenaline and substances linked to inflammation, such as C-reactive protein and interleukins.

STRESS REDUCTION WORKS

We can only partly control our emotional environments—stress-causing events can't always be avoided. But we can greatly change the ways in which we react to stress. People who do this can significantly lower their cardiovascular risks.

In one study, patients with heart disease were divided into three groups and followed for up to five years. Those in one group practiced stress reduction. Those in the other groups were treated either with an exercise program or with standard medical care. (The standard-care group maintained their regular medical regimen and did not participate in an exercise or stress-management program.)

Only 10% of those in the stress-control group had a subsequent heart attack or required bypass surgery or angioplasty, compared with 21% in the exercise group and 30% in the medical-care group.

BREATHE

The traditional techniques for reducing stress, such as yoga, are helpful but typically too complicated and time-consuming for most people. My colleagues and I have developed a simpler approach that anyone can do in about 15 minutes a day. It goes by the acronym

B-R-E-A-T-H-E, which stands for Begin, Relax, Envision, Apply, Treat, Heal and End.

• **Begin.** Pick a time of day when you won't be interrupted for 15 minutes. Find a comfortable location. Many patients use their bedrooms, but any quiet, private place will work.

• **Relax.** This phase of the exercise is meant to elicit the relaxation response, a physiological process that reduces stress hormones, slows electrical activity in the brain and reduces inflammation.

Sit or lie quietly. Focus so completely on your breathing that there isn't room in your mind for anything else. Inhale slowly and deeply through your nose. Then exhale just as slowly through your mouth. Each inhalation and exhalation should take about seven seconds.

Repeat the breathing cycle seven times. You'll know you're ready to go to the next step when your body is so relaxed that it feels as if all of your weight is supported by the chair or bed rather than by your muscles.

• **Envision.** Spend a few minutes imagining that every part of your heart—the arteries, muscles, valves and the electrical system—is strong and healthy. Form a mental picture (it doesn't have to be anatomically accurate) of the heart pumping blood and sending nourishment throughout your body. Hold the mental image for several minutes.

Studies using PET scans show that people who imagine that they are performing an action activate the same part of the brain that is involved when they actually do that action. Imagining a healthy heart literally can make the heart healthier.

• **Apply.** It's up to you when (and how often) you perform this relaxation exercise. Most people can find 15 minutes a day to take a mental break from stress to keep their hearts healthy. Others also use this technique when they notice that their stress levels are rising.

During a hectic day at work, for example, you might take a break for 15 minutes to calm down with conscious breathing and visualization.

• **Treat and heal.** I encourage patients to embrace the pleasurable aspects of this exercise. Don't consider it a chore. It's more like a spa treatment than a physical workout.

The healing aspect can be strongly motivating, particularly if you already have a history of heart disease. Every time you do this exercise, you are strengthening the neural networks that connect the heart and brain. This can lead to a decrease in heart arrhythmias (irregularities), an increase in immune-cell activity and even better sleep.

• **End.** Finish each relaxation session by making a mental checklist of what you have achieved. You have imagined that your heart and arteries are healthy. You have reduced stress hormones, and you are feeling more relaxed and energized than you did before.

The results are long-lasting. People who practice this for a few weeks will find themselves dealing with unexpected stressful events productively and in a calm, focused manner.

11

Hypertension

6 Dangerous Myths About Your Blood Pressure

About one of every three adults in the US has high blood pressure (hypertension). But only about half of these people have it under control. This unfortunate statistic is due, in part, to some common misconceptions about hypertension.

Six myths—and the facts...

MYTH #1: In-office blood pressure tests are the gold standard. The automated devices in most doctors' offices are convenient, but they're not as precise as the manual (mercury) blood pressure kits. It's common for automated office blood pressure machines to give readings that are off by several points. The old-fashioned monitors tend to give more precise measurements, since doctors use a stethoscope to listen to the sound of blood flowing.

To get an accurate blood pressure reading, the patient should have rested in a seated position for at least five minutes, and his/her arm should be supported on a table or held by the person giving the test.

Important: Both types of monitors can give a skewed reading due to "white-coat hypertension," higher readings that result from anxious feelings during a doctor's visit.

Fact: You can get accurate blood pressure readings at home as long as you use an automatic, cuff-style monitor that properly fits over your upper arm (not over your wrist or finger) and follow the instructions. The device should be approved by the Association for the Advancement of Medical Instrumentation (AAMI). This ensures that the device has undergone extensive studies to validate its accu-

Mark C. Houston, MD, an associate clinical professor of medicine at Vanderbilt University School of Medicine in Nashville and director of the Hypertension Institute of Nashville at Saint Thomas Hospital. He is also a member of the American Heart Association Council on Arteriosclerosis, Thrombosis and Vascular Biology and the author of *What Your Doctor May Not Tell You About Hypertension* and *What Your Doctor May Not Tell You About Heart Disease*.

racy. To tell if a monitor has AAMI approval, check the label on the device's package.

MYTH #2: It's fine to check your blood pressure now and then. Checking your blood pressure every few days or just once a week is fine for maintaining good blood pressure readings but not for achieving good control in the beginning.

New approach: 24-hour ambulatory blood pressure monitoring (ABPM). It's done routinely in the UK but is still a novelty in the US. That's likely to change because studies show that it's the most effective way to measure blood pressure.

With ABPM, patients wear a device (usually around the waist) that controls a blood pressure cuff that measures brachial pressure (inside the arm at the elbow crease). ABPM, which takes readings every 15 to 60 minutes over a 24-hour period, allows your doctor to choose medications and doses more precisely. The test costs $100 to $350, but it is usually covered by insurance with proper diagnostic coding (such as labile, or "episodic," hypertension or resistant hypertension).

My advice: Have the test once when diagnosed with hypertension, and repeat it once or twice a year to see how treatment is working.

MYTH #3: It's OK to take blood pressure medication at your convenience. Blood pressure normally drops 10% to 20% during sleep. But about 25% of blood pressure patients (known as nondippers) don't experience this nighttime drop. Their blood pressure is always elevated, and they need to time their medications accordingly.

If a 24-hour test shows that you're a nondipper, your doctor will probably advise you to take medications at night. Taking medications at night—say, at about 9 pm—can reduce the risk for cardiovascular events (such as a heart attack) by 61% compared with taking them in the morning. Nighttime medications can also help lower the surge in blood pressure that occurs in the morning.

MYTH #4: Sodium isn't a big deal for everyone. Much of what we hear or read about blood pressure these days includes references to "salt sensitivity." For people who are salt-sensitive, even small amounts of sodium can cause a rapid rise in blood pressure. But don't assume that you're safe just because your blood pressure doesn't seem to rise when you consume sodium.

Fact: Excessive salt causes vascular damage even in people without hypertension...and it increases the risk that you'll eventually develop high blood pressure.

The recommended daily limit for sodium is 1,500 mg for adults age 51 and over. People who are salt-sensitive should get even less. People who cut back on salt usually see a drop in systolic (top number) blood pressure of six to seven points and a drop in diastolic (bottom number) pressure of three to four points.

Also: Don't assume that sea salt is safe. It has only slightly less sodium chloride than table salt.

MYTH #5: You need drugs to control blood pressure. If your blood pressure is 140/90 or higher, your doctor will probably prescribe one or more medications.

But certain nutritional supplements can help boost the effectiveness of those drugs. One study found that 62% of patients who used the DASH 2 diet, exercised, lost weight and took specific supplements for six months were able to reduce or stop their use of blood pressure medications.* *Supplements to discuss with your doctor...*

- **Coenzyme Q10 (CoQ10) reduces blood pressure by an average of 15/10 points.** About half of people who take it can eventually discontinue blood pressure medications.

Typical dose: 120 mg to 225 mg daily.

- **Taurine, an amino acid, can lower blood pressure by 9/4.1 points.**

Typical dose: 2 g to 3 g daily. Larger doses may be needed in some cases.

- **Lycopene is an antioxidant in tomatoes, grapefruit and other fruits.** It reduces blood pressure, blood fats and inflammatory markers such as C-reactive protein. Consider taking this supplement if you don't eat a lot of lycopene-rich foods.

*For more details on the DASH 2 diet, go to *www.hypertensioninstitute.com* and search under "Nutritional Services."

Typical dose: 10 mg to 20 mg daily.

MYTH #6: Food won't help your blood pressure. Foods rich in potassium can reduce blood pressure. Try to get at least two-and-a-half times more potassium than sodium in your diet—the ratio that blocks sodium's negative effects.

Good high-potassium foods: A medium-sized potato with skin has 926 mg of potassium, and a medium-sized banana has 422 mg.

When Your Blood Pressure Just Won't Go Down

David A. Calhoun, MD, professor of medicine in the Vascular Biology and Hypertension Program at the University of Alabama in Birmingham. He was chair of the committee that wrote *Resistant Hypertension: Diagnosis, Evaluation, and Treatment*, published in *Hypertension*.

High blood pressure (hypertension) is widely known as a "silent" disease because it increases the risk for health problems ranging from stroke and heart attack to erectile dysfunction—often without causing symptoms. For this reason, half of people with hypertension don't even seek treatment.*

A more challenging health threat: There are many people who are trying to lower their blood pressure—but they are not successful. In fact, an estimated 20% to 30% of people being treated for high blood pressure are said to have resistant hypertension because their blood pressure remains high even though they are taking three or more medications simultaneously.

How to avoid—or overcome—this problem...

WHY TREATMENT MAY NOT WORK

Resistant hypertension is on the rise in the US, in part due to the dramatic increase in overweight individuals and those with diabetes and chronic kidney disease—all of which make high blood pressure harder to treat. When other health problems are diagnosed and effectively treated, blood pressure usually drops.

Other conditions that can play a role in resistant hypertension...

- **Obstructive sleep apnea.** In one study, 83% of people with resistant hypertension suffered from sleep apnea (the airway relaxes and shuts during sleep, causing a temporary drop in oxygen).

Symptoms to watch for: Snoring, gasping for air during sleep and daytime drowsiness.

- **Aldosteronism.** This condition occurs when the adrenal glands secrete too much of the hormone aldosterone, leading to fluid retention, which raises blood pressure. Aldosteronism is much more common than previously thought—it affects about 20% of people with resistant hypertension. Potassium levels often drop as a result of aldosteronism.

Symptoms to watch for: Weakness, muscle spasms and temporary paralysis—all of which can occur with low potassium.

DRUGS THAT MAY INTERFERE

Drugs taken for other health problems can interfere with blood pressure treatment. *For example...*

- **Nonsteroidal anti-inflammatory drugs (NSAIDs)**—over-the-counter (OTC) painkillers such as *ibuprofen* (Motrin, Advil) and *naproxen* (Aleve)—often are overlooked as a factor in resistant hypertension. NSAIDs promote fluid retention. If you have trouble controlling your blood pressure, *acetaminophen* (Tylenol) often is a better choice for pain relief.
- **Decongestants and diet pills,** including OTC versions, can raise blood pressure by causing vasoconstriction (narrowing of blood vessels).
- **Stimulants and amphetamines may elevate blood pressure,** also through vasoconstriction. Such drugs—*methylphenidate* (Ritalin) and *dextroamphetamine* and *amphetamine* (Adderall), for example—are taken for attention deficit disorder.

*For most people, hypertension is defined as blood pressure of 140/90 mmHg or higher. Optimal blood pressure is lower than 120/80 mmHg. More than one reading is needed to make a determination.

• **Oral contraceptives may keep blood pressure high,** likely by promoting fluid retention.

LIFESTYLE CHANGES THAT HELP

Factors that often contribute to resistant hypertension...

• **Salt is a double threat.** A high-sodium diet not only increases blood pressure in many people, but also blunts the effectiveness of many antihypertensive drugs.

Not everyone with high blood pressure is sensitive to sodium, but nearly all people with resistant hypertension would benefit from cutting back to less than 2,300 mg daily.

• **Potassium in your bloodstream can become depleted if you take a diuretic (water pill).** If you develop symptoms of low potassium (described earlier), ask your doctor to check your potassium level with a blood test—and then take a potassium supplement if needed.

Otherwise, include potassium-rich foods (such as citrus fruits, bananas, dried apricots and avocados) in your diet.

Caution: Chronic kidney disease patients, who are at higher risk for hyperkalemia (abnormally high blood levels of potassium), should ask their nephrologist (kidney disease specialist) about an appropriate diet.

• **Physical activity has been shown to produce a small but significant drop in blood pressure**—4 mm Hg in systolic (top number) pressure and 3 mm Hg in diastolic (bottom number) pressure, on average. Exercise at least 30 minutes, most days of the week.

WHICH DRUGS ARE BEST?

Drugs work in different ways to lower blood pressure and may be tried in different combinations. For example, if an angiotensin converting enzyme (ACE) inhibitor doesn't do the job, a calcium channel blocker or diuretic, rather than another ACE inhibitor, might be added to the regimen. *Two kinds of medications that are particularly important for resistant hypertension...*

• **Thiazide diuretics** lower blood pressure by ridding the body of excess water and salt and also appear to increase the effectiveness of other types of blood pressure medications. If you take two or three blood pressure drugs, one should be a thiazide diuretic, such as *hydrochlorothiazide* or *chlorthalidone.*

• **Mineralocorticoid receptor antagonists,** such as *spironolactone* (Aldactone) and *eplerenone* (Inspra), have been shown to reduce blood pressure substantially when added to combinations of other drugs that haven't done the job.

Important: Even the most effective medications won't work if they stay in the bottle. If your blood pressure remains high despite treatment, make sure you take all the pills, all the time.

Smart idea: A pill-organizer box may help you stick to your medication schedule.

DO YOU NEED A SPECIALIST?

If your blood pressure is still high after six months of treatment by your regular doctor, it may be time to see a hypertension expert. The American Society of Hypertension (ASH) maintains a directory of clinical hypertension specialists at *www.ash-us.org*. Or call the ASH at 212-696-9099. Your doctor also may know of a cardiologist or nephrologist with expertise in treating resistant hypertension.

Keep trying until you've found a treatment that works. All too often, resistant hypertension goes untreated, causing steady, silent damage for years.

---

5 Foods That Fight High Blood Pressure

Janet Bond Brill, PhD, RD, a nationally recognized nutrition, health and fitness expert who specializes in cardiovascular disease prevention. She has authored three books on the topic, including *Blood Pressure DOWN, Prevent a Second Heart Attack* and *Cholesterol DOWN. DrJanet.com*

Is your blood pressure on the high side? Your doctor might write a prescription when it creeps above 140/90—but you may be able to forgo medication. Lifestyle changes still are considered the best starting treatment for mild hypertension. These include not smoking, regular exercise and a healthy diet. *In addition to eating less salt, you want to include potent pressure-lowering foods, including...*

RAISINS

Raisins are basically dehydrated grapes, but they provide a much more concentrated dose of nutrients and fiber. They are high in potassium, with 220 milligrams (mg) in a small box (1.5 ounces). Potassium helps counteract the blood pressure–raising effects of salt. The more potassium we consume, the more sodium our bodies excrete. Researchers also speculate that the fiber and antioxidants in raisins change the biochemistry of blood vessels, making them more pliable—important for healthy blood pressure. Opt for dark raisins over light-colored ones because dark raisins have more catechins, a powerful type of antioxidant that can increase blood flow.

Researchers at Louisville Metabolic and Atherosclerosis Research Center compared people who snacked on raisins with those who ate other packaged snacks. Those in the raisin group had drops in systolic pressure (the top number) ranging from 4.8 points (after four weeks) to 10.2 points (after 12 weeks). Blood pressure barely budged in the no-raisin group. Some people worry about the sugar in raisins, but it is natural sugar (not added sugar) and will not adversely affect your health (though people with diabetes need to be cautious with portion sizes).

My advice: Aim to consume a few ounces of raisins every day. Prunes are an alternative.

BEETS

Beets, too, are high in potassium, with about 519 mg per cup. They're delicious, easy to cook (see the tasty recipe on page 354) and very effective for lowering blood pressure.

A study at The London Medical School found that people who drank about eight ounces of beet juice averaged a 10-point drop in blood pressure during the next 24 hours. The blood pressure–lowering effect was most pronounced at three to six hours past drinking but remained lower for the entire 24 hours. Eating whole beets might be even better because you will get extra fiber.

Along with fiber and potassium, beets also are high in nitrate. The nitrate is converted first to nitrite in the blood, then to nitric oxide. Nitric oxide is a gas that relaxes blood vessel walls and lowers blood pressure.

My advice: Eat beets several times a week. Look for beets that are dark red. They contain more protective phytochemicals than the gold or white beets. Cooked spinach and kale are alternatives.

DAIRY

In research involving nearly 45,000 people, researchers found that those who consumed low-fat "fluid" dairy foods, such as yogurt and low-fat milk, were 16% less likely to develop high blood pressure. Higher-fat forms of dairy, such as cheese and ice cream, had no blood pressure benefits. The study was published in *Journal of Human Hypertension.*

In another study, published in *The New England Journal of Medicine,* researchers found that people who included low-fat or fat-free dairy in a diet high in fruits and vegetables had double the blood pressure–lowering benefits of those who just ate the fruits and veggies.

Low-fat dairy is high in calcium, another blood pressure–lowering mineral that should be included in your diet. When you don't have enough calcium in your diet, a "calcium leak" occurs in your kidneys. This means that the kidneys excrete more calcium in the urine, disturbing the balance of mineral metabolism involved in blood pressure regulation.

My advice: Aim for at least one serving of low-fat or nonfat milk or yogurt every day. If you don't care for cow's milk or can't drink it, switch to fortified soy milk. It has just as much calcium and protein and also contains phytoestrogens, compounds that are good for the heart.

FLAXSEED

Flaxseed contains alpha-linolenic acid (ALA), an omega-3 fatty acid that helps prevent heart and vascular disease. Flaxseed also contains magnesium. A shortage of magnesium in our diet throws off the balance of sodium, potassium and calcium, which causes the blood vessels to constrict.

Flaxseed also is high in flavonoids, the same antioxidants that have boosted the popularity of dark chocolate, kale and red wine. Flavonoids are bioactive chemicals that reduce inflammation throughout the body, including in the arteries. Arterial inflammation is thought to be the "trigger" that leads to high blood pressure, blood clots and heart attacks.

In a large-scale observational study linking dietary magnesium intake with better heart health and longevity, nearly 59,000 healthy Japanese people were followed for 15 years. The scientists found that the people with the highest dietary intake of magnesium had a 50% reduced risk for death from heart disease (heart attack and stroke). According to the researchers, magnesium's heart-healthy benefit is linked to its ability to improve blood pressure, suppress irregular heartbeats and inhibit inflammation.

My advice: Add one or two tablespoons of ground flaxseed to breakfast cereals. You also can sprinkle flaxseed on yogurt or whip it into a breakfast smoothie. Or try chia seeds.

WALNUTS

Yale researchers found that people who ate two ounces of walnuts a day had improved blood flow and drops in blood pressure (a 3.5-point drop in systolic blood pressure and a 2.8-point drop in diastolic blood pressure). The mechanisms through which walnuts elicit a blood pressure–lowering response are believed to involve their high content of monounsaturated fatty acids, omega-3 ALA, magnesium and fiber, and their low levels of sodium and saturated fatty acids.

Bonus: Despite the reputation of nuts as a "fat snack," the people who ate them didn't gain weight.

The magnesium in walnuts is particularly important. It limits the amount of calcium that enters muscle cells inside artery walls. Ingesting the right amount of calcium (not too much and not too little) on a daily basis is essential for optimal blood pressure regulation. Magnesium regulates calcium's movement across the membranes of the smooth muscle cells, deep within the artery walls.

If your body doesn't have enough magnesium, too much calcium will enter the smooth muscle cells, which causes the arterial muscles to tighten, putting a squeeze on the arteries and raising blood pressure. Magnesium works like the popular calcium channel blockers, drugs that block entry of calcium into arterial walls, lowering blood pressure.

My advice: Eat two ounces of walnuts every day. Or choose other nuts such as almonds and pecans.

More from Janet Bond Brill, PhD, RD

DR. JANET'S ROASTED RED BEETS WITH LEMON VINAIGRETTE

Beets are a delicious side dish when roasted, peeled and topped with a lemony vinaigrette and fresh parsley. This recipe is from my book *Prevent a Second Heart Attack.*

6 medium-sized beets, washed and trimmed of greens and roots

2 Tablespoons extra-virgin olive oil

2 teaspoons fresh lemon juice

1 garlic clove, peeled and minced

1 teaspoon Dijon mustard

¼ teaspoon kosher salt

¼ teaspoon freshly ground black pepper

¼ cup chopped fresh flat-leaf Italian parsley

Preheat the oven to 400°F. Spray a baking dish with nonstick cooking spray. Place the beets in the dish, and cover tightly with foil. Bake the beets for about one hour or until they are tender when pierced with a fork or thin knife. Remove from the oven, and allow to cool to the touch.

Meanwhile, in a small bowl, whisk together the olive oil, lemon juice, garlic, mustard, salt and pepper for the dressing. When the beets are cool enough to handle, peel and slice the beets, arranging the slices on a platter. Drizzle with vinaigrette, and garnish with parsley. Serves six.

Popcorn Lowers Blood Pressure

In a new study, researchers who reviewed health and nutrition data for 31,684 men found that those who consumed the most whole grains (about 52 g daily) were 19% less likely to develop high blood pressure than those who consumed the least whole grains (about 3 g daily).

Best sources: Oatmeal (instant or cooked)—one cup, 30 g to 35 g...popcorn—one cup, 10 g to 12 g...whole-wheat bread—one slice, about 15 g...and bran cereal—one cup, 5 g to 10 g.

Alan Flint, MD, DrPH, research scientist, department of nutrition, Harvard School of Public Health, Boston.

Hibiscus Tea Lowers Blood Pressure

Herbal tea containing hibiscus seems to relax the blood vessels, having an effect similar to that of the hypertension medicines called ACE inhibitors. Hibiscus also is thought to be a diuretic—and removing water from the body can reduce blood pressure. Talk to your doctor about drinking hibiscus tea for high blood pressure.

Diane L. McKay, PhD, FACN, is a scientist at the Antioxidants Research Laboratory of the Jean Mayer USDA Human Nutrition Research Center on Aging at Tufts University, Boston, and leader of a study of 65 people, published in *Journal of Nutrition*.

New Hope for Pulmonary Hypertension

James Calvin, MD, professor of medicine, director, section of cardiology, department of internal medicine, Rush University Medical Center, Chicago.

Sometimes it is not technology or a new medication that makes the greatest difference in medical care but something far simpler. A new approach to treating pulmonary hypertension—a particularly dangerous type of high blood pressure that affects the arteries leading from the heart to the lungs—puts top specialists together as a "team" to work collaboratively with patients, with the goal of delivering a far better quality of care.

While specialists have always discussed their patients with one another, this approach takes the concept much further, according to James Calvin, MD, director of the section of cardiology at Rush University Medical Center and a cardiologist at the new Rush Pulmonary Hypertension Clinic in Chicago, which offers this type of multidisciplinary care. Dr. Calvin said that teamwork is built into every aspect of a patient's care to comprehensively address the many different causes of this complex disease. He said that the doctors' combined specialized training and clinical experience leads to more accurate diagnoses and more successful treatment.

Patients can even schedule appointments with several different specialists on the same day in the same office, and the doctors can conveniently consult with one another to, as Dr. Calvin puts it, "put our heads together to come up with a solution."

HARD TO DIAGNOSE

Pulmonary hypertension is not uncommon, and doctors are well aware of its signs and causes, but it can nonetheless be tricky to diagnose because its symptoms mimic those of so many other heart and lung diseases.

This condition develops in people whose hearts have had to pump especially hard to push blood through increasingly stiff and narrow arteries. It has many causes, including heart, lung and liver problems...living at altitudes higher than 8,000 feet...and heredity in some cases can contribute, too. When the body must expend intense effort to bring blood through the lungs to the left side of the heart the eventual result is weakening of the heart muscle on the right side leading to heart failure or other potentially fatal complications. Shortness of breath is usually the first warning sign of pulmonary hypertension, but other common symptoms include fatigue...dizziness...fainting...chest pain...leg and ankle swelling...palpitations (fast heartbeat)...and bluish lips and skin.

How pulmonary hypertension is diagnosed: An echocardiogram, a form of ultrasound that enables your doctor to get a good look at your heart and pulmonary arteries, is usually the first step toward diagnosis. If "problems" are found, the next step is right heart catheterization, to measure how well blood moves through and to look for blockages or other abnormalities. Doctors often order other tests to obtain additional information on the extent of the patient's problem, possibly a chest X-ray, CT scan, MRI and/or pulmonary function assessment (a measure of how well the lungs take in and release air).

LIFE WITH PULMONARY HYPERTENSION

While treatment is complex, inroads have been made. A variety of medications may be used, and together, they can allow many patients to continue to live their lives fairly normally. *These may include...*

- **Vasodilators.** These drugs—including *epoprostenol* (Flolan) and *iloprost* (Ventavis)—widen blood vessels and reduce scarring in them. Patients used to have to come to the hospital or a doctor's office for intravenous (IV) administration of this therapy, but now new drugs can be taken orally by patients at home.
- **Endothelin Receptor Agonists.** ERAs—such as *bosentan* (Tracleer) or *ambrisentan* (Letairis)—block endothelin, a substance in blood vessel walls that causes them to narrow.
- **Calcium channel blockers.** Though these were once the first line of treatment, they work only 5% of the time.
- **Other drugs.** Your physician may also prescribe an anticoagulant such as *warfarin* (Coumadin)...a diuretic to prevent fluid accumulation...*sildenafil* (Revatio) to relax smooth muscle in pulmonary arteries...digoxin to help the heart pump blood...and/or oxygen to help you breathe.
- **Surgical treatments.** If drugs alone cannot control your condition, options include open-heart surgery to create an opening between the right and left chambers of the heart and relieve pressure on the right side...and, in very severe cases, a lung or heart-lung transplant (in patients with a diseased lung).

PUT YOURSELF ON THE TEAM

When you have pulmonary hypertension, it's vital to control any other underlying conditions (for example, religiously take your blood pressure medications).

Dr. Calvin also says that for the best quality of life, keep your focus on making sensible, healthful daily lifestyle choices....

- **Get lots of rest.** Listen to your body. When you are tired, take a nap.
- **Follow a healthy diet.** In particular, avoid salt—which can increase swelling in your legs. Eat more whole foods and fewer salt-laden processed products.
- **Stay active.** Ask your doctor what level of exercise is safe for you.
- **Don't smoke.** Smoking severely damages your arteries, heart and lungs.
- **Avoid stress.** Improve your quality of life by meditating or practicing yoga or tai chi.
- **Eliminate saunas and hot baths.** These can cause your blood pressure to drop dangerously low.
- **Avoid high altitudes (including air travel).** Low oxygen levels worsen symptoms such as shortness of breath.

Pycnogenol: Can It Lower Your Blood Pressure?

Mark A. Stengler, NMD, naturopathic medical doctor and author of *The Natural Physician's Healing Therapies*, founder and medical director of the Stengler Center for Integrative Medicine in Encinitas, California. *MarkStengler.com*

When a nutritional supplement is said to provide a multitude of health benefits, it is reasonable to ask if the claims are too good to be true. That is why I have taken a close look at Pycnogenol (pronounced pik-NOJ-en-all), the brand name of an extract from the bark of the maritime pine tree that grows in France. .

The flavonoids (plant pigments) in Pycnogenol are potent anti-inflammatories and antioxidants (chemicals that protect cells from harmful molecules called free radicals). *Studies show the extract to be effective in treating...*

- **Hypertension** (high blood pressure).

Evidence: In a study published in the peer-reviewed international journal *Life Sciences*, 58 participants who were on prescription hypertension medication took either a placebo or 100 mg per day of Pycnogenol. After 12 weeks, 57% of the Pycnogenol users were able to halve their drug dosage while continuing to take the extract.

Bonus: Among Pycnogenol users, blood tests showed that LDL "bad" cholesterol dropped by 10% and antioxidant levels increased.

Studies suggest that Pycnogenol also may alleviate...

- **Circulatory problems,** including varicose veins, coronary artery disease, congestive heart failure, erectile dysfunction and retinopathy (a disorder of the retina).
- **Respiratory disorders,** such as allergies and asthma.
- **Pain in muscles and joints, such as postexercise soreness and osteoarthritis.**
- **Lymphedema** (abnormal swelling due to accumulation of lymph fluid), common among postsurgical breast cancer patients.

Bottom line: Dosage varies depending on your overall health, so talk to a holisitic physician.

Important: Check with your doctor before using Pycnogenol if you take blood-thinning drugs, such as aspirin or *warfarin* (Coumadin), because it also thins blood...if you take drugs for diabetes, because Pycnogenol can lower blood sugar...or if you are pregnant or nursing, as a general precaution. Otherwise, Pycnogenol generally is safe to take indefinitely. Side effects may include hives and tightness in the chest or throat.

Pycnogenol products are sold in health-food stores. Prices start at around $30 for 60 capsules of 50 mg to 100 mg. High-quality brands include Source Naturals (800-815-2333, *www.sourcenaturals.com*) and Country Life (800-645-5768, *www.country-life.com*).

Reduce High Blood Pressure By Tapping Your Toes

Ann Marie Chiasson, MD, family practitioner and clinical assistant professor of medicine, Arizona Center for Integrative Medicine, University of Tucson. She is the author of *Energy Healing: The Essentials of Self-Care*. Her video *Energy Healing for Beginners: Ten Essential Practices for Self-Care,* which includes a tapping demo, can be downloaded from *AnnMarieChiassonMD.com/Publications.html.*

There's a killer running rampant amongst us—and its name is high blood pressure. Overly dramatic? I don't think so.

High blood pressure increases your risk not only for heart attack, heart failure and stroke, but also for grave maladies that you may never have considered, such as kidney failure, dementia, aneurysm, blindness and osteoporosis.

Medications help reduce blood pressure... but their nasty side effects can include joint pain, headache, weakness, dizziness, heart palpitations, coughing, asthma, constipation, diarrhea, insomnia, depression and erectile dysfunction!

There's a promising alternative therapy that's completely risk-free—and costs nothing—so there's pretty much no excuse not to try.

The therapy is tapping, which is based on the principles of Chinese medicine. *Here's how it works...*

SOMETHING OLD, SOMETHING NEW

Ann Marie Chiasson, MD, of the Arizona Center for Integrative Medicine is a practitioner of the tapping method. For her own patients with high blood pressure, Dr. Chiasson has adapted a tapping technique that is part of the ancient Chinese practice called qigong.

Qigong involves simple movements, including tapping on the body's meridians, or "highways" of energy movement. These meridians are the same as those used during acupuncture and acupressure treatments. According to a review of nine studies published in *The Journal of Alternative and Complementary Medicine*, qigong reduced systolic blood pressure (the top number) by an average of 17 points and diastolic blood pressure (the bottom number) by an average of 10 points. Those are big reductions! In fact, they are comparable to the reductions achieved with drugs—but the qigong had no unwanted side effects.

Though Dr. Chiasson has not conducted a clinical trial on her tapping protocol, she has observed reductions in blood pressure among her patients who practice tapping. The technique she recommends also could conceivably benefit people who do not have high blood pressure if it reduces stress and thus helps lower the risk of developing high blood pressure.

TAP AWAY

Some tapping routines are complicated, involving tapping the top of the head, around the eyes, side of the hand and under the nose, chin and/or arms. But Dr. Chiasson's technique is a simpler toe-and-torso method that is quite easy to learn. It is safe and can be done in the privacy of your own home.

First, you may want to get a blood pressure reading so you can do a comparison later on. If the tapping technique is helpful, you eventually may be able to reduce or even discontinue your high blood pressure drugs (of course, for safety's sake, you should not stop taking any drugs without first talking to your doctor about it).

Dr. Chiasson's plan: Each day, do five minutes of toe tapping (instructions below)...five minutes of belly tapping...and five minutes of chest tapping. You may experience tingling or a sensation of warmth in the part of the body being tapped and/or in your hands, which is normal. You can listen to rhythmic music during your tapping if you like. As you tap, try to think as little as possible, Dr. Chiasson said—just focus on your body, tapping and breath.

Rate: For each tapping location, aim for a rate of about one to two taps per second.

- **Toe tapping.** Lie flat on your back on the bed or floor. Keeping your whole body relaxed, quickly rotate your legs inward and outward from the hips (like windshield wipers), tapping the sides of your big toes together with each inward rotation. Tap as softly or as vigorously as you like.
- **Belly tapping.** Stand with your feet a little wider than shoulder-width apart. Staying relaxed, gently bounce up and down by slightly bending your knees. At the same time, tap softly with gently closed fists on the area below your belly button and above your pubic bone. Try to synchronize your movements to give one tap per knee bend.
- **Chest tapping.** Sit or stand comfortably. Using your fingertips, open hands or gently closed fists, tap all over your chest area, including the armpits. Tap as softly or as vigorously as you like without pushing past your comfort level.

Cautions: If you are recovering from hip or knee surgery, skip the toe tapping (which might strain your joint) and do only the belly tapping and chest tapping. If you are pregnant, stick with just the chest tapping—lying on your back during toe tapping could reduce blood flow to the fetus...and tapping on your belly may not feel comfortable and could stimulate the acupressure points used to induce labor, Dr. Chiasson said.

Follow-up: Continue your tapping routine for eight weeks, then get another blood pressure reading to see whether your numbers have improved. If they have—or if you simply enjoy the relaxing effects of the tapping—you might want to continue indefinitely.

Blood Pressure–Lowering Juice

In a study of 14 healthy adults, participants' blood pressures dropped by an average of 10.4 mmHg systolic (top number) and 8 mmHg diastolic (bottom number) within a few hours of drinking two cups of beet juice (the effect lasted up to 24 hours).

Theory: Bacteria on the tongue convert chemical compounds found in beet juice into nitrites, which help keep blood vessels healthy. (The beet juice used in the study was sweetened with apple juice.)

Amrita Ahluwalia, PhD, professor of vascular pharmacology, Barts and The London School of Medicine, UK.

Probiotics Help Reduce Blood Pressure

A recent Australian study found that people who regularly ate dairy products containing live probiotic bacteria had a modest but significant reduction in blood pressure. They lowered systolic (top) pressure by 3.56 millimeters of mercury and diastolic (bottom) pressure by 2.38 millimeters.

Best: Aim for one serving of yogurt with live probiotic cultures every day.

Janet Bond Brill, PhD, RD, LDN, is a nutrition, health and fitness expert in Valley Forge, Pennsylvania, and author of *Blood Pressure Down*.

Blood Pressure Medication Breakthrough

Michael H. Alderman, MD, former president of the American Society of Hypertension, professor of medicine at Albert Einstein College of Medicine of Yeshiva University, the Bronx, New York.

People who take blood pressure medications may not realize how unscientific doctors have been in their approach to finding the right drug or drugs for their condition—in fact, the expression, "Throw enough mud at the wall and some is bound to stick," seems an apt description. Commonly, drugs for hypertension are prescribed on top of others in the hope that the growing pile will keep blood pressure under control. As a result, many patients end up taking three or even more different drugs daily to manage their blood pressure.

Drugs aren't the only tool that people can use to get blood pressure under control, of course. Many patients find that losing weight, exercising and making other lifestyle changes can do the trick. But for those who do require blood pressure medication, scientists have now developed a more precise method of predicting which drug will control hypertension in a particular individual—and this could be very good news for drug-saturated blood pressure patients!

ABCS OF HBP

Let me start by introducing you to renin, an enzyme produced by the kidneys that plays a critical role in modulating blood pressure. Renin regulates blood volume and vascular resistance as the body's needs change—but having too much renin is one cause of hypertension. Until recently, doctors have had no way to identify the patients in whom this is the root cause of the problem.

Of the two types of drugs that treat hypertension, there is one category called "R" drugs (beta-blockers and ACE inhibitors) that works to control pressure by blocking the effect of blood renin levels. The other type, called "V" drugs (diuretics and calcium channel blockers), controls pressure by reducing blood volume. Since doctors have not had any easy techniques to help them determine whether a patient would benefit more from one or the other, some people with hypertension end up taking both types. For instance, they may take a pill that combines an R and a V drug along with another that is either an R or a V on its own. This new research may dramatically reduce the need for such guesswork.

BETTER THAN A CRYSTAL BALL

Done at the Albert Einstein College of Medicine of Yeshiva University, New York City, this recent research was published in the *American Journal of Hypertension*. Researchers measured renin levels in 945 previously untreated participants diagnosed with hypertension (a systolic, or top blood pressure, reading of at least 140 mmHg) before assigning them to either a V or R drug. A follow-up blood pressure reading was done one to three months later, and researchers found that the patients who had had high renin levels (more than 2.5 ng/mg/h) at the start of the study achieved better blood pressure control with an R drug, while those who had had low renin levels (below about 0.74 ng/mg/h) did better on a V drug. The conclusion—renin levels can indeed be useful as a predictor of how a particular patient will respond to a particular type of blood pressure drug.

A very important finding: For some patients, being on the wrong drug actually elevated their blood pressure, making the situation especially dangerous. The researchers found that 16% of patients with the lowest levels of renin who took an R drug experienced an increase of 10 or more points in their blood pressure. This rise, called a "pressor response," is not at all uncommon—doctors have tended to assume it was caused by "noncompliance," blaming the patients for failing to take their medications. The study shows, though, that the pressor response often is caused by giving patients the wrong drug.

TALK TO YOUR DOCTOR

Based on these findings, Michael Alderman, MD, former president of the American Society of Hypertension, said that he recommends that doctors measure renin levels in newly diagnosed hypertension patients as well as in those now taking multiple antihypertensive medications—most particularly when the drugs don't seem to be helping. Dr. Alderman said that it will likely be a few years before testing renin levels in advance of prescribing blood pressure medications becomes a standard practice, but he expects that it eventually will. If you need blood pressure medications, ask to have your renin level tested before you get a prescription—trial and error is not the way you want to find out what works!

Monitor Your Blood Pressure

Monitoring blood pressure at home instead of only in the doctor's office is more effective for diagnosing and treating hypertension.

Bonus: A new study found that patients using home blood pressure–monitoring kits saved insurance companies up to $1,364 over 10 years, which could translate into lower premiums. Home blood pressure monitoring is also helpful for those at risk for hypertension.

Alejandro Arrieta, PhD, assistant professor of health policy and management, Florida International University, Miami.

No More High Blood Pressure?

An experimental vaccine immunizes against angiotensin II, a protein that constricts blood vessels. The vaccine, given a few times a year, could potentially replace traditional blood pressure medications.

The Lancet, TheLancet.com.

Do Good...To Lower Blood Pressure

People who volunteered an average of four hours a week reduced their risk for hypertension by 40%, a new four-year study of adults over age 50 has found. Volunteers also reported being more satisfied with their lives and having greater self-esteem and fewer symptoms of depression than those who didn't volunteer.

Possible explanation: Volunteering helps improve ties to the community, which can reduce stress. So choose a volunteer commitment you enjoy!

Rodlescia Sneed, MPH, researcher, department of psychology, Carnegie Mellon University, Pittsburgh.

New Device Lowers Resistant Hypertension

A small, implantable "Coupler" device shows early promise in the treatment of resistant hypertension. In a six-month trial of 83 patients with persistent high blood pressure, significant reductions were seen in the group using the Coupler (26.9 mmHg systolic) compared with a control group (3.7 mmHg). According to study principal investigator Melvin Lobo, PhD, the Coupler targets the mechanical aspects of how blood circulation works and once placed, the results are immediate.

If you've been unable to control your high blood pressure with medication: Ask your doctor about enrolling in a clinical trial or go to ClinicalTrials.gov and search Coupler device.

Study of 83 patients with uncontrolled hypertension, funded by Rox Medical, published in *The Lancet*. Reported in *Forbes.com*

Munch on This for Lower Blood Pressure

Jamey Wallace, ND, a naturopathic physician and chief medical officer at Bastyr Center for Natural Health, the teaching clinic of Bastyr University, in Kenmore, Washington.

If you've got high blood pressure or want to prevent it, you may want to stock up on celery. Why? Celery contains *phthalides*, chemicals that dilate the blood vessels and act as a diuretic, actions found in certain blood pressure–lowering drugs.

Some risks of high blood pressure are widely known (such as increased risk for heart attack and stroke). But high blood pressure also makes you more likely to develop dementia, kidney disease, eye disease, sleep apnea and sexual dysfunction. Normal blood pressure is less than 120/80.

What to do: For a consistent blood pressure-lowering effect, eat four medium-sized celery stalks per day. One easy way is to cut them into snack-sized pieces to munch on throughout the day—at midmorning, midafternoon and bedtime. (Talk to your doctor, though, if you have sun sensitivity—celery can increase skin reactions.)

Even better: Liven up your celery with other blood pressure–lowering foods—for example, hummus or nut butter (such as almond). People who eat these foods have lower blood pressure—possibly due to the foods' fiber and protein content.

Important: Four stalks of celery a day won't completely control high blood pressure. Use this remedy as part of an overall plan that includes increasing your intake of vegetables and fruits...exercising regularly...controlling your weight...reducing stress...and taking blood pressure medication, if necessary.

Also: Consult a physician familiar with natural therapies, if possible. Or talk with your regular doctor before you try this remedy—celery can interact with some medications.

Lower Blood Pressure With Even a Small Reduction in Salt

University of London researchers have determined that even a slight reduction—from two teaspoons to about one-and-a-half teaspoons of salt daily—can help lower blood pressure. For those who have moderate-to-high blood pressure, aim to reduce the table salt you add to food to less than one teaspoon—and ideally one-half teaspoon—daily.

Mark A. Stengler, NMD, is a naturopathic medical doctor and author of *The Natural Physician's Healing Therapies*, founder and medical director of the Stengler Center for Integrative Medicine in Encinitas, California, and adjunct associate clinical professor at the National College of Natural Medicine in Portland, Oregon. *MarkStengler.com*

12

Infectious Diseases

How to Wreck Your Immune System

Nobody wants to spend time sick in bed feeling miserable with a cold, the flu or any other illness.

But here's the catch: Even if you stay well rested, exercise and eat healthfully, you still could be sabotaging your immune system. Most people are unknowingly making it harder for their bodies to fight off illnesses. *How to stop hurting your immune system…*

• **Skip the germ-killing soaps.** Studies now show that triclosan, the key ingredient in many antibacterial hand soaps (as well as some shaving gels, shampoos, cosmetics, deodorants and other personal-care items), fuels the growth of antibiotic-resistant bugs in the public at large. With frequent use, triclosan also can hurt you personally by setting up your body to develop a secondary "superinfection" that can occur as a complication of colds, the flu or viral pneumonia.

Among the best ways to prevent colds and the flu: Vigorous, frequent hand-washing with plain soap is all you need, but here's the key—you need to scrub long enough (count to 20).

If you like the reassurance offered by a hand sanitizer, products with at least 60% alcohol, such as Purell or Germ-X, are widely recommended. However, the alcohol in such hand sanitizers can lead to dry, cracked skin, which provides an entry point for bacterial or fungal skin infections. Alcohol-based products are supported by strong research, but if dry skin is a problem, rely on hand-washing

Robert Rountree, MD, a family physician in private practice and owner of Boulder Wellcare in Boulder, Colorado. He is coauthor of numerous books, including *Immunotics: A Revolutionary Way to Fight Infection, Beat Chronic Illness and Stay Well.* He is also medical editor of the journal *Alternative and Complementary Therapies* and a faculty member at the Institute for Functional Medicine, based in Federal Way, Washington.

and/or a hand sanitizer that contains natural antibacterial plant oils such as citrus, oregano, rosemary and/or thyme.

Good choice: CleanWell, $15.81 for six one-ounce spray bottles, *www.cleanwelltoday.com.*

• **Take a pass on sugar.** Sugar, refined carbohydrates and high-fructose corn syrup can impair the effectiveness of our immune cells. As soon as you notice cold or flu symptoms, cut these foods out of your diet.

Beware: The caramelized sugar found on cinnamon rolls, donuts or sticky buns is particularly harmful to our immunity. Certain molecular structures in this type of sugar resemble bacteria, and our immune system receptors mistakenly bind to them, interfering with their ability to respond effectively to true infections.

If you need a sweetener: Try raw honey, which has immune-building properties.*

• **Watch out for pesticides.** Most nonorganic produce gets showered with pesticides, which damage your immune system.

What to try instead: Load up on fresh, organic fruits and vegetables to arm your immune system with disease-fighting vitamins and nutrients. Organic berries, citrus fruits, grapes and spinach are especially rich in antioxidants that support immune function. When fresh berries aren't available, try frozen organic berries. You can save money by opting for nonorganic citrus fruits and other peelable items (such as bananas) that are less likely to harbor dangerous pesticides than produce without peels.

POWER UP YOUR IMMUNITY

Many people rely on well-known immunity boosters such as vitamin C and/or echinacea, but you're likely to get better results from using the following on a daily basis as a preventive during cold and flu season (or year-round if you work directly with the public)...**

*Infants under age one and people who are allergic to pollen or immune compromised should not consume honey.

**Consult your doctor before trying dietary supplements—especially if you take prescription medication and/or have a chronic medical condition.

• **Probiotics.** By far, probiotics are the best way to enhance your immunity. These "good" bacteria, including Lactobacillus and Bifidobacterium, reside in your digestive tract, where they keep intestinal microbes in check and elevate your number of infection-fighting T cells.

Fermented foods, such as kefir, yogurt, kimchi, sauerkraut and kombucha, are all naturally rich in probiotics. Aim for two (four- to six-ounce) servings a day.

In general, however, probiotic supplements are more potent and may be more reliable than probiotic-rich foods. If you opt for a supplement, use a combination of Bifidobacterium and/or Lactobacillus species.

A probiotic found in studies to boost immunity: Culturelle, $33.49 for 80 capsules, *www.amazon.com.*

• **N-acetylcysteine (NAC).** The body easily converts this amino acid into a usable form of glutathione, an immunity-protecting antioxidant that itself is poorly absorbed from the gastrointestinal tract.

Scientific evidence: Italian researchers found that taking 1,200 mg daily of NAC throughout flu season reduced the frequency, severity and intensity of flulike symptoms.

Typical dose: 600 mg to 1,200 mg daily as a preventive...at the first sign of infection, increase the dose to 3,000 mg daily (taken in doses of 600 mg each throughout the day).

• **Elderberry syrup.** When used within the first 48 hours of feeling flu-ish, this syrup (made from naturally antiviral elderberries) has been shown to relieve symptoms four days faster than a placebo.

If you are not taking elderberry syrup as a daily preventive, start using it within the first two days of developing cold or flu symptoms. Follow label instructions.

Good choice: Sambucol Black Elderberry Immune System Support, $19.99 for 7.8 ounces, *www.drugstore.com.*

DON'T GO IT ALONE!

What do close relationships have to do with immunity? A lot, according to research.

When researchers exposed 276 adults to a rhinovirus (a cause of the common cold), subjects with only one to three relationships (such as fulfilling marriages or friendships with colleagues, neighbors and religious community members) were four times more likely to get sick than those who had more than six relationships.

Possible explanation: Social interactions help ease the negative effects of stress—a known threat to immunity.

What a Top Naturopath Has in His Own Medicine Cabinet

Mark A. Stengler, NMD, is a naturopathic medical doctor and author of *The Natural Physician's Healing Therapies*, founder and medical director of the Stengler Center for Integrative Medicine in Encinitas, California, and adjunct associate clinical professor at the National College of Natural Medicine in Portland, Oregon. *MarkStengler.com*

Sometimes you need powerful, fast-acting medications. But prescription and over-the-counter drugs can present serious risks. It's estimated that more than 2 million adverse drug reactions occur in the US every year and are responsible for more than 100,000 deaths annually.

I strongly recommend and use natural remedies. They contain lower doses of chemically active agents. They're less likely than drugs to cause dangerous side effects. And they often work just as well, sometimes better. All are available at health-food stores and online.

Important: Always check with your doctor before taking any new medication or supplement.

INFLUENZA FIGHTERS

A healthy immune system is the best way to protect against flu. *Starting at the beginning of flu season (typically early October), take...*

- **Influenzinum,** a homeopathic remedy that I've recommended for more than 15 years. The makers of influenzinum reformulate it annually based on the flu viruses that are expected to predominate that year.

Dose: Three pellets (of a 9C potency) dissolved under the tongue, once a week for six weeks.

- **N-acetylcysteine (NAC),** an antioxidant, reduces both the chance that you will get the flu and the severity of symptoms if you do get sick. An Italian study found that only 25% of older people who were injected with flu virus after taking NAC for six months experienced flu symptoms, versus 79% who took a placebo.

Dose: 1,000 mg daily in tablet form for prevention during the flu months (typically October through April). If you get the flu, increase the dose to 4,000 mg daily until you recover.

Also helpful: 2,000 international units (IU) of vitamin D daily. During the peak flu months, increase the dose to 5,000 IU.

COLD RELIEF

Don't waste your money on often ineffective over-the-counter cold medicines. *Instead...*

- **Pelargonium sidoides,** a South African plant, has been tested in more than 20 clinical studies. It relieves congestion, sore throat and other cold symptoms. It is available in syrups, lozenges, capsules and tablets. Follow the dosing instructions on the label.

LESS JOINT PAIN

Aspirin and related painkillers often irritate the stomach and increase the risk for ulcers. Natural analgesics are much gentler and just as effective.

- **Boswellia,** a tree found in India, Africa and the Middle East, has a milky resin that inhibits the body's production of inflammatory molecules. A study that looked at patients with osteoarthritis of the knee found that boswellia extract relieved pain and stiffness as effectively as the drug *valdecoxib* (Bextra), which has been withdrawn from the market because of side effects. A small percentage of boswellia users experience digestive upset. If that happens, reduce the amount. If you don't start to feel better within 48 hours, stop taking it. If you are taking it for chronic pain, give it two weeks.

Dose: 750 milligrams (mg), two to three times daily during flare-ups.

• **Curcumin is the active ingredient found in the spice turmeric.** In a study, rheumatoid arthritis patients reported that it helped relieve morning pain and stiffness.

Caution: Taking curcumin with blood thinners can increase the risk for bleeding.

Dose: 500 mg, three times daily. You can take it every day to keep pain and inflammation down or just take it during flare-ups.

MIGRAINE RELIEF

There are many drugs for treating migraines, but they're rife with side effects—and may increase the risk for liver damage or even a heart attack.

• **Butterbur,** a member of the daisy family, is an effective alternative. It contains two potent anti-inflammatory compounds, petasin and isopetasin, which may help blood vessels in the brain dilate and contract more normally.

A study published in *Neurology* found that people who used butterbur had a 48% reduction in the frequency of migraines. You also can use butterbur to reduce migraine intensity.

Dose: For prevention, take 50 mg of Petadolex (a butterbur extract) three times daily, with meals, for one month. Then reduce the dose to twice daily. For treating a migraine, take 50 mg three times daily until the migraine is gone.

EASE MUSCLE SORENESS

For an aching back or sore arms, apply an ice pack or a heating pad...or alternate cold and warmth. *Also helpful...*

• **Arnica is a plant in the daisy family that reduces muscle soreness and swelling.** It also helps bruises heal more quickly.

A new study from the Australian Institute of Sport in Canberra, Australia, published in *European Journal of Sport Science*, found that the topical application of arnica reduced the level of achiness for up to three days after a vigorous workout. The participants included men who ran in five bouts of eight-minute bursts on a treadmill, followed by two minutes of walking on a flat surface. They applied arnica gel or a placebo gel every four hours.

How to use it: Apply a small amount of cream or tincture to the sore areas. Repeat every hour as necessary. Don't apply if the skin is broken.

Helpful: If a large area is sore, you can take arnica orally instead. Take two pellets of a 30C potency three times daily for one to two days.

Natural Infection Fighters

Steven Sandberg-Lewis, ND, naturopathic physician and clinical and professor of naturopathic medicine at the National College of Natural Medicine in Portland, Oregon. He is author of *Functional Gastroenterology.*

Antibiotics enable millions of people to survive infections that used to be fatal. However, the widespread use of these drugs has increasingly led to antibiotic resistance—some harmful organisms can keep making people sick even when treated with the newest, most powerful antibiotics.

We tend to hear a lot about the overuse of antibiotics, but medications used to treat viruses and fungi also can be harmful.

For example, over-the-counter and prescription drugs used to treat yeast infections have the potential to cause side effects ranging from headache to seizures, while anti-viral medications can lead to gastrointestinal problems, dizziness and difficulty breathing in those with lung disease. Overuse of prescription drugs to treat viruses or fungi, such as *oseltamivir* (Tamiflu) and *acyclovir* (Zovirax), also can lead to resistance to these medications.

Little-known fact: Because the immune system of a healthy adult is quite effective at eliminating many types of bacteria, viruses and fungi, many infections can be successfully treated with natural products that strengthen immunity and fight microorganisms.

Important: Always see a doctor if the affected area is becoming more inflamed... seems to be spreading...is accompanied by a fever...or is not improving.

Conditions that typically improve within 24 to 48 hours when treated with natural antimicrobial agents (unless indicated otherwise, all can be found in health-food stores)...*

BRONCHITIS

Bronchitis is inflammation of the lining of the bronchial tubes, which carry air to the lungs. Acute bronchitis is usually due to a virus and often develops in conjunction with a cold or some other upper-respiratory tract ailment.

Natural treatment: Add 10 drops of liquid allicin (an active antibacterial and antiviral compound in garlic) to the reservoir of a portable nebulizer (a device that converts liquid into a fine mist that can be inhaled). Breathe the mist until all of the extract is gone. Repeat the treatment once or twice a day until the infection is gone.

Also helpful: Take eight (180 mg) capsules daily of Allimax, fresh-garlic supplements that can shorten the duration of the illness.

SORE THROAT

Most sore throats are caused by viruses, such as those that also cause the common cold or flu.

Natural treatment: Perform a yoga exercise known as the Lion Pose to increase blood and lymph circulation at the back of the tongue. This movement promotes the migration of immune cells to the area to help fight the infection.

What to do: Stick out your tongue as far as it will go, and hold it there for three to four seconds. Repeat the movement five or six times daily until your sore throat is gone.

Also helpful: Most people know that gargling with saltwater helps ease sore throat pain.

For better results: Add a few drops of bitter orange oil to a mixture of one-quarter teaspoon salt and one-half cup warm water to help kill bacteria, including some organisms that cause strep throat.

Important: Use a "bass voice" when you gargle the mixture (every few waking hours). The lower-pitched gargling sound causes more of the solution to get into the throat.

SINUSITIS

Infections of the sinus cavities typically cause headache, facial pain or pressure and a loss of smell and taste. Antibiotics can help in some cases, but most sinus infections are caused by organisms, such as viruses or fungi, that aren't killed by antibiotics.

Natural treatment: N-acetyl-cysteine (NAC), an amino acid that promotes the drainage of mucus and mobilizes infection-fighting white blood cells.

Typical dose: 600 mg, three times daily.

BLADDER INFECTION

Virtually every woman gets an occasional urinary tract infection (UTI), either in the urethra (the tube that allows urine to leave the body) and/or the bladder. Though relatively rare in men, UTIs become more common in those over age 50—a time when prostate enlargement tends to occur and can lead to an infection when urine fails to drain properly from the bladder. Antibiotics work for both women and men but often lead to yeast infections and other side effects.

Natural treatment: Unsweetened cranberry juice (one eight-ounce glass daily)** is widely used to help prevent UTIs. Cranberry contains anthocyanidins, compounds that are thought to help prevent Escherichia coli (E. coli), the cause of most UTIs, from adhering to tissues in the urinary tract.

For better results: Also take an herb called uva ursi (500 mg three to five times daily). If symptoms do not significantly improve within 24 hours, consult a physician before continuing this treatment.

Important: Drink a minimum of six glasses of water daily (in addition to the juice) until the infection is gone. It dilutes the concentration of bacteria in the bladder...reduces irritation...and helps flush out harmful organisms.

*Caution: If you have an allergy to a particular natural substance (such as garlic), do not use a remedy that contains the substance.

**If you take *warfarin* (Coumadin), consult your doctor before drinking this amount of cranberry juice—the juice may increase the effects of blood-thinning medication.

EAR INFECTION

Several studies in children show that most ear infections don't require antibiotics. It's likely that the same is true for adults, particularly for infections affecting the ear canal (swimmer's ear).

Natural treatment for swimmer's ear: Use a clean bulb syringe or eyedropper to administer three to five drops daily of a 50-50 mixture of distilled water and hydrogen peroxide, followed by three to five drops of a 50-50 solution of white vinegar and distilled water.

Also helpful: A combination supplement that includes echinacea, goldenseal and berberis (such as Source Naturals' Wellness Formula), along with a multisupplement containing bioflavonoids, zinc and vitamins C and A. Follow the dosage instructions on the label.

Important: Patients who get frequent ear infections should try eliminating dairy and bananas from their diet. These foods are believed to lead to the production of thicker-than-normal mucus that inhibits normal ear drainage.

Foods and Supplements Can Work as Well as Any Antibiotic

Joseph Kellerstein, DC, ND, a chiropractor and naturopathic and homeopathic physician who lectures at the Canadian College of Homeopathic Medicine and internationally. He has private practices in Toronto and Oshawa, Ontario, Canada. *DrJoeND.com*

Most likely you've been taught that if you have any type of bacterial infection, you must take an antibiotic. But overuse of antibiotics is increasingly rendering them ineffective and contributing to the rise of deadly drug-resistant superbugs. Not only are new strains of MRSA now emerging, but other types of bacteria, including Clostridium difficile and Salmonella, are becoming increasingly difficult to treat.

What's more: Antibiotics inhibit the growth of nearly all bacteria in the body that they come into contact with (good and bad), often causing annoying side effects such as diarrhea and yeast and intestinal infections.

Time to change your thinking: For many minor infections, natural antibiotics found in foods, supplements and herbs can eliminate harmful microbes just as well as prescription antibiotics—without side effects. Plus, if you do need a prescription antibiotic, natural products can often help these medications work more effectively.

If you think you have an infection: See your doctor.* He/she can tell you whether antibiotics are necessary or if it is safe to try natural products—some may interact with medications you are taking. (A high fever—with or without chills—is one sign you may need an antibiotic.) If you are cleared to try a natural regimen, check back with your doctor if the infection does not improve within 48 hours.

PROBIOTICS FOR RESPIRATORY INFECTIONS

You probably already know to take probiotics or eat yogurt to reduce the chance of side effects when you are on antibiotics. What you might not know is that probiotics also can help prevent and treat infections. And yogurt isn't the only food source. Little-known probiotic-rich alternatives include fermented vegetables (such as sauerkraut and kimchi)...fermented soy foods (such as miso and tempeh)...and kefir, a fermented milk product. When you eat these foods, their beneficial bacteria displace some of the disease-causing bacteria and secrete substances that inhibit or kill harmful germs.

A study found that individuals who took daily supplements of Lactobacillus reuteri (a common probiotic) were less than half as likely to take sick days for upper-respiratory or gastrointestinal illnesses than those who took placebos.

Natural approach: Regularly consuming probiotic foods helps prevent and treat infections. If you get recurrent infections and/or frequently use antibiotics, a probiotic supplement may be advised as well. Check with your doctor for the best probiotic and dosage for you.

*To find a naturopathic or homeopathic doctor near you, go to *www.naturopathic.org* or *www.homeopathyusa.org*.

COLLOIDAL SILVER FOR EAR INFECTIONS, MORE

The antibiotic properties of colloidal silver were first described nearly 2,000 years ago. It comes as a suspension—microscopic bits of silver are suspended in water or a gel-like substance—and can be used for ear, nose, throat and eye infections. Another silver product, silver sulfadiazine cream, is used to prevent and treat skin and wound infections.

Natural approach: Colloidal silver can be used orally or topically, depending on the condition being treated. Use a product that contains "true silver particles" rather than "ionic silver," which may be less effective at killing pathogens.

Caution: Colloidal silver can cause argyria, a grayish or bluish skin discoloration that may be permanent if you take massive doses (38 g per day). A standard colloidal silver product has less than 1 mg of silver per dose.

OIL OF OREGANO FOR THROAT AND BLADDER INFECTIONS

Oregano contains carvacrol, a powerful antimicrobial chemical compound. In a lab study, even low doses of oregano oil inhibited the growth of staph (Staphylococcus aureus) as effectively as streptomycin and other antibiotics. I recommend this oil for throat and bladder infections.

Natural approach: Add one or two drops of concentrated oregano oil to one teaspoon of olive or coconut oil to avoid burning your mouth. Take once a day during an infection.

GARLIC FOR DIARRHEA, MORE

Garlic has allicin, a broad-spectrum antimicrobial agent that fights a variety of bacteria, viruses and fungi. It's been found to be effective against Helicobacter pylori, a bacterium linked to stomach ulcers and cancer, and against certain bacteria that cause diarrhea.** Even some antibiotic-resistant strains of H. pylori responded to garlic in studies. And in both World Wars, garlic was used to prevent wound infections.

Natural approach: For prevention and treatment of the infections above, take deodorized garlic capsules (such as Vitacost Deodorized Garlic Ultra). They're more convenient—and less smelly—than eating lots of fresh garlic. Follow label directions. For a topical solution for wounds, mix one part garlic juice (found in health-food stores) with three parts water. Apply to gauze and place on skin. Never put garlic juice or crushed garlic directly on the skin—it can cause irritation.

HOMEOPATHY FOR SKIN INFECTIONS

Silica, a homeopathic remedy, helps treat painful skin infections—such as boils, inflamed acne and skin wounds—that seem to take forever to heal.

Natural approach: Take one pellet (6C concentration) every day for seven to 14 days until the area is about 80% healed. After that, watch the area for a few days to make sure it finishes healing.

Caution: If, at any point, the wound gets very red and inflamed...if redness spreads quickly...or if you have a high fever and/or chills, see your doctor immediately. Also, see your doctor if the wound does not finish healing after using the silica. These are signs that you may need an antibiotic.

**Caution: If diarrhea lasts for more than 24 hours in a child or more than two days in an adult, see a doctor. Also, see a doctor if diarrhea is accompanied by blood in your stool, severe abdominal pain or signs of dehydration, such as dry mouth and/or low urine output.

Easy Way to Prevent Hospital Infections

There's an easy way to prevent the spread of disease in the hospital...open a window.

Recent finding: Wards in an old-fashioned hospital wing with large windows that could be opened had greater ventilation and therefore reduced risk of tuberculosis infection compared with modern hospitals with mechanical ventilation systems.

Rod Escombe, MD, PhD, department of infectious diseases and immunity, Imperial College London, England, and leader of a study of natural ventilation, published in *PLoS Medicine*.

Beating the Flu Just Became Easier

William Schaffner MD, professor of preventive medicine and infectious disease specialist, Vanderbilt University School of Medicine, Nashville. Dr. Schaffner is an associate editor of *Journal of Infectious Diseases*, past president of the National Foundation for Infectious Diseases and winner of numerous research awards.

Mention the subject of flu vaccination in a group discussion and at least one person will swear that he or she caught the flu from a flu shot. Sorry—that's not possible. But it is possible—and even expected—that some people will catch the flu despite getting vaccinated because their immune systems need more protection than what a regular flu vaccine can provide, and they may be exposed to a strain not covered by the vaccine. People age 65 and older are particularly vulnerable.

"Older people—those 65 and older—don't respond as strongly as younger people to any vaccine, including the flu vaccine, because their immune systems simply have become weaker from aging," said William Schaffner, MD, a professor of preventive medicine and infectious disease specialist at Vanderbilt University School of Medicine. But good news—getting stronger immunity to avoid the flu just became easier for older adults thanks to a new high-dose vaccine that packs more immune-producing antigens into the shot than standard-dose vaccines. The high-dose trivalent vaccine, which protects against three flu strains, became available a few years ago, and research is now showing that it really does deliver in terms of better protection against the flu for older adults.

MORE VACCINE, BETTER PROTECTION

A two-year research study to track the effectiveness of the new high-dose flu vaccine involved 32,000 men and women age 65 and older. The study participants were randomly assigned to receive either the standard-dose trivalent vaccine or the high-dose trivalent vaccine.

After vaccination, the participants (who didn't know which vaccine they had received) were instructed to report any illness to the research team. Participants also received weekly or twice weekly phone calls from the researchers from the time they were vaccinated until the end of flu season in April. If a participant came down with flulike symptoms, the research team took a cell swab from inside the nose to see whether the influenza virus was the cause.

At the study's end, researchers found that the high-dose vaccine was 24% more effective than the standard vaccine in preventing flu in these older adults. This means that among older people who get vaccinated, the new vaccine can keep an additional one-quarter of them from getting the flu. That's a lot of people!

"The extra protection did come with some extra 'ouch,' though," said Dr. Schaffner. There were slightly more sore arms and short-term fevers after the high-dose vaccine, as the higher dose kicks the immune system in the shorts more briskly!

SOMETHING TO CONSIDER

More recent flu vaccines include a newly developed type with quadrivalent (four-strain) protection, though it has been in scant supply. In 2014 and 2015, more standard-dose vaccines offered quadrivalent protection. The high-dose vaccine, though, will offer only trivalent protection because the manufacturer is, so far, unable to squeeze all the antigen needed for a high-dose quadrivalent vaccine into a syringe that won't terrify people with its size.

If you are 65 or older, you may now be wondering whether you should get the standard-dose quadrivalent vaccine (for protection from four strains) or the high-dose trivalent vaccine (for extra-strong protection against three strains). Dr. Schaffner recommends the latter. "If you have a choice between the quadrivalent vaccine or the high-dose vaccine, opt for the high-dose vaccine. Although the quadrivalent vaccine has broader protection against flu strains, the high-dose vaccine has been proven, in the two-year study described, to provide more optimal protection against the flu in older people. The same kind of documented proof isn't yet available for the quadrivalent vaccine," he said.

"Let's acknowledge that the flu vaccine is good but it's not perfect," said Dr. Schaffner. "It's the best protection we currently have." Recent vaccines prevented between 50% and 60% of potential flu illnesses. The extra protection provided by the high-dose vaccine for people 65 and older boosts that number to 62% to 74%, and that's a very significant bonus. It may mean the difference between life and death for you or a loved one.

Antianxiety Drugs May Increase Pneumonia Risk

Recent finding: People who took benzodiazepines, such as Valium and Xanax—sedatives commonly prescribed for anxiety and insomnia—were 54% more likely to get pneumonia...22% more likely to die within 30 days of being diagnosed with pneumonia...and 32% more likely to die within three years of diagnosis than people who did not take the medications.

Study of almost 5,000 people by researchers at Institute of Cognitive Neuroscience, University College London, published in *Thorax*.

The Nutrient That Beats Pneumonia

James Tumwine MBChB, M.Med, PhD, professor of pediatrics and child health, School of Medicine, Makerere University, Kampala, Uganda, whose study was published in *BMC Medicine*.

Pneumonia is the sixth-leading cause of death in the US. Sadly, antibiotics alone often aren't enough to save the lives of pneumonia patients when their immune systems are so weak.

The good news is that adding a nutrient "booster" to the antibiotics has been shown to prevent more pneumonia deaths, according to a new study.

The best part is that this nutrient is both cheap and easy to find.

ONE MIGHTY MINERAL

The study took place in a developing country, Uganda, and it looked only at kids under five years old, but the researchers said that its findings apply to people of all ages all over the world—even those in developed countries. Researchers looked at 352 male and female children between six months old and five years old who were suffering from severe pneumonia. In addition to getting the prescribed antibiotics, half of the children received a daily supplement pill that contained the current Ugandan Recommended Daily Allowance (RDA) of zinc (10 milligrams per day for children under one year old and 20 milligrams per day for older children) and the other half received a daily placebo pill. (The US RDA is slightly lower.) Before starting treatment, the average level of zinc in the blood of all the children was measured and found to be below the normal range.

Findings: Children receiving zinc supplements were much less likely to die from the pneumonia. Within seven days, about 4% of the children receiving zinc died, while 12% of the children receiving the placebo died. (Remember, all received the same antibiotic treatment.) Researchers followed the children for only seven days, because due to past research they suspected that a child who survived pneumonia would likely have recovered by the seventh day of treatment. But they did not track how many (if any) children died after seven days.

According to one of the study authors, James Tumwine, MBChB, MMed, PhD, a professor of pediatrics and child health at the School of Medicine at Makerere University in Uganda, zinc increased survival because the children were deficient in zinc and the added zinc may have helped boost their immune systems. For example, zinc increases the function of T-cells (types of white blood cells), as well as the hormone thymulin, both of which help increase immunity.

CHEAP & EASY TO FIND

If you think that the only people who are deficient in zinc are those in developing countries or are young children, think again. For example, the ongoing National Health and Nutrition Examination Survey has found that about 35% to 45% of Americans age 60 or older aren't getting as much zinc as they should. And vegetarians also are at risk for zinc deficiency—not only because they do not consume the foods that are high in zinc (such as oysters and meat), but also because two staples of their diets, legumes and whole grains, contain phytates which inhibit zinc absorption.

Many people do not know whether they're zinc deficient. And you can have a healthy level for years and then it can suddenly drop once an infection such as pneumonia develops, said Dr. Tumwine, so asking a doctor to check your level at your annual checkup doesn't necessarily do any good.

If you get pneumonia, ask your doctor whether taking a daily zinc supplement or getting more of it through foods including red meat, poultry, oysters, nuts and zinc-fortified cereals may boost recovery. The RDA for zinc in the US for adults is 11 milligrams (mg) per day for men over age 19 and 8 mg per day for women over age 19. *For kids, it varies...*

- **7 months to 3 years old:** 3 mg
- **4 to 8 years old:** 5 mg
- **9 to 13 years old:** 8 mg
- **14 to 18 years old:** males, 11 mg; females, 9 mg
- **19 and older:** males, 11 mg; females, 8 mg

Fortunately, zinc is a mineral that's cheap and widely available. The cost of a zinc supplement is just pennies per tablet, and you can find zinc wherever nutritional supplements are sold.

Don't Sleep with Your Dentures

According to a recent study, adults who wore dentures during sleep were twice as likely to develop pneumonia as those who removed their dentures before bedtime.

Why: Bacteria grow more rapidly on dentures that are worn constantly and can spread to the lungs. The denture-wearers were also more likely to have dental plaque, gum inflammation and oral fungus.

What to do: Remove dentures at night and clean them thoroughly.

Toshimitsu Iinuma, DDS, PhD, assistant professor of complete denture prosthodontics, Nihon University School of Dentistry, Tokyo, Japan.

How NOT to Get a Deadly Infection

Susan Kellie, MD, associate professor of medicine in the division of infectious diseases at University of New Mexico (UNM) Health Sciences Center and hospital epidemiologist for the UNM Health Sciences Center and the New Mexico Veterans Administration Healthcare Systems, Albuquerque.

The virulent strain of methicillin-resistant *Staphylococcus aureus* (MRSA) continues to cause dangerous infections in otherwise healthy adults and children.

Several years ago, MRSA made headlines when a Virginia high school student died after MRSA spread quickly through his internal organs. Local officials closed 21 schools for disinfection.

The good news is that infections are on the downslide. Looking at data from 2005, government researchers estimated that were more than 94,000 life-threatening MRSA infections in the US annually, contributing to the deaths of an estimated 19,000 Americans per year. The most recent figures from the Centers for Disease Control (CDC), reported in the September 16, 2013 issue of *JAMA Internal*

Medicine, found that 30,000 fewer MRSA infections occurred in 2011 compared to 2005.

MRSA is considered a "superbug" because it's resistant to nearly all treatments, including the powerful antibiotic methicillin.

RISK STILL EXISTS

The ordinary Staphylococcus aureus (staph) bacterium is among the most common causes of infection. Up to one-third of Americans have a relatively innocuous form of staph in the nose or on the skin. It usually causes nothing more serious than boils or a hair-follicle infection.

MRSA is a strain of this organism that is resistant to certain antibiotics and has long been a problem in hospitals. The *JAMA* study, conducted by researchers at the CDC, found that about 85% of MRSA cases are connected with hospitals and other health-care settings—after surgery, in dialysis patients, etc.—but the more recent form of MRSA, known as USA 300, can be found in healthy Americans. *Examples...*

- **The Veterans Administration in Pittsburgh recently reported a four-fold increase** in emergency room treatments for skin and soft-tissue (tissue under the skin) infections caused by MRSA.
- **A study in *The New England Journal of Medicine*** found that nearly 60% of skin and soft-tissue infections at 11 university-affiliated emergency rooms were caused by MRSA.
- **In 2005, researchers investigated an outbreak of skin infections among the St. Louis Rams** and found that 9% of the football players had MRSA skin infections. In addition, 42% of nasal swabs taken from the players and staff members tested positive for MRSA. All carried the USA 300 form of MRSA, which was simultaneously being discovered throughout the country. This suggests rapid, widespread transmission.
- **Studies indicate that 1% of healthy Americans are colonized with MRSA**—bacteria are present but haven't caused infection. In group-living settings, such as prisons and military training camps, the colonization rate is as high as 2.5% to 3%. Among hospitalized patients, the rate of colonization is eight to 10 times higher than previously suspected.

WHAT TO LOOK FOR

MRSA—particularly the USA 300 variant—can be a serious public health threat, but while MRSA is resistant to some antibiotics, it is still vulnerable to others, such as *vancomycin.* Most patients, including those with systemic infection, can be treated successfully if they get an antibiotic promptly.

Infection with MRSA usually starts with the skin. Patients often notice what looks like a spider bite. There will be a small, swollen area with a halo of redness around it. The area will be tender...might become a larger abscess... and the middle area might turn black from tissue breakdown. Sometimes, the bacteria remain confined to the skin—but they also can burrow deep into the body, causing potentially life-threatening infections.

If you suspect that you have a staph infection, call your doctor. If he/she is not available, go to an emergency room.

PREVENTION

The CDC has identified five conditions, known as the 5 Cs, that increase the risk for MRSA—crowding...contact (usually skin to skin)...compromised skin...contaminated surfaces...and cleanliness (or the lack of it).

Patients in health-care settings have the highest risk, followed by those who spend time in communal settings—team locker rooms, prisons, etc. But the emergence of the community-acquired USA 300 form of MRSA means that everyone is potentially at risk.

Important steps to protect yourself...

- **Wash your hands with friction.** Most people with MRSA carry it in the nose, and people tend to touch their noses frequently. Wash your hands at least four times a day, rubbing them together briskly for at least 15 seconds and applying friction to all surfaces. Be sure to do this before meals and after touching gym equipment, shaking hands, etc. Use regular soap—antibacterial soap isn't necessary.

If you are in the hospital or another health-care setting, insist that doctors, nurses and technicians wash their hands before touching you—even if they wear gloves while doing the procedure.

• **Dry your hands with an air blower or a disposable paper towel.** Don't share towels with others, even at home.

• **Use an alcohol-based hand-cleaning gel.** Look for a product that contains at least 62% alcohol. A thorough application of the sanitizer takes only a few seconds and is a highly effective alternative to hand washing.

• **Cover wounds.** Damaged, open skin is the main pathway to infection. Wash cuts and scratches carefully...and keep them covered until they're completely healed.

• **Stay safe in gyms and locker rooms.** Wipe down sweaty equipment (barbells, exercise benches and exercise machine handles) with disinfectant before using...shower after exercise...wear flip-flops to protect your feet in the shower and locker room...and sit on your own towel, rather than on a bare bench.

• **Get vaccinated.** People who have had the flu are vulnerable to post-influenza MRSA pneumonia, which is potentially deadly. In older adults, an annual flu vaccination can reduce mortality from all causes by 50%.

• **Don't take unnecessary antibiotics.** In hospitals and nursing homes, between 20% and 30% of MRSA infections are attributed to antibiotic use.

Reason: Antibiotics kill many of the normal, healthy bacteria in the body. Eradicating "good" bacteria can allow MRSA to proliferate.

Patients often ask their doctors for antibiotics when they have a cold or another viral illness—and doctors often give them to keep their patients happy. But antibiotics are useless for viral infections.

Antibiotic Creams May Increase MRSA Resistance

Over-the-counter triple-antibiotic creams and ointments, such as Medi-Quik and Neosporin, seem to be leading to the emergence of a form of methicillin-resistant Staphylococcus aureus (MRSA) that resists *bacitracin* and *neomycin*—two of the antibiotics found in the creams.

Self-defense: Washing with soap and water is all that many scrapes and cuts require. If you do use an antibiotic cream, apply only a small amount and use it for as short a time as possible.

William Schaffner, MD, professor of preventive medicine, Vanderbilt University School of Medicine, Nashville, commenting on a study by Japanese researchers, published in *Emerging Infectious Diseases.*

Germy Airplanes

How can you keep from getting sick from all those germs on an airplane?

It's wise to try to protect yourself. Up to 20% of airplane passengers report coming down with a cold in the weeks after travel. Researchers recently found that some germs can live for up to one week on armrests, plastic tray tables and in seat pockets. *Examples...*

Methicillin-resistant Staphylococcus aureus (MRSA), which can cause life-threatening infections, and *Escherichia coli,* often the cause of severe diarrhea and vomiting.

Since most of the infections you are likely to pick up on these surfaces are transmitted via your hands, the best way to protect yourself is to bring a small, two-ounce bottle of alcohol-based hand sanitizer on the plane with you and use it frequently. You can also bring disinfecting wipes to use on tray tables and armrests.

Charles Gerba, PhD, professor of microbiology and environmental sciences, The University of Arizona College of Public Health, Tucson.

The African Virus You Should Worry About

William Schaffner, MD, professor of preventive medicine and infectious diseases, Vanderbilt University School of Medicine, Nashville, and a past president of the National Foundation for Infectious Diseases.

Many Americans haven't even heard of Chikungunya (CHIKV)—pronounced "chik-un-GUHN-ya"—but it's worth knowing about. This mosquito-borne virus originated in Africa, spread to Southeast Asia and now also exists in the Caribbean and the Americas.

CHIKV is rampant in the Caribbean because of local living conditions—open windows without screens and no air-conditioning—which leave people vulnerable to mosquitoes. Because more than 12 million Americans travel to the Caribbean each year, it's important that they understand how this virus is transmitted (via mosquitoes, not person to person) and take appropriate precautions.

At press time, 640 cases of travel-related CHIKV had been reported in 43 states and the District of Columbia this year. Mosquitoes infected with the CHIKV virus also were documented in Florida this July, and four cases had been reported there in people who had not traveled outside the US.

What are the symptoms? While CHIKV is rarely fatal, it is extremely painful and debilitating. In fact, its name roughly translates to "Bent Over in Pain," due to the severe discomfort it causes in the small joints of the hands and feet. Other symptoms of CHIKV include fever and sometimes a reddish rash with slight bumps that may occur on the face, trunk, arms and legs. For most people, CHIKV lasts one to two weeks. But 10% of sufferers may have painful joints for up to a year.

What's the best way to prevent infection? No matter where you live, it's important to avoid mosquito bites. Mosquitoes can infect you with CHIKV, West Nile Virus and other diseases.

Prevention of CHIKV depends on avoiding mosquito bites, especially in the daytime when CHIKV-carrying mosquitoes are most likely to be out. However, these mosquitoes also bite at dawn and dusk.

The most basic precaution is to keep mosquitoes outdoors by closing windows and running the air-conditioning if possible...or putting mesh screens on your windows. Be sure to also open and close the door as quickly as possible when entering or leaving the house.

In addition...

- **Wear bug repellent.** For your skin, products containing DEET, IR3535 or picaridin offer long-lasting protection. Opt for products containing permethrin if you're using repellent on your clothing. If you're using both sunscreen and insect repellent, apply sunscreen first.
- **Get rid of standing water, where mosquitoes breed.** Common sources are birdbaths and empty flowerpots. But don't forget to look for house gutters with the wrong pitch.
- **Stay indoors if you have CHIKV.** If you get bitten by a mosquito when you're sick, the virus will be spread to the mosquito...and possibly to many other people, creating an even bigger problem.

When Exotic Travel Turns Deadly

Richard O'Brien, MD, associate professor of emergency medicine at The Commonwealth Medical College of Pennsylvania in Scranton. Dr. O'Brien, who died in 2015, was also a spokesperson for the American College of Emergency Physicians, ACEP.org, and a recipient of the group's Communications Lifetime Achievement Award.

Not long ago, Shannon, an exceptional laboratory tech at the hospital where I work, joined a group of medical professionals from her church to volunteer in a small hospital in Haiti. A few days after her return home, I met Shannon in the hospital elevator. She looked exhausted and described the almost primitive conditions under which she had lived and worked in Haiti—grueling hours in 100-degree temperatures and incessant biting of mosquitoes and stinging ants. Realizing where my mind was going, she assured me that she had gotten the proper immunizations before her trip and had also taken chloroquine, the antimalaria medication that is commonly used as a preventive therapy. I was glad to hear that she had taken those steps but also knew that there had been reports of chloroquine not working. I warned Shannon to keep an eye on any symptoms that might develop.

So unless you're headed to Haiti, why should Shannon's saga matter to you? Even though more than 600,000 die of malaria worldwide each year, it's rare in the US, with only about 2,000 cases annually. But travelers to many places, such as Africa and South Asia, are prime targets. There are literally dozens of countries where an American could contract malaria—even if all the proper precautions are taken.

Now back to Shannon. Within moments of getting off the elevator, she developed chills—a common symptom of malaria. Once she reached the lab, she calmly asked a colleague to draw her blood and prepare several slides to examine under the microscope. Shannon's blood sample showed that she was indeed infected with one of the tiny parasites that causes malaria. A proper diagnosis is imperative so that the parasite is killed and the patient doesn't get worse because the wrong drugs are used. With further lab analysis, we were able to tailor Shannon's therapy with confidence.

After being admitted to the hospital, Shannon was seen by an infectious disease specialist and started receiving a combination of antimalarial medications. Even so, she ran high fevers and soaked her bed linens several times with perspiration. Without IV fluids, such sweating would have caused dehydration. Fortunately, Shannon improved dramatically over the next 48 hours and was sent home on oral medication. She's now back to excellent health. Shannon was lucky to have been back in the US when she got sick, since the medical facilities in Haiti are sorely lacking. Even more important, Shannon knew enough to not dismiss her symptoms as "just a virus"—a potentially deadly mistake made by many people, since malaria symptoms mimic a number of seemingly benign illnesses, such as influenza or food poisoning.

Lessons learned: Even if you've taken precautions before traveling, remember that no preventive medication is 100% effective against any disease. Always consult the CDC travel website, *www.CDC.gov/travel*, before visiting any underdeveloped country, and give yourself plenty of time to prepare—learn what symptoms you could develop if you get sick (with malaria, an infected person might get sick within seven days or up to a year later), and ask a travel professional for practical advice on how you would deal with a medical crisis if one occurred while you were still away. With a deadly disease like malaria, there's no time to spare!

Is Your Shower Water Dangerous?

Leah M. Feazel was the lead researcher on the showerhead study. She was head technician at the Pace Laboratory, University of Colorado-Boulder, and is currently a graduate student in Environmental Science and Engineering at the Colorado School of Mines, Golden, Colorado.

A recent study reported that in some communities people regularly shower with a dangerous microbe called *Mycobacterium avium*—a cousin of the tuberculosis-causing bacteria and one that is quite infectious in its own right.

The University of Colorado-Boulder study is part of a larger research project focused on bacteria we're exposed to in daily life. This particular study examined showerheads because they provide ideal conditions for the formation of slimy biofilms—an assemblage of bacteria that attach themselves to a surface and excrete a protective mesh layer around themselves (dental plaque is an example), making them difficult to eradicate. Theorizing that the shower might be the point of entry for this infection, lead researcher Leah Feazel said that researchers collected samples from the insides of 45 showerheads in nine US cities one, two or three times over two and one-half years. They found M. avium in both Denver and New York showerheads.

Confirming the finding, small amounts of M. avium were also detected in the water systems in both Denver and New York City. In those cities, the concentration of Mycobacteria (of which M. avium is one species) in some showerheads was more than 100 times that in the background water. Researchers theorize that this happened because the biofilms were able to establish colonies of such significant size that they could not be dislodged even by water regularly flowing through. Both municipalities treat their water systems with chlorine, ostensibly to eradicate such dangers, but M. avium are known to be resistant, so the bacteria that survive become even stronger. Since many species of Mycobacteria have been implicated in respiratory and other kinds of infections, this is a cause for concern.

WHY SHOWERS ARE ESPECIALLY RISKY

M. avium is common in soil and water, but it's especially dangerous in showerheads because it is dispersed in aerosol form, which is inhaled and can travel deep into the lungs. Like its relative, Mycobacterium tuberculosis, M. avium primarily causes lung disease, but it has also been known to cause digestive and lymphatic system infections. According to Feazel, M. avium infections are rare in people with healthy immune systems and "fairly rare" among the immune-compromised—but they're on the rise here in the US as well as in the rest of the developed world. The infections caused by M. avium can lead to especially severe illness for people with compromised immune systems, often requiring antibiotic treatment that may be only marginally effective.

HOW TO BE SURE YOU'RE SAFE

Since M. avium is so difficult to kill, individuals known to be immune deficient—including pregnant women...people with asthma or bronchitis...those who've had an organ transplant...and those with cancer or other chronic disease—should ask their doctors whether they should bathe instead of showering. Alternatively, Feazel suggests that people with compromised immune systems would do well to change their showerheads every six months (researchers found no M. avium in showerheads less than six months old) and to choose metal ones, which are less hospitable to biofilms than plastic.

MRSA at the Beach—How to Protect Yourself

You can catch MRSA anywhere—even at the beach. *Methicillin-resistant Staphylococcus aureus* (MRSA) is an antibiotic-resistant strain of bacteria that can cause difficult-to-treat skin and systemic infections. Staphylococcus bacteria are everywhere—many people carry them without realizing it. Beachgoers may pick up bacteria left behind in sand or water by other visitors.

Self-defense: Shower with soap after leaving the beach. Consider staying out of the water if you have an open cut or sore—these can be bacterial entry points.

Lisa Plano, MD, PhD, associate professor, departments of pediatrics and of microbiology and immunology, Miller School of Medicine, University of Miami, Florida, and leader of a study of 1,303 people, presented at a meeting of the American Association for the Advancement of Science.

Is It Safe to Swim in the Ocean?

Yes, it is safe for the vast majority of people. However, it's wise to take precautions. In a new study, 1,303 healthy adults swam at a South Florida beach for 15 minutes. When water samples were analyzed, 37% of them contained Staphylococcus aureus (staph) bacteria, which can cause a serious infection. People at highest risk for staph and other bacterial infections include older adults, young children and those with weakened immune systems.

Theory: Some swimmers may deposit staph bacteria—which is present on the skin of many healthy people—in the water. To protect yourself and others, shower with soap both before and after swimming in subtropical waters, including at beaches in South Florida, Southern California and the Caribbean.

Lisa Plano, MD, PhD, associate professor of pediatrics and microbiology, University of Miami.

Aquariums Harbor Dangerous Bacteria That Cause Severe Skin Infections

George Alangaden, MD, senior staff physician, division of infectious diseases, Henry Ford Hospital, and professor of medicine, Wayne State University, both in Detroit. His research was presented at the recent annual meeting of the Infectious Diseases Society of America.

Aquariums can be mesmerizingly beautiful...and healthful, too. Watching the colorful fish and rippling water can reduce blood pressure, heart rate, stress and anxiety. But aquariums also can present a hazard that few people—and few doctors—are aware of.

The danger: Some home aquariums harbor a bacterium that can lead to a dreadfully painful, unsightly and long-lasting infection that typically goes undiagnosed for many months, according to a new report from Henry Ford Hospital in Detroit.

FISHY CONNECTION

Mycobacterium marinum is a bacterium sometimes found in fish and in nonchlorinated water. When skin that has been "traumatized"—even by something as minor as a paper cut, splinter, hangnail or overzealous fingernail clipping—is exposed to M. marinum, the bacterium can find its way inside and set up an infection. Typically this happens when home-aquarium owners clean their freshwater or saltwater tanks and/or handle their fish (though it also can occur through contact with barnacles or infected fish in the wild).

The problem: It takes two to four weeks after the initial infection begins for the telltale symptoms to appear—and by then, any association with the aquarium typically has long been forgotten. The aquarium-lover is left with a growing number of painful, red, swollen bumps and open sores as large as quarters...which progress up his arm from his hand all the way to his armpit. This is highly unpleasant for anyone—but for a person with a compromised immune system (for instance, due to an autoimmune disorder, HIV, chemotherapy or drugs to prevent organ transplant rejection), M. marinum can even lead to a severe bone marrow or blood infection.

The study: Doctors at Henry Ford reviewed 10 years' worth of records on patients who were treated for M. marinum and discovered that the average length of time it took from symptom onset to correct diagnosis and treatment was a staggering 161 days! By that time, the infection typically had spread from the initial site far up the arm...and patients had already been on multiple ineffective treatments, each with its own potential side effects.

In each of the cases at Henry Ford Hospital, the correct diagnosis was ultimately made after a skin biopsy was performed and the culprit bacterium was finally identified. Only then was the correct treatment initiated, typically using a combination of several different antibiotics that needed to be taken for about two months.

Self-defense: If you have an aquarium, go fishing or clean barnacles, be on the lookout for any redness, swelling or bumps on your hands or forearms. If you develop such symptoms, see your doctor without delay and ask whether you may be infected with M. marinum. Remember, many doctors are unfamiliar with this infection, so bring this article along to your appointment. Treating the problem properly from the start can spare you needless pain and useless medication.

Reassuring: Handling fish bought from the grocery store or swimming in open water would not transmit the M. marinum infection, researchers said.

The Killer Lurking in the Water...And Two Other Dangerous Diseases on the Rise

John Galgiani, MD, professor of medicine at University of Arizona College of Medicine, Phoenix, and director of the Valley Fever Center for Excellence, Tucson, Arizona.

Richard S. Ostfeld, PhD, a senior scientist and disease ecologist at Cary Institute of Ecosystem Studies in Millbrook, New York. He is author of *Lyme Disease: The Ecology of a Complex System*.

Jonathan S. Yoder, MSW, MPH, team leader for the Domestic Water, Sanitation, and Hygiene Epidemiology Team in the National Center for Emerging Zoonotic and Infectious Diseases at the Centers for Disease Control and Prevention, Atlanta. *CDC.gov/naegleria*

Raoult Ratard, MD, MPH, Louisiana State Epidemiologist, Louisiana Department of Health and Hospitals, and adjunct associate professor, New Orleans School of Public Health, Louisiana State University, New Orleans.

The earth is getting warmer, on average—and that is leading to more cases of certain infectious diseases.

Here, three experts explain what you need to know now about three dangerous diseases on the rise...

VALLEY FEVER: GROWING DANGER IN THE DUST
John Galgiani, MD

More than half of people who live in or travel to the dry areas of the country—parts of Arizona, California, Nevada, New Mexico, Texas and Utah—run the risk of being infected with *Coccidioides*, a fungus that lives in the soil.

Coccidioidomycosis, also known as valley fever, causes no symptoms in 60% of people who get it—the immune system eliminates the infection, and no harm is done. But 35% will develop pneumonia, and 5% will become extremely ill when the fungus travels to the brain, bones or other parts of the body. The disease kills more than 150 people a year.

You literally can catch valley fever from the wind. Summer winds that create dust storms scoop up fungal spores from the soil and shoot them downwind. A rainy winter promotes fungal growth and can increase infections the following summer and fall. The number of infections decreases during the wet seasons, then spikes upward in the hot months. You cannot catch the disease from someone who is sick with it.

Between 1998 and 2011, the total number of reported infections increased tenfold. Though valley fever is common in parts of California and the Southwest, infections in the last dozen years have been reported to the CDC from 28 states and the District of Columbia.

Self-defense...

See a doctor if you have flulike symptoms—such as fever, a cough, chest pain, headache and fatigue—that don't start to improve in about a week. Some patients will have painful red bumps on their chest, arms, back or lower legs. Symptoms usually start about one to three weeks after you have been exposed to the fungus.

Tell your doctor about recent travels. Even in areas where valley fever is common, only about 25% of patients get an accurate diagnosis, partly because the infection has symptoms common to other illnesses. The misdiagnosis rate is higher in areas where doctors don't think to test for it.

Antifungal medications, such as *fluconazole* (Diflucan), will control the infection. You might need to take medications for about six months. More serious infections may require amphotericin B, an intravenous antifungal medication.

TICKS ON THE MOVE
Richard S. Ostfeld, PhD

People who live in the northeastern states are accustomed to checking their skin (and their pets) for ticks. It's a routine that's going to become more common in other states. The blacklegged tick that transmits Lyme disease is taking advantage of warmer temperatures.

It has been reported in many parts of the US and is moving into areas where it wasn't seen before, including the colder parts of Maine, Vermont and even Canada.

Other ticks are thriving, too. The American dog tick, for example, which transmits Rocky Mountain spotted fever, is found in every state. The Lone Star tick, found in the eastern and southeastern states, carries ehrlichiosis and tularemia.

The extreme weather that has been linked to climate change is a boon for ticks. The long summer droughts that are natural to some areas served to reduce tick populations. In recent years, some of the same areas have had shorter dry seasons or heavier-than-expected rains, which may have caused an uptick in ticks.

In some parts of the country, tick season appears to be starting earlier and ending later. It's not merely that summers are getting warmer. Winters, on average, are less cold than they used to be. Warmer winters are known to allow tick populations to expand northward and to higher elevations.

Self-defense...

• **Check for ticks.** Check yourself, your children and your pets after spending time outdoors. To reduce risk on hikes, stay on trails. If you plan to leave the path, wear light-colored clothing to make ticks easier to spot. Wear long sleeves, and tuck long pants into your socks.

• **Also, use insect repellent containing DEET on exposed skin.**

• **Know the symptoms.** Tick-related illnesses often are accompanied by flulike symptoms such as fever, fatigue, and aches and pains. Lyme and other tick diseases also can cause distinctive rashes. See your doctor if you develop any of these symptoms, particularly if you develop flulike symptoms when it's not flu season.

Most victims of tick-borne illnesses can be cured with antibiotics, particularly when the infection is detected and treated early.

BRAIN-EATING AMOEBA
Jonathan S. Yoder, MSW, MPH

This single-cell organism *Naegleria fowleri* is found in freshwater lakes, rivers, streams and hot springs. It is not found in the ocean or other bodies of saltwater. It rarely causes infection—but when it does, the infection is deadly.

This amoeba thrives in warm, untreated water and can survive in temperatures up to 115°F. It has been identified most often in southern states in the US.

But in 2010, a young girl was infected while swimming in a lake near her home in Minnesota—an area that's typically too cold for the amoeba to survive. Cases also have been reported in Indiana and Kansas. Scientists aren't sure if the warming of the planet has extended the amoeba's range, but it is one possibility.

The infection is rare. Only 31 cases were reported in the US between 2003 and 2012.

What happens: The amoeba enters the body through the nose, usually when people are swimming or diving in contaminated water. It then travels to the brain, where it literally consumes brain tissue.

Symptoms start one to seven days after exposure. The disease progresses rapidly, and there are no effective treatments. The fatality rate is more than 99%.

The organism can cause infection only when it enters the nasal cavities. There is no risk from drinking a glass of water or from typical showering.

In 2011, officials found Naegleria in a municipal water system in Louisiana, where it caused two deaths—in both cases, the patients had performed nasal flushing using a neti pot. *Self-defense...*

CAUTIONS FOR NETI POT USERS

Use only sterile or distilled water in your neti pot or in a bulb syringe. If you want to use tap water, first boil it for one to three minutes to kill any amoebae. Then, of course, let the water cool before putting it in the neti pot and using it.

Clean your neti pot thoroughly by washing it with soap and hot water or by running it through the ultra-high temperature water of a dishwasher to kill any amoebae. Let it air-dry thoroughly between uses, because amoebae can't survive long on a dry surface.

EXTRA PROTECTION FOR FRESH WATER SWIMMING
Raoult Ratard, MD, MPH

Millions of people all over the US swim in warm fresh water (over 77°) that contains amoebae—such as lakes, ponds, rivers and unchlorinated pools (chlorine at high concentrations kills amoebae)—without getting infected. But a very few do get infected.

Unfortunately, there are no key warning signs that a body of water has amoebae in it. It doesn't look, feel or smell any different. Some towns test certain bodies of water, but these tests are not very reliable because the amount of amoebae in the water varies day to day and it can take weeks for the test results to be processed. So if you find yourself in a warm body of water that's not chlorinated, try to keep your head above water and don't dive in. If you do go under, hold your nose or wear a nose clip and try not to snort any water up your nose.

How to Get Rid of Funky Fungus

Jamison Starbuck, ND, is a naturopathic physician in family practice and a guest lecturer at the University of Montana, both in Missoula.

No doubt about it, fungus is funky. Whether it's mold on that forgotten piece of fruit in the fridge…mushrooms sprouting in your lawn…or the flaky, itchy rash on your body—fungi are prevalent in our lives. Among the most widespread external fungal infections in humans are "athlete's foot" and "jock itch." There's also "yeast," the layman's term for the fungal infection–causing organism known as candida. You can be pretty sure that you have a fungal infection if you notice a few key signs—an area of scaling, peeling skin that may itch, burn, even crack and be very sore…or nails that are discolored (usually yellow or white), brittle, thick, cracked and crusty.

Conventional medical providers prescribe topical or oral antifungals such as *clotrimazole* (Lotrimin), *fluconazole* (Difulcan) or *griseofulvin* (Grifulvin V). These drugs can reduce the problem, and I sometimes prescribe them myself when the infection is severe. However, unless you strengthen your resistance to fungal intrusion, your problem will likely return when you stop the medication and you're exposed to fungi again. *For better results…*

- **Load up on probiotics.** Fungi—like bacteria—are found in and on our bodies at all times, but they cause problems only when their populations get out of control due to such factors as diet. Having lots of healthful bacteria throughout your body will take up much of the cellular space and nutrition the fungi need. That's why I often prescribe the healthful bacteria in probiotics—sometimes up to 30 billion colony-forming units (CFUs) of acidophilus and bifidus per day—for fungal infections. This dose is safe for most adults, though some people can get a loose stool or diarrhea. If this occurs, reduce or discontinue the probiotic.

- **Eliminate all simple sugars.** Forgive me, sugar lovers, but giving up simple sugars for at least 14 days will help reduce the fungi in your body. This means no candy, cookies, desserts, bread, muffins, bagels, pastries or any sort of alcohol. Fungi feed on simple sugars and refined carbohydrates. To help starve out the excess fungi in your system, keep these items out of your diet for two weeks (eat them only sparingly thereafter).

- **Use vinegar and sunlight.** Fungi, which usually thrive in dark, moist areas of our bodies, don't do well in an acidic environment. If you have a topical infection, swab it with a solution of white vinegar and water three times a day. Start with a 50/50 vinegar-water solution, and increase the vinegar strength until it stings. If your fungal rash is cracked, sore or bleeding, topical vinegar can be painful, so avoid it. If possible, also expose your rash to direct sunlight for about 10 minutes, twice daily. These approaches are cheaper than drugstore antifungals and often more effective.

When a fungal infection affects your nails: Fungi often hide beneath the nail (in the nail bed), where it is almost impossible to apply medicine. For this reason, I often prescribe liquid ketoconazole, in addition to the recommendations above, and advise patients to apply it at the edges and as far underneath the nail as is possible. Toenails need to be treated on a daily basis for six months...fingernails require at least three months of treatment.

Best Way to Fix Toenail Fungus

This common infection—often due to athlete's foot, which can be contracted by walking barefoot in a public shower, for example—causes thickened, disfigured toenails that sometimes curl inward.

You'll need a doctor's prescription for antifungal cream, such as Ertaczo or Naftin...or maybe even oral medication, such as *terbinafine* (Lamisil). *To speed the recovery process and help prevent recurrences, try this nail cream...*

• **Kerasal's Fungal Nail Renewal Treatment** ($27.49 for 0.33 ounce, *www.cvs.com*) contains acids and other ingredients that soften the nail, reduce its thickness and improve its appearance, usually within two weeks of nightly use.

Johanna S. Youner, DPM, podiatric surgeon in private practice and attending physician at New York–Presbyterian/Lower Manhattan Hospital, both in New York City. *HealthyFeetNY.com*

The Metal That Heals

Mark A. Stengler, NMD, naturopathic medical doctor and author of *The Natural Physician's Healing Therapies*, founder and medical director of the Stengler Center for Integrative Medicine in Encinitas, California, and adjunct associate clinical professor at the National College of Natural Medicine in Portland, Oregon. *MarkStengler.com*

What precious metal is an industrial commodity and a powerful healing agent? If you guessed silver, you're right. Silver has antimicrobial and antibacterial properties, and it has been used through the ages to cure infections and help heal wounds. Now interest in silver is growing in the mainstream medical community because new studies have found that it can kill a wide range of bacteria and viruses, including the very dangerous *E. coli* and *Staphylococcus*. You're sure to hear more about silver as more doctors start using it.

The form of silver generally used as medicine is colloidal silver, which is a suspension of microscopic particles of silver in liquid.

Healing with silver goes back a long time. Before the advent of antibiotics, colloidal silver was used to treat infections. Silver utensils and vessels (with silver linings) were known to kill germs better than utensils and vessels made of other materials. But after antibiotics came into vogue, silver went out of favor with conventional doctors except for a few uses—as a salve for burns and wounds...in nitrate eye solutions to prevent blindness in newborn babies...and as an antibacterial coating in the lining of catheters.

Holistic physicians, however, never stopped prescribing colloidal silver to prevent many types of viral, bacterial and fungal infections, with generally excellent results. In a Taiwanese study published in the journal *Colloids and Surfaces B: Biointerfaces*, colloidal silver was found to kill the potentially deadly superbug methicillin-resistant Staphylococcus aureus (MRSA) and Pseudomonas aeruginosa, another dangerous superbug, on surfaces (such as doorknobs and light switches, where it is known to colonize and spread among people). A study in *Current Science* found that colloidal silver can boost the effectiveness of standard antibiotics when used in combination with them. Colloidal silver's effectiveness against a range of viruses, including hepatitis C, herpes and HIV, also has been shown in both laboratory tests and in people.

HEALING WITH SILVER

I recommend colloidal silver in liquid form, drops or spray to many of my patients with infections of all kinds, including those of the eyes, ears, throat, respiratory tract, digestive tract or urinary tract. To determine how to use each form of colloidal silver, follow the instructions on the label. *For example, it can be...*

• **Ingested**—one teaspoon of the preparation four times daily, up to seven days.

• **Put into a saline solution to treat pinkeye**—two drops in one-half ounce of saline solution, and rinse the eye with the solution three times daily for seven days.

• **Placed directly in the ear**—two drops in the affected ear three times daily for seven days.

• **Sprayed on cuts.**

Other uses: Colloidal silver often is used by holistic physicians to fight infection intravenously. I frequently prescribe colloidal silver to be taken for several months by patients with Lyme disease...or I recommend it instead of antibiotics for infections. For these types of uses, it is best taken under a doctor's supervision (see below for the risks).

Brand to try: Sovereign Silver (888-328-8840, *www.natural-immunogenics.com*). This high-quality solution contains the smallest particles of any colloidal silver product on the market, with an average diameter of 0.8 nanometers (8 angstroms) per particle. Small particle size is important for several reasons. It enables the particles to penetrate and kill microbe cells more easily...and makes it easier for your body to flush them out of your system once they've done their job.

SAFETY ISSUES

Colloidal silver is safe for children, but it is not recommended for women who are pregnant or breast-feeding, because it has not been studied in these populations.

Ingesting silver products has, in rare cases, been linked to an irreversible condition called argyria, in which the skin turns bluish gray. While this is clearly a side effect that no one wants to encounter, case studies show that this condition occurs only when silver products are consumed for a year or more and/or as a result of ingesting very large amounts—at least one gram, which would require drinking an absurd amount of properly prepared colloidal silver solution (more than 100 quarts daily).

Do not attempt to make a colloidal silver product yourself, and do not ingest someone else's homemade product. A variety of do-it-yourself kits are available. However, these kits create silver particles that are quite large, making them less effective at killing microbes and more difficult for the body's cells to eliminate than smaller particles. Large silver particles are more likely to produce argyria with long-term use.

Parasites: Your Body May Be Hosting These "Stealth Germs"

Erno Daniel, MD, PhD, an internist and geriatrician at the Sansum Clinic in Santa Barbara, California, and a former clinical assistant professor of medicine at the University of Southern California in Los Angeles. He is the author of *Stealth Germs in Your Body.*

Most people think that parasitic infections are a problem only in less-developed countries. Not true. Up to 40% of US adults harbor *Toxoplasma gondii*, the parasite that causes toxoplasmosis, an infection marked by flulike symptoms. Meanwhile, the Centers for Disease Control and Prevention estimates that more than 100,000 cases of *giardiasis*, a parasitic infection that causes watery diarrhea, occur annually in the US.

Many parasitic infections cause only mild symptoms or no symptoms at all. But some organisms can cause brain and nervous system damage or long-lasting symptoms such as chronic fatigue or muscle aches. Some of these infections can turn deadly, especially in people whose immune systems are suppressed by illness or chemotherapy.

Good news: Once you're diagnosed (usually with a stool sample), most parasites can be eliminated with medication. Virtually all can be prevented with good hygiene and the safe handling of food and water. However, parasitic infections are notorious for going undiagnosed—largely because symptoms can be mistaken for other illnesses, and many doctors underestimate their presence in developed countries.

Common parasites in the US...

TOXOPLASMA GONDII

Healthy adults with this potentially dangerous single-celled organism typically have no symptoms. Occasionally, however, a scar can form on the retina. During a routine eye exam, the scar can be noted and serve as a clue to previous exposure. In people with impaired immunity, such as those undergoing chemotherapy or AIDS patients, untreated toxoplasmosis can suddenly reemerge and cause brain or nervous system damage and even can be fatal.

Although medications are usually recommended for those with compromised immunity, symptoms usually go away without treatment in people who are otherwise healthy. However, the dormant organism may reemerge.

T. gondii is often present in the feces of otherwise healthy-appearing cats. People may get infected while cleaning a cat's litter box or working in the yard and touching soil where a cat has defecated.

Be sure to wash your hands thoroughly after contact with a cat or its feces and after yard work or gardening. The disease also can be contracted by eating any type of undercooked contaminated meat, which can harbor the organism.

Symptoms: Swollen lymph nodes, headache, fever, body aches and sometimes a sore throat.

Treatment: *Pyrimethamine* (Daraprim), an antimalaria drug that also kills T. gondii. It's combined with an antibiotic to increase the effectiveness of the treatment. Treatment usually lasts several weeks, but those with compromised immunity may need to continue for the rest of their lives.

Important: Pyrimethamine inhibits the absorption of folate (folic acid). Patients who take high doses for extended periods are usually advised to supplement with 400 micrograms (mcg) of folic acid daily.

Toxoplasmosis can cause problems with pregnancy, including miscarriage. Pregnant women should speak to their doctors for precautions to take.

GIARDIA LAMBLIA

Cysts of the parasite *Giardia lamblia* are excreted in the feces of people who are infected with the organism. Infection can result from ingesting as few as 10 of these cysts. This might occur, for example, if someone uses the bathroom, doesn't wash his/her hands and then deposits the cysts on an object such as a cutting board.

The infection, known as giardiasis, can also be contracted by drinking contaminated water or eating contaminated food. Though the organism can survive in tap water, in most communities tap water is free of infectious agents, including G. lamblia. With untreated well water, not even a water filter will reliably kill G. lamblia.

Hikers, hunters, campers and anyone who spends a lot of time in nature should avoid drinking untreated water from or swimming in unclean streams, lakes or rivers.

Best: Pack your own purified water.

Symptoms: Gastrointestinal upset, such as severe diarrhea, cramping and sometimes nausea, often occurs upon first exposure. Later, the symptoms may be mistaken for irritable bowel syndrome or chronic acid indigestion. Some experience fatigue and weight loss.

Treatment: The drug *metronidazole* (Flagyl), taken three times daily for five to seven days. Side effects include a metallic aftertaste and nausea. Avoid drinking alcohol when taking Flagyl. Combining the two can cause upset stomach, vomiting and abdominal cramps.

CRYPTOSPORIDIUM PARVUM

This one-celled parasite—and its close relative *Cyclospora cayetanensis*—infects the small intestine. People with this infection, known as cryptosporidiosis, release enormous quantities of the parasite in their stools. People may get infected if they drink (or swim in) contaminated water, eat uncooked foods that were prepared by someone with the infection, or touch their mouths after touching a contaminated surface or object.

Note: Chlorination of water will not kill this organism.

Symptom: Watery diarrhea. This may continue for one to two weeks—or even up to a month—in people who are otherwise healthy. The infection is potentially deadly for those with weak immune systems.

Treatment: Patients who are generally healthy don't require treatment and usually recover within two weeks. In those with compromised immunity, in addition to treating the underlying illness if possible, fluid/electrolyte replacement may be required as well as antidiarrheal medications and/or antiparasitic medications to reduce symptoms.

TAPEWORMS AND LARVAE

The largest intestinal parasite is the tapeworm. It can survive in the intestine for more than a decade and can potentially reach up to 50 feet in length. Infection is usually caused by eating infected raw or undercooked pork, beef or fish.

Symptoms: Most people have no or only mild gastrointestinal symptoms, such as occasional diarrhea. Equally important, tapeworm larvae can migrate to parts of the body outside the intestine and cause seemingly unrelated symptoms, such as seizures (if they enter the brain).

Depending on the species and the nature of the infection (worm or larval), some patients may suffer damage to the central nervous system.

Treatment: *Praziquantel* (Biltricide) kills adult tapeworms. A stool sample is usually taken one to three months after the initial treatment. If the parasite is still present, the drug is repeated.

It also may be useful to take probiotics to ease severe diarrhea—speak to your doctor.

PARASITE SELF-DEFENSE

Food and water sanitation, as well as good hygiene, are the best ways to prevent parasitic infections. *Recommended...*

- **Use a countertop or under-the-sink activated carbon water filter** to trap cryptosporidium, giardia and other parasites.
- **Wash your hands not only after using the bathroom,** but also after working in the yard or handling laundry—particularly when the laundry includes underwear or bedsheets. You would be surprised at how many people don't follow these simple guidelines.
- **Always rinse fresh fruits and vegetables.** This will remove most organisms. In high-risk areas (such as tropical or underdeveloped countries), soak these foods in water disinfected with iodine. Add five to 10 drops per quart of water. Let the food soak for about 20 minutes.
- **Wash knives, cutting boards and other kitchen equipment**—as well as your hands —with warm, soapy water before and after handling raw meats.
- **Wear gloves when cleaning a litter box,** and wash your hands afterward.
- **Don't walk barefoot in the yard/garden,** particularly if you have cats (or livestock).

The Danger Growing in Your Fridge

C. Leigh Broadhurst, PhD, research scientist at a government agriculture research lab and research associate in the department of civil and environmental engineering at University of Maryland, College Park. She is author of *Natural Relief from Asthma: Breathe Freely, Naturally.*

When you see greenish spots on the surface of cottage cheese or a patch of fuzzy nastiness on a tomato, you know that you're dealing with mold. But a lot of people don't know about mold inside food—including hidden mold. And what about mold you may find growing on a piece of bread—does that mean you must throw out the entire loaf? *Here are answers to the moldy bread dilemma and eight other common questions...*

If I eat something moldy by mistake, how dangerous is it?

Some food molds can trigger sinusitis, asthma and allergies. Mold also can cause, in susceptible people, a host of less serious but uncomfortable symptoms, including cramps, headaches and nausea. The people who are most at risk are those with compromised immunity due to chronic illnesses (especially of the lungs), organ transplants, treatment with chemotherapy, etc.

What about the moldy yogurt scare earlier this year? Is yogurt more likely to have mold?

In September 2013, there was a recall of a popular brand of yogurt after the FDA received reports that the yogurt had mold that might have been causing cramps, diarrhea and other symptoms.

In general, if you or someone in your family has an illness that suppresses the immune system or you take medications that have a similar effect, be particularly careful with yogurt that contains fruit. Some fruits contain naturally occurring yeasts (a type of mold) that thrive in yogurt. Even if the fruit doesn't contain these yeasts, the combination of "sugaryness" and yogurt's soft texture creates an environment for other mold spores. It can grow overnight. Signs of mold include a swelled container... off colors or flavors...fermented or mildewy smell...and/or black or green spots.

Are any food molds deadly?

Some mold species produce poisonous substances called mycotoxins. The most dangerous of these is aflatoxin. It's typically found in grains and peanuts, mainly in developing parts of the world. With repeated exposure, it can cause liver cancer as well as a severe form of fungal hepatitis. It's rare in the US because manufacturers test for it constantly.

Important: If you buy a bag of peanuts and notice a moldy smell...blackened areas on any of the nuts...or a very foul taste, throw it away. You don't want to take chances with aflatoxin.

If I cut off the moldy part, can I still eat a food?

No one likes to throw away food that has a few spots. It's tempting to just skim or trim off small areas of mold. In general, I don't recommend that.

Molds are filamentous organisms. They have long, threadlike structures beneath the part that you can see on the surface. The threads grow rapidly, particularly in soft foods with a high liquid content. That's why it is much better to assume that the mold has spread throughout a container even if you can't see it. The same goes for bread. If a slice of bread has mold, throw out the entire loaf.

Exception: It's safe to trim the mold from hard foods, such as cheddar cheese. Cut off at least one inch around (and below) the mold spot. Be sure to keep the knife out of the mold so that it doesn't contaminate the rest of the food.

But some cheeses are supposed to be moldy. Can these cheeses grow harmful molds on them?

Some molds taste delicious. The white coating on Brie cheese, for example, is a surface mold. Other cheeses, particularly the blue-veined varieties, such as Roquefort and Gorgonzola, are laced all the way through with mold. These cheeses are highly protected by their specific culture, and as long as they are refrigerated and sealed, they will keep without growing anything harmful for many months. But the cheese may develop a sharp, almost alcoholic, taste.

I have had honey in my cabinet for years. Why doesn't that get moldy?

Foods such as honey that have a 50% or higher sugar content do not have enough water to grow most molds. Very salty foods, such as some preserved meats, also are unlikely to grow mold.

What's the best way to keep mold from growing on food?

Many people think refrigeration is the best way to deter mold, but that's actually the opposite of what you should do in many cases. Instead, store fresh foods in the same environment that they were in when you bought them. If you bought berries from the refrigerator case at the supermarket, keep them in the refrigerator at home. If you bought tomatoes at room temperature, keep them on the counter.

Exposing foods to different temperatures—and changing levels of humidity—can encourage mold growth.

Also important: Buy whole, fresh produce whenever possible. The risk for mold is much higher in precut foods.

Is it true that one bad apple can spoil the bunch?

When you buy produce by the box or in large bags, you often will find at least one moldy item, usually somewhere in the middle. If you don't get rid of it quickly, the mold will spread.

What to do: When you come home with a bulk container such as a bag of oranges, dump it out. Spread out the produce, and inspect each piece. Look for discolored or mushy areas. Throw out the bad ones.

Important: Berries are particularly susceptible to mold because they have a soft skin, plenty of moisture and contain sugar. Homegrown berries are less likely to get moldy than supermarket varieties because they're fresher. You might want to buy berries from a farmers' market—and buy only as much as you'll use in the next few days.

Sometimes I see mold on the door seal of my refrigerator. Could that spread to the food inside?

Yes. Mold that grows inside the grooves of the refrigerator door seal could eventually migrate to the inside of the refrigerator. Wash the seal and the inside of the fridge with a mild bleach solution.

Also, wash the inside of crisper drawers if any moldy produce has been in them. (If gaskets on food-storage containers have mold, wash those, too.)

If food in your fridge seems to get moldy quickly, check the internal temperature of the refrigerator with a thermometer. The ideal temperature is between 35°F and 38°F.

If adjusting the temperature setting doesn't help, you might need to repair or replace your refrigerator. If the door seal has gone bad, or if the air inside isn't circulating the way that it's supposed to, you might notice that your refrigerator is "sweating." The increased moisture is ideal for mold growth.

5 Top Myths About Lyme Disease

Richard I. Horowitz, MD, an internist, integrative medicine practitioner and medical director of the Hudson Valley Healing Arts Center in Hyde Park, New York. He is the author of *Why Can't I Get Better? Solving the Mystery of Lyme & Chronic Disease. CanGetBetter.com*

Your risk of getting Lyme disease is higher than you might think. Until recently, it was estimated that about 30,000 new cases occurred in the US each year. A report, released by the Centers for Disease Control and Prevention (CDC) in 2013, stated that the number of Lyme cases is roughly 10 times higher—about 300,000 per year.

If you assume that you're safe from Lyme, consider this: Although many people think that this disease occurs in isolated pockets around the country, it's actually now been reported in most parts of the US.

"The great imitator": Lyme, the most common disease that's spread by ticks, causes dozens of symptoms that can easily be mistaken for other conditions, such as chronic fatigue syndrome, fibromyalgia and autoimmune diseases including multiple sclerosis. Many patients with Lyme suffer unnecessarily because they never even know that they have the disease—and those who are diagnosed often are not given the best treatments.

Leading misconceptions about Lyme—and the facts...

MYTH #1: Lyme always causes a bull's-eye rash. People who live in areas where Lyme disease is common are taught to look for a red, expanding rash called erythema migrans. It resembles a bull's-eye and generally appears about seven days after a bite from an infected tick.

Fact: About half of Lyme patients develop a rash. But even when the rash is present, it resembles a bull's-eye in only about half of those cases. It's just as likely to appear as a "simple" rash that's easily mistaken for a spider bite or skin infection.

MYTH #2: Joint pain is the telltale symptom of Lyme. Many Lyme patients will develop Lyme arthritis, severe joint pain and swelling that usually affects the knees or other large joints. But not every Lyme patient develops this symptom—so you can't assume that the absence of joint pain and swelling means that you don't have Lyme.

Fact: Most Lyme patients have at least a dozen different symptoms, but there is no one symptom that everyone with Lyme has. Among the most common symptoms are fatigue, migratory joint and muscle pain, tingling, numbness and burning sensations, a stiff neck, headache, memory and concentration problems and sleep disorders. These symptoms can range from mild to severe. The constellation of symptoms and ruling out other disorders point to Lyme.

MYTH #3: Lyme is fairly easy to diagnose with a blood test. If you have Lyme symptoms, your doctor will probably recommend two-tiered blood testing—the ELISA test, which measures the total amount of antibodies produced by the body in response to the Lyme bacterium (*Borrelia burgdorferi*)... and if that test is positive, the Western blot, which looks for specific protein patterns that are characteristic of Lyme.

Fact: The tests are not very accurate. One study, conducted by the New York State Department of Health, looked at more than 1,500 patients who had been diagnosed with Lyme disease. Two-tiered testing missed 81% of the cases. If tests are done early in the course of the disease or if the patient has received an antibiotic, test results may indicate a false-negative.

Important: I recommend getting both the ELISA and Western blot tests. If your Western blot shows a 23, 31, 34, 39 and/or 83-93 band, this indicates Lyme. Other tests, such as a DNA test called polymerase chain reaction (PCR) and antibody titers, to check for other common tick-borne infections, such as Babesia (a malaria-like parasite) and Bartonella (which causes cat scratch fever), also can be helpful in diagnosing resistant symptoms.

MYTH #4: Doxycycline always cures Lyme quickly. When Lyme is diagnosed and treated within two to four weeks of the tick bite that transmitted the disease, about 75% of patients will be cured with tetracycline antibiotics such as doxycycline or other antibiotics such as penicillin or cephalosporin.

But about one-quarter of these patients—and a higher percentage of those who don't get quick treatment—will develop a chronic infection that doesn't respond to simple antibiotic therapy. Although some doctors don't think Lyme bacteria survive after 30 days of antibiotic treatment, many studies have shown that they can.

MYTH #5: Medication is the only treatment. Antibiotic therapy is the mainstay of Lyme treatment. But it's usually not enough.

Fact: Many Lyme symptoms—such as fatigue, muscle and joint pain, and memory loss—that persist despite antibiotics may be caused by more than one organism. Chinese herbs such as coptis, artemesia and cat's claw may help treat Lyme and these co-infections.

I often advise patients also to take low-dose naltrexone, a medication that helps reduce inflammation. A combination of naltrexone, curcumin (an anti-inflammatory compound found in the spice turmeric) and antioxidants like glutathione have helped relieve fatigue, pain and cognitive difficulty in my patients.

Also helpful: Diet is important. Some people feel better avoiding gluten, and for others, an alkaline diet with lots of fruits and vegetables counteracts the acidity and inflammation caused by infection.

BETTER TICK PROTECTION

People can prevent some cases of Lyme by carefully checking their skin and removing ticks with tweezers after spending time outdoors—but don't count on it.

Fact: The black-legged tick that causes Lyme is about the size of a sesame seed. Most people never see the ticks that bite them.

My advice: Whenever possible, wear long pants and high socks when you go outdoors during tick season. Spraying your clothing with a product that contains permethrin, a flower-based insect repellent, can help repel ticks. If it's just too hot and you prefer shorts or other summer clothes, you can apply the stronger insect repellent known as DEET to your skin, but wash it off as soon as you are out of the tick-infested area to reduce exposure to the chemical.

Herbal Help for Chronic Lyme Disease

Richard Horowitz, MD, is a board-certified internist and medical director of the Hudson Valley Healing Arts Center, an integrative medical center based in Hyde Park, New York, that specializes in the treatment of chronic Lyme disease and other tick-borne disorders.

Prompt antibiotic treatment often cures Lyme disease—but when it doesn't, certain herbs can help get rid of the infection and its nasty symptoms.

Frighteningly, experts now report that the deer tick bite can transmit not only the infamous spirochete (spiral-shaped bacterium) but also multiple infectious agents. Richard Horowitz, MD, a board-certified internist whose Hyde Park, New York, clinic has treated more than 12,000 Lyme disease patients in the past 20 years, says the disease is more complicated to treat than had previously been understood.

A PERSISTENT PROBLEM

If acute Lyme disease goes untreated or if antibiotic treatment is unsuccessful, patients can develop an array of persistent symptoms in the following weeks and months. The CDC's symptom list includes palsy (loss of muscle tone) on one or both sides of the face...severe headaches and neck stiffness due to meningitis (inflammation of membranes covering the brain and spinal cord)...heart palpitations... dizziness due to changes in heartbeat...severe joint pain and swelling...shooting pains, numbness or tingling of the hands and feet... irritability...and problems with concentration and memory.

Though some patients have symptoms that last for years, chronic Lyme disease is a controversial issue. In fact, *The Journal of Pediatrics* recently reported that half of physicians surveyed question the existence of chronic Lyme disease—even though, as Dr. Horowitz pointed out, there are numerous scientific articles proving the existence of persistent infection despite both short-term and longer-term antibiotic use.

HERBS IN ACTION

Numerous clinical studies have demonstrated the effectiveness of including certain herbs in the treatment of chronic Lyme disease. Why do herbs help achieve what antibiotics alone cannot? Because chronic Lyme disease can involve not only the main spirochetal infection, but also multiple bacterial, viral and/or parasitic coinfections transmitted by the same tick bite, Dr. Horowitz said. Herbs typically prescribed for chronic Lyme are able to combat these various infections because they have antispirochetal, antibacterial, antiviral, antiparasitic and/or antimalarial properties. They also help reduce inflammation...protect the heart...support the liver...aid kidney function....provide antioxidants...and/or boost the immune system.

Herbs to ask your doctor about: Herbal extracts usually are taken in capsule or tablet form. *Among the herbs most commonly prescribed for chronic Lyme are...*

- **Andrographis paniculata**
- **Astralagus**
- **Banderol**
- **Polygonum cuspidatum**
- **Samento**
- **Sarsaparilla**

Dr. Horowitz emphasized that Lyme patients should take herbs only under the guidance of a health-care practitioner who knows their benefits, side effects and interactions... who can determine which of the various herbal protocols that have been developed for Lyme would be most appropriate for an individual patient...and who can prescribe the right dosages.

Referrals: Visit *www.lymediseaseAssociation.org* and click on "Doctors"

Note: Certain herbs should not be used by patients who have particular medical conditions (such as gallbladder disease), who take certain medications (such as cyclosporine, cortisone drugs or blood thinners), who are or plan to get pregnant, or who are breastfeeding.

Some herbs initially can cause gastrointestinal side effects, such as constipation or nausea, so patients may start with a small dosage and increase gradually over several weeks... maintain the top dose for several months or so...then reduce the dosage incrementally as their chronic Lyme disease symptoms subside at last.

Superbugs Hide in Homes

Methicillin-resistant Staphylococcus aureus (MRSA) once was confined to hospitals and nursing homes, but it has been found in homes—specifically, strain USA300, the primary cause of community-acquired MRSA infections throughout the US. MRSA is resistant to common antibiotics and can cause pneumonia, blood infections and other serious illnesses. The infection is spread through skin-to-skin contact or by sharing personal hygiene items, such as razors or towels.

If you have a MRSA infection: Keep the wound covered, and wash your hands frequently to prevent MRSA from spreading to family members. Wash bedding and clothes with hot water.

Study led by researchers at Columbia University Medical Center, New York City, reported in *Proceedings of the National Academy of Sciences.*

Pneumonia Protection for People Age 65 and Over

The Centers for Disease Control recommends PCV13 (Prevnar 13) for all adults 65 years or older to protect against infection by Streptococcus pneumoniae bacteria, which can cause pneumonia, meningitis, and blood and middle-ear infections. Prevnar lasts longer than the older vaccine, Pneumovax, and has been given to children for several years. Now it is approved for older adults as well.

For more information visit *www.cdc.gov/pneumococcal/vaccination.html*

Centers for Disease Control, *UC Berkeley Wellness Letter. BerkeleyWellness.com*

Diseases You Get from Pets (Even a Deadly Staph Infection)

Jon Geller, DVM, is a veterinarian at Veterinary Emergency Hospital, Fort Collins, Colorado. Dr. Geller writes for numerous pet magazines and answers dog owners' questions online at *DogChannel.com.*

In recent years, the drug-resistant bacteria methicillin-resistant Staphylococcus aureus (MRSA), which used to be found exclusively in humans, has turned up in pets. Humans can acquire MRSA (often pronounced "mersa") during a hospital stay, then pass it on to their pets, where it can live for several months before being passed back to humans that have close contact with the pets. Dogs and cats both appear to be potential carriers of the bacteria, which can cause severe skin infections, pneumonia and even death in both humans and pets. For protection, always wash your hands after handling a pet, and don't let a pet lick your face. Take your pet to the vet if he/she has any sign of a skin infection.

Other diseases that you can get from your pets...

DOGS

• **Roundworms.** Toxocariasis is an infection acquired from the roundworm parasite that lives in the feces of infected dogs. Roundworm eggs find their way into the soil and can be ingested after gardening in infected soil or petting a dog that has been rolling around on the ground. Once ingested, the eggs develop into worms that migrate around the human body. Roundworm infections are more common in arid areas, where the eggs can survive in soil for years.

Human symptoms: Mild infections may not cause symptoms. More serious infections may cause abdominal pain, cough, fever, itchy skin and shortness of breath.

Human treatment: Antiparasitic drugs.

Dog symptoms: Diarrhea, weight loss.

Dog treatment: Deworming medication.

Prevention: Wash hands thoroughly after working in the garden or petting your dog.

• **Hookworms** are in the feces of infected dogs. Hookworm larva can penetrate the skin and develop into worms that tunnel under the skin, creating itchy red tracks.

Human symptoms: Itching, rash, abdominal pain, diarrhea, loss of appetite.

Human treatment: Antiparasitic drugs.

Dog symptoms: Diarrhea, weight loss.

Dog treatment: Deworming medication.

Prevention: Avoid bare-skin contact with soil or beaches where dogs may have defecated.

• **Leptospirosis** is a bacterial infection that affects the urinary tracts of dogs and other animals that acquire the infection through their noses or mouths after spending time in habitats shared by raccoons and other wildlife. Humans acquire it when an open sore or mucous membrane comes in contact with the bacteria.

Human symptoms: Some infected people have no symptoms. Others have high fever, severe headache, chills, vomiting and sometimes jaundice.

Human treatment: Antibiotics.

Dog symptoms: Lethargy, loss of appetite, jaundice.

Dog treatment: Fluids and antibiotics.

Prevention: Wear gloves when working around soil or a habitat shared with raccoons. Avoid swimming or wading in water that might be contaminated with animal urine.

CATS

• **Ringworm** is not a worm but a fungal infection named for the circular rash it causes on humans. Ringworm is transmitted via direct contact with an infected animal's skin or hair.

Human symptoms: Ring-shaped rash that is reddish and often itchy.

Human treatment: Antifungal ointment.

Cat symptoms: Hair thinning and loss.

Cat treatment: Antifungal ointment.

Prevention: Keep your cat inside to minimize the risk for skin parasites.

• **Toxoplasmosis.** Some cats shed a potentially infectious organism in their feces that can be particularly dangerous if ingested by pregnant women and people with compromised immune systems. Cats typically become infected when they eat infected prey, such as mice or birds. Humans can accidentally ingest the parasites after cleaning out a litter box.

Human symptoms: Most people never develop symptoms. Those who do may have headache, fever, fatigue, body aches.

Human treatment: Certain medications can reduce the severity.

Cat symptoms: Often no signs.

Cat treatment: Antibiotics.

Prevention: Pregnant women should avoid cleaning litter boxes. Keep your cat indoors.

• **Cat scratch fever.** This is a bacterial disease caused by *Bartonella henselae*. The organism usually is carried by fleas that live on the cat.

Human symptoms: Swollen lymph nodes, fever and malaise.

Human treatment: Antibiotics.

Cat symptoms: Most cats don't show any signs of illness.

Cat treatment: Flea medication.

Prevention: Promptly wash and disinfect any cat scratches. (See the following article for more ways your cat can harm you.)

BIRDS

•**Psittacosis.** Some birds carry bacteria that cause a bacterial respiratory infection in humans, acquired when they inhale dried secretions from infected birds.

Human symptoms: Fever, chills, headache, muscle aches and dry cough.

Human treatment: Antibiotics.

Bird symptoms: Typically no symptoms, though some birds show signs of respiratory illness, such as lethargy and discharge from eyes and nasal airways.

Bird treatment: Antibiotics.

Prevention: Use extreme care in handling any pet bird showing signs of respiratory illness.

---

6 Ways Your Cat Can Make You Sick—or Even Kill You

Richard O'Brien, MD, emergency physician, associate professor of emergency medicine at The Commonwealth Medical College of Pennsylvania, Scranton. He is a spokesperson for the American College of Emergency Physicians, Scranton, and a recipient of the group's Communications Lifetime Achievement Award.

There are few things in life that can beat the comfort of snuggling with pet cats. One in three households in America has at least one kitty roaming through it.

But there are also risks—big risks—to sharing space with cats. Richard O'Brien, MD, an emergency physician based in Scranton, Pennsylvania, admits that he loves cats and has had a few himself, but he's also seen firsthand how dangerous they can be. How can your own pet cat hurt you? Dr. O'Brien tallied up the six ways your cat can make you sick—or even kill you—and what you and your family need to know to protect yourselves.

•**By mouth and teeth.** A cat's mouth is a literal reservoir of bacteria, and you might have had firsthand experience of how very sharp the slender pointy teeth of a cute little cat are. If you've been bitten by a cat and didn't get a raging infection, consider yourself lucky. Puncture wounds from cat bites are usually very deep, sending bacteria deep into human flesh as if by needle injection. "Because of the shape of the cat's teeth, the deepest part of the wound is also the narrowest, so it's virtually impossible to clean the wound before it starts closing up," said Dr. O'Brien. "It's the perfect set-up for a nasty infection."

Because about 90% of cats carry a type of infectious bacteria called *Pasteurella multocida*, which can cause severe skin infections that can even spread to the heart (endocarditis) or protective tissue of the brain (meningitis), Dr. O'Brien treats every cat bite he sees with antibiotics—and a tetanus shot, too, if the bitten person hasn't had one in the past 10 years.

Many people who have been bitten by cats wait until redness and swelling start to appear before they decide to seek treatment, but by then it may be too late. P. multocida infections can worsen and spread very fast—within 24 hours.

Bottom line: When a cat bites, see a doctor right away for appropriate treatment.

A note about rabies: Although it's reassuring to know that the rabies virus, which is transmitted in the saliva of an infected animal, is rare in domesticated cats, all bets are off for feral or stray cats. This makes bites from strays, or just outdoor cats, a medical urgency—meaning you don't need an ambulance or emergency room visit, but you do need to get to a doctor as soon as possible. If you've been bitten by a cat and are not absolutely sure that it has been vaccinated against rabies, thoroughly wash the area with lots of soap and water and contact animal control, which will try to locate the cat and find out whether it's healthy or rabid. If there's any doubt about the creature, you'll need to be vaccinated for rabies within 10 days after the bite.

•**By claws and paws.** As you know from watching cats preen, they always have their paws in their mouths. A cat scratch can transmit bacteria that was originally in the cat's mouth to your skin. Usually, superficial love-tap scratches can be successfully cleaned with soap and water and then covered with antibiotic ointment for good measure. But a puncture wound from a cat's claw should be treated with prescription oral antibiotics for many of the same reasons mentioned above.

A note about cat scratch fever: About 40% of cats carry *Bartonella henselae*, the bacteria that causes cat scratch fever, which can be transmitted to humans not only by cat scratch but by a cat or flea bite as well. Common symptoms include bumps or blisters and/or swollen glands around the wound and, as the name suggests, fever. Although antibiotics are sometimes used to treat cat scratch fever, it often goes away on its own, but why not do what you can to avoid it altogether by remembering to thoroughly wash even simple cat scratches and daub them with a basic antibiotic ointment, such as bacitracin or bacitracin/polymyxin.

• **By fleas and ticks.** Both fleas and ticks can transmit nasty bacteria, viruses and even parasite larva, but only if they've bounced off an infected animal and onto you. "The biggest risk from fleas," said Dr. O'Brien, "is a very itchy rash from a mass of flea bites. If your cat has fleas, then your house has fleas, and they're very hard to get rid of because they breed abundantly, frequently and exponentially. If they are left unchecked, you could have many thousands of them in your home and yard. Avoiding them in the first place is much easier than trying to rid your carpet, upholstery and bedding of them, which might require the services of a professional exterminator to be sure that you're safely rid of them. So garland kitty with a flea collar and examine the cat regularly, especially outdoor cats, to make sure fleas aren't hitching a ride on them.

As for ticks, you know they can carry Lyme disease—among other diseases that can infect humans—and they can take a ride from your outdoor cat to you. Doing what you can to protect your cat from ticks by, for example, using a flea and tick collar is good for your health and safety, too.

A note about tapeworms: You can be infected with a tapeworm from a cat if a flea that's got tapeworm larvae attached to it ends up inside you. Yuck! How's that going to happen? Well, since tiny fleas can be missed by the naked eye and are always jumping into airborne flight, they can end up wafting into a person's mouth—usually that of a child—where they are unwittingly swallowed, allowing tapeworm larva to travel through the digestive tract to set up camp in the intestines.

As gross as it sounds, the type of tapeworm infecting most cats in the US, *Dipylidium caninum*, generally doesn't cause sickness in humans if ingested via an infected flea but just passes out in stool. If there are symptoms, they include stomach pain, diarrhea and anal itch. Fortunately, the tapeworm infection is easily treated with the prescription antiparasitic medication *praziquantel*. (The human formulation of this drug is marketed as Biltricide and the cat formulation as Droncit.) So for the health of your cat and home and for peace of mind, get your cat to a vet for treatment if it has symptoms of tapeworm infection, such as gassiness or passing tiny worms in the stool. And if you want to be really careful, have your cat examined for tapeworm during an annual vet exam.

• **By poop.** Up to 40% of domestic cats host a tiny parasite called *Toxoplasma gondii*, responsible for a flulike infection in humans called toxoplasmosis, which can lead to very serious complications in certain people. One way that humans are exposed to T. gondii is by cleaning cat litter boxes, as the parasite passes out of kitty in its feces.

The good news is that, if your body has already encountered T. gondii and fought it off, as is the case with about one-third of Americans, you're immune to it and probably never knew that you came across the critter in the first place. The bad news is that it can do damage in people with compromised immune systems, such as transplant patients or people with cancer or HIV infection, so they should steer clear of litter box areas. And as you probably already know, pregnant women are warned to stay away from cat litter because, if they become infected, the infection can cross the placenta and cause neurological and eye problems in the baby.

But T. gondii isn't the only disease-causing nasty thing in cat poop. Cat feces also harbors infectious bacteria such as Salmonella and Campylobacter, most famous for causing stomach and intestinal infections. Although getting these kinds of infections from cats is uncommon, Dr. O'Brien suggests that animal waste be handled like any hazardous waste. "Ideally, use gloves when cleaning the litter box. If you can't bother with this, at least wash with soap and water immediately afterward." Because cats—including strays over which you have no control—are also doing their business outdoors, you ought to also wear gloves when doing yard work and thoroughly wash your hands right after, he added.

- **By dander.** About 10 million Americans, including some cat lovers and owners, are allergic to cat dander, the tiny flecks of skin shed by the animal. Allergic reactions can range from watery eyes to severe breathing difficulty. It's virtually impossible to remove cat dander from a home that a cat lives in, so cats should never be allowed in a home with someone who is allergic to them. You also can never know where you will encounter cat dander, so if you're allergic to cats, it might be a good idea to carry an antihistamine with you and, if you have asthma, make sure you have your inhaler within reach.

- **By cuddling.** Yep, even cuddling with your cat can be hazardous to your health, believe it or not. For one, cats can harbor fungi that cause ringworm and can do so whether they themselves have symptoms of ringworm or not. Ringworm symptoms in both humans and cats include an itchy, scaly, bumpy rash that spreads with a ringlike formation at the borders. Cats also can easily pick up ringworm from infected people, so to keep ringworm from spreading if someone in the family has it, treat your cat as well. Also, if the ringworm in a pet or person is severe or keeps coming back, you've got to treat your house for ringworm, too. *Tips to get the fungus out of your house include...*

  - Vacuuming daily (throw out the vacuum cleaner bag after each vacuum).
  - Washing hard surfaces and cat-grooming equipment with diluted bleach (1.5 cups bleach per gallon of water)
  - Steam cleaning carpets and soft furnishings
  - Using disinfecting cleaners for bedding (yours and kitty's) and kennels.

Another cuddling hazard is bed-sharing with a cat. Dr. O'Brien was very firm about this danger—never let a cat sleep with you or a child, he said. It isn't because you or your child will be smothered, as folk wisdom tells us (although this has happened). The risk is simpler—the cat might scratch or bite while you're sleeping. Why would your darling kitty do such a thing? A sleeping cat might startle and reflexively extend its claws when you turn over in your sleep. If you're sleeping face-to-face with a cat, you could even end up with a corneal abrasion and infection that threatens your eyesight.

TAKE SIMPLE, COMMONSENSE PRECAUTIONS

Despite all these dangers associated with cats, Dr. O'Brien is certainly not suggesting we banish our furry friends from our homes. First, remember that they're animals uniquely made to react to stimuli in certain ways—usually to protect themselves. Respect that, and don't test a cat's limits of composure (or let a visitor do so). Also, protect your pet, yourself and your household by controlling for fleas, ticks and infections...setting boundaries about contact (such as keeping cats out of your bed)... and keeping up with vaccinations for a long, happy life with your animal companion.

Should You Be Concerned About Germs at the Gym?

Yes! In a study in the *Clinical Journal of Sports Medicine*, cold viruses were found on 63% of equipment in fitness centers. And 80% of infectious diseases are transmitted by contact—either direct (such as kissing, coughing or sneezing) or indirect (for example, touching a contaminated surface, such as gym equipment, and then touching your eyes, nose, mouth or a wound, which are considered portals of entry for germs).

Always make sure to wash your hands with soap and water for at least 20 seconds before eating or drinking anything or before touching those portals of entry. If you're not near a sink, use a hand sanitizer that contains at least 60% alcohol.

Philip M. Tierno, PhD, clinical professor of microbiology and pathology, New York University School of Medicine, New York City.

Your Church or Synagogue Can Make You Sick

William Schaffner, MD, professor, department of preventive medicine and medicine/infectious diseases, Vanderbilt University School of Medicine, Nashville. Dr. Schaffner also is an associate editor of *Journal of Infectious Diseases*, past president of the National Foundation for Infectious Diseases and winner of numerous research awards.

We don't mean to cast aspersions on anyone's religious practices, but a recent study will make you think twice about following one particular common custom.

The problem: With this custom, worshippers often unknowingly rub bacteria—including the kind found in fecal matter!—on their own faces.

What's more, a number of other hazards lurk in our churches and synagogues—toxins, allergens, irritants, germs, etc.—that can undermine the health of unwary worshippers.

William Schaffner, MD, professor in the department of preventive medicine and medicine/infectious diseases at Vanderbilt University School of Medicine in Nashville, discussed how to stay safe during services...

• **Contaminated holy water.** Researchers from the Institute of Hygiene and Applied Immunology at the Medical University of Vienna in Austria tested samples of holy water from 39 churches and shrines in that country. Christian churches use holy water for baptism. In addition, in Catholic churches and certain other denominations, there is a permanent font (basin) at the church entrance. Worshippers dip their fingers into the holy water, then anoint themselves by touching their faces, chests and shoulders to make the sign of the cross.

Study findings: All holy water samples from churches and hospital chapels showed extremely high concentrations of heterotrophic plate counts (used to measure microorganisms such as bacteria, molds and yeasts in water)...frequently visited churches also showed signs of fecal contamination as well as staphylococcus and other bacteria. The likely source was worshippers' hands. (We can't be sure that holy water in this country has the same problem, but there's no reason to assume that it doesn't.)

Among the waters tested were those from "holy springs," which are literally springs in the ground from which water flows (like in the famous grotto at Lourdes). The belief that these springs have healing powers is largely a Catholic tradition, but people from all faiths sometimes drink from or bathe in these springs. (The researchers suggested that holy springs acquired their healing reputations because they actually did provide water that was cleaner than the water available in cities and towns centuries ago—but of course, that is no longer the case.)

New findings: Only 14% of holy springs met the microbiological and chemical requirements for modern drinking-water regulations. Many springs were contaminated with E. coli and Campylobacter, which can cause severe diarrhea.

Self-defense: If you want to anoint yourself with holy water, dip only a fingertip, then when you touch your face, touch only your forehead—your risk is minimized as long as you avoid your lips and eye area, Dr. Schaffner said. Wash your hands or use a hand sanitizer as soon as possible afterward. Also, ask your priest or church sexton how often the fonts are emptied, cleaned and disinfected—your concern may encourage increased attention to this matter. If you have an infant who is going to be baptized, make certain that the special font used for baptism will be disinfected right before the service. And never drink the water from a holy spring even if you see others doing so.

• **Communal communion chalices.** Most Christian denominations include the sacrament of communion, in which wine and bread are shared—and often worshippers drink from a single large cup called a chalice. When offering wine using a communal chalice, officiants generally wipe the rim with a cloth before serving the next person. This reduces the chances of spreading colds, flu, oral herpes and other viruses—but it certainly doesn't eliminate the risk.

Safer: Many churches offer the option of receiving communion from tiny individual cups, Dr. Schaffner noted. If your church does not do this, speak to the minister or priest about implementing this practice.

• **Shared yarmulkes.** Most synagogues have a basket of the traditional head coverings for men who forget to bring their own. But just as schoolchildren are at risk for catching head lice when they share hats, there is a chance of getting lice by wearing a yarmulke from the communal basket. Yes, lice generally are more common among kids than adults—but the yarmulkes that wind up in the "take one if you need one" basket often are leftovers from a recent bar mitzvah or bat mitzvah (a coming-of-age ritual traditionally done at age 13)—so they were worn mostly by preteens and teenagers.

Lice avoidance: Remember to bring your own yarmulke! If you are the forgetful type, keep a few spares in places like the glove compartment of your car, your briefcase, coat pockets, etc. (One of my colleagues keeps a yarmulke in his wife's purse—with her permission, of course.)

• **Burning candles and incense.** According to a study from Maastricht University in the Netherlands, after candles and/or incense were burned in the usual manner in chapels and churches of various sizes, the concentration of toxic polycyclic aromatic hydrocarbons (PAHs) in the air increased by a factor of four to 10. PAHs and other types of particulate matter that form when certain substances are burned have been linked to increased risk for lung cancer and other pulmonary diseases. The irritants in smoke from candles and incense also can also trigger asthma attacks in susceptible people, Dr. Schaffner added.

Smoke screen: If your place of worship is not well ventilated and you have any sort of pulmonary condition or extra sensitivity to airborne irritants, sit as far away from the candles or incense source as possible, preferably near an open window or door. If a lit candle or incense thurible is carried around the church, hold a clean handkerchief over your mouth and nose as it passes your pew.

• **Molds.** This hazard isn't limited to houses of worship, of course. But many churches, synagogues and mosques are located in old buildings, and old buildings frequently are contaminated by mold...and even newer buildings aren't immune. Plumbing leaks, poor insulation, large carpets that are shampooed frequently—all of these factors may turn churches and synagogues into "petri dishes" for mold. Some molds can trigger allergic reactions or asthma attacks in sensitive people...others are known to produce potent toxins and/or irritants, Dr. Schaffner noted.

Best: If you find that you often have respiratory symptoms after visiting your house of worship, talk to the trustees about having the premises inspected by mold-remediation experts—so that you and your fellow worshippers can breathe easier.

Bottom line: There's no need to let concerns about getting sick from your church or temple deter you from your religious observances, Dr. Schaffner said. Your risk is very low if you follow the common-sense precautions above.

---

6 Surprising Places Where Mold Lurks

Jeffrey C. May, a certified indoor air-quality professional (CIAQP) and founder and principal scientist of May Indoor Air Investigations, LLC, an air-quality-assessment company located in Tyngsborough, Massachusetts. He is also the author of several books, including *The Mold Survival Guide. MayIndoorAir.com*

We all know that mold thrives in obvious places such as damp basements, steamy bathrooms and storage areas with piles of old books and/or clothing. But there are plenty of other spots you'd never suspect that also can harbor these nasty fungal spores.

For the 10% to 15% of Americans who are allergic to mold, inhaling (or ingesting) the spores can trigger symptoms such as sneezing, runny nose, swollen eyelids, an itchy throat and wheezing.

Six surprising mold hot spots...

Hot Spot #1: Your coffeemaker. In one study, mold was found in the water reservoirs of about half of the tested drip-type coffeemakers.

What to do: Once a month, fill your coffeemaker's reservoir with a 50/50 mixture of water and white vinegar. Turn the coffeemaker on, just as you would if you were brewing a pot of coffee. When the reservoir is half emptied, turn off the coffeemaker. Wait 30 minutes and then finish the brewing cycle. Rinse the machine by running plain, cool water through the cycle twice (or check manufacturer's instructions). When you finish your coffee each day, allow the reservoir to dry completely by leaving the lid open.

Hot Spot #2: Your washing machine. Mold has no problem growing inside the rubber gaskets on the doors of front-loading machines. Those gaskets prevent water from pouring through the door, but water is often trapped inside the rubber folds. In all kinds of machines, detergent trays can stay damp between cycles, and the agitators of top-loading machines can be an area for mold growth, too.

What to do: Keep the door and detergent tray open when you're not using the washing machine. For front-loaders, wipe the inside of the gasket bottom with a rag or paper towel to dry it if no more loads will be done that day.

If you think you have mold, run an empty cycle with the machine on its hottest setting, using a mixture of one cup of baking soda, one cup of bleach and one-half cup of powdered dishwasher detergent. Some front-loading washers have a separate cycle for washing the inside of the machine. If a top-loading washer smells musty, the agitator may have to be removed and the shaft and agitator cleaned.

Hot Spot #3: Under your refrigerator. Keep an eye on frost-free refrigerators and freezers.

Here's why: Your freezer section isn't actually frost-free. Frost is automatically melted during a heating cycle, and then the water accumulates in a pan at the bottom. The heat released from the condenser coils is supposed to speed up this evaporation, but often there is standing water in the pan. This water allows bacteria, yeast and mold to grow in the dust in the pan, and air movement can disperse these organisms into your kitchen.

What to do: Keep the condenser coils on your refrigerator clean by removing the grille at the bottom or back of the appliance and vacuuming the dust from the coils. A 36-inch Flexible Crevice Tool is available at *www.amazon.com* for $12.99. Cleaning the coils once a year improves the efficiency of the refrigerator and can eliminate dust-containing pollen, mold spores and pet dander.

Cleaning the drip pan might not be as easy—with some refrigerator models, the pan is accessible only from the back of the fridge and/or may be attached to the condenser. Check the refrigerator manufacturer's instructions for proper cleaning of the condenser coils and drip pan.

Hot Spot #4: The underside of the toilet tank. You probably don't look, but moisture often lingers here—and so does mold.

What to do: If it's easy enough, get on the floor (otherwise, use a mirror and flashlight) and take a look at the underside of each toilet tank in your home. If there's mold, mix one cup of bleach with one gallon of water, open a window or door for ventilation and scrub the moldy areas with gloved hands. Clean these areas with a nonabrasive bathroom cleanser once a month during times of high outdoor humidity.

Also helpful: Use a squeegee (found at home-supply stores) to remove moisture from the shower walls. A ceiling fan or oscillating fan that directs air at the shower walls will also help dry surfaces and reduce the threat of mold. Generally, small exhaust fans commonly used in bathrooms do not effectively remove moisture—but they do help, so if you have one, use it when showering and for about an hour afterward.

Hot Spot #5: Your Waterpik and toothbrush. The water reservoir of your Waterpik or other water-jet appliance may not dry out between uses, and mold may grow on rubber gaskets and/or the water reservoir. Toothbrushes generally dry too fast for mold to grow, but it can grow inside the hollow heads of electric toothbrushes.

What to do: After each use of your Waterpik, remove the water reservoir, invert it and let it dry. To drain the pump, lower the sprayer in the sink so that it is below the level of the pump. Gravity will allow the water to drain. To clean electric toothbrush heads, soak in diluted bleach, 3% hydrogen peroxide or vinegar for a few minutes once a month.

Hot Spot #6: Your dehumidifier. Dehumidifiers are designed to remove moisture and help prevent mold. But condensed water accumulates on cooling coils and can lead to mold growth in any dust trapped on the cooling-coil fins.

What to do: Empty the water basin at least weekly. During hot, humid weather, empty it daily. A few times a year, wash the plastic filter in a sink, scrub the inside of the bucket with nonabrasive cleanser (use diluted bleach if it is moldy) and spray any dust off the fins with water. Before storing the dehumidifier when it's not in use, wash and dry all of the parts carefully. Follow the manufacturer's instructions for cleaning the machine.

The Jekyll-and-Hyde Bacteria

Martin J. Blaser, MD, the Muriel G. and George W. Singer Professor of Translational Medicine and director of the Human Microbiome Program in the departments of medicine and microbiology at New York University School of Medicine, New York City. He is author of *Missing Microbes: How the Overuse of Antibiotics Is Fueling Our Modern Plagues.*

Doctors have long been prescribing antibiotics to anyone with gastric discomfort, including ulcers. The goal was to eliminate the bad guy—the *H. pylori* bacteria. But over time, scientists have discovered that the bad guy actually is a good guy as well. On the one hand, H. pylori increases your risk for ulcers and then later for stomach cancer, but on the other hand, it is good for the esophagus, protecting you against GERD and its consequences, including a different cancer, and it may even protect against asthma and weight gain.

Renowned scientist Martin J. Blaser, MD, has studied H. pylori for nearly 30 years and is the author of the recent book *Missing Microbes. Here he explains what this means for you...*

MICROBES IN DECLINE

Antibiotics are effective at killing bacteria and stopping infections. But they're not very discriminating. Each dose kills many different organisms, including ones that you may need to stay healthy.

In 2010, health-care practitioners in the US prescribed 258 million courses of antibiotics—about 833 prescriptions for every 1,000 people. The average child in the US receives about 17 courses of antibiotics before he/she is 20 years old.

Do we need all of these drugs? Absolutely not. In Sweden, where doctors are slower to write prescriptions, antibiotic use is only about 47% of US levels. Swedish children, in the first three years of life, are receiving less than one-and-a-half courses of antibiotics versus about four in US children—and the death rate in Swedish children is lower than in US children.

In the US, doctors routinely prescribe antibiotics for infections that usually are caused by viruses (which aren't affected by the drugs) or for conditions that usually get better with no treatment.

Result: Many people no longer have the bacteria that they may need to stay healthy. *Examples...*

HEARTBURN AND CANCER

In the 1980s, researchers discovered that most ulcers were caused by H. pylori, a common stomach organism. Doctors can test for it using a blood test or a stool test. Now ulcers are routinely cured with antibiotics that kill the bacterium.

The catch: The same microbe that causes ulcers is simultaneously protective. Researchers speculate that diminished populations of H. pylori—caused by improved sanitation as well as antibiotics—could explain why heartburn, known as gastroesophageal reflux disease (GERD), now affects about 18.6 million people in the US.

What's the connection? In the past, most people lived with H. pylori all their lives. It gradually damaged stomach cells and reduced acid levels. Less acid meant that GERD was less common, and less severe, than it is today.

This paradox is one of nature's trade-offs. People who take antibiotics to eliminate H. pylori won't have ulcers, but they're twice as likely to develop GERD. They also have an increased risk for Barrett's esophagus, tissue damage that can lead to esophageal cancer.

You should take antibiotics if you've been diagnosed with an ulcer. But the majority of patients with ulcerlike symptoms don't actually have ulcers. They're far more likely to have non-ulcer dyspepsia, a condition that isn't helped by antibiotics.

OBESITY

There's some evidence that the nation's obesity epidemic is caused in part by antibiotics. In laboratory studies, mice given antibiotics have increases in body fat even when their diets stay the same. Livestock producers routinely give antibiotics to uninfected animals not to ward off illness but because it increases their body weight.

The same bacterium that causes ulcers (and protects against GERD) also appears to regulate the activity of two stomach hormones—ghrelin, a hormone that triggers appetite when your stomach is empty, and leptin, a hormone that signals the brain when it's time to stop eating.

Children who get the typical courses of antibiotics may grow up without any H. pylori in their stomachs. This could increase their appetites by causing ghrelin levels to remain steady even after they've already eaten.

Antibiotics are just one factor that could affect bacteria and, in turn, contribute to obesity. Another is the increasing use of Cesarean-section childbirths. When researchers reviewed data from 15 separate studies with more than 38,000 participants, they found that babies delivered by Cesarean section—who aren't exposed to the same bacteria as those delivered vaginally—are 26% more likely to be overweight as adults.

ASTHMA AND ALLERGIES

Many patients with GERD also develop wheezing, constricted airways and other asthmalike symptoms. Once again, a missing bacterium might be to blame. In one study, researchers collected blood samples from more than 500 people. They found that those who tested positive for H. pylori were 30% less likely to have asthma than those who didn't have H. pylori.

It is possible that stomach inflammation triggered by some strains of H. pylori triggers the activity of immune cells that help prevent asthma and allergies. Also, it is possible that the higher acid levels (discussed above) in those without H. pylori could lead to asthma symptoms.

ANTIBIOTIC CAUTION

Antibiotics can be lifesaving drugs. I don't advise people to never take them. But doctors need to prescribe antibiotics more judiciously. *Important...*

- **Don't insist on antibiotics just because you (or your child) has an ear, sinus or upper-respiratory infection.** The vast majority of these infections are caused by viruses. Even when bacteria are to blame, the infections usually clear up on their own. Ask your doctor if he/she is sure that an infection needs to be treated.
- **Ask for a narrow-spectrum drug.** Doctors often prescribe high-powered, broad-spectrum antibiotics (such as the Z-Pak) because they knock out many common infections. But the broad-spectrum drugs also kill more innocent organisms.

When possible, it's better to take a narrow-spectrum antibiotic (such as penicillin) that's less likely to kill beneficial organisms. It's not a perfect solution, because all antibiotics kill multiple strains of bacteria. But "targeted" drugs may be somewhat less likely to cause long-term problems than broad-spectrum antibiotics.

On the horizon: In 1998, I predicted in the *British Medical Journal* that we would one day be giving H. pylori back to our children. Since then, the support for this idea has only grown deeper, but we are not there yet.

13

Kidney, Bladder and Liver Disorders

Deadly Kidney Disease Is on the Rise

Even if you feel fine right at this moment, your kidneys could be gradually failing.

Recent finding: Nearly six in 10 Americans will develop kidney disease in their lifetimes, according to a recent analysis published in *American Journal of Kidney Disease*. In comparison, lifetime risk for diabetes, heart attack and invasive cancer is approximately four in 10.

As a result of this and other findings, the National Kidney Foundation recently called for health-care professionals to screen patients in specific high-risk groups for chronic kidney disease (CKD)—those age 60 or older and those with high blood pressure or diabetes—by adding a simple urine albumin test for kidney damage to annual physical examinations.

My advice: Get checked even sooner, at about age 50, and then yearly after that. If you have been diagnosed with diabetes or hypertension, then you should get tested annually regardless of your age. If your doctor finds any sign of impairment, get a referral to a nephrologist to see if anything should be done.

Here's what else you need to know now about CKD...

A DISEASE ON THE RISE

CKD is the result of damage to the kidney's one million-plus filtering units (kidney nephrons). This damage impairs the body's ability to remove wastes as well as to do many other functions that the kidney does, such as regulating the amount of fluid in your body and the amount of critical chemicals, including sodium, potassium, calcium, phosphate and more. Typically there are no symptoms until 75% to 80% of kidney function is lost. At that

Robert C. Stanton, MD, principal investigator in the section on vascular cell biology and chief of the nephrology section at Joslin Diabetes Center and Joslin Clinic. He is associate professor of medicine at Harvard Medical School and a staff member at Beth Israel Deaconess Medical Center, all in Boston.

point, eventual kidney failure is likely, with dialysis and/or a transplant being the only treatment options.

Unfortunately, kidney disease is on the rise. In the mid-1980s, about 70,000 Americans were getting dialysis for kidney disease. In the years since, the number has risen to about 450,000, a sixfold increase. And millions of people with CKD aren't even aware that they have it.

The number of people with kidney disease is rising partly because the American population is aging, and older people get more chronic diseases, including CKD. There also has been an enormous increase in diabetes, which is the leading cause of CKD, followed by high blood pressure. More than one-third of people with diabetes and more than 20% of patients with high blood pressure show signs of kidney damage.

Smoking, obesity and high cholesterol also increase the risk.

You can reduce damage and slow the progression of CKD with medications and by treating the conditions that cause it. Once the disease has progressed, your options are limited—and the risks are high. Among dialysis patients, there is a 15% to 20% death rate every year. Worsening kidney function increases the risk of dying from cardiovascular disease. It also can lead to bone weakness, anemia and other complications.

It's critical to get diagnosed while the kidneys still are working well.

SIMPLE TESTS

Most cases of CKD can be detected with a few basic (and inexpensive) tests. If your doctor finds any sign of impairment, a referral to a nephrologist is a good idea to determine what is causing the kidney disease.

Be sure to ask your doctor about this test: A urinalysis, sometimes dubbed the "dipstick" test, checks more than a dozen components in urine, such as pH level, protein, glucose, nitrites and ketones. The presence of urine protein, in particular, offers an immediate clue that kidney damage may have occurred. If your doctor doesn't ask you for a urine sample to perform a urinalysis during your yearly checkup, talk to him/her about getting the test. *Routine tests to screen for kidney disease...*

- **Serum creatinine and estimated glomerular filtration rate (eGFR).** The latter test estimates how well your kidneys are filtering blood. As kidney disease worsens, your level of creatinine goes up and your eGFR goes down. An eGFR of less than 60 (for three months or longer) indicates CKD.

Caution: Creatinine alone is not a perfect measure of kidney health. If your creatinine is elevated, you will need additional tests to confirm—or rule out—CKD. For example, your creatinine can rise due to dehydration.

- **Urinary albumin-to-creatinine ratio (UACR).** Albumin, a protein in the blood that passes through the kidneys' microscopic filtering cells, signals kidney damage. The lower the number the better, with a normal UACR being less than 30.

Important: Exercising strenuously or eating a lot of meat before a test could raise creatinine levels, erroneously signaling a problem. Herbal supplements containing creatinine also can falsely elevate levels. This naturally occurring substance, which helps muscles make energy, often is taken by weight lifters.

NEXT STEPS

There isn't a cure for CKD, and the damage can't be reversed. However, you can slow the rate at which the disease progresses and possibly avoid dialysis/transplantation. *Important...*

- **Strict glucose control.** Since most cases of CKD are caused by diabetes, it's essential to maintain healthy blood sugar levels. Elevated glucose damages the blood vessels that are used by the kidneys to filter wastes. If you have diabetes, follow your doctor's instructions about when and how often to test your blood sugar. Eat a healthy diet...exercise most days of the week...and take medications as instructed.

- **Better blood pressure.** The same factors that are good for diabetes (and your heart) also will improve your blood pressure.

Important: Even if your blood pressure is normal or just slightly elevated, your doctor still might prescribe a drug called an ACE inhibitor (such as Vasotec) or an angiotensin II receptor blocker (such as Cozaar or Diovan) if you have elevated urine albumin levels. Blood pressure–lowering medications can slow the progression of CKD by lowering urine albumin levels, even if your blood pressure is normal.

• **Less salt.** Limit your daily salt consumption to 1,500 mg (about two-thirds of a teaspoon) or less if you have high blood pressure, take a diuretic or have swelling in your legs.

• **Not too much protein.** Animal studies indicate that a high-protein diet causes more serious illness in those with kidney disease. It's not clear whether it has the same effect in humans—but moderation makes sense.

You don't have to follow a very-low-protein diet—you just don't want too much protein. In my view, if you have CKD, it is likely that a protein intake of up to 56 g/day for men and 46 g/day for women is safe. Ask your doctor for a referral to a dietitian. He/she will help you calculate how much protein you need.

• **Be careful with painkillers.** People who regularly take large doses of painkillers—such as aspirin, ibuprofen or acetaminophen—have an elevated risk for CKD. If you depend on these medications—to control arthritis, for example—talk to your doctor. This is particularly important if you already have been diagnosed with CKD.

PROTECTING THE KIDNEYS

People with CKD also should take special precautions with…

• **Painkillers.** This includes over-the-counter NSAIDs, such as ibuprofen (Motrin) or naproxen (Aleve)—especially if used regularly, these drugs may hasten kidney deterioration. Acetaminophen (Tylenol) is usually a better option for people with CKD.

• **Dyes injected for contrast during radiographic procedures,** such as angiography and CT scans. These may injure kidneys that are weakened by disease. When arranging these tests, tell your doctor if you have CKD.

• **Surgery and anesthesia,** which may affect kidney function, require special precautions, such as careful monitoring of fluids. If you have CKD, tell your surgeon.

Best Dietary Strategies to Beat Kidney Disease

Alexander Chang, MD, a nephrology fellow in the department of nephrology and hypertension at Loyola University Medical Center in Maywood, Illinois. He is a member of the American Society of Nephrology, the National Kidney Foundation and the American Society of Hypertension.

We hear a great deal about the best dietary strategies to help prevent heart disease and diabetes. But what about kidney disease?

Recent development: For the first time, researchers have identified some of the key eating habits that help prevent the onset of kidney disease.

Why this is important: Kidney disease, which affects all the body's main physiological functions, significantly increases one's risk for serious medical conditions such as cardiovascular disease, including heart attack and stroke…sexual dysfunction…and bone fractures.

KEY FACTS ABOUT THE KIDNEYS

The kidneys are fist-size organs that remove waste (about two quarts) from the approximately 200 quarts of blood that are processed daily. Each kidney contains about one million filtering units—tiny, delicate networks of blood vessels and tubes that are easily damaged by diabetes, high blood pressure and other chronic diseases.

What you need to know…

KIDNEY DAMAGE OCCURS SLOWLY

Like hypertension and diabetes, kidney disease can progress over decades. Patients can lose up to 75% of their kidney function without experiencing kidney disease's eventual symptoms, which include fatigue and loss of appetite, difficulty concentrating, muscle cramps, swelling in the feet and/or ankles and/or low urine output. Increased risk for heart attack and stroke begins when kidney function has declined by about 50%—further declines usually require medication, dialysis or a kidney transplant.

Losing weight if you're overweight and following very specific dietary strategies are among the best ways to prevent kidney disease—and to minimize further damage if you are one of the 26 million Americans who already have it. Obesity increases the risk for hypertension and diabetes, which are the two most common causes of kidney disease.

Key dietary approaches recently identified by researchers...

• **Drink fewer sugar-sweetened drinks.** In a recent unpublished analysis of data from a 25-year study of young adults, Loyola researchers found that those who drank just 3.5 soft drinks or other sweetened beverages, such as energy drinks or fruit drinks, per week were 150% more likely to develop kidney disease than those who didn't drink them.

It's possible that the sweet beverages' high concentration of fructose, in particular (in refined sugar and high-fructose corn syrup) is responsible for the increased risk.

My advice: In general, Americans consume too much sugar. Switch to diet soft drinks.

Even better: Choose unsweetened beverages, such as water with a lemon slice.

• **Get less animal protein.** In our analysis, people who ate an average of more than 1.5 servings a day of red meat or processed meat were 139% more likely to develop kidney disease than those who ate less than that. In patients with kidney disease, reducing overall protein intake lessens stress on the kidneys and can delay disease progression and the need for dialysis.

My advice: If you have kidney disease, consider working with a nutritionist to find healthful ways to limit daily protein to 40 g to 50 g. Fish (salmon, herring, mackerel and sardines) and lean meats provide high-quality protein with less saturated fat than you would get from typical red meat. Some research suggests vegetarian diets are especially beneficial for people with kidney disease.

For prevention: Include the most healthful protein sources. For example, beans and whole grains provide not only high-quality protein but also antioxidants, vitamins and minerals.

• **Consume much less salt.** For many people, a high-salt diet is a main cause of high blood pressure—a leading risk factor for kidney disease.

My advice: Even though some recent research raises questions about universal sodium restrictions, most health organizations recommend limiting daily sodium intake to 2,300 mg.

For some people with hypertension, reducing salt to 1,500 mg daily can lower systolic (top number) and diastolic (bottom number) pressure by about 11 points. That's comparable to the reduction that typically occurs with the use of antihypertensive medications.

• **Drink low-fat milk.** A study published in the *American Journal of Clinical Nutrition* that looked at 2,245 participants found that those who consumed the most low-fat milk, along with other low-fat dairy products, reduced their risk of developing hypertension by about 7%. Keeping one's blood pressure under control also contributes to healthy kidneys.

It's possible that the proteins and minerals (such as calcium) in dairy foods are responsible. Even though full-fat dairy contains the same minerals and proteins, the higher level of saturated fat may offset the benefits.

My advice: Check the USDA's website, *www.choosemyplate.gov*, for general guidelines regarding daily intake of low-fat or nonfat dairy.

• **Limit phosphorus intake.** The RDA for phosphorus in adults is 700 mg daily. However, the average adult consumes about twice as much because phosphorus is found in nearly every food—and it's added to processed foods to preserve colors and improve taste and/or texture.

Healthy adults excrete excess phosphorus. But in those with impaired kidney function, phosphorus can accumulate and cause conditions such as hyperphosphatemia, a buildup of this naturally occurring element that can lead to accelerated bone loss.

My advice: If you have kidney disease, ask your doctor if you need to lower your phosphorus levels—and work with a nutritionist to find the best ways to stay within healthy limits. It's wise for everyone to stay away from processed foods. In general, foods that are high in protein, such as meats, are also high in phosphorus. So are cola soft drinks, starchy vegetables and hard cheeses.

Important: To avoid high-phosphorus processed foods, look for "phos" on food labels. High-phosphorus additives include phosphoric acid, calcium phosphate and monopotassium phosphate.

For more information on kidney disease, consult the National Kidney Foundation's website, *www.kidney.org*.

5-Cent Cure for Kidney Disease

Magdi Yaqoob, MD, professor of renal medicine, The Royal London Hospital, London, England.

Finally—some great news for the 26 million people with chronic kidney disease! Because the problem is progressive and incurable, it can seem hopeless, but new research shows that a natural remedy that is safe, effective and costs just a few pennies a day can dramatically slow down kidney decline. What is it? Baking soda, believe it or not—or, if you want to be technical, sodium bicarbonate.

Though it may well be the most medically important, this is hardly the first unconventional health-related use for this simple and inexpensive kitchen ingredient—some swear by it as a remedy for acid indigestion, while others use baking soda to brush their teeth or in lieu of antiperspirant or to soothe rashes and skin eruptions. For people with chronic kidney disease (CKD), however, it is important to take this only under your doctor's close supervision—read on to learn why.

RATE OF DECLINE SLOWED BY TWO-THIRDS

CKD affects one in nine adults. It runs the gamut from poor function and minor discomfort to end-stage renal disease that requires dialysis (getting hooked up to a machine to filter blood when your kidneys can no longer do so). The body naturally creates bicarbonate to help maintain the correct acid-alkaline balance (or pH), and insufficient levels can cause problems ranging from minor all the way to death. A low bicarbonate level (the condition is called metabolic acidosis) affects 30% to 50% of advanced CKD patients, and doctors have long speculated that baking soda might help boost kidney function by bringing up the level.

In a study of 134 people with advanced CKD and low bicarbonate levels, Magdi Yaqoob, MD, a professor of renal medicine at The Royal London Hospital in England and his colleagues put this theory to the test. They gave half the participants a small daily dose of sodium bicarbonate in tablet form at mealtime while also continuing their regular medical care.

Over a two-year period, investigators discovered that people who took the sodium bicarbonate experienced...

- **A two-thirds drop in kidney decline.** They lost kidney function at the rate of just 1% per year, compared with 3% in those who didn't take sodium bicarbonate. Though these percentages sound tiny, they are quite significant for people losing kidney function.
- **A dramatic decrease in the need for dialysis.** Only 6.5% in the bicarbonate group required dialysis, compared with 33% in the untreated group.
- **Better nutrient absorption.** Nutritional parameters, including the ability to metabolize protein effectively, improved in those who took bicarbonate tablets. While sodium levels rose, blood pressure did not.

Sodium bicarbonate seems to help people with CKD by suppressing production of ammonia and endothelin (proteins that constrict blood vessels and raise blood pressure), which in turn discourages scarring and dysfunction in the kidneys, Dr. Yaqoob explains. These findings were published in the *Journal of the American Society of Nephrology* (JASN). They require further validation in a larger, multicenter study but are very significant and encouraging, Dr. Yaqoob said.

ASK YOUR DOCTOR

If you have CKD, Dr. Yaqoob recommends asking your doctor about incorporating sodium bicarbonate into your medical care—but stresses this should not be attempted on your own. Though easily available and very helpful for particular people, sodium bicarbonate is not an innocuous substance. Dosage must be carefully calibrated to keep blood levels within normal limits. Excess can lead to milk alkali syndrome (calcium deposits in kidneys and other tissue), especially for kidney patients—but also in otherwise healthy people who consume excessive amounts.

That said, sodium bicarbonate may be a simple and inexpensive treatment to add to our medical arsenal against CKD. Talk to your doctor about it.

Better Kidney Cancer Treatment

In a study of 104 patients with a type of kidney cancer known as renal cell carcinoma (RCC), participants were treated with radiofrequency ablation (RFA), in which a needle-like probe heats and destroys cancerous tissue. A single treatment destroyed all tumors smaller than 3.7 cm (about 1.5 inches).

Self-defense: If you have been diagnosed with RCC and are not a good candidate for surgery because of high risk for surgical complications, ask your doctor about RFA.

Ronald J. Zagoria, MD, professor of radiology, Wake Forest University Health Sciences, Winston-Salem, North Carolina.

A Walk Does Wonders for Chronic Kidney Disease

Che-Yi Chou, MD, PhD, Kidney Institute, division of nephrology, department of internal medicine, both at China Medical University Hospital, Taiwan. Dr. Chou's study appeared in the *Clinical Journal of the American Society of Nephrology.*

It will seem astounding...but based on new research, if you have chronic kidney disease (CKD), there is a stone simple way that you might save yourself from needing dialysis or a kidney transplant. And this is a very big deal, because dialysis and transplantation are tough stuff. CKD, a condition in which the kidneys struggle to filter waste from the blood, is a silent health threat that you can be completely unaware of until serious damage is done. One in three adults with diabetes and one in five with high blood pressure has CKD, and like so many illnesses, incidence increases after age 50. If left unchecked, end-stage renal disease—kidney failure—occurs. That's when you'll need to be hooked up to a dialysis machine to filter your blood or will require a kidney transplant to stay alive.

Although there is no cure once CKD sets in, it can often be kept from advancing, and now doctors have confirmed that a certain simple exercise can not only help you avoid dialysis or transplantation but also add years to your life. And that exercise is...walking! *Here's what to do...*

A PROVEN BENEFIT

We all know that exercise improves cardiovascular fitness, and researchers had already confirmed that it improves fitness in people with CKD. But could walking actually help with the disease itself—and in a significant way? That question had never been tested by research...so a group of Taiwanese researchers decided to find out.

The study started out with 6,363 patients whose average age was 70. All had moderate to severe CKD, and 53% had CKD severe enough to need dialysis or a kidney transplant. The researchers recorded and monitored exercise activity and a range of other health and medical measurements in the group and identified 1,341 people who walked as their favorite form of exercise. These patients were compared with patients who did not walk nor exercise in any other way.

The results: Walkers were 33% less likely to die of kidney disease and 21% less likely to need dialysis or a kidney transplant than nonwalkers/nonexercisers. And the more a person walked, the more likely he or she was not on dialysis or in need of a kidney transplant and still alive when the study ended. So, for example, someone who walked once or twice a week for an average 30 minutes to an hour had a 17% lower risk of death and a 19% lower risk of needing dialysis or a kidney transplant compared with someone who didn't walk or exercise. And someone who walked for an average 30 minutes to an hour seven or more times a week had a 59% lower risk of death and a 44% lower risk of needing dialysis or a kidney transplant.

Now, when researchers see this kind of dramatic result, they always should explore whether there was some reason other than the activity that was studied (in this case, walking) that could explain things. These are called confounding factors—for example, could it be that walkers walked because they were healthier, as opposed to being healthier because they walked? But no confounding factors were found. The average age, average body size and degree of kidney disease was the same in the two groups, as was the prevalence of diabetes-associated coronary artery disease, cigarette smoking and use of medications for CKD.

The bottom line for people with CKD...walk! Walk everywhere! Walk often! Even a 30-minute walk once or twice a week can help. The more you walk, the greater the benefit.

ARE YOU AT RISK?

If you have diabetes or high blood pressure, your doctor should give you a simple blood test to see whether CKD is developing. Otherwise, here are telltale signs to keep an eye out for—these may signal that you should be evaluated for CKD...

- **Unexplained fatigue**
- **Trouble concentrating**
- **Poor appetite**
- **Trouble sleeping**
- **Nighttime muscle cramps**
- **Swollen feet and ankles**
- **Eye puffiness,** especially in the morning
- **Dry, itchy skin**
- **Frequent urination, especially at night**

Be sure to tell your doctor what medications you're on when you are examined for CKD. Because the kidneys also filter medications out of your body, meds can build up to toxic levels in your system if the kidneys aren't doing their job. If you have CKD, your doctor may take you off some medications and lower the dose of others.

There's no cure for CKD once it sets in, but it need not advance to severe and deadly stages that require dialysis or a kidney transplant. Besides exercising and keeping the underlying cause (whether it be diabetes, high blood pressure or something else) in check, mild CKD is managed by diet. *To do it right...*

- **Make walking a priority.** Walk first thing in the morning, or immediately after work.
- **Work with your doctor to manage the underlying cause,** and work with a dietitian to manage your nutrition requirements. A dietitian will plan a regimen that controls the amount of protein, salt, potassium and phosphorus you consume, all of which can build up to toxic levels in people with CKD. A dietitian will also balance your CKD diet needs with those related to glucose control or whatever condition may be associated with your CKD.

Better Kidney Disease Test

Researchers stored blood samples from 2,300 adults with healthy kidneys for 10 years, then tested the samples for six biomarkers.

Results: Levels of three of the biomarkers, when considered together, identified people at high risk for chronic kidney disease.

Theory: Screening for these biomarkers (homocysteine, aldosterone and B-type natriuretic peptides), along with known risk factors (such as diabetes and high blood pressure), could identify 7% more adults at risk for the disease. Early detection can help prevent full-blown kidney disease.

Caroline Fox, MD, assistant clinical professor of medicine, Harvard Medical School, Boston.

Do This to Beat Kidney Stones

Exercise reduces risk for kidney stones.

Recent finding: Active postmenopausal women were 16% to 31% less likely than sedentary women to develop kidney stones over an eight-year period. Maximum effects were found at the equivalent of three hours a week of moderate-paced walking, one hour of moderate-paced jogging or four hours of light gardening.

Study of 84,225 women led by researchers at University of Washington School of Medicine, Seattle, published in *Journal of the American Society of Nephrology.*

Best and Worst Drinks for Preventing Kidney Stones

Pietro Manuel Ferraro, MD, physician, department of internal medicine and medical specialties, Catholic University of the Sacred Heart, Rome, Italy. His study was published in *Clinical Journal of the American Society of Nephrology.*

Mention kidney stones and everyone within earshot winces—because we've all heard how painful these stones can be. So if you want to be stone-free, you're probably following the common advice to drink lots of liquids. But instead of focusing on how much you drink, the crucial question is what you drink, a new study reveals. Certain beverages—including some very surprising ones, such as beer!—are particularly helpful in protecting against stones, while other drinks do more harm than good.

Unfortunately, kidney stones are common, plaguing 19% of men and 9% of women in the US at least once in their lifetimes—and recurrences are quite common. Drinking plenty of water helps prevent stones from forming...but actually, there are other fluids that can be even more effective.

DRINK THIS, NOT THAT

Using data from three large studies, researchers followed 194,095 people, none of whom had a history of kidney stones, for more than eight years. Participants periodically completed questionnaires about their diet and overall health. During the course of the study, there were 4,462 cases of kidney stones.

Researchers adjusted for health factors (age, body mass index, diabetes, medications, blood pressure) as well as various dietary factors (including intake of meat, calcium and potassium) known to affect kidney stone risk. Then they calculated the stone risk associated with various types of beverages.

How the comparison was done: For each analysis, the effects of drinking an average of one or more servings per day were compared with drinking less than one serving per week. Because data from three different studies were used, serving sizes were not necessarily alike across the board. But in general, a serving was considered to be 12 ounces of soda or beer...eight ounces of coffee, tea, milk or fruit punch...five ounces of wine...and four to six ounces of juice. The researchers' findings were eye-opening.

- **Kidney stone risk boosters...**
  - Sugar-sweetened noncola sodas increased kidney stone risk by 33%.
  - Sugar-sweetened colas increased risk by 23%.
  - Fruit punch increased risk by 18%.
  - Diet noncola sodas (but, surprisingly, not diet colas) increased risk by 17%.
- **Kidney stone risk reducers...**
  - Beer reduced kidney stone risk by 41%.
  - White wine reduced risk by 33%.
  - Red wine reduced risk by 31%.
  - Caffeinated coffee reduced kidney stone risk by 26%.
  - Decaf coffee reduced risk by 16%.
  - Orange juice reduced risk by 12%.
  - Tea reduced risk by 11%.

Consumption of milk and juices other than orange juice did not significantly affect the likelihood of developing kidney stones.

Theories behind the findings: Because sugar-sweetened sodas and fruit punch are associated with higher risk, researchers suspect that their high fructose concentration may increase the amount of calcium, oxalate and uric acid in the urine—and those substances contribute to kidney stone formation. So how to explain the beneficial effects of orange juice, which is also high in fructose? Perhaps orange juice's high concentration of potassium citrate offsets the fructose and favorably changes the composition of urine.

Regarding the beneficial effects of coffee and tea, it could be that their caffeine acts as a diuretic that promotes urine production and thus helps prevent stones. Tea and coffee, including decaf, also contain antioxidants that may help combat stone formation. Alcohol, too, is a diuretic, and wine and beer contain antioxidants as well—though of course, with any type of alcoholic beverage, moderation is important.

Belly Fat Could Mean Kidney Problems

Researchers measured the kidney function of 315 healthy normal-weight adults and their waist-to-hip ratios.

Result: Healthy adults with an apple-shaped body—belly fat and higher waist-to-hip ratios—had lower kidney function, lower kidney blood flow and higher blood pressure in the kidneys.

Theory: Belly fat may trigger insulin resistance and low-grade inflammation, which may lead to kidney disease.

If you have an apple-shaped body: Ask your doctor to monitor your kidney functioning and suggest treatment, if needed.

Arjan Kwakernaak, MD, researcher, University Medical Center Groningen, the Netherlands.

Prolonged Sitting Linked to Kidney Disease

In a recent finding, women who sat a total of eight hours or more daily were about 30% more likely to develop chronic kidney disease than women who sat for three hours or less. Men who spent the most hours sitting had 19% increased risk.

Thomas Yates, PhD, senior lecturer at University of Leicester, Leicester, England, and lead researcher on a study of 6,379 people, published in *American Journal of Kidney Diseases.*

Better Dialysis

In a one-year study of 224 kidney disease patients, those who received eight hours of dialysis overnight (while sleeping) had a 78% lower death rate than those who received conventional dialysis (four hours, three days weekly).

Theory: Overnight dialysis patients are less likely to experience blood pressure drops, which can lead to complications.

Ercan Ok, MD, professor of internal medicine and nephrology, Ege University Hospital, Izmir, Turkey.

A Probiotic for Kidney Disease

Mark A. Stengler, NMD, licensed naturopathic medical doctor in private practice, Stengler Center for Integrative Medicine, Encinitas, California...adjunct associate clinical professor at the National College of Natural Medicine, Portland, Oregon...author of many books, including *The Natural Physician's Healing Therapies* and coauthor of *Prescription for Natural Cures. MarkStengler.com*

Patients with chronic kidney disease (CKD) often ask me about natural treatments that can help them. There's a new probiotic product called Renadyl that can help kidney function. I'm a great believer in probiotics—ingesting "good" bacteria daily inhibits growth of harmful bacteria and enhances immune function. There now are probiotic combinations targeted to help specific conditions—and one of these is for compromised kidney function.

In CKD, the kidneys no longer filter toxins efficiently. As a result, toxins accumulate in the bloodstream where they can damage a wide range of organs. Renadyl contains three strains of probiotics—Streptococcus thermophilus...Lactobacillus acidophilus...and Bifidobacterium longum. These bacteria strains metabolize toxins and convert them into nontoxic substances that then are excreted by the colon. In essence, this probiotic enables the colon to remove more toxins, thus reducing the kidneys' exposure to this substance.

By lessening the kidneys' workload and reducing the buildup of toxins in the blood, probiotics offer significant benefits for people with Stage 3 or Stage 4 kidney disease, whose kidneys still are functioning to some degree. It also helps reduce strain on the kidneys for those with Stage 1 or Stage 2 kidney disease. But it won't help people who are undergoing dialysis because their kidneys have failed completely.

In a 2010 study published in *Advances in Therapy*, researchers from the company that makes the probiotic and outside researchers gave patients with Stage 3 and Stage 4 CKD three capsules (equaling 90 billion colony-forming units) daily of this probiotic combination. After taking the probiotic for six months, about 63% of the study participants had decreased levels of blood urea nitrogen (which means that this toxin was being eliminated), and 86% reported substantially improved quality of life, which for CKD patients means eating more of the foods they want, sleeping better and having more energy because they don't have to urinate as many times at night.

Renadyl can be purchased from Kibow Biotech (888-271-2560, *www.kibowbiotech.com*). Cost is $135 for a three-month supply. Patients with CKD should speak to a holistic doctor before taking this probiotic or any other supplement.

Surprising Ways to Avoid Kidney Stones

Mathew D. Sorensen, MD, assistant professor of urology at the University of Washington School of Medicine in Seattle and director of the Comprehensive Metabolic Stone Clinic at the Puget Sound VA. His specialties include the treatment and prevention of kidney stones.

Plenty of people who develop kidney stones are shocked when this common condition occurs. How do these extremely painful stones take hold—and what can be done to prevent them?

Before you tell yourself that kidney stones are something that you'd never suffer, consider this—one of every 10 people is destined to develop at least one of these excruciating stones in his/her life. Each year, more than one million people see their doctors because of kidney stones. Already had a kidney stone? You're not off the hook—about half of kidney stone sufferers will develop another stone in five to seven years. *How to stay in the stone-free zone...*

HOW STONES FORM

The good news is that kidney stones can usually be prevented by making the right changes to your diet and lifestyle. The problem is that many of the prevention strategies are counterintuitive...and involve some surprising approaches, such as cutting back on foods that are widely considered to be healthful.

The majority of kidney stones are made of calcium and oxalate. During normal digestion, oxalate (found in many healthful foods, such as spinach and beets) combines with calcium (another generally healthful nutrient) and makes its way through the digestive system before being excreted.

If there is excess oxalate, however, it gets absorbed into the bloodstream and carried to the kidneys, where urine is produced. Most of the time, oxalate is removed in the urine, but if the urine becomes saturated with oxalate, stones can develop. *Surprising ways to stop stones from forming...*

STEP #1: Add just two daily servings of fruit and vegetables to your diet. When researchers at the University of Washington recently analyzed the diets of more than 80,000 postmenopausal women, they found that women who consumed the most fiber, fruits and vegetables had a 6% to 26% lower risk of developing kidney stones than women who ate the least. Good news: Just two additional servings a day were enough to make a big difference.

Simple way to get two more fruit/veggie servings daily: Have an extra apple and a handful of carrot sticks.

STEP #2: Consume calcium. You might be wondering why foods that contain calcium—a main constituent of kidney stones—would help reduce your risk of developing the stones. Here's why: Calcium gives the oxalate something to latch on to in the stomach. Otherwise, the oxalate ends up in the urine, where stones are more likely to form. Good sources of calcium: Yogurt, kale, bok choy and calcium-fortified foods.

Exception: People who use calcium supplements may face a higher risk for kidney stones. If you use calcium supplements, take them with meals. That way, the calcium can bind with any oxalate that may be in the food.

STEP #3: Go easy on oxalates. Eating oxalate-rich foods in moderation usually doesn't promote kidney stones. But if you start getting large amounts of these foods—for example, by regularly using lots of spinach or beets in homemade juices—you might have a problem.

If you have had kidney stones—or your doctor believes that you may be at increased risk for them due to such factors as a strong family history of the condition—talk to your doctor about limiting your intake of oxalate-rich foods such as spinach...Swiss chard...rhubarb...beets...all nuts (including almond milk)...chocolate (especially dark) ...and soy/tofu products.

STEP #4: Eat less fish and other animal protein. Wait a minute—isn't fish good for you? Fatty, omega-3-rich fish usually is healthful, but people at increased risk for kidney stones (including anyone with a history of stones) should limit their intake of fish and any type of meat to six ounces a day.

Here's why: Protein is made up of amino acids and gets broken down into uric acid. Eating lots of animal protein acidifies the urine and can increase uric acid levels in the blood, leading to gout...or in the urine, leading to calcium-based or uric acid kidney stones.

STEP #5: Drink the right beverages. Staying well hydrated is crucial—drink enough water and other fluids so that your urine is clear or light yellow. But pay attention to what you drink. One very large study showed that drinking sugar-sweetened sodas and punches increased risk for kidney stones by a whopping 33%. However, orange juice, coffee (both decaf and caffeinated) and tea decreased risk by varying amounts...beer cut risk by 41%...and wine reduced risk by 33%. Even so, these fluids should be consumed in moderate amounts.

Make lemonade: About one-third of stone formers are low in citrate (your doctor can test your levels), which is a known stone inhibitor. Since lemons have more citrate than any other citrus fruit, low-citrate patients may benefit from drinking a mixture of one-half cup of fresh or bottled lemon juice and seven and one-half cups of water (sweetened to taste). Consume the entire batch throughout the day to keep a steady stream of citrate flowing through the kidneys.

STEP #6: Watch your salt intake. Sodium causes the kidneys to excrete more calcium into the urine, and many studies show that increased salt consumption raises the likelihood of kidney stones. Don't get more than 2,000 mg of sodium per day.

STEP #7: Get moving! You might not think that exercise would affect your risk for kidney stones, but it does. A new study showed that even a small amount of physical activity reduced risk for kidney stones in women with no history of stones by 16%. Moderate activity (four hours of gardening or three hours of walking a week) reduced risk by 31%. There's no added benefit to very strenuous exercise.

Physical activity, especially weight-bearing exercise, may increase calcium absorption into bones, which means less calcium is excreted in the urine.

Lemonade for Kidney Stones

Roger L. Sur, MD, is a urologist, assistant professor of surgery and director of the University of California, San Diego (UCSD), Comprehensive Kidney Stone Center. He serves on the International Evidence Based Urology Working Group, which promotes evidence-based clinical practice of urology, and recently received a UCSD academic senate grant to fund his kidney stone research.

More than half a million Americans go to emergency rooms each year due to kidney stones, and about one in 10 Americans will suffer a kidney stone at some time in his/her life.

Simple home remedy: Drink lemonade. A study I published in *The Journal of Urology* found that patients who drank a little more than two quarts of lemonade (made with about four ounces of lemonade concentrate) daily for an average of 44 months had an increase in urinary citrate that was comparable to the increase in a group taking oral potassium citrate, which is commonly prescribed for kidney stones. More urinary citrate means a lower risk for calcium kidney stones, the most common form. Drinking water alone has not been found to raise urinary citrate levels.

If you've had kidney stones in the past, you have a 50% chance of getting one or more additional stones within five to 10 years. Drinking two quarts of lemonade daily could reduce this risk by 90%—without the expense or side effects of medication. I advise using an artificial sweetener or honey instead of refined sugar.

Other citrus juices, including orange and grapefruit juice, also contain citrate, but not as much as juice made from lemons.

One-Cut Kidney Surgery

A new procedure allows surgeons to use a single incision when removing a kidney, compared with the three to five holes used in conventional laparoscopic surgery. This technique reduces the need for pain medication and results in only one scar.

University of California, San Diego Medical Center.

Plastic Dishes May Cause Kidney Stones

Recent finding: When volunteers ate hot soup from plastic bowls made with melamine, levels of the chemical in their urine were up to 6.4 times higher than in people who ate soup from ceramic bowls.

Theory: Melamine-containing dishes release large amounts of the chemical, which has been linked to kidney stones, when used to serve high-temperature foods.

Best: Serve hot food in ceramic dishes. Check for melamine on the label when purchasing plastic dishes.

Ming-Tsang Wu, MD, ScD, professor and attending physician, Kaohsiung Medical University Hospital, Taiwan.

Don't Let Your Bladder Run Your Life!

Holly Lucille, ND, RN, a naturopathic doctor based in West Hollywood, California. She is the author of *Creating and Maintaining Balance: A Woman's Guide to Safe, Natural Hormone Health* and serves on the Institute for Natural Medicine Board of Directors. *DrHollyLucille.com*

Women and men who scout out restrooms wherever they are may think that others don't have to worry so much about their bladders. But that's not true.

Eye-opening statistic: One in every five adults over age 40 has overactive bladder... and after the age of 65, a whopping one in every three adults is affected. If you regularly have a strong and sudden urge to urinate and/or need to hit the john eight or more times a day (or more than once at night), chances are you have the condition, too.

Men with prostate enlargement and postmenopausal women (due to their low estrogen levels) are at increased risk of having overactive bladder. Urinary tract infections, use of certain medications (such as antidepressants and drugs to treat high blood pressure and insomnia) and even constipation also can cause or worsen the condition.

But there is a bright side. Research is now uncovering several surprisingly simple natural approaches that are highly effective for many people with overactive bladder. *Among the best...**

START WITH YOUR DIET

Most people don't connect a bladder problem to their diets. But there is a strong link. *My advice...*

- **Take a hard line with irritants.** Alcohol, caffeine and artificial sweeteners can exacerbate the feeling of urgency caused by overactive bladder. Cutting back on these items is a good first step, but they often creep back into one's diet over time.

What helps: Keep it simple—completely avoid alcohol, caffeine (all forms, including coffee, tea and caffeine-containing foods such as chocolate) and artificial sweeteners. Stick to decaffeinated coffee and herbal teas, and use agave and stevia as sweeteners.

Many individuals also are sensitive to certain foods, such as corn, wheat, dairy, eggs and peanuts. They often trigger an immune reaction that contributes to overall inflammation in the body, including in the bladder. If your symptoms of urinary urgency and/or frequency increase after eating one of these (or any other) foods, your body may be having an inflammatory response that is also affecting your bladder. Eliminate these foods from your diet.

- **Keep your gut healthy.** The scientific evidence is still in the early stages, but research now suggests that leaky gut syndrome, in which excess bacterial or fungal growth harms the mucosal membrane in the intestines, is at the root of several health problems, including overactive bladder.

The theory is that an imbalance of microbes, a condition known as dysbiosis, can irritate the walls of the bladder just as it does in the gut.

What helps: Probiotics and oregano oil capsules. Probiotics replenish "good" bacteria, and oregano oil has antibacterial properties that help cleanse "bad" bacteria and fungi from the gut.

- **Drink up!** People with overactive bladder often cut way back on their fluid intake because they already make so many trips to the bathroom. But when you don't drink enough fluids, urine tends to have an irritating effect because it becomes more concentrated. This increases urgency.

What helps: Drink half your body weight in ounces of water or herbal tea daily. Do not drink any fluids after 5 pm to help prevent bathroom runs during the night.

THE RIGHT SUPPLEMENTS

Cranberry supplements (or unsweetened cranberry juice) can be helpful for bladder infections, but they're usually not the best choice for overactive bladder. *My advice...*

- **Try pumpkin seed extract.** These capsules help tone and strengthen the tissue of your pelvic-floor muscles, which gives you better bladder control.

Typical dosage: 500 mg daily.

- **Consider Angelica archangelica extract.** This herb has gotten positive reviews from researchers who have investigated it as a therapy for overactive bladder.

Recent finding: When 43 men with overactive bladder took 300 mg of the herb daily, they had increased bladder capacity and made fewer trips to the bathroom.

*Talk to your doctor before trying any of these herbal remedies, especially if you take medication or have a chronic health condition. You may want to consult a naturopathic doctor. To find one near you, check *www.naturopathic.org*.

Typical dosage: 100 mg daily.

OTHER WAYS TO KEEP YOUR BLADDER HEALTHY

• **Kegel exercises, which help strengthen the pelvic-floor muscles, are essential for getting control of overactive bladder symptoms.** Unfortunately, most people who try doing Kegels end up doing them the wrong way.

How to do Kegels: Three to five times a day, contract your pelvic-floor muscles (the ones you use to stop and start the flow of urine), hold for a count of 10, then relax completely for a count of 10. Repeat 10 times. If you're a woman and aren't sure if you're contracting the right muscles, there is a possible solution.

New option for women: A medical device called Apex acts as an automatic Kegel exerciser. It is inserted into the vagina and electrically stimulates the correct muscles ($249 at *www.incontrolmedical.com*—cost may be covered by some insurance plans). Check with your doctor to see if this would be an appropriate aid for you.

Even though there's no handy device to help men do Kegels, the exercises usually reduce urgency when they're performed regularly.

Kegels can easily be part of anyone's daily routine—do them while waiting at a red light, after going to the bathroom or while watching TV.

• **Try acupuncture.** An increasing body of evidence shows that this therapy helps relieve overactive bladder symptoms. For example, in a study of 74 women with the condition, bladder capacity, urgency and frequency of urination significantly improved after four weekly bladder-specific acupuncture sessions.

• **Go for biofeedback.** Small electrodes are used to monitor the muscles involved in bladder control so that an individualized exercise program can be created. Biofeedback is noninvasive and is most effective when used along with other treatments. To find a board-certified provider, consult the Biofeedback Certification International Alliance, *www.bcia.org*.

Overactive Bladder

Over-the-counter treatment for overactive bladder is available for women, reports Leslie M. Rickey, MD, MPH. Oxytrol is a thin, flexible transdermal patch that releases oxybutynin, which is effective at controlling overactive bladder and decreasing urinary leakage. Side effects such as constipation, dry mouth and skin irritation usually are mild. But check with your doctor before using.

Leslie M. Rickey, MD, MPH, is assistant professor in the departments of surgery and obstetrics and gynecology, division of female pelvic medicine and reconstructive surgery, University of Maryland School of Medicine, Baltimore.

Solution to Nocturia—Get Moving

Study titled "Physical Activity and Benign Prostatic Hyperplasia-Related Outcomes and Nocturia," by researchers in the department of public health sciences and surgery, Loyola University, published in *Medicine & Science in Sports & Exercise.*

Are you a man who has a buddy who is sleep-deprived—not because he's living the high life but because he admits to visiting the "john" to pee several times a night? Or does that describe you?

Having to urinate repeatedly during the night is called nocturia, and it's a common symptom of benign prostatic hyperplasia (BPH), the medical term for enlarged prostate. It starts showing up in middle age, and by the time a man hits 80, the likelihood that he has nocturia is more than 90%. But even if you can't avoid BPH, you can avoid nocturia if you get serious about one thing, says a recent study that analyzed data from a huge, ongoing program called the Prostate, Lung, Colorectal, and Ovarian Cancer Screening Trial (PLCO, for short).

It's exercise. Although being physically active does not necessarily prevent BPH, studies show that exercise can delay its development and help keep symptoms—especially nocturia—to a minimum if BPH does set in.

The study looked at 28,404 men who had long-term BPH and 4,710 participants with newly diagnosed BPH. The men ranged in age from 55 to 74 at the start of the study. All kinds of information related to prostate health, outcomes related to BPH (whether a man had surgery for it, for example), exercise habits and other lifestyle habits were analyzed to better understand the role of exercise in preventing nocturia and other symptoms of BPH. Exercise included activities such as walking, jogging and bike riding.

A TRUE BATTLE OF THE BULGE

The study findings were an eye-opener about BPH, exercise habits and nocturia. Although exercise had little impact on other symptoms and issues related to BPH, it did make a difference in whether nocturia developed and the degree of severity if it did. For example, men who had long-time BPH and nocturia but got at least one hour of exercise per week were 35% less likely, on average, to need to urinate more than twice per night (severe nocturia) than men who got less than one hour of exercise per week.

Among those in whom BPH developed during the study, those who exercised at least one hour per week were an average 13% less likely to report nocturia than were inactive men—and that rate didn't much differ whether men got in one hour or more than four. And among those men who did have nocturia, those who exercised at least one hour per week were an average 34% less likely to need to make a bathroom run more than twice per night compared with men who were inactive—in other words, their nocturia was far less disruptive to their sleep. In this case, men who got more rather than less exercise were better off. For example, compared with men who didn't exercise, men who got one hour of exercise were 25% less likely to need more than two bathroom runs whereas men who got three hours of exercise were 43% less likely.

Researchers recorded exercise levels going back to when each participant was 40 years old. Men who had stayed physically active at least since their 40s were (no surprise) better protected against nocturia than men who only recently started exercising or never exercised. But don't think that it's ever too late to get some control over nocturia. Men who were currently exercising—even if they hadn't in the past—were better protected than men who were once physically active but stopped.

HOW IT WORKS

Physical activity gives you a triple whammy of goodness—it promotes weight loss in those who are too heavy...works off stress...and reduces inflammation, which all have an impact on nocturia, according to the researchers. They also noted that exercise probably has a stronger effect on nocturia and even BPH than what was seen in their study because it is likely that many of the participants exaggerated when reporting the amount of exercise they actually got. Studies show that most American men are sedentary, and this fact should have been more strongly represented in the study population, considering that the large majority of participants were overweight. Still, the take-home message is, if you are more active by day—if you make a habit of brisk walks or jogs, bicycling or gym workouts—you can help your bladder be less active at night when you want to sleep. It's easy and powerful.

The "Other" Bladder Problem

Michael B. Chancellor, MD, a urologist and director of neuro-urology at the Beaumont Health System in Royal Oak, Michigan. He is coauthor of *Atlas of Urodynamics* and a founding member of the Congress of Urologic Research and Education on Aging Underactive Bladder, which is spearheading research on novel therapies for treating UAB.

Ask anyone who is health conscious to name some common bladder problems, and you can bet that "overactive bladder" will be near the top of the list.

What few people realize: An estimated 20 million Americans are living with a different condition, which actually has the opposite effect on the bladder, but the problem is not getting diagnosed or treated by most doctors.

Known as underactive bladder (UAB), this disorder can make something as simple as going to the bathroom a chore...damage the kidneys...and even land a person in a nursing home.

RED FLAGS OF UAB

UAB occurs when the bladder loses its ability to contract and fully empty. Part of what makes this condition so vexing is that the symptoms can come and go, and they often mimic those of other diseases, such as prostate enlargement and urinary tract infections—both of which can cause frequent urination, another UAB symptom.

With UAB, sufferers have a hard time telling when their bladders are full. When they do have the urge to urinate, it may be painful, the urine may dribble or it may not come at all. In fact, it may take several minutes to start a stream of urine. They also may feel that there's urine left behind and end up heading to the bathroom again a short time later.

Of course, when the bladder does not completely empty, urine builds up. This can lead to embarrassing episodes of leakage from overflow incontinence...recurring urinary tract and kidney infections...and, in severe cases, kidney damage.

WHAT CAUSES UAB?

As we age, the muscles of the bladder lose some of their elasticity and ability to contract. However, UAB is not a normal part of aging.

When messages between the brain and the bladder are short-circuited in any way, your body doesn't register the normal urge to urinate when the bladder is full.

This breakdown in communication may be triggered by a stroke, Parkinson's disease, acute urinary tract infection, radiation therapy to the pelvic area, nerve damage after pelvic surgery or even a herniated disk. In people under age 40, multiple sclerosis is a common culprit, as is diabetes, which can damage peripheral nerves in the lower spinal cord that supply the bladder.

Even overactive bladder can be a trigger: In some cases, overactive bladder thickens the bladder wall in a way that interferes with the bladder's ability to contract during urination...leading to underactive bladder.

Certain medications can also lead to UAB: These may include antidepressants, antihistamines, blood pressure drugs and cholesterol-lowering statins.

DO YOU HAVE UAB?

If you're suffering from any of the symptoms of UAB, see your primary care doctor soon. He/she may refer you to a specialist—either a urologist or a uro-gynecologist, who treats urologic problems in women.

To find out whether you have UAB, the specialist will take your medical history...do a physical exam...and order blood and urine tests to see how well your bladder and kidneys are functioning. A cystoscopy, ultrasound or CT scan might also be ordered to determine whether your bladder muscles and nerves are working normally.

Helpful: Keeping a diary that lists how often and how much you urinate (using a measuring cup) can give your doctor valuable information. For a free online diary to track your bladder activity, go to *www.urodaily.com.*

HOW TO COPE WITH UAB

Doctors are still clearly defining UAB and working to understand what therapies are most effective. But if you've got this condition, you want help now! The research is ongoing, but here are some ways to cope with the condition—go ahead and bring up these approaches with your doctor. *Not all physicians are familiar with them...*

- **Double-voiding.** This technique gives you extra time to empty your bladder.

What to do: After urinating, stay at the toilet for a few additional minutes. After this short break, try to urinate again. If your bladder has not fully emptied, you will often be able to pass more urine.

- **Triggered-reflex voiding.** This involves the use of various stimulation techniques to trigger the brain signals that jump-start contractions of the bladder and the flow of urine.

The technique may work for anyone with UAB but can be especially useful for a person with a spinal cord injury who still has some reflexes but may not be able to feel whether the bladder is full.

What to do: Rub the area just above the pubic bone…tug on your pubic hair…or gently squeeze the head of the penis. Test different trigger zones to see which one might work for you.

- **Medications.** Men with UAB may get relief from a drug often used for prostate enlargement, such as *doxazosin* (Cardura). It helps a man empty his bladder by relaxing the muscle of the urethra (the tube through which urine flows).
- **Catheterization.** This is another way to empty the bladder. With self-catheterization, you insert a catheter, a strawlike tube, into your urethra to drain urine from your bladder. For people who are unable to do this, an "indwelling" catheter can be inserted into the urethra by a health-care professional to automatically drain urine into a pouch for a set period of time. However, if the catheter is not changed every two to four weeks, it can injure the urethra and/or cause infection.

For people who can't tolerate an indwelling catheter, a suprapubic catheter may be used. It requires a surgical procedure to insert it through a small hole in the abdomen directly into the bladder.

- **Surgery.** When the therapies described above are not effective or practical, the only option is surgery—either to enlarge the bladder by using a small section of the stomach or bowel that helps the bladder to stretch more easily…or to insert a mesh stent that allows the bladder to empty into a pouch outside the body.

Promising new approach: Stem cell therapy is being studied as a possible treatment for UAB. Researchers theorize that transplanting stem cells to help the bladder regenerate new, fully functioning tissue could be an effective solution for UAB sufferers.

New Urine Test Predicts Bladder Cancer Recurrence

A urine test that measures genetic biomarkers was 80% successful in predicting when bladder cancer would return in a recent study of 90 cancer survivors. Current tests, which include biopsy and cystoscopy, are 15% to 35% successful in predicting cancer recurrence. The new urine test may become available in the next year or two. To participate in a clinical trial for this urine test, go to *www.clinicaltrials.gov*.

Gangning Liang, PhD, associate professor of urology, USC Norris Comprehensive Cancer Center, Los Angeles.

Keep Your Bladder Healthy

Jamison Starbuck, ND, a naturopathic physician in family practice and a guest lecturer at the University of Montana, both in Missoula. She is past president of the American Association of Naturopathic Physicians and a contributing editor to *The Alternative Advisor: The Complete Guide to Natural Therapies and Alternative Treatments*.

If you're age 50 or older and haven't had a bladder infection, count yourself lucky. The reality is that these infections are among the most common complaints of the AARP crowd.

Here's why: With age, women—and men—are at increased risk because tissues in the bladder weaken, making it more difficult for it to fully empty…so bacteria have more time to proliferate and cause a urinary tract infection (UTI). As we age, our immune systems also don't work as well.

Interestingly, the symptoms of bladder infection become less apparent with age. Instead of the burning, cramping pain and bloody urine that generally accompany a UTI in younger people, only a modest increase in urinary frequency and a dark urine color may indicate a bladder infection once you're middle-aged or older. After about age 70, confusion, agitation, balance problems and falling may be a physician's only clues of a bladder infection.

Fortunately, there are some highly effective natural approaches to help prevent UTIs. *My favorite UTI-fighting strategies...*

• **Stay hydrated.** You must drink a minimum of two quarts of plain water daily—no matter what other beverages you consume. If you take a prescription medication, you may need even more water. Diuretics and some other drugs will make you lose water, so you'll need to drink more than usual. Discuss this with your pharmacist.

• **Use good hygiene.** OK, you might find this is a little embarrassing, but make sure that you wipe from front to back after a bowel movement...wash your genitals before and after sex...and change your undergarments regularly, particularly if you have incontinence or are sedentary (small amounts of stool on a person's underwear can increase infection risk).

• **Load up on cranberry.** Everyone knows that cranberry is supposed to be good for the bladder, but recent research made some people doubt its effectiveness. One study found that cranberry may not be very effective at preventing UTIs. But don't write off cranberry. The same research showed that compounds in cranberry do prevent infections by making it difficult for bacteria to stick to the walls of the bladder. Because most brands of cranberry juice (perhaps the most convenient form of the fruit) have added sugar to make them less tart, I usually advise people who develop more than one bladder infection a year to take 600 mg of a freeze-dried cranberry extract daily.

Caution: People with a history of calcium oxalate kidney stones or who take *warfarin* (Coumadin) or regularly use aspirin should avoid cranberry—it can increase stone risk and interact with these medications.

• **Get more probiotics.** The beneficial bacteria found in yogurt and other cultured foods, such as kefir and miso, reduce risk for bladder infection. Eat one cup of plain yogurt, kefir or miso soup daily or take a probiotic supplement.

• **Do Kegel exercises.** Women—and men—listen up! Strong pelvic muscles allow for more complete bladder emptying and reduce infection risk.

What to do: At least once daily, contract and release the muscles of your pelvic floor (the ones that stop urine flow) 10 times while seated or standing.

Help for Bladder Infection

If you're looking for a natural solution for bladder infections, try D-mannose.

Why it's effective: *Escherichia coli* (E. coli) bacteria stick to mannose molecules on cells that line the bladder, causing most bladder infections. D-mannose coats each E. coli bacterium and prevents it from sticking to the bladder wall. The E. coli bacteria then wash out of the body during urination. Follow label instructions.

If there is no significant improvement in symptoms after using D-mannose for 24 hours, you should consult your doctor, since it's likely that the infection is not caused by E. coli.

Jonathan V. Wright, MD, medical director, Tahoma Clinic, Tukwila, Washington. *TahomaClinic.com*

Treating a UTI Without Antibiotics

Sergei Frenzel, ND, MD, is the founder of Integrative Natural Health, a clinic in Milford, Connecticut. *CTinHealth.com*

Is there any good way to get rid of urinary tract infections without taking antibiotics?

One good approach is to increase your urine flow, which helps by pushing harmful bacteria out of the urinary tract, giving them less time to multiply. To achieve this, boost your fluid intake. You should be drinking about two quarts (eight cups) of water per day when healthy, so try increasing this—up to four quarts per day if you can—when you have a urinary tract infection (UTI).

Second, you want to adjust your urine's pH (a measure of acidity or alkalinity). The types of bacteria that cause UTIs tend to thrive in a more alkaline environment, so the goal is to make your urine more acidic. Taking 1,000 mg of vitamin C every four to six hours during a UTI helps move urine pH in the right direction. Drinking unsweetened cranberry juice or taking cranberry capsules also makes urine more acidic.

Third, you can supplement with herbs that have antibacterial qualities, such as echinacea, hydrastis (goldenseal) and/or uva ursi (bearberry). Herbal teas and tinctures are sold in health-food stores...or you can use a combination herbal product designed to improve urinary tract health, such as Wise Woman Herbals Urinary Tract Formula Liquid Extract Compound (*www.wisewomanherbals.com*).

See your doctor if you are not feeling better within several days or if you experience any worsening of UTI symptoms (such as increased urinary discomfort, fever or back pain). At that point, you may need antibiotics or you may benefit from a more individualized approach to UTI treatment.

No More UTIs!

Tomas L. Griebling, MD, MPH, the John P. Wolf 33° Masonic Distinguished Professor of Urology at The University of Kansas (KU) School of Medicine in Kansas City. He is a professor and vice-chair in the department of urology and faculty associate in The Landon Center on Aging.

Anyone who has ever had a urinary tract infection (UTI) knows that it's extremely unpleasant. The first clue may be that your urine is smelly and/or looks cloudy. You could also suffer burning or pain during urination, have blood in your urine and a fever or chills. To make matters worse, many people suffer repeated UTIs, and some doctors don't do much more than prescribe an antibiotic each time.

Good news: Studies now show that there are some surprisingly simple steps you can take to help guard against UTIs—whether you have suffered them repeatedly or never even had one.

WOMEN AND MEN GET UTIS

Even though UTIs are commonly considered a "women's problem," men develop them, too.

What men need to know: About 12% of men will suffer a UTI at some point in their lives, but men over age 50 are at increased risk. Common causes include prostatitis, a bacterial infection of the prostate gland that can also enter the urinary tract...and the use of urinary catheters in medical procedures.

What women need to know: More than 50% of women will experience a UTI at some point in their lives, and one-third of them will suffer recurring infections. Women are more prone to infection around the time of sexual activity due to the spread of E. coli bacteria to the vagina. In postmenopausal women, lower levels of estrogen decrease the amount of Lactobacillus, a "good" bacteria that grows in the vagina and serves as a natural defense against UTIs.

Symptoms are sometimes puzzling: Diagnosis of a UTI can be difficult in older men and women because they often don't suffer the classic symptoms but instead have atypical symptoms such as lethargy, confusion, nausea, shortness of breath and/or loss of appetite. If you suspect a UTI, ask that your doctor perform a urine culture.

STOP A UTI BEFORE IT STARTS

When a woman or man suffers from recurring UTIs (three or more infections in a one-year period), these steps will help break the cycle...

- **Go to the bathroom often.** Many people hold their urine longer than they should. This is a bad idea because the bladder may distend, making it more difficult to empty the bladder and preventing bacteria from being flushed out. To protect yourself, try to urinate roughly every four waking hours.

Important: People who are rushed when they are going to the bathroom may not fully empty their bladders. Take your time when urinating.

Helpful: When you think you are finished, give yourself another moment to see if there's any urine remaining before leaving the toilet.

- **Drink a lot of water.** You probably know that drinking water is a good way to help flush bacteria from the urinary tract. However, few people drink enough—you need to consume eight to 10 eight-ounce glasses of water each day. Water is best because it's pure and has no calories. Caffeine, soda and alcohol can aggravate the bladder.

Other preventives include...

- **Yogurt.** A 2012 study suggested that lactobacilli, found in probiotic supplements and yogurt, may be an acceptable alternative to antibiotics for the prevention of UTIs in women (with recurring infections, medication may be used for this purpose). The additional lactobacilli are believed to displace E. coli and stimulate the immune system to fight back against the infectious bacteria.

My advice: Consume a cup of yogurt each day—it should be low in sugar (avoid any yogurt that lists sugar as the first or second ingredient) and make sure it contains live cultures. Or take two probiotic capsules each day containing Lactobacillus rhamnosus GR-1 and Lactobacillus reuteri RC-14—the probiotic strains used in the study mentioned earlier. Probiotic supplements with these strains include Pro-Flora Women's Probiotic from Integrative Therapeutics, *www.integrativepro.com*...and UltraFlora Women's from Metagenics, *www.metagenics.com*.

- **Cranberry juice or cranberry supplements.** Research has been mixed, but several studies have shown that drinking at least one to two cups of cranberry juice daily may help prevent UTIs. Just be sure to drink real cranberry juice—not cranberry juice cocktail, which has lots of sugar, is diluted with other juices and provides minimal amounts of the actual berry that contains protective compounds known as proanthocyanidins.

You may want to try a cranberry supplement if you have diabetes (even real cranberry juice contains carbohydrates) or if you don't like cranberry juice. Do not exceed label instructions on dosage—research suggests that high doses may increase the risk for kidney stones.

- **Estrogen creams.** For postmenopausal women, a small amount of estrogen cream applied inside the vagina several times per week has been shown to significantly reduce the risk for recurrent UTIs. The cream thickens the walls of the urinary tract, making it more difficult for bacteria to penetrate.

Important: Most women who take estrogen in pill or patch form can safely add an estrogen cream—the amount absorbed into the bloodstream is negligible. Women with a history of uterine cancer or certain breast cancers may not be suitable candidates for any form of estrogen therapy. Ask your doctor.

WHEN YOU NEED AN ANTIBIOTIC

If the steps above do not prevent recurring UTIs, you may need a long-term course (six months or longer) of a low-dose antibiotic. To minimize the development of bacterial resistance, it's wise to start with a milder antibiotic, such as *sulfamethoxazole* and *trimethoprim* (Bactrim), if possible. However, more powerful antibiotics, such as *ciprofloxacin* (Cipro), may be needed to help prevent or treat stubborn infections.

Important: Many women self-diagnose a UTI, call up their doctors and receive a prescription for an antibiotic when in fact they may have a condition, such as vaginitis, that mimics UTI symptoms. Urinalysis and/or a urinary culture is necessary to get an accurate diagnosis.

Coffee and Tea Are Good for the Liver

Caffeine has been found to stimulate the metabolization of lipids (fats) stored in liver cells and decrease the fatty liver of mice. People at risk for or diagnosed with nonalcoholic fatty liver disease could benefit from drinking up to four cups of coffee or tea a day.

Study by researchers at Duke-NUS Graduate Medical School's Cardiovascular and Metabolic Disorders Program, Singapore, and Duke University School of Medicine, Durham, North Carolina, published in *Hepatology*.

The Breakthrough That Can Save Your Liver and Your Life

Jonathan Fenkel, MD, an assistant professor of medicine at Thomas Jefferson University in Philadelphia, where he directs the Jefferson Hepatitis C Center and is the associate medical director of liver transplantation.

As more and more people are getting tested for hepatitis C, new advances are making it easier than ever to eliminate the virus and its potential to cause deadly diseases such as cirrhosis and liver cancer. In case you missed it, in 2012, the CDC advised that everyone born between 1945 and 1965 get tested for hepatitis C —along with people of any age who have risk factors.

Why the CDC took action: Even though hepatitis C can strike at any age, more than two million US baby boomers are infected with the virus—and most don't realize it or even think they're at risk.

But the fact remains that anyone can be infected with hepatitis C. People at greatest risk include those who received blood transfusions before 1992 (when screening became more advanced) or anyone who used self-injected drugs with possibly contaminated needles. In some cases, people are believed to have become infected with the virus while getting tattoos or piercings done with contaminated ink or equipment or when being stuck with an infected needle in a health-care setting.

You can be vaccinated for hepatitis A and B, but there is no vaccine for hepatitis C.

AN EXCITING ADVANCE

Antiviral medication and immune therapy that requires self-injections have long been the main treatments for chronic hepatitis C. However, these drugs often cause grueling side effects, such as debilitating fatigue, headaches, depression, muscle aches and anemia. Also, the drugs need to be taken for at least 24 weeks or up to 48 weeks.

What's new: The FDA has recently approved two new medications that block enzymes that the hepatitis C virus needs to survive. Now patients are given a two- or three-drug cocktail that includes a new drug—*sofosbuvir* (Sovaldi) or *simeprevir* (Olysio)—combined with the antiviral ribavirin and sometimes interferon, which tends to have the most side effects. For the first time, some patients may be eligible for interferon-free therapies if they have a favorable hepatitis C genotype.

With the new regimen, 80% to 90% of patients will be completely cleared of the virus and often in as little as 12 weeks. Previous combination therapies had cure rates of 40% to 80%. Plus, even with interferon, the side effects of the new drug cocktail, such as stomach upset, fatigue and headache, last about half as long as they do with older regimens.

WHO NEEDS TREATMENT?

Some experts argue that the high cost of the new medication—a full course of treatment can cost roughly $100,000—means that it should be given only to those who have already developed liver disease.

My advice: Everyone with chronic hepatitis C should consult a doctor who is familiar with the risks and benefits of treatment, because even if your liver is healthy, you may still benefit from treatment, especially if the virus is causing joint pain, rashes, kidney disease or certain types of cancer such as lymphoma. Check with your insurance company to see if treatment is fully covered.

TIMING IS FLEXIBLE

Because chronic hepatitis C progresses slowly, you could potentially wait months or even years before starting treatment. Interferon-free treatments are expected to be available within the next year or two, so some doctors advise patients to delay getting treatment—both to avoid the side effects of interferon and to take advantage of an all-oral treatment plan (interferon is given by injection once a week). To determine the treatment schedule that's best for you, discuss all the options with your doctor.

FOLLOW-UP CARE

Even when hepatitis C is cured, many patients still have liver damage—and a higher-than-average risk of developing liver cancer.

How I advise my patients: Get screened (with ultrasound) for liver cancer one year after treatment and every few years after that. Those who have cirrhosis will need an ultrasound every six months and an upper endoscopy every two to three years. A low-sodium (less than 2,000 mg a day) diet is also recommended, and raw shellfish, which can cause sepsis, should be avoided.

If you have liver damage: Don't drink alcohol. If you take *acetaminophen* (Tylenol) for pain, don't use more than 2,000 mg daily.

Also, make sure your vitamin D levels are checked at your annual physical—liver damage can cause vitamin D deficiency.

A LETHAL VIRUS

Because hepatitis C has an uncanny ability to elude the immune system, most people exposed to the virus develop a chronic infection that, without treatment, never goes away.

Between 5% and 20% of people with chronic hepatitis C develop liver scarring (cirrhosis)—typically decades after the initial infection. Hepatitis C also is the leading cause of liver cancer and liver transplants in the US.

More from Dr. Fenkel...

Testing You Need

A simple blood test reveals if you ever have been exposed to the hepatitis C virus, but a second test is needed to determine if you're still infected.

Shocking: About half of individuals who test positive on the first test do not follow up with the second test, meaning that they probably won't get the treatments that can save their livers—and their lives.

TEST #1: An initial antibody test will reveal if you've been exposed to the virus at any time in your life. If the test is positive, you'll need a second test (see below). If test #1 is negative, you can relax and will not need testing again unless you're possibly exposed to the virus in the future (for example, you find out that you have shared a razor or toothbrush with someone who has hepatitis C). Even if results were negative to test #1, test again in six months if you have hepatitis risk factors.

TEST #2: A viral load assay, also a blood test, will reveal if the infection is chronic (still active in the body). If it is, discuss treatment options with your doctor and be tested for the strain—or genotype—of the virus, which will help determine the most effective medication.

Vitamin E: The Best Treatment for Fatty Liver Disease

Joel Lavine, MD, chief of gastroenterology, hepatology and nutrition at New York-Presbyterian/Morgan Stanley Children's Hospital in New York City, and a faculty member in the Department of Pediatrics at Columbia University College of Physicians and Surgeons.

Pat Robuck, PhD, senior advisor, National Institute of Diabetes and Digestive and Kidney Diseases, Bethesda, Maryland.

The liver is the biggest organ in the body—because it has a lot to do! Among other activities, it pumps out the bile acid that digests fats...processes protein...stores glucose, vitamin B12, iron and copper...generates blood-clotting factors...metabolizes medications and breaks down toxins...and removes waste products from the blood.

But as Americans get fatter—with nearly 7 out of 10 of us overweight—our livers are getting fattier. And sicker.

Key fact not widely reported: An estimated one-third of Americans have nonalcoholic fatty liver disease (NAFLD), with at least 20% of liver cells filled with fat globules. (Another 10 million have alcoholic fatty liver disease caused by heavy drinking—more than 2 drinks a day for a woman and more than 3 drinks a day for a man.)

For millions with NAFLD, the condition advances to nonalcoholic steatohepatitis (NASH), where many liver cells are not only fat-filled but also inflamed and possibly scarred.

"There is an increasing prevalence of NASH in this country, something that is directly related to the obesity epidemic," says Joel Lavine, MD, chief of gastroenterology, hepatology and nutrition at New York-Presbyterian/Morgan Stanley Children's Hospital in New York City.

And NASH is often a precursor of liver problems that are a whole lot worse.

One out of 7 people with NASH eventually develop cirrhosis—irreversible scarring of the liver, with symptoms that can include indigestion, fatigue, fluid retention and confusion. Cirrhosis can lead to liver cancer or liver failure.

NASH is also linked to an increased risk for heart attack and stroke.

Problem: There aren't any medications that control or reverse NASH.

Solution: A recent study in the *New England Journal of Medicine* shows that a vitamin can effectively treat the disease.

VITAMIN E BEATS THE DRUG

The study involved 247 people with NASH, which is diagnosed with a liver biopsy. They were divided into three groups.

One group took 800 milligrams (mg) daily of vitamin E, a powerful antioxidant that can protect liver cells. A second group took the diabetes drug *pioglitazone* (Actos), which earlier studies showed might help the liver. A third group took a placebo.

Results: After two years, 43% of those taking vitamin E had dramatic improvements—less fat in the liver, less inflammation, and less liver degeneration.

Although Actos outperformed the placebo, it didn't produce "statistically significant" improvements in NASH—which vitamin E did. (And those taking Actos gained an average of 10 pounds, a known side effect of the drug.)

"This study is an important landmark in the search for effective treatments for NASH," says Patricia Robuck, PhD, senior advisor at the National Institute of Diabetes and Digestive and Kidney Diseases.

"The good news is that cheap and readily available vitamin E can help many of those with NASH," adds Dr. Lavine.

In a similar study, presented at the annual meeting of the American Association for the Study of Liver Disease, vitamin E controlled NASH in overweight children with the disease. "This study reinforces the earlier finding that vitamin E improves NASH in adults," says Dr. Lavine.

And a study by Malaysian researchers showed that taking 400 mg daily of vitamin E for one year can help NAFLD, completely curing the condition in 15 of 30 people taking the nutrient and improving it in five.

Important: When people in the NASH study who were taking vitamin E stopped taking the nutrient, their level of liver enzymes started to rise, an indication of returning liver problems. People with NASH need to stay on vitamin E for the treatment to work, says Dr. Lavine.

NATURAL THERAPY FOR NASH

Anyone who is overweight or has a family history of liver disease should ask their doctor to be tested for NASH with a liver biopsy, says Dr. Lavine.

If the disease is present, he recommends medically supervised treatment with vitamin E, at the same dosage used in the study.

Natural Ways to Protect Your Liver

Gerard E. Mullin, MD, an internist, gastroenterologist and nutritionist. He is an associate professor of medicine at Johns Hopkins University School of Medicine and director of Integrative Gastroenterology Nutrition Services at The Johns Hopkins Hospital, both in Baltimore. Dr. Mullin is also author of *Integrative Gastroenterology* and *The Inside Tract*.

When it comes to vital organs in the body, it often seems like the heart and brain get all the attention.

But the liver also plays a crucial role in maintaining good health. Liver disease, which affects one person in 10, is among the top 12 causes of death in the US (primarily from cirrhosis).

Fortunately, there are plenty of steps you can take to help safeguard the health of your liver. *What you need to know...*

ANTIOXIDANT-RICH FOODS

All tissues of the body are subject to damage by highly reactive molecules known as oxygen free radicals, which are produced by natural metabolic processes. In the liver, free radicals can trigger an inflammatory response that may result in scarring and culminate in the tissue destruction that characterizes cirrhosis.

The body has built-in defenses against free radicals—enzyme systems that neutralize these dangerous chemicals. But they can be overwhelmed without the help of additional antioxidant compounds provided by the diet. To help protect your liver, make sure that your daily diet includes at least some of the foods with the highest antioxidant levels—especially if you have liver disease or are at risk for it (due to such factors as obesity or alcohol abuse)...*

- **Cinnamon.**
- **Berries** (especially wild blueberries, which are particularly high in antioxidants), cranberries, blackberries, raspberries and strawberries (frozen berries also are a good choice).

*There are no current guidelines on the amounts of these foods to consume for liver protection—add them to your diet in liberal amounts whenever possible.

- **Red, kidney or pinto beans.**
- **Pecans.**
- **Artichoke hearts.**
- **Russet potatoes** (with the skin).
- **Apples.**
- **Plums.**

Also: For a concentrated source of liver-shielding antioxidants, drink fresh raw juices made from beetroot, dandelion leaf, wheatgrass and/or barley grass. Antioxidant-rich green tea also promotes liver health.

DETOXIFYING FOODS

The liver plays a central role in ridding the body of toxins produced by bacteria and derived from external sources such as air pollution, heavy metals, pesticides, hormones in foods and natural wastes such as metabolic by-products.

The liver's detoxification process is complex. Enzymes first alter the toxic chemicals into more reactive compounds that can ultimately dissolve in bile for excretion through the digestive tract.

Certain foods stimulate the enzymes that catalyze detoxification. These include cruciferous vegetables, such as broccoli, cauliflower, cabbage and kale.

A key ingredient of cruciferous vegetables, sulforaphane, also protects the liver as an anti-inflammatory and antioxidant. Sulfur-containing foods that have a similar effect include eggs, garlic, onions, leeks and shallots.

The amino acid L-arginine also stimulates the liver's detoxification mechanism. Kidney beans and peanuts are good sources of L-arginine.

Bile flushes toxins out of the liver into the intestine en route to excretion. Choloretic foods—artichokes and ginger, for example—help stimulate the production and flow of bile.

HEALTHFUL BACTERIA

Regularly taking medications including nonsteroidal anti-inflammatory drugs, such as *ibuprofen* (Motrin), can create inflammation that may allow bacterial toxins to leak through the intestinal wall, triggering oxidative stress that can progress to scarring and even tissue destruction of the liver. Excessive alcohol consumption aggravates this disruption of the intestinal lining.

Beneficial bacteria found in the large intestine help keep harmful germs and their toxins from seeping through the intestinal wall. Probiotics (foods and supplements containing "good" bacteria) and prebiotics (foods that feed these bacteria) protect the liver indirectly by promoting the overall growth of healthful bacteria. Prebiotics include bananas, artichokes and fermented foods such as miso.

You can also use probiotic supplements, such as lactobacillus gg, or eat yogurt containing live cultures.

HEALTHY LIVER LIFESTYLE

Excessive alcohol disrupts the liver's metabolism and causes inflammation that leads to fatty deposits, scarring and the irreversible tissue destruction of cirrhosis.

While moderate alcohol intake (up to two drinks daily for men and no more than one drink daily for women) offers general health benefits for most people without endangering the liver, excessive amounts must be avoided.

Also: Exercise and watch your weight. Obesity and diabetes increase the risk for nonalcoholic fatty liver disease, which affects up to 23% of the population. Although it usually causes no symptoms, this buildup of fat deposits in the liver can, over time, lead to inflammation, a condition called nonalcoholic steatohepatitis (NASH) that may ultimately cause the same kind of lasting liver damage as alcohol.

Exercise goal: Two and a half hours of moderately strenuous exercise per week—spread over four or more days—will protect your liver while also improving your overall health.

KEY SUPPLEMENTS

There is no definitive research to support vitamin or herbal supplements to preserve liver health, but some studies suggest that they may help in treating liver disease. *If you are being treated for liver disease, ask your doctor about...*

- **Vitamin E.** Previous research is mixed, but a major two-year clinical trial recently published in *The New England Journal of Medicine* found significant improvement in NASH symptoms among patients who took 800 international units of vitamin E daily, compared with those who were given placebos or received a diabetes drug used to treat NASH.
- **Betaine.** A pilot study involving seven patients with NASH suggested that a year of treatment with this nutritional supplement could reduce fatty deposits, inflammation and fibrosis in the liver.

The Truth about Herbal Supplements and Your Liver

Andrew L. Rubman, ND, naturopathic physician and founder and medical director of the Southbury Clinic for Traditional Medicine, Southbury, Connecticut. *SouthburyClinic.com*

People were using herbs and other plants to stay healthy way before pharmaceutical companies showed up with synthetic products and their dangerous side effects. But you know that just because something is "natural" doesn't mean that it's safe.

Like synthetic prescription drugs that change body chemistry, herbal products also can hurt your liver, especially if they contain impurities...aren't really what they claim to be...or are just not used properly. Some herbs have been associated with liver injuries so often that they've been banned in the United States. But, in these cases, was the herb itself really bad or were other factors causing the problem?

"Although some of the concerns we are seeing about herbal supplements and liver toxicity are valid, most herbal products pose no harm when taken properly. 'Properly' means at the right dosages, for the right reason and for the right length of time," said naturopathic physician Andrew L. Rubman, ND, founder and medical director of the Southbury Clinic for Traditional Medicine in Southbury, Connecticut.

But the trend, unfortunately, is not making herbal supplements look good. Research compiled from a large database that tracks liver injuries caused by either prescription drugs or herbal supplements shows that the proportion of liver injuries associated with herbal and dietary supplements has increased over the past 10 years from 7% to 20%.

One study based on data from this research summarized the dangers of several different herbs and herbal formulations implicated in liver injuries. Dr. Rubman here supplies the lowdown on seven commonly known herbs that were on the list. *Some of these herbs definitely should be avoided...others used with caution...and others have just gotten a bum rap...*

• **Comfrey.** Comfrey has been traditionally used, often in the form of a tea, to soothe an upset stomach. It also has been used topically to treat wounds and skin inflammation because it is rich in tannins and other substances that promote skin repair. But because comfrey contains pyrrolizidine alkaloids, compounds that are toxic to the liver, products containing it that are meant to be drunk or eaten are now banned for nonprescription use in the United States.

Comfrey is now available only in the form of creams and ointments for treatment of skin wounds and inflammation, and because its harmful alkaloids can penetrate the skin, consumers are warned to not overdo use of these products—do not use on open wounds or broken skin and do not use for longer than 10 days at a time or for more than four to six weeks total in one year.

But the concern about comfrey's liver-harming properties might be overblown, according to Dr. Rubman. Other compounds in the herb that are beneficial to the liver may offset the dangers of the pyrrolizidine alkaloids, he said. Although in Dr. Rubman's view, the herb could probably be safely used while in the care of a naturopathic doctor who would monitor liver health, there are certainly plenty other safer remedies for soothing an upset stomach.

• **Kava.** Kava comes from the root of a type of pepper plant. On the tropical islands of the Pacific Ocean where the plant is native, kava has been used as a mild intoxicant, similar to alcohol. In Western herbal medicine, however, it has found a place, in pill form, in the relief of anxiety and insomnia. Liver damage, including hepatitis and liver failure, has been associated with kava use. This has led several countries, including the United Kingdom, Poland and France, to restrict or ban it. But researchers have been debating whether kava is, indeed, toxic or whether nontraditional ways of preparing it are causing liver injury.

It's neither banned nor restricted in the United States. Although the FDA acknowledges that kava is useful for managing anxiety, it has issued a warning that it has been linked to serious liver damage.

According to Dr. Rubman, kava's predicament is a perfect example of why herbs should be used in their traditional ways. When extracts are prepared in the traditional manner from the entire plant, they are generally safe, he said, but when an isolated chemical from the plant is commercially sold in capsule form, problems can occur. Why? Because other beneficial parts of the plant that act in a check-and-balance way are left out. For this reason, Dr. Rubman may prescribe the kava extract manufactured by Eclectic Institute in Sandy, Oregon, which is produced using the original extraction method. This brand of kava is widely available in nutrition stores and online through *www.amazon.com*, *www.vitacost.com*, and other sellers.

• **Green tea extract.** Green tea extract is on store shelves everywhere, frequently marketed as a weight-loss product. But when green tea extract is taken while fasting, as some people using weight-loss supplements may be doing, the liver may be overwhelmed by the high volume of antioxidant compounds, resulting sometimes in serious liver injury.

Taking weight-loss or other potent supplements while fasting is unwise, according to Dr. Rubman. "When someone adopts an unusual diet or fasts, the body's metabolism is thrown off. The change can cause the liver to go into overdrive to adjust," he said. "In the case of green tea extract, the same compound that is protective for someone with a normal metabolism can harm someone whose metabolism is not working at its best." Green tea extract, thus, is normally safe when taken in between meals but should not be part of a fasting or cleansing regimen.

• **Germander.** Germander actually refers to about 250 species of plants in the mint family that have been used to treat high blood pressure, gout, diabetes and other conditions, but it is known to be potentially poisonous to the liver. It should be used only under direct supervision of a naturopathic doctor or other knowledgeable health-care provider who can monitor the supplement's impact on the liver, according to Dr. Rubman. He cautioned that germander has been finding its way into weight-loss supplements and is also often added to supplements made from skullcap—an herb belonging to the mint family—or even substituted for skullcap in supplements claiming to contain skullcap. This unethical behavior by some supplement companies has put skullcap into a predicament. See the next section for details.

• **Skullcap.** Skullcap, also called asafetida, produces stalks of delicate flowers—usually purple although violet and red varieties also exist. American skullcap (*Scutellaria lateriflora*) is generally used to calm the nerves and relax muscles. Chinese skullcap (*Scutellaria baicalensis*) is used to treat allergies, infections, inflammation and headaches. Some studies have suggested that skullcap can cause hepatitis, but it's not known whether the blame lies with the herb itself or with one of the other products it is often mixed with (or replaced by)—namely germander.

As far as Dr. Rubman is concerned, skullcap is an innocent bystander, guilty only of being associated with or replaced by germander. In this instance, reading labels is not enough. Choosing high-quality supplements and not any eye-catching bottle on a store shelf is essential for your safety. Products manufactured by Eclectic Institute and HerbPharm are among those Dr. Rubman uses in his clinical practice.

• **Celandine.** From the poppy family, celandine has traditionally been used as a mild sedative and treatment for digestive problems. Blockage of bile ducts and other liver problems can develop in people who regularly use the herb for too long (three months or more). How celandine does its damage, which goes away once celandine use is stopped, isn't known.

Dr. Rubman has yet to encounter problems with celandine in his practice, but he prescribes the herb only in moderation and not on a regular basis. He also notes that it should be used only under the guidance of a naturopathic physician who will decide what the appropriate dosage for an individual patient is and how long it should be taken.

• **Chaparral.** High in antioxidants, chaparral refers to the leaves of the creosote bush, which is an evergreen shrub native to southwest deserts. Chaparral has been used to treat bronchitis, skin conditions and pain, but it very commonly causes bile ducts to become blocked after three weeks of use. Although the damage usually clears up quickly after chaparral is stopped, severe liver damage, including cirrhosis (a common cause for liver transplantation), has been associated with chaparral. As with green tea extract, an overload of an antioxidant compound may be behind the liver damage caused by chaparral. This is another herb that should be taken only under the guidance of a knowledgeable health-care provider, according to Dr. Rubman.

STAYING SAFE

How would you know if a supplement is hurting your liver? "Fatigue, loss of appetite, looking sick and pale and/or noticing a strong body odor can be signs of liver trouble," said Dr. Rubman. "You may become gassy, and your stools may be paler than usual." If you have any of these symptoms, stop taking the supplement and make an appointment to see your doctor as soon as possible. In extreme cases, jaundice may occur. Signs of jaundice include itchiness, yellow eyes and skin, dark urine, and yellow stools. If this happens, get to a doctor—or hospital emergency room—immediately.

"The liver is a very resilient organ," said Dr. Rubman. If a drug or supplement harms the liver, the damage is frequently—but not always—reversed once you stop taking the offending drug or supplement. To avoid liver problems that might be set off by herbs and herbal supplements, Dr. Rubman's advice, in addition to taking swift action if the symptoms described above occur, is to not be like the approximately 40% of supplement users who hide use from their doctors. He urges you to tell your health-care provider about everything you're taking so that your doctor will know what to do to prevent complications—such as not prescribing a drug that might interfere or interact with a supplement.

Most importantly, buy your herbs and supplements from a licensed naturopathic doctor. Naturopathic practitioners have access to the best, professional-grade products that are free from contaminants and sneaky substitutions. And naturopathic professionals can best advise you about the safe and effective use of a botanical remedy.

Watch Out for Itchy Feet

Johanna S. Youner, DPM, a podiatrist and podiatric surgeon in private practice and attending physician at New York-Presbyterian/Weill Cornell Medical Center, both in New York City. *HealthyFeetNY.com*

Pruritus (itching) of the feet can be extremely annoying for anyone who suffers from this problem.

It is associated with a number of different disorders. For example, it could be caused by a simple infection, which is typically treatable with topical medication or, in more severe cases, an oral medication.

To find out what's going on, see a podiatrist. He/she can take a skin scraping to determine whether you have an infection or another skin condition such as severe foot dryness, allergies or contact dermatitis.

Once skin disorders have been ruled out, your regular doctor can then check for any underlying health problem that could be triggering severe itchiness. This may include a wide range of conditions such as liver disorders like cholestasis (a blockage of the flow of bile)...diabetes...lymphoma...uremia (an electrolyte and hormone imbalance that can develop as a result of kidney disease)...iron-deficiency anemia...and human immunodeficiency virus (HIV).

Once the underlying condition is identified, treatment will help ease the itchiness.

Simple lifestyle changes, such as using a thick emollient or Benadryl cream, keeping showers brief and changing into clean socks twice a day, also can go a long way to help relieve the itching.

14

Respiratory Conditions

4 Secrets to Easier Breathing...Simple Ways to Help Yourself

If you can't catch your breath, walking, climbing stairs or simply carrying on a conversation can be a challenge.

When breathing is a struggle, you wouldn't think that exercise is the answer. But it can be a solution for people with chronic obstructive pulmonary disease (COPD) or heart failure or even for healthy people who occasionally become short of breath.*

Four better-breathing techniques that really help...

PURSED-LIP BREATHING

When you're feeling short of breath, inhale through your nose for two seconds, then pucker your lips as if you were going to whistle or blow out a candle. Exhale through pursed lips for four seconds.

How it helps: It prolongs the respiratory cycle and gives you more time to empty your lungs. This is particularly important if you have emphysema. With emphysema, air gets trapped in the lungs. The trapped air causes the lungs to overinflate, which reduces the amount of force that they're able to generate. This results in a buildup of carbon dioxide that makes it difficult to breathe.

You may need to do this only when you're more active than usual and short of breath. Or you may breathe better when you do it often.

CHANGING POSITIONS

Simply changing how you stand or sit can improve breathing when you're feeling winded.

*If you don't have COPD, you should see a doctor if you have shortness of breath after only slight activity or while resting, or if shortness of breath wakes you up at night or requires you to sleep propped up to breathe.

Gerard J. Criner, MD, a professor of medicine and director of pulmonary and critical care medicine at Temple Lung Center at Temple University School of Medicine in Philadelphia. He is codirector of the Center for Inflammation, Translational and Clinical Lung Research.

How it helps: Certain positions (see below) help muscles around the diaphragm work more efficiently to promote easier breathing.

Examples: While sitting, lean your chest forward...rest your elbows on your knees... and relax your upper-body muscles. When standing, bend forward at the waist and rest your hands on a table or the back of a chair. Or back up to a wall...support yourself with your hips...and lean forward and put your hands on your thighs.

CONTROLLED COUGHING

Your lungs produce excessive mucus when you have COPD. The congestion makes it harder to breathe. It also increases the risk for pneumonia and other lung infections. A normal, explosive cough is not effective at removing mucus. In fact, out-of-control coughing can cause airways to collapse and trap even more mucus. A controlled cough is more effective (and requires less oxygen and energy). You also can use this technique to help clear mucus from the lungs when you have a cold.

How to do it: Sit on a chair or the edge of your bed with both feet on the floor. Fold your arms around your midsection...breathe in slowly through your nose...then lean forward while pressing your arms against your abdomen. Lightly cough two or three times. Repeat as needed.

Important: Taking slow, gentle breaths through your nose while using this technique will prevent mucus from moving back into the airways.

COLD-AIR ASSISTANCE

This is a quick way to breathe better. When you are short of breath—or doing an activity that you know will lead to breathlessness, such as walking on a treadmill—position a fan so that it blows cool air on your face. You also can splash your face with cold water if you become short of breath.

How it helps: Cool air and water stimulate the trigeminal nerve in the face, which slows respiration and helps ease shortness of breath. That's why the treadmills and exercise bikes used in respiratory-rehabilitation facilities are often equipped with small fans.

More from Dr. Criner...

When to Get Breathing Help from a Professional

You can do many breathing exercises on your own without the help of a health professional. For the techniques below, however, it's best to first consult a respiratory therapist (ask your doctor for a referral) to ensure that you know how to do the exercise properly. You can then continue on your own.

• **Paced breathing for endurance.** This technique is useful for people who have COPD and/or heart failure, since it improves lung capacity and heart function.

How it helps: With practice, this technique can increase your cardiorespiratory endurance by 30% to 40%. To perform the exercise, a metronome is set at a rate that's faster than your usual respiratory rate. Your therapist will encourage you to breathe as hard and as fast as you can for, say, about 15 minutes. (Beginners might do it for only a few minutes at a time.)

Example: The metronome may be set for 20 breaths per minute to start, and you may eventually work up to 40 breaths per minute.

You'll notice that breathing becomes easier when you're doing various activities—for instance, when you're exercising, climbing stairs or taking brisk walks.

• **Inspiratory muscle training.** Think of this as a workout for your breathing muscles. It is especially helpful for people with COPD or other lung diseases and those recovering from respiratory failure. People who strengthen these muscles can improve their breathing efficiency by 25% to 30%.

How it helps: For this breathing exercise, you'll use a device known as an inspiratory muscle trainer, which includes a mouthpiece, a one-way valve and resistance settings. When you inhale, the one-way valve closes. You're forced to use effort to breathe against resistance. Then, the valve opens so that you can exhale normally. This breathing exercise is typically performed for 15 minutes twice a day. You can buy these devices online.

Good choice: The Threshold Inspiratory Muscle Trainer, available at *www.fitnessmart.com* for $47.50.

Strengthen Your Lungs—Turn Back the Clock

Mike Moreno, MD, who practices family medicine in San Diego, where he is on the board of the San Diego Chapter of the American Academy of Family Physicians. He is also the author of *The 17 Day Plan to Stop Aging.*

What is it that allows some people to remain robust and healthy well into their 80s and 90s while others become frail or virtually incapacitated? It's not just luck. New studies indicate that aging is largely determined by controllable factors.

To turn back your biological clock...

CHALLENGE YOUR LUNGS

You shouldn't be short of breath when you climb a flight of stairs or have sex, but many adults find that they have more trouble breathing as they age—even if they don't have asthma or other lung diseases.

Why: The lungs tend to lose elasticity over time, particularly if you smoke or live in an area with high air pollution. "Stiff" lungs cannot move air efficiently and cause breathing difficulty.

Simple thing you can do: Breathe slowly in and out through a drinking straw for two to three minutes, once or twice daily. Breathe only through your mouth, not your nose. This stretches the lungs, increases lung capacity and improves lung function.

Helpful: Start with an extra-wide straw, and go to a regular straw as you get used to breathing this way.

DRINK THYME TEA

When the lungs do not expand and contract normally (see above), or when the tissues are unusually dry, you're more likely to get colds or other infections, including pneumonia. The herb thyme contains thymol, an antioxidant that may help prevent colds, bronchitis and pneumonia and soothe chronic respiratory problems such as asthma, allergies and emphysema.

Simple thing you can do: Add a cup of thyme tea to your daily routine. If you have a chronic or acute respiratory illness, drink two cups of thyme tea daily—one in the morning and one at night.

To make thyme tea: Steep one tablespoon of dried thyme (or two tablespoons of fresh thyme) in two cups of hot water for five minutes, or use thyme tea bags (available at most health-food stores).

If you take a blood thinner: Talk to your doctor before using thyme—it can increase risk for bleeding. Also, if you're allergic to oregano, you're probably allergic to thyme.

Another simple step: Drink at least six to eight eight-ounce glasses of water every day. This helps loosen lung mucus and flushes out irritants, such as bacteria and viruses.

Garlic for Bronchitis

Steven Sandberg-Lewis, ND, is a naturopathic physician and a clinical professor of naturopathic medicine at the National College of Natural Medicine (NCNM) in Portland, Oregon. He is the author of *Functional Gastroenterology* (NCNM) and was awarded the NCNM's Lifetime Achievement Award in 2003.

Bronchitis usually occurs after a cold or other upper-respiratory infection. Antibiotics may be helpful—but many people don't need them because bronchitis is often due to a viral infection rather than a bacterial infection.

Simple home remedy: An inhalation of liquid allicin, an active compound in garlic with antibacterial and antiviral effects.

To use liquid allicin, add about 10 drops (my favorite allicin extract is called Allimax Liquid) to the reservoir of a portable nebulizer, which is available at most drugstores. Breathe the mist until all of the extract is gone—about 10 minutes. Repeat the treatment one to three times daily until you're feeling better.

Also helpful: Fresh garlic cloves (two per day) or garlic supplements. I recommend Allimax capsules with 180 mg of allicin per capsule. I advise my patients with bronchitis to take two capsules three to four times daily for five to seven days.

Best Exercise for COPD Patients

Renae McNamara, BAppSc (Phty), clinical specialist physiotherapist, pumonary rehabilition, clinical and rehabilitation sciences, University of Sydney, and department of respiratory and sleep medicine and department of physiotherapy, Prince of Wales Hospital, New South Wales, Australia.

A recent Australian study shows that aquatic exercise builds more endurance and decreases fatigue and shortness of breath more substantially for people with COPD than land exercise—and this finding may apply to people with other sorts of respiratory problems and chronic conditions, too.

Water workouts: Less Pain, More Gain

The research focused specifically on people who had both COPD, an all-too-common respiratory problem that is the third-leading cause of death in the US, and an additional chronic condition that makes exercise difficult—such as obesity, joint problems or back pain. But there's every reason to think that the study's results will apply to people with other sorts of medical issues, especially those with respiratory conditions, said lead researcher Renae McNamara, BAppSc (Phty), a respiratory physiotherapist in Australia. Future studies will need to examine that.

Researchers were interested in finding out which type of workout would help people find the most relief—land-based exercise (a mixture of walking, cycling, aerobics and dumbbell lifts) or water-based exercise (aquatic calisthenics done in chest-to-neck high water in a pool heated to 93°F).

The patients were split into three groups. One group did one-hour water exercises three times a week for eight weeks with a trained physiotherapist. Another group did land exercises for the same amount of time with the same trained physiotherapist. And a third group performed no exercise (the control).

At the end of the study, when each group was asked to perform a walking test to measure endurance, members of the water group could walk 118% farther than they could at the start of the study, on average...the land group's distance improved, too, but by only 53%...and the control group actually got weaker—their distance was 13% shorter.

Also, the people who had been exercising in a pool saw a 9% decrease in shortness of breath and a 13% decrease in fatigue by the end of the study...while the people who had been exercising on land saw only a 4% decrease in shortness of breath and a 3% decrease in fatigue.

CONTRA-CONVENTIONAL WISDOM

So why did water workouts come out on top? "Water may have helped more for a few reasons. First of all, you have the effect of buoyancy, which supports your weight and reduces impact on your joints," said McNamara. "Warm water also helps with pain control and increases blood flow to muscles. Plus, water offers resistance to all your movements, so your muscles work harder, and that strengthens them."

What's ironic is that it wasn't all that long ago that people with COPD were warned not to do water-based exercise. Doctors worried that the water would compress the chest and that the exertion would stress the heart. But studies that have analyzed COPD and water exercise under controlled conditions (as in, when patients were under the watchful eye of a health professional) have shown that these fears are unfounded, said McNamara.

GET YOUR GOGGLES ON!

Now that we have these study results, if you suffer from COPD as well as obesity, joint problems or back pain, you owe it to yourself to talk to your doctor or physical therapist about trying pool-based therapy with a trained health professional. (If you have COPD but none of those other conditions...or if you have one of the other conditions but not COPD...or if you suffer from a different type of respiratory problem...you may still find pool-based therapy to be more beneficial than land exercises, so it's worth a try, said McNamara.)

Group classes are usually easier to find than individual classes (plus, they tend to be cheaper and more fun). But either type of class is useful. To find one, call your local YMCA (*www.ymca.net*) or a community recreation center that has a pool or a hospital with an aquatic rehab center.

You might find, like my friend's dad, that all it takes is a little water to ease your pain and help you stay active.

Herbal Paste Applied in Summer Eases Breathing in Winter

Yongjun Bian, MD, is a clinical researcher in the respiratory department of Guang'anmen Hospital in Beijing, China, and a research fellow for a study of 125 COPD patients.

For people with chronic obstructive pulmonary disease (COPD), an incurable condition characterized by chronic bronchitis and/or emphysema, winter often brings a worsening of symptoms such as coughing, wheezing, shortness of breath, fatigue and recurrent respiratory infections. Steroids help control symptoms but can have side effects... antibiotics fight infection but increase the risk for antibiotic resistance. So it was welcome news when a recent study provided scientific evidence of the effectiveness of a topical herbal remedy called Xiao Chuan paste (XCP), which has been used in China for more than 1,000 years to treat COPD and other breathing problems.

Researchers randomly assigned COPD patients to receive either XCP or a placebo paste. As is traditional, the paste was applied to three specific pairs of acupuncture points on the back...the treatment was given four times during an eight-week period in July and August. Then participants were monitored from November through February.

Results: Compared with patients who received the placebo, those who received XCP were significantly less likely to experience an exacerbation of symptoms requiring steroids, antibiotics and/or hospitalization...and they reported a significantly higher quality of life. The only side effect—a mild skin reaction that cleared up without treatment once XCP was discontinued—occurred in just 2% of users.

XCP is made from herbs native to China, including Asarum heterotropoides, Ephedra vulgaris and Acorus gramineus Soland. Researchers theorize that the herbs have properties that affect immune regulation.

You can learn more about XCP by consulting a practitioner of traditional Chinese medicine who is knowledgeable about herbal therapies.

Referrals: National Certification Commission for Acupuncture and Oriental Medicine (*www.nccaom.org*) or American Association of Acupuncture and Oriental Medicine *(www.aaaomonline.org*).

The Supplement That Everyone Should Know About—NAC

Richard Firshein, DO, is founder and director of The Firshein Center for Comprehensive Medicine in New York City. *FirsheinCenter.com*

You know all about the benefits of fish oil...and magnesium...and vitamin D. But here's a supplement that far fewer people are taking—but many could benefit from. It's called n-acetylcysteine (NAC)—and it's especially helpful during cold and flu season since it can combat respiratory ailments. But wait, there's more. NAC also can ease lung and liver problems. To get this amazing remedy on your radar, we turned to Richard Firshein, DO, director of The Firshein Center for

Comprehensive Medicine in New York City, and asked him why he recommends NAC to so many of his patients. *Here's what he said...*

WHY IT'S SO POWERFUL

NAC is an amino acid—and a building block of glutathione, one of the most powerful antioxidants in the body. It helps the body combat damaging free radicals and stimulates other antioxidants in the body to do their beneficial work. In addition, NAC has many uses in the body. *Specifically, it can help you...*

- **Fight colds and flu.** NAC is a remedy often recommended by holistic doctors to prevent—and reduce symptoms of—the flu. A well-known Italian study published in *European Respiratory Journal* found that only 25% of people who took NAC and were injected with a flu virus developed flu symptoms compared with 79% who received a placebo. You also can consider taking NAC when you notice the first signs of a cold.

- **Protect your lungs.** NAC protects the lungs by helping to make glutathione in the lining of the lungs. NAC also can act as a buffer against pollution. When you have a cold, taking NAC can protect your lungs from complications such as bronchitis. In people who have chronic obstructive pulmonary diseases such as emphysema, NAC can help reduce the buildup of mucus and congestion, which, in turn, can help relieve the chronic cough that often accompanies emphysema. NAC also is recommended for people with pulmonary fibrosis, since it may slow the disease.

- **Detox the liver.** NAC is known to help cleanse the liver—it helps people whose livers are damaged either because of alcoholism or elevated liver enzymes. Elevated liver enzymes can occur in people who have hepatitis or heart failure or who are obese.

USING NAC

NAC is found in small amounts in some protein-rich foods such as pork, poultry and yogurt. But to really get its health benefits, you have to take it as a supplement. NAC is available at most health-food stores and drugstores.

Dr. Firshein usually recommends that his patients take between 500 mg and 1,000 mg daily of NAC to fight the common cold or flu...protect lungs...and detox the liver. Since every patient is different, it's important to check with your own holistic doctor about the amount of NAC that's right for you. This is especially important for patients with liver or lung diseases.

There are no side effects associated with NAC, although higher doses can cause digestive upset. People with heart or kidney disease should speak to their doctors first before taking NAC.

NAC can be taken on its own, but it's best to take it with other antioxidants, such as vitamin C, since NAC works better in conjunction with other antioxidants. The detoxification process may create toxic by-products that linger in the body. If there's a lot of toxicity, the other antioxidant can lend a hand clearing out the excess toxins.

Vitamin E Prevents COPD...and Other Natural Solutions

Anne Hermetet Agler, Division of Nutritional Sciences, Cornell University, Ithaca, New York.

Chris Burtin, PT (MSc), a hospital-based physical therapist in Katholieke Universiteit Leuven, Belgium.

Robert J. Green, ND, naturopathic physician and author of *Natural Therapies for Emphysema and COPD.*

We hear a lot about preventing heart disease, the number-one cause of death in America. And cancer, the number-two cause. And stroke, at number three.

But we rarely hear about preventing the seldom-discussed number-four cause of death in the US—chronic obstructive pulmonary disease (COPD), also known as emphysema and chronic bronchitis, which affects 16 million Americans and kills 122,000 yearly.

Now: Results from a new study provide a nutritional strategy that may help ward off COPD—take vitamin E.

E IS FOR EASIER BREATHING

Researchers from Cornell University and Harvard Medical School analyzed data from a seven-year study on nearly 40,000 women aged 45 and older who took either 600 international units (IU) of vitamin E or a placebo every other day.

Results: Those who took the nutrient had a 10% lower risk of developing COPD—even if they smoked, the main risk factor for the disease.

"As lung disease develops, damage occurs to sensitive tissues through several processes, including inflammation and damage from free radicals," says Anne Hermetet Agler, study researcher in the Division of Nutritional Sciences at Cornell University. "Vitamin E may protect the lung against such damage."

"Vitamin E is a powerful antioxidant, which makes it quite useful in counteracting oxidative damage in the lungs," agrees Robert J. Green, ND, a naturopathic physician and author of *Natural Therapies for Emphysema and COPD*.

And Dr. Green says you may want to take vitamin E if you already have COPD.

"Take 400 IU three or four times daily," he advises. "Take it with 50 to 100 milligrams (mg) of vitamin C to enhance absorption. You may need higher doses for therapeutic benefit, but don't exceed 1,600 IU daily without your physician's recommendation and supervision."

RECENT FINDINGS

The earliest symptoms of COPD might be a chronic cough and airway-clogging mucus (sputum). Later, you may find yourself unexpectedly short of breath while carrying groceries, climbing stairs or going for a brisk walk. As the disease advances, respiratory difficulties can turn into disasters. Eventually, your best friend could be an oxygen tank.

Good news: Recent research shows there are natural ways to control these and other symptoms of COPD.

- **A more active lifestyle.** In a study reported at an international conference of the American Thoracic Society, researchers found that people with COPD who had a more active lifestyle—more moving around during the day—performed better on a six-minute walk test (the distance they were able to walk in six minutes).

Recommendation: "COPD patients who wish to improve their ability to perform daily tasks may be better served by increasing their normal daily activities, such as walking to the post office, working in the garden, or doing housekeeping, rather than performing intense exercise once in a while," says Chris Burtin, PT, a hospital-based physical therapist in Belgium and the study leader.

"Daily walking is one of the best exercise activities for a person with COPD," adds Dr. Green. "Walking will help build your circulation and increase your stamina, and it will help build activity tolerance. Start out by walking half a block or less. Every other day, you should increase your walking distance a little bit. After a few months, you could be walking up to a mile without gasping."

- **Tai chi.** Researchers at Harvard Medical School studied 10 people with COPD, dividing them into two groups.

Five people took a twice-weekly, one-hour class in tai chi (gentle, meditative exercises that use flowing, circular movements, and balance and breathing techniques). Five didn't.

After 12 weeks, those taking tai chi had improvements in breathing capacity, walking distance and depression compared with those who didn't take the classes.

Recommendation: "Tai chi may be a suitable exercise option for patients with COPD," wrote the Harvard researchers in the journal Respiratory Care.

Resource: To find an accredited tai chi teacher near you, visit the website *www.taichichih.org*, and click on "find a teacher."

- **Singing.** "Despite optimal pharmacological therapy and pulmonary rehabilitation, patients with COPD continue to be breathless," noted a team of UK researchers in the journal *BMC Pulmonary Medicine*. "There is a need to develop additional strategies to alleviate symptoms. Learning to sing requires control of breathing and posture, and might have benefits that translate into daily life."

To test their theory, the researchers studied 28 people with COPD—half took twice-weekly singing classes and half didn't.

Results: After six weeks, those taking the classes had better physical functioning and less anxiety about breathlessness, compared with the non-singers.

"Singing classes can improve quality-of-life measures and anxiety, and are viewed as a very positive experience by patients with respiratory disease," concluded the researchers.

Resources: Ways to learn to sing include...

- *www.takelessons.com*, a website that connects you to singing teachers in any one of 2,800 cites across the US. Phone: 800-252-1508.
- *www.singingvoicelessons.com*, a website that offers the Singing Voice Lessons Series on CD, from voice coach Shelley Kristen.
- *www.easysinginglessons.com*, a website providing downloadable "Singing Is Easy" lessons.
- *Singing for the Stars: A Complete Program for Training Your Voice* by Seth Riggs, a book and 2-CD set.
- *Singing for Dummies (for Dummies)*, a book by Pamela S. Phillips.

Breathe Easier with Acupuncture

Masao Suzuki, LAc, PhD, is an associate professor in the department of clinical acupuncture and moxibustion at Meiji University of Integrative Medicine and the department of respiratory medicine at the Graduate School of Medicine at Kyoto University, both in Kyoto, Japan, as well as lead author of a study on acupuncture and COPD published in *Archives of Internal Medicine.*

Imagine being so short of breath that you can barely walk half a block without coughing, wheezing, getting tight in the chest or feeling too fatigued to go on. For people with chronic obstructive pulmonary disease (COPD)—a progressive and incurable lung condition characterized by chronic bronchitis and/or emphysema—such symptoms are a sad fact of life, as are recurrent respiratory infections. Steroids help control symptoms but can have side effects...antibiotics fight infection but increase the risk for antibiotic resistance.

So it was welcome news when a recent study from Japan showed that acupuncture helps relieve symptoms and improve quality of life for COPD patients. Women especially should take note because, despite COPD's reputation as a "man's disease," women account for the majority of US cases.

About the study: COPD patients were randomly assigned to one of two groups. Once a week for 12 weeks, one group received acupuncture at the standard "acupoints" traditionally used for lung problems. The other group got sham acupuncture at the same acupoints, performed with blunt needles that appeared to but did not actually enter the skin. All patients continued with their usual medication throughout the study.

Before treatment began, participants rated their degree of breathlessness after a six-minute walk test, using a scale of zero (breathing very well) to 10 (severely breathless). They also rated their typical level of breathlessness during daily activities...and underwent tests to measure blood oxygenation and other indicators of lung function. Tests were repeated at the end of the 12 weeks.

Results: Breathing scores and test results remained essentially the same for COPD patients who got sham acupuncture. But in the real acupuncture group, the average breathlessness score after the six-minute walk improved from 5.5 to 1.9...tests showed significant improvement in lung function...and patients reported markedly better quality of life. There were no significant adverse side effects. Researchers speculated that acupuncture helps relax the muscles involved in breathing.

Interested patients: It is important to note that the study participants received acupuncture as a complement to, not a replacement for, their usual COPD medication. To find a licensed acupuncturist (LAc) in your area, visit the website of the National Certification Commission for Acupuncture and Oriental Medicine (*www.nccaom.org*) or the American Association of Acupuncture and Oriental Medicine (*www.aaaomonline.org*).

Fun Way to Fix Your Lungs

Playing the harmonica promotes lung health. Blowing into the instrument lowers air pressure in the airways and expands the air sacs in the lungs, reducing the risk that they will narrow or collapse, as occurs in patients with asthma or emphysema. It also forces you to frequently change the pace and depth of your breath, which strengthens the diaphragm (a muscle separating the lungs from the abdomen).

If you have asthma, chronic bronchitis or emphysema: Consider learning to play the harmonica.

Dan Hamner, MD, a physiatrist and sports medicine physician, New York City.

Better Inhaler Use

Researchers asked 100 hospital patients with asthma or another lung disease, such as emphysema, to demonstrate using their inhalers.

Finding: Patients misused them up to 86% of the time—often forgetting to exhale completely before inhaling. People with poor vision, who had trouble reading the directions, were most likely to misuse inhalers.

If you use an inhaler: Read the instructions or ask a friend to read them to you. Also ask your doctor to demonstrate how to use your inhaler.

Valerie Press, MD, instructor of medicine, The University of Chicago Medical Center, Illinois.

You Could Have Asthma

Shortness of breath is not a symptom of aging. Asthma in older patients often is assumed to be bronchitis or emphysema, but at least 40% of patients have their first asthma attack at age 40 or older. Older adults are the only age group in which asthma is getting worse—60% of asthma deaths occur in people age 65 or older.

Self-defense: If you have shortness of breath, get tested for asthma.

Raymond Slavin, MD, allergist and professor of internal medicine, Saint Louis University School of Medicine, and author of a summary of allergic rhinitis, published in *Allergy and Asthma Proceedings*.

Heartburn Can Kill—Here's How to Get Relief…

Jamie Koufman, MD, professor of clinical otolaryngology at New York Medical College in Valhalla, New York, and founder and director of the Voice Institute of New York in New York City. She is coauthor, with Jordan Stern, MD, and Marc Bauer, of *Dropping Acid: The Reflux Diet, Cookbook and Cure*.

If you have heartburn, you feel a burning sensation in your chest, usually after eating a meal. Right? Not necessarily.

What you may not realize: Heartburn can occur without causing typical symptoms. With a "silent" form of heartburn known as laryngopharyngeal reflux (LPR), a chronic cough, hoarseness, frequent throat-clearing, difficulty swallowing and/or asthmalike symptoms, such as noisy breathing, are among the red flags to watch for.

Unfortunately, many patients with LPR suffer for years because their doctors mistakenly blame these symptoms on allergies, postnasal drip or other common health problems. Don't let this happen to you or a loved one. Untreated LPR increases risk for asthma, pneumonia—and even potentially deadly esophageal and throat cancers.

WHAT HAPPENS

It's normal for acids and enzymes in the stomach to surge upward (reflux) into the esophagus (the muscular tube that connects the throat to the stomach). This happens up to 50 times a day in the average adult, often without causing any symptoms or long-term damage. The esophagus is designed to withstand these assaults. But tissues in the throat are more sensitive.

Each episode of reflux causes material from the stomach to surge upward at incredibly fast speeds. At this high velocity, liquid droplets can spray past a valve called the upper esophageal sphincter and into the throat.

Doctors often refer to LPR as acid reflux, but this is somewhat misleading. Some acid does surge upward—but so does pepsin, an enzyme that breaks down proteins during digestion. The actual damage to the throat is caused by pepsin.

When you have an episode of reflux, pepsin molecules cling to tissues in the throat. The pepsin is harmless until it's activated by acid.

It takes only trace amounts of acid to activate pepsin. As long as you continue to consume acid-containing foods and beverages, the pepsin will stay in an active state.

HOW TO AVOID MISDIAGNOSIS

The prevalence of reflux disease, including LPR, has increased by about 4% every year in the last few decades. This increase is thought to be due to obesity, a risk factor for reflux, and higher levels of acidic foods and beverages in the American diet.

Despite the increasing prevalence of LPR, it still can be tough to get a correct diagnosis. You should suspect that you have it if you experience frequent or intermittent difficulty swallowing, hoarseness, persistent postnasal drip and/or the sensation of a lump in the throat. A cough that often occurs after eating or when lying down is another sign of LPR.

Important: Your family doctor might not be familiar with the symptoms of LPR or its treatments, so it is wise to go to an otolaryngologist (ear, nose and throat doctor) if you think that you may have the condition. He/she will probably be able to diagnose LPR from your medical history and a description of your symptoms.

Most patients with LPR are advised to take standard heartburn medications, such as *cimetidine* (Tagamet) or *omeprazole* (Prilosec). However, these medications only partially relieve symptoms for most LPR patients.

BEST TREATMENT OPTION

A reduced-acid diet is the most effective treatment for LPR. Pepsin is activated at a pH of 5 or lower. (A lower pH indicates a higher acid concentration.)

The majority of patients who follow a low-acid diet (see description at the end of this article) for two weeks, then continue to restrict acidity by mainly eating low-acid foods, can greatly reduce or even eliminate their symptoms. *To begin...*

- **Give up certain beverages.** Soft drinks are one of the main causes of LPR because they're highly acidic.

Examples: Coca-Cola has a pH of 2.5... and Tab and Diet Pepsi are each 2.9. Even less acidic beverages, such as sparkling water, can lead to reflux due to the carbonation.

I advise patients to avoid all carbonated drinks, fruit juice and alcohol. You can continue to drink coffee—but have no more than one cup each day. If you prefer tea, try chamomile.

- **Avoid canned and bottled foods and beverages.** The FDA requires that these foods and beverages (except water) be acidified to pH 4.6 or lower to prevent bacterial growth and prolong shelf life. However, this particular practice is believed to be one of the main reasons for the rise in LPR.

- **Drink Evamor water.** It's an alkaline bottled water with a pH of 8.8. It contains bicarbonate, which neutralizes acids. Research shows that the pepsin in throat tissues can't survive at pH levels above 7.7. Patients who drink this water regularly may recover more quickly than those who drink tap water. You can purchase Evamor Natural Artesian Water online at *www.evamor.com* or at most health-food stores and many major grocery stores.

- **Reduce fats.** Even when they're not high in acid, high-fat foods weaken the "holding" power of the esophageal muscle that prevents reflux. All high-fat foods will increase risk for LPR—and fried foods are particularly bad.

My advice: Don't give up fats entirely—just use them in smaller amounts, as though they're seasonings rather than main ingredients.

Example: All the fat in an egg is in the yolk, but a plain egg-white omelet is too bland for most people. For more richness while reducing reflux, add one egg yolk to three egg whites. You also should cut back significantly on cheese, meats, butter, etc.

- **Balance acids.** After following the low-acid diet for two weeks, most LPR patients can have acidic foods as long as they eat small amounts and combine them with nonacidic foods to keep the overall pH at safe levels.

Examples: Combine strawberries (which are too acidic to eat alone) with low-fat milk. The milk will buffer the acid and keep the total pH where it should be. Similarly, you could combine apple slices (which are acidic) with low-fat cheese.

My favorite combo: A smoothie with bananas, a cup of skim milk and a little plain yogurt (all nonacidic) with some strawberries (acidic).

- **Learn your particular trigger foods.** Most patients with LPR have more episodes/symptoms when they eat tomatoes, onions, garlic or peppers.

Also a problem: Fatty nuts (such as macadamia nuts and walnuts) and chocolate.

Other foods are idiosyncratic: They cause symptoms in some patients, but not in others. You will have to experiment with foods to discover what causes symptoms and what does not.

A LOW-ACID DIET

People who have LPR will need to follow a strict, low-acid diet to give damaged tissues time to heal and to deactivate any remaining pepsin molecules.

What to do: For two weeks, avoid carbonated beverages, fruit juice and alcohol. During this time, eat only low-acid foods (with a pH higher than 5).

Examples: Fish...tofu...poultry...egg whites ...bananas...melon...potatoes (plain or salted, no butter)...vegetables (raw or cooked, no onions, tomatoes or peppers)... milk (low fat, soy or Lactaid Fat Free)...chamomile tea...and water. You can find the pH levels of foods at a number of websites, such as *www.pickyourown.org/ph_of_foods.htm.*

After this period, you can gradually reintroduce other foods, as long as your diet consists primarily of low-acid foods.

Shocking News About Allergies and Asthma

Mark A. Stengler, NMD, a naturopathic medical doctor and author of *The Natural Physician's Healing Therapies*, director of the Stengler Center for Integrative Medicine in Encinitas, California, and adjunct associate clinical professor at the National College of Natural Medicine in Portland, Oregon. *MarkStengler.com*

Millions of people are walking around suffering from respiratory allergies... asthma...recurring colds...and bronchitis—and they don't have to be.

Let me give you an example: Pam, a woman in her 40s, had three colds in a row that turned into bronchitis. Another doctor had given her an asthma diagnosis. When she came to see me, she told me that she had been struggling with allergies and persistent fatigue for most of her adult life. I see so many patients with this combination of symptoms that I immediately suspected that she had an altogether different problem. It is called adrenal fatigue (AF), a collection of symptoms that occur when the adrenal glands, which produce stress- and inflammation-fighting hormones, no longer function properly.

You might wonder what AF has to do with these other conditions.

My answer: Everything. What's really going on is that AF is masquerading as allergies or asthma. Once AF is properly diagnosed and treated, these other conditions quickly clear up. I prescribed a treatment plan for Pam designed to get her adrenal glands functioning normally again. After just two months on the program, her respiratory problems disappeared and her energy level was higher than it had been in years.

What you need to know: AF is most often associated with a wide range of symptoms, including lack of energy, insomnia, blood sugar swings, cognitive impairment and depressed mood. But AF also can have a significant impact on your immune system. In addition, it often is not recognized by conventional physicians because it doesn't show up on regular lab tests. As surprising as it may sound, if you suffer from a respiratory allergy to dust, pollen, ragweed, pet dander or other environmental allergen—or if you have asthma that recurs despite treatment—there's a chance that your real problem is improperly functioning adrenal glands. (I have even found that AF is associated with asthma in some children, although it is more common in adults with asthma.)

AF CAN BE THE ROOT OF OTHER PROBLEMS

The adrenal glands are responsible for producing the hormone cortisol (released into the bloodstream in response to stress) and dehydroepiandrosterone or DHEA (a precursor to hormones such as estrogen and testosterone). AF usually occurs when patients undergo extended periods of stress, which cause levels of DHEA and cortisol to become elevated for long periods of time, usually four months or longer (although this varies by patient). The surplus production of DHEA and cortisol overtaxes the adrenals, resulting in a sharp drop in DHEA and cortisol levels.

What AF does to the immune system: Both cortisol and DHEA modulate the immune system's inflammatory response. When the glands no longer produce sufficient amounts of these hormones, the immune system becomes overactive, producing inflammatory responses even when there's no real threat or infection looming.

Result: Allergic responses...respiratory infections...and asthma. Most conventional medical doctors treat these conditions by prescribing antihistamines for allergy symptoms and corticosteroids to ward off asthma. In other words, they treat the symptoms, not the disease.

DIAGNOSIS AND TESTING

If you suspect that you have AF, it's best to see a naturopathic physician and have your adrenal function tested. My preference is a saliva test, which is more accurate than a blood or urine test. Your physician will retest you three or four months after treatment begins to see if your levels have improved.

HOW TO HEAL THE ADRENALS

My treatment protocol for AF involves supplements to boost adrenal function and/or increase resistance to stress. Patients follow the protocol for four to six months, which is the time it usually takes to get the adrenals working properly again. Most patients begin to feel better within the first month or two. When patients are doing well, I help wean them off their allergy or asthma medications during this time. People with very severe cases usually stay on my regimen for eight to 10 months. After treatment, patients either take lower doses or stop taking these supplements altogether, depending on their overall health. The supplements that I recommend below include herbs (which are most important in helping this condition) and B vitamins. There are no side effects except as noted.

- **Ashwagandha.** This herb, used in Ayurvedic medicine to treat inflammation, is a potent adaptogen, an herb that helps to bring physiological processes into balance and enhances the body's ability to handle stress. It has a strong effect on the adrenal glands and normalizes production of cortisol.

Dose: 250 milligrams (mg) daily of ashwagandha standardized to contain 8% of the active ingredient anolide.

- **Rhodiola.** Another adaptogen, rhodiola is an herb that has been used for centuries in Eastern Europe and Asia as an energy and mood enhancer. It boosts adrenal function, and studies show that it also improves the body's resistance to stress.

Dose: 300 mg daily of rhodiola standardized to contain 3% of the active ingredient rosavin.

- **Siberian ginseng (Eleutherococcus).** Another adaptogen, this herbal extract has been used for centuries in Russia and Asia to boost energy and fight stress.

Dose: 150 mg to 200 mg daily of Siberian ginseng extract standardized to contain 0.8% eleutheroside.

Side effects: Can cause insomnia if taken before bedtime and can affect some diabetes drugs. Should not be used during pregnancy.

- **Vitamin B-5 (pantothenic acid).** Vitamin B-5 helps adrenal function and is used by the body to manufacture cortisol.

Dose: 250 mg to 500 mg of vitamin B-5 daily.

- **Vitamin B-12.** This vitamin helps boost resistance to the effects of stress.

Dose: 50 micrograms (mcg) to 100 mcg of vitamin B-12 daily.

Finally, I advise my patients to take steps to reduce stress in their daily lives.

Recommendations: Get enough sleep (seven to eight hours a night)...take a 30-minute midday nap, if possible...eliminate all refined sugars from your diet...take regular vacations...and minimize daily stress by exercising or participating in relaxing activities, such as listening to calming music.

CART: A Better Way to Catch Your Breath If You Have Asthma

Study titled "Controlling Asthma by Training of Capnometry-Assisted Hypoventilation (CATCH) Vs Slow Breathing: A Randomized Controlled Trial," by researchers in the department of psychology and the Anxiety and Depression Research Center at Southern Methodist University, Dallas, published in *Chest.*

Asthma. The very mention of the word can make you feel like you have a boa constrictor wrapped around your chest. If you have asthma, chances are that when you feel that squeezing, suffocating feeling of an attack, you take deep breaths—gasping for air—but this is actually wrong. Or maybe you have heard that taking deep, slow and paced breaths is the right way to go. But the latest research shows that there really is a much better way to catch your breath.

WHEN LESS IS MORE

In an attempt to catch their breaths, asthmatics gulp air and breathe too rapidly during an attack. It's a natural reaction, but this can cause a decrease in the body's level of carbon dioxide (CO2), resulting in hyperventilation and its characteristic symptoms of dizziness, breathlessness and pins and needles. The lungs become hyperreactive, stuffy and dry, making the asthma attack far worse and scarier than it needs to be.

Now consider this: Shallow breathing does the opposite...it increases CO2 levels. Knowing this and knowing that shallow breathing helps people with panic disorder (who also tend to hyperventilate), researchers from Southern Methodist University in Dallas decided to test the effectiveness of a shallow-breathing technique, successfully used in people with panic disorder, in adults with asthma.

They randomly assigned 120 asthma sufferers to receive either a standard breathing therapy called slow-breathing and awareness training (SLOW) or a therapy called capnometry-assisted respiratory training (CART). SLOW teaches asthmatics to take slow, full breaths through awareness and control of their respiratory rate (the number of breaths they take per minute). CART also trains its users to control their respiratory rate but encourages shallow breathing and control of CO2 levels through use of a device called a capnometer. The capnometer provides feedback about CO2 levels so that a person can practice how to breathe to prevent CO2 from dipping too low.

The study participants practiced their therapies for four weeks on their own and with respiratory therapists and used their asthma medications as needed. The researchers monitored asthma attacks, need for medication and various aspects of respiratory function during this time and for six months' follow-up—and patients kept journals of the impact of SLOW or CART therapy on their asthma.

The results? Whereas both techniques resulted in an 81% improvement in lung function, the CART group was in better shape six months down the road than the other group. Their airways had become more widened and their CO2 levels were more normalized than those of patients practicing SLOW, and that difference remained consistent throughout further follow-up. Patients practicing CART also coped better when under the stress of an acute asthma attack because they felt more in control of their symptoms and what exactly was happening in their bodies during attacks.

LEARNING TO BREATHE

If you have (or know someone who has) asthma and are unfamiliar with breath retraining therapies, such as SLOW and CART, it's a good idea to ask your doctor for a referral to a respiratory therapist—especially someone who knows about CART. These therapies are not a substitute for asthma medication, but they clearly work as add-ons and can help you improve lung function so that you can possibly rely less on medication. As for which therapy is better for long-term improvement, this study, at least, points to CART.

How to Survive an Asthma Attack Without an Inhaler

Richard Firshein, DO, board-certified in family medicine and certified medical acupuncturist and founder and director of The Firshein Center for Comprehensive Medicine, New York City. He is author of *Reversing Asthma: Breathe Easier with This Revolutionary New Program.*

If you have asthma, then you know how scary it can be when you have an attack and have trouble breathing for anywhere from a few minutes to a few days, depending on its severity.

So you're probably careful to keep your rescue inhaler with you at all times—in case of an emergency.

But what happens if an attack starts and you discover that your inhaler is empty or you don't actually have it?

How can you lessen the severity of an asthma attack and/or stop it altogether without your trusty inhaler?

Richard Firshein, DO, director and founder of The Firshein Center for Comprehensive Medicine in New York City and author of *Reversing Asthma: Breathe Easier with This Revolutionary New Program*, provided some very interesting advice…

DO YOU NEED TO GO TO THE ER?

First off, quickly determine whether you're in immediate danger, said Dr. Firshein. If you have a peak-flow meter—a device that measures how much air you can expel from your lungs and that many asthmatics keep around the house—use it. If you're less than 25% off your normal mark, go on to the following steps, but if your number is off by more, get to an emergency room, he said, because this indicates that there is a serious problem—one that could be life-threatening, he said. If you don't have a peak-flow meter, then think about your symptoms. For example, if your lips or fingernails turn blue…if you can't stop coughing…if you feel soreness or tightness around the ribs…if you feel like you're having a panic attack…or if you're so exhausted from the effort of breathing that you can't finish a short sentence or stand up, then you need help fast—get to an ER.

HOW TO BREATHE EASIER

If you're not in immediate danger, try these tricks, below, from Dr. Firshein. Some of these techniques may help within minutes, while others may take a few hours to kick in, but since it's possible for an attack to last for days, try all of them to play it safe. During a typical asthma attack, the airways are constricted, muscles all over your body become tense and your body produces extra mucus—all of those things make it harder to breathe. So Dr. Firshein's advice addresses all of those problems. You know your body best, so if you try all of these tips but your attack still gets worse, go to a hospital.

- **Change your location.** Asthma is typically triggered by an irritant—either an allergen or toxin—that inflames the airways. So remove yourself from the environment that contains the trigger (if you know what it is) as fast as you can. If you're reacting to dust, pets, mold or smoke, for example, get away from it…or at the very least, breathe through a sleeve, a scarf or your jacket collar to reduce your exposure.

• **Tell someone.** Talking to someone may reduce your anxiety, and that's especially helpful, because anxiety can make your asthma attack worse. Also, if your asthma attack becomes more severe later on, you may need a ride to the hospital, so it's always good to keep someone else in the loop.

Also consider taking an over-the-counter decongestant (such as pseudoephedrine/Sudafed) and/or an expectorant (such as guaifenesin/Mucinex) or a drug that's a combination of the two (ephedrine + guaifenesin/Primatene Asthma), because these loosen mucus and make coughs more productive so you can rid your body of more phlegm.

• **Sip hot coffee or nonherbal tea.** Have one or two cups right away (but no more than that in one sitting, or your heart rate might spike too high—this is true among all people, not just asthmatics). Caffeine is metabolized into theophylline, which is also a drug that's used to prevent and treat asthma by relaxing the airways and decreasing the lungs' response to irritants. Getting caffeine from any source (a soda, an energy drink, a supplement, etc.) will likely help, but tea and coffee have other compounds that act similarly to caffeine (plus, liquids—especially hot liquids—help loosen mucus), so getting your caffeine in this form is best.

• **Practice breathing exercises.** Many people panic when they have an asthma attack and start breathing quickly, but that only restricts the amount of oxygen that the lungs get—in other words, it makes the attack worse. So breathe in through your nose to the count of four and then out to the count of six. Pursing your lips as you exhale will help slow the exhalation and keep the airways open longer. Continue breathing this way for as long as you need.

• **Press on some acupressure points.** The front parts of your inner shoulders (just above the armpits) and the outer edges of the creases of your elbows (when your elbows are bent) are "lung points." Pressing on one area at a time for a few consecutive minutes may relax muscles that have tightened up.

• **Steam things up.** Take a hot shower or stay in the bathroom with the hot water running from the showerhead or tub or sink faucet. Steam or warm moisture is better than cold moisture because it loosens mucus, so using a cool-air humidifier, although helpful, is not ideal.

• **Ask your doctor about taking magnesium and vitamin C.** Taking 500 milligrams (mg) of magnesium and 1,000 mg of vitamin C during an asthma attack may help if you're an adult. (Children ages 10 to 17 should take half the doses and children between the ages of five and nine should take one-third of the doses.) Magnesium is a bronchodilator that relaxes the breathing tubes, and vitamin C has a slight antihistamine effect.

• **Take medications.** The prescription corticosteroid prednisone, available in pill form, is used only for acute problems, such as during an attack, because it helps reduce inflammation—so if your doctor has already prescribed it to you and you have it on hand, use it. "This medication will not work as quickly as an inhaler, but it may prevent the problem from getting out of hand if you're having a lengthy attack," said Dr. Firshein. Just call your doctor and let him or her know that you're taking it, so your doctor can supervise your dosing.

Surgical Cure for Severe Asthma

Sumita B. Khatri, MD, MS, codirector, Asthma Center, The Respiratory Institute, Cleveland Clinic Foundation, Cleveland, Ohio.

A relatively new surgical procedure may be life-changing—even potentially lifesaving—for people with chronic asthma who haven't been able to get relief from the standard treatments. Called bronchial thermoplasty, the procedure was approved by the

FDA in 2010 and is now available in several hospitals around the country. It is worth exploring as a treatment if you or someone you are close to is suffering recurrent asthma attacks that have not been helped by traditional treatments. Thus far, the evidence suggests that this procedure, the first nondrug treatment for asthma, dramatically reduces the occurrence of asthma attacks and improves asthma-related quality of life.

It's estimated that more than 23 million Americans (including seven million children) suffer from asthma, a chronic disease that inflames and narrows airways. Some individuals are born with a predisposition to asthma due to allergies or develop it from exposure to secondhand smoke, while in others the causes may be more unpredictable, such as viral illnesses.

In people with asthma, the layer of smooth muscle that surrounds the airways becomes thicker and more reactive to certain triggers, explained Sumita B. Khatri, MD, codirector of the Asthma Center at the Cleveland Clinic's Respiratory Institute. When a person with asthma has an attack, the muscles around the airways constrict and go into spasms, narrowing the airways and leading to shortness of breath, tightness in the chest and other distressing symptoms.

REDUCES SWELLING IN AIRWAYS

In contrast to asthma medications that target inflammation and may secondarily reduce some of the muscle thickening, bronchial thermoplasty treats the airways directly with heat created by radiofrequency waves.

The treatment is apparently quite effective. A randomized, double-blind controlled study of about 300 patients found that those who underwent bronchial thermoplasty experienced vastly improved asthma-related quality of life in the 12 months afterward, including...

- **32% reduction in asthma attacks, on average.**
- **84% drop in visits to hospital emergency rooms.**
- **66% reduction in lost work or school days.**
- **73% decline in hospitalizations for respiratory problems.**

Dr. Khatri said that two years after the first clinical trials, the improvements are still in place—including not only a reduction in symptoms overall but also in the frequency of severe asthma flare-ups and hospitalizations. Many patients also have reduced their need for rescue/emergency medications as well, she said.

TREATMENTS AREN'T PAINFUL

Bronchial thermoplasty takes place over three one-hour sessions scheduled three weeks apart. In each procedure, the patient receives light sedation—many actually fall asleep. Each of the three treatments targets a different area of the lungs—in the first session, the airways of the right lower lobe...in the second, the left lower lobe...and in the third, the airways in both upper lobes.

What's involved: The pulmonologist threads a long, flexible tube called a bronchoscope down the mouth or through the nose and into an airway in the lung. Inside the bronchoscope, a special thermoplasty catheter contains electrodes that are heated with radiofrequency energy. This shrinks the muscle, which is believed to prevent the extreme airway muscle contractions during asthma attacks. "This result is expected to be permanent, but there is still not enough data yet to know for sure," Dr. Khatri said.

There are no pain-sensing nerves in the airways, so the application of thermal energy does not hurt, notes Dr. Khatri. Patients are monitored for several hours afterward because symptoms sometimes worsen in the short term. To reduce the likelihood that this will happen, patients take a five-day course of steroids before and after surgery.

Though bronchial thermoplasty often is done as an outpatient procedure, Dr. Khatri said that the Cleveland Clinic keeps patients overnight as an added safety precaution. She added that in the immediate post-procedure period, some patients experience discomfort similar to an asthma flare-up, requiring use of rescue/symptom-relieving medications. Also, many patients have a sore throat from the bronchoscope, while other possible transitory side effects are chest discomfort or pain, partial lung collapse (serious but treatable), headaches, anxiety and nausea.

ARE YOU A CANDIDATE?

Bronchial thermoplasty is FDA-approved only for people age 18 and older with severe ongoing symptoms from asthma that are not well controlled with regular asthma medications. It can't be performed on smokers, people with active respiratory infections or people who have heart arrhythmias or have implanted pacemakers, defibrillators or other electronic devices.

Bronchial thermoplasty is expensive and since it is still considered experimental, Medicare doesn't cover it and neither do most insurers. However, Dr. Khatri expects this to change as time goes on and more and more patients experience significant health benefits after bronchial thermoplasty.

Visit the website *www.btforasthma.com* for more information and to locate a hospital that performs this procedure.

Surprising Condition That Chiropractors Can Treat

James N. Dillard, MD, DC, CAc, a pain and integrative medicine specialist in private practice in New York City and East Hampton, New York, *DrDillard.com*. Dr. Dillard is coauthor of *The Chronic Pain Solution*.

If you were asked to name a condition commonly treated by chiropractors, chances are neck and back pain would come to mind. But the list could be much longer.

Even though 11% of Americans seek the services of a chiropractor each year, most people are unaware that chiropractic care—a more than 100-year-old hands-on discipline that focuses primarily on manipulation of the spine—can be used to treat discomfort in many parts of the body, including muscles that are affected by asthma.*

The goal of treating people with asthma is to stimulate the rib cage muscles to ease breathing, optimize blood and lymph flow and enhance nervous system activity, all of which help reduce symptoms such as chest tightness and shortness of breath. In treating asthma, chiropractors typically use not only spinal manipulation but also other modalities such as stretching and/or trigger-point massage. Exercise, good eating habits and meditation also may be discussed. Additionally, chiropractic and acupuncture can be an effective combination for asthma.

Scientific evidence: A study in *The Journal of the Canadian Chiropractic Association*, which compiled data from eight scientific articles, showed improvements, based on pulmonary function tests, in 5,882 asthma patients who underwent chiropractic care.

To find a chiropractor near you: Consult the American Chiropractic Association, 703-276-8800, *www.acatoday.org*.

*Chiropractic care is safe for most people. However, people who have osteoporosis or take blood-thinning medications could be at increased risk for bone fractures and/or internal bleeding, while in extremely rare cases, those with a history of stroke may have an increased risk for a subsequent stroke. If you have these conditions or any other chronic health problem, consult your doctor before seeking chiropractic care.

Killing You While You Sleep

Chris Meletis, ND, former chief medical officer for the National College of Naturopathic Medicine and currently the executive director of the Institute for Healthy Aging and a physician on the staff of Beaverton Naturopathic Medicine in Oregon. He is author of 18 books on health and healing, including *The Hyaluronic Acid Miracle*. *DrMeletis.com*

Twenty-eight million Americans have sleep apnea, a sleep disorder in which breathing repeatedly stops and starts. More than 80% of these people don't know they have it. And every year, an estimated 38,000 Americans die in their sleep because sleep apnea has exacerbated a circulatory problem, causing a fatal heart attack or stroke.

Bottom line: Diagnosing and treating sleep apnea can save your life. And now there's an exciting new treatment that's available. *What you need to know...*

THE DANGER

For people with sleep apnea, nighttime levels of blood oxygen can plummet from an optimal saturation of 100% to below 65%. This oxygen-robbing disorder can contribute to extreme daytime sleepiness, as well as high blood pressure, heart attack, stroke, congestive heart failure, type 2 diabetes, Alzheimer's disease, erectile dysfunction, depression, anxiety and gastroesophageal reflux disease (GERD). In fact, if you have sleep apnea, you have a nearly five times higher risk of dying overall.

What happens: During sleep, the muscles at the back of the throat relax, which relaxes the soft palate and the uvula, a small, triangular piece of tissue hanging from the soft palate.

When you have obstructive sleep apnea, the most common kind, this tissue doesn't just relax, it sags, plugging the airway—and breathing stops. You may snort, grunt, gasp or cough as the body rouses itself—and breathing restarts. Then you fall back to sleep, never remembering that you woke up.

This mini-suffocation and awakening can occur over and over—from as few as five times an hour (the criteria for being diagnosed with "mild" sleep apnea) to dozens of times each hour.

Risk factors for obstructive sleep apnea include snoring (a sign of a thickened soft palate), being male, being 65 or older (for women, risk rises after menopause) and obesity. But some people with sleep apnea have none of those risk factors.

DO YOU HAVE IT?

Several daytime symptoms are possible signs of sleep apnea. You might wake up with a headache and a dry mouth. You could be intensely tired during the day—even falling asleep at a red light. You might be irritable and depressed and find it hard to think clearly.

If your doctor suspects sleep apnea, he may recommend a "sleep study" conducted in a sleep disorder center. This overnight test—polysomnography—monitors and measures breathing patterns, blood oxygen levels, arm and leg movement, and heart, lung and brain activity. *But there are several downsides to a study in a sleep center...*

It's expensive, costing $1,500 to $2,500—which could be out-of-pocket if your insurance has a high deductible.

It's inconvenient. You're spending the night in a strange place with a video camera focused on you and personnel walking in and out.

Instead, I often recommend a sleep study at home. Using a portable device, it provides the same information as a study at a center—for a fraction of the cost ($450 to $650). It is becoming the preferred method of testing for many doctors and often is covered by insurance. I prefer the home test by SleepQuest.

For more information: 800-813-8358, *www.sleepquest.com.*

EXCITING NEW TREATMENT

Up until now, the standard treatment for sleep apnea has been a continuous positive airway pressure (CPAP) machine. This device uses tubing and a mask worn over the nose... over the nose and mouth...or directly in the nose (via what is called a nasal pillow). The mask continuously pumps air into the airway, preventing the soft palate from sagging. But the mask often is uncomfortable. In one study, nearly half of people prescribed a CPAP device stopped using it within one to three weeks.

The exciting news is that there's a convenient treatment for sleep apnea called Provent. A small, disposable patch fits over each nostril. The treatment uses your own breathing to create expiratory positive airway pressure (EPAP)—just enough to keep the throat open.

Recent scientific evidence: In a three-month study involving 250 people with sleep apnea, 127 used Provent and 123 used a fake, look-alike device. The people using Provent had a 43% decrease in nighttime apnea events, compared with a 10% decrease for those in the fake group. Over three months, there was also a significant decrease in daytime sleepiness among Provent users.

A 30-day supply of the patches costs about $70. They are prescription-only and currently are not covered by insurance or Medicare.

My perspective: Provent is an excellent new option for many people with obstructive sleep apnea, but it is not for mouth breathers, people with nasal allergies or those with severe apnea.

Information: 888-757-9355, *www.proventtherapy.com.*

CUSTOMIZED MOUTH GUARD

If the nasal patch is not an option for you, a customized oral appliance may be best. It moves the lower jaw forward, opening the throat. It usually is covered by insurance, either partially or totally.

I was diagnosed with severe obstructive sleep apnea six years ago—and I've had very good results with a customized oral appliance. In a recent sleep test, I used CPAP half the night and my oral appliance the other half—my blood oxygen levels were higher while using the appliance.

Red flag: Over-the-counter oral appliances for snoring are available, but for optimal results, you need an oral appliance created for your mouth and jaw by a dentist trained to make such a device.

Important: No matter which device you use, you need to get tested first and then retested after you start using the device to make sure that you are getting the oxygen you need.

LIFESTYLE CHANGES

Self-care strategies...

• **Sleep on your side.** This helps keep airways open.

• **Lose weight,** because extra pounds mean extra tissue in the throat. Just a 10% weight loss can decrease apnea events by 26%. However, thin people and children can have apnea, too.

• **Don't drink alcohol within three hours of going to bed.** It relaxes the airway.

• **Sing some vowels.** In a study by UK researchers, three months of singing lessons helped decrease snoring, which could in turn decrease apnea.

What to do: Sing the long vowel sounds a-a-a-e-e-e, taking two or three seconds to sing each vowel. Do this once or twice every day for five minutes a session.

Oral Appliance for Sleep Apnea Is a Low-Tech Lifesaver

Ali El Solh, MD, MPH, professor of medicine, The State University of New York at Buffalo School of Medicine and Biomedical Sciences, and physician, Veteran's Administration Western New York Healthcare System, both in Buffalo, New York. His research was published in *Respirology*.

Sleep apnea can contribute to serious cardiovascular problems and other chronic ailments, doubling the risk for sudden cardiac death and tripling the risk of dying from any cause within a given time frame.

The gold-standard treatment is continuous positive airway pressure (CPAP), an electrical appliance attached to a mask worn over the nose and mouth while sleeping. It provides a constant flow of air that keeps the patient's airway open.

Problem: 46% to 83% of patients don't comply with treatment because they find CPAP too uncomfortable or noisy.

There's a low-tech treatment that many patients find more tolerable—a custom-made mandibular advancement device (MAD), which fits in the mouth and is worn overnight like an orthodontic dental retainer. It holds the lower jawbone forward to keep the throat's soft tissues from collapsing into the airway and blocking it. In past studies, MAD hasn't performed quite as well as CPAP on most measurements, so it's usually reserved for mild-to-moderate sleep apnea.

Good news: According to a recent study, even for patients with severe sleep apnea, MAD is comparable to CPAP on the most important benchmark—reducing cardiovascular mortality.

ORAL VS. ELECTRICAL APPLIANCE

The new study involved patients with severe sleep apnea who were prescribed CPAP. After three months, 57% of the participants were no longer complying with CPAP treatment. Most of this noncompliant group refused further treatment (and thus were designated the "untreated" group), but some opted to try MAD. The final analysis included four groups—177 patients using CPAP...72 using MAD...212 who were untreated...and 208 people without sleep apnea, who served as controls. Participants were followed for an average of 6.6 years. During this follow-up period, 42 of the 669 participants died from cardiovascular causes—stroke, heart attack, cardiac arrest or cardiac arrhythmia.

Results: Not surprisingly, the highest cardiovascular mortality rate was among the untreated apnea patients, with 2.1 deaths per 100 person-years (the number of years patients were followed multiplied by the number of people in the group)...and the lowest rate was among the healthy control group, with just 0.28 cardiovascular deaths per 100 person-years. What was surprising was how well the MAD group did—their cardiovascular death rate was 0.61 per 100 person-years... very nearly as low as the CPAP group's rate of 0.56 per 100 person-years.

The fact that MAD reduced cardiovascular mortality on par with CPAP was particularly interesting given that the oral appliance did not actually control sleep apnea as well as CPAP. Prior to treatment, patients experienced an average of about 44 episodes of interrupted breathing per hour. With MAD, the average number of such interruptions fell to 16.3 per hour...while with CPAP, the average number fell all the way to 4.5 per hour. Where the MAD patients had an advantage—one that probably contributed to their impressive reduction in mortality risk—was in the amount of time they were willing to wear their devices. On average, CPAP patients used their devices for 5.8 hours per night, while MAD patients wore their devices for 6.5 hours per night. The researchers suggested that the increased treatment time with MAD helped compensate for the fact that the dental appliance isn't quite as effective as CPAP in controlling apnea episodes.

Compliance reality check: Given that many people simply cannot or will not put up with CPAP—in which case it hardly matters how superior CPAP is, because no treatment will help you if you don't use it!—MAD offers a very attractive alternative. Research has shown that patients generally do prefer MAD over CPAP. In fact, in this study, only 6% of the MAD group gave up the treatment.

Caveat: Some patients using MAD experience jaw discomfort.

Bottom line: If you (or your bed partner) have sleep apnea and can't tolerate CPAP, speak with your doctor about being fitted for MAD. These types of dental appliances can be custom-made by dentists who specialize in sleep disorders...cost between $300 to $2,500...and usually are covered by medical insurance (not dental). To be eligible for MAD, patients generally must have a certain level of gum, jaw and tooth health—your dentist can check you out for that.

$50 Fix Reduces Sleep Apnea by 36%

Stefania Redolfi, MD, university researcher, Respiratory Medicine Department, University of Brescia, Italy.

Would you rather wear a strange-looking and uncomfortable mask while you sleep...or tight stockings during the day?

The obvious answer is "um, neither"...but it is entirely possible that people who have a certain type of chronic obstructive sleep apnea may be presented with exactly this choice, based on recent European research. A study published in the *American Thoracic Society's American Journal of Respiratory and Critical Care Medicine* reports that wearing compression stockings can reduce sleep apnea episodes significantly for one-third of the people whose apnea is caused by chronic venous insufficiency—a pretty dramatic difference for such an easy treatment. Since it was a small, brief and preliminary study focused on just this one cause of obstructive sleep apnea, it's entirely possible that longer treatment may yield even more impressive results that are helpful to even more patients.

OUT FROM BEHIND THE MASK

Continuous positive airway pressure (CPAP) masks are bulky and uncomfortable and force many wearers to sleep in positions they'd rather not sleep in. Many people who need them refuse to wear them. That's why the news that there is a safe, easy-to-use and inexpensive treatment option for a good portion of people with sleep apnea is quite welcome.

Stefania Redolfi, MD, of the University of Brescia in Italy, lead researcher of this practical and surprisingly promising study, explained that chronic venous insufficiency is a vascular problem in which veins (primarily in the legs) can't efficiently pump blood back to the heart. Fluid builds up in the legs during the day and then shifts at night to the neck, bloating tissue there. This causes the person to experience the partial collapse of the pharynx in between breaths during sleep—and so begins the loud, unpleasant "gasp and snore" pattern that characterizes obstructive sleep apnea in these patients.

What does wearing tight stockings during the day have to do with insufficient oxygen at night? It is actually quite ingenious. "Wearing compression stockings during the day helps to reduce the daytime fluid accumulation in the legs," Dr. Redolfi explained, "which in turn reduces the amount of fluid flowing into the neck at night." Absent the pressure created by that fluid, the respiratory system does not narrow as much and, for many people, this intervention is enough to allow them to get adequate oxygen into their lungs by breathing—and sleeping—normally. This is a wonderful thing, because sleep apnea and the constantly interrupted sleep that goes with it can severely undermine a person's health.

WHAT THE RIGHT SOCKS CAN DO

The study was small, involving 12 patients—half randomly assigned to wear compression stockings during the day (putting them on as soon as they awakened and taking them off only after getting into bed for the night) for a week, while the other half served as the control, with the two groups switching places after the first week. Subjects spent their nights at a sleep center, where their physiological signs (including brain waves, respiration and eye movements) were measured continuously. Researchers also measured each person's overnight changes in leg fluid volume and neck circumference at the start of the study and at the end of both the compression-stocking and control periods.

Dr. Redolfi said that the researchers expected the compression stockings would help—but they were somewhat surprised by the degree to which they helped! Wearing the stockings resulted in...

- An average of a 62% reduction in overnight leg fluid volume change, as compared with when subjects did not wear the stockings.
- A 60% reduction in neck circumference increase (used as a proxy measurement to estimate fluid shift into the neck).
- A 36% reduction in the number of apnea episodes.

EFFECTIVE AND INEXPENSIVE

This is a very basic intervention that has the potential to make a big difference for patients who are struggling with obstructive sleep apnea. The stockings cost less than $50 and, though they aren't exactly cute or comfortable, Dr. Redolfi said that all the study participants preferred them to the CPAP mask. As simple as it sounds, though, she said that people with sleep apnea shouldn't try this on their own—she said it is important to have a sleep study done to measure whether the stockings are making a difference and if so, how much. Talk to your doctor about this. Dr. Redolfi plans further research to ascertain whether wearing the stockings for longer than a week shows more significant results...to learn whether other measures, such as using diuretics or exercises to reduce fluid volume, are useful... and also to examine whether wearing compression stockings can help people with sleep apnea due to other causes, such as obesity.

Male Hot Flashes Can Indicate Sleep Apnea

Steven Y. Park, MD, sleep medicine physician in New York City and author of *Sleep, Interrupted.*

Can men get hot flashes? Yes. Aging men with declining hormone levels can experience the same symptoms as menopausal women—weight gain, lower sexual desire and hot flashes, which are called night sweats when they happen during sleep. Hot flashes are much less common in men than in women, though, since hormone levels usually decline more gradually in men.

An overlooked cause of hot flashes in both sexes is sleep apnea, a condition in which the airway partially collapses during sleep, causing breathing to pause. It can trigger heart palpitations, severe sweating and frequent awakenings.

Men (and their female partners) can get some relief by using cooling gel pillows (such as the Chillow) and avoiding any food, caffeine or alcohol within four hours of bedtime. Talk to your doctor about hormone replacement therapy for both sexes. Men experiencing hot flashes and night sweats should also see a sleep specialist, who can test for sleep apnea.

Alternative Treatments to CPAP for Sleep Apnea

People who have obstructive sleep apnea stop breathing for very short intervals during the night, disrupting sleep and increasing the risk for diabetes, heart attack and stroke. In addition to conventional treatments such as continuous positive airway pressure (CPAP) machines and oral mouthpieces that advance the jaw, newer treatments include Provent Sleep Apnea Therapy (*www.proventtherapy.com*), which is a small disposable patch that fits over each nostril. A central valve produces pressure in the airway so that it remains open during sleep. The Winx Sleep Therapy System (*www.Apnicure.com*) uses a soft mouthpiece that is connected to a small vacuum console. The device creates suction to open the throat.

David Rapoport, MD, professor of medicine and director of the Sleep Disorders Center, New York University Medical Center, New York City.

An Implantable Alternative to CPAP for Sleep Apnea

Study titled "Upper-Airway Stimulation for Obstructive Sleep Apnea," published in *The New England Journal of Medicine.*

If you or your bedmate suffers from obstructive sleep apnea and you're using a continuous positive airway pressure (CPAP) device, you know it works well, but you probably can't stand it. As much as you would like to fantasize that you are geared up for a scuba-diving adventure as you lapse off to dreamland with that mask and hose attached to your face, the CPAP contraption is uncomfortable, noisy and unattractive. You wonder whether the remedy is worse than the disease. In fact, maybe you have a CPAP machine that you simply no longer use. Even though obstructive sleep apnea is associated with cardiovascular disease, liver disease, fatigue and cognitive impairment, you've decided not to wear that thing.

Finally, there is an alternative to a CPAP machine.

BE THE BIONIC MAN, NOT JACQUES COUSTEAU

As you may know, in obstructive sleep apnea (OSA), breathing temporarily stops several times a night—even several times an hour. It happens because the throat muscles relax too much, allowing the soft palate, the uvula and tongue to sag and block airways. OSA episodes usually last 10 to 20 seconds, sometimes much longer, and this loss of breath can cause dangerous drops in blood oxygen levels. When your brain senses the blocked breathing, it's rigged to wake you up. So you'll find yourself waking with a snort, a gasp or a reflexive jerk to kick-start the breathing process again. And this is the cycle over and over again all night for people with OSA who don't get treatment or who get a CPAP device but don't wear it.

AN ALTERNATIVE FOR THE STUBBORN

Although CPAP has a near 100% rate of effectiveness in preventing OSA, it's not effective unless it is actually used, of course. "Nonadherence"—the medical term for flipping off doctors' orders—is high when it comes to CPAP use. Up to 83% of CPAP owners use the device less than four hours per night. That's nowhere near enough to be protected against OSA complications already mentioned—cardiovascular disease and liver dysfunction, daytime sleepiness and fatigue and problems with memory and concentration.

If you have OSA and you're having trouble sticking with CPAP, an alternative now is available called Inspire Upper Airway Stimulation. It's not as effective as CPAP but may be close enough and much easier to live with—and it's far better than nothing at all.

There is a drawback—the Inspire device requires a two-and-a-half-hour surgical procedure in which a small neurostimulator is implanted into a spot on your chest just below the collar bone. The device is then literally wired to your hypoglossal nerve and intercostal muscles. (The hypoglossal nerve runs along the jawline and controls the movement of the tongue, and the intercostals surround your ribs and control the movement of the chest wall.)

The device is calibrated, adjusted and controlled via telemetry, which means that you and your doctor communicate with it via radio waves. You also have to learn how to use a handheld controller to turn it on and off. (Yes, now you are part machine.) When the device senses a problem with your breathing, it stimulates the hypoglossal nerve and intercostal muscles to make your tongue and chest move to keep airways open.

A recent study of 126 patients with moderate-to-severe OSA who would not use CPAP showed that the Inspire device was effective in preventing OSA episodes. It reduced sleep apnea by 68%—from an average of 29 events per hour to nine events. In turn, it prevented dangerous dips in blood oxygen levels by 70%. The oxygen desaturation index (ODI), a measure of how often blood oxygen levels fall four or more points below normal, decreased from an average 25 episodes per hour to seven.

As for more on the surgical rigmarole, 95% of patients in the study went home the same day or the day after the procedure. Not bad. The device was activated a month after implantation, which was when patients were trained in how to use the controller.

Most adverse effects had to do with weakness or soreness of the tongue because of stimulation of the hypoglossal nerve or from rubbing continually over the lower teeth or else general discomfort from nerve stimulation, but these problems went away either after patients adjusted the device or simply got acclimated to it. Two patients experienced serious discomfort, which was remedied by adjusting the placement of the device, which required another surgical procedure.

IS IT RIGHT FOR YOU?

The Inspire device was recently approved by the FDA for people with moderate-to-severe OSA. The implantation procedure is performed by an otolaryngologist, who will also calibrate and adjust the device. Be forewarned that the doctor you consult—whether it be an otolaryngologist or respiratory or sleep specialist—will first either want you to try CPAP if you haven't already or else try to optimize your CPAP by seeing if you need a better-fitting or quieter model or more training in how to most effectively use your CPAP machine. That's because CPAP, as mentioned, is the most effective way to control OSA and is less expensive and less risky than surgery.

That said, if you are averse to dealing with CPAP but have the motivation to undergo a surgical procedure that will implant a device in your chest that you need to remember to turn on each night, and off each morning, Inspire may be right for you.

Deadly Link to "Mother's Little Helper"

Robert D. Sanders, PhD, is a senior clinical research associate in the Wellcome Department of Imaging Neuroscience at the Institute of Cognitive Science at University College London in the UK and coauthor of an article on benzodiazepines and pneumonia published in *Thorax*.

Doctors often prescribe such drugs as *lorazepam* (Ativan), *diazepam* (Valium) or *temazepam* (Restoril) to relieve insomnia, anxiety or muscle spasms. These medications do have their place, particularly when limited to the recommended short-term use of about two to four weeks. However, longer-term use raises grave concerns—not only because these drugs are addictive but also because they increase the risk for potentially deadly pneumonia. The danger is widespread, considering that in the US, 2% of the population and up to 10% of elderly patients have taken benzodiazepines for 12 months or more.

Earlier research demonstrated an association between benzodiazepine use and an increased risk for infection and death among critically ill patients. So researchers in the UK set out to discover whether risks also applied to people who were not critically ill. They analyzed health records of nearly 5,000 patients of all ages who were diagnosed with pneumonia during a one-year period. Then they compared each pneumonia patient with six similar people, matched by age and sex, who had not had pneumonia during the study period (so overall, the study was based on data from almost 35,000 people).

What they found: Benzodiazepine use was associated with a 54% increased risk for pneumonia...a 22% increased risk of dying within 30 days of the pneumonia diagnosis...and a 32% increased risk of dying within three years. The results held even after researchers adjusted for patients' history of respiratory problems, heart attack, depression, smoking, age and other risk factors.

Worrisome: Most of the participants who had used benzodiazepines had done so chronically, meaning for at least three months.

Researchers suggested that the increased risks may be due to the drugs' effects on the immune system. Of course, the study does not prove that chronic benzodiazepine use causes pneumonia, simply that there is an association. Even so, the findings deserve to be taken quite seriously.

Self-defense: If you have been taking a benzodiazepine for more than a few weeks, do not stop taking it on your own—this could cause withdrawal symptoms (dizziness, headache, numbness, tremors, hallucinations) and/or sudden worsening of the condition being treated. Instead, contact your doctor without delay to discuss alternative treatment options and determine the safest way to be weaned off the sedative.

15

Stroke

How to Survive a Stroke

Stroke is the fifth-leading cause of death (according to the Centers for Disease Control and Prevention) in the US and second only to Alzheimer's disease as the most common cause of disabling neurological damage.

What to do if it happens to you...

CALL 911—NOT YOUR DOCTOR

The majority of strokes, known as ischemic strokes, are caused by a clot in a blood vessel in the brain. The main treatment is tissue plasminogen activator (tPA), a clot-dissolving drug. It must be given intravenously within three hours (preferably, within 90 minutes) of a stroke to help prevent permanent brain damage that can result in such problems as difficulty moving an arm or leg and trouble speaking or understanding spoken or written words.

Recent research: In two different studies, researchers found that patients with stroke symptoms who call their doctors instead of dialing 911 risk dangerous delays in treatment.

Take-home message: Symptoms of stroke are always an emergency. Patients who receive tPA within three hours of a stroke are 11% to 13% more likely to survive, and experience fewer complications, than those who delay treatment.

OVERLOOKED SYMPTOMS

People who experience certain common stroke symptoms, such as sudden confusion or weakness, are more likely to call 911 than those who suffer sudden numbness or visual disturbances—stroke symptoms that are less well-known.

New study: Researchers looked at data from 2,056 patients who had suffered a stroke or a transient ischemic attack ("mini-stroke"). People who had a "dramatic" symptom, such as falling to the ground, were far more likely to get emergency help than those who suffered

Philip B. Gorelick, MD, MPH, the John S. Garvin Professor and director of the Center for Stroke Research in the department of neurology and rehabilitation at the University of Illinois College of Medicine in Chicago.

numbness, visual disturbances or other "mild" symptoms.

Take-home message: Many Americans still aren't familiar with the full range of stroke symptoms. Someone who suddenly falls to the ground knows that something is wrong...and bystanders will be quick to call 911. A symptom such as numbness or a visual disturbance is more subjective and easier to miss—or to ignore.

Self-defense: If you experience any stroke symptoms, including unexplained numbness or visual disturbances, call 911.

MIDDLE-AGED WOMEN AT RISK

Men, on average, have a greater risk for stroke than women, but the risk is approximately the same five to 10 years after a woman undergoes menopause—perhaps due to physiological changes that occur when estrogen levels decline. Recently, however, stroke risk has tripled among younger women.

New study: Data collected between 1999 and 2004 found that nearly 2% of American middle-aged women (ages 45 to 64) had suffered a stroke, compared with only about 0.5% between 1988 and 1994. The stroke rate among middle-aged men (approximately 1%) has stayed about the same.

What accounts for the increased risk? Abdominal fat, researchers theorize. The average woman's waistline increased by nearly two inches in the decade between the surveys, while the average body mass index (BMI)—a weight-to-height ratio widely used to determine healthy body weight—increased from 27 to 29, probably due to higher calorie consumption and less exercise.

Take-home message: Abdominal obesity is an emerging risk factor for stroke. Reasons: Belly fat secretes inflammatory substances that have been linked to cardiovascular disease, including stroke. Also, women with abdominal obesity are more likely to have other stroke risk factors, such as high blood pressure and diabetes.

Today, middle-aged women may have a greater stroke risk than middle-aged men. Abdominal obesity may be largely to blame.

Self-defense: Maintain a healthy weight. For women and men, this means a BMI of less than 25. To check your BMI, go to the National Heart, Lung and Blood Institute website (*www.nhlbi.nih.gov/health/educational/lose_wt/BMI/bmicalc.htm*). Also, a woman should not allow her waist size to exceed 35 inches... for a man, it's 40 inches.

DANGER OF DAYTIME DOZING

Short naps (30 minutes or less) during the day improve energy and alertness, and might even be good for the heart by reducing blood pressure and overall stress. Unintentionally falling asleep (dozing), on the other hand, has been linked to an increased risk for stroke.

New study: Researchers followed 2,153 men and women for an average of 2.3 years. Those who reported "some" dozing were 2.6 times more likely to have a stroke than those who didn't doze.

Take-home message: People who fall asleep without meaning to may be suffering from sleep apnea, a condition in which breathing intermittently stops and starts during sleep. Sleep apnea has been linked to stroke risk factors, including high blood pressure and an increased tendency of blood to clot.

Self-defense: Anyone who regularly dozes off should ask his/her doctor about undergoing sleep testing to detect apnea or other sleep-related breathing disorders.

MODERATE EXERCISE IS ENOUGH

It's no surprise that people who engage in strenuous aerobic workouts have a lower risk for stroke than those who are sedentary. Now, research suggests that less-intense exercise provides similar benefits.

New study: When researchers looked at data from more than 60,000 people, the risk for stroke in those at moderate levels of cardiorespiratory fitness was nearly the same as in those who exercised more intensely. Such moderate fitness could be achieved by, say, engaging in brisk walking for at least 30 minutes, five days per week.

Take-home message: When it comes to exercise, you don't need to adhere to the cliché of "No pain, no gain" to reduce your stroke risk.

Self-defense: Engaging in nothing more vigorous than brisk walking most days of the week can substantially lower stroke risk.

Stroke Symptoms May Pass Quickly...Don't Ignore!

Get emergency help if you have stroke symptoms—even if they last only a few minutes. If symptoms pass quickly, don't conclude "it was nothing" and forget it.

Danger: "Mini-strokes," or transient ischemic attacks, that pass quickly often are precursors to imminent serious strokes. If the risk is recognized, medication may prevent a serious stroke later on—but if ignored, the worst is more likely to happen.

Symptoms: Sudden numbness or weakness in the face, one arm or one leg...sudden mental confusion or trouble speaking...sudden dizziness, trouble walking or coordination problems...sudden severe headache with no apparent cause.

Keith A. Siller, MD, medical director, Comprehensive Stroke Care Center, New York University Medical Center, New York City.

Prevent a Stroke: Be Vigilant About These Risk Factors

Louis R. Caplan, MD, senior neurologist at Beth Israel Deaconess Medical Center and a professor of neurology at Harvard Medical School, both in Boston. He has written or edited more than 40 books, including *Stroke (What Do I Do Now?)* and most recently *Navigating the Complexities of Stroke.*

What if there were more to preventing a stroke than keeping your blood pressure under control...getting regular exercise...watching your body weight...and not smoking? Researchers are now discovering that there is.

New thinking: While most stroke sufferers say that "it just came out of the blue," an increasing body of evidence shows that these potentially devastating "brain attacks" can be caused by conditions that you might ordinarily think are completely unrelated.

Once you're aware of these "hidden" risk factors—and take the necessary steps to prevent or control them—you can improve your odds of never having a stroke. *Recently discovered stroke risk factors...*

INFLAMMATORY BOWEL DISEASE

Both Crohn's disease and ulcerative colitis can severely damage the large or small intestine. But that is not the only risk. Among patients who have either one of these conditions, known as inflammatory bowel disease (IBD), stroke is the third most common cause of death, according to some estimates.

During flare-ups, patients with IBD have elevated blood levels of substances that trigger clots—the cause of most strokes. A Harvard study, for example, found that many IBD patients have high levels of C-reactive protein (CRP), an inflammatory marker that has been linked to atherosclerotic lesions, damaged areas in blood vessels that can lead to stroke-causing clots in the brain.

If you have IBD: Ask your doctor what you can do to reduce your risk for blood clots and inflammation. Some patients with IBD can't take aspirin or other anticlotting drugs because these medications frequently cause intestinal bleeding. Instead of aspirin, you might be advised to take an autoimmune medication such as *azathioprine* (Azasan, Imuran), which suppresses the immune system and reduces inflammation. During flare-ups, some patients are given steroids to further reduce inflammation.

Side effects, including nausea and vomiting with azathioprine use and weight gain and increased blood pressure with steroid use, usually can be minimized by taking the lowest possible dose.

Some physicians recommend omega-3 fish oil supplements for IBD, which are less likely to cause side effects. Ask your doctor whether these supplements (and what dose) are right for you.

Important: Strokes tend to occur in IBD patients when inflammation is most severe. To check inflammatory markers, CRP levels and erythrocyte sedimentation rate (ESR) can be measured. Tests for clotting include fibrinogen and d-dimer. The results of these tests will help determine the course of the patient's IBD treatment.

MIGRAINES

Migraine headaches accompanied by auras (characterized by the appearance of flashing lights or other visual disturbances) are actually a greater risk factor for stroke than obesity, smoking or diabetes (see below), according to a startling study presented at the American Academy of Neurology's annual meeting earlier this year.

When researchers use MRIs to examine blood vessels in the brain, they find more tiny areas of arterial damage in patients who have migraines with auras than in those who don't get migraines. (Research shows that there is no link between stroke and migraines that aren't accompanied by auras.)

If you have migraines with auras: Reduce your risk by controlling other stroke risk factors—don't smoke...lose weight if you're overweight...and control cholesterol levels.

Also: Women under age 50 who have migraines (with or without auras) may be advised to not use combined-hormone forms of birth control pills—they slightly increase risk for stroke. In addition, patients who have migraines with auras should not take beta-blockers, such as *propranolol* (Inderal), or the triptan drugs, such as *sumatriptan* (Imitrex), commonly used for migraine headaches. These drugs can also increase stroke risk. For frequent migraines with auras, I often prescribe the blood pressure drug *verapamil* (Calan) and a daily 325-mg aspirin. Ask your doctor for advice.

RHEUMATOID ARTHRITIS

Rheumatoid arthritis, unlike the common "wear-and-tear" variety (osteoarthritis), is an autoimmune disease that not only causes inflammation in the joints but may also trigger it in the heart, blood vessels and other parts of the body.

Arterial inflammation increases the risk for blood clots, heart attack and stroke. In fact, patients with severe rheumatoid arthritis were almost twice as likely to have a stroke as those without the disease, according to a study published in *Arthritis Care & Research*.

If you have rheumatoid arthritis: Work with your rheumatologist to manage flare-ups and reduce systemic inflammation. Your doctor will probably recommend that you take one or more anti-inflammatory painkillers, such as *ibuprofen* (Motrin). In addition, he/she might prescribe a disease-modifying antirheumatic drug (DMARD), such as *methotrexate* (Trexall), to slow the progression of the disease—and the increased risk for stroke. Fish oil also may be prescribed to reduce joint tenderness.

Strokes tend to occur in rheumatoid arthritis patients when inflammation is peaking. Ask your doctor if you should have the inflammation tests (CRP and ESR) mentioned in the IBD section.

DIABETES

If you have diabetes or diabetes risk factors—such as obesity, a sedentary lifestyle or a family history of diabetes—protect yourself. People with diabetes are up to four times more likely to have a stroke than those without it.

High blood sugar in people with diabetes damages blood vessels throughout the body, including in the brain. The damage can lead to both ischemic (clot-related) and hemorrhagic (bleeding) strokes.

If you have diabetes: Work closely with your doctor. Patients who achieve good glucose control with oral medications and/or insulin are much less likely to suffer from vascular damage.

Also important: Lose weight if you need to. Weight loss combined with exercise helps your body metabolize blood sugar more efficiently. In those with mild diabetes, weight loss combined with exercise may restore normal blood sugar levels...and can reduce complications and the need for medications in those with more serious diabetes.

CLOTTING DISORDERS

Any condition that affects the blood's normal clotting functions can increase risk for stroke.

Examples: Thrombocytosis (excessive platelets in the blood)...an elevated hematocrit (higher-than-normal percentage of red blood cells)...or Factor V Leiden (an inherited tendency to form blood clots). Clotting tests (fibrinogen and d-dimer) are recommended for these disorders.

If you have a clotting disorder: Ask your doctor what you can do to protect yourself from stroke. Example: If you have an elevated hematocrit, your doctor might advise you to drink more fluids.

This is particularly important for older adults, who tend to drink less later in the day because they don't want to get up at night to urinate. I recommend that these patients drink approximately 80 ounces of noncaffeine-containing fluids during the day, stopping by 7 pm. People who don't take in enough fluids can develop "thick" blood that impedes circulation—and increases the risk for clots.

Never Have a Stroke

Lori Mosca, MD, PhD, MPH, director of the New York–Presbyterian Hospital Preventive Cardiology Program in New York City, *HeartHealthTimes.com*. She is professor of medicine at Columbia University Medical Center, past-chair of the American Heart Association Council on Epidemiology, and author of *Heart to Heart: A Personal Plan for Creating a Heart-Healthy Family*.

For women, stroke prevention is even more important than it is for men. There are steps you can take now to reduce your risk.

Reasons: Between the ages of 45 and 54, women are more than twice as likely as men to have a stroke, according to a new study from the University of California, Los Angeles. Even when treated with state-of-the-art medication, women of all ages are at greater risk than men for suffering serious disability after a stroke. And regardless of age, female stroke patients are more likely to die than male stroke patients are. *What you need to know...*

STROKE PREVENTION STRATEGIES

A stroke is a "brain attack" that occurs when a blood vessel that carries oxygen and nutrients to the brain gets blocked by a clot (an ischemic stroke) or leaks or bursts (a hemorrhagic stroke). Either way, cells in the affected area of the brain are starved of oxygen. This can impair a person's ability to function, often irreparably.

Risk factors for stroke build up over years, even decades. *To slash your stroke risk...*

1. Know your numbers. Get a checkup that includes tests for the risk factors below. *Discuss with your doctor how your results compare with these ideal measurements...*

- Blood pressure—less than 130/80.
- Total cholesterol—less than 200.
- LDL (bad) cholesterol—no more than 100 for most women.
- HDL (good) cholesterol—greater than 50.
- Triglycerides (blood fats)—less than 150.
- Fasting blood glucose (sugar)—less than 100.
- Body mass index (a ratio of height to weight)—18.5 to 24.9, with higher numbers indicating excessive weight. Calculate your body mass index at *www.nhlbi.nih.gov/health/educational/lose_wt/BMI/bmicalc.htm*.
- Waist circumference—35 inches or less.

2. Determine your risk level based on new American Heart Association (AHA) guidelines. This will help you and your doctor develop a personalized prevention program.

- You're at high risk if you've already had a stroke...or have diabetes or coronary heart disease.
- You're at risk if you smoke...have high blood pressure...or have a condition called metabolic syndrome, characterized by symptoms such as a thick waist, higher-than-normal blood glucose, high triglycerides and low HDL cholesterol.
- Your risk factor level is optimal if you eat a heart-healthy diet...exercise regularly...and have none of the risk factors listed above.

For more risk-assessment tools, visit *www.hearthealthtimes.com*, the website for the

New York–Presbyterian Hospital Preventive Cardiology Program.

3. Exercise every day at moderate intensity. Being active helps lower blood pressure and keeps your weight in check.

Concern: Being overweight by as little as 10 pounds boosts stroke risk. To lose weight, you should log 60 to 90 minutes of exercise daily. Consistency is important because it keeps blood vessels healthy and metabolism functioning optimally.

4. Eat to beat stroke. Build your diet mostly on fruits, vegetables and whole grains. Eat fish twice a week, preferably fatty kinds, such as herring. Limit sodium to less than 2,300 mg a day by reducing salt added to foods and avoiding high-sodium prepared foods (check nutrition labels). Avoid trans fats, such as partially hydrogenated vegetable oils and shortening. Keep saturated fat low—less than 7% of total calories if possible—by limiting meats and nonskim dairy foods. Consume no more than 300 mg daily of dietary cholesterol. Limit alcohol to one drink daily. Avoid fried foods. Opt for baked, boiled, broiled, steamed or sautéed foods.

5. Make informed decisions about medications that affect hormones. Taking estrogen for menopausal symptoms or a selective estrogen receptor modulator (SERM), such as tamoxifen, for breast cancer treatment may raise stroke risk. The longer you take such medications, the greater your risk.

6. Consider aspirin. For women age 65 and over, taking aspirin daily (typically 75 mg to 162 mg) may prevent the blood clots that cause the most common type of stroke and may protect against heart disease. Aspirin therapy also may make sense for women under age 65 who are at high risk for stroke.

Do not take aspirin without first discussing it with your doctor. Aspirin therapy can increase your risk for stroke if you have uncontrolled high blood pressure. It also can cause gastrointestinal bleeding. That's why women under age 65 who are not at high risk for stroke generally are advised against taking daily aspirin—the risks may outweigh the benefits.

7. Stop smoking. Smoking increases blood pressure and blood clotting, both of which can set the stage for stroke. Women who smoke and take oral contraceptives are at even greater risk for stroke. Studies show that the more individual, group or telephone smoking-cessation counseling you get, the better your chances of quitting.

Helpful: Use medication, such as nicotine replacement, to reduce cravings.

8. Don't ignore troubling symptoms, such as heart palpitations. A common risk factor for stroke is atrial fibrillation (AF)—an irregular, rapid heart rhythm that causes abnormal blood flow and increases the likelihood of a clot. AF increases a woman's stroke risk fivefold. Other AF symptoms include light-headedness, weakness, confusion and/or difficulty breathing. If you have symptoms of AF, see your doctor—blood-thinning drugs, such as aspirin or *warfarin* (Coumadin), can lower your risk for clots and stroke.

9. Talk to your doctor about other medications that reduce risk factors. If efforts to improve your lifestyle habits aren't enough to reduce your risk, talk to your doctor about adding drug therapy. For instance, thiazide diuretics and other prescription drugs can help control blood pressure...niacin or fibrate medication can increase HDL (good) cholesterol.

More from Dr. Lori Mosca...

One Word That Can Save a Life—FAST

Stroke is a medical emergency that requires immediate care. Brain cells starved of oxygen die and do not regenerate. *To remember the sudden symptoms of stroke, think of the word "FAST"...*

- **Face.** Sudden numbness or weakness of the face, especially on one side...severe headache...dizziness...vision trouble.
- **Arm and leg.** Sudden numbness or weakness of the arm and/or leg, especially on one side...trouble walking...loss of coordination.
- **Speech.** Sudden confusion and trouble speaking or understanding speech.

- **Time.** Time is critical—if you think you or someone else is having a stroke, call 911.

Better Stroke Prevention

In a study of 451 patients at high risk for stroke, those who took medication to lower cholesterol, blood pressure and clotting were 9% less likely to have a stroke within three years than those who took the same drugs and had stent surgery in the brain to open narrowed arteries.

Possible reason: Complications from surgery in small brain arteries can lead to stroke.

Colin Derdeyn, MD, director, Center for Stroke and Cerebrovascular Disease, Washington University School of Medicine, St. Louis, Missouri.

Drug-Free Stroke Fighter: Red Peppers

Eating red peppers and other vitamin C–rich fruits and veggies may reduce your risk for intracerebral hemorrhagic stroke (a blood vessel rupture in the brain). And what's so great about red peppers? At 190 mg per cup, they contain three times more vitamin C than an orange. Other good sources of vitamin C—broccoli and strawberries. Researchers believe that this vitamin may reduce stroke risk by regulating blood pressure and strengthening collagen, which promotes healthy blood vessels.

Stéphane Vannier, MD, neurologist, Pontchaillou University Hospital, Rennes, France, from research being presented at the annual meeting of the American Academy of Neurology.

Do You Get Enough of the Anti-Stroke Mineral?

Susanna Larsson, PhD, is an associate professor at the Institute of Environmental Medicine at the Karolinska Institutet in Stockholm, Sweden, and lead author of a study on dietary magnesium.

Our moms always told us to eat our greens and beans...and now a new study reveals yet another important reason why these wise women were right. People who consume plenty of foods rich in magnesium—such as leafy green veggies and legumes—appear to have fewer strokes.

Researchers analyzed data from seven studies involving a total of 241,378 people from the US, Europe and Asia who were followed for an average of nearly 12 years.

What they found: For every additional 100 mg of magnesium consumed daily, a person's risk for ischemic stroke (the most common type, which is caused by a blood clot) was reduced by 9%.

Concern: Study participants from the US fell far short of the ideal, consuming foods that provided, on average, just 242 mg of magnesium per day—though the RDA is 320 mg for most adult women and 420 for most adult men.

Because this study focused specifically on food, researchers did not make a recommendation regarding the use of magnesium supplementation. However, it is easy to boost your intake of the brain-protecting mineral with food. *For instance, you can get about 100 mg of magnesium each from...*

- **Beans** (black, lima, navy, white), 1 cup.
- **Beet greens,** 1 cup cooked.
- **Bran cereal,** ½ cup.
- **Brazil nuts,** 1 ounce.
- **Cashews,** 1¼ ounces.
- **Halibut,** 3 ounces.
- **Lentils,** 1¼ cups.
- **Okra,** 1 cup cooked.
- **Spinach,** ⅔ cup cooked.

Drink Tea to Guard Against Stroke

Do you love a cozy cup of tea? If not, there is a good reason to develop a taste for it.

Researchers from the University of California, Los Angeles, analyzed data from nine studies involving a total of nearly 195,000 people.

Findings: Compared with people who drank less than one cup of tea daily, those who drank at least three cups daily of green or black tea (both of which come from the Camillia sinensis plant) had a 21% lower risk for stroke...risk dropped 42% for those who drank six or more cups of green or black tea daily. It is the flavonoid epigallocatechin gallate and the amino acid theanine, both of which are found in green and black teas, that might reduce stroke risk, researchers say.

Note: Though not included in the study, oolong tea and white tea (but not herbal teas) also come from the Camillia sinensis plant and therefore may have similar stroke-preventing benefits. There was not enough data on decaffeinated tea to include it in the study.

Lenore Arab, PhD, is a professor of medicine at the David Geffen School of Medicine at the University of California, Los Angeles, and lead author of a review of studies published in *Stroke*.

Vitamin E and Stroke Risk

Mark A. Stengler, NMD, naturopathic medical doctor in private practice, Encinitas, California...adjunct associate clinical professor at the National College of Natural Medicine, Portland, Oregon...the author of many books, including *The Natural Physician's Healing Therapies* and coauthor of *Prescription for Natural Cures*.

Many of my patients have asked me whether they should continue to take vitamin E after hearing media reports that vitamin E increases stroke risk. You might have the same question.

So to set the record straight, vitamin E protects against the most common type of stroke, ischemic stroke (which is caused by an obstruction in a blood vessel in the brain). There is little controversy about this—and the study published in *BMJ* (*British Medical Journal*) that sparked the concern about vitamin E confirmed the validity of this even though the media didn't highlight this finding. The researchers found that people who took vitamin E supplements had a 10% lower risk for ischemic stroke than those not taking vitamin E.

The finding that the media chose to focus on from the *BMJ* study and that caused all the controversy was this—in an analysis of nine previously published studies, people taking vitamin E had a 22% greater risk for a different type of stroke, hemorrhagic stroke (caused when a weakened blood vessel in the brain ruptures) than those not taking vitamin E. This finding shouldn't be ignored, but it would have been more responsible reporting to also remind the public that vitamin E protected against the most common type of stroke.

In addition to my objections to the way this study was reported, I have concerns about the analysis itself. There were a number of variables in the nine studies analyzed, including a wide range of vitamin E doses...the type of supplement taken (natural and synthetic)... and varying ages and health of the study participants. I don't think anyone can draw conclusions from all this disparate information.

My view: Most people are far more likely to suffer an ischemic stroke than a hemorrhagic stroke. Since vitamin E supplements will help reduce your risk for this most common type of stroke, the benefit-to-risk ratio of taking a vitamin E supplement is in most people's favor. That's why I'm still taking my vitamin E—and recommending it to my patients. My preference is a vitamin E brand that contains both tocopherols and tocotrienols. A good dose to maintain health is 400 international units (IU) daily. If you are taking blood-thinning medication, consult with a doctor before taking vitamin E because it has a blood-thinning effect. To decrease your risk for any type of stroke, maintain a healthy blood pressure and practice good diet and exercise habits.

Avoid a Stroke by Avoiding Shingles

Maria A. Nagel, MD, department of neurology, University of Colorado School of Medicine, Aurora. Her expert commentary and the study on shingles and stroke appeared in *Current Neurology and Neuroscience Reports*. The study, titled "Risk of Stroke Following Herpes Zoster: A Self-Controlled Case-Series Study," by researchers on the faculty of epidemiology and population health at the London School of Hygiene and Tropical Medicine, United Kingdom, was published in *Clinical Infectious Diseases*.

The chronic pain and unsightly rash of shingles is bad enough, but now there's increasing evidence that you're at much higher risk for stroke in the first few weeks following the onset of a shingles attack. Protect yourself by knowing which shingles symptom is most associated with stroke and how you can lower your risk of shingles and shingles-related stroke.

Shingles, also known as herpes zoster, is caused by varicella zoster virus (VZV)—the same virus that causes chicken pox. Decades after infection, when a person's immune system is weakened by age, disease or medications, the virus can reactivate. Shingles' main symptoms are shooting pain, burning, numbness, itchiness and a rash and blisters on one side of the body, which usually last about two weeks but can become chronic.

Shingles usually affects the skin, but the virus can also affect blood vessels, the brain, eyes and spinal cord, leading to inflammation of the brain (encephalitis), inflammation of the membranes around the spinal cord and brain (meningitis), blindness or stroke. The new study examined more than 6,500 patients and showed that the risk of stroke increased by 63% during the first month following the first symptoms of shingles. The increased risk gradually lessened—to 42% during the second and third months and to 23% during months four through six.

One specific form of shingles greatly increased stroke risk. Herpes zoster ophthalmicus (HZO)—where the shingles rash occurs around one or both eyes—turned out to be a telltale risk factor for stroke in the study. Patients with HZO had a greater than threefold increased risk of stroke. That's because HZO is a sign that the herpes virus has reactivated from a cluster of neurons in the head called the trigeminal ganglia. "When the virus reactivates here, it not only travels along nerve fibers that go straight to the area around the eye, but also has potential to travel along nerve fibers directly to blood vessels in the brain," explained Maria Nagel, MD, a specialist in viral infections of the nervous system who provided expert commentary that accompanied the study.

BEST DEFENSE AGAINST SHINGLES

Getting the shingles vaccine (Zostavax) is no guarantee that you won't get shingles, but it does cut your risk in half. The US Centers for Disease Control and Prevention recommends the vaccine for adults 60 years of age and older, but it is FDA-approved for anyone over 50.

The vaccine is not recommended for every older adult. *Avoid it if you...*

- **Are allergic to gelatin,** the antibiotic neomycin or any other component of the vaccine.
- **Have a weakened immune system,** either due to a medical condition such as diabetes, kidney failure, sickle-cell anemia, cirrhosis or HIV infection...because you are receiving treatments that modify or suppress your immune system such as chemotherapy or radiation or are on immunosuppressive therapies for an autoimmune disease such as rheumatoid arthritis, multiple sclerosis and Crohn's disease...or take certain medications including corticosteroids, *infliximab* (Remicade), *adalimumab* (Humira) and *etanercept* (Enbrel).

BEST DEFENSE IF YOU GET SHINGLES

If you do get shingles, even after vaccination, take action. Antiviral therapy such as *acyclovir* (Zovirax), *valacyclovir* (Valtrex) or *famciclovir* (Famvir) not only relieves symptoms, but can lower your risk of stroke. In the study on stroke and shingles, patients who were treated with antiviral therapy for shingles were still at increased stroke risk but at a much lower rate—28%—than patients who did not receive antiviral therapy.

"I treat all my shingles patients with a full two-week course of antiviral therapy, taking into consideration their kidney function and any medical conditions that need to be monitored while on antiviral therapy," said Dr. Nagel. "The rash usually resolves within two weeks or less if antivirals are used, but pain can persist for up to three months."

If you haven't already been vaccinated for shingles, this study is a good reason to stop procrastinating. If shingles does happen to erupt, discuss antiviral therapy with your doctor instead of just toughing it out—especially if you develop a rash around your eyes. Also, be on the lookout for strokelike symptoms, such as drooping or numbness on one side of the face, weakness or numbness in an arm or leg, slurred speech or sudden loss of vision or dimness of vision, in the first few months after a shingles outbreak. If these occur, seek urgent medical care and be sure to let your doctor know about your recent history of shingles.

Better Stroke Prevention

Fewer than one in three stroke survivors are able to consistently control their blood pressure. But those who can keep blood pressure below 140/90 mmHg most of the time reduced their risk for a second stroke by 54%, according to a recent study of 3,680 stroke survivors.

Best practices: Check blood pressure twice a day at home and share logs of your readings with your doctor. Also, lower your salt intake... eat a healthful diet...exercise regularly...and be sure to take all prescribed medication.

Amytis Towfighi, MD, assistant professor of neurology, Keck School of Medicine, University of Southern California, Los Angeles.

Catching a Stroke Before It Starts

Fiona Webster, PhD, is an education scientist and assistant professor in the department of family and community medicine at the University of Toronto in Ontario and lead author of a study on stroke prevention clinics published in *Stroke*.

When you think of saving lives that would otherwise be lost to stroke, you probably imagine frightened but clear-thinking family members calling 911 or efficient ER doctors administering crucial medication just in the nick of time. Those things matter, of course—but a lifesaving approach that often is overlooked is the stroke prevention clinic.

Researchers recently compared the medical records of 16,468 patients who had experienced either an ischemic stroke (caused when a clot blocks blood flow to the brain) or a transient ischemic attack (TIA), often called a "mini-stroke." TIAs produce symptoms that are similar to stroke—sudden weakness or numbness on one side of the body, slurred speech, dizziness, vision problems—but usually last a much shorter time and often cause no permanent damage. However, the risk of having a full-blown and potentially fatal stroke within three months after a TIA is as high as 20%.

Study findings: TIA and ischemic stroke patients who were referred to stroke prevention clinics that aimed to identify and address risk factors were 26% less likely to die of stroke in the following 12 months than patients who did not attend such programs. These findings underscore the importance of secondary prevention for at-risk patients, researchers said.

Why it works: Many factors that place a person at increased risk for stroke are modifiable. When a patient learns which particular risk factors are putting her in danger and takes steps to control those, her risk is significantly reduced. A stroke prevention clinic is an outpatient program staffed by medical professionals trained to assess, diagnose and treat stroke risk factors. *The treatment dura-*

tion and exact services provided vary, but typically patients...

• **Have their blood monitored** to measure how well any medications they take are working to control clotting, modulate blood pressure and/or regulate cholesterol.

• **Receive support to exercise more,** lose weight, reduce stress and/or quit smoking, as needed.

• **Are assessed and treated as necessary for heart conditions,** sleep apnea and other chronic conditions that contribute to stroke risk.

Not all hospitals have stroke prevention clinics—and not all doctors refer their TIA or stroke patients to such programs. If you have had a TIA or stroke, talk to your doctor about whether a stroke prevention clinic could benefit you...and ask your insurer whether your policy covers the cost.

New Life After Stroke

Joel Stein, MD, chief medical officer at the Spaulding Rehabilitation Hospital and an associate professor in the department of physical medicine and rehabilitation at Harvard Medical School, both in Boston. Dr. Stein is coauthor of *Life After Stroke* and the author of *Stroke and the Family*.

Until recently, if you lost the use of an arm or leg due to a stroke, doctors assumed that the disability was permanent.

Now: Sophisticated imaging tests have shown that the brain can "rewire" itself and compensate for some of the brain damage caused by a stroke (often resulting in paralysis or problems controlling movement of a limb).

This exciting, new understanding of brain physiology means that the estimated 700,000 Americans who suffer a stroke each year will now have a much better chance of regaining their independence.

Joel Stein, MD, a renowned expert in the field and chief medical officer at one of the country's leading rehabilitation centers, discusses the latest advances in stroke rehabilitation...

A "BRAIN ATTACK"

Our body movements are controlled by brain cells called neurons. During a stroke, a blood clot blocks blood supply to an area of the brain (ischemic stroke) or a broken or leaking blood vessel causes bleeding into or around the brain (hemorrhagic stroke). In both cases, neurons die, and areas of the brain that are responsible for movement or other functions do not send and receive information correctly as a result.

Dead brain cells can't be revived, but the brain's ability to "rewire" itself—a quality known as plasticity—means that it is possible for new brain connections (also known as pathways) to take over and do the job of the nonfunctioning neurons.

Even though some stroke-induced brain damage is too great to repair, state-of-the-art stroke rehabilitation helps maximize the brain's power to create new connections and improve control over body movement.

EXERCISE THE BRAIN AND BODY

Supervised physical therapy should begin, if possible, within a week of suffering a stroke. Movement reinforces brain communication pathways—the more you "work" these pathways, the stronger they become and the easier it is to move the body. The goal of exercise after stroke is to practice movements and to help the brain regain as much function as possible.

The best type of physical therapy depends on the stroke survivor's abilities and on the resources of the rehabilitation facility. The therapies described in this article are usually used for weeks to months (at least three times weekly for one-hour sessions) as part of an overall rehabilitation program that includes occupational therapy and, in some cases, speech therapy. If you or a loved one is recovering from a stroke, talk with your stroke rehabilitation physician—generally a physiatrist (a physician who specializes in rehabilitation medicine) or a neurologist—about how these breakthrough techniques might fit into your program...*

*To locate a stroke rehabilitation center near you, contact the Commission on Accreditation of Rehabilitation Facilities (888-281-6531, *www.carf.org*).

• **Constraint-Induced Movement Therapy (CIMT).**

Recommended for: People who have limited use of an arm due to a stroke.

After recovery, stroke survivors often depend on the more functional, "good" arm to perform daily functions. That causes the affected arm to regress and lose even more function. CIMT forces use of the affected arm.

In a typical two-week course of CIMT, the good arm is restrained in a sling or mitt for nearly all waking hours, including during six hours of daily intensive physical therapy. Research shows that CIMT gives lasting improvement in movement and usage and enhances emotional well-being and quality of life.

• **Robotics.**

Recommended for: People with partial use of an affected arm or leg who may need help completing movements, such as using eating utensils. Rehabilitation robotics are sophisticated, programmable mechanical exercise devices. *For example...*

• InMotion2 shoulder-elbow robot. With your arm in a brace attached to the arm of a robot, you "play" adaptive video games that require arm movements. The games get progressively more difficult as your abilities improve. They work by encouraging intense repetition of movements, which strengthens brain connections.

• Myomo e100 NeuroRobotic System. This assistive elbow brace straps onto the stroke patient's affected arm. It works by "reading" your muscle signals and then completing the motion—for example, bending your elbow to lift an object—even if you don't have complete control yet.

Because you perform the full movement (albeit with help), new brain communication pathways are formed, and eventually you may be able to complete the movement without the mechanical brace.

• Hocoma Lokomat. This robot helps with walking. You are strapped into a large machine that supports your body and legs. The robot guides your legs as you walk on a treadmill. It works by helping brain cells reestablish a communication pathway that governs walking.

ELECTRICAL STIMULATION

Just as electrical impulses allow cells in your brain and other parts of your body to communicate with one another, the use of electrical stimulation devices may help the brain restore connections.

Limb systems strap onto an affected arm or leg and deliver mild electrical stimulation to the skin to improve motor abilities. Arm stimulation allows you to grab a glass or write with a pencil. Leg stimulation prevents "foot drop" to make walking easier.

Brain systems work by electrically encouraging the brain to rewire itself. The two main techniques are transcranial magnetic stimulation (TMS), which uses a powerful magnetic pulse to stimulate the part of the brain affected by the stroke...and direct electrical current, a noninvasive technique in which a current passes through the skull and into the brain. These brain systems are still being researched, but scientists hope that electrical stimulation might be enough to help connect the circuits that were damaged during a stroke.

Music Speeds Stroke Recovery

In a recent finding, stroke victims who listened to their favorite music daily during the first months after a stroke showed faster and more significant improvements in memory and attention than stroke victims who did not listen to music or who listened to audio books. Three months after a stroke, verbal memory improved by 60% among music listeners, compared with 18% for audio book listeners and 29% for nonlisteners. Similar differences were found six months after a stroke.

Teppo Sarkamo, PhD student, cognitive brain research unit, department of psychology, Helsinki University of Finland, and leader of a study of 54 stroke patients, published in *Brain*.

Rx: Take a Walk and Call Me in the Morning

Jordan D. Metzl, MD, a sports medicine physician at the Hospital for Special Surgery in New York City. The author of *The Exercise Cure: A Doctor's All-Natural, No-Pill Prescription for Better Health & Longer Life*, Dr. Metzl maintains practices in New York City and Greenwich, Connecticut, and is a medical columnist for *Triathlete Magazine*. He has run in 31 marathons and finished 11 Ironman competitions.

A recent study made international headlines when it found that exercise was just as effective as—or sometimes even outperformed—drugs when treating such conditions as heart disease and stroke.

The details: After examining about 300 medical trials involving more than 330,000 patients, Harvard researchers found that frequent exercise and powerful drugs, such as beta-blockers and blood thinners, provided very similar results. And in the case of stroke recovery, regular workouts were actually more effective than taking anticoagulant medications.

A troubling fact: Only one-third of clinicians "prescribe" exercise, which could not only boost the health of Americans significantly but also save the average patient thousands of dollars a year in medical costs.

My recommendations for condition-specific routines that contribute to a healthy, disease-free future...*

HEART ATTACK AND STROKE

Drugs such as beta-blockers help treat heart disease, but side effects can include fatigue, dizziness, upset stomach and cold hands. Meanwhile, a single 40-minute session of aerobic exercise has been shown to lower blood pressure for 24 hours in hypertensive patients, and regular workouts can reduce both systolic (top number) and diastolic (bottom number) blood pressure by five to 10 points. Consistent exercise also can improve cholesterol levels.

Why exercise works: The heart is a muscle, and cardiovascular exercise forces it to pump longer and eventually makes it stronger, preventing the buildup of plaques that can rupture and lead to a heart attack or stroke. Many heart attack and stroke survivors are afraid to exercise, but it's crucial that they move past this fear. Those who exercise require less medication...need fewer major surgeries such as bypasses...and are 25% less likely to die from a second heart attack than their couch potato counterparts.

What to do: Five times a week, do 30 to 40 minutes of cardiovascular exercise at a "Zone 2" level of exertion (see the next page). You have lots of choices for this exercise. Options include very fast walking, jogging, swimming, using an elliptical machine or recumbent bike, or taking an aerobics class. Pick an activity you enjoy to help you stay committed. After just six weeks, you'll likely have lower blood pressure, and by three months, your cholesterol levels should be improved.

Note: People with heart failure, a condition in which the heart cannot pump enough blood to the rest of the body, should avoid resistance exercises, such as push-ups and heavy weight lifting, that force muscles to work against an immovable or very heavy object. Such activities can put an excessive burden on the heart and cause further injury to it.

DEPRESSION

Exercise really is nature's antidepressant. Several studies have shown that working out is just as effective, if not more so, than medication when it comes to treating mild-to-moderate depression. Exercise also can help reduce the amount of medication needed to treat severe cases of depression...and even prevent depression in some people.

A Norwegian study that tracked about 39,000 people for two years found that those who reported doing moderate-to-high physical activity, including daily brisk walks for more than 30 minutes, scored significantly lower on

*Be sure to check with your doctor before starting any fitness program. If your condition is severe, he/she may initially want you to use exercise as an adjunct to medication, not as a replacement. Never stop taking a prescribed drug without talking to your doctor. *Caution:* With any of these workouts, seek immediate medical attention if you experience chest pain, shortness of breath, nausea, blurred vision or significant bone or muscle pain while exercising.

depression and anxiety tests compared with nonexercisers.

There are many effective antidepressant drugs, but they are frequently accompanied by bothersome side effects, including sexual dysfunction, nausea, fatigue and weight gain. And while most of these drugs can take a month to work, a single exercise session can trigger an immediate lift in mood, and consistent aerobic exercise will make an even more lasting positive impact.

What to do: The key is to boost your heart rate high enough to trigger the release of endorphins, feel-good chemicals that elicit a state of relaxed calm. Spend 30 to 45 minutes at a "Zone 3" level of exertion (see below), three to five days a week, to benefit.

You also may want to try exercising outdoors. A study published in *Environmental Science & Technology* found that outdoor exercise produces stronger feelings of revitalization, a bigger boost of energy and a greater reduction in depression and anger than exercising indoors.

Strength training also is effective in treating depression—lifting weights releases endorphins and builds a sense of empowerment. For a strength-training program, ask your doctor to recommend a physical therapist or personal trainer.

If it's difficult to motivate yourself to exercise when you're depressed, relying on a personal trainer—or a "workout buddy"—can help.

BACK PAIN

Back pain strikes roughly half of Americans. Pain medications are available, but many are addictive and merely mask the symptoms rather than address the underlying problem. Muscle relaxants cause drowsiness...overuse of nonsteroidal anti-inflammatory drugs (NSAIDs), such as ibuprofen, can lead to ulcers...and steroid injections, which can be given only a few times per year, can cause infection or nerve damage and long-term side effects such as osteoporosis or high blood pressure.

What to do: There's a very powerful low-tech solution—a foam roller. Widely available at sporting goods stores, these cylindrical rollers have a record of preventing and relieving back pain. With the cylinder on the floor, move various muscles (your hamstrings, quadriceps and lower back) back and forth over the foam roller slowly. Roll each area for one to two minutes. If you hit an especially tender spot, pause and roll slowly or hover in place until you feel a release. The entire routine should take about 10 minutes.

Note: Rolling muscles can feel uncomfortable and even painful at first. But the more painful it is, the more that muscle needs to be rolled. Frequency eases discomfort.

In addition to rolling your muscles, start a back- and core-strengthening program. Avoid using heavy weights, especially within an hour of waking—that's when your muscles are tighter and you're more likely to strain a muscle.

Instead, opt for higher repetitions (three sets of 15) with lighter weights (three to five pounds for women and eight to 10 pounds for men) to build endurance in your back and core, which is more protective than sheer strength.

A good core-strengthening exercise: The plank. In a push-up position, bend your elbows and rest your weight on your forearms (your body should form a straight line from shoulders to ankles). Pull your navel into your spine, and contract your abdominal muscles for 30 seconds, building up to a minute or two at a time. Perform the plank once a day.

THE 3 EXERCISE EXERTION ZONES

There are three main levels of exertion that are based on how easy it is for you to talk...

Zone 1: Talking is easy while moving. An example of Zone 1 exertion might be a moderate-paced walk.

Zone 2: Talking is tough but manageable. In Zone 2, there should be a little huffing and puffing but no gasping for air.

Zone 3: Carrying on a conversation is quite difficult at this level of exertion due to panting.

Stroke Patients May Improve Years After Their Strokes

Even two to three years after their strokes, patients still can learn to use undamaged areas of the brain to perform tasks, especially if their physical therapy includes long-term, supervised walking on a treadmill.

Physical therapy typically is prescribed for only 30 to 60 days following a stroke because, until recently, it was believed that patients could make significant improvements only within that time frame.

Daniel F. Hanley, MD, department of neurology, Johns Hopkins University School of Medicine, Baltimore, and leader of a study published in *Stroke*.

Magnets May Help Stroke Patients

In a procedure called repetitive transcranial magnetic stimulation, electromagnets are strategically placed on a stroke patient's head. The magnets deliver tiny electric currents to the area of the brain affected by the stroke, reducing muscle weakness and improving overall motor function.

Recent finding: Patients given this treatment in addition to physical therapy showed significant improvement in motor function, compared with those who did not receive brain stimulation. Study participants had strokes between one and 36 months before starting this treatment.

Anwar Etribi, PhD, emeritus professor of neurology, Ain Shams University, Cairo, Egypt, and leader of a study published in *European Journal of Neurology*.

This Treatment Is Better Than Stents

Aggressive nonsurgical treatment prevents stroke recurrence more effectively than stents.

Recent finding: People at high risk for a second stroke who received anticlotting medications and intense management of cardiovascular risks (blood pressure and cholesterol) and who strictly adhered to a lifestyle-modification program (diet and exercise) had fewer incidences of stroke recurrence than patients who received this treatment in addition to receiving a stent.

Colin P. Derdeyn, MD, is professor of radiology, neurology and neurological surgery at Washington University School of Medicine in St. Louis and lead author of a study published in *The Lancet*.

Breakthroughs in Stroke Recovery

Murray Flaster, MD, PhD, an associate professor of neurology and neurological surgery and director of Loyola Outpatient Clinics at Loyola University Chicago Stritch School of Medicine, where he specializes in vascular neurology and neurological intensive care. He is also the lead author of a recent review article in *MedLink Neurology* covering the latest techniques for caring for ischemic stroke patients.

Physician scientists have now discovered that a series of surprisingly simple treatments—performed in the first 24 to 48 hours after a stroke—can prevent additional brain damage and help reduce the risk for disability and complications, including cognitive impairments.

Important: The recommendations described in this article apply only to patients who have had an ischemic stroke (caused by a blood clot). Almost 90% of all strokes are ischemic. Unless it's otherwise noted, these recommendations do not apply to patients who have suffered a hemorrhagic (bleeding) stroke.

Most important treatments following stroke...

• **Maintain or raise blood pressure.** It sounds counterintuitive because high blood pressure is one of the main risk factors for stroke—and because most stroke patients have a spike in blood pressure of about 20 points. But studies have shown that higher-than-normal blood pressure can help patients recover faster, with less brain damage.

Giving blood pressure–lowering drugs in the hospital can cause a decrease in cerebral perfusion pressure (a measurement of blood flow to the brain) that can increase damage.

Recommended: As a general rule, your blood pressure should not be lowered immediately after a stroke, even if you have existing hypertension. As long as your blood pressure reading is below 220/120 (normal is about 120/80), it should be left alone.

In some patients, particularly those with a blockage in a major blood vessel, it might be advisable to actively raise blood pressure with a vasopressive medication, such as *phenylephrine* (Neo-Synephrine).

Exceptions: Blood pressure may still need to be lowered in patients who have had a hemorrhagic stroke (caused by bleeding in the brain) or in those who are taking clot-dissolving drugs. Raising blood pressure in patients who are actively bleeding or at risk for bleeding can potentially cause more bleeding.

• **Reduce body temperature.** Fever is common in stroke patients due to infection or the stroke itself, with up to 25% having a temperature of 100.4°F or higher within 48 hours after being admitted to the hospital. A fever is dangerous because it increases the metabolic demands of damaged brain tissue—energy that should go toward healing. It also triggers the release of inflammatory substances that can cause additional damage.

Recommended: *Acetaminophen* (Tylenol) and hydration. Cooling blankets may be used for fever above 101°F. An experimental treatment called therapeutic hypothermia involves rapidly lowering body temperature with a cooled saline solution given intravenously.

• **Rehydrate.** Dehydration is common in stroke patients because fever and other complications can reduce the body's fluids. If you've had a stroke and are dehydrated, your risk of forming additional blood clots is increased by fivefold.

Reason: Dehydration reduces the volume of blood in the body. This, in turn, reduces blood pressure and increases the tendency of blood to clot.

Recommended: Intravenous (IV) saline solution for at least 24 to 48 hours.

• **Lower the bed.** When the head of the bed is raised, the increased elevation can decrease cerebral blood flow, particularly when the stroke affects the middle cerebral artery, which is common in ischemic stroke.

Important finding: Studies suggest that lowering the head of the bed from 30 degrees to 15 degrees increases blood flow through the middle cerebral artery by 12%. There's an additional 8% increase when the bed is flat.

The trade-off: Many patients aren't comfortable when the bed is completely flat. They also have more trouble swallowing, which increases the risk that they'll get pneumonia after inhaling (aspirating) foreign material from the mouth. Therefore, the head of the bed should initially be elevated to about 15 degrees. If the patient doesn't improve, the bed can be lowered.

• **Use an insulin drip.** It's common for stroke patients to have high blood sugar because of preexisting diabetes or prediabetes. In addition, the stroke itself can temporarily raise blood sugar (in fact, any major stressor in the body can raise blood glucose levels). High blood sugar, or hyperglycemia, is associated with a 2.7-fold increase in poor outcomes following stroke. Poor outcomes could include language difficulties, paralysis, cognitive impairments, etc.

Recommended: Stroke patients should be tested for hyperglycemia immediately after arriving in the hospital emergency department and then as frequently as needed. If blood sugar is higher than 155 mg/dL, insulin should be administered intravenously.

Important: To help prevent stroke-related complications that are worsened by elevated blood sugar, these patients should not be given saline that contains glucose—even if they could benefit nutritionally from the additional sugar.

- **Give a statin quickly.** Stroke patients routinely have their cholesterol tested in the hospital.

Recommended: There's no need to wait for the results before giving patients a cholesterol-lowering statin drug, such as *atorvastatin* (Lipitor) or *pravastatin* (Pravachol).

Reason: Even if your cholesterol is normal, statins reduce the inflammatory brain damage that's caused by stroke. Giving these medications quickly can help patients recover more promptly. Continuing statin therapy (if you have high cholesterol and are already taking a statin) can help prevent a subsequent stroke.

- **Start activity early.** Hospitalized patients who are physically active to any degree—even if it is just sitting up in bed—improve more quickly and have fewer complications than those who are initially immobile.

Other benefits: Physical activity also reduces the risk for pneumonia, deep-vein thrombosis, pulmonary embolism and bedsores.

Recommended: Some form of activity within hours after having a stroke if the patient is neurologically stable. We encourage patients to spend as little time in bed as possible even if their mobility is impaired and to do as much as they can tolerate.

Important: Activity should always be carefully guided by nurses, therapists or other members of the hospital team to avoid injury.

Foods That Fix Your Body After a Stroke

Foods that may reduce brain damage from stroke: Blueberries, spinach and spirulina, a type of green algae. These foods have high levels of antioxidants that help neutralize damaging free radicals.

Recent study: Rats that were fed diets enriched with these foods for one month prior to inducing a stroke had only half as much brain damage as rats that were not fed these foods. This study suggests that including these foods—one cup of blueberries, a big spinach salad or a few teaspoons of spirulina powder—in your daily diet may make a difference in the severity of a stroke.

Paula C. Bickford, PhD, professor of neuro-surgery, University of South Florida, and James A. Haley VA Hospital, both in Tampa, and leader of the study published in *Experimental Neurology*.

Walk to Recover from a Stroke

When 128 adult stroke survivors were divided into two groups, those who took a brisk outdoor walk for 30 minutes three times a week for three months reported a 16.7% greater improvement in their general health and ability to perform everyday physical activities, compared with those who had therapeutic massage but did no exercise. The walking group also was able to walk farther during a six-minute endurance test, indicating better mobility and physical fitness. Those who walked for 20 minutes daily also showed improvement.

Carron Gordon, PhD, lecturer in physical therapy, The University of the West Indies, Mona, Jamaica.

Anti-Depressants Can Help Stroke Victims

Stroke victims' learning and memory skills can be improved by the antidepressant Lexapro.

Recent finding: Stroke patients given a 12-week course of *escitalopram* (Lexapro) after a stroke had higher scores on tests of verbal and visual memory. The drug, a selective serotonin reuptake inhibitor (SSRI), helped stroke recovery even if given as much as three months after the stroke, although it should be administered as soon as possible.

Ricardo E. Jorge, MD, associate professor of psychiatry, Carver College of Medicine, University of Iowa, Iowa City, and leader of a study of 129 nondepressed stroke patients, published in *Archives of General Psychiatry*.

Device Helps Muscle Movement After Stroke

In a small six-week study of patients who had suffered a stroke at least six months earlier, those who used a portable exercise device called the Tailwind three times weekly improved control of their arm muscles.

Theory: Because the device requires the use of both sides of the brain and mimics natural arm functions, it has the potential to "rewire" the brain's motor control circuitry.

If you have lost the use of an arm due to a stroke: Ask your doctor about the Tailwind.

Jill Whitall, PhD, professor of neuromotor control and rehabilitation, University of Maryland School of Medicine, Baltimore.

How Brain Scientist Jill Bolte Taylor Came Back From a Stroke

Jill Bolte Taylor, PhD, a neuroanatomist affiliated with the Indiana University School of Medicine in Indianapolis. She is a national spokesperson for the Harvard Brain Tissue Resource Center, which collects human brain tissue for research, and the author of *My Stroke of Insight: A Brain Scientist's Personal Journey*.

In 1996, Jill Bolte Taylor, PhD, a 37-year-old brain scientist, had a severe hemorrhagic (bleeding) stroke in the left hemisphere of her brain.

Dr. Taylor's cognitive abilities degenerated rapidly in the hours following the stroke. Bleeding affected the motor cortex (paralyzing her right arm)...the sensory cortex (making it difficult for her to see or hear)...and the brain's language centers (making it difficult for her to speak).

After struggling to call for help, she was taken to the hospital, where she underwent surgery two-and-a-half weeks later to remove a golf ball–sized blood clot in her brain.

Today, Dr. Taylor is completely recovered—all of her physical, cognitive and emotional abilities are intact. Her recovery refutes the widely held belief that if a stroke survivor doesn't regain a particular ability within six months, it will never be regained.

Dr. Taylor, a neuroanatomist (a scientist specializing in the anatomy of the brain) lectures widely about her stroke recovery. The strategies she shares here can be used by all those who have had a debilitating ischemic stroke (in which a blood clot stops blood supply to an area of the brain) or any severe brain injury...

STEP 1: MOVE TO RECOVER

People who survive a stroke often experience crushing fatigue due to the damage that occurs to brain cells (neurons)—this affects their energy levels and abilities to process information. Simple tasks, such as changing the position of your body or even opening your eyes, are extraordinarily difficult. But the same activities that restore physical strength also force individual neurons to reconnect and communicate with one another—a process that is essential for post-stroke neurological recovery.

Helpful: Any physical activity is beneficial—even basic movements, such as standing up or sitting down.

Important: When you feel rested and capable of expending the necessary energy, you should push yourself to do more and more physically each day. As I gained strength, I progressed to trying more difficult activities, such as standing at the sink and doing dishes.

STEP 2: ESCAPE THE MENTAL NOISE

Neurons that are damaged by a stroke are unable to process normal stimuli, such as bright lights or the sound of a television. As a result, visual or auditory distractions may be interpreted by the brain as mental "noise." Saturating the brain with such stimuli may make it much harder for the neurons to recover and may impede the retention of new information.

Helpful: After any kind of stroke or other brain trauma, alternate periods of sleep with briefer periods (about 20 minutes) of learning and cognitive challenges (such as those described below). Periods of sleep (as much as needed until waking up naturally) allow the brain to assimilate information that is gleaned during periods of wakefulness.

STEP 3: WORK THE MIND

The brain has remarkable "plasticity" (the ability to form new connections between the surviving neurons). After a stroke, if there is damage to the brain areas that control movement, sensory perceptions and cognition, you need to challenge these areas.

Examples...

- **Multiple-choice questions.** My mother, who was my primary caregiver, understood that asking "yes" or "no" questions didn't force me to think hard enough. That's why she asked me multiple-choice questions—for example, did I want minestrone soup or a grilled cheese sandwich? Each question forced me to relearn words.
- **Simple puzzles.** If you've had a serious stroke, putting together a simple jigsaw puzzle may be a huge challenge. You might not recognize shapes or colors. You might not have the dexterity to put the pieces together. But doing such a puzzle is a superb exercise because it forces you to work different parts of the brain at the same time.
- **Reading.** It's among the hardest tasks because, for many stroke patients, the entire concept of letters and words is lost—temporarily for some stroke survivors, but permanently for others. I had to relearn everything from scratch—that the squiggles that make up letters have names...that combinations of letters make sounds...and that combinations of sounds make words.

Helpful: I started with children's picture books, which would be appropriate for most stroke patients who are relearning to read.

STEP 4: THE SIMPLEST STEPS

Healthy people can't begin to comprehend how complicated things seem after a stroke. When I first started walking, for example, I didn't understand the concept of sidewalk cracks. Each time I saw one, I had to stop and analyze whether it was important.

Helpful: Caregivers need to break down tasks to the simplest levels. For example, a stroke patient might not understand how to sit up in bed. He/she might need to spend days just learning how to shift body weight. In my case, I had to learn to simply hold an eating utensil before I could imagine raising it to my mouth.

STEP 5: FOCUS ON ABILITIES

When you've had a stroke, the extent of your disabilities can be overwhelming. It took me eight years before I was fully recovered. Patients can easily get frustrated and quit trying. At that point, if a patient is not aware of what recovery step needs to be taken next, he may never actually take that next step. It's normal for a stroke survivor to reach a recovery plateau, to continue to learn, then hit another plateau. There are many plateaus along the way.

Helpful: Even if progress seems exceptionally slow, remind a person who has had a stroke of the smallest successes—it may be something as simple as once again being able to hold a fork securely.

If you are the stroke survivor, use small triumphs as inspiration. In my case, it was embarrassing to drool in front of strangers, but I reminded myself that I had managed to swallow.

After my stroke, I never imagined that I would regain enough of my abilities to return to a career as a scientist and teacher. I've managed to do both—in fact, at the same level and intensity. My stroke recovery gave me an opportunity to start my life again.

Two-Pill Treatment Cuts Stroke Risk by One-Third After a TIA

S. Claiborne Johnston, MD, PhD, director, Clinical and Translational Science Institute, University of California, San Francisco. His study was published in *The New England Journal of Medicine.*

My friend Donald recently suffered a transient ischemic attack (TIA), also known as a mini-stroke or warning stroke. His strokelike symptoms lasted only a few minutes, and he emerged without permanent damage. But he's not home-free—because 10% to 20% of TIA patients go on to have a full-blown stroke within 90 days.

Breakthrough: Now there's a way to reduce that risk by one-third. It involves adding a second type of pill to the standard pill that TIA patients take. But to work best, the dual treatment should begin right away after a TIA. That's why you need to know about it—so you'll be prepared in case you or a loved one ever suffers a TIA.

DYNAMIC DRUG DUO

The vast majority of strokes are ischemic strokes, the type caused by a blood clot. That's why it's standard for TIA patients to start taking a daily aspirin, because aspirin is known to help prevent clots. Aspirin's benefits in this regard, though, are rather modest. So researchers set out to determine whether adding the anticoagulant drug *clopidogrel* (Plavix) would help. Like aspirin, clopidogrel works by preventing platelets (a type of blood cell) from collecting and forming clots. Clopidogrel is not risk-free—it can cause significant bleeding—but researchers wanted to see whether its benefits outweighed its risks for TIA patients.

The recent study included 5,170 people who had had a TIA or a similar kind of mini-stroke called an acute minor ischemic stroke within the previous 24 hours. All patients received aspirin right away. The first dose ranged from 75 milligrams (mg) to 300 mg, depending on their doctors' decisions, then the dose was dropped to 75 mg from day two onward.

Patients were randomly divided into two groups. In one group, patients received daily aspirin plus a placebo through day 90. In the other group, patients received clopidogrel at a dose of 300 mg on day one and 75 mg on days two through 90, plus daily aspirin for 21 days. In this dual-therapy group, aspirin was discontinued after 21 days to minimize the risk for bleeding.

Here's what happened over the course of the 90 days...

- **Stroke occurred in 12% of patients in the aspirin-only group,** but in only 8% of the patients in the clopidogrel-plus-aspirin group—meaning that the likelihood of suffering a stroke was one-third lower in the clopidogrel-plus-aspirin group.
- **Fatal or disabling stroke occurred in 7% of aspirin-only users...**but in only 5% of clopidogrel-plus-aspirin users.
- **Hemorrhagic stroke (the type caused by bleeding rather than a clot) occurred at an identical rate of 0.3% in both groups...** and other severe bleeding events (such as bleeding that required surgery or transfusion) occurred at an identical rate of 0.2% in both groups. This was important—because it meant that adding the 90-day clopidogrel therapy to the 21-day aspirin therapy did not increase patients' risk for hemorrhagic stroke or other severe bleeding problems. The rate of mild bleeding events (such as bruising or oozing from puncture sites) was slightly higher among the clopidogrel-plus-aspirin users.

TIMING MATTERS BIG TIME

Because this study was conducted in China, some experts would like to see the results confirmed before the two-pill therapy becomes the standard of care in the US. It's also worth noting that, because the study follow-up period lasted 90 days, it's not known whether any participants went on to have strokes later—but remember, the riskiest period for stroke occurs right after a TIA. That's why the researchers said that starting treatment with clopidogrel-plus-aspirin as soon as possible after TIA symptoms appear is likely to produce the greatest benefit. Note that doctors generally recommend that TIA patients stay on antiplatelet therapy indefinitely.

What to watch for: The most typical warning signs of a TIA are exactly the same as those of a stroke—sudden numbness or weakness of the face, arm or leg, especially on one side of the body...sudden confusion or trouble speaking or understanding speech...sudden loss of balance or coordination or difficulty with walking...sudden problems with vision in one or both eyes...and/or a sudden, severe headache with no known cause.

As soon as symptoms appear: Seek emergency medical help without delay! If it turns out that you are having a TIA, ask your doctor whether the dual clopidogrel-plus-aspirin therapy is right for you. Remember, the sooner you get started on the treatment, the better your chances of avoiding a full-blown stroke.

Better Stroke Follow-Up

Monitoring a stroke patient's pulse at home may help guard against a second stroke—and you don't have to be a doctor to do it. Pulse can reveal an irregular heartbeat, a major cause of second strokes. When patients and family members were trained to properly take a pulse in a study of 256 stroke survivors, their measurements were almost as accurate as those taken by health-care professionals and correctly identified most arrhythmias, which can be treated with medication.

Bernd Kallmünzer, MD, stroke unit physician, University of Erlangen-Nuremberg, Germany.

Anxiety/Stroke Link

People with high levels of anxiety were 33% more likely to have strokes than those with low levels, according to a recent 22-year study of 6,000 adults.

Possible reasons: Higher levels of stress hormones, elevated heart rate and blood pressure, as well as anxiety-related behaviors such as smoking and physical inactivity, may be to blame.

Maya Lambiase, PhD, postdoctoral fellow, University of Pittsburgh.

Exciting Treatment for Stroke Victims

Randolph S. Marshall, MD, chief, stroke division, The Neurological Institute of New York at Columbia University Medical Center in New York City.

Imagine looking at a wall clock and seeing only the right half of the face...or hearing only sounds that come from your right. Not seeing or responding to stimuli on the left side is a fact of life for about 50% of stroke patients due to a brain condition called hemispatial neglect ("hemineglect"). Only about half of hemineglect patients go on to recover without treatment, and recovery can take days to years, depending on the severity of the stroke. Now a recent study brings good news...it reveals that applying magnetic stimulation daily for just two weeks to certain areas of the brain may jump-start recovery and help stroke survivors see, hear and respond normally.

This technique, called continuous theta-burst stimulation or TBS, was developed about 15 years ago primarily to treat depression. But if future research confirms the new findings, it could soon be used to treat stroke victims, too. Researchers at the Santa Lucia Foundation in Rome performed the study, which was published in December 2011 in *Neurology*.

REBALANCING THE BRAIN

When a stroke affects the right side of the brain, it causes hyperactivity on the left side of the brain, and this is what leads to an inability to see, hear and/or respond to stimuli on the left. Hemineglect can technically occur on either side of the brain, but because of the brain's anatomy, the sensory deficit most often occurs on the left.

The traditional treatment for hemineglect consists of mental rehab tasks, for example, matching objects on a computer screen, completing paper-and-pencil tasks to improve visual scanning (for example, the ability to find a friend in a crowded restaurant) and doing physical therapy exercises (such as repetitive movements of the arm or leg) to improve motor skills. Researchers wanted to investigate whether several weeks of TBS therapy would promote faster and longer-term recovery.

A STIMULATING STUDY

Twenty patients who had had strokes causing hemineglect participated in the four-week study. Five days a week, all participants took part in standard mental and physical rehab sessions. For the first two weeks of the study, though, on weekday mornings, all patients had 15 minutes of either "real" or "sham" TBS sessions. Then, to measure whether participants had improvement in their ability to perceive stimuli that take place on their left sides, researchers gave participants the Behavioral Inattention Test (BIT), which covered such tasks as drawing, dialing a phone and reading a menu.

The results: Researchers found that test scores for those who received real TBS treatment improved by 16% immediately following the two weeks of therapy, revealing that perception and response to left-side stimuli had improved. After four weeks, TBS patients showed a 23% improvement in test scores, indicating that TBS benefits continued after treatment had ended—and grew. On the other hand, participants receiving sham TBS showed no clinically significant improvements in test scores after two or four weeks.

A TREATMENT OF THE FUTURE

To see what these findings might mean for readers, we spoke with Randolph S. Marshall, MD, chief of the stroke division at The Neurological Institute of New York at Columbia University Medical Center in New York City. He coauthored the accompanying editorial in the journal. Dr. Marshall said that this study showed the longest-lasting effect of TBS thus far and that once patients with hemineglect start to improve, the improvement usually continues. No one knows exactly how TBS works in the brain, but Dr. Marshall said it seems to make neuron firing less frequent and thus calms the overexcitability in the brain.

Psychiatrists who administer TBS for depression conduct treatments in their offices and clinics, but for now, TBS for hemineglect is taking place only for research at some teaching hospitals, said Dr. Marshall. So you can't even ask for it off-label right now, unfortunately. More research will help discover how to maximize the treatment's effectiveness, figure out which patients are most likely to benefit from it and identify potential side effects—and it will help persuade insurance companies to cover the cost. (TBS sessions for depression run from about $200 to $300 each.) Dr. Marshall anticipates that within a few years, the country's network of specialized stroke centers will have doctors trained and ready to put TBS therapy into practice.

The Missing Piece to Stroke Recovery

Michael C. Munin, MD, an associate professor at the University of Pittsburgh School of Medicine and vice-chair for Clinical Program Development in the department of physical medicine and rehabilitation, also at the medical school. Dr. Munin has authored recent studies in the *American Journal of Physical Medicine & Rehabilitation* and *Archives of Physical Medicine and Rehabilitation*.

Imagine yourself attempting to open a jar if your hand were bunched in a fist or trying to walk if one of your arms were clenched across your chest.

This type of uncontrollable muscle tightness is a constant challenge for an estimated one million Americans affected by upper limb spasticity. Typically resulting from a stroke, multiple sclerosis, cerebral palsy or an accident that affects the brain or spinal cord, upper limb spasticity most often affects the elbows, wrists and fingers.

Unlike paralysis, which causes loss of muscle function, upper limb spasticity is marked by uncontrollable muscle tightness and/or a lack of muscle inhibition. With upper limb spasticity, a person's elbow might not bend without forcing it down with the other hand, or spasms might cause the arm to recoil as though a spring had been released.

Problem: About 58% of stroke survivors experience upper limb spasticity. Of those, only about half get appropriate treatment—often because the condition develops slowly, and patients assume that it's a complication they have to live with.

Good news: Most people with upper limb spasticity can achieve better muscle control, and even increase their muscle strength, with a combination of medical treatments and specialized physical and/or occupational therapy.

AN UNDERTREATED PROBLEM

Upper limb spasticity often goes undiagnosed because it may not develop until weeks, months or even years after a person has a stroke or is diagnosed with a condition that leads to the spasticity.

Best treatment: People with upper limb spasticity have the best chance of regaining mobility and functional ability when therapy combines repetitive task training exercises with injections of botulinum toxin type A (Botox), which was approved by the FDA to treat upper limb spasticity. (Botox was approved earlier by the FDA to help remove wrinkles and ease migraine pain.)

Research shows that when used for upper limb spasticity, Botox injections combined with repetitive task training can bring about a 30% improvement, on average, within 12 weeks and, in some cases, an improvement of up to 54%. Benefits typically last about three months. However, patients must have some arm function remaining after a stroke to benefit from the training.

The repetition involved in repetitive task training strengthens the brain's ability to communicate with different muscles. And even though the exercises won't eliminate spasticity, they can make it easier for patients to perform daily tasks, such as cooking meals, buttoning a jacket, even hugging loved ones.

Important: The sooner a person with upper limb spasticity starts the repetitive training, the better—if too much time passes, the muscles atrophy to such an extent that recovery becomes more difficult. Still, it's never too late. What's imperative is to use the affected limb and not ignore it due to disability.

Ideally, patients meet with a physical or occupational therapist at least once a week for about 30 to 60 minutes, often for several months.* Then they practice at home what they've learned. Important: The goal of therapy is to enable people with upper limb spasticity to do the types of activities that they need to do—for example, watering plants, buttoning clothes, etc.

When starting treatment, it's important to tell the therapist what activities you enjoy most or find most important. You're more likely to stay motivated and keep practicing when you see a clear benefit. *Repetitive task training may include...*

- **Stretching exercises.** Spasticity often leads to a shortening of tendons and/or ligaments, which interferes with normal motions. Stretching can lengthen these tissues. Someone with hand spasticity might be advised to open the hand and extend the fingers...hold the stretch for several seconds...and then repeat.
- **Putting lids on jars.** There are more steps to this than you might think. The patient has to expand the fingers to grip the lid...grip the jar with the other hand...then contract the fingers to grip the lid and screw it on.
- **Folding laundry.** This uses muscles in the fingers, wrists, elbows, etc. Studies have shown that many patients who couldn't fold laundry are able to do it on their own, comfortably, after a few months of repetitive task training.

BEST MEDICAL TREATMENTS

New advances are now making upper limb spasticity more treatable than ever before.

*To find an occupational therapist near you, contact the American Occupational Therapy Association, Inc., 301-652-6611, *www.aota.org*. To find a physical therapist, consult the American Physical Therapy Association, 800-999-2782, *www.apta.org*.

Even though oral medications can be given to treat "global" spasticity that affects multiple regions, such as the arm, head and neck, these drugs often cause unwanted sedation even at low doses. Some of these drugs, such as *tizanidine* (Zanaflex), block nerve impulses. Others, such as *baclofen* (Lioresal) and *diazepam* (Valium), act on the central nervous system to relax muscles.

Recent development: The FDA's approval of Botox to treat upper limb spasticity is an important development because Botox reduces muscle tension without the systemic side effects of oral drugs. Botox allows doctors to treat smaller muscle groups in specific areas, such as in the fingers or elbows.

How it works: Botox selectively weakens (it doesn't paralyze) affected muscles. An injection of Botox into a hand, for example, can loosen a clenched fist and allow more normal motions. Someone whose left arm is clenched across his/her body can get an injection of Botox to relax the limb and, say, get his arm into a coat sleeve.

An injection usually starts working within three days but could take up to two weeks. It keeps working for three to four months. The main risk—unintended temporary muscle weakening—is rare and can be corrected with future dose adjustments.

Other approaches...

- **Phenol injections.** For years, doctors have used a type of alcohol known as phenol to reduce muscle contractions and spasms, but phenol is mainly used to block specific nerves that operate large muscle groups. Because it is a nerve block (injected just above the nerve) rather than a muscle weakener (such as Botox), nerves have to be easily accessible, and these typically are the ones that supply the large muscle groups. Unlike Botox, a phenol injection starts working immediately.

The effects of each phenol injection last four to six months. Patients who get a phenol injection may also be treated with a low dose of Botox. The main side effect of phenol is a burning/tingling sensation at the injection site.

- **Orthotic devices are sometimes used to hold limbs in a desired position.** For example, a patient with hand tightness might wear a "resting splint" at night to keep the fingers open and straight. This may also improve the patient's muscle function during the day. Or a splint might be used to keep the ankle from twisting.

NEW TYPES OF SURGERY

In the past, patients with spasticity often underwent surgery to cut the spinal nerves that caused muscle tightness. This is rarely done anymore.

Now: Surgery is mainly used to lengthen the tendons/ligaments attached to a spastic area. This procedure increases the patient's range of motion.

Surgery also is used to implant a computerized pump that delivers a steady dose of the muscle-relaxing drug baclofen. The pump, which is implanted in the abdomen, can give patients with severe spasticity long-lasting relief. Pump implants are best suited for people who have global spasticity, which covers too many areas to inject. Infection risk is roughly 1%.

Benefit: Because the drug is delivered directly to the spinal area, the required dose can be up to 1,000 times lower than oral medications. This minimizes grogginess and other side effects.

Dry Brushing for Stroke

What could help immobility after a stroke? Immobility affects blood circulation and impairs the delivery of nutrients to cells and the elimination of toxins and waste products—both essential for good health. Dry brushing, massage and reflexology will help stimulate a patient's circulation.

Dry brushing, a rubdown of the body with natural-bristle brushes, can activate circulation of the lymphatic system, which is necessary for warding off infections.

Massage also can help to activate circulation and eliminate waste products, such as lactic acid, that cause muscle stiffness and pain. Reflexology (pressure to trigger points on hands, bottoms of the feet and other areas) and acupuncture may also be effective.

Mao Shing Ni, DOM, PhD, LAc, Oriental medicine practitioner at Tao of Wellness, Santa Monica, California.

Stroke Prevention Drug

An alternative to *warfarin* is available to prevent stroke in people with atrial fibrillation and at least one other stroke risk factor. *Apixaban* (Eliquis) is more effective for patients in this group than the traditional medicine warfarin. It was approved by the FDA in 2012. It is not approved for use in patients who have had a recent hemorrhage or who have faulty or artificial heart valves. Ask your doctor for details.

Rafael Alexander Ortiz, MD, director of Center for Stroke and Neuro-Endovascular Surgery, Lenox Hill Hospital, New York City.

Yoga Boosts Balance Long After a Stroke

Arlene A. Schmid, PhD, OTR (occupational therapist registered), is an assistant professor in the department of occupational therapy at Indiana University and a rehabilitation research scientist at Roudebush VA Medical Center, both in Indianapolis. She is the lead author of a study on yoga and balance published in *Stroke*.

Many people think of yoga as exercise for the limber-limbed young. So you may be happily surprised to learn that yoga can help stroke survivors improve their balance and become more active—even if they start practicing yoga long after their strokes occurred.

This news from a small but encouraging study is important because stroke victims often are left with long-term balance problems that contribute to disability and increase the risk for potentially fatal falls. What's more, the study results challenge the discouraging yet common notion that significant improvement in motor skills is unlikely when more than six months have passed since a patient's stroke.

Study scoop: Participants included 47 adults, average age 63, who had suffered strokes anywhere from six months to more than 11 years earlier. All had finished their stroke rehabilitation programs...could stand on their own or with a device...and continued to receive usual medical care throughout the study. For eight weeks, one group of participants attended twice-weekly hour-long group classes involving modified yoga postures, breathing techniques and meditation, with classes growing more challenging over time. A second "yoga-plus" group took the same yoga classes and also received an audio recording of yoga/relaxation techniques to use three times weekly at home. A third group, which served as a control, received no yoga instruction. All participants completed tests of balance, independence and quality of life at the start and end of the study.

Results: No significant changes were seen in the control group. In contrast, members of both the yoga and yoga-plus groups experienced significant improvement in their ability to balance and raised their scores on tests of independence and quality of life. Yoga participants also felt less afraid of falling and reported attempting more challenging activities because of their improved balance—for instance, they talked about walking through a grocery store instead of using a motorized scooter...being able to take a shower...and feeling inspired to visit friends. (Comparing the two yoga groups, the addition of the audio recording did not change the results significantly, though the yoga-plus people did report enjoying listening to it.)

How does yoga work its magic? Researchers suggested that yoga's mind-body connection may make it more therapeutic than traditional exercise...and that yoga is especially effective in improving poststroke function because it promotes coordination of complex movements, balance, strengthening and breathing.

Stroke patients: Ask your doctor or occupational therapist whether yoga is appropriate for you. If so, request a referral to a registered yoga therapist who is experienced in working with stroke survivors.

Instant Help for Stroke Victims

When researchers reviewed 14 studies involving 429 stroke patients, they found that a lower-leg splint supporting the foot and ankle—designed to keep joints properly aligned—immediately helped patients walk faster and improved balance, while an upper-limb splint (such as a wrist splint) did not improve function.

If a loved one has suffered a stroke: Ask his/her physical therapist or podiatrist whether a lower-leg splint might improve your loved one's mobility and balance.

Sarah T. Tyson, PhD, physiotherapist, School of Health, Sport and Rehabilitation, University of Salford, Greater Manchester, England.

Virtual Stroke Rehab

A virtual-reality program makes stroke rehabilitation more fun. Patients wearing goggles see bugs flying nearby. When they successfully "smack" them, the bugs move farther away, improving the patients' range of motion.

University of Central Florida.

Index

D

E

F

G

H

M

Q

R